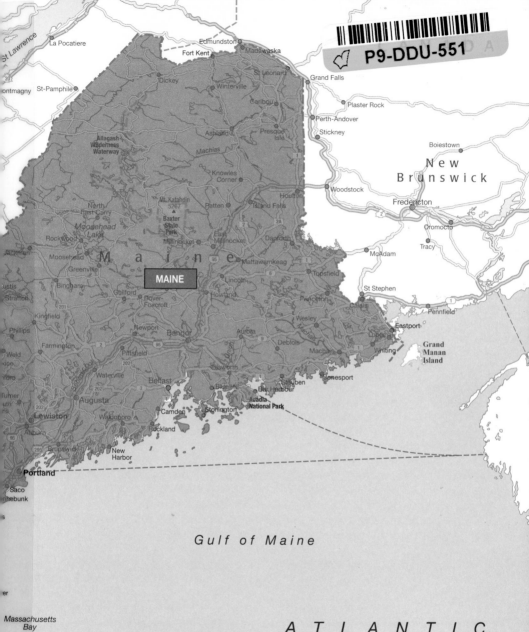

La Pocatiere

St Lawrence

ontmagny   St-Pamphile

Edmundston
Fort Kent
Madawaska

Dickey

St Leonard

Grand Falls

Winterville

Caribou

Plaster Rock

Perth-Andover

Stickney

Ashland

Presque
Isle

Boiestown

New
Brunswick

Allagash
Wilderness
Waterway

Machias

Knowles
Corner

Houlton

Woodstock

Fredericton

North
East Carry

Mt. Katahdin
5267

Patten

Island Falls

Baxter
State
Park

2A

Oromocto

Moosehead
Lake

Rockwood

East
Millinocket

Danforth

McAdam

Tracy

Millinocket

Moosehead

M a i n e

95

Mattawamkeag

MAINE

Greenville

Lincoln

Topsfield

St Stephen

Bingham

Guilford

Dover-
Foxcroft

Howland

Princeton

Calais

Pennfield

Stratton

Eustis

201

Wesley

Eastport

Kingfield

Newport

Bangor

Aurora

Deblois

Lubec

Grand
Manan
Island

Phillips

Farmington

95

Pittsfield

Ellsworth

Machias

Whiting

Weld
xico

202

Steuben

Jonesport

ord

Waterville

Belfast

Blue Hill

Turner
uth
ris

Augusta

Camden

Stonington

Bar Harbor

**Acadia
National Park**

Lewiston

Waldoboro

Auburn

90

Rockland

Brunswick

295

New
Harbor

Portland

Saco
hebunk

Gulf of Maine

Massachusetts
Bay

A T L A N T I C

O C E A N

rincetown
ape Cod
Bay

Cape Cod

Chatham

annis

Monomoy Island

**APE COD AND
HE ISLANDS**

ucket

Nantucket

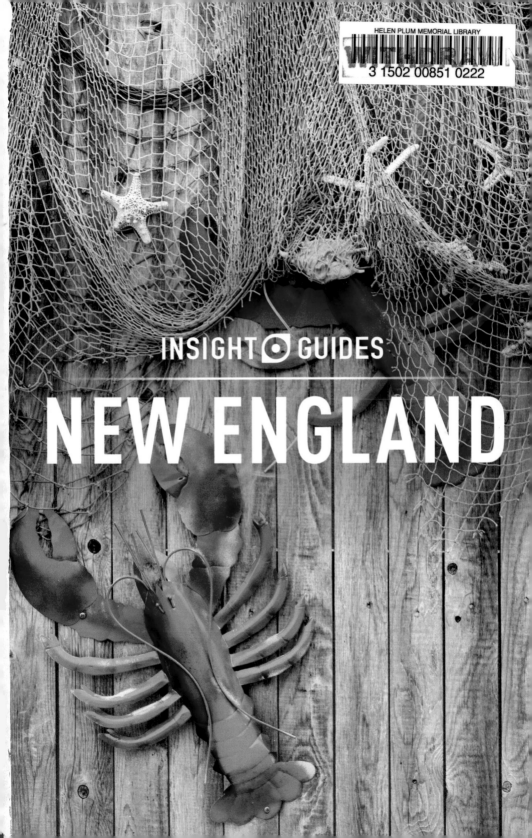

INSIGHT ⊙ GUIDES

NEW ENGLAND

Walking Eye App

YOUR FREE DESTINATION CONTENT AND EBOOK AVAILABLE THROUGH THE WALKING EYE APP

Your guide now includes a free eBook and destination content for your chosen destination, all for the same great price as before. Simply download the Walking Eye App from the App Store or Google Play to access your free eBook and destination content.

HOW THE WALKING EYE APP WORKS

Through the Walking Eye App, you can purchase a range of eBooks and destination content. However, when you buy this book, you can download the corresponding eBook and destination content for free. Just see below in the grey panels where to find your free content and then scan the QR code at the bottom of this page.

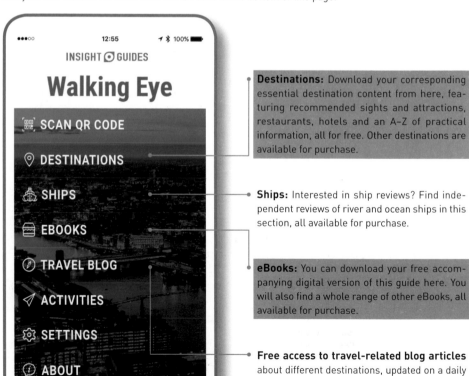

Destinations: Download your corresponding essential destination content from here, featuring recommended sights and attractions, restaurants, hotels and an A–Z of practical information, all for free. Other destinations are available for purchase.

Ships: Interested in ship reviews? Find independent reviews of river and ocean ships in this section, all available for purchase.

eBooks: You can download your free accompanying digital version of this guide here. You will also find a whole range of other eBooks, all available for purchase.

Free access to travel-related blog articles about different destinations, updated on a daily basis.

HOW THE DESTINATION CONTENT WORKS

Each destination includes a short introduction, an A–Z of practical information and recommended points of interest, split into 4 different categories:

- Highlights
- Accommodation
- Eating out
- What to do

You can view the location of every point of interest and save it by adding it to your Favourites. In the 'Around Me' section you can view all the points of interest within 5km.

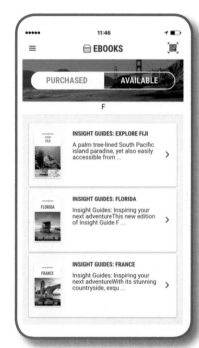

HOW THE EBOOKS WORK

The eBooks are provided in EPUB file format. Please note that you will need an eBook reader installed on your device to open the file. Many devices come with this as standard, but you may still need to install one manually from Google Play.

The eBook content is identical to the content in the printed guide.

HOW TO DOWNLOAD THE WALKING EYE APP

1. Download the Walking Eye App from the App Store or Google Play.
2. Open the app and select the scanning function from the main menu.
3. Scan the QR code on this page – you will then be asked a security question to verify ownership of the book.
4. Once this has been verified, you will see your eBook and destination content in the purchased ebook and destination sections, where you will be able to download them.

Other destination apps and eBooks are available for purchase separately or are free with the purchase of the Insight Guide book.

CONTENTS

Introduction

The best of New England 6
Yankee country 19
The lay of the land 21

History & features

Decisive dates 28
Beginnings 30
Birth of a nation 36
   ○ The Shakers 43
Evolution and reinvention 44
New England's people 53
The bountiful sea 59
The Puritan tradition.................................64
Teaching New England's minds....................69
Literary utopia..74
Lobsters and locavores..............................81
   ○ Sweet treats 85
Building New England 86
Sports and outdoor activities......................92

Places

Introduction...107
■ BOSTON 113
   ○ Boston's literary trail 132
◎ Boston's Freedom Trail...........................138
■ AROUND BOSTON 141
   ○ The Salem witch trials 146
◎ Fall foliage 160
■ CAPE COD AND THE ISLANDS.............162
   ○ Nantucket's stormy past..................185
◎ Covered bridges 186
■ CENTRAL MASSACHUSETTS 188
■ THE PIONEER VALLEY 195
■ THE BERKSHIRES................................202
■ RHODE ISLAND 213
◎ Newport's mansions 230
■ CONNECTICUT 232
   ○ Connecticut's nicknames..................254
   ○ The coming of the casinos 257
■ VERMONT 261
   ○ Green New England 264
   ○ The Appalachian Trail 288
■ NEW HAMPSHIRE 295

○ Farmers, produce, and eating local .**314**
○ Pioneers and revolutionaries **319**
◉ Flora and fauna......................................**320**
■ MAINE...**323**
○ Maine's lighthouses.........................**346**

Travel tips

TRANSPORTATION

Getting there **354**
By air **354**
By train...**354**
By boat **354**
Getting around **354**
Boston **354**
New England................................**355**

A – Z

Accommodations **357**
Age restrictions **357**
Budgeting for your trip **357**
Children **358**
Climate..**358**
Crime and safety......................................**359**
Customs regulations................................**359**
Disabled access **359**
Eating out **360**
Electricity **360**
Embassies and consulates **360**
Emergencies **360**
Festivals **360**
Health and medical care..........................**361**
Internet **361**
LGBTQ travelers **361**
Media...**361**
Money **362**
Opening hours...**362**
Pets **363**
Postal services...**363**
Public holidays **363**
Religious services **363**
Shopping **363**
Smoking **364**
Tax **364**
Telephones..**364**
Time zone..**364**

Tourist information **364**
Tour operators and travel agents **364**
Visas and passports **365**
Websites..**365**

FURTHER READING

History and culture **366**
Landscape and natural history.................**366**
Architecture **367**
Fiction **367**
Movies set in New England.......................**367**
Other Insight Guides.................................**367**

Maps

New England..**108**
Boston **110**
Cambridge **134**
Boston daytrips...**142**
Salem **144**
Lexington and Concord **153**
Plymouth..**157**
Cape Cod and the Islands **164**
Central Massachusetts.............................**189**
Worcester **190**
Springfield...**196**
Pioneer Valley **198**
The Berkshires..**205**
Rhode Island **214**
Providence **216**
Newport **220**
Connecticut **234**
Hartford...**236**
Vermont and New Hampshire **258**
Burlington **280**
Portsmouth **296**
Manchester **300**
Maine...**324**
Portland **328**
Mount Desert Island **340**
Inside front cover New England
Inside back cover Boston Subway and Boston

LEGEND
○ Insight on
◉ Photo story

THE BEST OF NEW ENGLAND: TOP ATTRACTIONS

△ **New England cuisine**. Lobsters, maple syrup, and organic produce create New England's culinary delights. See page 81.

△ **Mystic Seaport, Connecticut**. An old whaling port, with vessels such as the *Charles W. Morgan*. See page 255.

▽ **White Mountains, New Hampshire**. A vast tract of rugged peaks, hiking trails, and ski slopes, and a unique cog railway. See page 311.

△ **Cape Cod National Seashore**. More than 40 miles (65km) of secluded beaches, vast stretches of sand dunes, crashing surf, and swimming in the bracing Atlantic. See page 168.

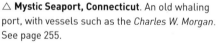

◁ **Acadia National Park, Maine**. The famed rock-bound coast of Maine preserved in a rugged 41,000-acre parkland. See page 339.

▽ **Freedom Trail, Boston, Massachusetts**. Follow the 2.5-mile (4km) red-brick path linking the major Revolutionary War sites. See page 138.

△ **Philip Johnson's Glass House**. The architectural innovator created a new way of considering buildings. See page 247.

△ **Shelburne Museum, Vermont**. Peerless collection of Americana, including the *Ticonderoga*. See page 283.

◁ **Fall foliage**. Leaf-peepers seek out the best spots to marvel at spectacular hues of red, yellow, and orange. See page 160.

▷ **Cottages of Newport, Rhode Island**. Extravagant mansions that are monuments to America's Gilded Age. See page 230.

THE BEST OF NEW ENGLAND: EDITOR'S CHOICE

BEST PARKS

Baxter State Park, ME. This wilderness tract deep in Maine's interior is crowned with Mt Katahdin, the northern terminus of the Appalachian Trail. This is the place to look for moose, black bears ... and supreme solitude. See page 347.
Acadia National Park, ME. Nowhere is the famed "rock-bound coast of Maine" better exemplified – and better preserved – than in this rugged parkland. See page 339.
Kent Falls State Park, CT. Fall Brook cascades down a series of waterfalls as it tumbles its way to the Housatonic River. The park has moderate hiking trails with spectacular views. See page 240.

The Minute Man memorial.

Salem's waterfront.

TOP HISTORIC SITES

Freedom Trail, Boston. Follow the red-brick path that links Boston's most important Revolutionary sites, including the Old State House, the Paul Revere House, the Old North Church, and the 1797 frigate Constitution, alias "Old Ironsides." See page 138.
Lowell National Historical Park, MA. With many of its massive textile mills still intact, the city's core is now a National Historical Park. Tour downtown by canal boat or trolley, and visit a mill where power looms still turn out cloth. See page 150.
Salem Maritime National Historic Site, MA. In the cradle of America's first mercantile fortunes, an old waterfront quarter contains an 1819 Custom House, the home of a merchant prince, and the replica of a 1797 sailing ship. See page 144.
Minute Man National Historical Park, MA. The events of April 18 and 19, 1775, are brought to life on Lexington Green, where Minutemen and British soldiers first exchanged fire, and at Concord's North Bridge, where Revolutionary hostilities began in earnest. See page 151.
Coolidge State Historic Site, VT. The preserved birthplace of President Calvin Coolidge isn't just a single home, but all of Plymouth Notch village. You can visit the house where Coolidge took the oath of office by kerosene lamp on learning of President Harding's death. See page 267.

FINEST MUSEUMS

Boston's Museum of Science

England architecture features the restored 1906 Lake Champlain steamer *Ticonderoga*. See page 283.

Isabella Stewart Gardner Museum, Boston. A Venetian palazzo with fine art, antique furniture, and a flower-filled interior courtyard. See page 130.

Massachusetts Museum of Contemporary Art, North Adams, MA. One of the world's premier venues for the arts of our times. Soaring galleries for visual arts; theaters for dance, music, and film. See page 209.

Springfield Museums, Springfield, MA. Wonderful gathering of five museums of art and history, plus the Dr Seuss Memorial Sculpture Garden, clustered around a park-like quadrangle. See page 195.

Museum of Fine Arts, Boston. One of the world's great museums, whose collections include some of the best Impressionist paintings outside Paris. See page 130.

Shelburne Museum, VT. This matchless collection of Americana, folk and fine art, and vernacular New

Playing at pirates on Cape Cod.

BEST FOR FAMILIES

Mystic Seaport, CT. In this re-creation of a 19th-century waterfront community, shops and chandleries line the narrow streets and the *Charles W. Morgan*, the last surviving American whaling vessel to sail under canvas, rests at wharfside. See page 255.

The "Big E," MA. There are state and county fairs all over New England, but the biggest is the region-wide Eastern States Exposition in West Springfield. Animal exhibits and judging, amusement rides, and big-name acts fill the 175-acre (71-hectare) grounds for 17 days in September. See page 196.

Ben & Jerry's Factory Tour, VT. The tour tells the story of how two

unlikely entrepreneurs created the famous ice cream, revealing the alchemy behind flavors such as Cherry Garcia and Phish Food. See page 272.

ECHO Lake Aquarium and Science Center, Burlington, VT. An all-day adventure that goes far beyond other science centers with its range of explorations from under Lake Champlain, to Native American life, to seeing what you look like as a frog. See page 281.

McAuliffe-Shepard Discovery Center, Concord, NH. Named for New Hampshire's space pioneers, Christa McAuliffe and Alan Shepard, it's a hands-on day of space discovery. See page 302.

Trails on Mount Vermont are popular with both hikers and bikers.

RECOMMENDED HIKES

Appalachian Trail. Linking every state except Rhode Island, the Georgia-to-Maine Appalachian Trail's northernmost portion offers opportunities for day or overnight hiking. See page 288.

The Long Trail. Vermont's rugged trail, which partly overlaps the Appalachian, scales the

Green Mountain peaks. See page 273.

Block Island, RI. Called "one of the 12 best unspoiled areas in the Western Hemisphere," the heritage trail crosses the island's rolling green hills and ends at the dramatic Mohegan Bluffs overlooking the Atlantic. See page 228.

Longfellow House.

TOP COLLEGE TOWNS

Cambridge, MA. Home to Harvard and the Massachusetts Institute of Technology (MIT), both have specialized museums, with Harvard's Fogg Museum (art) and Peabody Museum of Archaeology and Ethnology among the region's finest. Harvard Square bustles with shops, bookstores, restaurants, and clubs; Central Square, near MIT, offers inexpensive eateries and eclectic shops. See page 133.
Hanover, NH. Here is one of the region's loveliest town greens, surrounded by the stately buildings of Dartmouth College. The school's Hood Museum of Art and Baker-Berry Memorial Library are cultural highlights. See page 307.
Burlington, VT. The architectural treasures of the University of Vermont dominate the hilltop above the state's largest city. Church Street Marketplace is lined with boutiques,

bars, and restaurants, and the waterfront sparkles with marinas, a natural history museum, and a bike path. See page 280.
New Haven, CT. This is home to some of America's most spectacular collegiate Gothic architecture, on the campus of Yale University. Yale's impressive array of museums includes a center for British art, a rare book and manuscript library, a museum of natural history, and even a collection of musical instruments. See page 249.
Worcester, MA. Home to 10 colleges, universities, and graduate schools, as well as the Worcester Art Museum and an indoor-outdoor natural history museum with a treetop trail. It is also the northern terminus of the Blackstone River Greenway, which runs from Worcester to Providence, RI. See page 190.

FINEST HISTORIC HOUSES

Gillette Castle, CT. A medieval stone mansion on a site overlooking the Connecticut River in East Haddam. See page 243.
Salem, MA. The homes preserved by the Peabody Essex Museum and Salem Maritime National Historic Site represent the pinnacle of the austerely beautiful Federal style of architecture. See page 143.
Longfellow House, Cambridge, MA. This spacious Georgian mansion was George Washington's headquarters early in the Revolution and was

later the home of Henry Wadsworth Longfellow. See page 137.
Portsmouth, NH. A treasure trove of Georgian and Federal architecture, including the one-time home of naval hero John Paul Jones. See page 296.
Newport Cottages, RI. The greatest monuments to America's Gilded Age are the extravagant mansions along Bellevue Avenue. The Breakers, Rosecliff, The Elms, and other monuments to untaxed riches were used for only a few weeks in summer. See page 230.

The Biological Sciences Building at Harvard.

Cape Cod National Seashore.

BEST BEACHES

Block Island, RI. It's worth the ferry ride to enjoy these uncrowded strands – remote Mohegan Bluffs, calm State Beach, and Surfers Beach. See page 228.

Plum Island, MA. Parking is limited, so there are never towel-to-towel crowds. A bonus: the island is one of the East's premier birding destinations. See page 148.

Cape Cod National Seashore, MA. Options for sunning and (brisk) swimming range from easy-to-reach Nauset in the south to the dune-circled Province Lands and Pilgrim Heights beaches in Provincetown and Truro. See page 168.

Hammonasset State Beach, CT. The gentle, generally warm waters of Long Island Sound wash this broad, superbly maintained beach that has plenty of parking, and changing facilities. See page 251.

TOP SKI AREAS

Stowe, VT. Some trails, including the famous "Front Four" on Mt Mansfield, date from the 1930s. The resort boasts spectacular terrain, aerial gondolas, and superb lodging. See page 273.

Killington, VT. New England's biggest ski area has over 200 trails and nearly three dozen lifts. The resort is a study in superlatives – steepest mogul run, a 3,050ft (930-meter) vertical drop, and a 10-mile (16km) downhill trail. See page 268.

Jay Peak, VT. The most reliable snow cover and a variety of trails: harrowing steeps, long cruising runs, and even a slow skiing zone. See page 277.

Sugarloaf, ME. Plenty of intermediate runs, but nearly half the trails are black diamonds. Glade action is terrific. See page 348.

Sunday River, ME. Offers great grooming, high-speed quad lifts, and a double-diamond mogul run as foil to its more forgiving cruisers. See page 349.

Snowboarding at Sunday River Ski Resort.

Fall foliage in the Berkshires.

Marshall Point Lighthouse, near Port Clyde in Maine.

YANKEE COUNTRY

Old World traditions blended with New World experiences have melded together to create a region with unique character.

Hartwell Tavern, Concord, Massachusetts.

No region in America has a longer or more impressive history than New England. Archeologists say the first "New Englanders" were living here as early as 9000 BC, and the Vikings stopped by briefly in AD 1000. But for most people, New England's history begins with the arrival of the Pilgrims in 1620. In the next 200 tumultuous years, it saw the faltering steps of tenuous settlements become the firm strides of healthy colonies and the creation of an education system unmatched in the other colonies or Mother England. Those led to the desire for self-determination that was so strong, it led to a revolution that created a new country and a new form of government.

The symbols of that history are all around: Plymouth Rock, Lexington, and the Old North Church; the whaling ports of New Bedford and Mystic, the fishing fleets of Maine. The literary world stretches from Mark Twain's Hartford home to Walden Pond and Robert Frost's Vermont cottage. And historic names: Adams (Sam and both Johns, and don't forget Abigail), Ethan Allen, and Nathan Hale.

While other areas respect their history, when a conflict arises between preservation and development the "practicality" of abandoning the old often wins. Not so much in New England, where there's an appreciation that the "old" is what

Exhibit in First Harrison Gray Otis House, Boston.

gives the current world its value. Every town has its historical society, protecting its past and telling its story. It relishes the stereotypes that charm visitors: vivid autumn leaves, patchwork quilts of farms, trim colonial towns, sailboats on its bays, crashing waves against the coast, lighthouses sending their beams of safety into a fog-shrouded night.

But while rooted in the past, New Englanders reach for the future. Its cities are testaments to reuse and renewal; its schools are magnets for innovation and intellectual achievement; its cultural venues pride themselves on their creative visions in music, dance, and theater.

Though small in size compared to the rest of the country, New England offers a vast range of experiences for visitors to enjoy.

The colors of fall melt into the blue hills.

THE LAY OF THE LAND

The Pilgrims believed in a stern, unforgiving God, so perhaps they were not surprised to find themselves in a stern, unforgiving land.

Rocky, infertile soil; treacherous coastline; short, unreliable growing seasons; long, harsh winters. You wonder if the *Mayflower* would have had any passengers if they'd known what awaited them. What was it like – this "new" England that the Pilgrims envisioned as the location of their new home?

New England encompasses 66,672 sq miles (172,680 sq km) and consists of the Commonwealth of Massachusetts and the states of Connecticut, Rhode Island, Vermont, New Hampshire, and Maine. It is bounded by Canada to the north, the Atlantic Ocean to the east, Long Island Sound to the south, and New York State to the west. Moving inland from the coastal lowlands in the south and east, the terrain gradually rises to forested hills and culminates in the weatherbeaten peaks of the Appalachian system, represented by the White Mountains to the north and the Green and Taconic mountains and Berkshire Hills to the west.

A model of the Mayflower in Plymouth, MA.

PANGAEA

The familiar New England landscape was formed by glaciers about 20,000 years ago, but what is now the North American continent started long before that. About 225 million years ago, the earth had just one giant land mass, called Pangaea, which was surrounded by one massive ocean. Through the constant shifting of the ocean floor – plate tectonics – Pangaea began to split apart and drift across the ocean to form the continents that we recognize today. How long Pangaea existed before it started to tear itself apart is unclear, but the granite gneiss and schist peaks of New Hampshire – like Mt Monadnock – are about 400 million years old, and the granite found in eastern Massachusetts is even older – by about another 200 million years. That "Dedham" granite is found in only one

other place – western Africa. Vermont's marble splits the difference. Geologists peg that at about 500 million years old.

THE GLACIAL EFFECT

The modern landscape of New England was created in the last ice age by its glaciers. About 18,000 years ago, the Laurentide ice cap was 2 miles (3km) thick in some places, and stretched as far south as Pennsylvania. As the massive sheet of ice was forced south by its own bulk and gravity, it pushed everything in front of it – rock, soil, and sediment – like a geological bulldozer. If you picture the side of the road after a snowplow has come through, you get an idea of what happened. The rocks and debris scraped up from the road surface at the bottom of the pile of snow are like what the glacier pushed along. And just as that debris is left when the snow melts, the rocks, soil, and sediment from the glacier remained as hills and valleys. Those were dry land on a vast landscape, but it did not stay that way for long. The glaciers did not "retreat" as much as melt, and the water began filling the empty spaces and causing more changes in the land as it coursed through and created the landscape.

Geologists have names for everything the glaciers created: "glacial moraines" are the hills

Bunker Hill. New Hampshire's "notches" – Franconia, Pinkham, and Crawford – are U-shaped valleys gouged by glacial movement. A "cirque" has nothing to do with the acrobats of Cirque du Soleil; it does come from French, however. It means an amphitheater-shaped basin with steep walls, usually found at the head of a glacially formed valley. Tuckerman Ravine is an example.

As the glaciers melted, the sea levels rose and played their own role in creating the landscape. Originally, fresh water filled the low areas of the moraines, like Block Island and Long Island

Sunlight filters through the fall foliage on a Vermont backroad.

of rubble and soil left behind as the glaciers retreated. When the melting water rose around them, the moraines became Cape Cod, Nantucket, and Block Island. Up in Maine, meltwater running along the ground that was under the ice created the finger-like spits of land north and east of Casco Bay – "eskers" – of the Boothbays and Bailey Island. Henry David Thoreau's Walden Pond is a glacial "kettle pond." Those are the holes left when a chunk of ice breaks off from a parent glacier, is surrounded by sediment and rocks, and then melts. Elsewhere, some geologists think the wave action of floodwaters of rapidly melting ice as it ran underneath the land created landforms that look something like solid waves. Called "drumlins," they're the Boston Harbor Islands and

sounds and Narragansett Bay. But the sea levels rose by as much as 400 feet (120m) and breached the moraines, filling them with salt water. Elsewhere, the weight of the glaciers pushed down the land in many places, which meant that seawater came far inland. Originally, Lake Champlain was an inland saltwater sea because the St Lawrence River connected it to the Atlantic. As the glacial debris closed off the ocean's access, the Champlain Sea drained and became the much smaller, freshwater Lake Champlain, but evidence of its former life remains, like the skeleton of a whale found encased in a 10,000-year-old layer of clay near Burlington.

The most famous and easily recognizable glacial landscape feature is "glacial erratics." The famous stone fences lining the pastures of Vermont are made of these – rocks transported and deposited by glaciers from distant geologic formations. The farmers – then and now – wrestling them from the ground undoubtedly thought (and think) of them as something other than merely "erratic."

As the glaciers melted 10,000 years ago, plants and animals suitable for cold climates appeared – caribou, grasses, the trees that would become sugar maples and pine. This was tundra, the same soil and climate found in Alaska and northern Canada. The first humans showed up at about the

were to dominate and tame it. It was a concept as alien to Puritan thinking as dressing in buckskins and using bear grease as a hair conditioner.

The Puritans didn't care that the treacherous shoals off the coast of Maine or the tricky navigation around Cape Cod were the results of eons of geologic activity or that the soil so hard to cultivate was barren because of the scouring action of blocks of ice. They needed to build shelters and plant crops if they hoped to survive. From a psychological perspective, their no-nonsense practicality and conviction that life is supposed to be difficult

The Portland Head Lighthouse in South Portland, Maine.

same time. The earth was warming, and it was gradually creating a climate hospitable for plants to grow and animals and humans to thrive.

THE PILGRIMS' ARRIVAL

By the time the *Mayflower* landed, the region was covered with dense forests filled with game; the rivers provided both drinking water and fish, but they were also the transportation routes and the location for most villages. The Indians did practice some agriculture, but they were a hunter-gatherer society, which practiced what we'd call today sustainable living – taking what was needed and no more and making sure there was enough left for it to regrow or repopulate. They believed in being part of a balance of nature, not that they

⊘ GEORGE PERKINS MARSH

Born in Woodstock VT in 1801, George Perkins Marsh is considered the first environmentalist. Growing up, he witnessed the effects of farming and logging practices. Later, he developed a theory that the actions of humans had a direct effect on the environment. The great civilizations of the Mediterranean, he suggested, had collapsed because of environmental degradation initiated by human activity. Until that time, common wisdom held that all changes were the result of natural phenomena. His 1864 book, *Man and Nature*, explored the interdependence between the natural and man-made worlds.

probably prepared them for the rigors, disappointments, and tragedies they faced. It's as though each obstacle to be overcome hardened them to the next. You have to wonder if they would have remained so stern and so obstinate for so long if they'd made landfall in the Chesapeake, where the 1634 Catholic colony thrived almost immediately, or if they had arrived in May and not November and had a chance to plant a few crops and gather enough food to sustain them over the winter.

Clearing the land was their first priority; without that, there would be no land to cultivate, no way

gone, victims of the changes the settlers were causing to the land.

The clear-cutting of the forest and establishment of agriculture had a profound effect on the region's ecological balance that no one would have understood. The colonists viewed the forests as both an impediment and a commodity; the trees needed to be cleared, but the wood built their houses and ships and was transported to a Europe which had denuded its vast forests centuries before. They believed that the resource was limitless, so they went about har-

George Perkins Marsh.

Storing up firewood for the long winter nights.

to plant crops. Trees were cut down, rocks laboriously dug from the ground and dragged from fields. Only the flat terrain near Lake Champlain was fertile, open farmland, but it was decades before there was any significant settlement there.

There was plenty of game to be had; the written records tell of groups of men leaving the settlement to go "fowling" and of hunting deer. There's no mention of moose; the behemoth wasn't found in the areas the Pilgrims first settled – Massachusetts, Rhode Island, and Connecticut. One wonders what they would have made of them. What they did have were catamounts – mountain lions. They were a real threat as they could attack people, although the animals more usually went after livestock. But within a century, the cats were

vesting it with the industriousness that typified everything about their lives. In the first 150 years of colonization, nearly half of Vermont's 6 million acres (2.4 million hectares) of forest had been cut down. The practice set off a disastrous ecological chain of events. In a land where topsoil was already scarce, clear-cutting led to soil erosion as the land had no protection from the effects of rainfall, snowmelt, or wind which made it even more difficult to farm the already challenging land. With their natural habitats, breeding areas, and food sources depleted or eliminated, wildlife declined or migrated elsewhere, upsetting the balance between prey and predator. That was further exacerbated by the settlers themselves killing wolves, mountain lions, and other predators.

Forage for wild creatures became annoying weeds; damaging insects which had been held in check could overpopulate when the birds which ate them flew away to find new nesting areas.

LOGGING

Like the Indians, the settlers built along what historians call "lines of least resistance," places where it was easiest to find suitable living conditions; notably along waterways. However, the Algonquin, Abenaki, and other native groups deliberately kept their populations small, split-

supplies and equipment needed to build houses and farms. They became a valuable resource in the Industrial Revolution, when the swiftly flowing water powered the machinery that powered the region's economic growth. That came at a cost as, once again, the resource was viewed as a commodity and was used to dispose of industrial waste as well as transport industrial production.

Vermont, to its credit, recognized the damage that had been done. It began a reforestation program in the 1920s. Today, much of the state looks as it did three centuries ago. Grassroots

A rainbow peaks above a New Hampshire valley.

The Pilgrims experienced harsh weather in their first year in New England, including severe rain and snow; although the reports sent back to England focused on the positive rather than dwelling on the harsh conditions.

ting into new groups when one village became too large, and migrated as seasons changed to give areas time to refresh themselves – not unlike modern ideas of crop rotation. The rivers were vital transportation, although in the earliest years, colonists cut crude roadways through the forests, since canoes could never carry the

and state-level programs clean up the waterways. Development is challenged to prove that it won't cause more environmental damage than create economic benefits. In Maine, the long-term efforts to establish a national park which would protect the vast forests from development and over-logging eventually bore fruit in 2016 when president Barack Obama celebrated the 100th anniversary of the National Park Service by creating America's newest reserve, the Katahdin Woods and Waters National Monument, comprising over 87,500 acres of land along the East Branch of the Penobscot River. It seems that the cycle has come full-circle; efforts to restore the forest, land, and water are being pursued with the same energy the Pilgrims and industrial magnates used to exploit them.

DECISIVE DATES

9000 BC
Earliest evidence of human activity in New England, at Shawville VT.

AD 1000
The Viking Leif Erikson discovers Vinland the Good, the location of which remains unknown.

14th–15th centuries
The Algonquin Indians arrive.

1524
Explorer Giovanni da Verrazano travels as far north as Narragansett Bay.

1609
Samuel de Champlain is the first European to visit the lake later named for him.

1620
The Plymouth Company finances a group of 66 Puritans to establish a permanent settlement in North America.

1630
The Massachusetts Bay Colony is founded by John Winthrop with the settlement of Boston.

1636
Harvard College is established. Reverend Roger Williams is banished from the Massachusetts Bay Colony and founds Providence RI.

1692
Salem witch trials: 400 stand accused of sorcery and other crimes. Of those found guilty, 20 are executed.

The pilgrims meet the Indians.

1764
The Revenue Act, imposed by Britain, taxes sugar, silk, and wine.

1765
The Stamp Act taxes commercial and legal documents, newspapers, and playing cards.

1767
The Townshend Acts place harsh duties on paper, glass, and tea. Two regiments of British troops land at Boston to impose order.

1773
Sixty men (disguised as Mohawk Indians) dump tea over the railings of three ships in Boston Harbor in protest against taxes on tea.

1774
Britain retaliates against the Boston Tea Party by closing Boston Harbor. The First Continental Congress convenes at Philadelphia.

1775
Britain and the colonists engage at Lexington in the first battle of the Revolution.

1776
George Washington drives the British from Boston. On July 4, the Declaration of Independence is adopted.

1789
The first cotton mill begins operating in Pawtucket RI.

1800
Poor conditions at Pawtucket lead workers to strike, in the nation's first industrial action.

1831
The abolitionist William Lloyd Garrison founds the weekly *Liberator* newspaper.

1833
New England's first steam railroad opens between Boston and Lowell MA.

1845
Henry David Thoreau builds his cabin at Walden Pond.

1845–50
More than 1,000 Irish immigrants fleeing from the Potato Famine at home arrive in Boston each month.

1852
Uncle Tom's Cabin, by Harriet Beecher Stowe, encourages the abolitionist movement.

1854
The Boston Public Library becomes the world's first free municipal library.

1876
Boston's Museum of Fine Arts opens.

1886
Great Barrington MA pioneers the use of street lights.

1891
Basketball is invented in Springfield MA.

1923
Vermont's Calvin Coolidge becomes US president when Warren Harding dies in office.

1929
The Wall Street crash and the resultant Great Depression hits New England hard. Its manufacturing industry begins a long decline.

1944
A conference at Bretton Woods NH creates the framework for a postwar world monetary system.

1954
The first nuclear submarine, the USS *Nautilus*, is launched at Groton CT.

1960
Massachusetts Senator John F. Kennedy is elected US president.

1992
The Mashantucket Pequot Indians open the controversial but very profitable Foxwoods Casino in Mashantucket CT. It is soon followed by the Mohegan Sun casino.

1997
Sebastian Junger's best-selling book *The Perfect Storm* tells the story of a doomed Gloucester trawler. Hollywood films it in 2000.

2000
Vermont advances gay rights by passing a civil union bill. By 2012 all six New England states recognize same-sex marriages or civil unions.

2002
Controversy rages over aesthetics vs. renewable energy as giant windmills for electrical generation are proposed for Vermont ridgetops and Nantucket Sound.

2003
New Hampshire's iconic rock formation, The Old Man of the Mountain, collapses.

2004
Boston's Red Sox, based at Fenway Park, take the World Series baseball crown for the first time in 86 years. They win again in 2007 and 2013.

2005
Completion of America's biggest-ever public works project, the "Big Dig," which moved Boston's Central Artery underground and added a third harbor tunnel.

2006
Massachusetts passes a health care reform act which mandates that nearly every citizen obtain health insurance.

2007
Massachusetts elects its first African-American governor, Deval Patrick.

2011
Hurricane Irene causes massive flooding and destruction, particularly in Vermont.

2013
Three people are killed and over 260 injured during the 2013 Boston Marathon when terrorists detonate two bombs in the crowd watching the event.

2014
Republican candidate Charles Duane Baker Jr. scores a narrow victory in Massachusetts general election to become the state's 72nd governor.

2016
Donald Trump elected 45th US president; Massachusetts is the first state on the East Coast to legalize recreational use of marijuana.

2018
Massachusetts to hold gubernatorial election in November.

Massachusetts senator Jack Kennedy's campaign buttons, 1960.

BEGINNINGS

The first people arrived in the region around 12,000 BC, but it was the landing of the Pilgrim Fathers in 1620 that changed the face of America.

Although, as the name suggests, it was the English who sowed the seeds of New England's fortune, they were not the first to gaze on these northern shores. Anthropologists generally agree that the first pilgrims reached North America overland from Asia via the then-frozen Bering Straits, arriving on the continent between 12,000 and 25,000 years ago.

The oldest fossil finds of human activity in New England, uncovered in Shawville VT and Wapunucket MA, date respectively to 9000 and 4000 BC and include a variety of spear points, knives, pendants, and ancient house floors. These early settlers were to witness the landing of the Vikings in AD 1000, the first documented European visitors to North America. Initially, the Vikings got on well with the Indians, cordially trading Viking cloth for local furs. But soon hostilities broke out, and the Vikings abandoned the New World.

THE ALGONQUINS

The Algonquins seeped into the New England forests probably sometime during the 14th or 15th century. They did not come in droves; by 1600, no more than 25,000 Indians populated New England, less than one for every 2 sq miles (5 sq km). Nor did this population comprise a unified culture: the Algonquins broke down into at least 10 tribal divisions. Some tribes had no more than 200 or 300 members.

Far from being the nomads of later characterizations, the Algonquins were agricultural and semi-sedentary. Tribal communities moved with the seasons, following established routes restricted to particular tribal domains. In the winter they occupied the sheltered valleys of the interior, in the warmer months the fertile coastal areas.

Early contacts with the local tribes were generally peaceful.

But the Indians had to toil year-round to feed and clothe themselves. With an excellent understanding of agricultural techniques, they grew crops such as beans, pumpkins, and tobacco, but relied most heavily on maize, the Indian corn. Meat and fish sufficiently balanced the vegetable fare. Plentiful moose and beaver, turkey and goose, lobsters and clams, salmon and bass, along with other delectables, made for a varied menu.

PATH TO SETTLEMENT

The early European explorers were not mere adventurers, but determined fortune-hunters seeking an easier passage to the Orient and its treasures. When the Genoese sailor Cristoforo

Colombo (Latinized as Christopher Columbus) was trying to finance his expedition, he spoke of riches and trade. So when he returned with news of an undiscovered continent, but without the gold and spices he promised, he was ridiculed and disgraced.

Columbus' countryman Giovanni Caboto (John Cabot), searching for the Northwest Passage to the East, received slightly better treatment from his patron, Henry VII of England. The first European since the Norse to visit America's northern shores (at Labrador, historians believe), Cabot was

seas. Recognizing conquest and colonization as a path to power, the late-starting English were to take over from the conquistadors as pioneers of the New World.

In 1583, equipped with a royal charter to discover "remote heathen and barbarious land not actually possessed by any Christian prince or people ... and to have, hold, occupy and enjoy" such territories, Sir Humphrey Gilbert was the first Englishman to attempt the settlement of North America. Sailing from Plymouth with his flagship *Delight* and three other vessels, Gilbert

Drawing of an Algonquin village, 1585.

blessed with a huge royal pension of £20 a year after his 1497 expedition. It was a good bargain for the Crown, considering that England based its claim to all America east of the Rockies and north of Florida on the extent of Cabot's exploration.

For most of the 16th century, Spanish conquistadors dominated the New World, where they profitably exploited resource-rich Central and South America. After Cabot's venture, the less inviting and accessible north was largely neglected and the Northwest Passage remained a merchant's dream.

THE ENGLISH TAKE OVER

In the closing decades of the 16th century, Elizabeth I's England eclipsed Spain as master of the

⊘ ALGONQUIN SOCIETY

Politics and state affairs were left in the charge of the *sachem*, a hereditary chief who commanded each tribe. The *powwows*, or medicine men, gained considerable political might as the vicars of Indian religion; they combined healing with religion through mystical rites, and held powerful positions in the tribe.

In no sense did the Algonquins comprise a united nation. Unlike their Iroquois neighbors to the west, no council, senate, or chief-of-chiefs disciplined the Algonquian tribes toward unified action. This lack of unity gave the European settlers an advantage.

intended to establish a trading post at the mouth of the Penobscot River. But after reasserting English control of Newfoundland, he sailed south to disaster: three out of the four ships sank and Gilbert himself died.

The first years of the 17th century saw a renewed interest in exploration. In 1606, James I granted charters for two new ventures, the Virginia Companies of London and Plymouth, giving the latter rights to found a colony somewhere between North Carolina and Nova Scotia. Loaded with the usual arms and foodstuffs, some livestock, and trinkets to trade with the Indians, the first band of 100 adventurers built Fort St George on Parker's Island in Maine. There they wintered but, finding no evidence of precious metals, and the weather "extreme unseasonable and frosty," the group left the following spring.

Recognizing the need to plan more carefully, the Plymouth Company next commissioned the experienced surveyor John Smith to take a critical look at the region's potential for settlement and profit. Smith is credited as the first to give the region its name of "New England."

Eight-year-old Anne Pollard sets foot in Boston (1630).

"Algonquin" is the French word for the tribe. It's thought to be a mispronunciation of elehgumoqik, the Algonquin word for allies. The Algonquin identify themselves as the Anishnabe, which means "original people."

ANSWERING A HIGHER CALL

The explorers of the 16th century were driven by the profit motive. Since they discovered neither the coveted Northwest Passage nor gold and diamonds, they couldn't discern the promise of the New World. Decades of work produced no more than a few crude maps and travelogues.

Renaissance Europe did not foster religious tolerance. Dissent was treason, and heretics mounted the same scaffolds as did traitors. To the Puritans, devotees of more extreme Protestant beliefs than their Church of England (Anglican)

⊘ THE CRUSADE TO CONVERT THE ALGONQUINS

Although the Puritans owed much to the Algonquins for their cooperation in the early days of settlement, and although they professed no racial prejudice against the Indians (one contemporary theory held that they were descended from a lost tribe of Israel), the Puritans soon assumed the task of converting their newfound neighbors from their heathen ways. The Bible was translated into the Algonquian language. The Reverend John Eliot set up a string of "Praying Towns" of Christian Algonquins. During the 1660s and early 1670s, these communities may have accounted for as many as one-fifth of all New England Indians. But the Puritans were looking for more than religious

fellow-travelers; they sought to create nothing less than a breed of neo-Englishmen.

As the historian Alden T. Vaughan concluded, the Indians would have had to "forsake their theology, their language, their political and economic structures, their habitations and clothing, their social mores, their customs of work and play" – in short, commit cultural suicide – to satisfy the Puritans. Several Algonquins were sent to Harvard to receive ministerial training, but only one, Caleb Cheeshahteaumuck, graduated. His portrait was hung in Harvard in 2010. *Caleb's Crossing* by Geraldine Brooks, a novel based on his life, was published in 2011.

countrymen, the symbols of papal domination – jeweled miters, elaborate rituals, and power-hungry bishops – were the devil's work, from which the Anglican establishment had not sufficiently distanced itself. Even more disturbing to the Puritans was the persecution they suffered under James I in his attempts to impose religious conformity.

A group of Puritans from Lincolnshire struck a deal with the Plymouth Company to finance a settlement in the unpopulated north of America. For the Plymouth Company, it was a chance to at least recoup its so-far-wasted investment in the region. If the colony succeeded, the company might actually turn a profit. For the Puritans, it was an opportunity to escape persecution and a corrupt environment and create their idealized society in an unsullied location. In 1620, 66 of these Pilgrims left from Plymouth on the 180-ton *Mayflower*, carrying everything they needed to start and maintain a self-sufficient community. The trip itself was no luxury cruise, and after more than two months at sea the travelers "were not a little joyful" to sight Cape Cod on November 11. Deciding that the sandy cape lacked fresh water and arable land, the group dispatched Captain Myles Standish (nicknamed "Captain Shrimp" because of his height) to find a more fertile site. In mid-December, the Pilgrims disembarked at Plymouth Rock.

The first winter was a miserable ordeal, testing fully the hardened Puritan will. Scurvy, pneumonia, and other infections killed more than half of the settlers, including Governor John Carver. At any one time, no more than six or seven remained in good health. But spring brought better times, notably the signing of a treaty of friendship with the local Indians, one of whom, Squanto, had been temporarily abducted to England by an earlier expedition and now acted as ambassador, recommending mutual cooperation.

HEAVENLY ASPIRATIONS

Acknowledging the contribution of the local people, the Pilgrims hosted a feast of celebration nearing the first anniversary of their arrival. In a three-day harvest celebration, similar to those they knew in England and Holland, both natives and newcomers enjoyed a meal of venison, lobster, clams, and fruits. A few weeks later, 35 freedom-seekers, well stocked with provisions, joined the *Mayflower* survivors, and by the spring of 1624, Plymouth was a thriving village of more than 30 cottages.

In 1628 another group of Puritans, led by Thomas Dudley, Thomas Leverett, and John Winthrop, obtained a royal charter as the Company of the Massachusetts Bay in New England. The next summer, 350 hopefuls arrived at Salem, followed by another 1,500 in 1630. Not only more numerous than the Plymouth Pilgrims but also better financed, the Massachusetts Bay Company founded the town of Boston that year on the Shawmut Peninsula – a neck of land whose only prior English inhabitant had been the scholarly hermit William Blaxton, who

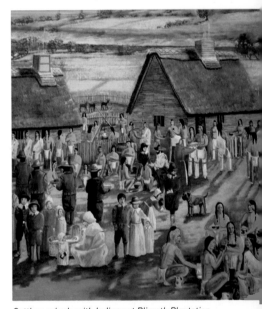

Settlers mingle with Indians at Plimoth Plantation.

promptly removed himself to Rhode Island. As Charles I and Archbishop William Laud tightened the screws of persecution back home, the Massachusetts Bay Colony grew quickly despite primitive conditions.

Growth was not limited to the area of the first landings on the Massachusetts shore. The reverends Thomas Hooker and Samuel Stone, along with former Bay governor John Haynes, left Cambridge for Connecticut, where they settled the towns of Hartford, Wethersfield, and Windsor. Two Londoners, Theophilus Eaton and John Davenport, soon after established themselves at New Haven. The Plymouth Colony had been operating a trading post on Maine's Kennebec River since 1627. The New World's first real estate developers, John Mason and Sir Ferdinando Gorges, tried to capitalize on their vast property grants in New Hampshire and Maine, but these ambitious ventures were humbled by the region's daunting inhospitability.

Elsewhere, groups of New Englanders helped expand the frontiers outside the region. Puritan communities transplanted to New York, North Carolina, and Georgia maintained ties with their old homes. One such group, from Westmorland CT, continued to send representatives to the Connecticut Assembly long after moving to Pennsylvania.

Roger Williams believed in fair dealings with the local people.

THE FOUNDING OF PROVIDENCE

In the early years of Massachusetts Bay, the Reverend Roger Williams took it upon himself to condemn the shackles of imposed religion, preaching from his pulpit in Salem that "forced worship stinks in God's nostrils." His compatriots in the General Court banished him from the colony in 1636.

But Williams did not return to England. He turned instead to Canonicus and Miantonomi, the two Narragansett leaders he had befriended in the course of studying the Indian population. The chieftains saw fit to grant him, gratis, a large tract on the Pawtuxet River. Here, Williams founded Providence. Fellow exiles joined him over the next

few years – Anne Hutchinson (who later died in an Indian attack on her final home on Long Island Sound) and William Coddington on nearby Aquidneck Island, and Samuel Gorton in Warwick.

Though the new settlement grew slowly – from fewer than 20 families in 1638 to no more than 1,000 individuals three decades later – the Providence and Rhode Island plantations proved an unholy thorn in Massachusetts' underbelly. No kind words here. The unholy partisan rhetoric makes Parliamentary and Congressional sniping sound like tributes to Mother Teresa. Hutchinson, with her "very voluble tongue," lambasted her former parish with "Call it whore and strumpet not a Church of Christ," while back in Massachusetts, the ordinarily restrained Cotton Mather continually insulted the colony as the "fag end of creation," "the sewer of New England," and, ever so cleverly, "Rogue's Island."

But Rhode Island lived up to its intent, and religious freedom was guaranteed by a 1663 royal charter. It welcomed New England's first Jewish émigrés in 1662, along with scores of Quakers and French Huguenots.

VIOLENCE BREAKS OUT

Missionary zeal alienated many of the Indians, but it was empire-building that led to bloodshed. At first, there was plenty of room for the Indians and settlers to coexist peacefully. About a third of the Algonquin inhabitants had fallen victim to a great plague in the early 1600s, which may have been illnesses brought by the first explorers and against which the Indians had no

⦿ PURITAN INTOLERANCE

The 19th-century social satirist Artemus Ward (real name: Charles Farrar Browne) once observed: "The Puritans nobly fled from a land of despotism to a land of freedom, where they could not only enjoy their own religion, but could prevent everybody else from enjoying his." Dictating rules of conduct not just for the church but for all worldly pursuits, the Puritans were far less tolerant of social or theological deviation than their oppressors back in England had been. Indeed, in 1661, the king himself intervened to protect Quakers in the Bay Colony after several were hanged publicly on Boston Common. As often the case in American history, injustice belied the slogans of liberty.

immunity, leaving their lands under populated when the *Mayflower* landed. But, as the ambitious English settlements expanded and pushed

> Mary Richardson was captured during King Philip's War (1675–76) and held for eleven weeks before being ransomed for £20. Her book, The Capture and Restoration of Mrs. Mary Richardson, was a best seller.

wigwams) in one of the fiercest battles ever fought on New England soil. The Indian will was broken; for them, the war had been a holocaust.

For the settlers, their initial ascetic zeal and belief that they could create an unchallenged theocracy had been tempered by the realities of life in a rugged wilderness, internal philosophical disagreements, and the worldly temptations of material gain and power. While religion still played an important role in setting the tone of discussions and decision, political power would be the rallying call of a new era.

King Philip's War, a vicious conflict in 1675–76, broke the Indian spirit.

south, friction between the two peoples was the inevitable result.

In 1636 war erupted with the Pequots (a fearsome tribe whose name means "destroyer" in Algonquian), and battles at Fort Mystic and Fairfield CT, saw several hundred lives lost on both sides. It was King Philip's War (1675–76), however, that marked the demise of Indian society in most of New England. The Nipmuc, Narragansett, and Wampanoag forces, nominally led by Philip (whose real name was Metacomet), suffered from chronic tribal disunity and were outnumbered by at least five to one. At the "Great Swamp Fight" near present-day South Kingston RI, 2,000 Narragansetts were slain (many of them women and children trapped in burning

⊘ ORGANIZING THE NEW WORLD

Some 2,000 immigrants arrived each year between 1630 and 1637, and new communities such as Ipswich, Dorchester, Concord (the first inland village), Dedham, and Watertown sprang up. In 1636, the Puritan clergy established Harvard College to train future ministers. The Great and General Court – to this day the name of the Massachusetts legislature – was formed to manage administrative and judicial affairs, a governor and deputy governor being indirectly chosen by the colony's freeholders. At the town level, landowners convened to discuss problems – a practical arrangement since, even as late as 1700, the average town included no more than 200 or 300 families.

BIRTH OF A NATION

Lexington Green's "shot heard round the world" in 1775 heralded the start of the American Revolution and the struggle for independence.

The colonies of New England had, for the most part, been left to their own devices from the first landing at Plymouth. Suffering serious political turmoil in the early 17th century, highlighted by the beheading of Charles I, England had little time to attend to the governing of dissident settlers 3,000 miles (4,800km) from London. The Puritans gladly filled the vacuum and took on the responsibilities of de facto autonomy.

PURITAN VALUES

Even before reaching their destination, the Pilgrims signed the famous Mayflower Compact, creating a government "to enact, constitute, and frame such just and equal Laws, Ordinances, Acts, Constitutions, and offices, from time to time, as shall be thought most meet and convenient for the general good." John Winthrop and his followers carried with them their royal charter when they sailed to Massachusetts, and in 1631 the freemen of the new colony gave an oath of fidelity not to the king but to the Bay Company and its officers. The settlers agreed that if England tried to impose its own governor on them, "we ought not to accept him, but defend our lawful possessions."

Fifty-five years later, they were given the chance. In 1686, James II unilaterally revoked the northern colonies' sacred charters and consolidated English holdings from Maine to New Jersey into a vast Dominion of New England in America. The monarch justified his decision as a security measure, a benevolent protection from the French and Indians. The Puritans were not convinced. They scorned the king's first envoy, Joseph Dudley, an avid Anglican, as having "as many virtues as can consist with so great a thirst for honor and

Patriot Paul Revere's famous ride.

power." They branded his successor, Edmund Andros, "the greatest tyrant who ever ruled in this country."

A strong cue from England itself moved New England to action and revolt. At the "Glorious Revolution" of early 1689, William and Mary, in cahoots with Parliament, seized the throne from James II. New England spontaneously erupted; Andros and his cronies were dragged from state house to jail cell. The old powers of self-government were largely restored, along with a certain mutual respect between Crown and colonies.

A later English king, George III, presided over the loss of Britain's New World empire. Initial attempts by London to raise taxes in

New England were successfully resisted. But in 1767 Britain's Chancellor of the Exchequer, Charles Townshend, boasted: "I dare

Paul Revere's famous ride ended when he was stopped by a British patrol just west of Lexington. Luckily, two men riding with him, William Dawes and Dr Samuel Prescott, were able to escape and warn the Minutemen.

orders, others followed, and, after the smoke had cleared, three colonists lay dead (including a black man named Crispus Attucks) and two were mortally wounded. The American revolt had its first martyrs, and the growing anti-British element in New England had a field day with the incident.

Tempers cooled briefly. Parliament struck down the Townshend Acts – all except one, that is. To assert the king's authority, and to try to raise at least some revenue, Britain maintained the tax on East Indian tea, a not insignificant

The Boston massacre of March 5, 1770.

tax America." Parliament passed the Townshend Acts, imposing duties on such imports as paper, glass, and tea. Two regiments of British troops landed at Boston to put some muscle behind the waning control of Governor Thomas Hutchinson.

THE BOSTON MASSACRE

The Redcoats were not well received. On the night of March 5, 1770, a crowd of several hundred rowdy Bostonians gathered to taunt a lone "lobster-back" standing guard outside the customs house on King Street (present-day State Street). When shouts turned to stones and snowballs, seven Redcoats came to aid the sentry. One fired into the melee without

gesture given that tea then was as important as a Starbuck's latté is now.

American addicts turned to smuggled Dutch blends or to "Liberty Tea," a nasty brew made from sage, currant, or plantain leaves. The British responded by subsidizing their brand and, in September 1773, flooded the market with about half a million pounds of their product, with shipments to ports all along the eastern seaboard. It didn't work.

Boston emerged once again as the focus of resistance. The Massachusetts Committee of Correspondence, an unofficial legislature, and the Sons of Liberty, a fast-growing secret society at the forefront of revolutionary activism, demanded that Governor Hutchinson send home the tea-laden *Dartmouth*.

When he refused, the protesters' reaction was swift and calculatedly theatrical. On December 16, 60 men (among them Sam Adams and John Hancock), disguised as Mohawk Indians, descended on the *Dartmouth* and two sister ships. Boston Harbor was turned into a teapot as they dumped 342 crates over the railings. The Boston Tea Party, as it came to be called, was a display of profound disrespect to parliament and the king. Parliament responded with the "Coercive" Acts. Most infamously, the Boston Port Act sealed off the city by naval block-

First News of the Battle of Lexington by William Tylee Renney (1813–57).

ade. The First Continental Congress convened angrily in Philadelphia on September 5, 1774. Revolution was at hand.

A SHOT HEARD ROUND THE WORLD

An uneasy stalemate prevailed until the spring of 1775. British garrisons controlled only the major towns. The countryside became virtually unpoliceable. New Englanders stockpiled arms and ammunition to prepare for the inevitable conflict.

In early April 1775, London instructed Boston commander General Thomas Gage to quash seditious activities in rural Massachusetts, where a Provincial Congress had

assumed de facto governmental control. Late on April 18, Gage dispatched a contingent of 700 soldiers to destroy a makeshift arms depot in Concord, 20 miles (32km) west of Boston. At Lexington, 70 citizen soldiers, the original Minutemen (those who could be summoned for duty at a minute's notice), lay in wait for the British, having been forewarned by the daring early-morning rides from Boston of patriots Paul Revere and William Dawes.

The two forces met on the town common. A musket was fired. Minutes later, eight Americans lay dead. The British continued on to Concord, where the colonial militia triggered, in Ralph Waldo Emerson's words, "the shot heard round the world." The Minutemen made up for their lack of numbers by employing unconventional guerrilla tactics, harassing the enemy with crack sniper fire. By nightfall they had killed 273 British soldiers.

As the British retreated to Boston, officers lost control of their men, who began ransacking homes and taverns, attacking those they found inside. "The devastation committed by the British troops on their retreat," reported one sensationalized and exaggerated account, "is almost beyond description, such as plundering and burning of dwelling houses and other buildings, driving into the street women in childbed, killing old men in their houses unarmed."

INDEPENDENCE IS DECLARED

The war's first year did not go well for Britain and on July 4, 1776, the Declaration of Independence was adopted by the Continental Congress. Of the signatories, 14 came from the charter states of Massachusetts, Connecticut, New Hampshire, and Rhode Island. Except for Newport RI, not taken from the British until October 1779, New England had achieved its independence.

After the Treaty of Paris ended the Revolutionary War in 1783, the magnates of New England's prosperous cities turned to protect their newly established interests as the 13 independent colonies hammered out an integrated union. Concerned that a centralized federal government would prove as insensitive to local sentiment as had the Crown, revolutionary heroes Sam Adams and John

Hancock gave only grudging support to the Constitution. Rhode Island, in more than a dozen votes between 1787 and 1789, voted it down and ratified it only after the Bill of Rights was added.

THE INDUSTRIAL AGE

New England's leaders became increasingly reactionary as they guarded their economic interests. In Massachusetts, poor hill farmers rose against the state government in Shays' Rebellion of 1786, demonstrating that genuine equality remained a dream. In 1812, fearing the loss of a thriving maritime trade, New England firmly opposed renewed and greater conflict with Great Britain.

But the first two decades of the 19th century showed how vulnerable maritime trade was to the whims of international politics. The Napoleonic Wars, President Thomas Jefferson's Embargo Acts, and the War of 1812 severely hampered New England's chase after an honest, apolitical dollar. Recognizing that it is best not to put all one's commercial eggs in one flimsy

Soldiers at the Battle of Bunker Hill, 1775.

⊘ THE BATTLE OF BUNKER HILL

The Battle of Bunker Hill broke out in June 1775 on the Charlestown Peninsula, across the Charles River from Boston. To consolidate control of overland access to the port city, Continental Army general Artemas Ward ordered the fortification of Bunker's Hill (as it was then known), although it was actually on adjoining Breed's Hill that the Americans dug in.

The British could not allow such a build-up if they were to entertain even the faintest hope of holding Boston. On June 17, Redcoats scaled Breed's slopes twice but were rebuffed. In a desperate third attempt they succeeded, but only because the colonial force had exhausted its supply of ammunition. It was for this reason, and not out of bravery, that Colonel William Prescott issued his famous command: "Don't fire until you see the whites of their eyes, men."

Bunker Hill was a costly victory for the Crown, which suffered more than 1,000 casualties. Optimism, seen in remarks like General John Burgoyne's "We'll soon find elbow room," was reduced to the doubting reflections of another British officer, "This victory has cost us very dear indeed... Nor do I see that we enjoy one solid benefit in return, or are likely to reap from it any one advantage whatever." Less than a year later, under siege by George Washington, Gage, General Gage evacuated his troops to Halifax.

basket, its merchants turned to the herald of a new industrial age.

THE MACHINE AGE

In the fall of 1789, a teenage Samuel Slater sailed from England to New York disguised as a common laborer, defying British laws forbidding the emigration of skilled mechanics. For seven years he had apprenticed to Jedediah Strutt, a partner of the famed innovator Richard Arkwright, and knew the specifications of Arkwright's factory-sized cotton-spinning machine.

The USS Constitution takes on the British Navy in 1812.

In America, the reduction of raw cotton was still being done by laborers working in their own homes on individual looms. An early attempt at consolidating the process, a mill at Beverly MA, had been a failure owing to the crudeness of its machinery. Arkwright's device, already proven across the Atlantic, was the answer, so Quaker financier Moses Brown engaged Slater to come to Providence and put his knowledge to use. Together, they built America's first successful cotton mill on the Blackstone River at Pawtucket.

With underpaid workers kept at the grind for 70 hours a week, Pawtucket became the site of the nation's first strike in 1800. It was left to Bostonian Francis Cabot Lowell (from the family that would later produce a Harvard president, a celebrated astronomer, and three poets) to take a more enlightened approach.

During a two-year visit to England, Lowell became an avid industrial tourist and, on his return to Massachusetts, he was determined to duplicate British weaving feats. Putting up $10,000 of his own money, he collected another $90,000 from the so-called "Boston Associates" – the families of Lawrence, Cabot, Eliot, Higginson, and others – to establish a small mill (with a power loom and 1,700 spindles) at Waltham.

A "COMMERCIAL UTOPIA"

Lowell died in 1817, but his plans were realized by his associates under the aegis of the Merrimack Manufacturing Company. In 1820, the mill

⊘ BOSTON: THE ATHENS OF AMERICA

Colonial New Englanders enriched their intellectual life by founding such pioneer colleges as Harvard, Yale, Dartmouth, and Brown. As the 19th century progressed, and with the interest on their old China Trade money compounded tremendously via investment in the new manufacturing technologies, Boston's first families sponsored a new round of institutions that would lend weight to the city's position as "the Athens of America."

The Handel and Haydn Society dates from 1815, the New England Conservatory of Music from 1867, and the Boston Symphony Orchestra – founded and supported for 40 years by the arch-Brahmin Major Henry Lee

Higginson – from 1881. The BSO is the parent organization of the less classically oriented Boston Pops, and makes its summer home at the renowned Tanglewood music festival in the Berkshires. Boston's magnificent Museum of Fine Arts (1876) evolved from a collection room in the Boston Athenaeum – itself a great New England Institution, founded in 1807 and still one of America's premier privately owned libraries (there are only 1,049 proprietary shareholders).

Governor John Winthrop believed strongly in aristocratic rule. He wrote: "A democracy is, among civil nations, accounted the meanest and worst of all forms of government."

was moved to a tract on the Merrimack River, just above the village of Chelmsford.

The Merrimack Company took care of its people. Though grievously overworked by modern standards, "mill girls" enjoyed clean, safe dormitory housing and opportunities for cultural enrichment. New England's first company town was, in the words of the English novelist Anthony Trollope, "the realization of commercial utopia." Soon the efficient new factory system – if not its early paternalism – would spread up the Merrimack River to Lawrence MA and ultimately to the vast Amoskeag mills at Manchester NH, destined to become the greatest producer of cotton cloth on earth.

LIFE ON THE FRONTIER

Not everybody shared in the boom. During the second half of the 18th century, the northern areas of New England had enjoyed a dramatic infusion of people, as land began to grow scarce in the densely populated coastal areas. More than 100 new towns were established in New Hampshire in the 15 years preceding the

Boston's Old State House, around 1801.

☉ TRADING IN RUM, MOLASSES, AND SLAVES

When not calling comrades to religious or political barricades, the colonial New Englander attended to the more practical pursuit of commerce: it was both out of the seas and on the seas that New England's money was made. Codfish provided a lucrative export to Catholic Europe, while whaling provided oil for lighting and lubricants.

New England was at the pivot of the profitable Triangle Trade: in harbors like Newport, a fleet of 350 ships unloaded West Indian molasses and reloaded the ships with tons of rum. From there, the rum was transported to Africa, where it was traded for kidnapped slaves who were shipped to the West Indies and, in

turn, traded for molasses. It was a cyclical venture that brought much profit to the New Englanders, and untold suffering to the trafficked slaves.

New England shipyards gained world fame for crafting swift, easily managed ocean-going vessels, a tradition launched even before Pilgrim settlement with the 1607 construction of the *Virginia* in the short-lived Popham colony in Maine. Although disrupted by the Revolution, maritime trade bounced back quickly, mining the riches of China and India so coveted by the early American explorers. In 1792, Boston's *Columbia* threaded the Straits of Magellan en route to Canton to trade for tea, spices, silk, and opium.

Revolution; between 1790 and 1800, the populations of Vermont and Maine nearly doubled.

On the craggy hillsides, the pioneers set up small farms, built their own houses and barns, and raised wheat, corn, pigs, and cattle to fill the dinner table. These rugged families prided themselves on being almost completely self-sufficient; in fact, it used to be said of upcountry farms that all they needed to import were nails and salt. This was a new frontier, New England's frontier.

But this frontier's potential was limited by nature. The climate was inhospitable: in 1816, for instance, a June snowfall resulted in total crop failure. Agricultural machinery could not plow the irregular farmland. As for those famous New England stone walls, they were in actuality a practical by-product of what many disillusioned farmers called the region's prime produce: rocks. Property consolidation was difficult, as families jealously guarded original claims; small-scale production could not compete with more efficient new suppliers elsewhere in the United States and around the world. As far as agriculture was concerned, northern New England had seen its zenith by 1850.

After that, a slow, sapping decline attacked upland vitality. By the turn of the century, population growth had leveled and agricultural production dived. More than half of New Hampshire's farmland lay abandoned. Cheese production in Maine, New Hampshire, and Vermont fell by 95 percent between 1849 and 1919. The

California Gold Rush of 1849 drew young men from the farms. The Civil War took away even more, with veterans often heading west to seek their fortunes rather than returning to their fathers' stony acres. And girls went to the Massachusetts mills.

ATHENAEUMS FOR ALL

Boston had become established as the center of cultural activities. Elsewhere, Salem's Peabody Essex Museum was founded, in part as a repository of curiosities brought home by the

One of an outstanding collection of 19th-century figureheads in Salem's Peabody Museum.

city's far-faring merchant captains. In Hartford, the Wadsworth Athenaeum was founded as an art museum in 1842 by local businessman Daniel Wadsworth ("atheneum" or "athenaeum" was a cultural catch-all title in the 19th century). New England was a leader in the concept of libraries being in the public domain. In 1854, the Boston Public Library became the world's first free municipal library. Cradle of the Revolution, pioneer in commerce and industry, and now America's cultural capital – New England had shown its leadership in one realm after another. But as the 20th century approached, it would have to face a challenge not of invention, but re-invention.

⊘ THE STAMP ACT

Needing to cover the cost of keeping troops in the colonies, Britain's parliament passed a Revenue Act in 1764 taxing on sugar, silk, and certain wines. The infamous Stamp Act followed a year later, requiring that all commercial and legal documents, newspapers, and playing cards be taxed. The measure was fiercely assailed. Stamp distributors were hanged in effigy and ridiculed at mock trials. Liberty was buried in symbolic funerals. New Englanders, who had no say in electing British parliamentarians, argued that there should be no taxation without representation. Britain's prime minister, William Pitt, responded by repealing the Stamp Act in March 1766.

THE SHAKERS

These disciplined people were famous for their unique way of life, their manner of worship, and their influential craftsmanship.

The founder of the United Society of Believers in Christ's Second Appearing was Ann Lee, born in 1736 in Manchester, England. An illiterate factory worker, she was a woman of deep convictions at a time of religious persecution. Lee became the spiritual leader of a group of dissidents from the Anglican Church called the "Shaking Quakers" because of the movements they made as the Holy Spirit took hold of them and purged their sins. They became known as the Shakers, and their cultural contributions to furniture design and music have lasted through the centuries.

Persecuted and sent to jail, Lee had a vision that she had a mission to teach a new way of life, one where men and women were equal, free from lust, greed, and violence, with their lives governed by material and spiritual simplicity. She was convinced that only through celibacy could men and women further Christ's kingdom on earth.

After a second vision, Lee and eight followers set sail for New York in 1770. It was not until the 1780s, however, that converts were attracted in great numbers. Mother Ann died in 1783, soon after a proselytizing tour of New England and before the full flowering of Shakerism. At its peak in the 1840s, more than 6,000 members lived in 19 communities.

The Shakers, officially known as the United Society of Believers in Christ's Second Appearing, aimed for perfection in life. Devoted to orderliness and simplicity, they were also dedicated to such progressive notions as sexual equality (facilities for men and women were identical and jobs were shared on a rotation), and they welcomed technological advances that might improve the quality of their work. They were inventors (of, for instance, the circular saw and clothes pegs).

The Shakers ran model farms and, as keen gardeners, were the first to packet and sell seeds; they also marketed medicinal herbs. They sold their meticulously crafted baskets, boxes, chairs, and textiles. By blending discipline, business acumen, ingenuity, and superb craftsmanship, they achieved prosperity, both spiritual and financial.

Celibacy, a key principle, made it difficult for communities to renew themselves, but their ranks were swelled by converts, and orphans were adopted. Numbers dwindled after the mid-1800s, though,

The Shaker dance was an integral part of worship.

and today just a handful of "Believers" remain, in Sabbathday Lake ME. Shaker ideals of simplicity and practicality live on, however, in a legacy of architecture, furniture, and crafts.

The villages at Canterbury NH and Hancock MA are preserved as museums, where visitors watch craftsmen make baskets, boxes, and chairs in the Shaker manner. In the Dwelling Houses they can see the efficient kitchens, the wall pegs on which chairs and utensils were hung, and the built-in cupboards designed so that no dust could accumulate on top or underneath.

The Shakers were one of the first societies to have gender equality, which was institutionalized in the 1780s, long before the concept became common elsewhere.

EVOLUTION AND REINVENTION

When jobs and political influence left the region, New England responded by developing new opportunities and addressing emerging economic and environmental concerns.

By the beginning of the modern era, New England had come to represent America's achievements and ideals – or, conversely, it could be said that America was New England writ large. But no one looking at the American social and economic landscape in 1900 could doubt that the nation's energy and drive now found their sources in other places – in the dynamo of New York, in the raw busy cities of the Midwest, and even in upstart California.

The changes began with the vanishing of the ethnic and religious homogeneity which had aided the old political consensus. Uprooted by the Potato Famine of 1845–50, the Irish sailed to the land of opportunity, arriving in Boston at a rate of more than 1,000 a month. Immigrants from Quebec and throughout Europe followed: Catholics, Jews, and Orthodox Christians upset Protestant homogeneity. The influx touched every corner of New England; the waves of immigration meant that "New Englanders" had adopted, not inherited, the American flag.

Mayor James Curley, a legend in Boston.

ELECTORAL CORRUPTION

In the wake of this human shock wave, an anti-immigrant backlash erupted among the established citizenry, whose forebears had ironically fought so hard to achieve democracy and equal rights. The doors of society were shut to even the most successful of the new arrivals, and their children and grandchildren. In the 1850s, openly racist legislatures controlled Massachusetts, Rhode Island, Connecticut, and New Hampshire. Anti-immigrant organizations, such as the American Protective Association and the Immigrant Restriction League, attracted substantial memberships in their efforts to limit the electoral power of the new arrivals.

Poverty was endemic. In 1930, only 81 out of 5,030 apartments in Boston's North End had refrigerators. Only one in two had bathrooms.

Their efforts failed. No matter how unfamiliar the immigrants were with the workings of democracy when they arrived, they soon learned the power of political organization – particularly the Irish. In 1881, John Breen, born in Tipperary, became the first Irish-born politician to take high office when he was elected as mayor of Lawrence MA. His triumph launched the Irish not only into political influence but also to political domination of Massachusetts and Rhode

Island politics. Hugh O'Brien, a journalist, won the mayoral election in Boston three years later, and Patrick Andrew Collin won a congressional seat in Washington. By the turn of the century, all levels of government were being run by what was, after all, the majority of the population.

But with newfound responsibility came insidious corruption. In Rhode Island, Providence was run by a political machine that openly paid between $2 and $30 per vote, depending on the candidate. Even astute leaders were often as corrupt as they were effective. James Michael

THE BULLDOZERS MOVE IN

By the 1950s, it was clear that the economic malaise was not confined to factories; New England's cities and towns were also showing their age. One remedy was renovation. Boston led the way by establishing a redevelopment authority. Without sacrificing the charm of its venerable Beacon Hill and Back Bay neighborhoods, the Massachusetts capital set about remaking its downtown into a new landscape of modern civic structures, office buildings, and apartments. Providence RI is considered the example of how to

A busy Boston wharf in the late 19th century.

Curley, major of Boston for five terms and governor of Massachusetts for one, improved the economic conditions of his less-privileged constituents. But he doled out jobs and money to community leaders who made sure voting in their neighborhoods went his way.

JOBS AND CAPITAL MIGRATE

Days of industrial glory passed as industrial jobs migrated south, where wages were 20–50 percent lower than in New England. The South also remained relatively free of labor unions, a distinct advantage to employers with bitter memories of the strikes that shut down textile mills in Lawrence MA in 1912 and at the Amoskeag mills in Manchester NH in 1922.

do it right; the revitalized downtown Riverwalk is a magnet for recreation, shopping, dining, and festivals like WaterFire. Yet in keeping with the sorry tradition, the mayor who supervised the resurrection – Buddy Cianci – was convicted of corruption.

Other cities followed suit, with greater and lesser degrees of success; from Portland ME to Rutland VT, noble old train stations and civic buildings came crashing down, with the wrecker's ball tearing all too freely into the downtown streets of Victorian-era buildings around them. Often, the result was a bland city center of sterile office plazas and suburban-style malls. The smaller and more economically disadvantaged cities usually came out best in the long run: places like Newburyport MA and New London

CT inadvertently saved their old downtowns by neglecting them until restoration and adaptive reuse had become popular.

Urban renewal would have been simply window dressing without a revival of the regional economy. Salvation would have to come through exploitation of New England's particular resources. But what were they? They certainly weren't oil, gas, or minerals. Just about the only thing of value taken from New England ground was the granite and marble and marble stone from the quarries of Vermont. Manufacturing

computer age. Schools already known for their liberal arts programs expanded into the new world of technology. MIT with its emphasis on research and innovation and Worcester Polytechnic Institute with its focus on practical application became leaders in evolving engineering and computer sciences.

By the 1970s, Route 128 – the beltway surrounding Boston and its inner suburbs – was touted on official road signs as "America's Technology Highway." Raytheon and Microsoft, among others, plugged in here. Massachusetts General

The Weave Room at the Boott Cotton Mills Museum.

hadn't disappeared altogether, either; the Bath Iron Works in Maine still built ships for the Navy, and there were still specialty textile, footwear, and machinery factories scattered throughout the six states. But these were hardly growth industries. When New England searched for the key to future prosperity, it looked to its most protean and dependable resource of all: its people.

More precisely, it looked to people and to education, one of the oldest New England pursuits. When it became clear that the high technology and financial service sectors would become prime drivers of the American economy, New England was ready. The concentration of colleges and universities in the Boston area provided a splendid resource at the dawn of the

Hospital and other medical institutions conduct research, often in conjunction with MIT's biotechnology labs and Harvard's medical school.

A NEED FOR NEW DIRECTIONS

High technology gave a boost to the burgeoning financial services industry. Boston became an investment banking capital, and the center of the mutual-fund business. John Hancock, Fidelity, Putnam, and MFS all headquartered here. In Hartford, two dozen insurance companies, dominated by titans such as Aetna, call the Connecticut capital home.

High technology and finance have been at the core of the boom-and-bust cycle of the past quarter-century. Both industries flew high in the mid-1980s and again in the late 1990s, and both hit the ground hard when the economy crashed in the 2000s. But while the cities are suffering severely, diversification is easing the effects regionwide. New England has not suffered as much as other regions of the country from the steep decline in housing values that accompanied the mortgage crisis of 2007 and 2008 – in large part, most analysts believe, because real estate prices in the six states simply hadn't gone along for as wild a ride during the boom that preceded the bust. There weren't many places here where developers had overbuilt, flooding the market.

The diversification of the region's economy ranges from "electronic cottages," in which

> "The political condition of Rhode Island is notorious, acknowledged and it is shameful," wrote influential journalist Lincoln Steffens. "Rhode Island is a State for sale and cheap."

Boston City Hall, built in the 1960s, was much criticized for its architectural style of New Brutalism.

⊘ THE GREAT DEPRESSION TAKES ITS TOLL

With few alternatives to manufacturing, New England was particularly hard hit by the Depression. Unemployment in factory towns left idle a quarter of the total labor pool. Even the mighty Amoskeag mills in New Hampshire finally closed their doors in 1935. In Boston it cramped even upper-class lifestyles, but the worst hardships were suffered in the already squalid working-class quarters. Here, wages halved, and unemployment was almost 40 percent after the 1929 Wall Street crash. By the end of 1935, nearly a quarter of Manchester's families were receiving public welfare.

Like the rest of the country, New England was rescued from the Depression by America's involvement in World War II. Shipyards hummed in Bath ME and Quincy MA. In Hartford, Springfield, and even Island Pond VT workers assembled machinery and weaponry for the Allied armies.

But the resurging economy slumped again after V-E and V-J Day. Peace came to a New England that still hadn't solved its core economic difficulties – the migration of jobs to states where labor was cheaper, the aging of the manufacturing infrastructure, and a location that was at the outer corner of America's transportation network, instead of at its center. New Englanders were forced to come up with creative solutions, taking advantage of the region's natural bounty.

individuals run publishing, consulting, and other businesses from their homes, to the traditional pursuits of farming, logging, and fishing.

Life hasn't been easy for people involved in those primary industries. Dairy farmers, mostly centered in Vermont, have seen their ranks dwindle as expenses spiral and milk prices stagnate. The forest products industry struggles against foreign competition and high energy costs; throughout northern New Hampshire and Maine, paper mills – once reliable blue-collar employers – have closed, while the vast tracts of woodlands

Lobsterman at Penobscot Bay, Maine.

owned by their parent companies increasingly have been sold, to face the possibility of subdivision and vacation-home development.

Alarmed by this threat to the integrity and wildness of the "Great North Woods" that ranges from northern Maine to New York State, activists have proposed – and, in the northeastern corner of Vermont, have accomplished – government purchase and protection of large swaths of forest. Despite opposition from some Maine senators and governors, the lobbying for the establishment of a preserved area that would take in much of the Maine woods proved successful and in 2016 president Barack Obama inaugurated the Katahdin Woods and Waters National Monument. It covers an area of more than 87,500 acres of forestland in

Maine's North Woods and the East Branch of the Penobscot River.

Along the Atlantic coast, fishing fleets have seen the depletion of the cod stocks, shrimp and lobster populations mainly due to overfishing and warming up of coastal waters. They are struggling to stay afloat in the face of high fuel costs, permit fees, and restrictions of the size of their catch. That same price spiral applies to heating and transportation, in a region more heavily dependent on oil for heat than any other in the United States. As for the third great consumer of energy, electrical generation, New Englanders are eager to innovate in a "green" direction, but argue as to which technologies to embrace. Controversy swirls around proposals to erect giant windmills in Nantucket Sound, where they would be visible from Cape Cod shores, and on ridgelines in northern Vermont, which might spoil famous views. Dozens of grassroots and more formally organized groups work to address the problems locally and network to develop a consensus and action plans to solve them on a regional level.

Once again, the region's educational institutions are playing a major role in addressing the ecological issues. With student bodies facing a future shaped by how the problems are solved, there's been a growth in courses of study which concentrate on ecological concerns. Scientific programs in everything from marine biology to forest management and sustainable agricultural practices are routinely offered at many schools, as are new fields like environmental economics.

PLENTY TO ARGUE ABOUT

Argument and controversy, of course, have long been bread and butter to New Englanders. Budget issues are always hot topics, even when the economy is booming. With the economic crisis hitting municipal and personal pocketbooks, passionate, often bitter, debates rage over how to balance the books – if that's even possible – while still providing essential services. The arguments revolve around the definition of "essential." On both the state and local levels, many expenditures are mandated by law – in some areas, as much as 80 percent of the budget is required to be spent on mandated programs and allocations, like Medicare (government-sponsored healthcare for senior citizens) and various welfare programs. That leaves little flexibility or cash to fund education, libraries, infrastructure maintenance, social programs, police and fire departments, or recreation. Each affected group makes a strong argument that budget-balancing should come at the expense of someone else. About the only common ground is the conviction that raising taxes to raise revenue is unacceptable. The polarization of political parties on the national level largely angers voters "back home." Most polls show that the voters want to see compromise and action on national issues, even as they often resist yielding on anything at their local level.

Wind power is being used in places as diverse as ski resorts in Vermont and wastewater treatment facilities in Massachusetts, but many opponents say they mar the mountain views so vital to New England's tourist economy.

Boston's modern waterfront.

⊘ ELECTION IMPORTANCE

"Independent" is the operative political word in New England, regardless of the conventional political labels worn by its leaders. This independent streak reveals deep divisions over many issues.

New Englanders have long led the way in protecting the environment, but every economic slump makes jobs vs. development regulations an issue in state elections. Education is a time-honored priority, but tempers flare over financing schools via property taxes rather than broad-based levies. Vermont bucked the trend in many states by recognizing same-sex civil unions and by 2012 all New England states had followed suit.

While strongly supporting the military, particularly troops in Afghanistan and Iraq and their families, the majority of the region's citizens staunchly opposed the Iraq War. At town meetings in 2008, two Vermont municipalities actually voted to indict President George Bush and Vice-President Dick Cheney for war crimes if they set foot within their jurisdictions.

In 2013 New Hampshire legalized the medical use of marijuana and decriminalized it four years later (Connecticut, Rhode Island and Vermont have also decriminalized marijuana, while Maine and Massachusetts legalized it in 2016). Conversely, New Hampshire is the only state in New England that has retained capital punishment, though it has not held an execution since 1939.

Decorative buoys on Cape Cod.

Re-creating the Puritan heritage at Plimoth Plantation.

NEW ENGLAND'S PEOPLE

It's easy to describe New Englanders by stereotype – stern Puritans, revolutionary patriots, aristocratic Bostonians, taciturn farmers, crusty fishermen, beefy Irish cops – but none of these people are that one-dimensional.

New Englanders often think of themselves as a nation within a nation. They are as likely to identify themselves with the region as with their individual state. In 1798, Yale's president, Timothy Dwight, said New Englanders were distinguished by their "love of science and learning, love of liberty, morality, piety, and unusual spirit of enquiry." That's as true now as it was then.

DEMOGRAPHICS

Nearly 15 million people call New England home. Over 22 percent of them are under the age of 18; 13 percent are over 65. Of these, the majority are Caucasian (83 percent), far outnumbering the next largest groups – Hispanic, African-American, and Asian-American – with a combined population of about 15 percent. Native Americans and Oceanic peoples largely complete the head-count. Nearly 2 percent describe themselves as multi-racial. Massachusetts has the largest population: over 6.8 million residents; Vermont has only 624,000.

Three-quarters of the population lives in Massachusetts, Connecticut, and Rhode Island. Most of them reside in metropolitan Boston and along the stretch of I–95 corridor from Massachusetts through Connecticut toward New York. Southern Connecticut's fortunes are so tied to those of New York that some demographers remove the state from many surveys of New England and use it as a source of information about New York.

Because of that urban concentration in a relatively small area, New England overall has the highest population density in the country, belying the image of an area of bucolic landscapes, vast tracts of mountain wilderness, and isolated

A man dressed as a Wampanoag Indian at Plimoth Plantation.

fishing villages. It's just one of the juxtapositions of the many facets of the region.

ORIGINAL PEOPLE

When the Pilgrims arrived they were met by members of the Wampanoag tribe. Before the arrival of the Europeans, there were an estimated 250,000 people of the Algonquian tribes scattered through New England. But the first explorers brought more than an avaricious interest in exploring, settling, and exploiting the New World; they also brought diseases against which the Native Americans had no immunity. The plagues wiped out as much as 90 percent of the population. Today, there are an estimated

37,000 American Indians in the region. A minority live on nine reservations; most live in the general community, with varying degrees of success. Decades of subtle and overt discrimina-

> *Just 48 miles (77km) long and 37 miles (60km) wide, Rhode Island – or little Rhody as it's known locally – is the smallest US state, but it boasts one fifth of the nation's historical landmarks.*

Visitors to Applefest, Vermont's biggest apple festival and craft show, held in October at South Hero.

tion are being replaced by a new sense of tribal identity and pride. The nations are fighting legal battles to regain land either taken outright by settlers or through violations of treaties.

SETTLERS

Of the European-originated population, English dominance has been superseded by those of Irish, French/French Canadian, and Italian descent. The centers of population break down along ethnic lines. Boston has a large Irish and Italian population which is more numerous now than those who trace their lineage to the city's British roots. Rhode Island has strong Italian connections, but Providence boasts a large

Portuguese neighborhood. Northern Vermont and New Hampshire have a strong French influence due to its proximity to Quebec. But there's also a French accent in central Massachusetts, stemming from the Industrial Revolution when large numbers of French Canadians migrated south to work in the factories.

Spiritually, the Pilgrims would be displeased, at best, by the region's religious affiliations. Given the influx of Irish, Italian, Portuguese, and Hispanic immigrants, it's no surprise that 36 percent of New Englanders are Catholic, with another 32 percent identifying themselves as Christian. But 25 percent claim no religious affiliation of any kind, one of the highest levels in the country. So much for the Puritans' determination to create a theocracy in which pleasing God – particularly the non-Papist God – was fundamental.

PATRIOTISM

It's a small wonder that the spark of independence was fanned into flame here. The nature of New England fostered self-reliance and a distrust of authority. Those were the driving motivations of the Pilgrims' self-imposed exile, after all. Once here, they found no land of milk and honey, but a wilderness that further tested their resolve.

Fiercely proud of their history as founders of the nation (dismissing Spanish explorers in 16th-century Florida and the 1607 Jamestown Colony in Virginia) and as the Cradle of Liberty and the Revolution (Franklin, Jefferson, and Washington are appreciated for their contributions, but New Englanders will aver that Samuel Adams, Ethan Allen, and Captain John Parker at the Battle of Lexington set the stage for the others' success), New Englanders are almost obsessively patriotic. Patriots Day – the observance of the Battles of Lexington and Concord – is a state holiday in Massachusetts, and the week surrounding the 4th of July is a city-wide festival in Boston. The first Independence Day parade was in Bristol RI in 1785. The town still displays the nation's colors everywhere – including on the main road through town, where the center line is painted red, white, and blue. They point with pride to Maine's Bath Iron Works and Electric Boat Company in Groton CT – both of which produce vessels for the US Navy

– the Naval War College in Newport, and the US Coast Guard Academy in New London. When the USS *Constitution* sails around Boston Harbor every 4th of July, many of those watching from shore and on the private boats escorting her are misty-eyed.

Presidential hopefuls ignore New England in general and New Hampshire in particular at their peril. New Hampshire's election primary, coming at the beginning of the official campaign season, is vital for contenders. A loss in New Hampshire usually means an end to the presidential dream, while a victory is a major boost to the campaign. The state bookends its importance in the presidential saga by being the first to open its polls on election day when the 30-odd registered voters of Dixville Notch cast their ballots at midnight. (In the primaries, the Dixville voters have chosen the eventual Republican candidate in every election since 1968; it's a bit spotty on the Democratic side, and the general election results are accurately predictive no more than half the time.)

COMMON PERSONALITY TRAITS

It's impossible to separate the New England mindset from the land and the climate. The region's personality was cast in years of digging rocks out of pastures, felling trees in the wilderness, and fighting ocean waves. It was hard to transport goods and supplies then; it's still not always convenient now. And no one has ever claimed to meet a rich or lazy fisherman or farmer. As a result, rural New Englanders – be they Vermont dairy farmers, Maine fishermen, or New Hampshire loggers – all share a certain fundamental sense of practicality and frugality. "Use it up, wear it out, make it do, do without" is a phrase often used to sum up the philosophy of New Englanders to material goods.

Small towns are often accused of being cool to outsiders, particularly "flatlanders" moving in from anywhere – particularly anywhere outside New England. The joke is that it takes at least 20 years of living in a town before you're no longer called "the new folks." It's not hostility, but another instance of practicality, this time merging with experience. New England doesn't grant its residents the leisure time to sip tea on a veranda and "visit" as they might in the South. There are always chores to be

done: livestock to feed and water; fishing gear to repair; the chain saw to tune; and the everpresent need to collect firewood. Towns are insular, and their people have come to know and rely on one another. Outsiders are kept at a distance until they prove themselves as a part of the community. In the meantime, their motivations, ideas, and attitudes are watched and weighed. Tensions arise when they propose ideas that are interpreted as changing the structure and functions of the community that attracted the newcomers in the first place.

Students at Harvard University, Cambridge.

⊘ VOTING IN DIXVILLE NOTCH

Every four years, the national media descend on the village of Dixville Notch, New Hampshire to watch as voters cast their ballots. This small village is among the first places in the country to declare its results in presidential elections and the New Hampshire primary. By mutual agreement, the entire roster (around 30 people) assembles in the Ballot Room of the Balsams Grand Resort Hotel where they each have a personal voting booth. By 12:01am they've all selected their candidate and by 12:05am, the world knows who won. Announcing the outcome is far from predicting the winner; their vote is accurate only about 50 percent of the time.

There's a level of community involvement in government that's not seen elsewhere. At annual town meetings, residents publicly debate and decide issues like the town budget, local ordinances, and canine leash laws. Everyone has his or her say, and the debates are generally conducted in an atmosphere of respect. While attendance has slipped over the decades, with some places seeing only a quarter of the residents showing up and others choosing to establish a more representative system, the town meeting is still a valued institution.

Dollar bills are pinned to a statue of San Gennaro at Boston's annual Little Italy street festival.

URBAN CENTERS

The urban centers of Boston, Providence, and southern Connecticut share, enjoy, and endure the same elements – major cultural and entertainment venues, traffic congestion and pollution, and more employment opportunities. They are as homogeneous as any cluster of cities can be, for reasons that reflect their history. Insulated from the rest of the country and seeing few new arrivals, they remained the enclaves of those who founded them for two centuries. Then came the waves of immigrants, starting with the Irish. Each group tried to re-establish a sense of what they left behind by living in the same neighborhood, going to the same schools and churches, developing a common shopping area. In every practical way, those neighborhoods are as much small towns as any place in the Berkshires or central Maine. The impact of the immigrants on the social and political establishment was another revolution, as they applied the same drive which led them to leave their old homes to gaining political and social power in their new one – not unlike the Pilgrims.

CONSERVATIVE IMAGE; MODERN IDEAS

The image of the dour, fundamentalist Puritans gives the region a reputation for conservative attitudes, but in practice it usually takes a liberal stand. Upon reflection, that's not unexpected; the Puritans were liberals in their own way, and the region's history is, after all, one of revolutionary ideas put into practice. A line from the play *1776* has Rhode Islander Stephen Hopkins admonishing the delegates to the Continental Congress that "there's no idea so dangerous that it can't be talked about."

In 2006 Massachusetts passed a revolutionary health care reform law designed to provide at least a minimum level of health insurance to nearly all of its residents. The law obliges employers with over ten full-time employees to provide health insurance, while residents with incomes below 150 percent of the federal poverty level are granted free insurance. As a result the number of uninsured Massachusetts residents dropped from 6 percent in 2006 to 2.5 percent in 2017.

⊘ SANCTUARY CITIES

As in many other areas of the country, immigration – particularly the arrival of undocumented immigrants – is a highly controversial issue. Federal law and the Department of Homeland Security both require local governments to cooperate with immigration enforcement policies, but some places object to the requirements, either for humanitarian or economic reasons. Maine limits state employees' ability to report the presence of illegal aliens, while Vermont maintains a bias-free policy in providing state services. Several municipalities in New England act as sanctuary cities, with police and municipal offices providing services without verifying immigration status.

IMPACT OF TOURISM

Inconvenient to the rest of the nation, far from transportation routes, with few manufacturing jobs, and few resources to export, New Englanders seek ways to achieve economic viability. Taking advantage of the wealth of universities and medical facilities, it is positioning itself as a leader in research and high-tech fields, areas that pay well and need less infrastructure to support. Tourism was a natural field to develop. Residents often spend their vacation time within the region, which keeps tax revenue and spending dollars in the local coffers. Attracting outside visitors, though, is in many ways more desirable, since it means the visitors are helping to foot the bill for things that sales and occupancy taxes typically cover, such as schools, social programs, police, and fire departments, without requiring those services themselves.

The impact of tourism in New England is significant. It is now the largest industry in Maine, generating $9 billion in sales and responsible for 28 percent of the state's sales tax and 15 percent of its jobs. In Vermont, it creates 11 percent of the jobs in the state, and over $470 million in business tax revenue. And it's a $20-billion industry in Massachusetts, generating over $4.8 billion a year annually in wages.

Most areas are well able to handle the visitors; there may be a lot of them, but they are either spread out or drawn to magnet areas that are able to handle the numbers. Peak times like fall foliage and very popular destinations like Martha's Vineyard and the Kennebunks in the summer are sometimes victims of their own success.

It's ironic that the forbidding land and conditions that so nearly defeated the Puritans were the very things that are the foundations for New Englanders' success: a tough spirit willing to take on challenges and adapt to change, a measure of common sense in deciding how to live, an appreciation of the beauty of the elements, and the willingness to rely on one another. While New England is a region of many differences, these are the traits its people share.

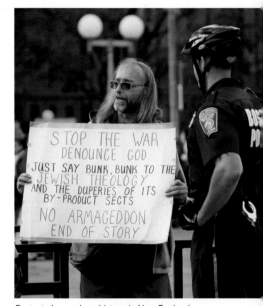

Protests have a long history in New England.

⊘ FESTIVALS FROM AROUND THE WORLD

Almost every weekend, you can hear the music, see the traditional costumes, shop for crafts, and taste the flavors of cultures the original Pilgrims never imagined. Some of the more interesting ethnic festivals are: the **La Kermesse Festival**, the largest Franco-American festival in the US, held every June in Biddeford ME (www.lakermessefestival.com); the **Cape Verdean Independence Day** celebration in Providence (http://www.ricapeverdeanheritage.org/), featuring live music, dance groups, parades, and arts and crafts shows; the **Southeast Asian Water Festival** (www.lowellwaterfestival.com), which honors the spirits and spirituality of water, held on the third Saturday in August in Lowell MA; and the largest Portuguese festival in the world, the **Feast of the Blessed Sacrament** (www.portuguesefeast.com) in late July in New Bedford MA. One of the largest West Indian communities holds its Taste of the **Caribbean and Jerk Festival** in Hartford CT in August (www.cayasco.org). Rhode Island celebrates the diversity of its population in September during the annual Rhode Island Heritage Day Festival in Providence with through crafts, dances, music, and food from African-American, Bolivian, German, Guatemalan, Indian, Irish, Laotian, and Puerto Rican groups (www.preservation.ri.gov/heritage).

THE BOUNTIFUL SEA

Even though the codfish has yielded to computer technology as the most important element in New England's economy, the sea still plays a central role in coastal life.

The first generation of Europeans in America all had the same "baptism by sea": a two-month voyage across the stormy North Atlantic. Most of the settlers who came were landlubbers; many had never seen the ocean before. But shipbuilding was one of the first enterprises the early colonists undertook. Ships maintained the connection to the homeland and provided an income from trade. The vast virgin forests of the New World supplied materials for their construction. One hundred years after the Pilgrims stepped onto Plymouth Rock, New England's coastal shipyards were launching a ship a day. With labor and lumber costs so much cheaper than those in England, American-made ships dominated the market.

For the early settlers, the sea brought news from home, fresh legions of colonists, and ships involved in the Triangle Trade (the transport of slaves, molasses, and rum between ports in Africa, the Caribbean, and New England). Early on, fishing was seen as a prime source of the region's prosperity. Codfish nourished not just New Englanders, but also colonists in Mid-Atlantic and Southern towns. One of the first important acts of the Great and General Court of Massachusetts was to set standards for the regulation and encouragement of the fishing industry.

THE WHALING BOOM

Lamps were fired by vegetable and animal oils; candles were made from animal tallow. The light was dim and the lamps were smoky until someone made the discovery that blubber from a beached whale could be rendered and the oil extracted would provide a clearer, brighter light.

Whales beached themselves frequently on the New England shores, and whaling began

Boston harbor in the late 19th century.

as a shore activity. Teams of townsfolk gathered whenever they saw a whale, tethering it to a stake to prevent the tide taking it out to sea. The blubber was cut away, rendered in the kettles of a "tryworks" set up on the beach and transformed into a high-quality oil which could be burned in the town's lamps or traded. Soon such business became an industry.

WATERY HIGHWAYS

In colonial times, overland routes were expensive to build and maintain, so coastal freighters and passenger boats regularly sailed from Boston to New York and Philadelphia. The more enterprising captains headed south, where they unloaded their cod at Philadelphia or Annapolis and took on corn and flour, beans, and barrels of pork, which could be sold at a great profit at home.

Though a boon to New England's maritime economy, the coastal trade, like fishing and whaling, was not an easy way to make a living. Every trip between Boston and ports to the south involved a voyage around Cape Cod, and the weather that had so discouraged the Pilgrims was a constant threat. Ships and men were regularly lost to the ravages of the sea.

Though fishing and the coastal trade helped New England employ its people and pay its bills,

Whalers might pursue their quarry for months.

the region was not a rich one. Because it always imported more goods than it exported, ways had to be found to reduce the trade deficit.

Merchants and sea captains decided that, if they couldn't produce goods from their rocky soil, at least they could transport the goods produced by others. New England merchant vessels undertook long and arduous voyages to Europe, Africa, and the Orient. And it was not only the cargoes that were put up for sale: the ships themselves were frequently on the auctioning block, bringing added revenue to their builders back home.

Trade was good to the region. While the pioneer towns of inland America were primitive and rough, New England seaports took on the polish of wealth and culture. Fortunes made at sea were translated into fine mansions and patronage of the arts. From the profits of their voyages, captains brought home art treasures, luxury goods, and curiosities from exotic destinations. The Peabody Essex Museum of Salem is filled with the wealth that came to New England on returning merchant ships.

CLOCKS, SHOES, AND ICE

As time went by, the new republic developed industries that produced goods for trade. Connecticut's household utensils, machines, clocks, pistols, and rifles, plus shoes and cloth from Rhode Island and Massachusetts, ultimately made their way around the world.

Perhaps the most ingenious export of all was ice. Cut from ponds, rivers, and lakes,

☉ LIT BY WHALE OIL

The demand for whale oil became so great that fishermen, hoping to get rich from its sale, began to pursue whales along the shore, thus initiating New England's whaling industry. The trade took a great leap forward in 1712, when Captain Christopher Hussey of Nantucket was blown off course into deep water and accidentally bagged the first sperm whale. Although it had teeth in lieu of coveted baleen – bony upper jaw slats useful as stays for collars and corsets – the spermaceti oil proved far superior to that of the already endangered "right" whale (so called because it was the right one to pursue). Nantucket whalers came to specialize in the pursuit of this purer, lighter, and more profitable oil.

Whalers out of Nantucket and New Bedford pursued their mammoth quarry for months, even years, as far as the Pacific, until their holds were filled with barrels of the oil that would fire the nation's lamps and illumine the capitals of Europe. The whaling ships themselves served as complete processing plants.

Until 1859, when petroleum was discovered in Pennsylvania and distillers began producing kerosene, the sea was the world's great proven oil reserve. For a closer look at this fascinating chapter in maritime history, see the last surviving whaler, the *Charles W. Morgan*, tied up at Mystic Seaport in Connecticut, or visit the whaling museums in Nantucket or New Bedford.

ice was packed in sawdust, loaded into fast clipper ships and sent off to Cuba, South America, and beyond. The rulers of the British Raj in India sipped drinks cooled by ice from New England. In exchange for a commodity that was free for the cutting, New Englanders brought back spices, fine porcelain, silks, and other items.

THE TAMING OF THE SEA

The War of 1812 sent New England's maritime commerce into depression, but by the mid-19th century its seaports returned to glory during the brief heyday of the clipper ship. "Never, in these United States, has the brain of man conceived, or the hand of man fashioned, so perfect a thing as the clipper ship," wrote the great Massachusetts historian Samuel Eliot Morison.

But the clippers' days were numbered, as were those of the larger, bulkier schooners carrying up to six masts, built to transport coal and other heavy loads that clippers, with their small holds, could never profitably carry. Neither clipper nor schooner could go anywhere when the wind failed – but the new steamships could travel even in a dead calm, and even keep to schedule. They could work their way around Cape Cod, ignoring the winds that had caused so much trouble since Pilgrim times. Steam also powered the new railroads that linked the Atlantic and Pacific coasts, putting the ships that had sailed all the way around South America to reach California out of business.

SAFER WAVES

Today, the sea is still a major source of income – and at a much lower price in lives lost to storms. A century ago whole families, even most of a town, might be lost to a single ferocious storm. There are still tragedies at sea, but radar, radio, and stricter safety precautions help prevent many accidents.

STILL A WORKING SEA

By the 1970s, New England fishermen, working from their small boats, were competing with large trawlers from Europe and Japan. In 1976, the US imposed new regulations prohibiting the foreign vessels from coming within 200 miles (320km) of the US coastline. Initially, that appeared to be a good thing, but the fleet soon

expanded exponentially and it became clear that the fishery was collapsing. Despite angry disagreements from the fishermen, regulations were imposed limiting the catch. These were largely ignored and rarely enforced, however. By 1989, the population of groundfish – cod, flounder, redfish, and other bottom dwellers – had dropped by 65 percent. Tighter regulations were established, aimed at better management of resources.

Today, the fishing fleet has largely consolidated. There are fewer ships and they are lim-

Elias Hasket Derby (1739–99), owner of the Grand Turk, the first New England vessel to trade directly with China.

Battered by storms that seemed endless, the tiny yet sturdy barque Mayflower was driven across Cape Cod Bay in November 1620 and into the mainland at a place the Pilgrims named Plymouth.

ited as to how many days they can fish and the size of their catch. There is less over-fishing and smaller hauls, but revenues are higher. But there are also fewer fishermen, and those who are on the water are aging. The average age of a fisherman in Massachusetts is 59; the number of young men seeking to make their living at sea is shrinking. The cost of a boat is upwards of $200,000; fuel is expensive; maintenance costs are high; permits are costly; income is spotty. Many fear that the future

> Boaters along the coast will often see the colorful bobbing floats that mark the location of the fish-baited traps on the bottom; each captain has his own float design.

"Widow's walks" were built on top of sea-facing houses so that sailors' wives could watch for their husbands' return.

of fishing lies in the hands of large corporate trawlers, which will destroy the economies of small fishing villages which depend on their large fleet of small boats.

And as for the lobster? The population was in steep decline in the 1980s, and then seemed to revive strongly. It's now shrinking, or so say the regulators. The lobstermen disagree, saying they see signs of a growing – albeit slowly growing – population.

There's one success story in the saga – scallops. When the 6,600-sq-mile (17,000-sq-km) George's Bank fishery was closed as a result of the cod limitations, the population of the bivalve increased dramatically. The fishery is now run on a rotating schedule, with some areas closed every year while others are harvested. It's become an example of a successful sustainable fishery. But it appears unlikely to win support from fishermen or lobstermen to try it elsewhere.

CRUISING THE COAST

In previous centuries, a New Englander either went to sea to earn a living, or remained a landlubber. But now New England's seacoast has become a major playground, and the variety of maritime sports seems limitless. As in so many other realms, the world of work has become the world of play, and places once associated solely with danger and hardship are visited just for fun.

Forty miles (64km) of Cape Cod's sandy beaches have been set aside as the Cape Cod National Seashore, one of the great tourist attractions of New England. The beaches of Connecticut, Rhode Island, New Hampshire, and Maine attract visitors. Reliable ferries carry vacationers to Nantucket, Martha's Vineyard, Block Island, and the outer islands along the Maine coast. Tourists stroll among the handsome sea captains' houses, and explore the world of the seafaring men who built them.

Perhaps the clearest indication of the taming of the sea is this: the perilous voyage undertaken by the Pilgrims in 1620 is now done for sport. Transatlantic yacht racing began in 1866

⊙ WOODS HOLE

Woods Hole (http://www.whoi.edu/) is the world's largest non-profit ocean research, engineering, and education organization. It's dedicated to research and higher education at the frontiers of ocean science. For many years, this facility on the western shore of Cape Cod was considered a source of interesting, if arcane, information. With increased concern about ocean pollution, fishery health, and global warming, its research is now widely reported. It supports four "ocean institutes" which encompass areas of concern for the public, other scientists, and policymakers: Coastal Oceans; Deep Ocean Exploration; Oceans and Climate Change; and Ocean Life.

when the *Henrietta* raced the *Vesta* to England. In 1851, the schooner *America* won the Royal Yacht Squadron Cup, and the America's Cup became the great event of yachting, with the first race held in Newport in 1870. The beauty and science of yacht design and racing is pursued passionately in Newport and in dozens of other ports along the coast.

New England's waters are particularly suited to yachting: Long Island, off the coast of Connecticut, protects spacious Long Island Sound; and Cape Cod Bay has provided calm sailing ever since the days of the Pilgrims. With the cutting of the Cape Cod Canal and the establishment of the Intra-coastal Waterway, coastal cruising has been made safer and more enjoyable than ever before.

The whalers that sailed out of New Bedford and Nantucket are long gone. Yet boats from a dozen ports still head out each day in search of whales, but now it's tourists' cameras, not harpoons, that are aimed at them. It's strange that the leviathans that once made New England "oil-rich" should still be helping its economy.

A cruiseship navigates the rocky shore with the help of a lighthouse.

⊘ LIFE-SAVING STATIONS

The waters off the New England coast were (and still are) treacherous. Many ships and crews floundered when they ran aground or were caught in fierce storms. In 1784, the Humane Society of the Commonwealth of Massachusetts was created to help ships in distress. Huts were built along the beach to provide shelter for shipwreck survivors. Those were followed by the use of whaleboats, rowed out to ships by 10-man crews. Those aids were only near major ports, leaving the rest of the coast unprotected.

In 1878, Maine native Sumner Kimball organized the US Life-Saving Service. He established a chain of life-saving houses along both coasts and the Great Lakes. These provided the first large-scale, round-the-clock lookout and rescue service. The life of the crews was strenuous. Sumner wanted physically fit fishermen who knew the idiosyncrasies of the local coastline. Their main piece of equipment was the surfboat, a 1,000lb (455kg) boat which they would hoist onto a wheeled cart. Every day, they would rehearse dragging it along the shore and across the beach and launching it in the surf. At night, two men would patrol the beach, looking and listening for any signs of a ship in trouble. When help was needed, the crews would launch the surfboats, usually in heavy seas, high winds, and driving rain. The Life-Saving Service merged with other agencies to become the US Coast Guard in 1915.

THE PURITAN TRADITION

H. L. Mencken once quipped that a Puritan is someone tormented by the fact that somebody, somewhere, is having fun, but there's no denying that the strength of character of the original settlers has molded the region.

The Puritans did more than settle New England; they created it. Yet today people laud their optimism and courage in deciding to risk everything for their ideals, while criticizing the methods they used to achieve them. "Puritanism" is a pejorative term denoting an excess of zeal in pursuing rigid ideas of morality and law. Nor is this a 21st-century judgment: in 1917 Mencken further dismissed Puritanism as "all that's unattractive about American culture, compounded over time by evangelism, moralism from political demagogues, and relentless money-grubbing."

Certainly, the creed was not a cozy one. Out of the Calvinistic doctrines regarding humanity's inherent evil and the predestination of the soul grew a society that was stern and uncompromising. Even at its best, the Puritans' dogma was a hard one, an ultimate faith that required everyone – from the most prominent minister to the humblest child – to strain toward an ineffable God.

Puritans argued that humans, in their fallen state, could never know God and could thus never truly know the state of their own souls. Salvation came not through human action, but through God's mysterious grace. Abject though we human creatures may be, we must always examine our conscience, always repent our inevitable sin, always attempt to lead a just life, and always know that no matter how sincere and devout our efforts, they will probably fall short.

John Winthrop, the Puritan leader who aimed to build an ideal society.

SPIRITUAL VALUES

The Puritans' difficult faith stood them in good stead, but it found little room for gentleness or pleasure. Regarding discipline and hard work as spiritual values, these early settlers labored long for the greater glory of God – while incidentally accumulating considerable wealth and building prosperous communities. Puritans came to identify worldly success with godliness, rewards bestowed by God as signs of His approval.

In America, as in England, class distinctions were important. But the Puritans, eschewing such worldly signs of status as expensive clothes and fancy carriages, had to devise other more subtle ways of indicating social class. Thus, the title "Master" was reserved exclusively for educated men.

THE SEARCH FOR PERFECTION

Education was essential to the Puritans' vision of what their new society in America was to be. Most of the settlers were well educated;

four officers of the Massachusetts Bay Colony – John Winthrop, Sir Richard Saltonstall, Isaac Johnson, and John Humphrey – had attended Cambridge University. For them, the journey to the New World was more than an adventure to a new frontier, it was a chance to transport their old society in purified form to a new land. Discontented in a country where they were persecuted for their religious practices, they came to America to build an ideal society, their "city on a hill." These men knew that unless they provided for the education of clergymen, they might quickly lose sight of the New (and perfect) England.

A society in which education established one's credentials before God and the world was destined to develop an impressive school system. As early as 1635, Boston voted a declaration that "our brother, Mr Philemon Pormont shall be intreated to become scholemaster for teaching and nourtering of children with us."

Pormont established Boston Latin School, the country's first secondary school and still one of Boston's finest high schools. And with the goal of educating a native New England ministry still in view, Massachusetts Bay Colony officials chartered the institution that was to become Harvard College in 1636. It was the first of a succession of New England colleges founded upon strong religious foundations but destined to provide a secular education for future generations.

THE WITCH HUNTS

In the mid-1600s, when the fever for witch-killing blew across the North Atlantic from Europe, the colonies of Rhode Island, Connecticut, and Massachusetts joined the pack with decrees of death. Non-conformity – which threatened the carefully constructed society – was now equated with devil worship. Connecticut quickly seized and executed nine victims. Bostonians hanged Margaret Jones of Charlestown on a bright June day in 1648, and for an encore on Boston Common they hanged the beautiful and cultured Ann Hibbins, widow of the colony's former representative to England.

Against that lunatic background, the fanatical Rev. Cotton Mather sensed a great opportunity for self-promotion and professional success. He was already the colony's most highly acclaimed clergyman. He was learned and brilliant, and he was also ambitious. He longed to succeed his father, the Rev. Increase Mather, as the president of Harvard. He decided it would boost his reputation and enhance his career if he could identify assorted witches and promote their executions. So he went to work and soon focused on a witch-suspect named Goodwife Glover, the mother of a North End laundress. With Mather's help, poor Mrs Glover quickly wound up in the noose of a Boston Common gallows rope.

The idealized First Thanksgiving (1914) by Jennie Augusta Brownscombe.

Arthur Miller's celebrated play The Crucible, based on the Salem witch trials, was written in 1953, at the height of McCarthyism. During that era, people were accused of supporting Communism, usually without any evidence.

The most notorious expression of religious hysteria emerged in the Salem witch trials of 1692, which the playwright Arthur Miller described as "one of the strangest and most awful chapters in human history." The trials grew from the feverish imaginations of adolescent girls who became swept up in tales of voodoo and mysticism as told to them by Tituba, a slavewoman from Barbados. All too eager to discover depravity in someone else, the

> *The early Puritans' strict beliefs in moral rectitude can still be sensed in the region's activists, who often campaign on social and environmental issues.*

The influential Puritan minister and educator, Rev. Increase Mather (1639–1723).

Puritans sat in eager judgment on the accused. Unrelenting in their desire to purge their world of evil and in their arrogant belief in their own righteousness, they sent 20 innocent people to their death.

CRADLE OF REFORMATION

As if to live down the small-mindedness of their predecessors and to return to their original ideals of creating a just society, the New England philosophers and legislators of the 19th century stood in the very vanguard of political reform. Having abolished slavery themselves by the end of the 18th century (but not before accumulating great fortunes

by providing the ships and transporting the rum and molasses which were all part of the Triangle Trade), high-minded New Englanders dedicated themselves to nationwide abolition. William Lloyd Garrison founded his weekly newspaper *The Liberator* in Boston in 1831 (not all shared his views at that time: he was nearly killed by a Boston mob in 1835) and persisted until 1865, when the 13th amendment was finally passed. Joining him in the struggle were writers such as Harriet Beecher Stowe, who delivered one of the abolitionist movement's most effective tracts in the form of her best-selling 1852 novel, *Uncle Tom's Cabin*.

After the Civil War, New England's reformists turned their attention to the labor abuses brought on by the Industrial Revolution and to the role of women in society. Susan B. Anthony turned her attention to women's rights from her home in Massachusetts. The first women's college to open in the US was Vassar Female College, founded in Poughkeepsie NY in 1861. By 1879, four outstanding colleges for women had been established in Massachusetts: Smith, Wellesley, Mount Holyoke, and Radcliffe.

Despite this growing willingness to entertain change – reinforced by decades of stability and prosperity – remnants of the Puritan strain persisted. For the most part, New England remained a deeply moral, and occasionally moralistic, society. At their worst, New Englanders suppressed books they deemed

⊘ WHERE DEMOCRACY MATTERS

Town meetings were central to the social and political structures of the Puritans. Unlike a representative governing body, these were public gatherings during which all local matters were discussed and decided. A serious attempt was made to introduce a high degree of participation and this principle is still pursued. Town meetings can be displays of democracy in its purest form; all town issues are on the agenda and they are decided after debates, which are often long and lively, usually respectful but sometimes acrimonious. It often takes several sessions to reach consensus on many matters, particularly budgetary ones.

offensive to public taste, and considered theater – and, worse yet, actors – a pernicious influence on impressionable minds.

THE DEMON DRINK

Blue laws, first introduced in Connecticut in 1781 to control public and private conduct, especially on the Sabbath, enjoyed regular revivals in the 19th and 20th centuries. Alcohol was frequently seen as a destructive influence, although Increase Mather wrote, "Drink is in itself a good creature of God, and to be received with thankfulness, but the abuse of drink is from Satan." To this day you cannot buy alcohol in Connecticut on Sundays, except in restaurants. In Massachusetts, would-be imbibers must wait until noon to purchase alcohol on Sundays, and large retail stores may not open on Thanksgiving and Christmas. Maine does not allow car dealerships to operate on Sunday.

What, then, is the true Puritan legacy? It's easy to grumble about arcane liquor laws, or to see the cold hand of Puritanism in each new dictum about what we should and shouldn't eat. But New England wasn't going to get settled by people out to have fun; the soil and the climate would not have cooperated. On the credit side, Puritan legal principles helped craft the Constitution, with its emphasis on the supremacy of law. Reinforced by the determination of immigrants who arrived in New England from the antebellum days onward, the fabled "Puritan work ethic" and a conviction in the ability to achieve self-determination is as much a part of New England as Thanksgiving.

As for the Puritan sense of rectitude and moral improvement, it survives today in activist movements – strong in New England – dedicated to social change and promoting environment-friendly policies. Same-sex unions are legal in all of the New England states; Massachusetts has established health benefits for nearly all citizens; groups throughout the region work on immigration issues. The Puritans' zeal to create a perfect society lives on in what has become one of the country's most progressive regions.

Salem witch trials, 1692.

⊘ THE TRANSCENDENTALISTS WHO PURSUED UTOPIA

The gradual liberalization of New England's churches and colleges in the 18th century gave way to a true intellectual flowering in the 19th century. Flushed with the success of the Revolutionary War and the founding of a nation that was growing prosperous from the lucrative China trade, the Puritan temperament was ready for an overhaul, perhaps even a transformation.

Many New Englanders were embracing the doctrines of Unitarianism, which taught that God was a single rather than tripartite entity, and rejected such old Calvinist mainstays as predestination and the innate baseness of the human personality. Henry Ware, who founded the Harvard Divinity School in 1819, was a Unitarian, as was the great

Boston pastor William Ellery Channing. Unitarianism's liberal cast of thought prepared the ground for the sweet optimism of Transcendentalism, a mystical philosophy which argued the existence of an Oversoul unifying all creation, and which preached the primacy of insight over reason and the inherent goodness of humankind.

The movement spawned several experiments in living, the best known being Henry David Thoreau's solitary retreat on Walden Pond, and short-lived communal farms at Brook Farm in Concord and Fruitlands in Harvard MA. Led by Ralph Waldo Emerson, the movement attracted some of the brightest minds of the day. Today, at www.transcendentalists.com, its ideas inhabit the internet.

University campus,
Haven, CT.

TEACHING NEW ENGLAND'S MINDS

The Puritans recognized that education was vital to their survival; that appreciation has made New England a magnet for the best in higher education.

New England is the cradle of American education. Although justly recognized as the home for many of the most respected and influential colleges and universities, learning at all levels has always been important.

In an age when literacy was largely a luxury, the religious reformers who created the first settlements in New England firmly believed that every church member – every citizen, in other words – should be able to read Scripture. By 1639, Boston and its neighboring communities of Charlestown and Dorchester had hired schoolmasters. Boston Latin School was established in 1635 and in 1642 education was decreed as compulsory for all males. By 1672, every colony except Rhode Island had adopted systems of compulsory elementary education.

The curriculum centered around the incorporation of Calvinist doctrine in every aspect of life. The first textbook was *The New England Primer*, which taught reading through rote memorization. A typical passage for the young scholars read, "In Adam's fall/We sinned all," a far cry from the innocent "See Dick. See Dick Run" readers of later years.

THE BIRTH OF THE IVY LEAGUE

References to New England's Ivy League schools are so pervasive that it is sometimes tiresome. Yet the schools had a profound effect on the early years of colonization, and their influence is equally profound nearly four centuries later.

In 1636, the Great and General Court of Massachusetts Bay had appropriated the sum of £400 for "a schoale or colledge," which was established the following year at New Town, across the Charles River from Boston. The first class assembled two years later.

A fencing lesson at Yale in the early 20th century.

In that same year of 1638, a young minister in nearby Charlestown died of consumption. Rev. John Harvard left his library of 400 books and half of his estate to the new college, which would thereafter bear his name.

YALE'S BEGINNINGS

In Connecticut, a group of 10 clergymen met in 1701 to found an institution called the "Collegiate School." Their impetus was in part a reaction against the perceived liberalization of the Harvard curriculum. It, too, benefited from a philanthropic gesture from an immensely wealthy, Boston-born ex-governor of the East India Company. His name was Elihu Yale, and so generous were his donations to New

Haven's fledgling school that it was named in his honor in 1718.

New England's third-oldest college was the fruit of a growing ecumenical spirit. It isn't surprising that a representative of the relatively new Baptist sect should have chosen to establish a college in Rhode Island, a colony devoted from its infancy to religious freedom. Rev. James Manning secured a charter for a "College of Rhode Island" in 1764, which included Baptists, Congregationalists, and Episcopalians. Established on College Hill in Providence by 1770, the college counted

> "I am obliged to confess I should sooner live in a society governed by the first two thousand names in the Boston telephone directory than in a society governed by the two thousand faculty members of Harvard University." William F. Buckley

among its 1783 class Nicholas Brown Jr, son of one of the four Brown brothers who dominated Rhode Island commerce in that era. Nicholas Jr would give his alma mater some $160,000 over his lifetime. Hence the institution's new name, from 1804 onward – Brown University.

One of the more unlikely locations for a college in the 18th century was the New Hampshire wilderness. In the 1760s, one Rev. Eleazar Wheelock was looking for a place to relocate a Christian school for Indians, which he had established in Connecticut. Having secured a pledge of £11,000 and the patronage of the Earl of Dartmouth, Wheelock's next step was to find a community that wanted the school. The most eager candidate was tiny Hanover NH, which offered 3,000 acres (1,200 hectares). The school, Dartmouth College, received its royal charter in 1769.

THE PREP SCHOOLS

Several "preparatory" boarding schools were established where sons could receive a better education than locally. Phillips Andover (1778), Phillips Exeter (1781), and Deerfield Academy (1797) served as feeders for the Ivy League schools. They went co-ed in the 1970s and are still elite and elitist in their student body and mission.

EDUCATION FOR WOMEN

Girls did not get much of the same consideration in education. While they were usually taught to read – because they needed to study the Scriptures, too – they were not taught to write. Activities requiring that talent were the purview of men. Other areas of study were deemed completely unsuitable for women. It was not uncommon for women who could read a contract to sign it with an "X."

In the 1800s, this began to change as women were seen as an important influence in building a society of strong, moral leaders. In 1825, Boston opened the first high school for women. That was followed by the establishment of Mount Holyoke

Serious study at Boston Public Library.

⊘ ENVIRONMENTAL STUDIES

With more than 100 colleges and universities, it's not surprising that nearly any course of study is available in New England. Most schools offer degrees in political science, history, and biology, but it's in the environmental field that New England's school excel. Some have programs which are focused on the region's unique attributes, particularly in regards to its vulnerable ecology. In addition to environmental engineering, geoscience, and maritime studies, there are concentrations in green building and community design, sustainable landscape horticulture, field naturalism, and even ecological economics.

Female Seminary in 1837 by Mary Lyon. Born in remote Buckland MA in 1797, she was unusual in that she attended school regularly until she was 13. The women were taught English, math, history, and geography. Her inspirational words, "Go

> "In New York," said Mark Twain, "they ask how much money a man has; in Philadelphia, what family he's from; in Boston, how much he knows."

The white colonists distrusted and discriminated against the Indians, setting up a pattern of displacement and poverty that still exists among the Algonquin and Abenaki people.

SCHOOL SEGREGATION

It was an equally grim situation for African-Americans. In 1800, Prince Hall began teaching black students in his Boston home, after the state legislature refused to extend public education to African-Americans. When abolitionists opened Noyes Academy in Canaan NH, a mob tore the building

Harvard University, Graduation Day.

where no one else will go, do what no one else will do," remain the school's philosophy. Notable graduates include Emily Dickinson; former Obama Deputy Chief of Staff Mona Sutphen, and Dulcy Singer, executive producer of *Sesame Street*.

NATIVE AMERICANS AT DARTMOUTH

While education was advancing for women, other groups were ignored. Although Dartmouth was founded with the express purpose of educating Native American males and incorporating them into "civilized" society, the effort largely failed. Few Indians arrived, and only one graduated. Many tribal members were not interested in assimilation and, even if they were, there were few schools in the areas where they lived.

down and fired cannons at the homes where the students were living. In 1849, Benjamin Roberts sued the City of Boston for the right of his daughter to attend high school. He lost the case, and it became the precedent which created the "separate but equal" concept of school segregation. In Canterbury CT, Prudence Crandall's decision to admit a black woman to her Female Boarding School in 1833 led to violent demonstrations and her arrest. The school was attacked by a mob following her acquittal, and she moved away. Even in more modern times, school busing – transporting children to schools in order to achieve racial balance – was met with rioting in Boston.

Ironically, many of the most vocal opponents of the busing program were descendants of Irish immigrants, who were not welcome in public schools when they arrived. The Irish established a system of parish schools (parochial schools) to provide elementary and secondary education, which became a mainstay of Catholic education.

THE LITTLE IVIES

New England is peppered with the campuses of the "Little Ivies" – schools which rival their better-known counterparts in excellence. The list of is long, with Bowdoin in Maine, Middlebury in Vermont, Wesleyan in Connecticut, and

TOWN VS. GOWN

Most of the colleges are in small towns, which reflect both the atmosphere of intellectual pursuits of the college and the youthful exuberance of their students. "Town–gown" issues arise over off-campus housing, loud parties and drinking, and parking congestion in residential areas near the schools. The towns are well aware of the positive economic impact the schools play in their community; the schools are aware of the need to maintain good relations with their non-collegiate neighbors. Compromises and conflict are constants in the

An exhibit at the Hart Nautical Museum, MIT campus, Cambridge, MA.

Amherst and Williams in Massachusetts the best known. The "Seven Sisters" are schools that were established when women were not admitted to other colleges. Mount Holyoke is one; the others in New England are Smith and Wellesley. Radcliffe was another, but has since been absorbed by Harvard and no longer exists as an independent entity.

The 19th century also saw the rise of the great public universities; each New England state supports one, with the University of Vermont (1791) occupying an unusual semi-private status. The Jesuit institutions Boston College and College of the Holy Cross (Massachusetts) and Fairfield University (Connecticut) are among the leaders in church-sponsored higher education.

communities. Most towns have only one school to consider. Some cities have several. Worcester MA is home to 10 colleges; Providence RI to six.

SPECIALTY SCHOOLS AND PROGRAMS

While New England's liberal arts schools are justly famous, the region also excels in the number of schools with specific concentrations.

Massachusetts Institute of Technology (MIT) enrolled its first students in 1865. MIT occupies an expansive campus along the Charles River in Cambridge. The Institute's graduates have been instrumental in making Boston a hub of the computer and other high-technology industries, an eastern counterpart to California's Silicon Valley. In nearby Worcester, Worcester Polytechnic Institute also opened in 1865. Its unique program sees students working on real-world projects from their first semester. Their incoming freshman student profile is actually better than that of MIT's entering class.

At the New England Conservatory of Music, students concentrate on orchestral music, voice, and composition. Berklee College of Music in Boston is the largest college of contemporary music in the world. Focusing on jazz and rock, it also offers courses in reggae and bluegrass. The New England Culinary Institute in Montpelier VT and Johnson and Wales University in Boston

In the recent past, Vermont and New Hampshire have grappled with the problem of school funding, with courts ruling that reliance upon local property taxes is unfair to children in towns with meager tax bases, and that revenue-sharing systems must be initiated. Even in more populous and urban Massachusetts, where professional educators are more likely to insulate citizens from education policy decisions, there have been heated public discussions over issues such as teacher competency tests, and the question of English-only instruction actually reached the ballot box in 2002 (and won).

An interior view of a modern science building on the campus of the University of Massachusetts-Amherst.

graduate highly trained chefs. Chester College in New Hampshire has a focus on creative writing as well as fine arts. Rhode Island School of Design and in Providence RI, the School of the Museum of Fine Arts in Boston, and Lyme Academy College of Fine Arts in Old Lyme, CT are all renowned for their visual arts programs.

THE FUNDING PREDICAMENT

Even in an era when public education largely fits a national rather than a regional mold, one strong aspect of the old colonial legacy robustly survives: a passionate grassroots involvement in education issues. Of the six New England states, only Rhode Island fails to make the Top Ten list of the best primary and middle schools in the nation.

⊘ HARVARD'S STATUS

Although it was technically not a religious but a civic institution, Harvard College served primarily to train ministers throughout the 17th century – a century which saw only 465 documented graduates. Harvard's greatest strides were taken during the four-decade presidency of Charles William Eliot (1869–1909), who introduced the elective system, modernized the teaching of law and medicine, and created a graduate school of arts and sciences. Born into an old Boston family himself, Eliot did more than any Harvard educator to elevate the university beyond its onetime status as a school largely attended by the local Brahmin class.

LITERARY UTOPIA

From Cotton Mather to Emily Dickinson and Robert Parker, New England writers have chronicled and commented on the region's people from Puritan times to modern day.

The Massachusetts Bay Colony was barely 10 years old when its first printing press turned out a new edition of the Book of Psalms. The 1640 *Bay Psalm Book* represented not only the beginning of American printing, but, as it was a fresh translation, of American literature as well. Along with Scriptures and sermons, 17th-century New England writers favored histories and biographies extolling the Puritan experiment.

The religious strain in early New England writing was the only approved context. The Puritan ethos had no room for a worldly focus. Even the poignant poems of Anne Bradstreet, which reflect on her life and family, are filled with religious imagery. (There are those who read into her works frustration and dissatisfaction with Puritan attitudes.)

THE SACRED AND THE SECULAR

The literary oratory of the Puritan preachers was as frightening as any Stephen King novel. Increase Mather's *An Essay for the Recording of Illustrious Providences* (1684) tells of the Devil tormenting Massachusetts villagers, and credits a Connecticut River flood as "an awful intimation of Divine displeasure." His son, Cotton Mather, was author of more than 400 works and a dogged chronicler of supernatural manifestations. His 1689 *Memorable Providences, Relating to Witchcrafts and Possessions* helped set the stage for the 1692 Salem witch hysteria. And staunchly orthodox Reverend Jonathan Edwards' 1741 sermon "Sinners in the Hands of an Angry God" must have made his congregation's blood run cold.

But it was also an era in which secular concerns became a part of the colonial life of letters. In Boston, James Franklin (brother of Benjamin) published one of New England's first successful newspapers, the *New England*

Cotton Mather, author of more than 400 works.

⊙ PIONEERING POETS

New England produced two poets of merit in the 17th century. Anne Bradstreet, who arrived with the first settlers of Boston in 1630, collected her early work in *The Tenth Muse Lately Sprung Up in America* (1650). She found inspiration in her own life experiences. Edward Taylor, a Massachusetts pastor, was the finest 17th-century American poet. His religious meditations have been compared to the English metaphysical poetry of his era; and his observations on commonplace subjects, as in "To a Spider Catching A Fly," reveal a talent for observation that transcend their purpose as religious metaphor.

Courant, beginning in 1721. Isaiah Thomas began publishing his *Massachusetts Spy* in 1770, airing revolutionary sentiments.

The early Federal period was the age of the "Connecticut Wits," a coterie noted for their fondness for formal Augustan poetry. Among them were lawyers John Trumbull and Joel Barlow, and longtime Yale president Timothy Dwight. The best remembered of their works is Barlow's *The Hasty Pudding*, a mock-heroic tribute to the simple cornmeal concoction that still appears on New England menus as "Indian Pudding."

Unitarian, found in that denomination's liberal humanism a cornerstone for the philosophy of Transcendentalism, which emphasized the unity of the individual soul with the rest of creation and with the divine. Its principles suffuse Emerson's poetry and essays such as *Self-Reliance*, as well as the work of Bronson Alcott (father of *Little Women* author Louisa May Alcott), Margaret Fuller, and Jones Very.

Emerson owned land just outside Concord, on Walden Pond. Here, his friend Henry David Thoreau built a cabin and spent two years living

An 1875 literary portrait in Boston includes Oliver Wendell Holmes (standing on left), and (left to right, seated) John Greenleaf Whittier, Ralph Waldo Emerson, John Lothrop Motley, Nathaniel Hawthorne, and Henry Wadsworth Longfellow.

Although he made his fame in New York City as a newspaper editor, Massachusetts-born William Cullen Bryant was still a New Englander when, in 1811, he wrote the first draft of his poem *Thanatopsis* at the age of 17. *Thanatopsis* (Greek for "a view of death") is noteworthy not only for reflecting the new romantic feeling in English poetry, but for presaging the influential role that nature would play in the Transcendentalist movement of the coming decades.

THE TRANSCENDENTALISTS

That era began with the 1836 publication of an essay called *Nature*, by Ralph Waldo Emerson, a young clergyman from Concord MA. Emerson, a

the life of rustic simplicity and contemplation which he chronicled in *Walden* (1854). Thoreau coupled the Transcendentalists' near-mystical sense of the oneness of man and nature with a naturalist's eye for observation and the fierce independence of conscience that blazes in his seminal essay *Civil Disobedience*.

FIRESIDE ENTERTAINMENT

New Englanders brought the Puritan's moral rectitude to the greatest national drama of their day, the struggle over slavery. The abolitionist movement had deep roots in New England, home of William Lloyd Garrison and his uncompromising newspaper *The Liberator*, and *Uncle Tom's Cabin* (1852) by author Harriet Beecher Stowe. William Wells Brown, an escaped slave, wrote *Clotel*, which deals with the destructive effects of slavery on slave and

---

The essay Civil Disobedience posits that individuals must not allow governments or actions to overrule their conscience. The essay influenced Mohandas Gandhi and Martin Luther King Jr.

A statue of Nathaniel Hawthorne in his hometown of Salem.

mulatto families. It is considered the first novel written by an African-American. John Greenleaf Whittier, a Quaker poet devoted to the cause, is today remembered less as an abolitionist than as one of the "fireside poets" of the post-Civil War years. Working in genres such as the pastoral (Whittier's 1866 *Snow-Bound*) and historical narrative (Henry Wadsworth Longfellow's *Evangeline* and *The Song of Hiawatha*), these created a common popular literature, often read aloud at the fireside.

One of the finest New England poets lived a secluded life in Amherst MA, far from literary salons. Emily Dickinson had a gem-cutter's way with language, crafting nearly 1,800 short lyric poems in which sharp observation of the material world was a prism for the timeless and universal. She shunned publication, and the first volume of her work didn't appear until 1890 – four years after her death.

The two New England giants of American literature in the mid-19th century defy any association with a school or movement of their day. Nathaniel Hawthorne had an early flirtation with Transcendentalism and radical communalism (his *The Blithedale Romance* is based in part on the Brook Farm commune is Massachusetts), but he was far too independent a figure to fit comfortably into Concord, where he spent part of his early career. Hawthorne mined the annals and mores of Puritan New England for the themes of guilt and consequence that inform *The Scarlet Letter* (1850) and *The House of the Seven Gables* (1851). His short stories,

⊘ NATHANIEL HAWTHORNE

The descendant of Salem Puritans, Hawthorne (1804–64) grew up with a family legend of a Judge Hawthorne, who, as a magistrate at the witchcraft trials, was cursed by a woman he convicted. Hawthorne would later use this story in *The House of the Seven Gables*.

In fact, much of Hawthorne's darkly romantic work was drawn from real life. In the 1836 tale, "The Minister's Black Veil," the protagonist explains: "If I hide my face for sorrow, there is cause enough, and if I cover it for secret sin, what mortal might not do the same." Hawthorne was no doubt familiar with the story of the Rev. Joseph Moody of York ME, who, after accidentally shooting and killing a friend on a hunting trip, became

morbidly frightened of having his friend's family and fiancée look upon him, and therefore covered his face with a black handkerchief.

"Young Goodman Brown," one of Hawthorne's greatest tales, also draws on his Salem heritage. In what may be a dream, Brown, wandering in the dark forest, comes upon the Devil, who leads him to a clearing where villagers are engaged in Devil-worship; among the congregation is Faith, Goodman's wife. In this tale, Hawthorne depicts a world sunk in evil: if Goodman Brown's vision is true, the Devil rules; if not, and if Goodman has imagined innocent people in Satan's service, he reveals, like the Salem Puritans, the depth of his own corruption.

many deeply allegorical, are often set in a mythic Puritan past.

Herman Melville was born in New York City, but spent much of his working life in New England. His masterpiece, *Moby-Dick*, employs the New England settings of New Bedford and Nantucket, both important whaling ports in the 19th century.

REGIONAL FOCUS

The post-Civil War era saw the rise of the Regional movement in American literature, represented in New England by figures such as Sarah Orne Jewett, a novelist of coastal Maine, and Rowland Robinson, a Vermonter with a

> *The House of the Seven Gables influenced the writings of horror and fantasy writer H. P. Lovecraft. The Pyncheon family did exist and are related to modern author Thomas Pynchon, whose writings as also dense and complex.*

The enduring image of Moby-Dick.

Author Herman Melville.

⊘ HERMAN MELVILLE

At the age of 20, Melville set sail on a packet to Liverpool in England, and two years later, in 1841, traveled to the South Seas on the whaler *Acushnet*. Although he later jumped ship to join the US Navy, it was to be a life-changing voyage, for it provided him with his first successful books, *Typee or a Peep at Polynesian Life* (1846) and *Omoo: A Narrative of Adventures in the South Seas* (1847).

He married Elizabeth Shaw and they had four children. He continued to write sea stories, mostly because he needed to earn money, but he was inspired by the dark genius of Nathaniel Hawthorne to attempt the epic narrative that became *Moby-Dick; or, The Whale* (1851). This masterpiece, written while he was living in Pittsfield MA,

draws upon the character of Yankee whalers Melville met during his own time in the "fishery," but the tale of Captain Ahab's relentless pursuit of the whale that had bitten off his leg assumes allegorical overtones as the crew of the *Pequod* are carried to their doom by Ahab's monomania.

Like much of his work, *Moby-Dick* was better received in England than in America. After a breakdown, Melville visited Hawthorne in Liverpool, where Hawthorne was serving as American consul. Later he worked as a customs officer in New York harbor. He died in 1891, his work largely forgotten.

In recent years, some critics have perceived homoerotic overtones in works such as *Pierre* and *Billy Budd*.

sharp ear for the dialect of upcountry Yankees and French-Canadian immigrants. William Dean Howells, who edited *The Atlantic Monthly*, made Boston the setting of *A Modern Instance* (1882) and *The Rise of Silas Lapham* (1885), both of which deal with men on the make in a city flush with prosperity.

Henry James (1843–1916) set many of his short stories in Boston's upper-class society, which also provided the milieu for *The Europeans* (1878) and for *The Bostonians* (1886), his satire on the city's radical and reformist circles.

often darkly conflicted individuals. Robert Frost (1874–1963), born in California of an old New England family but a resident of rural Vermont and New Hampshire for much of his life, created a universal language out of dry, economical Yankee speech. Edith Wharton was the first woman to win the Pulitzer Prize for fiction in 1920 for *The Age of Innocence*.

In the theater, Eugene O'Neill (1888–1953), brought up partly in Connecticut and associated as a young man with the Provincetown Players on Cape Cod, offered the bleak *Desire Under the*

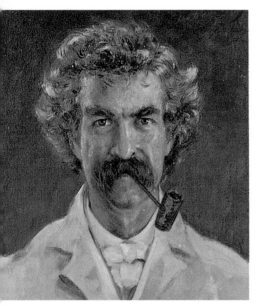

Mark Twain, professional wit and master storyteller.

John Irving with the Oscar he won for adapting his novel The Cider House Rules for Hollywood.

It was an age that saw one writer who belonged to a world far from New England happily set down roots in the region: Samuel Langhorne Clemens, better known as Mark Twain, built a sprawling mansion in Hartford CT and transported a representative native of the state to medieval England in *A Connecticut Yankee in King Arthur's Court*.

MODERN TRENDS

By 1900, New England had ceased to be the most socially and economically vigorous part of the United States, but it still provided fertile ground for writers. Edward Arlington Robinson (1869–1935) drew upon characters of his native small-town Maine to create incisive portraits of

Elms and the uncharacteristically comic *Ah, Wilderness*, both with New England settings.

Local fiction in the 20th century ranged from John P. Marquand's skewering appraisal of the Boston Brahmin class run to ground in *The Late George Apley* (1937) to philosopher George Santayana's darker analysis of a similar scion of the old order in *The Last Puritan* (1936). John Cheever may have moved from his native Massachusetts to New York, but his morally struggling suburbanites traded heavily in the old New England themes of guilt and redemption. John Updike, a New Englander by choice, presented the quandaries of his characters in early novels and stories set in the suburbs of Boston. And, far from the middle class of Cheever and Updike, Jack Kerouac set several autobiographical novels in the French-Canadian quarter of his native Lowell MA.

TODAY'S TOP WRITERS

With its scores of colleges and universities, the region has attracted authors not necessarily rooted in the region and its traditional concerns. Jhumpa Lahiri, London-born but Rhode Island-raised and educated, uses Boston as a setting for some of her short stories which explore conflicts and confusion of Indians adjusting to new cultures in her 1999 book *Interpreter of Maladies*, for which she garnered a Pulitzer Prize. In 2009 Pulitzer Prize was awarded to Portland-native Elizabeth Strout for her Maine-set collection of short stories *Olive Kitteridge* while Boston-born Paul Harding won the 2010 Pulitzer Prize for his powerful portrayal of New England father and son in *Tinkers*.

Even a small state like Vermont can boast internationally recognized names such as Julia Alvarez, Jamaica Kincaid, and David Mamet. Native or not, though, many writers fasten quickly to New England locales and themes. Boston lawyer George V. Higgins gave us the rough side of his city's life and language via *The Friends of Eddie Coyle* (1972). Dennis Lahane does much the same with *Mystic River* (2001) and *Gone, Baby, Gone* (1998). In *Empire Falls* (2001) Richard Russo serves up his characters in the matrix of a decaying Maine mill town. John Irving, who lives in Vermont, made the quirks of New Englanders part of *The Hotel New Hampshire* (1981), *The Cider House Rules* (1985), and *Last Night in Twisted River* (2009). Another Vermont resident, Jodi Picoult, places many of her 24 novels in New England.

Howard Frank Mosher, also a Vermonter, lovingly portrays the vanishing world of the backcountry yeomen and eccentrics of the state's remote Northeast Kingdom in *Where the Rivers Flow North* (1978) and *On Kingdom Mountain* (2007). Another Vermont author, Chris Bohjalian, has set moral dilemmas in small towns in novels such as *Midwives* (1996) and *The Law of Similars* (1998).

New England academia has provided the setting for works such as Yale professor Stephen L. Carter's *New England White* (2007) and Philip Roth's *The Human Stain* (2001), both dealing with the complexities of race on campus.

In the realm of popular reading, Robert B. Parker's Spenser detective novels have a vivid Boston setting. And, up in Bangor, in a big Victorian house behind an iron fence festooned with bats and spiderwebs, lives a native son who uses nondescript Maine settings while scaring his readers out of their wits. His name is Stephen King.

Author Stephen King at a book-signing in 2014.

⊘ STEPHEN KING'S MAINE

Stephen King has done for Maine what Charles Dickens did for Victorian London, and fans of the prolific writer have fun trying to identify the real-life locations that turn up, thinly disguised, in his creepy tales. Indeed, there's a nascent Stephen King Trail, taking in Kezar Lake, near Lovell (Dark Score Lake in *Bag of Bones*), Bridgton (setting for *The Mist* and *The Body*), Hampden (*Carrie*), Orrington (*Pet Sematary*), Long Lake (*The Shining*), and Durham (*Salem's Lot*). King, born in 1947, has a summer lodge near Lovell and an old lumber baron's mansion near Bangor (a town disguised as Derry in *It*). To locate the mansion, look for a locked gate decorated with a bronze vampire.

LOBSTERS AND LOCAVORES

A new generation of chefs with fresh ideas and a novel appreciation for locally sourced ingredients is whetting appetites from the Maine coast to the Berkshire Mountains.

If it weren't for codfish, New England might never have been settled. It was the abundant cod that initially lured English fishermen, and eventually settlers, to this land. New arrivals quickly learned to appreciate oysters, clams, and the many types of fish that swam in the offshore waters. The unforgiving land was hard to till, but the Indians taught them how to cultivate corn and wheat and which plants and berries were edible. All healthy, to be sure, but not exciting. Even when the maritime trade brought in spices and ingredients from around the world, New England had a reputation for dull food.

That's changing as creative chefs – like groundbreaker Lydia Shire (often considered the first of the truly inventive New England chefs) at Scampo, Tiffani Faison at Tiger Mama or Juan Pedroso at Ivonne's, all in Boston; Matthew Varga at Gracie's in Providence; or Doug Mack at Mary's in distant Bristol VT – with a passion for fresh, local, organic ingredients find surprisingly fertile ground in New England's rocky soil.

HARVEST FROM THE SEA

The sea is where the new New England cuisine started and it still provides the primary offering on most menus. The Pilgrims wouldn't have known what to make of our mania for lobster. They considered the crustaceans fit only for pig food, or bait; well into the 19th century, boatloads of lobsters sold for pennies, and prisoners rioted at the prospect of yet another lobster dinner. But lobster has gone upscale. While creative preparations abound, menus retain traditional boiled lobsters, lobster ravioli, lobster macaroni and cheese, and "lobster rolls" – toasted hot dog buns filled with chunks of lobster meat, tossed with celery and mayonnaise or melted butter.

Cape Cod is world-renowned for its oysters.

New England's fabled clam chowder got its name from the French settlers of Canada, who simmered their soups in a *chaudière* (cauldron). Such long, slow cooking is needed to render large hard-shell quahogs (pronounced "ko-hogs") palatable. Small and medium-size clams – cherrystones and littlenecks – are delectable served raw on the half-shell. Soft-shell, long-neck clams – commonly known as "steamers" – are a favored repast all along the coast, dipped first in their own broth (to wash off the grit), then melted butter. Clam shacks fire up their fry-o-lators to prepare another favorite: clams batter-coated or simply rolled in cornmeal and fried.

Clambakes were once a New England tradition, especially on Cape Cod. The customary

Once thought too cold for planting vineyards, New England now has several wineries. Experts say it's a sign of global warming – that once-frigid New England is developing a climate favorable for growing grapes.

procedure was to dig a pit on the beach, line it with stones, build a driftwood fire, cover the hot stones with seaweed, add clams and their

exposure to European traditions has introduced two relatively new seafood treats: mussels, long ignored by New England restaurants, are now very nearly ubiquitous, while scallops are finding favor in the kitchen.

FAVORITES FROM THE HEARTH

Not all New England culinary standards come from the sea. New Englanders ate pot roasts, potpies, and stews – the sort of things people living a demanding physical life needed to keep themselves going. They're still found on the

Serving Boston's theater district since 1868.

accompaniments (typically, lobsters, potatoes, corn on the cob), and then top it all off with more seaweed, a sailcloth tarp, and plenty of sand, leaving the whole to bake for about an hour. Most restaurants these days dispense with clambake per se, and just serve what's called a "shore dinner" – steamed.

Oysters are a popular dish in New England, and have been from the very beginning. As early as 1601, Samuel de Champlain had singled out the area now known as Wellfleet, on Cape Cod, for its exceptional beds. To this day, Wellfleet and Cotuit, on Cape Cod, are world-renowned for their oysters.

Fillet of young cod, haddock, striped bass, and bluefish still grace traditional menus, although

menus of traditional restaurants specializing in "comfort food."

Boston has its famous baked beans, more commonly found in northern Maine and New Hampshire. For dessert, try Indian pudding, based on cornmeal and molasses; you'll soon notice that Vermonters will add maple syrup to almost anything. Blueberries ripen in early summer, and cranberries star in fall festivals from Plymouth to Nantucket.

LOCAVORES AND LOCAL SOURCING

Despite its relatively short growing season, New England has become a center for the "locavore" movement. Advocates obtain most, if not all, of their foods locally. They promote the value of eating foods grown without chemicals (whether pesticides or fertilizers), supporting local farmers (which supports the local economy), and reducing the environmental impact of transporting foods over long distances. Pick-your-own farms and farm stands proliferate throughout the region from early summer to early autumn, as fruits and vegetables come into season.

Artisan cheese-making is all the rage in upcountry New England, particularly in Vermont. Shelburne Farms and Grafton cheddars,

restaurants, steak houses, and Chinese takeaway were standard. Mexican restaurants with combo platters of burritos and refried beans were considered exotic. Aside from a few ethnic islands like the Portuguese enclaves in Providence, there was little to distinguish one town's cooking from another. The shift to an interest in flavorful dining coincided with the waves of immigrants arriving not just from Europe, but from Asia, Latin America, and the Caribbean. Japanese, Thai, and Vietnamese restaurants opened to serve the new communities, and the enticing aromas drew

Boston's Cheers Bar, inspiration for the classic television series Cheers (1982–93).

Bayley Hazen and Green Mountain blue cheeses, and sheep's milk cheese from Willow Hill Farms and Three Shepherds of the Mad River Valley are all worth seeking out.

Chefs eagerly support the "locally sourced" concept, for many of the same reasons consumers like it. Many menus brag about their use of local ingredients. The "Vermont Fresh" program gives restaurants buying locally a decal to display, while Massachusetts "Culinary Cuisine" tourism initiative directs visitors to locavore-minded restaurants.

DISCOVERING FLAVORS

For decades, American palates accepted bland staples as de rigeur when dining out. Italian

⦿ EASTIE FOODS

A stroll through the streets of East Boston is a culinary walk around the world. Usually referred to as "Eastie," East Boston was the first neighborhood where each arriving group of immigrants settled. Starting with the Irish in the 1840s, it's seen Italians, Jews, Russians, and Poles. More recently, Pakistanis and Indians, Asians, and Latinos have arrived. Although most nationalities move to other areas as their finances allow, the restaurants they opened often remain behind. You can start with Lolly's Bakery on Bennington Street, have lunch at a Salvadoran, Vietnamese, or Italian place, and finish with ice cream from Frio Rico (www.friorico.com) in Bennington Street.

customers for whom chicken korma and lobster sautéed with ginger and scallions were a revelation. It didn't take long for the trend to extend to New England's ingredients.

Chefs transform traditional New England products into creative new "fusion" preparations. Adventurous eaters can have salad of Maine rock crab with lobster knuckles and fried taro, crispy squash risotto cakes, pumpkin ravioli with mussels marinière, lightly fried lobster with lemongrass and Thai basil, or seared scallops in cider sauce.

TAKING IT NATIONAL

Some of the specialty foods made in New England are distributed nationally. In Connecticut, the late actor Paul Newman's "Newman's Own" brand of salad dressing, pasta sauces, popcorn, and cookies still donates its profits to charities. Vermont's maple syrup and Waterbury-based Ben and Jerry's Ice Cream are found in groceries nationwide. That may violate the tenets of the culinary environmentalists, but it's a boon to the region's economy and promises that a taste of New England can be had anywhere.

Craft beer selection.

⊘ NEW ENGLAND'S BREWERY SCENE

New England was at the forefront of the microbrew revolution, which began in the early 1990s. Starting in garages and basements, the fledgling brewmasters found appreciative audiences and quickly expanded their offerings and the availability of their product. While some limit their production strictly to brewing beer, many others operate brewpubs serving a range of regional and international beers.

Vermont has more microbreweries (meaning a very small output) per capita than any other state. Its most popular labels include Otter Creek, Long Trail, Magic Hat, Catamount, Rock Art, Trout River, and Wolaver's (organic). New Hampshire holds its annual brewfest of

beers from throughout New England every June in Lincoln. Redhook, Smuttynose, and Shipyard are all "craft brewers," which generally and informally means their output is fairly large and is distributed throughout New England and often beyond. It also means that if you like it, you can probably find it wherever you travel.

Although Boston sports bars like The Fours on Canal Street or Mike's on Davis Square sell a lot of the national brands, like Budweiser and Coors, it's no longer unusual for someone who drifts in to watch a BoSox game on the big screen to have a critical conversation with the bartender about the "hoppiness" of what's on tap.

🔍 SWEET TREATS

These sweet New England treats will make you say "Whoopie" for Whoopie Pies and other tasty concoctions.

A favorite confectionary treat all over New England, the Whoopie Pie is the state's Official Treat. The "pie" is really two round, mound-shaped pieces of chocolate cake with a sweet, creamy filling sandwiched inside. Just the right size to fit in your hand, it's a caloric, teeth-decaying bit of happiness.

Its origins are obscure and the subject of some culinary controversy. Maine claims the cookie/cake as its own, although it's not clear how it got there. The Amish in Pennsylvania claim it's one of their creations. Mainers suggest that perhaps Amish moving up north to live Downeast brought it with them. It's never actually come to blows, but residents of each state are quick to claim the original recipes.

Maine's Official State Dessert, meanwhile, is the blueberry pie. Considering that Maine is the primary grower of blueberries in the country, it seems fair. The berry is often used in one of the region's other famous desserts: pandowdy (or pan dowdy, the spelling varies; it's also sometimes called grunt, cobbler, crumble, or buckle). It's a pie plate filled with apples or berries sweetened with maple syrup, honey, or molasses, with a crumbled crust baked on top. Blueberry pie is frequently served warm with vanilla ice cream on top, in a combination that wins hearts around the world.

New Englanders have a passionate love of ice cream. Although vanilla is almost always the favorite in polls, you should try Grape-Nuts ice cream. The crunchy cereal (which has neither grapes nor nuts) is mixed into the ice cream before it freezes. (It is also particularly good on pan dowdy.) The United States leads the world in per capita ice cream consumption, and New Englanders are said to eat 14 pints more of the stuff every year than the average American.

Strawberry shortcake is also popular treat, but New Englanders make theirs with a biscuit, not shortcake. For overseas visitors, this can be a bit confusing, because a biscuit is a cross between a roll and a crumpet – a far cry from the traditional cookie. The basic concept of the strawberry shortcake has been expanded to include cakes, cookies, and even cartoon characters.

Perhaps the dessert with the most valid historical pedigree is Indian Pudding. Also called Hasty Pudding, it was one of the first desserts the Pilgrims made. Used to creamy concoctions they left behind in England, they were thrilled when milch cows finally arrived in the New World. They blended milk with cornmeal, eggs, butter, cinnamon, ginger, and molasses and baked it. Boston Cream Pie (the State Dessert of Massachusetts) also has Colonial origins. The early colonists put cream filling between two cakes; in 1855, a chef at the Parker House Hotel

A Whoopie Pie makes for a tasty treat.

in Boston added the chocolate icing and renamed it.

The sweetest of all New England ingredients is maple syrup. The Indians taught the Pilgrims how to tap the sap from maple trees and turn it into a thick, sweet syrup. Traditionally, buckets are hung from tubes drilled into trees, collected and drained by hand, with the sap being boiled for hours until it reaches the desired consistency. Modern methods reduce some of the labor, and you can visit "sugar shacks" in the spring to see how it's done. It takes about 40 gallons of sap to make one gallon of syrup, so that bottle of syrup can be quite valuable. Maple syrup and its by-products are used almost everywhere and in everything: maple syrup over pancakes, maple-cured sausage and bacon, maple ice cream, maple candy.

BUILDING NEW ENGLAND

Shingles and clapboards, gables and steeples; New England's buildings reflect the beauty of its landscape and the practicality of its people.

Tourists visiting the full inventory of historic homes in New England hear a lot of architectural terms – Palladian, neoclassical, Greek Revival, Federalist. If asked, only a few could define them and fewer could explain why they matter. But the buildings of New England say as much about the people and their history as the events that took place in and around them. If you can read New England's architecture, you come close to reading New England itself.

PURITAN PRACTICALITY

No original examples of the very first New England architecture remain. Those were the steep-gabled, one-room huts the Pilgrims shivered in during the winter of 1620–21. They understandably built something more substantial as soon as they could.

Their new homes were not built with an eye towards beauty, although there is something stirring and attractive in their stark simplicity. These "first period" houses are heavy and medieval and almost entirely without ornamentation. Simple oblong boxes, they were framed and filled with the waddle-and-daub that was left visible on half-timbered houses in England. That stemmed equally from the Puritan's distain for worldly affectations and the sheer practicality of their situation. Faced with the rigors of simply surviving in the harsh New England environment, they did not have the time or inclination to spend on anything that was unnecessary. Clapboards provided a thin blanket of protection against winter's snow and cold. Combined with the steep roof and massive central chimney shared by rooms on both levels of the house, the early dwellings of the stern Pilgrims reflected their authoritative character. (Good examples of these are the 1640

The 1683 Capen House, Topsfield, Massachusetts.

Whipple House in Ipswich MA and the 1641 Wing Fort House in East Sandwich MA).

In many of the early homes, the upper floor extended slightly beyond the lower. This overhang mimicked the practical design of townhomes in English cities, where the lower floor entrance was set back from the busy, dirty, congested street. In the colonies, however, space was not at a premium and houses could be set back easily. Within a few years, that style was abandoned and both levels of the houses were flush with each other. (The 1683 Parson Capen House in Topsfield MA is an example of this design.)

Seventeenth-century public buildings – called meetinghouses – were equally without embellishment. The large rooms often served as both the town hall and center for worship, reflecting the early ties between church and state. While most houses of this period are gone, many of the meetinghouses remain. (The Old Ship Meetinghouse in Hingham MA is one.)

THE GEORGIAN STYLE

As survival became more assured and their finances improved, the colonists began to indulge themselves by adding flourishes to their humble homes. In heavily Puritan-influenced areas, those were modest touches, justified by

Although there are subtle variations in the specifics, only a dedicated historian or obsessed amateur can tell the difference. These are the buildings you are likely to think of when you imagine the homes of patriots in powdered wigs. The overall concept of the design is symmetry: Everything is in balance; the proportions are equal; the construction is solid. The buildings exude stability, serenity, elegance, and wealth. The style has a staying powder that has far outlasted its origins; "Colonial"-style homes are the most frequently built and most popular in the US real estate market.

A classic Georgian-style building in Deerfield Village.

deciding the improvements were rewards from God for living a properly sacred life.

At the turn of the 18th century, settlements were being established away from the original towns, and commerce was developing with other locations even farther afield. These drew the more adventurous spirits and those who chafed at the rigid religious principles which limited personal expression. Along the coast, where maritime trading and fishing were making their mark, money and exposure to influences from abroad combined to weaken the religious hold on taste and propriety and allow for displays of success in the form of impressive mansions.

Pre-Revolutionary architecture is called variously "Georgian," "Colonial," and "Palladian."

"Gingerbread" is the architectural term describing elaborate ornamentation, particularly hand-carved wooden latticework on verandas of houses built in the latter part of the 19th century. The village of Oak Bluffs on Martha's Vineyard is almost entirely filled with "gingerbread" houses.

The inspiration for the style came from the 16th-century Italian architect Andrea Palladio (hence the term "Palladian"). His designs were used extensively as London was rebuilt following the 1666 fire which reduced much of the city to ashes. It was only natural that what was popular in England would make its way to the colonies, where the people were eager to imitate the latest fashions of the Mother Country.

The term "Georgian" came into use a bit later. It refers to the time of the three English King Georges (1714–1820). Given the souring of relations between the colonies and the kings during that time frame, it wasn't a term used often by 17th-century realtors.

One distinguishing feature of a typical Colonial/Georgian/Palladian house was its size.

Georgian homes, with wood-paneled walls and broad stairways, had larger rooms and more privacy. Four full rooms, both upstairs and down, were the norm. Two separate chimneys serviced the two, now larger, halves of the house. These two leaner towers added to exterior elegance and richness while leaving room for a deep hallway where the massive chimney had been.

Old Deerfield MA has several fine examples of Georgian houses which managed to survive the frequent raids by Native Americans during

A Federal-style home in Newburyport.

⊘ VILLAGE DESIGN

Just as houses reflect the New Englander character, so did the arrangement of their villages. The idea of a planned community is not unique to 20th-century developers. Early settlements were compact, practical affairs, with houses nestled around a village green, which was dominated by a church, demonstrating the supremacy of religious authority. The green served several purposes. It was a common grazing area for livestock; it was safer to let the animals graze there than to let them roam freely. It was a community gathering place, and criminal punishments like floggings and hangings were big draws.

the early days of settlement. The 1733 Ashley House and 1743 Sheldon-Hawks House stand at the north end of Deerfield's main thoroughfare.

By mid-century, coastal ports were very profitable, as sea captains' and merchants' houses showed. Many of these were later remodeled, making it difficult to find a "purebred" house of the period. Portsmouth NH is blessed with two unsullied originals – the 1763 Moffatt-Ladd House and the 1760 Wentworth-Coolidge House.

By the end of the Revolution, architectural tastes were changing. The new nation sought new expressions of its personality. Perhaps deliberately, perhaps subliminally, during the first decades of the new republic, it developed a distinctive architectural appearance.

THE FEDERAL STYLE

Following the Revolution, optimism was palpable in harbors from Boston to Bath, Salem to New Bedford. Even inland, whaling, shipbuilding, and the expansion of trade around the globe brought the influence of the sea to many New Englanders as the coastal merchants commanded the goods and natural resources of the whole region. Fine houses were built in towns far from the seaports by prospering local businessmen. But no country carpenter could rival the skills of Salem's Samuel McIntire or Boston's Charles Bulfinch.

built in the early 1800s when the sea captains decided to move away a little from the noise and clutter of the port. (To see McIntire's interior artistry, tour the Gardner-Pingree House.)

Salem stands as a success in the often-heartbreaking saga of period buildings being discarded and destroyed in the face of newer architectural styles and community needs. Both there and in nearby Newburyport, preservation-minded private owners and community groups buy and restore the old buildings and lead efforts to rejuvenate historic town centers by

The Massachusetts State House.

Back Bay brownstones.

Their combined work represents the finest of the period. McIntire's inspiration was Robert Adam, the Scottish architect who raised the art of interior decoration to exquisite heights with his dainty stucco reliefs. Such detailing, along with free-standing curved stairways and delicate fireplace mantels, characterize Federal interior design. The structural design is a square, three-story building with chimneys on the outer walls and a portico over the entrance. McIntire introduced these elements in Salem.

The full impact of McIntire's work in Salem is best grasped on Chestnut Street, which in its entirety has been designated a National Historic Landmark. Up and down both sides of this majestic street are stunning Federal-style mansions,

putting them to new uses and promoting them as the historic landmarks they are.

BULFINCH'S MASTERPIECES

The Federalist era peaked with the work of Charles Bulfinch (1763–1844). The jewel of his New England portfolio is the Massachusetts State House, standing atop Beacon Hill. (The claimant for the top spot in his showcase is the US Capitol in Washington DC). Majestic in scope and symbolism now, it was even more so in 1798 when it was surrounded by open land and dominated the city by its visibility from anywhere.

The neoclassical State House, very Palladian in inspiration, has been extended twice in two contradictory styles. The 1890 addition to the back of the building is a lumpish but highly mannered Baroque echo of its opposing side. The second addition in 1914 neutralized the first by blotting it out from view. The two massive marble wings serve as a neutral backdrop for the golden-domed Bulfinch original.

Bulfinch was in on the beginning of the Beacon Hill speculation, and the three homes he built for developer Harrison Gray Otis in 1796, 1802, and 1805 reflect the evolution of the Federal residential style. Several other Bulfinch-designed rowhouses grace Chestnut Street.

GREEK GRANDEUR

Along with covered bridges, the white steeples of village churches are a symbol of rural New England. Their design can be traced to Asher Benjamin, an influential force in New England architecture at the beginning of the 19th century. In his first architectural handbook, he rendered a steepled church which became the prototype for hundreds of buildings. Although the fundamental design has never changed, the detailing gives clues as to when a church was built.

In 1830, Benjamin encouraged New England to adopt the Greek Revival style, which was popular elsewhere. Identified by the grand size and use of massive columns, its most popular use is for civic buildings and institutions. In Boston, the Quincy Marketplace building and the 1828 Arcade in Providence RI are sterling examples of the style.

FORM VS. FUNCTION

The beginning of the Industrial Age saw a shift in the principles of the region's architecture. Houses were primarily shelter; industrial buildings were sturdy and practical. By 1850, something had changed. Perhaps for no other reason than boredom with symmetry, scale, and four-square plans, architecture took off in a riot of historic revivals.

Gothic, Italianate, Renaissance, and Romanesque are among the eclectic labels attached to the late 19th-century designs. Descriptions are lengthy and confusing; visual examples provide a better frame of reference. The Connecticut capitol in Hartford is Gothic; so are the "gingerbread" cottages on Martha's Vineyard. Boston's Trinity Church is an outspoken example of Romanesque design (by Henry Hobson Richardson); Boston Public Library is Renaissance Revival as interpreted by McKim, Mead & White.

For an immersion course in all the variations and applications, tour the summer "cottages" built by the elite on Newport. The mansions reflect

> *Often considered the enfant terrible of modern architecture, Philip Johnson was instrumental in starting a revolution in American architecture by forcing designers to rethink their concepts of style, ornamentation, and use of space.*

Boston's Trinity Church, built in 1872–77.

everything from Italian Renaissance to Beaux Arts, Rococo to the Palace of Versailles. Far from being an evolutionary development growing out of New England's personality, these were imports reflecting mainstream American trends.

INFLUENCE OF PHILIP JOHNSON

Architect Philip Johnson (1906–2005) profoundly influenced architectural styles and philosophy in the 20th century. His principles of clean lines with no applied decorations and volume over mass inspired a generation of modern buildings, used extensively in inner-city urban-renewal projects – accused as often of being soulless and sterile as they are inspiring and ethereal. His first major work was his personal residence. The "Glass

House" in New Canaan CT is the ultimate example of his concept. It uses the landscape to create the "walls" which set the visual and mental limitations of space. His works in the region include the List Art Gallery in Providence RI and the Kline Science Center at Yale. (He graduated from rival Harvard.)

INTERNATIONAL INPUT

Johnson's ideas as interpreted by both domestic and non-native architects play an important part in the look of 20th-century New England. Harvard University boasts the only Le Corbusier building in the United States (the Carpenter Center), and Walter Gropius built a model Bauhaus house in the Boston suburb of Lincoln. At MIT, Eero Saarinen designed the striking Kresge Auditorium and Chapel. I.M. Pei designed Boston's Hancock Tower, a cool glass 60-story rhomboid that reflects its surroundings and constantly changing cloudscapes above; other Pei projects in the city include an addition to the Boston Public Library which quotes the original's mass without copying its rich ornamentation – a direct line between Johnson's ideas and practical application. Pei is

Lowell's sturdy, practical industrial buildings.

⊘ CHARLES BULFINCH

Even in an age where success often came young, Charles Bulfinch (1763–1844) was exceptional. Often considered America's first professional architect, he had his first major commission at the age of 25, when he designed the Hollis Street Church in Boston. His works are noted for their simplicity and balance, creating an aura of good taste and respectability in residences, honor and high values in public structures. His most famous work in Boston is the Massachusetts State House (1798); Boston Common and University Hall at Harvard show his influence. But his most important work is the US Capitol Building in Washington DC.

also responsible for the Christian Science Center.

More recently, British architect James Stirling chose a postmodernist–Egyptian motif for Harvard's Sackler Museum of ancient, Islamic, and Asian art; and Japanese architect Tadao Ando took his inspiration from mid-century's austere International style in his 2008 Stone Hill Center at the Clark Institute in Williamstown MA. Like Ando, the New York firm of Diller Scofidio + Renfro places great emphasis on sleekly framed outdoor vistas in its 2006 Institute of Contemporary Art (ICA) on the Boston waterfront. With its top floor cantilevered over the harbor's edge, the ICA is, in the words of *Boston Globe* architecture critic Robert Campbell, "intensely involved with the sea." As, indeed, nearly all of New England once was.

SPORTS AND OUTDOOR ACTIVITIES

One of the biggest reasons to visit New England is to enjoy its great outdoors; you don't have to go far to get close to nature, and the possibilities for exploration are endless.

Regardless of ability or interest, New England is the place to get outdoors and enjoy nature. You can explore on foot, by bicycle, or on back of a snowmobile. With a variety of activities in every kind of weather, make sure your trip to New England takes advantage of the great sports and outdoor activities.

MOUNTAIN BIKING

Everywhere you go in New England, you see bicycles. Even in busy Boston, the HubWay (www. thehubway.com) bike-rental program encourages people to pedal around town. It's certainly the most relaxing way to view the countryside. Forget the traffic: on a bike, you're able to really enjoy the scenery, stop when and where you want to look at a view or watch a moose grazing in a marsh by the roadside, park the bike for an impromptu stroll up the beach or splash in the ocean, pause at a covered bridge for pictures, pedal past stately sea captains' mansions and back roads where cows look up from their grazing to watch you roll by. It's particularly nice during fall foliage season; on a bike, you don't have to deal with the heavy traffic and can really slow down, take side roads on a moment's whim, and savor the views.

You can plan a trip to go inn-to-inn, staying somewhere different each night or use one town as a base and explore the area in a different direction every day. There are at least a half-dozen companies offering guided biking tours in New England. That's a good choice if you don't know the area and are not comfortable with making your own arrangements. Most of them concentrate on tours of three to six days on the Maine Coast and Acadia, Martha's Vineyard and Nantucket, or Rhode Island's coastline, all of which are easy rides, although some are more

Mountain biking near the village of Bethel, in Maine.

challenging. One treks through the Berkshires, one along the Champlain Valley, and a more strenuous one bikes in the White Mountains. Their itineraries all include stops at museums and extra activities like kayak excursions. Several of them also offer self-guided tours, making all arrangements for accommodations and providing you with detailed maps and cue sheets. Bike trails – like the Blackstone River Greenway which will run 48 miles (77km) from Providence RI to Worcester MA, or the Cape Cod National Seashore biking trails – are developed routes bikers can enjoy for a day or longer. Mountain bikers consider New England to have some of the best trails in the eastern US, particularly in the White Mountains and Maine. Many ski resorts (like Jiminy Peak) offer mountain biking during the summer, which is a great introduction to the sport. There are no organized tours, but several websites connect bikers. For tour companies, visit www.CTbiketours.com, www.bikethewhites.com, or www.bikeandthelike.com. If mountain biking is more your style, visit www.bustedspoke.com.

CAMPING

Camping means many things to many people. For the purists, it's pitching a tent along a mountain trail far from any human influence. For others, it's water nearby. Others accommodate RVs. The best resource for detailed information on campsites on national property is the *U.S. National Forest Campground Guide* (www.forestcamping.com), which lists complete details of every site, however humble and remote. Private campgrounds are equally diverse, some striving to create as "natural" an experience as they can, while others have pools, game rooms, and planned activities. The Good Sam Club (www.goodsamclub.com) produces an excellent directory for the RV community. Backpackers, thru-hikers, and tent campers use

Camping in the backwoods of Maine.

hooking up a motor coach with air-conditioning and a flat-screen TV at an RV park with resort amenities. And there's a vast middle ground of "pop-up" campers, cabin stays, and "sleep in the back of your SUV" adventures. Most campers want some chance to get closer to the outdoors; campgrounds are usually in or near places for hiking or along beaches. Some are on the outskirts of tourist-popular areas – like the towns of Mystic or Shelburne – which give the best of both worlds. All of those options are met by state parks and national parks and forests, although what options are offered varies greatly, depending on the location. Some "primitive" sites are just that: a clearing along a trail that might or might not have a portable toilet or pump for drinkable resources like the Appalachian Mountain Club (www.outdoors.org) as a starting point for information. KOA campgrounds (www.koa.com) are particularly welcoming to tent campers; some of their facilities have on-site cabins, vintage trailers, yurts, and tepees for rent.

DOG SLEDDING AND SKIJORING

There are few more thrilling ways to experience the backcountry than by being a passenger in a dog sled gliding over the snow, powered by a team of incredibly strong, deliriously happy huskies. Most people are happy with a ride, but if you want to imagine yourself in the Iditarod, consider a course in dog mushing. Lasting from one to three days, you learn all about the care and feeding of the dogs; how to harness and hitch the team; how to drive, steer, and – hopefully – how to stop. The longer courses usually involve overnight trips, staying at lodges. A lack of snow doesn't end the fun. Most places use wheeled carts in spring and summer and during fall foliage. An increasingly popular human-canine activity is skijoring, which is dog-assisted Nordic skiing. Human and dog are harnessed together and the dog helps pull the skier. The Vermont Outdoor Guide Association (www.voga.org) has a detailed directory of dog-sled operations. New

region itself, there are a nearly infinite number of possibilities: the scenic Cliff Walk in Newport; through the woods to a stunning waterfall in a state park in Massachusetts; learning to iden-tify trees and birds on marked trails near towns in Vermont; scrambling up rockfalls on rugged trails in New Hampshire. During fall foliage, it's the overwhelming beauty of walking through a tunnel of brilliantly colored maple trees; in winter, the quiet serenity of snow-shrouded pines. Hike-it-yourselfers can be overloaded with the sheer number of trails anywhere there are hills – from

Huskies pull a sled on winter snow.

Trail markers in Acadia National Park, Maine.

England Dog Sledding (www.newenglanddogsled-ding.com), located on the Maine–New Hampshire border, has all sorts of packages and courses.

GEOCACHING

Consider it a high-tech scavenger hunt. Using a hand-held GPS, geocachers look for a "cache" at coordinates. It can be as large as a shoebox or as small as a matchbox. They log their finds online. It's a growing family, group, and indi-vidual sport.

HIKING

The other popular self-propelled way to explore New England is on foot. Like biking, you very lit-erally set your own pace and itinerary. Like the

the relatively gentle Berkshires and western Con-necticut to the fierce passes in the White Moun-tains. Cape Cod and Block Island have their own rugged beauty that's best appreciated on foot. The most comprehensive website for trails, directions, and contacts is www.hikenewengland.com. The inter-active site breaks everything down by region and difficulty. Most casual hikers are happy with day trips, but hiking vacations are a nice option if you aren't trying to cram in seeing all of New England in one week. Some use one inn as a base and take day trips, returning to the inn each night. Others are inn-to-inn, with hikers exploring new areas every day. Your luggage is moved for you; you carry a day pack with water and sunscreen. These are good if you don't know an area and don't want to make your own accommodations. Most are for casual or intermediate hikers (www.thewayfarers.com), but a few are multiday, strenuous excursions

> By far the most undemanding way to enjoy the water is with a "float trip." Sitting on an oversize inner tube, you drift down the river, letting the current set the pace. A second tube holds a cooler with sandwiches and drinks.

are docile and well-trained. Rides rarely move faster than a walk and last between one and two hours. There are frequent stops to enjoy the scenery and take photos. Rides are particularly nice during fall foliage. Most stables are open from mid-May through October, but a few offer winter rides. Those are not to be missed. Some resorts have sleigh rides in the winter, which are pure magic. If you want an overnight experience, Berkshire Horseback Adventures (www.berkshirehorseback.net) has an overnight camping trip which is suitable for beginners.

Ice fishing is a favorite pastime in winter.

(www.distantjourneys.com). Options are fewer if you are looking for a simple day trip. Northwoods Outfitters (www.maineoutfitter.com), based in Greenville ME, has guided hikes lasting a few hours. One of the most popular is the wildlife tour that specifically looks for moose. In winter, they'll teach you how to snowshoe.

HORSEBACK RIDING

Why should you do all the work going up the mountain? Let a sure-footed, well-trained horse do it for you and you just go along for the ride. Stables offering trail rides know that most people aren't experienced riders; for many people, the ride is the first time they've touched a horse, much less ridden one, so the mounts

ICE FISHING

Truly obsessed anglers know that fishing doesn't end when the lakes freeze over; the fish are still waiting to be caught. They bundle up, pack a thermos of hot chocolate or coffee, slide a hut across the ice, auger through the ice, and drop a line. For those huddled around the hole sitting on wooden crates or folding chairs while jigging their lines, it's a bonding experience that will never be forgotten. It's also a lot of quirky fun. The Fly Rod Shop (www.flyrodshop.com) in Stowe has half-day tours and free ice fishing clinics every Saturday morning from January through mid-March. Pickett Hill Guide Service (www.pickethillguideservice.com) in Bennington serves a full meal in a warm shanty; it is worth rising very early to enjoy the fragile beauty of the winter sunrise in Vermont as part of the ice-fishing experience.

PADDLE SPORTS

Traveling New England's inland waterways has always been done by paddle. Canoes carried the Abenaki and Algonquin, French trappers, and English explorers along Lake Champlain and the region's rivers. Many of those waterways are still as undisturbed now as they were then. Red-eyed, brilliantly spotted loon glide across your path; egrets stand in the grasses; you may

before descending to Lake Champlain and continuing into New York. Another famous trail is the Allagash River Waterway in Maine, which is protected as a national Wild and Scenic River. Overnight guided tours along this waterway run from two to eight days; Northwoods Outfitters (www.maineoutfitter.com) has complete packages for that trip and several others in Maine. All trips have dozens of photo opportunities, but the moose and wildlife overnight trip by New England Outdoor Center (www.neoc.com) is particularly designed to get you to the most scenic

Sailing on the Charles River in Boston.

spot the occasional moose in the swamp or eagle overhead. It's as far removed from the hustle and hassle of the "real world" as it gets. You can rent canoes and kayaks by the hour or day at lakes, rivers, and coastal areas. Many of the outfitters offer instruction and guided tours. The nature tours are especially fun, since birds and other wildlife are easier to spot and approach by canoe or kayak. If nature's not your thing, there are also tours that stop at wineries and ice cream stands.

There are several well-documented long-distance trails: the Northern Forest Canoe Trail (www.northernforestcanoetrail.org is an excellent resource) runs from the very northern tip of Maine along the US–Canada border (with a short stretch into Quebec; bring your passport)

spots and promises plenty of moose sightings.

Stand-up paddling can be described as surfing with training wheels, although you provide the propulsion, not the waves. Standing, sitting, or kneeling on a very wide, very stable board, you use a modified kayak paddle to move. It takes about 10 minutes to learn and is an easy work-out. Umiak Outdoor Outfitters (www.umiak.com) in Stowe VT has the equipment and location to try out this fast-growing, family-friendly, fitness-not-required sport. Rocky stretches of New England's rivers create some exciting white-water rafting. From gentle riffles to full-fledged, hold-your-breath-'til-it's-over rapids, rafting is a drenching, exhilarating adventure. New England Outdoor Center (www.neoc.com) has a full range of options from "soft adventure" trips that are ideal introductory afternoons to the "full river" experience, which is not for the faint-hearted.

Sea kayaking takes paddling into another dimension, since you're dealing with waves and tides and ocean currents. Most day trips stay close to shore and sheltered waters, making the paddling relatively easy. The best trips are around Acadia National Park (www.acadiafun.com and www.mainekayak.com have all the options), where guided trips routinely spot harbor seals – who sometimes decide to swim alongside the

ON THE WATER

With hundreds of miles of coastline dotted with fine harbors, sailing is a natural part of any vacation. With the snap of canvas as it fills with wind and the feel of the salt spray as you move almost effortlessly across the water you understand the lure of the sea that called men to the water and away from more mundane (although usually safer) lives ashore. Experienced sailors can rent vessels in Newport in Bristol RI or charter a boat with a crew (www.bareboatsailing.com; www.sightsailing.com). Sailing schools gen-

A kayaker navigates the falls at Rocky Gorge near the Kancamagus Pass, New Hampshire.

Non-skiers find plenty to do at most ski resorts, which have almost all developed into one-stop destinations with spas, entertainment, and plenty of non-slope diversions.

paddlers – porpoises, osprey, and sea birds. The sunset cruises are especially nice, as the tempo of the day slows and the nesting birds swoop past you to settle in for the night. Overnight camping trips let you watch the stars as you lie on the beach on an uninhabited island or spend several days working up the coast on an inn-to-inn adventure.

erally have three- to six-day courses, but there are a few with one-day instruction and sails. If you'd rather someone else do all the water work, scenic cruises take you around Boston Harbor, close to lighthouses, to Connecticut's Thimble Islands, and along Lake Champlain. Seeing a whale breach the water is breathtaking. The power and beauty are unforgettable. Whale-watching trips sail daily from Boston, Gloucester, Nantucket, Portland, Provincetown, and Plymouth MA.

SKIING

There aren't quite as many ski resorts as there are snowflakes in a blizzard, but it sometimes seems that way. Although a few try to keep the simple, rustic ambience of the first ski lodges, most are major resort destinations with a range of activities, not just downhill skiing but snowboarding, tubing, snowshoeing, and Nordic (cross-country) skiing. There are après-ski massages, spas, dining, dancing, indoor pools, retail shops; Jay Peak even has an indoor water park. Towns like Stowe and Killington VT and North Conway NH thrive during the winter as the restaurants, shops, B&Bs, and bistros welcome the skiers. Although most ski resorts are in Vermont, New Hampshire, and Maine

Skiing in Stowe, Vermont.

(Sugarloaf is the largest ski area east of the Rockies), western Massachusetts has several respectable slopes. Most people stick to the groomed trails at ski centers; there's always a variety from "bunny trails" for the novices to triple black diamonds for those with great skill (or great bravado or both). Experienced skiers with winter survival skills try backcountry skiing. Pinkham Notch and Tuckerman Ravine are both popular areas for the sport. Great Glen Trails (www.greatglentrails.com), in Gorham NH, is a good place to connect with others heading for the wilderness on skis. Cross-country skiers looking for a challenge take on the Catamount Trail (www.catamounttrail.org), which runs the length of Vermont.

SNOWMOBILING

Vermont has 5,000 miles (8,000km) of groomed trails for snowmobilers which lace through the mountains and valleys. Smuggler's Notch Snowmobile Tours (www.sterlingridgeresort.com) leads one- and two-hour trips; Vermont Outdoor Guides Association (www.voga.org) has a list of rental outlets. The Katahdin region in Maine has a reputation for some of the finest snowmobiling trails (www.neoc.com), while the northernmost woods of New Hampshire have trails that link with those in Vermont, Maine, and Canada (www.nhconnlakes.com).

SPECTATOR SPORTS

Boston is home to professional teams in sports, both well-known and rarely followed. The Red Sox, Celtics, and Bruins play baseball, basketball, and hockey, respectively. The New England Patriots are the National Football League team, based in Boston, but drawing from a regionwide fan base. Soccer has the New England Revolution and the Breakers, the women's professional soccer team. There are lacrosse (including the Cannons), as well as softball (Riptides teams.

Baseball's minor league has a charm of its own. In small towns from Pawtucket to Pittsfield, young players hone their skills and hope for their big break. Cape Cod has its own league, with 10 teams. Minor-league ball is a family night out; the small stadiums often have playgrounds and pre-game entertainment for kids.

College teams also have dedicated followers, although most New England schools are not powerhouses on the national level. The exceptions there are the University of Connecticut's Huskies, who consistently go to the NCAA men's and women's basketball playoffs. The men's team won in 2011 and 2014, while the women are the nation's most successful female team. They can claim a record 11 national championships, and their 2016 victory saw the Huskies become the first women's team to win the title four years in a row. The University of Connecticut is also strong in soccer and baseball. The University of Vermont, meanwhile, also has strong basketball, hockey, and soccer programs. The Ivy League schools may be intellectual champions, but on the athletic field only Brown is notable, with lacrosse, football, hockey, and basketball teams of note.

A baseball game at Fenway Park.

A view over Boston at night.

Annisquam Yacht Club,
Massachusetts.

Boston Light, Little Brewster Island.

INTRODUCTION

A detailed guide to the six New England states, with principal sights clearly cross-referenced by number to the accompanying maps.

Although America's Industrial Revolution started in New England, it's the region's flaming fall leaves and charming white-steepled churches that local tourist boards promote. Certainly, the six states are bursting with 300 years of historical sights and influence – considerably more than any other place in America. But they are also remarkably vital: attend a town meeting in one of the superficially sleepy rural communities and you'll find that the robust tradition of democracy bequeathed by the Founding Fathers lives on, making many a town manager's life little easier than the president's.

It is precisely this juxtaposition of past influence and present prestige that is so compelling. What's more, each state has retained a well-defined identity, teasing visitors into testing their preconceptions against 21st-century reality – Maine associated with solitude and contemplation; Massachusetts with bustle and culture; Vermont with beauty and peace; Connecticut with carefully kept, white clapboard homes; Rhode Island with its renowned sailing; and tranquil New Hampshire, whose bellwether presidential primary every four years encourages the pollsters to predict the political fortunes that are about to be won and lost.

Celebrating Halloween.

A trip to New England can mean finding a priceless antique in an out-of-the-way backwoods store or dining in a sophisticated Boston bistro. It can mean rafting down a Maine river or skiing down a New Hampshire mountain, lounging on a Nantucket beach, or picnicking on the harbor in Newport RI. Yet the region is surprisingly compact.

State boundaries have more political significance than practical importance to the visitor. But, for convenience, each state is explored in depth in the following pages as a self-contained unit. Massachusetts, the most populous, has been divided into separate chapters: Boston, the areas surrounding Boston, Cape Cod and the islands of Martha's Vineyard and Nantucket, central Massachusetts, the Pioneer Valley, and the Berkshires.

New England

0 _____ 50 miles
0 _____ 50 km

N

Riviere aux Rats

Québec ✈

Scott

Q u é b e c

C A N A D A

St Michel des Saints

Trois-Rivieres

St François

St-George

Victoriaville

Black Lake

St-Ludg

St Jovite

St-Jeróme

Drummondville

Lachute

Acton Vale

Asbestos

Windsor

Cookshire

Woburn

Hawkesbury

Montreal

Ontario

Pike River

Sherbrooke

Cornwall

Lacolle

Rock Island

Longfellow Mountains

Ran

Masséna

Richford

Newport

Colebrook

Wilsons Falls

Errol

Potsdam

Malone

Plattsburgh

St Albans

100

111

Me

Clayburg

Lake Champlain

Mt. Mansfield ▲4393

Lancaster

Berlin

Bethel

Sevey

Tupper Lake

Saranac Lake

Burlington

Stowe

St Johnsbury

Mt. Washington 6288▲

Gorham

Bridgto

Waterbury

Montpelier

White Mountains

A d i r o n d a c k
Park

Verennes

Barre

Middlebury

Green Mountain National Forest

Randolph

Bethel

Hanover

White Mountain National Forest

Conway

Eagle Bay

Blue Mountain Lake

Indian Lake

Schroon Lake

Plymouth

Wolfeboro

A d i r o n d a c k

Fair Haven

V e r m o n t

Woodstock

Lebanon

Laconia

Sanford

M o u n t a i n s

Speculator

Rutland

Danby

4

Concord

Rochester

Higgins Bay

N e w   Y o r k

Glen Falls

7

Chester

91

10

N e w

Dover

Middleville

U N I T E D   S T A T E S   O F   A M E R I C A

Hillsborough

H a m p s h i r e

Portsmouth

Gloversville

Amsterdam

Green Mountain National Forest

5

Keene

293

Manchester

Salem

Har

Richfield Springs

Schenectady

Troy

Bennington

North Adams

101

202

Nashua

Lowell

Andover

Newbur

Oneonta

20

87

Mt Greylock 3491▲

Windsor

2

10

Westminster

Fitchburg

495

Gloueste

Bev

Albany

Pittsfield

112

Greenfield

Worcester

Sale

Stamford

Dalton

Lenox

Northampton

Amherst

Cambridge

Boston

Catskill Mountains

Catskill

Hillsdale

Great Barrington

90

146

95

Conset
Scituate

Fleischmanns

Canaan

Springfield

Brockton

Plymouth

Slide Mt. 4202

Kingston

Millerton

44

Enfield

84

Woonsocket

Taunton

Fall River

Liberty

44

Winsted

91

Hartford

44

Providence

West Warwick

New Bedford

Monticello

Poughkeepsie

202

6

395

Rhode
Island

Warwick

New Palm

Middletown

84

Connecticut

Waterbury

2

Norwich

95

Kingston

Newport

Viney
Ha

Port Jervis

6

8

New London

Rhode Island Sound

Marth
Vineya

Milford

Newburgh

Danbury

15

New Haven

95

Block Island Sound

Block Island

Peekskill

7

Milford

Long Island Sound

Orient Point

Montauk

New Jersey

Suffern

95

Stamford

Bridgeport

25

27

Long Island

15

St-Jovite

50

15

540

30

3

87

9

7

89

91

25

93

16

2

16

25

11

8

4

4

91

10

2

9

5

6

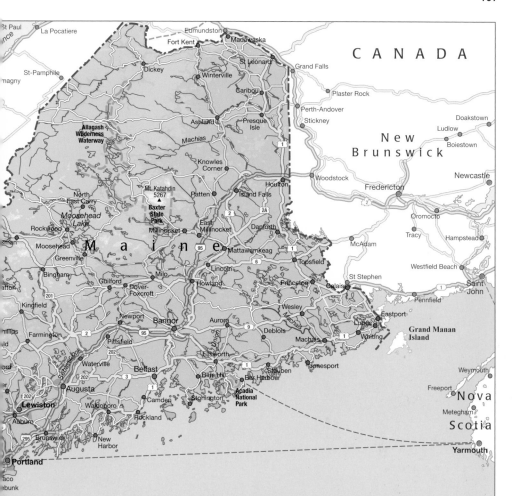

Boston

0 ___ 500 yds
0 ___ 500 m

N

Cambridge Street

Cambridge Street

Monsignor O'Brien Highw

Winter Street

Gore Street

Lechmere

Lech
Sc

DONNELLY
FIELD

Sacred
Heart

Holy Cross
Polish Church

Middlesex County
Courthouse

Thorndike Street

Spring Street

Otis St

Hurley Street

EAST
CAMBRIDGE

Cambrid
G

AHERN
FIELD

Charles Street

Rogers

Street

EDWARD J.
SENNOTT PARK

Broadway

Binney

Street

Harvard

Central

Broadway

Massachusetts Avenue

CAMBRIDGE

Technology
Square

Munroe

Potter
St

Athenaeum
St

Main Street

Main Street

Kendall/MIT

Main Street

Long

CAMBRIDGEPORT

Ray and Maria
Stata Center

List Visual
Arts Center

Harvard
Boat Club

MIT
Museum

Massachusetts Institute of
Technology (MIT)

Great
Court

Memorial Drive

MIT
Chapel

Steinbrenner
Stadium

Kresge
Auditorium

Hart
Nautical
Gallery

Harvard
Bridge

Memorial Drive

Charles

Esplanade

Lagoon

In

Storrow

Storrow Drive

Beacon Street

Dartmouth

Hunnew
Mansi

Ames-Webster
Mansion

Marlborough

Fir
Bapt
Chur

Boston
University

Back Street

Storrow Drive

John F.
Andrews
House

BACK BAY

Old South
Church

Copi

Boston University
East

Commonwealth

Kenmore Square

Commonwealth

Commonwealth

Newbury

Street

Boston
Public
Library

Kenmore

Newbury

Street

Burrage
House

Boylston

Lord &
Taylor

Massachusetts

Turnpike

Hynes Convention
Center

Institute of
Contemporary Art

John F. Kennedy NHS

Landsdowne Street

Performance Center

Berklee

Prudential
Center

Sak's

Copley
Place

Fenway
Park

FENWAY

Prudential
Tower

Landmark
Center

Fenway

BACK BAY
FENS

Publishing
Co. Bldg

Christian
Science
Center

Prudential

Mother
Church

HARRIET
TUBMAN
PARK

Horticultural
Hall

Symphony Hall

Museum of Fine Arts

Isabella Stewart Gardner Museum

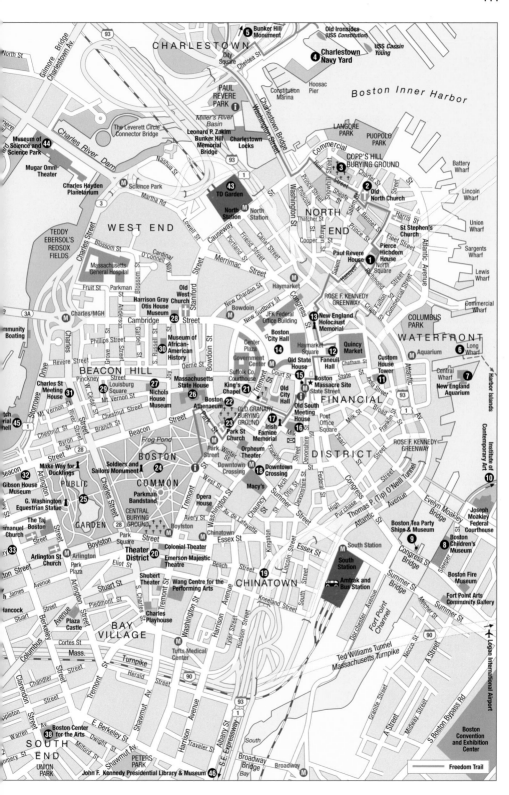

High-rise office buildings in Boston.

BOSTON

Boston has always taken itself seriously; it does, after all, have Revolutionary history, famed universities, vibrant arts, creative cuisine, and the legendary Red Sox.

The poet and essayist Ralph Waldo Emerson wrote: "This town of Boston has a history... It is not an accident, not a windmill, or a railroad station, or a crossroads town, but a seat of humanity, of men of principle, obeying sentiment and marching to it..." It might be fair to say that Boston does not have a history, but rather that it is history. New York may be more dynamic, Washington more imposing, and Seattle more gorgeously situated, but no city in America so nobly mingles its past with its present, or a history of tradition with a future of innovation.

A WALKING CITY

Despite urban development, Boston changes so abruptly in mood and nuance from one street to another that it cries out to be explored on foot. The city is charmingly, perversely bereft of a main drag, and its streets practice the old European vices of waywardness and digression. The visitor should, too.

Every day hundreds of visitors walk the red line on the sidewalk that marks the 2.5-mile (4km) **Freedom Trail**, a self-guided, or narrated, 90-minute tour (tel: 617-357 8300; www.freedomtrail.org – three-hour Audio Guide also available online) that takes in the major sites of the city's momentous Revolutionary history. Note that the Freedom Trail guided tour price

Acorn Street, Beacon Hill.

does not include admission to sites along the way. If you want to visit several locations, buy a combination, reduced-price admission ticket. There are several commercial tour operators who conduct guided tours along the Trail (and other Boston itineraries).

THE NORTH END

This picturesque neighborhood is Boston's original heart, and to walk its streets is to walk among legends. The Freedom Trail threads through the North End on its way between Boston

Main Attractions
The Freedom Trail
New England Aquarium
Faneuil Hall and Quincy
  Market
Old Granary Burying
  Ground
Museum of Fine Arts
Isabella Stewart Gardner
  Museum
Fenway Park
Museum of Science

Maps on pages
110, 134

Common and the Bunker Hill Monument in Charlestown.

The North End was the original nub at the end of the Shawmut Peninsula where the first settlers planted their town. Later, it became Boston's immigrant core: once Irish, then Jewish, and now Italian. Gentrification has homogenized this ancient quarter, but many older Italians remain – along with fragrant Italian grocery stores, bakeries, restaurants, and festivals.

A stroll through the North End can start at the **Paul Revere House ❶** (19 North Square; tel: 617-523 2338; www. paulreverehouse.org; daily mid-Apr–Oct 9.30am–5.15pm, Nov–mid-Apr 9.30am–4.15pm, Jan–Mar closed Mon) in North Square. Built around 1680, it is the city's oldest building, and its period furnishings include some items owned by the Reveres. The age and architecture of the place are the main attractions; for Revere's exquisite work in silver, visit the Museum of Fine Arts. A new visitors' center and museum adjacent to the house – opened in 2016 – provides well-curated information about Paul Revere's legendary midnight ride and the Revolution, as well as Revere's work as a silversmith.

From here, head north toward Hanover Street and the Revere Mall, with its equestrian statue of Revere. (Ironically, Revere did not reach his destination on that fateful night. He was captured by the British a few miles from Concord. A fellow rider, William Dawes, spurred his horse over a stone wall and rode on to alert the Minutemen.) At the end of the tranquil, tree-shaded mall stands Boston's oldest church, the 1723 **Old North Church ❷** (193 Salem Street; tel: 617-523 6676; www.oldnorth.com; daily mid Nov–Mar 10am–4pm, Apr–mid Nov 9am–6pm; voluntary donation), where beneath the graceful spire the sexton Robert Newman famously hung two lanterns on April 18, 1775, on the orders of Paul Revere, to signify to the citizens the British plan to move troops inland by boat rather than on foot. Inside, the stately pulpit and a bust of George Washington preside over the original box pews. The beauty of this space finds lovely accompaniment in the "royal peal" of its eight

The USS Constitution in Charleston Navy Yard.

bells, one of which is inscribed, "We are the first ring of bells cast for the British Empire in North America, Anno 1774." Nearby, between Hull and Charter streets, stand the weathered headstones of **Copp's Hill Burying Ground ❸** (daily 10am–5pm), where many early Bostonians are buried and where several gravestones bear evidence of British soldiers' musket practice.

CHARLESTOWN

Across Charlestown Bridge from the North End a famous bit of history lies at anchor in the **Charlestown Navy Yard ❹** (tel: 617-242 5585; free entrance 24 hours, bring valid photo ID), which opened during the War of 1812 and functioned until 1974. The USS *Constitution* (1 Constitution Road; hours subject to change, see www.navy.mil/local/constitution/visitors.asp; free), the venerable frigate known as "Old Ironsides," was built in 1797 and is the world's oldest commissioned vessel. It fought over 40 battles in the War of 1812 and won them all. Tours of the vessel, given by US Navy sailors every half hour, illustrate the cramped and dangerous world of a man o' war in the days of sail. On July 4, when the *Constitution* makes its annual turn-around cruise (no public allowed), there's a 21-gun salute; on July 5, the public is invited to a sunset parade.

Other sites in the Navy Yard include: The **USS *Constitution* Museum** (Building 22; tel: 617-426 1812; https://ussconstitutionmuseum.org; daily Nov–Mar 10am–5pm, Apr–Oct 9am–6pm; voluntary donation), which tells the ship's story through uniforms, weapons, paintings, and artifacts, and the **Boston Marine Society** (tel: 617-242 0522; www.bostonmarinesociety.org; Mon–Fri 10am–3pm by appointment), the oldest association of sea captains in the world, housed in the old octagonal Muster House, which contains a diverse collection of nautical art and artifacts. Of these three, children will most enjoy the USS *Constitution* Museum, with its interactive exhibits. Also in dock: the World War II destroyer USS *Cassin Young* (tel: 617-242 5601; May–Sept daily; for guided tours check www.dd793.com). Inside the Yard, stop for information and brochures at the Boston National Historical Park

The Bunker Hill Monument as seen from Charlestown Marina.

Old North Church, Freedom Trail.

⊘ Fact

The name's the same: Boston's trolley, trams, trains, and ferries are all known as the "T."

Navy Yard Visitor Center (55 Constitution Road; tel: 617-242 5601; May–Nov daily, Dec–Apr Tue–Sun).

The Freedom Trail continues to the **Bunker Hill Monument** (Monument Square; tel: 617-242 5641; daily; free), a granite needle 221ft (67 meters) high, commemorating the battle. There are 294 steps to the top, where there's a panoramic view of the harbor and city. **The Bunker Hill Museum** across the street from the monument (43 Monument Square; daily) has exhibits about the battle, the building of the monument, and the history of Charlestown.

THE WATERFRONT

The eastern boundary of the North End is the Waterfront District. The great wharves of windjammer days remain, many now supporting apartments, shopping arcades, and upscale restaurants. At the center of it all is Columbus Park, part of a green space linking the Waterfront with the downtown area.

Close to the Aquarium subway station, **Long Wharf** ⑥, the hub of Boston's shipping industry in the 17th century, is now the starting point for harbor cruises and the high-speed harbor islands ferry. Alternatively, you can get harbor views for free by strolling along the walkway southwards to Rowes Wharf. This is a section of the 47-mile (76km) **Harbor-Walk** (www.bostonharborwalk.com), nearly 39 miles (63km) of which have been completed. Connecting the water's edge to the city's open spaces, it stretches from Chelsea Creek to the Neponset River, passing through East Boston, Charlestown, the North End, downtown Boston, South Boston, and Dorchester.

THE AQUARIUM

The **New England Aquarium** ⑦ (1 Central Wharf; tel: 617-973-5200; www.neaq.org; July–Aug Sun–Thu 9am–6pm, Fri–Sat until 7pm, Sept–June Mon–Fri 9am–5pm, Sat–Sun until 6pm; discount combination ticket to aquarium and IMAX Theater or aquarium and whale-watch cruises) is extremely popular; try to visit on a weekday if possible. It has a gargantuan four-story, 200,000-gallon (760,000-liter) cylindrical tank in which sharks, sea turtles, moray eels, and

Postal inspector Anthony Cornstock.

⊘ BANNED IN BOSTON

The phrase "banned in Boston" generally refers to something controversial, particularly if it has sexual content. In the late 19th and early 20th centuries, authorities could prevent books, plays, and movies from being seen or distributed in Boston. The practice, however, goes back to much earlier times.

In 1651, William Pynchon wrote "The Meritorious Price of Our Redemption," which was highly critical of the Puritans' religious views. The General Court, which effectively ruled Massachusetts as a theocracy, was not amused. It burned the book and "encouraged" Pynchon to return to England, which he did.

In the 1870s, along came Anthony Comstock. A postal inspector with moral views that made the Puritans look like Romans at an orgy, he engineered the passage of the Comstock Act, which prohibited the distribution of "obscene, lewd, or lascivious" material through the mail. Even medical students' anatomy textbooks were outlawed. After hearing Comstock speak, the Watch and Ward Society formed in Boston. For decades, it dictated the cultural scene in Boston. Many publishers and theatrical troupes publicized their "banning" to attract more readers or a larger audience. Not until the Supreme Court limited the ability of local authorities to regulate content did "banned in Boston" cease to be meaningful.

other tropical species glide in never-ending circles in a simulated Caribbean coral reef. The tank is so large that it was built first and the rest of the aquarium was constructed around it. African penguins greet visitors as they arrive, and northern fur seals cavort in their open-air tank. The Aquarium operates three-to four-hour whale-watch cruises from late May through late October (tel: 617-973-5206), with researchers and naturalists on board, and its **Simons IMAX Theater** shows 3-D movies with digital sound on New England's largest screen.

CHILDREN'S MUSEUM

Follow HarborWalk southwards past Rowes Wharf towards the Fort Point/Seaport neighborhood. The fast development of the area was made possible by the Big Dig project and the demolition of the John F. Fitzgerald Expressway, which left space to create the **Rose Fitzgerald Kennedy Greenway** (www.rosekennedygreenway.org; see page 128), a chain of five parks featuring fountains, sculptures, an urban arboretum and the open-air Beer Garden, featuring draft beers by Trillium Brewing Company (summer only).

Cross Northern Avenue/Evelyn Moakley Bridge (Seaport Boulevard) to the **Boston Children's Museum** ❽ (308 Congress Street; tel: 617-426 6500; www.bostonchildrensmuseum.org; daily 10am–5pm, Fri until 9pm). Housed in a renovated warehouse, it is a hands-on adventure where children can climb a 3-D maze and visit an authentic Japanese house transplanted from Boston's sister city, Kyoto. New England's maritime traditions are reflected in hands-on boating exhibits and environmental exhibits. Like the Aquarium, the museum makes a good, if not centrally located, respite for kids getting "historied out" by Freedom Trail attractions. At the nearby building shaped like a milk bottle, Hood Milk Bottle, you can indulge in some excellent ice-cream.

Nearby, on Congress St Bridge, is the **Boston Tea Party Ships & Museum** ❾ (306 Congress Street; tel: 866 955 0667; www.bostonteapartyship.com; daily, tours every 30 minutes). It has full-size replicas of three 18th-century ships – *Beaver*, *Dartmouth*, and *Eleanor* – whose cargo of tea was thrown overboard on the chilly night of December 16, 1773, by 60 whooping patriots dressed as Mohawk Indians. They were protesting Britain's having imposed taxes on such cargos without granting the colonists representation in Parliament.

CONTEMPORARY ART

The whole Fort Point and Seaport area has been busy reinventing itself over recent years as one of Boston's hippest districts. Once an industrial center, former warehouses have been converted and fashionable restaurants and coffee houses – as well as a large artist community – have moved in. With more than 300 artists setting up in the area's old warehouses, it's well worth visiting the **Fort Point Arts Community gallery** on Summer Street (FPAC; www.fortpointarts.

A statue of Samuel Adams outside Faneuil Hall.

The New England Aquarium.

org), which has public art displays and its own store, Made in Fort Point, selling local art works.

The four-story **Institute of Contemporary Art** ❿ (100 Northern Avenue; tel: 617-478 3100; www.icaboston.org; Tue–Wed and Sat–Sun 10am–5pm, Thu–Fri until 9pm) cantilevers starkly over the waterfront. The permanent collection features contemporary artists who've exhibited at the ICA. A comprehensive venue for the arts, it has exhibits, performances, indie films, speakers, and family activities. There's a free summer concert series on the piazza in the summer.

CUSTOM HOUSE TOWER

Just west of the New England Aquarium rises the 26-story **Custom House Tower** ⓫ (3 McKinley Square), for many years Boston's tallest building. It's certainly the city's quaintest high-rise, with the c.1910 clock tower placed somewhat incongruously on the 1847 Greek Revival-style building. It now houses the Marriott Custom House Hotel.

The Irish Famine Memorial.

FANEUIL HALL

Close by is **Faneuil Hall** ⓬ (parking lot: 75 State Street; tel: 617-523 1300; daily 9am–6pm, tours daily), donated to Boston in 1742 by merchant Peter Faneuil to give the city a central marketplace and enlarged in 1805 by Charles Bulfinch. Patriot orators stirred the embers of the Revolution in the early 1770s here, earning the hall the name "Cradle of Liberty." A visitors' center is open daily 9am–6pm.

Facing it is the **Faneuil Hall Marketplace** (www.faneuilhallmarketplace.com) – also called **Quincy Market** – with a domed granite arcade built in 1826. It's a 6.5-acre (2.6-hectare) complex of flower stalls, jewelry stores, pushcarts, restaurants, and shops. Several dozen food stands line the long hall of the central building, offering everything from freshly shucked oysters to French pastry. Jugglers, mimes, acrobats, and other street performers contribute to the festive atmosphere.

The Rotunda of Faneuil Hall has photos and old signage showing the history of the hall. The fourth floor is home to the museum of the Ancient and Honorable Artillery Company (tel: 617-227 1638; www.ahac.us.com; Mon–Fri 9am–3pm). Two of Boston's landmark restaurants are also two of the oldest dining spots in the country: **Durgin Park** (http://arkrestaurants.com/durgin_park), in the marketplace, which opened its doors in 1827, and the **Union Oyster House** (41 Union Street; www.unionoysterhouse.com), one block from Faneuil Hall, which started serving in 1826.

In Carmen Park on Congress Street six glass towers comprise the **New England Holocaust Memorial** ⓭ (www.nehm.org). Six luminous towers, each 54ft (16 meters) tall, internally lit to shine at night, sit atop dark chambers from which smoke rises. The towers are etched with six million numbers, reminiscent of the numbers tattooed on the arms of the victims of the Nazis. Every Friday and Saturday fruit and vegetable vendors pack nearby **Haymarket**

Square's outdoor marketplace (www.hay marketboston.org) to sell their wares.

GOVERNMENT CENTER

Looming just inland from Faneuil Hall is **Government Center** ⑭. Here, in the 1960s, the Boston Redevelopment Authority razed buildings and removed streets to create a huge open space – some 56 acres (23 hectares). The centerpiece of this plaza is a massive concrete **City Hall** in the cheerless brutalist style, described as an "Aztec temple on a brick desert." The plaza is used for outdoor concerts in the summer months, but it has never become the civic gathering place its creators envisioned.

To the southeast rise the banks and office towers along Franklin, Congress, Federal, State, and Broad streets. Soaring confidently from a primitive warren of jumbled byways, these behemoths constitute the hub of business.

OLD STATE HOUSE

To the southwest lies downtown's retail heart, as well as some buildings illuminated brightly in history.

At the intersection of Washington and Court streets stands the **Old State House** ⑮ (206 Washington Street; tel: 617-720 1713; www.bostonhistory.org; daily 9am–5pm), once the seat of British rule. It was here that cousins Sam and John Adams, James Otis, and John Hancock led the arguments against continued British rule over its North American colonies. The museum works hard to be more than yet another collection of colonial artifacts. The multimedia presentation on the Boston Massacre (which took place just outside) illustrates an early example of "media hype." There are lots of hands-on activities and a few historic artifacts, such as tea from the Boston Tea Party.

The handsome, gambrel-roofed brick building at the corner of School and Washington streets was once the Old Corner Bookstore, a gathering spot for such writers and thinkers as Hawthorne, Emerson, and Thoreau.

OLD SOUTH MEETING HOUSE

Continue down Washington Street to the **Old South Meeting House** ⑯ (310

Steamed dumplings in a Chinatown restaurant.

⊘ EATING IN CHINATOWN

No visit to Chinatown would be complete without having lunch at one of its myriad restaurants, and the dim sum "palaces" – always good value – are among the most authentic. Waitresses push carts laden with appetizer-size dishes such as steamed buns, spare ribs, and, yes, chicken feet, through vast, cavernous rooms packed with tables. Diners point at the dishes they want, are charged for each (it's OK if you don't speak the language, because pointing is universal), and pay at the end of the meal. Literally, dim sum means "touch your heart." Favorite dim sum eateries include Empire Garden at 690 Washington Street (http://empiregardenboston.com), China Pearl at 9 Tyler Street (http://chinapearlboston.net), and Winsor Dim Sum Café at 10 Tyler Street (http://winsordimsumcafe.com).

Three signers of the Declaration of Independence are buried in the Old Granary Burying Ground, as are five victims of the Boston Massacre.

The Albert Gordon reading room at the Boston Athenaeum.

Washington Street; tel: 617-482 6439; www.osmh.org; daily Apr–Oct 9.30am–5pm, Nov–Mar 10am–4pm), scene of scores of protest meetings denouncing British policy. From here on December 16, 1773, the 60 patriots set off to conduct the Boston Tea Party. A stunning state-of-the-art audio exhibit, "If these Walls Could Speak," sets the scene (free with admission on your own smartphone or alternative device). It's the headquarters for the annual re-enactment of the Tea Party, usually held the weekend closest to December 16.

Nearby, at Washington and School streets, the **Irish Famine Memorial** 🄸, a pair of sculptures by Robert Shure, commemorate the immigrants driven to America by the Potato Famine of the 1840s. Set in a small plaza one sculpture depicts a desperate family about to leave Ireland, and the other shows the three hopeful and determined immigrants arriving in Boston.

DOWNTOWN CROSSING

A little farther to the south is the city's mercantile heart, the pedestrian-friendly **Downtown Crossing** 🄸 (www.downtownboston.org). Roughly bordered by Boston Common, and Essex, Devonshire, and Court streets, it's filled with retail shops and restaurants, office buildings and hotels, student housing, and residential space.

The Art Deco **50 Post Office Square,** former headquarters of the New England Telephone Company (now Verizon Communications) at 185 Franklin Street, rises 298ft (91 meters) in the heart of the Financial District. After the building changed hands in 2011 it got a complete makeover, but most of the original features were preserved. Sadly, the 160ft (50-meter) mural in its lobby, which payed homage to telephone history, has been removed.

CHINATOWN

Continue on Washington Street to Beach Street into the heart of **Chinatown** 🄸. The Asian-American quarter saw its population boom in the first decade of the 21st century with the arrival of citizens from countries including Vietnam, Thailand,

and Cambodia. The narrow, crowded streets are packed with tiny restaurants and shops selling everything from back scratchers to thousand-year-old eggs, and is a wonderful place to wander for a few hours.

THEATER DISTRICT

The **Theater District** ⑳ runs along Washington and Tremont streets, then follows Boylston and Stuart streets almost to Back Bay. The performance season runs from early fall through late June, with some acts in July and August. More than a dozen performance venues are along this route, including the magnificently opulent **Opera House** (539 Washington Street; www.bostonoperahouse.com) and **Boch Center** (270 Tremont Street; www.boch center.org), which encompasses the 1925 **Wang Center for the Performing Arts**, and the 1910 **Shubert Theater**.

Nearby Bay Village is a six-block neighborhood adjacent to Park Square and along Stuart Street whose homes are diminutive versions of those on Beacon Hill. The reason: many of the Hill's craftsmen and builders lived in the village and designed their homes in a similar fashion.

KING'S CHAPEL

Back on School Street, pass the **Old City Hall**, a grand affair now leased as office space, and turn right at Tremont Street to look into **King's Chapel** ㉑ (64 Beacon Street; tel: 617- 523 1749; www. kings-chapel.org; services Wed 6pm and Sun 11am, visits Mon–Sun 10am–4pm, Sun 1.30–4pm, winter closed Tue–Thu; guided tours of the church's crypt and bell tower available daily; voluntary donation). The congregation was established in 1686 as the first Anglican church in Boston. Built in 1754 of Quincy granite, it retains its crisp white box pews. Paul Revere said the bell he cast for the church was "the sweetest I ever made." You can hear it on Sunday mornings. Its burial ground is Boston's

oldest. Among those interred here are colonial governor John Winthrop and Mary Chilton, the first woman to step off the *Mayflower* (daily 10am–5pm).

On Tuesdays at 12.15pm the church hosts a 30- to 45-minute recital series featuring a variety of performers and repertoires from jazz to medieval. Admission is by donation (tel: 617- 227 2155). Crossing over Tremont Street, head left to the **Old Granary Burying Ground** (tel: 617-635 4505; daily 9am–5pm), founded in 1660, a pleasant glade where Peter Faneuil, John Hancock, Samuel Adams, Paul Revere, and the victims of the Boston Massacre are interred.

BOSTON ATHENAEUM

Overlooking the burial ground are the windows of a private library, the **Boston Athenaeum** ㉒ (10½ Beacon Street; tel: 617-720 7612; www.boston athenaeum.org; Tue noon–8pm, Wed– Sat 10am–4pm; guided tours, including floors otherwise off-limits to the public: Tue at 5.30pm, Thu 3pm, and sat at 11am, reservations required). There are reading rooms, marble busts, and

The State House, built on land used as a cow pasture by John Hancock.

An 1869 bronze of George Washington presides over the Commonwealth Avenue entrance to the Public Garden.

Stained-glass roof in the Hall of Flags, Massachusetts State House.

prints and paintings, as well as books from George Washington's library. The Athenaeum is one of the best places to spot specimens of the species known as the Proper Bostonian, short of joining an exclusive Beacon Hill club.

A few more paces down Tremont Street, at one corner of the Boston Common, is Peter Banner's elegant 1809 **Park Street Church** 🅫 (1 Park Street; tel: 617-523 3383; www.park street.org; tours mid June–Aug Tue–Sat 9.30am–3pm). On July 4, 1829, William Lloyd Garrison made his first anti-slavery speech here, launching his far-reaching emancipation campaign.

BOSTON COMMON

Every American city has a great park, but only Boston can claim the oldest, the venerable **Boston Common** 🅬, a magical swath of lawn and trees and benches. Sitting in the sun-mottled shade, watching pigeons strut and children frolic around Frog Pond, out-of-towners can understand how Bostonians might mistake this spot for the very center of the world.

The land that was to become the Common originally belonged to Boston's first English settler, one Reverend William Blaxton, who had made his home in 1625 on the western slope of what is now known as Beacon Hill. His life was interrupted in 1630 by the arrival of a band of settlers led by Governor John Winthrop of the Massachusetts Bay Company. The new Bostonians were nobly determined, as Winthrop had written, to "be a City upon a hill," and in 1634 he sold his land to the town for around $150 and fled farther into the wilderness.

The 45 acres (18 hectares) he left behind quickly became a versatile community utility. During the next 150 years, it was used for pasturing livestock, as a militia drilling ground, and as a convenient place to whip, pillory, or hang people. As a military post, the Common put up the Redcoats all through the Revolution.

Now the Common is "just" a park: glorious when the magnolias bloom or when snow at sunset evokes the impressionist paintings of Childe Hassam.

PUBLIC GARDEN

Just across Charles Street, the elegant **Public Garden** ㉕ strikes a more formal pose. These variegated trees, meandering paths, and ornate beds of flowers were once part of the fetid Back Bay marshes; but by 1867, the Garden had taken its present graceful shape, complete with weeping willows, a bridge for daydreamers, and a shallow 4-acre (1.6-hectare) pond.

In summer, swan boats (tel: 617-522 1966; www.swanboats.com; mid-Apr–mid-Sept daily) carry happy tourists across the placid waters of the garden's lagoon. At the Commonwealth Avenue entrance, an equestrian George Washington bronze by Thomas Ball presides, while a row of bronze ducks on the north side pays tribute to Robert McCloskey's classic 1941 children's picture book, *Make Way for Ducklings*. Real ducks, too, inhabit an island in the pond and paddle about to toddlers' delight.

BEACON HILL

Back up at the east end of the Common, the gold dome of the **Massachusetts**

State House ㉖ (24 Beacon Street; tel: 617-727 3676; www.sec.state.ma.us; Mon–Fri 9am–5pm; guided tours: 10am–3.30pm, reservations required; free) gleams atop Beacon Hill on land once owned by John Hancock. Completed in 1798, this peerless Federal-style design by Charles Bulfinch, with less successful but happily unobtrusive additions by several others, symbolizes the eminence of politics in Boston. The approach to the legislative chambers passes through a series of splendid halls leading to the Senate Staircase Hall and the Hall of Flags, both symphonies of fin de siècle marble opulence.

One of the highlights is the House Chamber, a paneled hall under a two-stage dome. Great moments of Massachusetts' history decorate the walls in a series of Albert Herter paintings, while above circles a frieze carved with a roll-call of the state's super-achievers. The portentous codfish known as the "Sacred Cod," a sleek, stiff carving in pine that commemorates Boston's great Federal-era fishing industry, was

Pedal-powered (and wheelchair-accessible) swan boats can carry up to 20 people around the Public Garden's lagoon.

Nineteenth-century Beacon Hill life as seen in the Nichols House Museum.

The first Harrison Gray Otis House. Otis (1765–1848) was mayor of Boston and a leader of America's first political party, the Federalists.

The Christian Science Center.

first hung in the Old State House. Without this old mascot, the house refuses to meet. Less recognized is the pine cone atop the gold dome. It symbolizes the importance of the logging industry to Boston in the 18th century. At the beginning of the 19th century, a large, steep three-peaked hill known as the Trimount dominated the area. In the 1780s, a primitive beacon atop one of the peaks warned ships against running aground. In 1795, Bulfinch and partner Harrison Gray Otis leveled 60ft (18 meters) of the Trimount, using it to fill in part of the Charles River. The newly accessible land quickly became the idyllic gas-lit neighborhood of bow-fronted town houses now known as "The Hill." At first, everyone expected that the new residences of Beacon Hill would be urban estates along the lines of Bulfinch's freestanding No. 85 Mount Vernon Street (1800) – his second house for Otis – which is to this day one of Boston's most majestic houses (not open to the public). But the mansion plans were quickly scaled down to today's smaller blocks.

At No. 55 Mount Vernon Street is the 1804 Bulfinch-designed **Nichols House Museum** 27 (tel: 617-227 6993; www.nicholshousemuseum.org; Apr–Oct Tue–Sat 11am–4pm, Nov–Mar Thu–Sat 11am–4pm; tours on the hour 11am–4pm). The former home of the philanthropist, suffragist, and landscape designer Rose Standish Nichols, it is a splendidly accurate portrayal of an early 19th-century Beacon Hill interior.

FEDERAL-ERA TASTES

To get a sense of The Hill, walk west down Beacon Street from the State House. At Nos 39 and 40 stand twin 1818 Greek Revival mansions, one built for Daniel Parker, owner of the Parker House, Boston's oldest hotel. At Nos 42 and 43, the Somerset Club, built in 1819 as a mansion for prominent merchant David Sears, was bought by the most exclusive of Boston social clubs in 1872. At 45 Beacon Street is the third house designed by Bulfinch for Otis (1805).

The first (1796) **Harrison Gray Otis House Museum** 28 at 141 Cambridge Street, just outside Beacon Hill proper (tel: 617-994 5920; www.historicneweng land.org/property/otis-house; Wed–Sun 11am–4.30pm, Apr–Nov only Mon and Tue; tours every half hour), is the last surviving mansion in what was Boston's most elite 18th-century neighborhood. It offers a glimpse into the elegant life of Boston's governing class immediately after the American Revolution.

Louisburg Square 29, developed between Pinckney and Mount Vernon streets around 1840, epitomizes the Beacon Hill style and its urban delicacy. Created as a model for town house development, it has long been *the* address in Boston. Louisa May Alcott (1832–88), author of *Little Women*, once lived here.

Another charming example of Beacon Hill's spirit is at Nos 13, 15, and 17 Chestnut Street, one of America's most beautiful residential streets, where Bulfinch built for the daughters of his

client Hepzibah Swan three exquisite town houses in a prim little row.

AFRICAN-AMERICAN HISTORY

During the 19th century much of Boston's free African-American population lived on the north side of Beacon Hill. The **Museum of African-American History** ⑳ (46 Joy Street; tel: 617-725 0022; http://maah.org; Mon–Sat 10am–4pm; self-guided tours available) encompasses two sites open to the public. The African Meeting House (8 Smith Court), dedicated in 1806, is the oldest black church building still standing in the United States. It was here that William Lloyd Garrison founded the New England Anti-Slavery Society in 1832. The Abiel Smith School (46 Joy Street) served as the country's first publicly funded grammar school for African-Americans from 1834 until 1855, when Boston's schools were integrated.

The museum also oversees a site on Nantucket and Boston's Black Heritage Trail with the assistance of the National Park Service.

CHARLES STREET

On the west side of Beacon Hill, Charles Street, with its restaurants, coffee houses, bakeries, and boutiques, is a prime spot to stroll, shop, and snack.

The street's principal landmark is the **Charles Street Meeting House** ㉛ at the corner of Charles and Mount Vernon streets. Built for the Third Baptist Church in 1807, it later served as the home of the First African Methodist Episcopal Church and the Unitarian-Universalist Church; over the years luminaries including Frederick Douglass and Sojourner Truth spoke here. It was converted into offices and retail space in the 1980s.

Wander off Charles onto the shady, peaceful streets that trail toward the Charles River or lead back up the hill. Many houses here are noteworthy for their former occupants. Polar explorer

Admiral Richard E. Byrd (1888–1957) lived in Nos 7–9 Brimmer Street, while No. 44 in the same street was the life-long home of the great historian Samuel Eliot Morison. The Victorian clergyman and philosopher William Ellery Channing lived at No. 83 Mount Vernon Street, next door to the second Otis mansion.

BACK BAY

From Beacon Hill, it's an easy transition both in distance and architectural feeling to the handsome streets of Back Bay. Although it epitomizes "Old Boston," this neighborhood dates only to the 1850s filling of a noxious tidal mudflat declared, in 1849, "offensive and injurious" by the Board of Health.

The legislature's grand 1857 plan for Back Bay, influenced by Baron Haussmann's recent rebuilding of central Paris, called for long vistas down dignified blocks, and a wide boulevard with a French-style park down the middle. In 1858 the first load of fill arrived by train from Needham, 10 miles (16km) to the southwest. During the next 20 years, 600 acres (240 hectares) of dry

> **⊘ Fact**
>
> The attractions of the Back Bay were not appreciated by some conservatives. Even in the 20th century, one Beacon Hill gentleman told his prospective son-in-law, who was hoping to build a house in the Back Bay, that he could not allow his daughter to live on "made land." He got his way: the couple elected to settle on Beacon Hill.

Open-air jazz on Newbury Street.

The view from Top of the Hub restaurant, on the 52nd floor of the Prudential Tower.

The altar of Trinity Church.

land emerged from the muck that was Back Bay.

Back Bay's imposing rowhouses, now nearly all divided into condominiums or apartments, line **Commonwealth Avenue**, a verdant 32-acre (13-hectare) promenade shaded by mature elms, sweet gum, ash, and linden trees. (Starting near the Charles River and going right to left, the axial thoroughfares are Beacon Street, Marlborough Street, Commonwealth Avenue, Newbury Street, and Boylston Street.)

Head west to 137 Beacon Street, between Arlington and Berkeley (the cross-streets ascend in alphabetical order), to visit the **Gibson House Museum** ❷ (tel: 617-267 6338; www.thegibsonhouse. org; Wed–Sun guided tours only at 1pm, 2pm, and 3pm). Built in 1859, the brick rowhouse has been left much as it was; it houses a museum whose furniture, paintings, books, clocks, and textiles recreate the feel of Back Bay living in its heyday, including the servants' "downstairs" world of kitchen and laundry.

In the block between Clarendon and Dartmouth, Commonwealth Avenue displays its most memorable structures. The romantic houses that march down this stretch perfectly justify the avenue's reputation as America's Champs-Élysées.

ALONG NEWBURY STREET

Newbury and Boylston streets are the only part of the Back Bay zoned for commerce. **Newbury Street** ❸, the "Rodeo Drive of the East," is lined with jewelers, day spas, restaurants, sidewalk cafés, designer boutiques, and art galleries, including the venerable Vose Galleries of Boston at No. 238 (www. vosegalleries.com), which specializes in American painting from 1669 to 1940.

COPLEY PLACE

Copley Place ❹ (100 Huntington Avenue; tel: 617-262 6600; www.simon. com/mall/copley-place) is a two-story megaplex occupying more than 9 acres (3.6 hectares) with two hotels, dozens of inviting restaurants, and all of the familiar retail stores: Neiman Marcus, Louis Vuitton, Barneys New York, Armani.

According to *Women's Wear Daily*, Prudential Center is one of the top five shopping centers for women in the country. With Saks Fifth Avenue and Lord & Taylor as anchor stores, who can argue? The south garden is an oasis where you can rest, recoup, and plan the rest of the shopping expedition. This is also the location for the Hynes Veterans Memorial Convention Center. The **Prudential Center** (www.prudentialcenter.com) is connected to Copley Place by a "skyway" in Boston's original skyscraper, the 52-story **Prudential Tower** ⑮ (800 Boylston Street). Its 50th-floor Skywalk Observatory (tel: 617-859 0648; www.skywalkboston.com; daily beginning Nov–beginning Mar 10am–8pm, mid-Mar–beginning Nov until 10pm) provides an exhilarating, map-like, four-way view of the city. An "Acoustiguide" audio tour details points of interest far below. It's available in English, Spanish, German, Mandarin, French Canadian, and Japanese. The Top of the Hub is an elegant, expensive spot to have lunch, or enjoy a cocktail and watch the sunset.

THE MOTHER CHURCH

In 1866, Mary Baker Eddy credited her rapid recovery from a serious accident to a glimpse of God's healing power. The religious movement that she founded in 1879 today has its world headquarters on 22 acres (9 hectares) immediately south of the Prudential Center on Huntington Avenue. The **Christian Science Center** ㊱ (175 Huntington Avenue; tel: 617-450 3423; www.christianscience.com/church-of-christ-scientist; Sunday services at 10am and 5pm; tours Tue–Sun, see website or call for times) complex includes three older buildings – the Byzantine-Renaissance Mother Church (1894), the Italianate Mother Church Extension (1904), and the Publishing Society (1933) – as well as I.M. Pei's 1973 additions.

In the publishing wing, the **Mapparium** (Mary Baker Eddy Library; tel: 617-450 7000; www.marybakereddylibrary.org; Tue–Sun 10am–4pm; tours only) is an extraordinary stained-glass walk-in representation of the globe. Visitors walk across a 30ft (9-meter) glass bridge to stand, literally in the center of the world. From there, they have a

The John Hancock Tower.

⊘ THE BRAHMINS

The fabled history of Boston, the Puritans' "City Upon a Hill," had a rather prosaic origin. The settlers were merely looking for good drinking water. When the final location was chosen, they believed that the site was divinely chosen. They also believed that the future success of the settlement depended on their acting in accordance to divine will. "The eies of all people are upon us," declared John Winthrop, their leader. God must have approved, because the "Bible Commonwealth" grew quickly. By 1700, its fleet was the third-largest in the English-speaking world, and its population the largest in North America. Bostonians developed the self-confidence that is a hallmark of self-reliant and self-made people.

During the decades following the Revolution, Boston's maritime domination created a "codfish aristocracy" of fortunes netted from the sea. They were the "Boston Brahmins," a name borrowed from the Hindu priestly caste. They funded institutions such as the Boston Public Library, the Massachusetts Institute of Technology, and Boston University.

When the Irish Potato Famine struck in 1845, thousands of impoverished Irish immigrants suddenly arrived, promptly constituting a new underclass. They were followed by Italians, Poles, and Russians. By 1900, Boston's population had swelled to more than half a million and the Puritan capital became a mostly Catholic metropolis. Newcomers and incumbents clashed, and Boston was divided into two distinct cultures. The established elite still maintained power even as it withdrew into its world of Back Bay addresses. But while the new citizens sweated in factories, they remade Boston – and its politics – in their own image: scrappy, practical, and anything but elite.

By the 1950s, Boston was in a slump. The population was shrinking as factories moved south and urban renewal programs destroyed old neighborhoods to create soulless government centers and the expansion of Massachusetts General Hospital. A furious backlash by residents started a rejuvenation of the established neighborhoods and the city itself. It finessed its surfeit of colleges and universities and Mass General to establish a reputation as a medical and technical research and high-tech center, second only to Silicon Valley.

Snack stand at Fenway Park.

The Rose Kennedy Greenway.

3-D view of the world's nations as they were in 1935, the year the globe was built. One presentation uses words, music, and LED lights to demonstrate how ideas travel through time and geography and influence the world. Another gives the background of the concept and construction of the Mapparium. The acoustics are disorienting, with whispers in one continent being clearly heard in another.

COPLEY SQUARE

Follow Dartmouth Street to Boylston for one of the city's most stimulating displays of architecture: **Copley Square** ➌⓻. First, there's Charles McKim's 1895 **Boston Public Library** (700 Boylston Street; general information: tel: 617-536 5400, tour information: tel: 617-859 2216; www.bpl.org; Mon–Thu 9am–9pm, Fri–Sat 9am–5pm, Sun 1–5pm; guided art and architecture tours available, see website or call for details; free). This Italian Palazzo masterpiece might well be the center of the Boston that claims to be the "Athens of America." With more than 6 million volumes and

a vast, ornate reading room, it is one of the great libraries in the world. But it's more than a building of books. There's art everywhere – murals by Sargent and Puvis de Chavannes, statues by Saint-Gaudens and Daniel Chester French – and, at the center of a maze of stairs and passages, a peaceful inner courtyard. Philip Johnson's massive 1972 addition "quotes" the original structure in a vastly simplified modern vernacular.

Across the square stands H. H. Richardson's 1877 masterpiece, **Trinity Church** (206 Clarendon Street; tel: 617-536 0944; www.trinitychurchboston.org; Tue–Sat 10am–4.30pm, Sun 12.15–4.30pm; free art and architecture tours after Sun 10am service in summer; guided and self-guided tours daily, see website or call for times). This is a tour de force in Romanesque inventiveness and a striking medievalist contrast to the Public Library's classicism. Inside, what impresses is the wealth of murals, mosaics, carvings, and stained glass. This is Boston's most sumptuous interior space. Organ concerts (by donation) are held Fridays 12.10pm.

Ⓞ THE GREENWAY

When the Big Dig buried the interstates that sliced through downtown Boston, it left a gaping hole in the cityscape. The solution was to create a mile-long chain of parks – The Rose Kennedy Greenway – built above the I-93 tunnel and reuniting neighborhoods long separated by the now-gone freeway. Named after the matriarch of the Kennedy clan, it reflects her love of Boston and of gardens. It takes about 30 minutes to hike the greenway, but the idea is to stroll, not powerwalk. Each of the five parks has its own personality, fountains, events, vendors, gardens, and artwork. The Conservancy which manages the Greenway hosts historical and horticultural tours. For details and a schedule, tel: 617-292 0020 or visit www.rosekennedygreenway.org.

200 CLARENDON STREET

Above everything looms I.M. Pei & Partners' magnificent blue-green mirror, **200 Clarendon Street** – previously the **John Hancock Tower**, built in 1976. The Tower initially had a propensity in windy weather to lose the huge sheets of glass covering it; miraculously, no one was hurt when the glass fell. That problem was solved after the tower was completed, when all 10,344 panes were replaced; the building also swayed in high winds and required more retrofitting to stiffen the building's core. The observation deck at the top of the building was closed after the terrorist attacks in New York City, Pennsylvania, and Washington, DC on September 11, 2001.

THE SOUTH END

To the south and east of the Christian Science Center and Copley Square sprawls the South End, an ethnically diverse but much gentrified quarter of Victorian bowfront town houses. Particularly pleasing architecturally are the areas around Worcester Square, Rutland Street, and leafy Union Park Square, where it's evident that London – rather than Paris, as in the Back Bay – was the developers' inspiration.

On Sundays from 10am to 4pm, the basement at 450 Harrison Avenue becomes the **lifestyle vintage market** (www.sowavintagemarket.com), as local artists and growers display their wares. Look for unique handbags and jewelry, paintings, and antiques, plus fresh produce and baked goods.

The **Boston Center for the Arts** ❸ (539 Tremont Street; tel: 617-426 5000; www.bcaonline.org) is a lively performing and visual arts complex encompassing the **Mills Gallery** (Sun and Wed noon–5pm, Thu–Sat noon–9pm), which mounts five large-scale expositions each year, and four theaters which present more than 50 productions yearly.

BOSTON'S GREATEST HALL

From the South End, Huntington Avenue leads southwest past several of Boston's greatest institutions. At the northwest corner of Massachusetts Avenue stands the majestic gable-roofed **Symphony Hall** ❸ (301 Massachusetts Avenue; tel: 888-266 1200; www.bso.org; free tours offered selected weekdays at 4.30pm and Sat at 3.30pm, see website or call 617-638 9391 to reserve). The acoustically impeccable, beautifully appointed 1900 building is home to the renowned Boston Symphony Orchestra and, in summer and during the Christmas holidays, its less formal offshoot, the Boston Pops Orchestra. Tickets can be hard to come by. Two options are "rush tickets" – a limited number of tickets set aside for Tuesday and Thursday evening and Friday matinee performances. They are deeply discounted, available a few hours before the show, and must be paid for in cash. Open rehearsals are also open to the public at discounted prices. Call for information.

Tip

Admission to the MFA on Wed after 4pm (except for special exhibits) is by donation. You can also purchase tickets online (www.mfa.org). Pay for parking at automated kiosks in the West Wing coatroom before leaving the museum.

Playing baseball at Fenway Park.

Exhibits in the John F. Kennedy Presidential Library and Museum.

The Zakim Bridge spans the Charles River.

THE MFA

Continue down Huntington Avenue to reach the **Museum of Fine Arts (MFA)** ❹ (465 Huntington Avenue; tel: 617-267 9300; www.mfa.org; Sat–Tue 10am–5pm, Wed–Fri 10am–10pm; entrance ticket allows for free return visit within 10 days). You'll need two days – at least – to even begin to see, much less appreciate, everything that the museum has on display. Built in 1909 and repeatedly enlarged since then, this incredible museum is perhaps best known for its Impressionists – including the largest number of Monets outside France. The Art of the Americas wing houses 55 galleries featuring pieces ranging from pre-Columbian to 20th-century. The museum also has the world's best collection of 19th-century American art. The finest collection of Egyptian Old Kingdom objects outside Cairo includes a statue of King Mycerinus, who built the Third Pyramid at Giza, and his queen Kha-merer-nebty II. There are gilded and painted mummy masks. Cyrus Edwin Dallin's elegantly poignant bronze *Appeal to the Great Spirit* is in the forecourt. Over 200 works by contemporary artists are on display in the seven galleries of the renovated I.M. Pei building (built in 1981).

There are almost as many tours available as there are galleries. Free guided tours and gallery walks are included in the admission price. Each focuses on a specific theme. The schedule is available at the admission desk, but check the website or call ahead for advance planning. Tours are available in several languages; again, call ahead to be sure a guide and the tour you want are available. An outdoor walking tour of the building and surrounding neighborhood is offered several times a week (call for schedule). Finally, a multimedia guide (charge) with details about 500 objects in the museum is available from the admission desk for do-it-yourself touring, as well as a mobile guide with highlights. The guide is available at the admission desk.

MRS JACK'S PALAZZO

Close to the MFA, the **Isabella Stewart Gardner Museum** ❹ (280 The

⊙ THE BIG DIG

The official name is the Central Artery/Tunnel Project, but to Bostonians, it's the Big Dig. The most ambitious highway project ever undertaken in the US, the project reconfigured the hugely complicated, congested, and confusing highway and interstate system in central Boston. The Big Dig moved the ground-level I-93, which sliced through downtown Boston, to a 3.5-mile (5.6km) tunnel, extended the I-90 to Logan International Airport, and built a new crossing over the Charles River – the Bunker Hill Memorial Bridge. Originally scheduled to be completed in 1998 for a cost of $2.8 billion, with cost overruns, design flaws, and construction delays, it was finally completed in 2007 at a cost of $14.6 billion. Although expensive, there is no doubt that the Big Dig has improved car travel in and around Boston.

Fenway; tel: 617-566 1401; www.
gardnermuseum.org; Wed–Mon 11am–
5pm) is an exquisite 1903 neo-Vene-
tian palazzo assembled by Boston's
most flamboyant grande dame. The
unstoppable "Mrs Jack" may have
scandalized Brahmin Boston when
she paraded two pet lions down Beacon Street, but she proved an astute
patron of the arts.

During the 1890s, she set her sights
on such masterpieces as Titian's *The
Rape of Europa*, Rembrandt's *The
Storm on the Sea of Galilee*, and Ver-
meer's *The Concert*. In 1896, when her
collection was outgrowing her home,
she commissioned her fantasy palace
at the very edge of town. Today her
eclectic collection constitutes one of
the world's great small museums.
A modern extension, designed by
prize-winning architect Renzo Piano,
opened in 2012, and connected by a
glass corridor to the main building,
includes a dedicated performance
hall for the Sunday afternoon concert
series and an exhibition space with a
retractable ceiling.

FENWAY PARK

North of the museums is another of
Boston's shrines, **Fenway Park** ㊷ (4
Yawkey Way; tel: 617-226 6666; www.
mlb.com/redsox). Built in 1912 and
famously called a "lyrical bandbox"
by novelist John Updike, the Red Sox's
home field is the oldest ballpark in the
major leagues. Book on to a behind-
the-scenes 50-minute tour (tel: 617-
226 6666; daily 9am–5pm on the hour,
winter from 10am, except on game
days when the last tour is 3 hours
before the game starts).

The home of the Boston Celtics, who
have been National Basketball Association champions 17 times, and the Bruins, Boston's National Hockey League
team, and the National Lacrosse
League Blazers, is the state-of-the-
art **TD Garden** ㊸ (formerly Banknorth
Garden; box office: tel: 617-624 1050;

www.tdgarden.com) at 100 Legends Way
near North Station.

THE CHARLES RIVER

Like many great cities, Boston lies in
the embrace of a great river. Along
Back Bay, the Charles River widens
into a large basin, like a giant mirror held up to the city's profile. It
was designed to do just that, by the
civic-minded citizens who created the
Charles River Dam in 1908.

The dam itself is home to Boston's
Museum of Science and Science Park
㊹ (1 Science Park; tel: 617-723 2500;
www.mos.org; July 5–Labor Day Sat–
Thu 9am–7pm, Fri 9am–9pm, Labor
Day–July 4 Sat–Thu 9am–5pm, Fri
9am–9pm; additional charge for Omni/
IMAX, butterfly garden, planetarium,
and 3-D cinema; combination tickets
available). Here, visitors can watch
simulated lightning, become sleuths at
CSI: the Experience, explore the potential of wind and solar power, design
nanobots, and enjoy a wide variety of
ever-changing hands-on exhibits and
live animal and bird demonstrations.

Tip

The information center at
MIT (77 Massachusetts
Avenue; tel: 617-253
4795; www.mit.edu; Mon–
Fri 9am–5pm) can provide
details of free 75- to
90-min tours (Mon–Fri
11am and 2.30pm) from
the lobby of Building 7
during the academic year.
To download a mobile
walking tour, search for
"MIT Mobile."

*A bug-eyed attraction
at the Museum of
Science.*

BOSTON'S LITERARY TRAIL

Boston's literary history is almost as long and storied as its Revolutionary one. Names like Emerson, Longfellow, and Alcott are as well-known as Adams, Revere, and Hancock.

Touring Boston and its environs should include visiting the places made famous by the authors – both historic and contemporary. You can explore the places that shaped them and are the settings for their novels, locations of their memoirs, or inspirations for their poetry. You can drink at their characters' favorite bars, channel their energy by visiting their homes, and pay your respects at their graves.

WALKING TOURS

The easiest way to get your literary bearings is with a walking tour. **Boston by Foot** (http://bostonbyfoot.org; tel: 617-367 2345) conducts a literary-themed stroll escorted by knowledgeable, entertaining guides. The "Literary Landmarks" tour focuses on the vibrant literary history of Victorian Boston and highlights the homes of Hawthorne, Longfellow, Emerson, Thoreau, Alcott, and other names familiar from required reading in school. The guides'

A vacant lot on West Street, near Brattle's Bookstore, is used as a temporary shop to sell overstock or used books.

enthusiasm and chatty stories explain why these people were the megastars of their time and why they matter now.

If you'd rather edit your own itinerary, grab a copy of *The Literary Trail of Greater Boston* by Susan Wilson, a lively romp through Boston, Cambridge, and Concord, visiting places as well-known as Walden Pond and as obscure as the site of the original Parker House Hotel. (Charles Dickens lived in the original building and first performed *A Christmas Carol* there.) There's a lot of insider gossip which is as entertaining as any of the books they wrote.

LITERARY LANDMARKS

No guidebook or tour can promise to point out sites associated with personally favorite writers, particularly the most contemporary ones. For that, you need to make notes, use a map, and do a little sleuthing. Fans of Robert Parker's Spencer series can sit on a bench in Boston's Public Park near the swan pond and the *Make Way for Ducklings* sculpture, just as the detective (and Parker) often did, then have a drink at the Bristol Lounge at the Four Seasons Hotel, Spencer's hangout. Dennis Lehane's troubled characters frequent any of the corner bars in South Boston.

In Gloucester, the Crow's Nest Bar is where the crew of the *Andrea Gail* drank before the "perfect storm." Linda Greenlaw, mentioned in the book (she was the skipper of a nearby boat) can direct you to the Dry Dock Bar in Portland ME, the setting for *All Fishermen are Liars*. New Bedford is no longer home port for a whaling fleet, but the ghosts of the ships and crews are at the dockside museum there. More ghosts are in Salem, of course, the setting for Arthur Miller's famous play *The Crucible*, which relates the tales of the Salem witch trials of 1672.

INDEPENDENT BOOKSTORES

True bibliophiles must make a pilgrimage to the **Brattle Bookstore** in Cambridge (9 West Street; www.brattlebookshop.com), one of the oldest and largest antiquarian bookstores in the country. And it's fitting to pause in front of the **Old Corner Bookstore** in Boston (Washington and School streets). It was once the gathering place for Victorian writers.

For reasonably inquisitive kids over 7, this temple of science and technology surpasses even the Children's Museum as a respite from history and art.

THE SHELL

The river's edge is one of the city's favorite places to stretch its legs. Roller skaters wired for sound, joggers, bike riders, and sunbathers all migrate here. So do the great crowds that turn out to hear the free concerts and watch movies under open summer skies at the **Hatch Memorial Shell** ⑮ (www.hatchshell.com). The Boston Pops' Fourth of July concert with fireworks is spectacular; get there very early and bring a blanket or chairs.

Every Wednesday evening from early July through late August the **Boston Landmarks Orchestra** (tel: 617-987 2000; www.landmarksorchestra.org) performs classical music at the Shell. It also puts on concerts for children and neighborhood concerts throughout the city.

JFK'S LEGACY

A short subway ride away is a point of pilgrimage for many people, the **John F. Kennedy Presidential Library and Museum** ⑯ (Columbia Point; tel: 617-514 1600 or 866-JFK 1960; www.jfklibrary.org; daily 9am–5pm; MBTA red line south to JFK/UMass and free shuttle bus marked "JFK"; GPS address: 220 Morrissey Boulevard, Boston). Set dramatically beside the ocean, the museum, dedicated to the life and legacy of JFK, makes excellent use of film, videos, and recreated settings (including the Oval Office) to evoke a masterful portrait of politics and society half a century ago. The building, designed by I.M. Pei, has a very large library and archive, and is surrounded by a 9.5-acre (3.8-hectare) park. An exhibit is based on the 1964 interviews with Jacqueline Kennedy by historian Arthur Schlesinger, Jr which covers her memories of the early campaigns through the Cuban Missile Crisis and

her role as First Lady, mother, and wife. Docent-led highlight tours and a presentation about PT-109 are included in the admission. Museum brochures are available in Chinese, Korean, Italian, Russian, French, Portuguese, German, Spanish, and Japanese.

CAMBRIDGE

Literary critic Elizabeth Hardwick once described Boston and Cambridge as "two ends of the same moustache." Indeed, across the Charles lies a separate city that is absolutely inseparable from its companion metropolis.

Just across Harvard Bridge is the **Massachusetts Institute of Technology (MIT)** Ⓐ. Housed in solid neoclassical buildings with the trim logic of natural laws, MIT almost routinely produces Nobel laureates, new scientific advances, and White House science advisors.

The Finnish architect Eero Saarinen designed two of its highlights: the inward-looking, cylindrical **MIT Chapel**, illuminated by light reflected from a moat, and the tent-like **Kresge**

Building 10 and the Great Dome form part of the Maclaurin Buildings on the MIT campus.

The inauthentic 1814 statue of John Harvard.

⊙ Tip

The Boston City PASS (www.citypass.com) saves 45 percent on admission to the Harvard Museum of Natural History (HMNH) and three other major Boston sites: the New England Aquarium, the Museum of Science, and the Skywalk Observatory. The pass costs $56 and is valid for nine days. It is also available from the HMNH admission desk.

A statue of conductor Arthur Fiedler near the Hatch Memorial Shell.

Auditorium, which rises from a circular brick terrace, its roof apparently balanced by slender metal rods on three points. The school welcomes visitors. The **visitor center** (77 Massachusetts Avenue; tel: 617-253 4795) has maps and directions, and is the starting point for tours. Display labs across the campus demonstrate engineering phenomena, artificial intelligence, and computer science. The **Visual Arts Center** is a venue for temporary exhibits. The permanent collection is spread out across campus.

Exhibits at the **MIT Museum** (265 Massachusetts Avenue; tel: 617-253 5927; https://mitmuseum.mit.edu; daily 10am–5pm, July–Aug until 6pm) explore inventions, ideas, and innovations in creative interactive exhibits, and include the world's largest holography collection. It's most suited for those above 12 years old. The **Hart Nautical Gallery** has ship models showing the development of 1,000 years of naval design and a mechanical engineering exhibit focusing on robotics, bioengineering, and ocean science.

Harvard Square Ⓑ, at the heart of Cambridge, is home to Harvard University and a playground of bookstores, coffeehouses, and shops to the west and north of the Yard. At its center is the international Out of Town News, housed in a historic kiosk and stocked with a mind-boggling array of national and international publications, and beside it, Dmitri Hadzi's gently humorous stone sculpture, *Omphalos*, suggesting that Harvard is, as its supporters have long held, the center (or navel) of the universe.

The venerable Harvard Cooperative Society ("Coop" for short; https://store.thecoop.com) was founded in 1882 as an alternative to overpriced local shops; both the Harvard and the MIT stores are the best places to buy souvenirs from either school.

HARVARD UNIVERSITY

Standing proudly above the redbrick and green ivy are the spires of America's oldest institution of higher learning, **Harvard University**. Self-confident and backed by enormous wealth – its

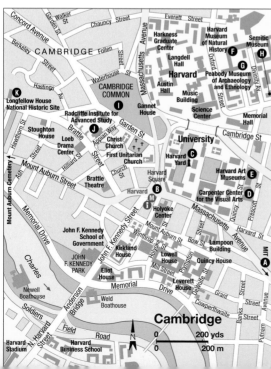

endowment exceeded $35 billion at last count – Harvard has been a world index of intellectual accomplishment almost since its 1636 founding. Eight American presidents and heads of state of some two dozen countries graduated from Harvard, and 48 Nobel laureates and 41 Pulitzer Prize winners have been among its faculty members.

The heart of the place is **Harvard Yard Ⓒ**, withdrawn tranquilly behind the walls that separate it from Harvard Square outside. Passing through the gate that proclaims "Enter to Grow in Wisdom," the visitor encounters a hallowed world of grass and trees, ghosts and venerable brick – a living, eminently walkable museum of American architecture from colonial times to the present.

Massachusetts Hall (1720), Harvard's oldest standing building, quartered Revolutionary troops, as well as housing a lecture hall, a famous drama workshop, and, since 1939, the offices of the university president. Nearby stands little **Holden Chapel** (1744), once described as "a solitary English daisy in a field of Yankee dandelions."

At the Yard's center stands Charles Bulfinch's **University Hall**, built of white granite in 1815. In front is Daniel Chester French's 1814 statue of John Harvard (1607–38), the young Puritan minister for whom the college was named after he left it half his estate and all his books. Since no likeness of John Harvard existed, French used a student as his model.

East of University Hall, three massive buildings set off the central green on which commencement is celebrated each June. These are H. H. Richardson's 1880 masterwork **Sever Hall**, with its subtle brick decorations; **Memorial Church** (1932), with its Doric columns; and the monumental **Widener Library**. Given by the mother of alumnus and bibliophile Harry Elkins Widener, who died on the *Titanic* in 1912, the library is the

center of Harvard's network of 92 libraries, which together house over 12 million volumes, America's third-largest book collection.

To the east of the Yard stands the **Carpenter Center for the Visual Arts** Ⓓ (24 Quincy Street; tel: 617-496 5387; https://carpenter.center/; Tue–Sun noon–5pm; free), a cubist, machine-like building constructed in 1963 that represents the only American work of the great French architect Le Corbusier. The five levels, a "synthesis of the arts," include the top-floor Sert Gallery exhibiting works by contemporary artists, and the Harvard Film Archive, which shows rare and experimental films (tel: 617-495 4700; http://hcl.harvard.edu/hfa/).

For decades, Harvard has been home to three art museums: the **Fogg** (European and American art), the **Busch-Reisinger** (northern European art), and the **Arthur M. Sackler** (ancient, Islamic, and Oriental art). In 2014, the renovated and expanded 1927 **Harvard Art Museums building** Ⓔ (32 Quincy Street; tel: 617-495 9400; www.

Ⓞ Tip

Free hour-long tours of Harvard leave from the Smith Campus Center (100 Elm Street; tel: 617-495 1573; www.harvard.edu; Mon–Sat several tours during the academic year, see website or call for details). Self-guided audio tours are available in several languages and mobile tours can be downloaded from www.harvard.edu/visitors/mobile-tour.

Harvard University campus.

Tip

It's easy to get to the Kennedy National Historic Site by public transportation (www.mbta.com). All routes require a walk of about four blocks from the "T" stop: take the MBTA's Green Line "C" Cleveland Circle train to Coolidge Corner or the "B" Boston train to Babcock Street; the Route 66 Bus from Harvard Square also goes to Coolidge Corner.

harvardartmuseums.org; daily 10am–5pm) brought the Fogg, the Busch-Reisinger, and the Arthur M. Sackler museums under the same roof, allowing the public greater access to the collections. A striking new wing, designed by the acclaimed Renzo Piano Building Workshop, was added.

A few blocks north on Oxford Street stands the **Harvard Museum of Natural History**  (26 Oxford Street; tel: 617-495 3045; www.hmnh.harvard.edu; daily 9am–5pm), a huge complex housing several museums. A major draw is the **Botanical Museum**, which features a multimedia exploration of New England forests, an African gallery concentrating on endangered species, a renovated Great Mammal Hall, and an exhibit on evolution research. The most enchanting and famous exhibit is "Glass Flowers," a collection of over 3,000 astoundingly accurate models of more than 830 plant species executed by Leopold Blaschka and his son Rudolph in 19th-century Dresden.

In the same building, the **Museum of Comparative Zoology** (www.mcz.

Harvard's Botanical Museum.

harvard.edu) includes George Washington's stuffed pheasants as well as the world's oldest reptile eggs. Also on the site is the **Mineralogical and Geological Museum** (http://mgmh.fas.harvard.edu), with over 5,000 samples of minerals, rocks, and meteorites (both daily 9am–5pm).

The **Peabody Museum of Archaeology and Ethnology**  (11 Divinity Avenue; tel: 617-496 1027; www.peabody.harvard.edu; daily 9am–5pm) is filled with fossils, dinosaurs, American Indian cultural objects, and wonders from ancient Egypt. A free audio tour is available via wand or MP3 download.

Nearby, the University's collection of Near Eastern archaeological artifacts is housed in the **Semitic Museum**  (6 Divinity Avenue; tel: 617-495 4631; https://semiticmuseum.fas.harvard.edu; Sun–Fri 11am–4pm; free). There are over 40,000 artifacts from Egypt, Israel, Syria, Iraq, Jordan, and Tunisia, which the museum uses to illustrate Near Eastern history, culture, and archaeology.

CAMBRIDGE COMMON

On July 4, 1775, George Washington assumed command of the Continental Army on **Cambridge Common** . A trio of cannons abandoned by the British when they left Boston in 1776 stand close to a bronze relief of Washington on horseback under an elm tree. On the south side of the Common, just across Garden Street, Christ Church (1761) was used as a barracks by patriots, and its organ pipes were made into bullets. Close by is an entrance to **Radcliffe Institute for Advanced Study** , formerly Radcliffe College (www.radcliffe.harvard.edu), the women's college that merged with Harvard in 1975.

LONGFELLOW'S LEGACY

In the 18th century, Brattle Street was home to so many British loyalists that it was known as Tory Row. Its handsome homes include No. 90, designed by H. H. Richardson of Trinity Church

fame, and No. 94, the 17th-century Henry Vassall House. Look out for the yellow clapboard Longfellow House at the **Longfellow House – Washington Headquarters National Historic Site** 🄚 (105 Brattle Street; tel: 617-876 4491; www.nps.gov/long; June–Oct Wed–Sun; guided tours several times a day; free). Ironically for its setting in the midst of British loyalists, this was the place where George Washington took command of the Continental Army in 1775 and which he used as his head-quarters during the Siege of Boston in 1775–76. This was the idyllic wedding present given to the poet Henry Wads-worth Longfellow and his wife, Fanny, by her father in 1843.

Little has changed inside; Longfel-low's library and furniture are here, including a chair made from the "spreading chestnut-tree," which stood at 56 Brattle Street and was immortal-ized in his poem *The Village Blacksmith*. Unhappily, Fanny was fatally burned in the house in 1861.

Periodically there are poetry read-ings, concerts, re-enactments, and other events. Check the website for schedules.

JOHN F. KENNEDY NATIONAL HISTORIC SITE

The nation's 35th president was born at 83 Beals Street in Brookline, now the **John F. Kennedy National His-toric Site** 🐼 (tel: 617-566 7937; www. nps.gov/jofi; late May–Oct Wed–Sun 9.30am–5pm, off season by appoint-ment only; free), where his family lived from 1914 to 1920. In 1967 his mother, Rose Kennedy, returned to the house and restored it to the way she recalled it looked in 1917, the year of his birth. An unprepossessing house typical of turn-of-the-century homes in Bos-ton's then-new "streetcar suburbs," the birthplace is surprisingly modest for a family later associated with its exclusive Hyannisport compound on Cape Cod – but then, even patriarch Joseph P. Kennedy had to start some-where. Guided and self-guided tours are available. The self-guided tours can be accessed by cell phone (usage charges apply).

⊙ THE HARBOR ISLANDS

Thirty-four islands, ranging from little more than piles of rock (The Graves) to 214-acre (87-hectare) Long Island, make up the **Boston Harbor Island National Recreation Area** (tel: 617-223 8666; www.bostonharboris-lands.org, the site has an excellent map), where visitors can camp, swim, hike, and bird-watch.

If you're already on location, the best place to get information is at the pavilion between Quincy Market and Long Wharf-North. There are also visitor centers on Spectacle and Georges islands.

For centuries, the islands have been used for civic punishment and isolation centers. They were used to incarcerate American Indians during the Puritan era, as a holding area for Irish immigrants, as the site of a hos-pital and a prison, and as the location of harbor defense forts during times of conflict. In 1996 Congress decided to support local and state efforts to turn them into a recreational state park. They are now prime examples of environmental stewardship.

The **Boston Harbor Islands Partnership** (www.

bostonharborislands.org; tel: 617-223 8666) coordinates the management of the island park. It also runs ferries from Long Wharf in Boston Shipyard to Georges and Spectacle islands.

Boston Harbor Cruises (tel: 617-227 4321; www.bos tonharborcruises.com) ferry people across from Boston's Long Wharf to Georges, Spectacle, and Peddocks islands and from Hingham and Hull (June–Oct). Lovells, Grape, and Bumpkin islands also make up part of the inter-island loop.

For those totally without sea legs, four of the islands are accessible by car: Deer Island from Winthrop; Nut, World's End, and Webb Memorial State Park from Quincy and Hingham. Access to these islands is restricted at times, and you'll have to check with the police station located on the causeway of the Squantum peninsula.

Some islands are accessible by private boat, but be sure to check the docking requirements with the harbor master before you travel.

📷 BOSTON'S FREEDOM TRAIL

Boston is rich in history and is small enough to navigate on foot. The Freedom Trail is a handy way for visitors to take in the most important sites of this historic city.

The Freedom Trail (www.thefreedomtrail.org), a 2.5-mile (4km) red-brick path linking 16 historic locations that all played a part in Boston's Colonial and Revolutionary history, was born in 1951. Aware that "Tourists were going berserk, bumbling around and frothing at the mouth because they couldn't find what they were looking for," newspaperman William Greenough Schofield suggested that the sites be linked in a numbered sequence. In 1974, part of the Trail became Boston's National Historical Park.

A LEISURELY PACE

It's tempting to see the city by tour bus, sightseeing trolley, or the amphibious vehicles called "duck boats". All provide quick introductions to some of the major sites and help you get your bearings as to where things are in relation to each other. But by walking you can choose your own pace, decide what you really want to see, when to eat, or take time to explore that interesting-looking building around the corner that isn't on the tour guide's itinerary. Good walking shoes and a map are a necessity. (Free Freedom Trail maps are available at www.freedomtrail.org, the National Park Visitor Center at 15 State Street next to the Old State House, or at the visitor center at the Boston Common on Tremont Street, near Park Street). The entire trail can be walked in one day, but it's much more satisfying to do it in a more leisurely fashion over two days.

The idea for the Freedom Trail was conceived by local journalist William Schofield in 1951, as a pedestrian trail to link important local landmarks.

In Boston's Veterans' Day parade, groups dress as Revolutionary War-period soldiers and march with flags from Boston Common to City Hall.

King's Chapel Burying Ground became the town's first cemetery in 1630. A chapel joined it in 1689. Many colonists are buried here, including John Winthrop, the colony's governor; Hezekiah Usher, its first printer; and Mary Chilton, the first woman to step off the Mayflower in 1620.

The Freedom Trail is marked by a red line of paint or brick running from Boston Common to the Bunker Hill Monument in Charlestown.

Paul Revere rides again

Boston misses few opportunities to relive its stirring history. On March 5, Boston Massacre Day, the Charlestown Militia leads a parade from the Old State House to City Hall Plaza. Patriots' Day, on the third Monday in April, is the year's biggest one-day celebration. Paul Revere's and William Dawes' rides are re-enacted, this time with a state police escort. After a parade in Back Bay, the first two battles of the Revolution are staged with gusto at Lexington Green and Concord. June sees the Ancient and Honorable Artillery Company parade, and the Battle of Bunker Hill is re-enacted at the Monument following a parade from Charlestown. And on December 16, the Boston Tea Party of 1773 is re-enacted. For a condensed version of all of the above, Boston Harborfest (www.bostonharborfest.com) is a nine-day festival that runs from late June through the July 4th weekend. There are British encampments on Boston Common, a replay of the Boston Tea Party, and the reading of the Declaration of Independence from the balcony of the Old State House. It culminates with the annual fireworks-enhanced outdoor concert by the Boston Pops.

The Freedom Trail has simple ground markers that note 16 significant historical sights, including graveyards, notable churches, and a historic naval frigate.

Charles Bulfinch designed the magnificent red-brick and domed State House ("the hub of the solar system") when he was only 24. Guided tours are available.

Statue on Paul Revere Mall depicting Paul Revere on his midnight ride.

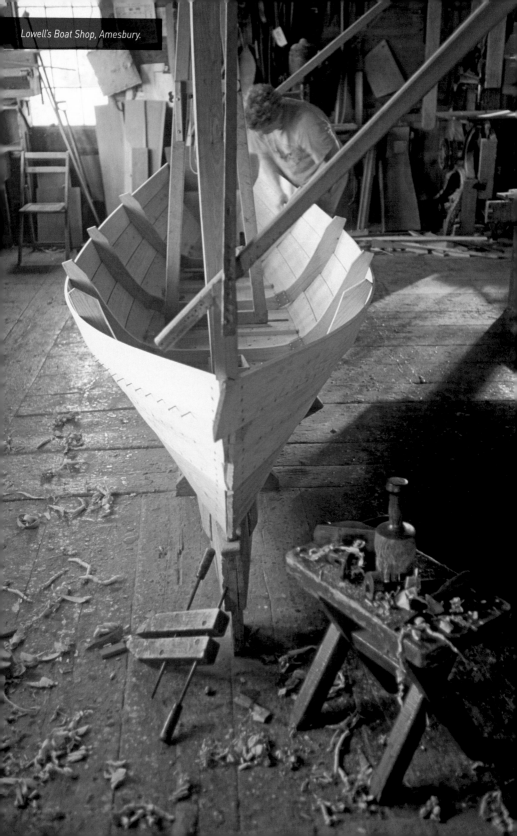
Lowell's Boat Shop, Amesbury.

AROUND BOSTON

The arc around Boston is filled with attractions and historical sites, where meadows are haunted with the echoes of musket fire and philosophers sought the meaning of life.

There are a number of historical sights that can be visited as day trips from the city. To the north of the city is the iconic seacoast, with its weathered villages, where fishing once dominated. To the west are vivid reminders of the American Revolution, while south of the city is a region with a rich legacy that includes Pilgrims, presidents, and whalers.

NORTH OF BOSTON

Just a few miles north of Boston via Route 1 (Main Street/Saugus Exit) is the **Saugus Iron Works National Historic Site ①** (244 Central Street; tel:781 816 7299; www.nps.gov/sair; May–Oct daily 9am–5pm). The buildings have been reconstructed as they were in 1646, with a blast furnace and forge, ironworks house, and a restored 17th-century home. The site was established by John Winthrop Jr and, though ultimately unprofitable, launched America's ironworking industry. On summer weekends, there are iron-casting demonstrations.

MARBLEHEAD

Take Route 1A north to Route 114 to **Marblehead ②**, founded as a fishing village in 1629. The narrow streets of the Historic District are lined with over 200 pre- and post-Revolutionary homes, many now chic B&Bs, shops, and galleries.

The Essex Shipbuilding Museum.

The **Marblehead Museum & Historical Society** (170 Washington Street; tel: 781-631 1768; www.marbleheadmuseum. org; 10am–4pm June–Oct Tue–Sat, Nov–May Tue–Fri) preserves the city's history; exhibits include a delightful collection of folk-art paintings by self-taught J.O.J. Frost, who first picked up a brush at age 70.

The original of Archibald Willard's painting *The Spirit of '76* (aka **Yankee Doodle**) is displayed in the Selectmen's Room of Abbot Hall (188 Washington

Main Attractions

Salem
Gloucester
Parker River National
  Wildlife Refuge
Lexington and Concord
Walden Pond
Plymouth
Fall River

Maps on pages
142, 144, 153, 157

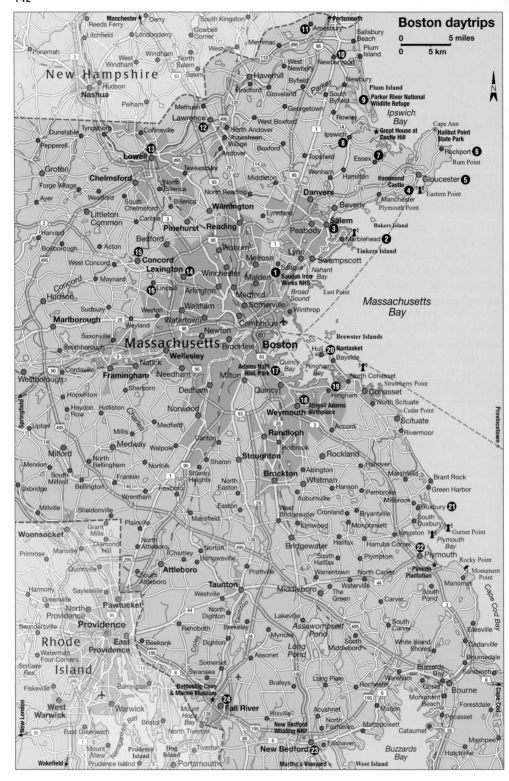

Boston daytrips

Street; tel: 781-639 3425; Mon–Fri, summer also Sat and Sun).

Old Burial Hill, overlooking the harbor, is the final resting place for 600 soldiers of the Revolution.

SALEM

Founded in 1626 as a seaport, the maritime history, cultural attractions, and colonial atmosphere of **Salem** ❸ rival any other town. A red line along the sidewalks marks the route linking the historic sites. Begin with a visit to **the National Park Service Regional Visitor Center** ❹ (2 New Liberty Street; tel: 978-740 1650; www.nps.gov/sama; daily, Nov–Apr closed Mon–Tue), located in the former armoury, which shows an excellent film detailing the area's history.

Most visitors will initially want to tour the scenes of the infamous witchcraft trials of 1692. When normalcy returned, the "witches" of Salem entered into fact and folklore which support a bewitchingly popular array of attractions. There's a sense of theme park in much of the town, with souvenir shops selling incense and potions, psychic readers, even a bronze statue of Elizabeth Montgomery in her role as Samantha in *Bewitched*.

For all of the frivolity, the trials were a horrific time. Particularly moving is the **Salem Witch Trials Tercentenary Memorial** ❸. The paving stones and walls surrounding the stark granite court are incised with pleas of innocence from the accused. Adjoining is Charter Street Burying Point, the final resting place of witch trials Court Magistrate John Hawthorne.

The **Salem Witch Museum** ❸ (19½ Washington Square North; tel: 978-744 1692; www.salemwitchmuseum.com; daily 10am–5pm, until 7pm July–Aug); **Witch Dungeon Museum** ❹ (16 Lynde Street; tel: 978-741 3570; www.witchdungeon.com; Apr–Nov daily 10am–5pm); **Witch History Museum** ❸ (197–201 Essex Street; tel: 978-741 7770; www.witchhistorymuseum.com; Apr–Nov daily 10am–5pm); and **Witch House** ❸ (310½ Essex Street; www.witchhouse.info; mid-Mar–mid-Nov daily 10am–5pm, rest of the year Thu–Sun noon–4pm), home of Judge Jonathan Corwin, all present

◔ Tip

It's easy enough to walk to all sites – both "witchy" and otherwise – but to get a comprehensive overview, hop on the Salem trolley (tel: 978-744 5469; www.salemtrolley.com) for an hour-long, historically accurate tour.

A statue outside the Salem Witch Museum.

Ship figurehead on display at the Peabody Essex Museum in Salem.

historically accurate, although often sensationalized, versions of the events.

NAUTICAL SALEM

It's a shame that witch kitsch dominates, because the area has much else to recommend it. Salem owes its restored grandeur to its former prominence as a seaport.

Salem Maritime National Historic Site G (160 Derby Street; tel: 978-740 1650, call for opening times) recreates Salem's rise as an important port. A short film explains how Salem opened up trade with the Orient, its role in the Triangle slave trade, and privateering. Visitors tour the Custom House, a public house, a goods store, and a merchant's mansion. The replica 1797 East Indiaman *Friendship* is magnificent. Admission to the site is free, but there is a charge for the ranger-led tours. You can also download an audio tour for MP3 players.

Commercial, but fun, the **New England Pirate Museum H** (274 Derby Street; tel: 978-741 2800; www.pirate museum.com; 10am–5pm May–Oct daily,

Apr and Nov Sat–Sun; combination tickets with Witch Dungeon and Witch History Museums available) brings to light a little-known piece of Salem history. In the 1690s, Capt. Kidd, Blackbeard, and other nefarious figures frequented the area. The museum displays recovered pirate loot; you'll also board a mock-up of a pirate ship.

PEABODY ESSEX MUSEUM

The **Peabody Essex Museum I** (161 Essex Street; tel: 978-745 9500; www. pem.org; Tue–Sun 10am–5pm, third Thu of the month until 9pm) began as a place for sea captains to show off the oddities and objects collected on their voyages. Its collections of Asian, maritime, and Oceanic art are extensive. The Yin Yu Tang house, a 200-year-old Chinese dwelling, was carefully dismantled and reconstructed in the museum's courtyard.

On Essex Street, the Museum preserves six houses that span two centuries of New England architecture; the McIntyre Historic District preserves Georgian and Federal-period houses

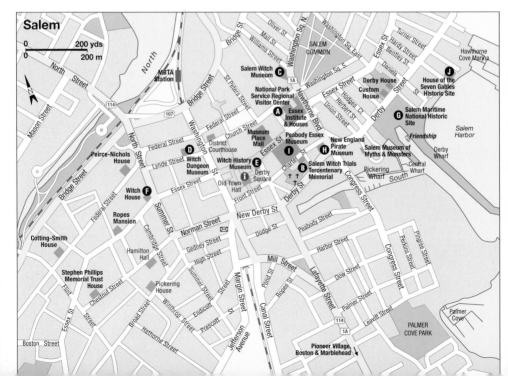

designed or inspired by architect and master builder Samuel McIntire. The district offers a tour de force for anyone interested in both architecture and American cultural history: this is where, and how, the nation's first millionaires lived.

New England's oldest remaining 17th-century wooden mansion is the forbidding-looking 1668 **House of the Seven Gables ❶** (115 Derby Street; tel: 978-744 0991; www.7gables.org; late May–late June Sun–Thu 10am–5pm, Fri–Sat until 7pm, late June–end Oct daily 10am–7pm, Nov–end Dec daily 10am–5pm, closed early Jan, mid Jan–mid Feb Fri–Tue 10am–5pm, Mid Feb–late May 10am–5pm; guided tour included in the price of admission). The structure is famous for more than mere antiquity, having been the inspiration for the house in the classic 1851 novel by Salem native Nathaniel Hawthorne. The house in which Hawthorne was born has been moved next door, and visitors can tour both houses as well as the handsome colonial revival gardens.

South of town in Forest River Park, **Pioneer Village** (tel: 978-744 8815; www.pioneervillagesalem.com or http://pioneervillagesalem.org; June–Sept Sat–Sun, tours at 12.30pm, 1.30pm, 2.30pm) is a re-created, living-history Puritan village which further helps explain the mindset of the Puritans.

ESSEX SCENIC BYWAY

Cross the Danvers River on Route 1A to Beverly, to Route 127, the Essex Coastal Scenic Byway. The route hugs the rocky shoreline, passing through 13 coastal communities filled with New England ambience and over 8,000 buildings on the National Register of Historic Places.

HAMMOND CASTLE

Just before Gloucester stands **Hammond Castle ❹** (80 Hesperus Avenue; tel: 978-283 2080; www.hammondcastle.org; Labor Day–Oct). This was the 1920s fantasy abode of the prolific inventor John Hays Hammond Jr – remote control via radio waves was his most important idea – who plundered

Salem Maritime National Historic site is home to the replica tall ship Friendship.

THE SALEM WITCH TRIALS

Behind the tawdry merchandising and overwrought re-enactments lies a dark episodes of religious intolerance in New England that culminated in the execution of 20 innocent people.

Since its founding in 1626, the town (whose name derives, ironically, from *shalom*, the Hebrew word for peace) had never been a bastion of tolerance and goodwill: it was from Salem that Roger Williams, the founder of Rhode Island, had been exiled for preaching religious freedom.

The townspeople's rigid ways took a destructive turn when Tituba, a Barbados slave serving the household of Salem's minister, Samuel Parris, began regaling his daughter, Elizabeth, and niece, Abigail Williams, with vivid accounts of voodoo. Fascinated, Elizabeth and Abigail invited a handful of their friends to listen to Tituba's tales.

Meetings of such a nature, being strictly forbidden in Puritan Salem, held an illicit appeal that the girls

Kitsch witch-themed toys boost the local economy.

must have found difficult to resist, but no doubt they also found their guilty pleasure difficult to live with, for all soon began to exhibit bizarre behavior: they would crawl on the floor, making choking sounds, and cry out that needles were piercing their flesh. The town doctor was called in to examine the girls and, after medicine failed to cure them, he diagnosed them as victims of witchcraft.

The Rev. Mr Parris suggested that Tituba might be their tormentor, and the slave was charged with witchcraft. In confessing, under pain of torture, she gave a lurid account of how a tall man from Boston, accompanied by witches, had molested the girls.

Satan himself, she claimed, had ordered her to murder the girls, and other witches had beaten her for her refusal to comply; she merely tormented them, trying to abate her own pain. In her stories, she pointed a finger at two women unpopular in the village, Sarah Osborne and Sarah Good, who were charged with everything from bewitching cattle to using voodoo dolls.

Inflamed by the oratory of such self-promoting preachers as Cotton Mather, subsequent accusations spread like wildfire. Ultimately, 400 people ended up accused – many of them marginal members of society, whose lack of prosperity the Puritans took to mean a lack of godliness.

Imprisoned in cold, damp cells, several of the accused women died while awaiting trial. Of those found guilty in Salem, 19 were hanged and one man was pressed to death beneath a wooden plank piled with rocks. These executions took place between June and September, and the terror might have continued through the fall had Governor General Sir William Phips not returned from the north woods, where he had been fighting an alliance of French and Native Americans, and put a stop to the madness. In December 1692, he ordered all the suspects released – including his own wife.

A number of literary works and films have been inspired by the Salem witch trials, including Henry Wadsworth Longfellow's play *Giles Corey of the Salem Farms* (1868) and Arthur Miller's powerful allegory of McCarthyism, *The Crucible* (1952), adapted for the screen in the eponymous movie (1996) starring Daniel Day-Lewis and Winona Ryder.

Europe for elements to work into his dreamhouse, including a medieval village facade to overlook the indoor pool.

The entire castle was built around the monumental 8,200-pipe organ (the largest organ in a private home in the US) that Hammond designed – although he is not the Hammond of Hammond Organ fame. Check the museum's website for a schedule of organ concerts.

GLOUCESTER

Approaching **Gloucester** ❺ from either Route 127 or Route 133, you pass the **Gloucester Fishermen's Wives Memorial**. Overlooking the harbor, the statue of a fisherman's family looking out to sea is a fitting complement to the famous *Fishermen's Memorial* (Route 127), the statue of a fisherman who grips the wheel and peers oceanward. The city's fishing fleet was immortalized in Sebastian Junger's 1997 bestselling novel and the subsequent movie *The Perfect Storm*. The bar where the movie was shot, the Crow's Nest, still looks much as it did during filming a decade ago.

The **Cape Ann Museum** (27 Pleasant Street; tel: 978-283 0455; www.capeann museum.org; Tue–Sat 10am–5pm, Sun 1–4pm) uses artwork to preserve and explore the history of Gloucester's mariners. **Maritime Gloucester** (23 Harbor Loop; tel: 978-281 0470; www. maritimegloucester.org; summer daily, fall and winter Tue–Sat) immerses visitors in the realities of fishing with displays about fitting out schooners and an operating marine railway. Underwater cameras allow for a virtual visit to the Stellwagen Bank National Marine Sanctuary, New England's only maritime sanctuary. Visitors can take a cruise on the center's schooner *Ardelle*.

The visitor center (9 Hough Avenue; tel: 978-281 8865; www.gloucesterma.com) has information about whale-watching cruises. Pick up a walking/driving tour of the galleries of the Rocky Neck Art Colony just east of town.

Overlooking Gloucester harbor is the wonderfully over-the-top **Beauport/Sleeper-McCann House** (75 Eastern Point Boulevard; tel: 978-283 0800; www.historicnewengland.org; late

> ⊙ **Tip**
>
> On the last Sunday in June, the fishermen of Gloucester participate in the Blessing of the Fleet. The unusual, Mission-style Our Lady of Good Voyage Church (142 Prospect Street; tel: 978-283 1490), overlooking the harbor, was built for the Portuguese community.

⊙ ROCKY NECK ARTISTS

A tiny spit of land less than 1 square mile (2.6 sq km) in size just outside Gloucester is the home of Rocky Neck Art Colony. The nation's longest continuously operating art colony, it has attracted a steady draw of realist painters, sculptors, and writers since the 1850s. Childe Hassan, Winslow Homer, Edward Hopper, and John Sloan all drew inspiration from the landscape and lighting. Many of their works hang in galleries and museums across the country and the world, bringing New England's nature and people to audiences far outside the region. A walking tour visits 12 sites used by the artists. For the most part, both the vistas they saw and the buildings where they worked are unchanged (www.rockyneck-artcolony.org).

Hawthorne's House of the Seven Gables.

May–mid-Oct Tue–Sat). Henry Davis Sleeper was one of the first professional interior decorators. Work started on his house in 1907 and continued for 27 years. Each of the 40 rooms is thematic and fanciful: one bedroom is in chapel style, the belfry is rich in chinoiserie, and the book tower has wooden "damask" curtains salvaged from a hearse.

ROCKPORT

Granite was shipped to ports around the world in the 19th century from **Rockport** ❻, a bustling former fishing village-turned-artists' colony and tourist attraction. The seagoers' cottages that crowded onto Bearskin Neck have become tourist-oriented shops. The red fishing shack on the harbor is known as Motif No. 1 because it is said to be more frequently painted and sketched than any other building in America.

Signposted off Curtis Street on the edge of the village, the **Paper House** (52 Pigeon Hill Street; tel: 978-546 2629; www.paperhouserockport.com; spring–fall daily 10am–5pm) is an endearing

oddity, built entirely of rolled-up newspaper reinforced with glue and varnish. Begun in 1922 by an inventor of office supplies, the project took 20 years, and includes a desk made of copies of the *Christian Science Monitor*.

ESSEX

Essex ❼ was a major shipbuilding center in the age of sail. The **Essex Shipbuilding Museum** (66 Main Street; tel: 978-768 7541; www.essexshipbuildingmuseum.org; late May–Oct Wed–Sun, rest of the year Sat and Sun) traces the region's rich boatbuilding history through thousands of photographs, documents, and shipbuilding tools. Two schooners – one authentic, the other a reproduction – share the dock. A burial ground full of interestingly designed 18th- and 19th-century gravestones is on the property. **Cogswell's Grant** (60 Spring Street; tel: 978-768 3632; www.historicnewengland.org; June–mid-Oct Wed–Sun 11am–4pm) is a fabulous collection of American folk art fittingly displayed in an 18th-century farmhouse.

IPSWICH

Continue on Route 133 into **Ipswich** ❽, which has more homes built between 1625 and 1725 than any other community in the country. The **Ipswich Museum** in the 1800 Heard House (54 South Main Street; tel: 978-356 2811; www.ipswichmuseum.org; late May–mid-Oct Thu–Sat 10am–4pm, Sun 1–4pm) has artifacts of the town's 400-year history. Nearby, the 1640 **John Whipple House** (same schedule as the Ipswich Museum) is a fine example of a Puritan homestead.

PARKER RIVER NATIONAL WILDLIFE REFUGE

On the way out to **Plum Island** along Water Street, the Massachusetts Audubon Society offers interpretive displays at their 54-acre (22-hectare) **Joppa Flats Education Center** (tel: 978-462 9998; Tue–Sun and Mon holidays).

Plum Island in the Parker River National Wildlife Refuge.

Just across the road, the **Parker River National Wildlife Refuge visitor center**  (6 Plum Island Turnpike, Newburyport; tel: 978-465 5753; www.fws.gov/refuge/Parker_River/; daily) offers interactive exhibits about the flora and fauna found in the 4,662-acre (1,887-hectare) refuge. There are ample opportunities for wildlife observation, paddling, and shellfishing. Depending on the season, the 6 miles (10km) of sand dunes and ocean beach yield a riot of false heather, dune grass, scrub pine, and beach plums. Geese, pheasants, rabbits, deer, woodchucks, turtles, and toads roam freely over the preserve. In March and October the skies are dark with migrating geese and ducks. From April through mid-August, large areas of the beach are roped off to permit the piping plovers – an endangered species of shorebirds – to nest and feed in peace.

NEWBURYPORT

Continue north to **Newburyport** ⑩. The "Clipper City," once home to a magnificent merchant fleet and a thriving shipbuilding industry, has benefited from careful preservation.

The **Market Square** is a symphony of brick and bustle with fine shops and restaurants adjacent to a waterfront promenade and piers where whale-watching tours embark. Newburyport is the birthplace of the US Coast Guard. Exhibits at the **Custom House Maritime Museum** (25 Water Street, tel: 978-462 8681; www.customhousemaritimemuseum.org; Jan–Apr Sat 10am–4pm and Sun noon–4pm, May–Dec Tue–Sat 10am–4pm and Sun noon–4pm) chronicle the history of the "Coasties" and the area's shipwrecks, as well as displaying maritime art.

The 1808 Federal-style **Cushing House** (98 High Street; tel: 978-462 2681; www.newburyhistory.org/cushing-house/; mid-May–Oct Wed–Sun) was once the home of lawyer and diplomat Caleb Cushing (1800–79), America's first ambassador to China. Artifacts on display include fine New England and Oriental silver, furniture, clocks, toys, and needlework.

AMESBURY

In nearby **Amesbury** ⑪, **Lowell's Boat Shop** (459 Main Street; tel: 978-834 0050; www.lowellsboatshop.com; call for opening hours) is the oldest continuously operating boat shop in the US and birthplace of the fishing dory. It continues to make dories and skiffs much as it did when it first opened its doors in 1793.

Close by is the **Whittier Home** (86 Friend Street; tel: 978-388 1337; www.whittierhome.org; May–Oct Sat). It was here that the "Quaker Poet" and abolitionist John Greenleaf Whittier (1807–92) lived as an adult. The house and furnishings have been preserved as they were during his life.

WEST OF BOSTON

Aside from Boston proper, this has probably the most historic real estate in the country. The colonial era ended and the Revolutionary era began here, but it also saw the birth of trade unions

A gallery in the Rocky Neck Artist Colony.

⊙ Tip

Like any paradise, the Parker River National Wildlife Refuge has its bugbears – in this case, small, flying insects called greenhead flies, whose bite is very painful. They're most common from July through mid-August.

– another revolutionary idea – as part of the aptly named Industrial Revolution.

LAWRENCE

North of Boston on I-93 is **Lawrence** , one of the country's first planned industrial cities. More than 30 immigrant populations worked in the city's mills. Their story is ably recounted at **Lawrence Heritage State Park** (1 Jackson Street; tel: 978-794 1655; www.lawrenceheritage.org; daily 9am–4pm). Exhibits at the visitor center, housed in a restored 1840 boarding house, recreate the living conditions of mill workers, and include a multimedia program about the Great Strike of 1912, also called the "Bread and Roses" strike.

The one-time model mill town of **Lowell** ⑬, southwest of Lawrence on I-495, is America's best brick-and-mortar chronicle of industrial history. The **Lowell National Historical Park** (246 Market Street; tel: 978-970 5000; www.nps.gov/lowe/; daily; charge for some tours) incorporates sites throughout the city which illustrate the history of the Industrial Revolution. Sightseeing

Guarding the approach to the mills in Lawrence MA, during the 1912 strike.

ferries ply the old canals and trolleys clang through the streets. At the **Boott Cotton Mills Museum** (115 John Street; tel: 978-970 5000; end Nov–end Mar Mon–Fri noon–4pm, Sat–Sun noon–5pm, rest of year daily 9.30am–5pm) authentic looms pound at full speed, while the typical boardinghouse for women workers who lived in appalling conditions is recreated in the Mill Girls and Immigrants Exhibit (40 French Street; end Nov–end Mar Wed–Sun 1.30–4pm, rest of year daily 1.30–5pm).

Jack Kerouac, the Beat Generation icon, was born, raised, and buried here. The **Kerouac Memorial**, in Kerouac Park on Bridge Street, is a series of metal tablets displaying his most poignant quotes. The website www.lowellcelebrateskerouac.org is informative about his local links.

The artist James Abbott Whistler (1834–1903) spent the first three years of his life in what is now the **Whistler House Museum of Art** (243 Worthen Street; tel: 978-452 7641; www.whistlerhouse.org; Wed–Sat 11am–4pm; voluntary donation). The collection of 19th- and

⊙ THE BREAD AND ROSES STRIKE

In 1912, Lowell MA had dozens of textile factories operating around the clock. While the mill owners prospered, their workers dealt with low pay, hazardous working conditions, and deplorable living conditions. Nearly 40 percent of the workers died before age 25.

When a new law went into effect lowering the work week from 56 to 54 hours, employers cut the workers' wages by a similar percent. The workers – mostly immigrant women – walked away from their looms and took to the streets, demanding better pay and dignified treatment.

Their cause inspired poet James Oppenheim to write *Bread and Roses*, which included the lines "We come marching, marching in the beauty of the day; A million darkened kitchens, a thousand mill lofts gray... Our lives shall not be sweated from birth until life closes; Hearts starve as well as bodies; give us bread, but give us roses." Within a month, 30,000 millworkers had joined the strike. The governor called out the militia which violently confronted the marching women. After 63 days, the owners and workers came to agreements. But the success was short-lived. The agreements were largely verbal, not written, and within a few years the working conditions and pay had deteriorated; employers thwarted efforts at union organizing; and a depression further undermined the gains.

20th-century New England representational arts includes his etchings.

It's appropriate that the center of the nation's textile industry is home to the **New England Quilt Museum** (18 Shattuck Street; tel: 978-452 4207; www.nequiltmuseum.org; May–Dec Tue–Sun 10am–4pm, Jan–Apr Tue–Sat 10am–4pm). It recounts the history of American quiltmaking with more than 150 traditional and contemporary quilts.

Hop aboard *New Orleans #99*, the trolley that inspired playwright Tennessee Williams' *A Streetcar Named Desire* for a 2-mile (3km) ride at the **National Streetcar Museum** (25 Shattuck Street; tel: 978-275 1821; www.trolleymuseum.org/lowell; Sat–Sun; streetcar rides weekends May–Oct).

THE SHOT HEARD ROUND THE WORLD

On April 19, 1775, British regulars clashed in a battle with militia and Minutemen in **Lexington** ⑭ and **Concord** ⑮, and "the shot heard round the world" launched the eight-year War for Independence. The route of the British advance from Boston is designated the **Battle Road**.

Chronologically, a visit to the Lexington and Concord battle sites should go east to west. From Lowell, take Route 3 to exit 31. From Boston, all of the revolutionary sites can be reached via Route 2. The best place to start a visit to the area is at one of the visitor centers at the **Minute Man National Historical Park** (Headquarters 174 Liberty Street, Concord; tel: 978-369 6993; www.nps.gov/mima); **Minute Man Visitor Center** (250 N. Great Road, Lincoln; Apr–Oct daily); and the **Hartwell Tavern** (Route 2A, Lincoln; mid-June–mid-Oct daily), a restored, 18th-century home and tavern where park rangers in colonial attire offer 20-minute programs daily. The **North Bridge Visitor Center** (174 Liberty Street, Concord; Apr–Oct daily, Nov–Dec and Mar Tue–Sat) has an excellent multimedia presentation, *The Road to Revolution*, which explains the events for those who aren't steeped in American history and those Americans who didn't pay attention in history class.

The iconic statue of John Parker on Battle Green, Lexington.

The Boott Cotton Mills Museum.

Tip

An easy way to take in all the sights without driving is to use the Liberty Ride Trolley (www.tourlexington.us; Apr–Oct). Costumed guides narrate a 90-minute tour of Lexington and Concord, covering 20 different sites.

LEXINGTON

Most of the important Lexington sites are within a musket shot of each other. The **Lexington Visitor Center Ⓐ** (1875 Massachusetts Avenue, across from the green; tel: 781-862 1450; daily) is a good place to get your bearings. Across the street is **Battle Green Ⓑ**, with the famous statue of Minuteman Captain John Parker. Seventy-seven militiamen faced 1,000 British regulars here. The remains of the eight Minutemen who died rest underneath the obelisk on the Green. **Buckman Tavern Ⓒ** (1 Bedford Street; tel: 781-862 5598; daily) was the place Captain Parker and his Minutemen sipped beer while waiting for the British.

The **Hancock-Clarke House Ⓓ** (36 Hancock Street; tel: 781-861 0928; June–Oct daily, Apr–May Sat–Sun) was Paul Revere's destination. He was trying to warn John Hancock and Samuel Adams with news of the British advance. A mile outside town, **Munroe Tavern Ⓔ** (1332 Massachusetts Avenue; tel: 781-862 0295; June–Oct daily, Apr–May Sat–Sun)

sheltered British Brigadier General Earl Percy and his troops during their retreat from Concord. A bit farther on, the **Scottish Rite Masonic Museum & Library Ⓕ** (formerly the National Heritage Museum; 33 Marrett Road, Route 2A; tel: 781-861 6559; www.srmml.org; Wed–Sat 10am–4pm, closed Fri in summer) focuses on the history of American freemasonry and fraternalism, as well as the period surrounding the American Revolution.

Leaving Lexington on **Battle Road** (aka Route 2A and Massachusetts Avenue), you'll pass the **Ebenezer Fiske House Site Farmhouse Ⓖ**, where a historical marker explains the course of the fierce fighting that broke out there. A section of the original road here is unpaved and closed to traffic, giving an idea of its original appearance.

CONCORD

Concord Museum Ⓗ (53 Cambridge Turnpike, Route 2A; www.concordmuseum.org; tel: 978-369 9763; Apr–Dec Mon–Sat 9am–5pm, Sun noon–5pm except June, July & Aug Sun from 9am,

A Patriots Day re-enactment on Concord's replica Old North Bridge.

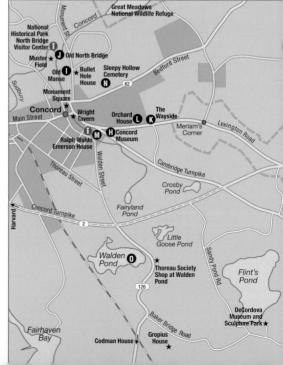

Jan–Mar Mon–Sat 11am–4pm and Sun 1–4pm) has excellent displays relating to Revolutionary Concord, including one of the two lanterns hung by Robert Newman in Old North Church in Boston. The town's literary legacy is also strongly covered. A gallery devoted to Concord's Henry David Thoreau (1817–62) has a superb collection of artifacts associated with the great author and naturalist, including furnishings from his cabin by Walden Pond. The construction of a new education center is due to finish in July 2018.

The **Old Manse** ⓘ (269 Monument Street; tel: 978-369 3909; tours mid Apr–Oct Tue–Sun, Nov–mid Apr Sat–Sun) was built by Minister William Emerson around 1770, and was used to shelter women and children during the battle. It became home to his grandson Ralph Waldo, who wrote *Nature* (1836) here, and was rented for three years to Nathaniel Hawthorne. There is a specialty bookstore on site.

At **Old North Bridge** ⓙ, rangers tell how the tide of the battle turned against the British here. Pass Daniel Chester French's *Minute Man* statue to reach the North Bridge Visitor Center.

CONCORD'S LITERARY ASSOCIATIONS

From 1845 to 1848 the writer Louisa May Alcott lived in **The Wayside** ⓚ (455 Lexington Road, Route 2A; tel: 978-318 7863; call for opening times). In 1852 it was bought by writer Nathaniel Hawthorne. He added the tower, but found it unsatisfactory for working in, and said he would happily see the house burn down.

From 1858 to 1877, the Alcott family lived at **Orchard House** ⓛ (399 Lexington Road, Route 2A; tel: 978-369 4118; www.louisamayalcott.org; guided tours daily), where Louisa May penned *Little Women* and *Little Men*. The house still has most of the family's furnishings and looks as it did when they lived here. There's an excellent orientation video and a self-guided tour of Bronson's School of Philosophy, which functioned from 1880 to 1888. Once a month, there is a living-history tour complete with a costumed guide (dressed as an Alcott

◉ **Where**

The Battle Road Trail is a 5-mile (8km) walking and biking trail which begins at the eastern boundary of the park in Lexington and ends at Meriam's Corner near Concord. It's more historically accurate than the highway with which it shares the name. The trail largely follows the road which existed in 1775, with a few detours through the fields and forests the Minutemen used.

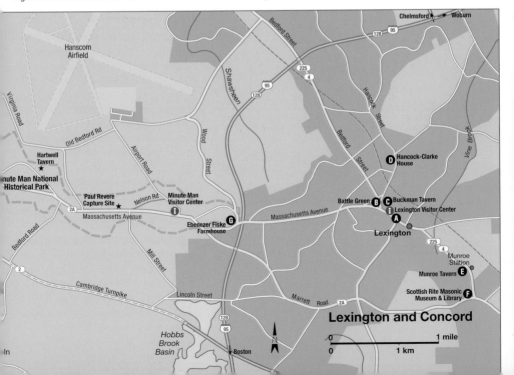

Lexington and Concord

Walden Pond is the birthplace of the conservatism movement.

family member or one of their famous friends), 19th-century games, and period songs (booking advised).

THOREAU AND EMERSON

Philosopher and author Ralph Waldo Emerson lived most of his adult life nearby; his house, furnished as it was when he died in 1882, is preserved as the **Ralph Waldo Emerson House** Ⓜ (28 Cambridge Turnpike; tel: 978-369 2236; mid-Apr–Oct Thu–Sun).

Sleepy Hollow Cemetery Ⓝ (Bedford Street, Route 62) is the resting place of most of the Concord big names, among them Hawthorne, the Alcotts, Emerson, and Thoreau.

WALDEN POND

South of Concord off Route 126, Thoreau spent 26 months in a one-room cabin (there's now a replica) by **Walden Pond** Ⓞ (tel: 978-369 3254; open year-round; parking fee) striving to be self-sufficient and recording the progress of nature, all of which he recounted in *Walden* (1854). A National Historic Landmark, the

Walden Pond.

pond and surrounding land are now a state reservation.

LINCOLN

Tiny, upscale **Lincoln** ⑯ just south of Lexington and Concord, has the superb **DeCordova Sculpture Park** (51 Sandy Pond Road; tel: 781-259 8355; www.decordova.org; mid-Oct–Apr Wed–Fri 10am–4pm, Sat–Sun until 5pm, May–Sept daily 10am–5pm). With around 75 large-scale contemporary outdoor American sculptures, the 35-acre (14-hectare) museum is the largest of its kind in New England. The house of the one-time estate, known as "The Castle," is now a museum of modern and contemporary American art. The café serves light lunches.

The **Gropius House** (68 Baker Bridge Road; tel: 781-259 8098; May–Oct Wed–Sun; Nov–Apr weekends) was built by the renowned 20th-century architect who helped launch the Bauhaus school in 1938 when he came to teach at the Harvard Graduate School of Design.

SOUTH OF BOSTON

The first settlers arrived in this part of the New World, hoping to establish a theocracy unfettered by outside influences. That drive for self-determination led a later resident, John Adams, to argue for establishment of an independent government for their descendants. The whalers and fishermen in New Bedford and Fall River continue that self-reliant life as they challenge the elements while earning their living from the sea.

From Boston, head south on I-93 to exit 12 and follow Route 3A to Quincy and the **Adams National Historical Park** ⑰ (visitor center at 1250 Hancock Street; tel: 617-770 1175; www.nps.gov/adam; houses open mid-Apr–mid-Nov daily, visitor center and park year-round). This was home to four generations of Adamses from 1720 to 1927. The site includes the birthplaces of America's first father-and-son

presidential pair – John Adams (second president of the US) and his son, John Quincy Adams (the sixth) – and Peacefield, the elegant home that John and his wife, Abigail, moved to in 1787.

High points of the tour are J.Q. Adams's library, with 14,000 volumes, and the formal garden, especially appealing when the daffodils bloom. Entrance to the buildings is by guided tour only, first-come, first-served: on weekends and holidays, waits of one to two hours are common.

ABIGAIL ADAMS

The second first lady, John Adams's wife Abigail, was born at the **Abigail Adams Birthplace** ⓲ (180 Norton Street; tel: 781-277 1271; www.abigailadamsbirthplace.com; call for tour information) in **Weymouth** in 1744. The house, built in 1685 and once referred to as "The Mansion," has been restored to its mid-1700s appearance.

HINGHAM

Farther down the coast off routes 1 and 3A is **Hingham** ⓳, beautified by Frederick Law Olmsted, creator of Boston's "emerald necklace" of parks and New York's Central Park; his handiwork here is the bucolic **World's End Reservation** (250 Martin's Lane; tel: 781-740 7233; daily), a 250-acre (100-hectare) harborside preserve with walking trails providing views of the Boston skyline and Hingham harbor.

NANTASKET

Enclosing Hingham Bay and curving toward Boston like a beckoning finger is the sandy spit of **Nantasket** ⓴, a long-time summer playground of which only a carousel has survived redevelopment. The classic 1928 **Paragon Carousel** (205 Nantasket Avenue; tel: 781-925 0472; www.paragoncarousel.com; mid-June–mid Sept Sun–Thu 10am–9pm, Fri–Sat until 10pm, mid Sept–Oct Sat–Sun 11am–5pm, Easter–end May Sat–Sun 11am–5pm, first half June Fri 5–10pm, Sat 10am–10pm, Sun 10am–9pm) is a gem. An "adopt a horse" program helps fund the restoration of the 66 horses that prance to the music of a Wurlitzer organ.

John Adams (1735–1826) served as ambassador to the Netherlands and Britain and became the second president of the United States.

A statue of Thoreau outside a replica of his cabin at Walden Pond.

Interpreting the past at Plimoth Plantation.

The **Hull Lifesaving Museum** (1117 Nantasket Avenue; tel: 781-925 5433; www.lifesavingmuseum.org; Sept–June Mon–Thu 10am–2pm, Sat 10am–4pm, July–Aug also Sun 10am–4pm), in a restored 19th-century lifesaving station at the mouth of Boston Harbor, gives visitors a good idea of the heroic measures required when the lighthouse warnings failed to stave off disaster. Hands-on exhibits focus on storms, lighthouses, wrecks, and rescues. There are fabulous views of Boston Light (America's oldest operating lighthouse) and Graves lighthouse from the observation cupola.

At the end of the Hull Peninsula, the observation deck at the top of the water tower in **Fort Revere Park** (tel: 781-925 1777; Memorial Day–Labor Day) offers a panoramic view from Cape Ann to Provincetown. There's also a small military museum.

DUXBURY

USS Lionfish, at Battleship Cove.

Just off gently meandering Route 3A to the south is **Duxbury** ㉑. It was settled in 1628 by Pilgrims, and they are well remembered here. A statue of Captain Myles Standish, *Mayflower* passenger and Plymouth colony leader, crowns a 125-step observation tower at the top of Captain's Hill in **Myles Standish Monument State Reservation** (Crescent Street; tel: 508-747 5360; daily). Fellow *Mayflower* passengers John and Priscilla Alden lived at the finely preserved 1653 **Alden House** (105 Alden Street; tel: 781-934 9092; www.alden.org; guided tours June–mid Oct Wed–Sat) and are buried, along with Myles, at the **Old Burying Ground** on Chestnut Street.

Wealthy shipbuilder/merchant Ezra Weston Jr, affectionately nicknamed King Caesar (New England's then-largest ship, *The Hope*, was constructed in his shipyard in 1841), built a stately Federal mansion in 1809 that today stands as a testament to his wealth and good taste. Highlights at the **King Caesar House** (120 King Caesar Road; tel: 781-934 6106; July–Aug Wed–Sun and Sept weekends) include rare French scenic wallpaper and a variety of 19th-century furnishings.

Carl A. Weyerhaeuser, the grandson of the founder of the hugely successful lumber company, began collecting art with a discerning eye while a student at Harvard. Today the **Art Complex Museum** (189 Alden Street; tel: 781-934 6634; www.artcomplex.org; Wed–Sun; free) houses his superb collection, including prints by Dürer; Shaker furniture; American paintings by artists such as Sargent, Cropsey, and Bellows; and Asian art. A Japanese teahouse occasionally hosts traditional tea ceremonies.

PLYMOUTH

Southward on Route 3 lies **Plymouth** ㉒, where the Pilgrims made landfall in 1620. **Plymouth Rock** Ⓐ, legendary 1620 landing place of the Pilgrims, enjoys a place of honor under an elaborate harborside portico which resembles Athens' Parthenon. The rock is... well, a rock, but even if taken with a

grain of salt as the actual landfall, it's an interesting example of origin mythology.

A stone's throw from the monument is the **Mayflower II** (State Pier, Water Street; tel: 508-746 1622; www.plimoth.org; late Mar–Nov daily). A replica of the original *Mayflower*, this was built in England and sailed to Plymouth in 1957. Actors on board the 104ft (32-meter) -long vessel portray the original passengers and field visitors' questions with accuracy and wit, vividly conveying the hardships that its 102 passengers endured on their 66-day voyage. Between now and 2020 *Mayflower II* will be undergoing restoration to its full glory to celebrate the 400th anniversary of the Pilgrims' voyage.

Across the road from the Rock is **Coles Hill** , where, during their first winter, the Pilgrims secretly buried their dead at night to hide the truth about their fast dwindling numbers from the Indians. **Pilgrim Hall Museum** (75 Court Street; tel: 508-746 1620; www.pilgrimhallmuseum.org; mid Feb–Dec daily 9.30am–4.30pm) displays such relics as John Alden's halberd; Myles

Standish's sword, razor, and Bible; and the cradle of Peregrine White, born aboard the *Mayflower*.

Farther east, beyond Main Street, is **Burial Hill** , with gravestones dating back to the colony's founding. "Under this stone rests the ashes of Willm Bradford, a zealous Puritan and sincere Christian, Governor of Plymouth Colony from April 1621–57 (the year he died, aged 69) except five years which he declined." The hill was the site of the Pilgrims' first meeting house, fort, and watchtower.

South of Burial Hill is the replica **Jenney Grist Mill** (tel: 508-747 4544; www.jenneymuseum.org; Apr–Nov Mon–Sat 9am–5pm), where corn is still ground as it was by the Pilgrims in 1636. A costumed guide gives 30-minute tours (reservations recommended).

PLIMOTH PLANTATION

South of town on Route 3, **Plimoth Plantation** (Warren Avenue; tel: 508-746 1622; www.plimoth.org; late Mar–Nov daily) is a painstaking reconstruction of the English settlement in 1627.

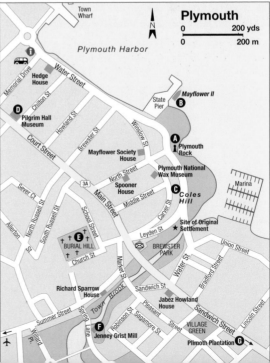

Mayflower II, a replica of the original Mayflower, moored at the State Pier, Plymouth.

Anchors aweigh at Battleship Cove.

Costumed re-enactors portray actual residents of the colony. Their homes are thatched huts; their crops and live-stock true to the era. Their accented English is the historically accurate Jacobean dialect, which is unlike the modern American or British mode of speaking, although Shakespeare and Queen Elizabeth I would have recognized it. As they go about their daily chores, they engage visitors in conversations about religion, child-rearing, relations with local Indian tribes, and village gossip. They stay true to their "character," only answering questions within the knowledge base of a person in their era. Other topics are met with incomprehension.

At the Wampanoag village on the banks of the Eel River, members of the Wampanoag nation – not re-enactors – plant crops, gather food, make tools and personal items, and maintain their dwellings. Although they wear traditional clothing, they are not role-playing, and converse from a modern perspective (and in modern English) about their history and culture.

Wild turkey.

The café serves food inspired by Wampanoag and English Colonial ingredients (as well as more usual fare); and a display at the Visitors' Center concentrates on the Puritans' most famous social event, the 1621 Thanksgiving (and how it has developed into the annual celebration of over-indulgence and postprandial football). It's all self-guided and tickets are good for two days. There are a variety of combination packages.

NEW BEDFORD

From Plymouth, take Route 44 to I-495 and I-195 to **New Bedford** , onetime whaling capital and today the East Coast's busiest fishing port. The narrow cobblestone streets and historic buildings of the old quarter have been incorporated into the **New Bedford Whaling National Historical Park** (33 William Street; tel: 508-996 4095; www.nps.gov/nebe; daily). A video explains the role of whaling in New Bedford's development. There's a Portuguese translation and devices for the hearing impaired. At weekends

⊘ THANKSGIVING

While both Florida and Virginia claim that "Thanksgiving" was first celebrated in their territory, the holiday is inextricably linked to Massachusetts and the Pilgrims. Far from realizing they were starting a national tradition, they were merely partaking in a familiar European harvest celebration. They had a lot to be thankful for. Nearly half of the *Mayflower*'s passengers died during the first winter. Only help from the Wampanoags saved the rest. But the harvest of 1621 was a good one and prompted celebrations lasting three days. The 53 surviving Pilgrims and about 100 men from Chief Massasoyt's tribe feasted on venison, fish, lobster, clams, berries, watercress, dried fruit, and plums. The next celebration was not held for several years, and by then relations with the local inhabitants had soured.

Making Thanksgiving a national holiday was the obsession of Sara Josepha Hale. Starting in 1827, she organized support and lobbied endlessly to have a national day of thanksgiving. In 1863, she finally succeeded when Abraham Lincoln issued a proclamation naming the last Thursday of November as a day of thanksgiving. But that was a one-time thing. It wasn't a permanent national holiday until 1941, when Franklin Roosevelt signed the paperwork.

in July and August, park rangers conduct Underground Railroad tours of the city, relating the history of the escaped slaves who fled to New Bedford for freedom and jobs.

The park incorporates several sites which operate independently. The **New Bedford Whaling Museum** (18 Johnny Cake Hill; tel: 508-997 0046; www. whalingmuseum.org; Apr–Dec daily 9am–5pm, Jan–Mar Tue–Sat 9am–4pm, Sun 11am–4pm; audio tour available) evokes the lifestyles of the whalers and fishermen, and has a huge collection of ship models – most memorably the *Lagoda*, a half-size replica of a 19th-century whaling vessel – plus a collection of scrimshaw, intricately carved out of whalebone by the sailors on their long voyages.

Across from the museum is the **Seamen's Bethel** (http://seamensbethel. org; daily; voluntary donation) with the "Whaleman's Chapel" mentioned by Herman Melville in *Moby-Dick*. The 156ft (47-meter) Grand Banks fishing schooner *Ernestina*, launched in Essex in 1894, sailed to within 600 miles (965km) of the North Pole and then brought immigrants from Europe. She's now moored at the State Pier.

Taking up a full city block, the 1834 **Rotch-Jones-Duff House & Garden** (396 County Road; tel: 508-997 1401; http://rjdmuseum.org; Mon–Sat 10am–4pm, Sun noon–4pm; free second Thu eve of the month) is a superb example of residential Greek Revival architecture. Originally built for a prominent whaling merchant, it chronicles life in New Bedford from 1834 to 1981. The gardens are equally magnificent, formally laid out with ornamental beds, graceful walkways, and an apiary garden.

FALL RIVER

Nine miles (14km) west of New Bedford, **Fall River** ㉔ is dominated by huge mills, reminders of the city's long-defunct cotton industry. The city's

life is told at **Fall River Heritage State Park** overlooking Battleship Cove (Davol Street; tel: 508-675 5759; daily). You can ride on a 1920 carousel (July–Aug), housed in a Victorian pavilion.

Battleship Cove (tel: 508-678 1100; http://battleshipcove.org; 9am–4pm Apr–Oct daily, Nov–Mar Fri–Sun; admission is good for two consecutive days) has the world's largest collection of historic naval ships. Among them are the submarine USS *Lionfish*, the 46,000-ton battleship USS *Massachusetts*, and the world's only restored pair of PT boats. The submarine and the battleship – "Big Mamie," a fighting veteran of World War II – can be visited.

Virtually adjacent, the **Marine Museum** (70 Water Street; tel: 508-674 3533; http://battleshipcove.org/maritime-museum; Apr–Sept Wed–Sun, Nov weekends; same ticket as for Battleship Cove) traces the history of the Fall River Line from 1847 to 1937, and is packed with nautical paraphernalia, including a major display about the *Titanic*, and an exhibit about the sinking of the liner *Andrea Doria*.

The replica of the Jenney Grist Mill.

FALL FOLIAGE

A revered ritual of New England life is leaf-peeping – driving to see the green leaves of summer turn to the vivid oranges, yellows, and reds of fall.

Droves of dedicated leaf-peepers come by the car- and busload every autumn. Time and place are everything when it comes to watching the fall colors change, and advance reservations at inns and restaurants are essential if you want to secure the best spots. In the far north of New England, leaves start turning mid-September, moving gradually farther south over the next few weeks. By the end of October, the show is pretty much over. Plan your travel accordingly, moving from north to south. New Hampshire and Vermont are most often linked with great foliage, but all six states have colorful fall vistas.

Virtually every ski resort transforms its lifts into "foliage" rides. Take a hike and surround yourself with the colors of the forest. An online fall foliage map which updates conditions regularly and suggests several driving routes is at www.discovernewengland.org.

Almost any highway route designated as "scenic" on a state map will yield bountiful leaf color. But while it may be fun to drive back roads in search of great fall color, Interstates often have the best foliage. In Maine, I–95 offers some great leaf-peeping in the 75-mile (120km) stretch from Augusta to Bangor. Similarly, in northeastern Connecticut, I–395 always puts on a fine leaf show. In Massachusetts, one of the best foliage drives is westward along the Mohawk Trail (Route 2, Greenfield to Williamstown). But it's virtually impossible not to see beautiful colors.

Foliage hot-lines: Connecticut, tel: 800-CT-BOUND; Massachusetts, tel: 617 626 1250; New Hampshire, tel: 800-258 3608; Vermont, tel: 800-828 3239; Maine, tel: 888-624 6345; Rhode Island, tel: 401 222 2601.

Day breaks on a sugar house and maple trees in the autumn countryside of Vermont. There are many historic wooden buildings and bridges that complement the fall colors.

On the road from the scenic town of Millinocket to Baxter State Park in Maine, you'll have the opportunity to see the golden leaves of fall, and perhaps a few moose or white-tailed deer.

The color of the fall leaves is largely determined by the quality of soil in which the plant grows. A plant with rich soil and many nutrients will remain slightly greenish, while a plant that is in poor soil will turn a bright and fiery red.

Leaf-peeping is a major economic activity in New England, and a number of locales have set up special "leaf watching" websites to help track the changing colors, to make sure you get the best experience possible.

Peak timing

As nature has one last fling before settling in for the long winter, the colors of autumn leaves are sometimes so vivid it seems they will shine in the dark.

By trying too hard to pinpoint the absolute peak of foliage, however, you risk missing the majesty of the leaf-changing phenomenon: If you're lucky enough to be in New England in October, you're sure to see peak foliage somewhere, because each tree changes its color according to an inner timetable that's affected by moisture, temperature, and the shorter days of fall.

Botanists call the color change "leaf senescence" – the process by which the green pigment chlorophyll is drawn back into the tree to nourish it. The tree is essentially turning off the system that carries nutrients to the leaves so that it can store the energy it needs to survive until spring. When chlorophyll is cut off, other pigments shine through. Brightest of all are red swamp maples and sumac. Aspen and birch turn yellow, sugar maples a peachy orange. Warm, sunny days and cool, crisp nights seem to be the recipe for the most spectacular colors.

When the summer months gently dwindle into fall, New Englanders call it an "Indian Summer;" it provides the opportunity to explore the great outdoors via the regions many accessible hiking and biking trails.

he Virginia Creeper (Parthenocissus quinquefolia) can urn a particular shade of crimson in the fall, and is equently seen in gardens throughout New England.

CAPE COD AND THE ISLANDS

This sandy summer playground has clam shacks, historic B&Bs, National Seashore beaches, and a lively arts scene, plus the islands of Martha's Vineyard and Nantucket.

⊙ Main Attractions

National Marine Life
  Center
Sandwich Glass Museum
Sandy Neck Beach
Cape Cod National
  Seashore
Provincetown
Woods Hole Oceanographic
  Institution
Martha's Vineyard
Oak Bluffs, Nantucket

Map on page 164

Bostonians consider Cape Cod their own private playground, but its fame has spread so far that it attracts international travelers. In high season, lodgings are filled to capacity, traffic on the Cape's few highways is heavy, and local merchants work hard to make the profits that will carry them through the virtually dormant winters. Even at the height of its summertime popularity, when the roads, restaurants, and beaches tend to be jammed, Cape Cod manages to preserve its wild charm and dramatic beauty.

Much of this quality is protected within the boundaries of the Cape Cod National Seashore, a vast 27,000-acre (11,000-hectare) nature reserve established by far-sighted legislators in 1961. Precisely because it has not been commercially exploited, this huge expanse of untouched dunes survives as one of the Cape's most alluring features.

GETTING YOUR BEARINGS

Shaped like the flexed arm of a body-builder, it's important to note the nomenclature of the island. "Upper Cape" refers to the portion nearest the mainland; "Mid-Cape" is roughly from Barnstable County eastward to Chatham and Orleans, where the "arm" bends; "Lower Cape" is the "forearm" jutting northward to East-ham, Truro, and Provincetown.

Technically, Cape Cod is an island. The **Cape Cod Canal** was built by New York financier August Belmont in 1914 to eliminate the need for ships to round the Cape via the often stormy Atlantic. Belmont ran the canal as a private endeavor until 1928, when it was purchased by the US Government. The US Army Corps of Engineers supervised the building of the two bridges and improvements to the waterway: by 1940 it was the widest sea-level canal (there are no locks) in the world. Two

Fishing charters are readily available.

7-mile (11km) service roads which parallel the canal are great for bicycling or hiking.

The **Cape Cod Canal Visitor Center** ❶ (60 Ed Moffitt Drive, Sandwich; tel: 508-833 9678: May–Oct daily), off Route 6A, recounts the history of the canal and the bridges. Park rangers conduct guided walks, bike hikes, and themed programs.

CHOOSE A BRIDGE

Expressways funnel traffic to the two access bridges over the canal. At the waterway's eastern end, Route 3 comes south from Boston and crosses the Sagamore Bridge to join Route 6, the Mid-Cape Highway.

The other span, the Bourne Bridge, is handy if you approach the Cape from the west. This is the crossing to use if you want to head south toward Falmouth and Woods Hole via Route 28. For those wishing to avoid the drive, there are summer ferries between Provincetown and Boston, Provincetown and Plymouth, and flights into Hyannis and Provincetown.

WHICH ROUTE?

Itineraries on the Upper and Mid-Cape offer a choice of speedy, featureless highways or scenic, meandering roads. Those intent on reaching the Outer Cape in a hurry generally opt for Route 6, the four-lane, limited-access Mid-Cape Highway; those headed for Falmouth, Woods Hole, and points along Nantucket Sound can take the equally speedy Route 28.

To get a true sense of the Cape, however, take the prettier back roads. Roughly parallel to the Mid-Cape Highway, two-lane Route 6A starts in Sagamore and runs eastward along the bay through old towns full of graceful, historic houses and crafts and antiques shops.

The same can be said of Route 28A, hugging the shore en route to Falmouth. As Route 28 veers northeastward from Falmouth to Chatham, it's marred by recurrent stretches of overdevelopment but, again, one has only to venture off the main road a bit to discover such towns as Osterville and Centerville, Harwich Port and Chatham itself.

The Sagamore Bridge over the Cape Cod Canal.

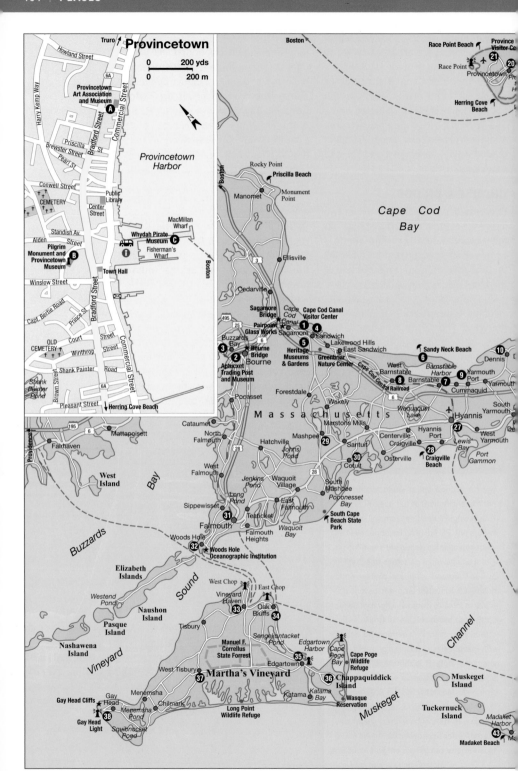

Provincetown

0   200 yds

0   200 m

Truro

Howland Street

Harry Kemp Way

6A

Provincetown
Art Association
and Museum

A

Provincetown
Harbor

Bradford Street

Commercial St

Priscilla
Street

Brewster Street

Pearl St

Conwell Street

CEMETERY

Public
Library

Center
Street

MacMillan
Wharf

Standish Av.

Alden   Street

Pilgrim
Monument and
Provincetown
Museum

B

Whydah Pirate
Museum

C

Fisherman's
Wharf

Winslow Street

Town Hall

Capt. Bertie Road

Prince St

OLD
CEMETERY

Court
Street

Winthrop

Street

Shank
Painter
Pond

Brown Street

Shank Painter   Road

Commercial Street

Bradford Street

Pleasant Street

6A

Herring Cove Beach

Providence

195   6

Fairhaven

Mattapoisett

West
Island

Buzzards   Bay

Elizabeth
Islands

Westend
Pond

Naushon
Island

Pasque
Island

Nashawena
Island

Vineyard   Sound

Gay Head Cliffs

Gay
Head

38

Gay Head
Light

Menemsha
Pond

Squibnocket
Pond

Menemsha

Chilmark

West Tisbury

37

Martha's Vineyard

Tisbury

West Chop

Vineyard
Haven

33

West Chop

East Chop

Oak
Bluffs

34

Manuel F.
Correllus
State Forrest

Sengekontacket
Pond

Edgartown
Harbor

35

Edgartown

Katama

Katama
Bay

Long Point
Wildlife Refuge

Cape
Poge
Bay

Cape Poge
Wildlife Refuge

36

Chappaquiddick
Island

28

Wasque
Reservation

Muskeget

Muskeget
Island

Tuckernuck
Island

Madaket
Harbor

43

Madaket Beach

Boston

Race Point Beach

Race Point

Province
Visitor Ce

21

Provincetown

20

Herring Cove
Beach

Cape   Cod
Bay

Rocky Point

Priscilla Beach

Manomet

Monument
Point

Ellisville

Cedarville

Sagamore
Bridge

495

25

Pairpoint
Glass Works

Buzzards
Bay

3

2

Bourne
Bridge

Aptucxet
Trading Post
and Museum

Bourne

Cape
Cod
Canal

Cape Cod Canal
Visitor Center

Sagamore

1

4

5

Sandwich

Lakewood Hills

East Sandwich

Heritage
Museums
& Gardens

Greenbriar
Nature Center

West
Barnstable

Barnstable

8

Sandy Neck Beach

6

Barnstable
Harbor

9

Yarmouth
Port

7

Cummaquid

Dennis

10

Yarmouth

South
Yarmouth

Pocasset

Cataumet

North
Falmouth

Forestdale

Wakely

Massachusetts

Mashpee

Marstons Mills

29

Santuit

Cotuit

Wequaquet
Lake

Centerville
Craigville

Osterville

Hyannis
Port

27

Hyannis

30

Hatchville

Johns
Pond

West
Falmouth

Jenkins
Pond

Waquoit
Village

South
Mashpee

Poponesset
Bay

Craigville
Beach

West
Yarmouth

Lewis
Bay

Port
Gammon

Sippewisset

Long
Pond

31

Teaticket

East
Falmouth

Falmouth

Woods Hole

32

Falmouth
Heights

Waquoit
Bay

South Cape
Beach State
Park

Woods Hole
Oceanographic Institution

Buzzards   Bay

Channel

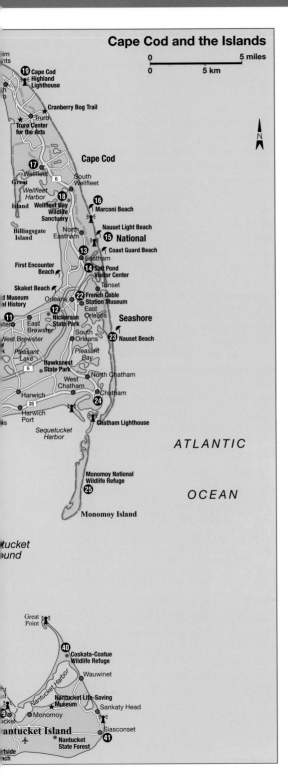

Cape Cod and the Islands

0   5 miles
0   5 km

19 Cape Cod Highland Lighthouse

Cranberry Bog Trail

Truro
Truro Center for the Arts

Cape Cod

17 Wellfleet
Great
South Wellfleet
Wellfleet Harbor
Island   Wellfleet Bay **18** Wildlife Sanctuary
Billingsgate Island
First Encounter Beach
Skaket Beach
Museum al History
11 East Brewster
ter
West Brewster
Pleasant Lake
Hawksnest State Park
Harwich
Harwich Port
Sequetucket Harbor

16 Marconi Beach
North Eastham
Nauset Light Beach
15 **National**
13 Coast Guard Beach
Eastham
14 Salt Pond Visitor Center
Tonset
22 French Cable Station Museum
Orleans
12 East Orleans
Nickerson State Park
South Orleans
23 Nauset Beach
Pleasant Bay
North Chatham
West Chatham
Chatham
24
Chatham Lighthouse

Seashore

ATLANTIC

OCEAN

Monomoy National Wildlife Refuge
25

Monomoy Island

tucket
ound

Great Point
40 Coskata-Coatue Wildlife Refuge
Wauwinet

Nantucket Life-Saving Museum
Sankaty Head
Monomoy
antucket Island
Siasconset
Nantucket State Forest
41
rfside

Once Route 28 and Route 6 merge in Orleans, Route 6 north is pleasant all the way to Provincetown, if traffic-clogged in summer.

ATTRACTIONS NEAR THE BRIDGES

On the Cape side of the Sagamore Bridge, glassblowers at the **Pairpoint Glass Works** (851 Sandwich Road; off Route 6A; tel: 800-899 0953; https://pairpoint.com; store Mon–Sat 10am–4pm, Sun 11am–4pm) give demonstrations on weekdays (10am–4pm).

West of the Bourne Bridge, on the mainland side near the canal, the Bourne Historical Society's **Aptucxet Trading Post and Museum** ❷ (24 Aptucxet Road, Bourne; tel: 508-759 8167; www.bournehistoricalsociety.org/aptucxet-museum; Memorial Day–Columbus Day Tue–Sun) is a replica of the first English-speaking trading post in North America, set up in 1627 to trade with the Wampanoag Indians, the Dutch in New York, and the Plymouth settlement.

Many of the houses along Sandwich Road and Keene Street in Bourne date to the 1800s. This includes the **Briggs-McDermott House**, restored to reflect the period of 1840 to 1910.

In nearby **Buzzards Bay** ❸, the **National Marine Life Center** (120 Main Street; tel: 508-743 9888; http://nmlc.org; 10am–5pm late May–early Sept daily, Labor Day–Columbus Day weekends; voluntary donation) rescues and rehabilitates stranded marine animals such as sea turtles, seals, dolphins, and terrapins.

THE BAY SIDE: SANDWICH TO BREWSTER

This region gained a reputation for its glass after Boston merchant Deming Jarvis founded a glass factory in **Sandwich** ❹ in 1825. It thrived until competition from plants in the Midwest, and a strike by exploited workers, shut the enterprise down in 1888. Outstanding examples of their output are found in the **Sandwich Glass Museum** (129 Main Street; tel: 508-888 0251; http://sandwichglassmuseum.org; Apr–Dec daily 9.30am–5pm, Feb–Mar Wed–Sun 9.30am–4pm), where there are demonstrations of the art of glass-blowing every hour.

⊘ Tip

A beach entrance fee is collected from late June through early September, and on weekends and holidays from Memorial Day through September. In 2017, vehicles were charged $20, motorcyclists $10 and bicyclists, and pedestrians $3. If you're going to be visiting for an extended period, a $60 vehicle pass covers all beaches on the National Seashore for the season.

Relaxing near Sandwich, the oldest town on Cape Cod.

Sandwich, the first town to be founded on the Cape, in 1637, is one of the prettiest and best-preserved. At its center stands the restored 1654 **Dexter Grist Mill** (mid-May–early Sept daily; stone-ground cornmeal available in summer), with a new watermill added in 2015, and the 1637 **Hoxie House** (Water Street; tel: 508-888 1173; mid-June–Sept daily; combination ticket for Dexter Mil and House available), a remarkably well-preserved saltbox reputed to be the Cape's oldest dwelling.

The woodland and wetlands around Sandwich were the inspiration for the tales of Peter Rabbit (the name borrowed from Beatrix Potter), Reddy Fox, Jimmy Skunk, and all of the other whimsical characters created by the author and naturalist Thornton Burgess (1874–1965). Peter Rabbit's favorite briar patch – a 57-acre (23-hectare) conservation area – is adjacent to **Greenbriar Nature Center** (6 Discovery Hill Road; tel: 508-888 6870; www.thorntonburgess.org; mid-May–Dec daily, Jan–mid-Apr Tue–Sat; voluntary donation), which has a room dedicated to Burgess' work.

HERITAGE MUSEUMS & GARDENS

For more glimpses into the American past, follow the signs – past a lovely historic cemetery overlooking Shawme Pond – to **Heritage Museums & Gardens** ❺ (67 Grove Street; tel: 508-888 3300; https://heritagemuseumsandgardens.org; mid-Apr–Oct daily, mid Nov–mid Dec Fri–Sun), a spacious complex of three museums of Americana that includes toys, military artifacts, folk art, and a working carousel (ride included in admission). A round stone barn (copied from the Shaker original in Hancock MA) houses an outstanding array of early cars. The grounds have the largest public garden in southern New England. In spring, they are awash in the vivid pinks and purples of flowering rhododendrons.

SANDY NECK AND BARNSTABLE

Motoring east along Route 6A, you'll pass the turnoff for the 6-mile (9km) **Sandy Neck Beach** ❻ (tel: 508-362 8300; parking fee), which is a favored habitat of the diamondback terrapin

and the endangered piping plover. Hikers and swimmers are welcome to explore, provided they don't disturb the birds' nesting sites.

Barnstable ❼ is also home to 4,000-acre (1,620-hectare) **Great Marsh**, the Cape's largest saltwater marsh. **Hyannis Whale Watcher Cruises** (tel: 800-287 0374; www.whales.net) depart from Barnstable Harbor May through October.

Just up the hill from the harbor, the **Coast Guard Heritage Museum** (3353 Route 6A; tel: 508-362 8521; www.coastguardheritagemuseum.org; May–Oct Tue–Sat 10am–3pm) tells the story of the Lighthouse Service, Lightship Service, Lifesaving Service, and Revenue Cutter Service – all predecessors of the Coast Guard.

In **West Barnstable ❽**, **West Parish Meetinghouse** is an outstanding example of early colonial architecture and has a Paul Revere bell cast in 1806. When the congregation grew too large in 1723, the parishioners cut the building in half, pulled the north end away, and added 18 feet (5.5 meters) to the middle.

East of Barnstable, **Yarmouth Port ❾** is a delightful village with fine old houses. The **Captain Bangs Hallet House** (11 Strawberry Lane; tel: 508-362 3021; www.hsoy.org; tours June–mid-Oct Thu–Sun) is the only sea captain's house open to visitors on Cape Cod; it's arranged as though the captain had just returned from a voyage to China, with silk, porcelain, and lacquered treasures on display. The **Edward Gorey House** (8 Strawberry Lane; tel: 508-362 3909; www.edwardgoreyhouse.org; mid-Apr–June Thu–Sat 11am–4pm, Sun noon–4pm, July–mid-Oct also Wed 11am–4pm, mid-Oct–Dec Fri–Sat 11am–4pm, Sun noon–4pm) exhibits possessions of the artist/illustrator who lived here and focuses on one of his lifetime passions: animal welfare. The 1889 **Hallet's Store** (139 Main Street; tel: 508-362 3362; www.hallets.com) claims to be the oldest soda fountain in America.

CAPE PLAYHOUSE

In the town of **Dennis ❿**, follow signs for the **Scargo Hill Tower**, a stone turret from which, on a clear day, you can see Cape Cod laid out like a map, with Provincetown visible at the northern tip. Dennis is home to America's oldest, and perhaps most outstanding, professional summer theater, **Cape Playhouse**.

On the playhouse grounds, the **Cape Cod Museum of Art** (tel: 508-385 4477; www.ccmoa.org; summer Tue–Sun, winter Thu–Sun; free Thu 5–8pm) restricts its permanent collection to works by artists with regional associations, although temporary exhibits may showcase artists whose work influences or is influenced by the Cape.

EAST TO BREWSTER

Brewster ⓫ is home to numerous fine old houses and inns. At **Stony Brook Mill** (830 Stony Brook Road, southwest off Route 6A; July–Aug Sat 10am–2pm; free) there is a small museum upstairs with a loom used for weaving demonstrations and freshly ground cornmeal for sale. Each spring, from mid-Mar to

⊘ Tip

Performances take place mid-June–mid-Sept at **Cape Playhouse** (Dennis, Route 6A; tel: 508-385 3911; www.capeplayhouse.com). Independent films and simulcasts of live performances at the National Theater and Metropolitan Opera are screened at the adjoining **Cape Cinema** (tel: 508-385 2503; www.capecinema.com). With leather armchairs and Art Deco frescoes by Rockwell Kent (1882–1971), the theater is a sensory treat.

Fishing in the shallows.

Scalloping at Wellfleet. Bay scallops are found in the low tide in eelgrass and tide pools.

Cape Cod National Seashore.

early May, schools of herring leap up a series of ladders to spawn in the freshwater pond behind the mill.

The **Cape Cod Museum of Natural History** (869 Main Street, Route 6A; tel: 508-896 3867; www.ccmnh.org; see website or call for opening times) explores 400 acres (162 hectares) of the local habitat through hands-on exhibits and nature trails.

Railroad magnate Roland Nickerson once owned 2,000 acres (800 hectares) of wooded land in Brewster, using them as a personal hunting and fishing preserve. In 1934 his widow donated most of this tract to the state; today **Nickerson State Park** ⑫ (Route 6A; tel: 508-896 3491) is a popular spot for camping, swimming, picnicking, and walks. The 8-mile (13km) bicycle trail connects with the **Cape Cod Rail Trail**.

THE LOWER CAPE: EASTHAM

Eastham ⑬, easily recognized by its 1793 windmill on the town green, has the **Swift-Daley House** (Route 6, next to post office; www.easthamhistoricalsociety. org; July–Aug Wed–Fri 10am–1pm;

voluntary donation), built in 1741 by a ship's carpenter and furnished with items from its long history; and, across from the Salt Pond Visitor Center, a **one-room schoolhouse** built in 1869 (www.easthamhistoricalsociety.org; July–Aug Wed–Fri 10am–4pm, Sat 11am–4pm; voluntary donation).

For a side trip into Cape Cod's history, head west to **First Encounter Beach**. It's here that a Pilgrim scouting party out of Provincetown first encountered a band of Indians, who, wary after earlier encounters with kidnappers, attacked the Pilgrims and were rebuffed by gunfire. This uneasy meeting is one of the reasons why the Pilgrims pressed on to Plymouth. Today, the historic site is a peaceful town beach (which, like most, charges a parking fee in summer).

CAPE COD NATIONAL SEASHORE

Established in 1961 when part-time Cape resident John F. Kennedy was president, **Cape Cod National Seashore** (headquarters: 99 Marconi Site Road, Wellfleet; tel: 508-255 3421;

www.nps.gov/caco) extends from Eastham to Provincetown and protects 27,000 acres (10,930 hectares) of land, including 40 miles (65km) of pristine beaches, lighthouses, cranberry bogs, marshes, ponds, hiking and biking trails, and sand dunes.

The **Salt Pond Visitor Center** ⓮ (Route 6; tel: 508-255 3421; daily) provides an excellent introduction to the area. Interpretive films and exhibits explain the ecology of the Cape, and a bicycle trail (bikes can be rented nearby) winds through pine forests and marshes to end at Coast Guard Beach, where, in 1928, writer-naturalist Henry Beston produced his classic book *The Outermost House*, chronicling a year spent living on the dunes. The 0.25-mile (0.4km) Buttonbrush Trail is a multisensory path with a guide rope and text panels in large type and Braille. Park rangers offer numerous outdoor programs and guided tours, including a visit to the 1730 **Atwood Higgins House**, a typical early settler's home in nearby Wellfleet and the **Capt. Penniman House**, home to a whaling family.

Farther north is **Nauset Light Beach** ⓯, graced with an 1877, 48ft (15-meter) lighthouse which was rescued from an eroding cliff in nearby Eastham in 1996 and moved to its present site. Tours (tel: 508-240 2612; www.nausetlight.org; voluntary donation) are given Sundays from early May through October, and Tuesdays and Wednesdays in July and August. Breeches buoy rescue demonstrations are held on Thursday evenings throughout the summer at the 1897 Old Harbor Life Saving Station on Race Point Beach.

At the Seashore's **Marconi Beach** ⓰, Guglielmo Marconi set up the first wireless station in the United States and transmitted the first transatlantic wireless message to Europe in 1903. **The Atlantic White Cedar Swamp Trail**, starting from the Marconi site, is especially beautiful.

WELLFLEET

Famous for its oysters, **Wellfleet** ⓱ is full of fine galleries and fun restaurants, and surrounded by inviting wildlife areas. Just south of town, off Route

The Wellfleet Drive-In Theater.

◔ WELLFLEET DRIVE-IN

For a bit of social and cinematic nostalgia, spend one evening at the Wellfleet Drive-In (www.wellfleetcinemas.com/drive-in-theatre). Built in 1957, it still shows a family-suitable double feature every night from late May through Labor Day. All of the elements are there: the mono-speakers you hang on your window (although the modern transmission with much better quality is available through your car's FM radio), the playground and mini-golf under the giant screen, the snack bar serving popcorn and hot dogs until the second feature starts, people setting up beach chairs and blankets in front of their vehicles. The drive-in is at 51 State Highway (Route 6) at the line between Wellfleet and Eastham. In one more nod to nostalgia, bring cash; they don't take credit cards.

Tip

On summer weekends, traffic jams in Provincetown can be frustrating. A good alternative is The Flex (tel: 800-352 7155; www.capecodtransit.org), a bus that runs between Harwich and Provincetown. You can buy a one-way fare, day pass, or multiple-use pass. You flag the driver down along the route (except along Route 6).

6, the Audubon Society maintains the 1,100-acre (445-hectare) **Wellfleet Bay Wildlife Sanctuary** ⑱ (tel: 508-349 2615; www.massaudubon.org; visitor center: Memorial Day–Columbus Day daily, rest of the year Tue–Sun). Five miles (8km) of walking trails lead from the visitor center which has two 700-gallon (2,650-liter) aquariums, which introduce both salt marsh and fresh-water habitats and residents.

TRURO

Farther north, the landscape becomes ever more wild and barren. Scrubby vegetation gives way to desert-like sand dunes. This is **Truro**, whose light and scenery led realist painter Edward Hopper (1882–1967) to make his summer home here for 30 years.

East of Truro, the **Cranberry Bog Trail** accesses the natural habitat of the tiny red fruit that proved such a boon to Cape Cod agriculture. Another road east leads to **Highland Light**, towering over Head of the Meadow Beach, which is the local name for the **Cape Cod Highland Lighthouse** ⑲ (tel:

On the beach at Provincetown.

508-487 1121; www.highlandlighthouse. org; mid-May–Oct daily). Erected in 1857, it is the peninsula's oldest lighthouse. From May to October, there are nighttime tours during the full moon.

The **Highland House Museum** (Highland Light Road; tel: 508-487 3397; www.trurohistorical.org; June–Sept Mon-Sat 10am–4.30pm) was built as a hotel in 1907. The museum offers an interesting look at the hardscrabble life of the Lower Cape before tourism, and even has a pirate's chest.

The **Truro Center for the Arts** (10 Meetinghouse Road; tel: 508-349 7511; www.castlehill.org) hosts a summer-long festival of craft workshops, concerts, and forums.

PROVINCETOWN

With its well-protected harbor, **Provincetown** ⑳ started out as a natural fishing port, settled by the Nauset Indians long before the Pilgrims came along. So it remains to this day. Portuguese fishermen, many from the Azores, came here in the heyday of the whaling trade and stayed on for the good fishing. Their descendants still make up a sizable proportion of the town's year-round residents. (Some of them conduct whale-watching cruises from April through October. MacMillan and Fisherman's wharves are where the boats dock.)

The subtle beauties and serenity of the National Seashore contrast dramatically with the blatant development and frenetic energy along Commercial Street. Shops thrive on tourists buying fine art and T-shirts, swanky barware and saltwater taffy, jewelry and kitsch souvenirs. There are bistros and hot dog stands, delightful old inns and inexpensive guest houses, tacky shacks, and beautiful landscaped captains' mansions. The town is proud of its fully open and integrated attitude, which has made it the Cape's pre-eminent destination for the LGBTQ community.

Led by painter Charles Hawthorne, who in 1899 founded the Cape Cod

School of Art, hordes of artists and writers flocked to Provincetown in the early decades of the 20th century, drawn partly by the area's stark beauty and largely by the cheap rents and food to be found here (thanks to the tourist boom they inspired, the latter are, of course, history).

Among the notables who passed through here, if only briefly, are dramatists Eugene O'Neill and Tennessee Williams and writers Sinclair Lewis, John Dos Passos, and Norman Mailer. A dozen or more illustrious painters, such as the abstract expressionist Robert Motherwell (1915–91), have left their mark. A number of galleries specialize in Provincetown art from the early 1900s onward.

The **Provincetown Art Association and Museum Ⓐ**, founded in 1914 (460 Commercial Street; tel: 508-487 1750; www.paam.org; Oct–May Thu–Sun noon–5pm, June daily 11am–5pm, until 10pm on Fri, July–Aug Mon–Thu 11am–8pm, Fri until 10pm, Sat until 6pm, Sun until 5pm, Sept Mon–Thu 11am–6pm, Fri, Sat and Sun as in summer) focuses on Provincetown and Cape Cod–inspired artists.

The lofty Italianate tower looming above the town is the **Pilgrim Monument Ⓑ** (High Pole Hill Road; tel: 508-487 1310; www.pilgrim-monument. org; daily April–May and Sept–Dec 9am–5pm, June–Aug until 7pm). It was built in 1892 to commemorate the *Mayflower* Pilgrims' first landing in the New World; they spent five weeks here before moving on to Plymouth. The determined climber (252 steps) will be rewarded with a panoramic view of the town and the entire Cape. At the monument's foot is the **Provincetown Museum** (same opening times as monument), whose intriguing exhibits document the town's colorful history. One ticket admits visitors to both sites.

Spoils from the *Whydah*, a pirate ship that sank in 1717 and was discovered off Wellfleet in 1984, are displayed at the **Whydah Pirate Museum Ⓒ** on MacMillan Wharf (tel: 508-534 9571; www.discoverpirates.com).

The very tip of Cape Cod – which is almost entirely within National Seashore boundaries – has a desolate beauty. The waters off **Race Point**

Chatham's Old Godfrey Windmill, built in 1797 to grind corn.

The Pilgrim Monument.

Beach experience rip tides, so it is more popular for sunbathing and off-road driving than swimming. **Herring Cove** is one of the Cape's most popular beaches; there's no undertow, which families appreciate. By custom, family activities are on the right hand of the beach, while the gay community relaxes on the left. It has the best sunsets on the Cape. Although officially forbidden, there are periodic reports of informal nude sunbathing in some of the more remote areas of the already remote sand dunes. For information, stop at the **Province Lands Visitor Center** ㉑ (171 Race Point Road; tel: 508-487 1256; May–Oct daily), which has a good viewing platform. This is the best place to get information about the dune shacks of the **Peaked Hill Bars Historic District**: 18 tiny dwellings (inhabited: please respect privacy) scattered throughout the Province Lands. There is a lottery for rentals of these bare-bones lodgings, several of which were once inhabited by seclusion-seeking writers and artists.

A Wampanoag Indian.

THE SOUND: CHATHAM TO FALMOUTH

Leaving Provincetown, turn left onto Route 28 at the junction with Route 6 to **Orleans**, called by its Indian name of Nauset until it was incorporated in 1797 and renamed for the Duke of Orleans (the future king of France), a recent visitor. Orleans has another "French connection" – it was the stateside terminus for a transatlantic telegraph cable to Brest in France.

The cable performed well from 1891 to 1959 before it become obsolete, and is now commemorated in the **French Cable Station Museum** ㉒ (41 South Orleans Road; tel: 508-240 1735; www.frenchcablestationmuseum.org; June–Sept Fri–Sun 1–4pm; voluntary donation). There are displays of the equipment used to test, install, and repair the underwater telegraph cable, worth a look for "look-how-they-did-it-then" enthusiasts.

Turn onto Route 6A through East Orleans to Nauset Beach Road and **Nauset Beach** ㉓ (parking fee). Almost 10 miles (16km) long, this is one of the Cape's best stretches of coast,

⊘ THE MASHPEE WAMPANOAGS

If it weren't for the Mashpee Wampanoag tribe, the history of New England would have probably been a lot different. These were the people who greeted the Pilgrims, taught them the basics of farming in the new colony, and helped them survive the first harsh winter. Initially the two groups enjoyed a cordial relationship, but as the colony grew, things deteriorated; between land grabs, wars, diseases inadvertently introduced by the Europeans, assimilation, and migration, the once-powerful, independent Mashpee tribe dwindled to almost insignificant numbers. In 2007, their decades-long fight for federal recognition as a tribe succeeded, bringing with it opportunities for economic development and cultural renewal. One of the most important projects is reviving the native language. Ironically, the English settlers' determination to "civilize" the tribe plays a key role in this. Because they wanted legal documents proving all transactions with the tribe, the Wampanoag developed an alphabet and written language, the first tribe to do so. Tribal members, historians, and linguists are using those deeds, contracts, wills, letters, translated scriptures, inventories, and bills of sale to develop dictionaries and reconstruct grammar and usage. The tribe sponsors an annual three-day powwow over the 4th of July weekend which attracts dancers and drummers from tribes across the country; visit www.mashpeewampanoagtribe.com.

popular for bathing as well as surfcasting for stripers and bluefish. Facilities include a concession stand and public restrooms. Gentler **Skaket Beach** (parking fee) on the bay side is popular with those who prefer calmer waters.

CHATHAM

Cape Cod's southern shore, from Chatham to Falmouth, is a zone where the battle for – and against – commercialization has raged for decades. Some pockets of subdued gentility still reign just off the honky-tonk stretches.

Chatham ㉔ at Cape Cod's "elbow" is one of the aristocratic enclaves. The "Old Village" and Chatham Historic Business District are classy examples of how to blend historic and commercial interests. The Chatham Fish Pier is a perfect spot to watch the fishing fleet bring in the daily catch. Seals sometimes follow the boats. The Fisherman's Monument on the pier shows a stylized hand raising a fishing net. The **Chatham Railroad Museum** (153 Depot Road; tel: 508-945 5100; www.chathamrailroadmuseum.com; mid-June–mid-Sept Tue–Sat 10am–4pm; voluntary donation) is housed in the town's ornate but defunct Victorian railroad station. Rail buffs will be interested in reminders of the days when passenger trains ran all the way to Provincetown. **Chatham Light** (tel: 508-945 5199; tours May–Sept Wed; free), an active Coast Guard station, overlooks South Beach. The Chatham Marconi Maritime Center (847 Orleans Road, also known as Route 28; tel: 508-945 8889; www.chathammarconi.org; late May–mid-Oct, mid Oct–early Dec Fri only) was part of the transatlantic underwater cable and early aviation radio communications systems developed by Guglielmo Marconi. It has a lot of original equipment and memorabilia of that era.

Bird fanciers will want to make a visit to **Monomoy National Wildlife Refuge** ㉕, a 7,600-acre (3,100-hectare) preserve which is a stopping point for hundreds of species of birds traveling the Atlantic Flyway. Continue past Chatham

Light to the refuge headquarters (Morris Island Road, Chatham; tel: 508-945 0594; refuge open daily; visitor center: Memorial Day–Labor Day Mon–Sat; other times as staff is available; www.fws.gov/refuge/Monomoy), where a 1,200-meter nature trail begins. But most of the refuge is accessible only by boat: Monomoy Island Ferry (tel: 508-237 0420; www.monomoyislandferry.com) offers transportation May–Oct, and walking tours to Monomoy Lighthouse, as well as seal-watching tours. Reservations for all services are essential.

HARWICH PORT TO HYANNIS

Picturesque Harwich and Harwich Port are the last peaceful settlements east of the Cape's commercial belt. From West Harwich to Hyannis, Route 28 is lined with motels, restaurants, businesses, and amusements. It's a long stretch, where traffic usually crawls all summer, making it seem even longer.

Detour a short distance to visit **South Dennis** ㉖, nicknamed "Sea Captain's Village." Many of the handsome homes built by prosperous

In summer, visitors need to guard against overexposure to the sun, wind, and biting insects.

Dressing up as pirates.

Memorial at the John F. Kennedy Hyannis Museum. JFK once said "I always go to Hyannisport to be revived."

The Cohoon Museum of American Art.

19th-century sea captains are preserved in the Historic District.

HYANNIS

Hyannis ㉗ is probably best known as the summer home of the Kennedy clan. In the old Town Hall, the highlight is the **John F. Kennedy Hyannis Museum** (397 Main Street; tel: 508-790 3077; www. jfkhyannismuseum.org; June–Oct Mon–Sat 9am–5pm, Sun noon–5pm, Nov Mon–Sat 10am–4pm, Sun noon–4pm). The museum displays photos and mementos of the president, who summered in adjoining Hyannis Port. Although the Kennedy compound is the object of many a pilgrimage, it is not open to the public and very little of it can be seen from the road. A small park dedicated to Kennedy's memory adjoins Veterans Beach, on Hyannis's harbor.

An "old-fashioned swashbuckling adventure" awaits kids and parents aboard the **Pirate Adventure on *Sea Gypsy*** (Ocean Street Docks; tel: 508-394 9100; www.capecodpirateadventures. com; mid-June–Labor Day daily; reservations essential).

Alternatively, you can take to the rails aboard one of **Cape Cod Central Railroad**'s excursions (252 Main Street; tel: 888-797 7245; www.capetrain.com). These include a scenic two-hour trip, an adults-only five-course dinner train, a Sunday brunch ride, and a family supper train.

More than 50 classic sports cars – mostly British, and all red – are on show in **Hyannis Port** on the grounds of the Simmons Homestead Inn (288 Scudder Avenue; tel: 508-778 4934; www.toadhallcars.com; daily). Visitors can also play with the more than 200 felines that roam the grounds, or sample some of the 700 single malt Scotch whiskeys in the bar.

CRAIGVILLE BEACH

West of Hyannis, the tide of commercialism subsides occasionally to provide glimpses of Cape Cod's beauty. Make a southward detour for Centerville. Here, relatively warm-watered **Craigville Beach** ㉘ (1050 Craigville Beach Road; tel: 508 790 6345; charge in summer) on Nantucket Sound, with lifeguards and bath houses, is one of the Cape's most popular.

MASHPEE INDIAN MEETINGHOUSE

Heading toward Falmouth, take a side trip north to **Mashpee** ㉙, located amid Wampanoag tribal lands which have been carved up by development. The **Old Indian Meeting House** (Meeting House Road at Route 28), the oldest church building on the Cape, built in 1684, and the burial ground next door, are well worth a look.

CAHOON MUSEUM

The contemporary primitive and very charming paintings of American folk artists Ralph and Martha Cahoon are on show, along with 19th- and early-20th-century American marine art, in **Cotuit** ㉚ at the **Cahoon Museum of American Art** (4676 Falmouth Road; tel: 508-428

7581; www.cahoonmuseum.org; Feb–Dec Tue–Sat 10am–4pm and Sun 1–4pm). The building is a 1775 farmhouse.

FALMOUTH

Falmouth ③ is a microcosm of Cape Cod life. The pretty town green, a Revolutionary militia training ground, is ringed by fine old houses, including several delightful B&Bs, and the Historical Society's **Museums on the Green** (Village Green; tel: 508-548 4857; www.museumsonthegreen.org; mid-June–mid-Oct Mon–Fri 10am–3pm, Sat 10am–1pm). The two 18th-century houses contain an extensive display about the people and practices of whaling and the story of Katherine Lee Bates, who wrote *America the Beautiful*.

Falmouth Harbor is filled with pleasure craft; swimmers and windsurfers favor the beaches and guest houses of Victorian-era Falmouth Heights overlooking Nantucket Sound. Spring, when thousands of daffodils and rhododendrons bloom, is the best time to visit the 6-acre (2.4-hectare) **Spohr's Gardens** (45 Fells Road; tel: 508-548 0623; www. spohrgardens.org; daily; voluntary donation) overlooking a scenic oyster pond.

WOODS HOLE

One of the most pleasant activities in Falmouth is to rent a bicycle and follow the old railroad bed, now a bike path, down to **Woods Hole ③**. Most travelers come here merely to board the ferry for Martha's Vineyard, a 45-minute voyage away, but Woods Hole itself warrants a stopover. It is devoted almost exclusively to maritime activities and has several excellent seafood restaurants.

The world-famous **Woods Hole Oceanographic Institution** (266 Wood Hole Road; tel: 508-548 1400; www.whoi. edu) maintains an Ocean Science Exhibition Center (15 School Street; Memorial Day–Aug daily, Sept–Oct Mon–Sat, Nov–Dec Tue–Fri) to describe its fascinating research with a mock-up of a deep water submersible and videos of exploration of the *Titanic*. Weekdays in July and August the institution offers free 75-minute tours of the dock area and restricted village facilities; reservations recommended. Visitors can tour

⊙ **Tip**

The Shining Sea Bikeway is a 10.7-mile (17.2km) paved bikeway that stretches from Falmouth to Woods Hole. It's the only one of the many bike trails on Cape Cod that skirts the shoreline. The name comes from *America the Beautiful* which was penned by Katherine Lee Bates, a Falmouth resident.

Research vessels moored at Woods Hole.

> **Tip**

Parking in Woods Hole (http://woodshole.com) is metered and can be extremely hard to find. During the summer Whoosh trolleys run between Falmouth (free parking) and Woods Hole on the half-hour (tel: 800-352 7155; www.capecodrta.org).

the **Marine Biological Laboratory** and learn about using marine organisms in research (127 Water Street; tel: 508-289 7623; www.mbl.edu; July–Aug Mon–Fri afternoons; note: children under the age of 5 cannot take the tour; reservations required). The visitor center (93 Water Street; open weekdays, call for information) has interesting displays about the research if you can't make a tour.

The small but intriguing **Woods Hole Science Aquarium** (166 Water Street; tel: 508-495 2001; http://aquarium.nefsc.noaa.gov; Tue–Sat 11am–4pm; voluntary donation) is home to 140 species of marine animals, mostly from northeast and mid-Atlantic waters

MARTHA'S VINEYARD

Over the decades, Vineyard residents have grown blasé about the celebrities in their midst, and precisely because of that laissez-faire attitude, the roster just keeps growing. The latest is (former) President Obama and his family, who have spent summer vacations at the Blue Heron Farm in Chilmark on the southwest coast.

Main Street, Falmouth.

Like Cape Cod, Martha's Vineyard is a geological remnant of the last ice age. Two advancing lobes of a glacier molded the triangular northern shoreline, then retreated, leaving hilly moraines, low plains, and many-fingered ponds. And Martha? She was the daughter of Thomas Mayhew, who bought a large tract of land in 1642, including Nantucket Island, for £40. (Mayhew named the nearby Elizabeth Islands after another daughter.) The "Vineyard" part of the name refers to once-abundant wild grapes.

Vineyard Haven, Oak Bluffs, and Edgartown, the three protected harbor towns of the northeastern portion of the island, have always been active and prosperous, although the main order of business is no longer shipping and whaling, but tourism and summer homes. By contrast, the sparsely populated "up-island" (that is, to the west and south) towns of West Tisbury, Chilmark, Menemsha, and Gay Head remain determinedly rural.

It may come as a disappointment to many visitors to find that, as a rule, Martha's Vineyard's extensive beaches are not accessible to outsiders but have been reserved for homeowners; the major exception, beyond the placid Joseph Sylvia State Beach on the bay side, is South Beach, fronting the rolling Atlantic south of Edgartown; other public beaches are Katama (good for surfing and for strong swimmers), Moshpu, Oak Bluffs, and Menemsha.

VINEYARD HAVEN

Known until 1870 as Holmes Hole, **Vineyard Haven** ㉝ (the official name of the town is Tisbury, but everyone calls it by the name of its primary village) blossomed into a busy port during the 18th and 19th centuries, with both maritime businesses and farmers profiting from the constant movement of ships. Today, the homey **Black Dog Tavern** (20 Beach Street Extension; tel: 508-693 9223; www.theblackdog.com), with its offshoot bakery, store, and catalog business, enjoys a similar relationship with the legions of vacationers who arrive by ferry from Woods Hole.

Handsome houses grace Williams Street, a block off Main Street.

Covering a swath of more than 5,000 acres (2,000 hectares) in the middle of the island, **Manuel F. Correllus State Forest** (tel: 508-693 2540), site of one of the largest environmental restoration projects in the country, is laced with 15 miles (24km) of walking, bicycling, and bridle paths. Take Edgartown Road out of Vineyard Haven to Barnes Road, then turn right (south) to the forest entrance. The park was originally created in 1908 as a refuge for the heath hen, in an attempt to prevent the bird's extinction. Initially successful, a disastrous wildfire, severe winters, and arrival of predators accounted for the death of the remaining birds. A sculpture of the bird is installed in the forest.

OAK BLUFFS

Religion tinged with tourism produced an unusual community in **Oak Bluffs**

34. The resort town has the largest marina on Martha's Vineyard, and boats at anchor bob at their moorings in front of gingerbread houses which face the water. It is also home to Martha's Vineyard Camp Meeting Association. In 1835, Edgartown Methodists chose a secluded circle of oak trees here as a site for a camp meeting. Twenty years later, there were more than 320 tents at Wesleyan Grove, as it was named, and thousands of people gathered here each summer. Small houses soon replaced the tents – tiny gingerbread cottages that are a riot of color and jigsaw carving with all manner of turrets, spires, gables, and eaves. They were laid out along circular drives known as **Trinity Park**. At its center is the "tabernacle" where the congregation gathers, a wrought iron-and-wood shelter that's nearly as elaborate as the cottages, with two clerestories with glass windows and an octagonal cupola. The building is used for both revival and worship services (Sun 9.30am) and secular community events. In mid-August,

> **Tip**
>
> Pie in the Sky Bakery & Café at the end of the Shining Sea Bike Trail in Woods Hole (10 Water Street; tel: 508 540 5475; https://piecoffee.com) opens at 5am with freshly brewed coffee and homemade croissants.

The Cape Cod Rail Trail.

○ THE CAPE COD RAIL TRAIL

In the Cape's early heyday, summertime visitors arrived by train. But, except for the excursion trains run between Hyannis and the Cape Cod Canal by the Cape Cod Central Railroad (tel:888 797 7245; www.capetrain.com), rail travel has disappeared from the Cape. However, at least one section of roadbed has been put to a pleasure-making use: the Cape Cod Rail Trail is a 25-mile (40km) paved recreational path located mid-Cape and stretching from South Dennis through Nickerson State Park to Wellfleet. Ideal for bicycling, skating, walking, and jogging, it's an intimate, relaxing way to discover and enjoy the "real" Cape. Along the way, it passes through quaint villages, salt marshes, pine forests, and cranberry bogs. The most scenic sections are the National Seashore spur trails in Eastham and Wellfleet that terminate at the Atlantic Ocean. You can rent bicycles at a number of places along the way, including Barbara's Bike & Sport (tel: 508-760 4723 www.barbsbikeshop.com) in Dennis, Idle Times Bike Shop (tel: 508-255 8281 North Eastham; 508-240 1122 Orleans; www.idletimesbikes.com) at the trail in North Eastham and Orleans, and Little Capistrano Bike Shop (tel: 508-255 6515 Eastham, 508-349 2363 Wellfleet; www.littlecapistranobikeshop.com) with locations in Eastham and at the trailhead in Wellfleet.

the **Grand Illumination** recreates the camp's traditional closing-night ceremony when colorful Chinese lanterns are hung on the porches of the cottages and in the trees. Visitors can tour **Cottage Museum** (2 Trinity Park; daily in summer), an 1867 home which recreates life at the Campground in the 1800s. **Union Chapel**, built in 1870 as a non-sectarian place of worship (55 Narragansett Avenue; tel: 508-627 4440; www.unionchapelmv.org), is as remarkable for its unique octagonal design and dormer-studded cupola as for its acclaimed acoustics.

Flying Horses Carousel (33 Lake Street; tel: 508-693 9481; http://mv preservation.org/properties/flying-horses-carousel/) is the oldest operating carousel in the country. Originally in Coney Island, it was moved to Oak Bluffs in 1884, and its horses have been giving rides ever since.

Many of the ever-expanding number of sites included in the island's **African-American Heritage Trail** (http://mvafricanamericanheritagetrail.org) are located in the area.

East Chop Lighthouse (East Chop Drive; tel: 508-627 4441; tours mid-June–mid-Sept Sun) was erected in 1878 and nicknamed "the Chocolate Light" because of its brown color.

EDGARTOWN

South of Oak Bluffs on Beach Road, **Edgartown** ❸ is the oldest settlement on Martha's Vineyard.

The imposing Greek Revival **Old Whaling Church** of 1843 (89 Main Street; tel: 508-627 4442), with enormous pillars and a soaring tower, is a rare instance of monumental scale in Edgartown. The church is now the venue for concerts, a film series, and community events. Tucked behind the church is the **Vincent House Museum**, the oldest house on the island (1672), furnished to show four centuries of life in the town.

The **Martha's Vineyard Museum** (59 School Street; tel: 508-627 4441; www.mvmuseum.org; mid-June–early Oct daily, rest of the year Mon–Sat) records the island's unique history, culture, and traditions on a pretty campus with several old buildings

Victorian architecture adds character to Oak Bluffs.

containing agricultural and nautical equipment. The **Ross Fresnel Lens Building** houses a 19th-century first-order Fresnel lens; the **Francis Foster Maritime Gallery** exhibits logbooks, ship models, and other nautical treasures; and the 1845 **Captain Francis Pease House** has exhibits about the island's history, a Native American Gallery, a book shop, and local crafts. In 2011 the museum bought the building of the former Marine Hospital (1895) in Vineyard Haven. It was remodelled, adapted to the museum's needs, and is set to open in 2018 – with the current museum being closed between May and October 2018 while the collection is transferred – see website for details.

The museum oversees **Edgartown Lighthouse** (tel: 508-627 4441; mid-June–Labor Day daily, end May–mid June and Labor Day–Columbus Day Sat–Sun).

CHAPPAQUIDDICK ISLAND

A stone's throw away from Edgartown, across a narrow neck of the harbor, is **Chappaquiddick Island** ③⑥. The island's original name means "The Separated Island," which it steadfastly remains. The Chappy Ferry (tel: 508-627-9427 or visit http://chappyferry.com for operating times and conditions; daily) carries cars (three or four at a time) and clusters of pedestrians over the 200-yard crossing. The main attraction on "Chappy," several miles from the ferry landing, is the **Wasque** (pronounced *way-skwee*) **Reservation** (east end of Wasque Road; tel: 508-627 3599; year-round daily; charge Memorial Day–mid-Oct), a 200-acre (80-hectare) preserve with walking trails, excellent bird-watching, and beach (be careful: there's a strong current).

Cape Poge Wildlife Refuge, at the island's eastern end, offers 6 miles (10km) of dunes, woods, salt marshes, ponds, tidal flats, a lighthouse, and beach. A variety of narrated tours (tel: 508-627 3599; www.thetrustees.org) are offered, including a 1.5-hour lighthouse trip and a 2.5-hour overland exploration.

UP-ISLAND ESCAPE

Tiny **West Tisbury** ③⑦ is home to Alley's General Store (1045 State Road; tel: 508-693 0088; daily), which opened in 1858 and still deals in "most everything." There's a lively farmer's market on Wednesday and Saturday mornings outside the 1859 **Grange Hall** (1067 State Road).

The popular agricultural fair (http://marthasvineyardagriculturalsociety.org/annual-fair/) held in town each August is a slice of old fashioned country fun, with fiddle and corn-shucking contests, horse pulls, and rides. The **Granary Gallery at the Red Barn** (636 Old County Road; tel: 508-693 0455; http://granarygallery.com/) exhibits photographs by Margaret Bourke-White and Alfred Eisenstaedt, a summer regular. It carries works by a long list of contemporary artists.

Highlights of a visit to **Long Point Wildlife Refuge** (tel: 508-693 3678; www.thetrustees.org/places-to-visit/cape-cod-islands/long-point.html; daily; charge

The shore at Chappaquiddick.

Edgartown, an old whaling port first settled by the English in 1642.

Brant Point Lighthouse at Nantucket Harbor.

mid-June–mid-Sept), part of a sand barrens ecosystem which exists in patches from New Jersey to Maine, include a lovely beach and an easy 2-mile (3km) nature trail. There are sheltered fresh and saltwater ponds, safe for exploring with kids.

CHILMARK TO GAY HEAD

Of the parallel roads traveling from West Tisbury to Chilmark, Middle Road traverses the most rugged, interesting glacial terrain. At **Chilmark Center** is Beetlebung Corner, a stand of tupelo trees from which "beetles" (mallets) and "bungs" (wooden stoppers) were once made. The residents of Chilmark (incorporated in 1694) built their dwellings at a generous distance from one another, and the once-inexpensive property and evocative natural settings attracted an influx of artists such as Jackson Pollock.

Nearby **Menemsha** is a tiny fishing village on Vineyard Sound, famed for its appearance in Steven Spielberg's ever-popular 1975 movie *Jaws* and prized for its technicolor sunsets. Fishing charters

operate from the harbor, which has a number of shops and restaurants.

One of the most spectacular natural sights on Martha's Vineyard is at its westernmost tip, looking out to the untamed sea. From Chilmark, follow the single hilly road that at several points offers breathtaking views of Menemsha Pond northward and Squibnocket Pond to the south.

At the end, **Gay Head Light** ➌ (aka **Aquinnah Light**; tel: 508-627 4441; www.gayheadlight.org; late May–mid-Oct daily, check website for hours) marks the western terminus of the island and the location of the stunning, ancient geologic strata that compose the majestic **Gay Head cliffs**. Clays of many colors – from gray to pink to green – are most vibrant towards late afternoon and represent eons of geological activity: fossils found amid the ever-changing contours of this 150ft (46-meter) promontory have been dated back millions of years. For sailors returning from a voyage, this magnificently colored embankment was the first sign they were home, thus giving Gay Head its "gaiety." Due to cliff erosion the lighthouse started to tilt dangerously and had to be moved farther inland in 2015.

NANTUCKET ISLAND

An Indian word meaning "that faraway land," Nantucket Island isn't too far away for the thousands of people who visit each year by ferry and airplane. The winter population of over 7,000 increases sevenfold when the "summer people" take over the sidewalks of town.

In sharp contrast to Martha's Vineyard, Nantucket's mid-island moors and miles of beautiful, unspoiled beaches are open to visitors, most of whom use the preferred island mode of transportation: bikes (several shops stand ready to equip tourists near the ferry dock). The harbor town of Nantucket, centrally located on the north shore, is unquestionably the focal

point of the island and its only commercial center.

NANTUCKET TOWN

The town of **Nantucket** 🔟 is a gem of 18th- and 19th-century architecture, from the dominant clapboard-and-shingle Quaker homes to the grandeur of the buildings lining **Upper Main Street**. Because the twists and turns can prove disorienting, it's best to tour with a street map (available from the bike shops, or in the free local newspapers distributed on the ferry).

As in whaling days, the waterfront is the focus of life in Nantucket town. Several wharves extend into the harbor, the most central of which – **Straight Wharf** – is an extension of Main Street. First built in 1723, rebuilt after an 1846 fire, and renovated in the late 1950s, it's now like a small village unto itself, surrounded by luxury yachts and sailboats, some of which are available for charter. (The untouched barrier beach of Coatue is an ideal destination.)

Old South Wharf has also been spruced up and rendered tourist-friendly with boutiques and cafés; it's possible – for a tidy sum – to rent tiny but picturesque wharfside cottages here.

Along Main Street up from Straight Wharf, a picturesque shopping district lines the gently rising cobblestone street. Although the 1-sq-mile (2.5-sq-km) **National Landmark Historic District** contains 800 pre-1850 buildings, the redbrick facades lining Main Street are relatively new. With its tree-lined, brick-paved sidewalks, Main Street is a hub of activity in summer, offering distractions from collectibles to edibles.

Nantucket is proud of its history, especially its grand old homes and museums. The **Nantucket Historical Association** (15 Broad Street; tel: 508-228 1894; www.nha.org) oversees more than a dozen properties on the island. Most are open daily from Memorial Day to mid-October. Among them are the **Whaling Museum** (13 Broad Street; early Feb–early Apr Sat–Sun 11am–3pm, late May–late Oct daily 10am–5pm, hours for the rest of the year vary, check the website), housed in a former spermaceti candle factory, which

Bringing a good catch to Menemsha, where Steven Spielberg's Jaws was filmed.

⊘ THE UNPROMISING PENINSULA THAT BECAME A PLAYGROUND

Shaped like a bodybuilder's flexed arm, Cape Cod extends 31 miles (50km) eastward into the Atlantic Ocean, then another 31 miles to the north. Well forested up to about the "elbow," then increasingly reduced to scrub oak and pitch pine, this sandy peninsula is lined with more than 300 miles (500km) of beaches. The crook of the arm forms Cape Cod Bay, where the waters are placid and free of often treacherous ocean surf.

Lighthouses guide mariners plying the cold Atlantic waters. The lighthouses are frequently photographed symbols of the Cape. Some of the most popular include Nauset Light, Chatham Light, Nobska Light, and Race Point Light. Most are operated by the U.S. Coast Guard, although a few function under independent groups.

In 1602, Bartholomew Gosnold, a British mariner sailing by this long arm of sand, noted a great many codfish in the waters and added the name "Cape Cod" to his map. In 1620, the *Mayflower* pulled into the harbor of what is now Provincetown and, before debarking to explore, its passengers drew up the Mayflower Compact for self-government.

This early constitution grew into the government of the Commonwealth of Massachusetts.

Before the advent of modern transport, Cape Cod was a hardscrabble area peopled by the Wampanoag tribes, hardy Yankees, and industrious immigrants from the coasts and islands of Portugal. Since the land supported only subsistence farming, most people earned their living from the sea.

The first hordes of tourists arrived in the late 19th century, brought by steamship and railroad. Escaping the summer heat of Boston, Providence, and New York for the cool sea breezes along the shore, they found low prices, inexpensive real estate, and simple pleasures in abundance. Real estate is no longer a bargain, but the location is priceless.

With almost 600 miles (965km) of coastline and 60 public beaches, Cape Code is one of the best places to get out on the water. The greens are also popular destinations, with 27 public and 15 private golf courses on the island. The peak seasons are from late-May to early-September, but if you can travel in the spring or autumn there are usually deals to be found.

The 1805 Old Gaol contained four barred cells. Prisoners were often allowed to go home each night, having no real chance of escaping from the island.

Provincetown Art Colony.

commemorates Nantucket's seafaring days with impressive displays, including the skeleton of a 43ft (13-meter) sperm whale. If your only exposure to old-time whaling was via a high-school reading of *Moby-Dick*, the museum will bring the hardship and heroics of the "fishery" vividly to life.

The 1686 **Jethro Coffin House** (www.nha.org/sites/oldesthouse.html), on the northwest edge of town on Sunset Hill Lane, is the oldest on the island. This plain saltbox design reflects the austere lifestyle led by the island's earliest settlers. Other attractions include the 1746 **Old Mill**, the oldest functioning mill in the country; the 1805 **Old Gaol**; and the 1838 **Quaker Meetinghouse**.

Climb up the tower of the **First Congregational Church** (62 Centre Street; www.nantucketfcc.org; tel: 508-228 0950) for a spectacular view of the island; Sunday service is at 10am.

The three-story red-brick **Jared Coffin House** (tel: 508-228 2400/800-248 2405; www.jaredcoffinhouse.com), at the corner of Centre and Broad streets, made its 1845 debut as the island's showiest dwelling; within two years it became a hotel, and today it remains one of the island's finest inns.

The family was so prolific that it accounted for half the island's population by the early 19th century, and two more Coffin residences stand at 75 and 78 Main Street, examples of the brick Federal style of architecture.

Farther up Main Street are the "**Three Bricks**," architectural triplets built by wealthy whaler Joseph Starbuck for his three sons. Across the street, and worlds apart in style, stand the "**Two Greeks**," Greek Revival mansions built for two Starbuck daughters. One, the **Hadwen House** (96 Main Street), showcases the affluent lifestyle of a wealthy whaling family.

Ralph Waldo Emerson gave the inaugural address at the 1847 Greek Revival **Nantucket Atheneum** (www.nantucketatheneum.org), now a public library and cultural center, at the corner of Lower India Street.

The **Museum of African American History** (29 York Street; tel: 508-228

Ⓞ PROVINCETOWN'S ART COLONY

Bay and ocean, sand and sky, the Mediterranean-like light: the natural beauty of Provincetown at the tip of Cape Cod has attracted artists since the town was little more than a fishing pier at the end of a sand spit.

The colony began in the late 1800s. Studios rented for as little as $50 a year, a boon to the "starving artists." In 1899, Impressionist painter Charles Webster Hawthorne opened the Cape Cod School of Arts. By 1916, the Provincetown Art Colony had matured, with more than 300 artists – many of them fleeing the war in Europe – attending six schools of art. The Bohemian atmosphere attracted poets, writers, and playwrights, leading the *Boston Globe* to dub Provincetown "the biggest art colony in the world." It was as renowned as the colonies in Taos NM and East Hampton on Long Island NY. The Great Depression and World War II weakened the colony, but it began to rebound in the 1950s. The community supported efforts to create affordable studio space (places were now renting for $1,500 for a season) and encourage artists to migrate to the area. Today, Provincetown has dozens of art galleries, many of which specialize in contemporary works by local painters, photographers, and sculptors such as Joel Meyerowitz, Paul Bowen, and Paul Resika.

9833; www.afroammuseum.org; Jan–May Fri–Sun 11am–4pm, June–Sept Tue–Fri 10am–4pm, Sat until 2pm, Sun noon–4pm, Oct–Dec Tue–Sun 11am–4pm) maintains two historic sites documenting the history of the island's African-American community: The **African American Meeting House** and the **Florence Higginbotham House**. The Black Heritage Trail is a guided or self-guided tour of 10 sites illustrating the heritage of African-Americans living on Nantucket, particularly in the 19th century. The map is available at the museum or for download.

No. 99 Main Street, with its detailed and finely proportioned facade, is one of the handsomest wooden Federal-style buildings on Nantucket; it was built by forebears of Rowland Macy, who left the island to seek his fortune and founded a rather well-known namesake store.

Overlooking the harbor from **Brant Point** is one of America's oldest lighthouses. Visitors departing by sea often toss the traditional penny into the water off Brant Point to ensure that they'll return to the shores of Nantucket.

A few blocks out of town, the **Maria Mitchell Association** (4 Vestal Street; tel: 508-228 9198; www.mmo.org; mid-June–mid-Oct, most facilities Mon–Sat, check the website for details) honors the local savant who discovered a comet at the age of 29 in 1847, garnering international acclaim. She became the first woman admitted to the American Academy of Arts and Sciences, and America's first female college professor, teaching astronomy at Vassar. The Association oversees several facilities: the Natural Science Center, which focuses on the natural world of and around Nantucket Island; two observatories which offer public tours, programs, and stargazing; Mitchell's home; and a seasonal aquarium at the harbor. Work is under way to bring all of the elements together in one building.

The classic and unique arts of the island, including basket-making and scrimshaw, are displayed at **the Nantucket Lightship Basket Museum** (49 Union Street; tel: 508-228 1177; www.nantucketlightshipbasketmuseum.org; late May–early Oct Tue–Sat 10am–4.30pm, call for off-season hours).

OUTSIDE NANTUCKET TOWN

"Nantucket! Take out your map and look at it," urged Herman Melville in *Moby-Dick*. An inspection of the map reveals an island with hamlets and hideaways sprinkled across its 14-mile (23km) length. Despite some mid-island development in recent decades, about one-third of the island is under protective stewardship. Although environmental restrictions limit activities on dunes and moors, much of the land can be explored. Wear long pants and use insect repellent; deer ticks carry Lyme disease.

Stretching northeast from the town of Nantucket is a 6-mile (10km) inner harbor, protected from Nantucket Sound by **Coatue**, a thin spit of land

The island has long attracted painters. The Artists Association of Nantucket has more than 500 members and runs a gallery.

A sea view from the White Elephant Inn.

⊙ Tip

The NRTA (tel: 508-228 7025; http://nrtawave.com/) runs shuttle buses from mid-May through Columbus Day/early Oct, usually 7am–11.30pm, and offers service throughout the island, stopping at beaches, towns, and attractions. All-day passes are available.

with flat white beaches. This sweep of land, encompassing the 1,117-acre (453-hectare) **Coskata-Coatue Wildlife Refuge** �40 (pronounced *co-skate-uh coat-oo*; Wauwinet Road; tel: 508-228 5646; www.nantucketconservation.org/property/coatue/; May–Oct), is accessible by boat or over-sand vehicle. The 16 miles (26km) of trails extend north to **Great Point**, where a lighthouse – a solar-powered 1986 replica of the 1818 original, swept away by a 1984 storm – warns boats away from the sandbars of Nantucket Sound. Gray and harbor seals rest here after they have fed on fish provided by the riptide. The refuge and beaches are patrolled from April to October. Nantucket Conservation Foundation (www.nantucketconservation.org), which administers the refuge, offers 2.5-hour guided naturalist-led excursions for foundation members June to Columbus Day weekend from 8.30–10.30 am (call for information on how to enrol at tel: 508-228 2884 – or consult the website).

The excellent **Nantucket Shipwreck and Life-Saving Museum** (158 Polpis Road; tel: 508-228 1885; Mon–Sat 10am–5pm, Sun from noon), en route to Great Point, presents fascinating exhibits, including artifacts from the Italian liner *Andrea Doria*, which sank not far from here in 1956.

Monomoy, the most populous settlement other than Nantucket town, affords spectacular views from its bluffs. From here, the Polpis Road leads across the rolling and delicate Nantucket Moors, which are carpeted with bayberry, beach plum, heather, and other lush vegetation – a lovely green and flowering pink in summer, brilliant red and gold in the fall.

SIASCONSET

Tourists discovered **Siasconset** �41 in 1848 when the first hotel opened in this easternmost town on Nantucket. By 1888, a clever entrepreneur had built a colony of fully equipped, fully furnished cottages, including a "spare room" on wheels, for vacationers. The Bluff Walk edges the ocean-facing side of the properties. Erosion from the unrelenting ocean waves is claiming the bluffs; each year, some of the dwellings tumble down the cliffs. The views are wonderful.

Nantucket's most popular beaches are located on the flat, windswept south shore, open to the cold, spirited waters of the Atlantic Ocean. At **Surfside Beach** �42, a colorful Victorian life-saving station serves nowadays as the island's only youth hostel. Surfers favor the beach at Cisco, a bit more remote, at the end of Hummock Pond Road, while **Madaket Beach** �43, at the south-western tip of Nantucket, is popular for swimming, fishing, and, especially, sunset-gazing.

The northern coast east of Madaket Harbor, heading back toward town, offers the gentle surf of **Dionis** and **Jetties** beaches. **Children's Beach**, tucked well inside the West Jetty near Steamship Wharf, is especially placid and enhanced by a playground.

Cranberries, cultivated in Cape Cod since 1816.

NANTUCKET'S STORMY PAST

The island's golden age didn't last long, but the handsome little town that whaling fortunes had built found new prosperity in tourism at the end of the 19th century.

In 1830 the whaling ship *Sarah* returned home to Nantucket Island, carrying 3,500 barrels of valuable whale oil after a voyage of nearly three years. On the island, stately mansions, decorated with silks and china from faraway lands, awaited the returning captains of such vessels. Schools, hotels, a library, and the commercial activity on Main Street were indications of a prosperous people.

There was no more glorious way for young men to seek their fortunes than aboard a whaling ship, but it was dangerous work. "For every drop of oil, a drop of blood," the whalemen's saying went.

Since its earliest days, Nantucket, which is thought to mean "faraway land" or "island" in Algonquian, has been populated by determined and spirited people. The first colonists, who arrived in 1659, were emigrants who chafed at the Puritan severity of towns on the North Shore of Massachusetts. Taught "onshore" whaling by the Algonquins, they traveled out in open boats to chase and harpoon whales sighted from land. By the beginning of the 18th century, offshore whaling had begun and with each generation of larger, more seaworthy craft, the whaling industry grew.

The Algonquins, however, lost out. Although they sailed on whaling boats, their way of life on the island was irreversibly changed by the colonists. By 1855, diseases (introduced to the country from Europe), alcohol, assimilation, and exile had taken the last of Nantucket's original residents.

Both the Revolutionary War and the War of 1812 battered Nantucket's whaling industry, but the islanders' tenacity brought it back to life. Nantucket ships again sailed throughout the world and brought back record quantities of oil. During this period the town acquired much of its urbanity, but the islanders' prosperity was short-lived: the Great Fire of 1846 razed the port, and in the 1850s kerosene replaced whale oil. Too heavily dependent on whaling, Nantucket was left in a permanent urban drydock.

From a peak of around 10,000, Nantucket's population dropped to 3,200 in 1875. Those who remained applied their ingenuity to a new venture, one that thrives today and continues to capitalize on the gifts of the sea. Tourism took off toward the end of the 19th century, as steamboats made the island more readily accessible. Land speculators built hotels and vacation homes, many of which now house the country's rich and famous.

Quaint Siasconset (pronounced Sconset), linked to the town by a narrow-gauge railroad built in 1884, was especially popular, drawing such luminaries as the popular actress Lillian Russell. The railroad is gone now – it was used for scrap metal during World War I – but tourism lives on.

The tourist season in Nantucket Island now runs from before Memorial Day to after Columbus Day. While Nantucket's permanent population numbers around 10,000, in summer it surges to over 50,000 with the arrival of tourists and seasonal residents, who come to enjoy its historic harbors, coastal scenery, and relaxed pace of life.

Harvesting cranberries, the focus of a Nantucket festival that kicks off the harvesting season each October.

COVERED BRIDGES

Masterpieces of folk technology, covered bridges were the creation of craftsmen who acted as designers, engineers, and builders.

New Englanders didn't invent covered bridges – they have been built in Europe for centuries – but they did perfect their design and engineering. The roofs covering the wooden supports extended the life of the bridge by as much as 40 years. And just as today's highway signs warn, the roadways on bridges freeze before those on solid ground, so the covered road was safer in winter.

Yankee bridge builders devised systems of load-bearing that still stand up to traffic. The "kingpost" design uses diagonal braces leading from a central upright towards the opposite shores. The "queen-post" elaborates on this with two parallel uprights, allowing for a longer bridge.

Perhaps the most elegant approach was devised in the 19th century by Ithiel Town. The "Town Lattice" truss incorporates a pair of crisscrossed diagonal members, which opened out like an old-fashioned laundry rack and were made rigid with wooden pegs. The Cornish-Windsor Bridge, spanning the Connecticut River between Vermont and New Hampshire, is a Town Lattice type and is the second-longest covered bridge in the US.

The Cornish-Windsor spans the river that separates Vermont from New Hampshire, and locals frequently argue about which state can claim the historic structure. (The state of New Hampshire owns and maintains the bridge.)

The Carleton Bridge in Swanzey, New Hampshire was built in 1789. The height and width of the bridge matches the dimensions of a small wagon of hay.

Originally known as the Bog Bridge, the Cilleyville Bridge tilts a bit to the left. Locals believe that the architects of the bridge had a disagreement, and one partner deliberately cut one set of timber supports shorter than the other.

Architectural traits

The image of the barn-red, wooden bridge over a rushing, rocky riverbed is a special icon in New England. Vermont alone has more than 100.

The design was based in practicality: covered bridges survived the New England weather better than open ones. The roofs were high and the roadways wide so that fully loaded hay wagons could pass through without difficulty. Bridges were also bulletin boards. The interior walls were covered with posters advertising everything from medicinal elixirs to religious revivals. And why are the bridges almost always painted red? The usual explanation is that it would trick skittish horses into thinking they were entering their familiar barn. Another – that red paint was available and protected the wood from the elements as effectively as any other coating – probably has just as much validity.

The worst enemy of wooden covered bridges is vandalism, usually in the form of fire. Most recently, Hurricane Irene in August 2011 completely swept away bridges in Bartonsville VT and the Turkey Jim Bridge in New Hampshire and left another 13 damaged, some beyond repair. But they are so well loved by their communities and aficionados that it's a rare occasion when a lost bridge isn't replaced. Within days of Irene, the Vermont Covered Bridge Society (www.vermontbridges.com) was organizing surveys of the damage and lobbying for funding to repair and rebuild these historic treasures.

The Groveton Bridge passes over the Ammonoosuc River near Northumberland, New Hampshire. The bridge was built with a Paddleford truss, and has several additional arches for support. There is a water supply suspended beneath the bridge, which is only accessible on foot.

This tiny and romantic structure is the Kent Falls covered bridge in Connecticut.

CENTRAL MASSACHUSETTS

Tucked between Boston and the western regions, the midsection of Massachusetts harkens back to an earlier era of agriculture and small-town industry.

Main Attractions
Fruitlands Museum
Blackstone River Valley
Worcester
Southwick's Zoo
Old Sturbridge Village
Quabbin Reservoir

Maps on pages 189, 190

West of Boston on Route 2 is the little town of Harvard. In the mid-19th century, idealistic self-improvement and social betterment advocates settled in the area. The **Fruitlands Museum** ❶ (102 Prospect Hill Road; tel: 978-456 3924; www.fruitlands.org; Nov–Mar Sat–Sun noon–5pm, check website for main season hours), set in a rustic, wooded 210-acre (85-hectare) campus, chronicles those efforts as well as American Indian and fine-art traditions. Between 1914 and 1945 Clara Endicott Sears, who had been born into a privileged

Boston Brahmin background, assembled an astonishing collection on the site. The result was one of America's first outdoor museums, now a National Register Historic District.

In 1843, Transcendentalist Amos Bronson Alcott, father of Louisa May Alcott (author of *Little Women*), left his Concord home to found an anti-materialist utopian community called Fruitlands, as one of the goals was to "live off the fruits of the land." Vegetarianism, asceticism, and a philosophical return to nature were their mandates, but the commune lasted barely six months. The Fruitlands Farmhouse details the community. The Shaker Office was built in 1794 at the now-defunct Shaker Community in Shirley MA. The building was moved to the Fruitlands where it displays ephemera about the Massachusetts Shakers. The Native American Gallery has cultural and archaeological materials from across the country. The Art Gallery concentrates on Hudson River landscapes and 19th-century portraits. Note that access to the buildings is via outdoor trails through uneven wooded terrain, so proper footwear is advised. There are 3.5 miles (5km) of nature trails on the property, giving fine views of the Nashua River valley.

The past is preserved at the Fruitlands Museum.

WACHUSETT STATE RESERVATION

For a bird's-eye view of the geographic center of the state, visit the **Wachusett State Reservation and Ski Area ❷** (345 Mountain Road, off Route 140; tel: 978-464 2987; www.mass.gov/locations/wachusett-mountain-state-reservation; summit open Memorial weekend–late Oct; road open daily parking fees) in Princeton. The visitor center (open daily) atop the 2,006ft (649-meter) summit provides maps of the hiking trails, which are open year-round. This is the nearest ski and snowboard center to Boston, an hour to the east.

BLACKSTONE RIVER VALLEY

Beginning in the mid-19th century, a swath of central Massachusetts extending from Worcester into Rhode Island was a bustling industrial center whose factories made everything from monkey wrenches to the whimsical Mr Potato Head toy. The **John H. Chafee Blackstone River Valley National Heritage Corridor** (www.nps.gov/blac/index.htm) links 24 communities from Providence RI to Worcester MA that were the birthplace of America's Industrial Revolution.

A non-traditional national park, it's a living landscape whose people and their environs tell a fascinating story of early industrial America. There are visitor centers in Massachusetts at the 1,000-acre (400-hectare) River Bend Farm in Uxbridge and in Worcester at Broad Meadow Brook Wildlife Sanctuary and the Worcester Historical Museum.

The Blackstone River Greenway (formerly "Bikeway") will be a 48-mile (77km) off-road trail running parallel to the Blackstone River and using the canal towpath to connect 15 communities from Worcester MA to Providence RI. So far, about 5 miles (8km) in Millsbury and Worcester have been completed. Another 3.5 miles (5.5km) from Blackstone to Millville were opened in 2017. In Rhode Island, about 12 miles (19km) are complete. For updates, check with www.cycleblackstone.com.

A statue at the Fruitlands Museum.

A ski instructor at Wachusett Mountain.

A red-winged blackbird calling from the bulrushes.

The Worcester Art Museum, which opened in 1898, contains more than 35,000 pieces.

WORCESTER

About 15 miles (24km) south of Princeton on Route 3 is **Worcester** ❸, the state's second-largest city. This gritty industrial center spawned the country's first park, first wire-making company, first steam calliope, first carpet loom, first diner manufacturer, first Valentine, and (suitably enough) first birth-control pill, not to mention the beginnings of liquid-fuel rocketry, female suffrage, and the Free Soil Party, precursor of the Republican Party. Twelve colleges and universities are here, including Worcester Polytechnic Institute, whose alumni include rocket scientist Dr Robert Goddard (and whose incoming freshman profile is better than that of MIT).

Goddard was a Worcester native. A fine collection of his rocketry patents and other memorabilia is exhibited at the **Goddard Library** ❹ at Clark University (950 Main Street; tel: 508-793 7163; http://www2.clarku.edu/research/goddard/; Mon–Thu 8am–midnight, Fri 8am–8pm, Sat 10am–8pm, Sun noon–midnight). Other notable Worcesterites include composer Stephen Foster, socialist leader Emma Goldman, humorist Robert Benchley, and 1960s radical Abbie Hoffman.

Publisher Isaiah Thomas, a Son of Liberty who fled Boston in advance of the British Army in 1770 and continued to publish his rabble-rousing revolutionary newspaper, the *Massachusetts Spy*, was from Worcester. In 1812 he established the **American Antiquarian Society** ❸; its Worcester headquarters, at 185 Salisbury Street, is now a research library whose vast collection focuses on American history, literature, and culture from 1640 through 1876 (tel: 508-755 5221; www.americanantiquarian.org; one-hour tours Wed). Tours include an especially interesting visit to the document preservation laboratories.

The city is a trove of antiquarian delights. The **Worcester Historical Museum** ❹ (30 Elm Street; tel: 508-753 8278; www.worcesterhistory.org; Tue–Sat 10am–4pm; children under 18 free) traces the city's industrial and cultural history and maintains

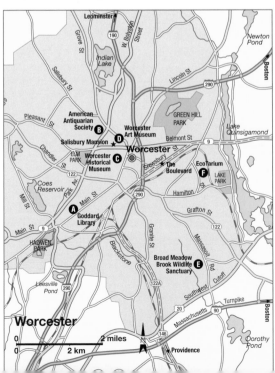

Worcester map

the splendid 1772 Georgian Salisbury Mansion (40 Highland Street; Thu–Sat 1–4pm; children under 18 free). The museum is also a visitor center for the John H. Chafee Blackstone River Valley National Heritage Corridor.

ANCIENT AND TRADITIONAL ART

The **Worcester Art Museum**  (55 Salisbury Street; tel: 508-799 4406; www.worcesterart.org; Wed–Sun 10am–4pm; free first Sat of the month 10am–noon) is the second-largest in New England. Its sponsorship of excavations at Antioch, Syria, in the 1930s yielded a remarkable collection of 2nd-century AD Roman mosaics. Equally appealing is the extensive gallery of 17th-, 18th-, and 19th-century American art, including paintings by John Singleton Copley, Winslow Homer, and John Singer Sargent. The museum also boasts an impressive collection of arms and armor acquired from the former Higgins Armory Museum.

More than 78 species of butterfly make their home at the 400-acre (160-hectare) **Broad Meadow Brook Wildlife Sanctuary** (414 Massasoit Road; tel: 508-753 6087; www.massaudubon.org/get-outdoors/wildlife-sanctuaries/broad-meadow-brook; Tue–Sat 9am–4pm, Sun 12.30–4pm). Some of the nature trails are accessible for physically and visually impaired visitors. The visitor center has a floor-to-ceiling map of the Blackstone River watershed. It's also an information center for the John H. Chafee Blackstone River Valley National Heritage Corridor.

Two miles (3km) from downtown Worcester, you can walk through treetops, visit a digital planetarium, ride on a narrow-gauge railway, and see a variety of animal species at the **EcoTarium** (222 Harrington Way; tel: 508-929 2700; www.ecotarium.org; Tue–Sat 10am–5pm, Sun noon–5pm). The unique indoor–outdoor center introduces visitors to the region's ecosystem and wildlife.

SOUTH TO RHODE ISLAND

South of Worcester on Route 122, tiny **Uxbridge** is home to the

Tip

In July and August the EcoTarium hosts a popular Summer Discovery Camp (tel: 508-929 2700), one of the longest-running summer camps in the US, for children aged 5–14. Excellent adventures guaranteed!

Johnny Appleseed.

JOHNNY APPLESEED

Born on a hardscrabble farm near Leominster, John Chapman became a legend as "Johnny Appleseed." The image of a barefoot man wearing ragged clothing with a tin pot on his head while randomly tossing apple seeds into the air is more accurate than most people might think. A follower of the Swedenborgian religion sect which believed that the more deprivations you endure in this life, the better your reward in the next, he did go barefoot – even in the winter, clothed himself in rags, and used a tin pot as a hat, drinking vessel, and cook pot. But his understanding of apple cultivation was as unsophisticated as his personal living habits were crude. As Chapman traveled through Ohio, Indiana, and Illinois, he planted apple nurseries, constructed fences around them to keep out livestock, instructed caretakers on how to tend to the saplings, sold half-grown trees for replanting, and returned every few years to maintain the nurseries. He did not graft his trees, however, which is the only way to develop edible varieties. His fruit could only be used to press cider. As much a spiritual missionary as an environmental one, Chapman would preach to farmers in exchange for a place to sleep and a meal. Much beloved for his gentle nature, eloquent sermons, and endearing eccentricities, he died in Fort Wayne, Indiana. A local family buried him in their family plot.

Blackstone River and Canal Heritage State Park (287 Oak Street, off Route 122; tel: 508-278 7604; www.mass. gov/locations/blackstone-river-and-canal-heritage-state-park; daily sunrise–sunset) on **River Bend Farm**. Displays at the visitor center tell the story of the area's canals; visitors can walk along restored sections of the towpath, and explore 1,000 acres (400 hectares) of natural area, including Rice City Pond, rich in wildlife.

Wildlife from around the world is found at **Southwick's Zoo** (2 Southwick Street, off Route 16; http:// southwickszoo.com/; tel: 800-258 9182; mid-Apr–Oct daily 10am–5pm) in **Mendon ❺**. The largest private zoo in New England has over 100 animals – from white rhinos and Bengal tigers to Barbary sheep and prairie dogs – in natural settings. A sky ride tracks above the enclosures and there are animal shows throughout the day.

OLD STURBRIDGE VILLAGE

Off Route 20, **Old Sturbridge Village ❻**, a recreated community of more than 40 period buildings scattered over 200 acres (80 hectares), offers a "you are there" take on New England rural life between 1790 and 1840 (tel: 800-733 1830; www.osv.org; Jan–mid-Feb Sat–Sun 9.30am–4pm, mid-Feb–late Nov Wed–Sun 9.30am–4pm, except during "by Christmas by Candlelight" in Dec, see website or call for details; entrance fee includes 2 days' admission within 10 consecutive days; discount for active-duty and retired military and their guests).

Visitors are given illuminating explanations, couched in modern parlance, as the interpreters go about the daily business of farm and town life, including cobbling shoes, making tin lanterns, and leading prayers.

Depending on the season, they also make soap, shear sheep, or laboriously build stone walls. Concepts of political freedom and discourse grew, in part, from the emergence of a free and vibrant press, and the activities of the Isaiah Thomas Printing Office are designed to show how printed communication became an integral and vital part of the new nation's growth.

QUABBIN RESERVOIR

Lying northwest of Sturbridge amidst rolling hills that are especially beautiful in autumn is the huge **Quabbin Reservoir ❼** (visitor center: Route 9, Belchertown; tel: 413-323 7221; www.mass.gov/locations/quabbin-reservoir; daily 9am–4.30pm). One of the country's largest man-made public water supplies, it comprises 128 sq miles (331 sq km) of flooded valley that holds 412 billion gallons (1.56 trillion liters) and supplies the drinking water to Greater Boston.

Four towns were flooded in 1939 to create this great body of water. Quabbin is prized as a place to fish, hike, canoe, and admire the bald eagles that breed here.

Demonstrating how to raise a barn in Old Sturbridge Village.

Fall colors surround Quabbin Reservoir.

THE PIONEER VALLEY

The Connecticut River passes through several counties in the western Massachusetts lowlands; in 1939 the area was dubbed "Pioneer Valley" in honor of the 17th-century settlers who tamed these wild lands.

The Pioneer Valley may be named for the early settlers who faced rugged mountains, fierce weather, and determined resistance from the native population, but it can apply equally to the people who followed. Pioneers in sports invented basketball and volleyball here; pioneers in engineering manufactured the first automobile; pioneers in thought graduate from its 14 colleges and universities. It's a mix of bucolic rural towns and sophisticated culture, modern amusement parks and classic carousels, iconic Americana and remnants of Eastern European culture.

Springfield ❶, the Pioneer Valley's largest city, was established as a trading post in 1636. Throughout its history Springfield has been a manufacturing hub: Indian motorcycles, Rolls-Royces, and Smith & Wesson revolvers have all been made here. But it was in 1892 that Dr James Naismith invented a game that would make possible the city's major attraction: the $103 million, interactive, state-of-the-art **Basketball Hall of Fame ❹** (1000 Hall Fame Avenue; tel: 877-446 6752; www.hoophall.com; daily 10am–4pm, subject to change based on events; three-day pass available). The 48,000-sq-ft (4,500-sq-meter), three-level facility fascinates the sport's aficionados: others may experience an information overload.

The Dr Seuss National Memorial Sculpture Garden.

In 1779 George Washington chose Springfield as the site of one of the nation's first two arsenals. The **Springfield Armory National Historic Site ❸** (Armory Square; tel: 413-734 8551; www.nps.gov/spar; 9am–5pm Memorial Day–Oct 31 daily, Nov–Memorial Day weekend Wed–Sun) now houses a museum featuring one of the world's largest historic firearms collections.

The **Springfield Museums at the Quadrangle ❻** (21 Edwards Street; tel: 413-263 6800 or 800-625 7738; www.springfieldmuseums.org; Tue–Sun

⊘ Main Attractions

Springfield
Holyoke
Smith College Museum of Art
Hadley Farm Museum
Amherst
Emily Dickinson Museum
Historic Deerfield

Maps on pages 196, 198

⊘ Drink

Springfield's Club Quarter is in the metro area surrounding Stearns Square. It's an eclectic social and entertainment area with an amazingly wide range of venues and themes – from dive bars to the Mardi Gras Club, an exclusive "gentlemen's club;" pool halls; Theodore's Blues Club (http://theodoresbbq.com), generally considered one of the best blues clubs in the country; hip dance clubs; and Shakago's (http://shakagomartinibar.com), a swanky, sophisticated jazz bar.

11am–5pm, Welcome Center open daily; one ticket covers all) oversees five museums clustered around a common square. The **George Walter Vincent Smith Art Museum** features Asian decorative arts. The **Science Museum** contains a planetarium and plenty of hands-on exhibits. The **Michele and Donald D'Amour Museum of Fine Arts** has an impressively broad collection, from traditional themes to contemporary shows. The Lyman and Merrie Wood **Museum of Springfield History** places the city's history in the larger context of America in the 18th and 19th centuries. The newest museum to open on the Quad, the **Amazing World of Dr. Seuss** is dedicated to the ingenious Springfield native Theodor Geisel (1904–91), aka Dr. Seuss, world-famous children's author and cartoonist. The museum offers interactive exhibits that let children – and adults – experiment with sounds, play rhyming games, and invent their own stories. The second floor displays memorabilia curated by Geisel's two step daughters and great nephew.

Sharing the Quad is also the **Dr. Seuss National Memorial Sculpture Garden**, a fanciful outdoor park with life-size bronze sculptures of characters created by the city's favorite son.

The 735-acre (300-hectare) **Forest Park ⓓ** (Sumner Avenue; daily) has a zoo (tel: 413-733 2251; www.forestparkzoo.org; Apr–mid-Oct) with more than 100 species, and a seasonal, child-size train tour.

The city's rich cultural life is headquartered in **Symphony Hall ⓔ** (1 Columbus Center; tel: 413-788 7646; www.symphonyhall.com), home of the Springfield Symphony Orchestra and CityStage Theater.

Follow State Street to Berkshire Avenue and then turn right on Main Street to the **Titanic Historical Society** (208 Main Street, Indian Orchard; tel: 413-543 4770; www.titanichistorical society.org; daily 10am–4pm). Modest in size, its collection of artifacts from the legendary shipwreck is – well – titanic in scope. Mrs Astor's lifejacket, the bell from the ship which recovered most of the victims, the wireless message sent to the ship warning of icebergs which never reached the bridge are all displayed.

THE "BIG E"

Across the river, in **West Springfield ❷**, the Theater Project at the Majestic Theater (131 Elm Street; tel: 413-747 7797; www.majestictheater.com) mounts live performances.

Every September, prize livestock and top-name talents entertain the crowds for just over two weeks at the **Eastern States Exposition** (the "Big E"; tel: 413-737 2443; www.thebige.com), New England's largest agricultural fair. The Storrowton Village Museum (tel: 413-205 5051; www.storrowtonvillage.com; audio and group tours as well as special programs, check the website for schedules), on the fairgrounds, is nine transplanted 18th- and early-19th-century

Springfield

buildings surrounding a traditional town green.

SIX FLAGS

In nearby **Agawam**, **Six Flags New England** ❸ (tel: 413-786 9300; www. sixflags.com; check website for hours) is New England's largest amusement park.

HOLYOKE

Head 8 miles (13km) north from Springfield on Route 5 or I-91 (exit 16) to **Holyoke** ❹, home to **Wistariahurst Museum** (238 Cabot Street; tel: 413-322 5660; www.wistariahurst. org; gardens and grounds open daily dawn–dusk, for tours and other events visit the website). The elegantly furnished mansion is a fine example of the Beaux Arts movement.

The visitor center at **Holyoke Heritage State Park** (221 Appleton Street; tel: 413-534 1723; www.mass.gov/loca tions/holyoke-heritage-state-park; sunrise–sunset) recounts the history of the city and its industrial heritage. Next to the center is a 1929 **merry-go-round** (www.holyokemerrygoround.org; Sept–June Sat–Sun noon–4pm, July–Aug Tue–Sat 10.30am–4pm, Sun noon–4pm).

Also in the park, the **Children's Museum** (444 Dwight Street; tel: 413-536 7048; www.childrensmuseumholyoke. org; Tue–Fri 9am–4pm, Sat from 10am, Sun from noon) has lots of hands-on activities. In the same building, the **Volleyball Hall of Fame** (tel: 413-536 0926; www.volleyhall.org; Thu–Sun noon-4.30pm) immortalizes William G. Morgan, who invented the game at the Holyoke YMCA in 1895.

NORTHAMPTON

Continue north alongside the Connecticut River to **Northampton** ❺. Surrounded by colleges – Amherst, Mount Holyoke, Hampshire, the University of Massachusetts, and Smith – Northampton's lively bistros, restaurants, and galleries reflect the youthful energy of the educationally elite. The area has attracted hundreds of artisans and artists, who showcase their wares at craft shops all over town.

Smith College Museum of Art (Elm Street, Route 9; tel: 413-585 2760; www. smith.edu/artmuseum; Tue–Sat 10am–4pm, until 8pm on Thu, Sun noon–4pm) focuses on American art and French impressionists. It also houses an impressive collection of Asian and African pieces. The college's **Lyman Conservatory** (tel: 413-585 2740; www. smith.edu/garden/plants/lyman-conserva tory; daily; voluntary donation) has an audio tour of the 1896 greenhouse. There's a brochure of the 127-acre (51-hectare) **arboretum and gardens**.

Calvin Coolidge (1872–1933), the governor of Massachusetts who became the 30th US president, began his law practice in Northampton. A collection of his papers is on exhibit in the **Coolidge Memorial Room** in the **Forbes Library** (20 West Street; tel: 413-587 1014; https://forbeslibrary.org/; Mon 9am–5pm, Tue and Thu 1–5pm, Wed 4–9pm).

That sinking feeling at the Six Flags amusement park.

A collection of historic wooden planes at the Hadley Farm Museum.

HADLEY

To the east along Route 9, between Northampton and Amherst, is **Hadley ⑥**, whose long history of farming from the 18th century onward is documented at the **Hadley Farm Museum** (Junction Routes 9 and 47; www.hadleyfarmmuseum.org; mid-May–mid-Oct Sat–Sun).

The nearby **Porter-Phelps-Huntington Historic House Museum** (130 River Drive; tel: 413-584 4699; www.pphmuseum.org; mid-May–mid Oct Sat–Wed 1–4.30pm) is a Georgian-style house, built in 1752 and structurally unchanged since 1799.

The museum hosts concerts and lectures in the summer. Just off Route 47 in nearby **J.A. Skinner State Park** (tel: 413-586 0350; www.mass.gov/locations/skinner-state-park), a road (Apr–Nov) climbs to a viewpoint immortalized in Thomas Cole's 1830 painting, *The Oxbow*. The **Summit House**, a former 19th-century hotel, reopened in 2014 after a four-year renovation project.

South on Route 116, in nearby **South Hadley, Mount Holyoke College ⑦** (tel: 413-538 2000; www.mtholyoke.edu) is America's oldest women's college. Its 400-acre (160-hectare) campus was the work of landscape architect Frederick Law Olmsted. Students run regular campus tours (see www.mtholyoke.edu/admission/visit for details).

The *Lady Bea*, a 49-passenger boat with indoor seating and sundeck departs Brunelle's Marina for narrated scenic cruises on the Connecticut River (tel: 413-315 6342; www.brunelles.com; Memorial Day–early Oct Thu–Sun afternoons and evenings).

AMHERST

Continue east on Route 9 to **Amherst ⑧**, long a hotbed of intellectual vigor and social independence. Lexicographer Noah Webster lived here, as did a reclusive genius of American poetry.

Visitors to the **Emily Dickinson Museum** can experience the spartan environment that housed a self-confined soul who poured her emotions solely into her poetry (280 Main Street; tel: 413-542-8161; www.emilydickinsonmuseum.org; Apr–Dec Wed–Sun 11am–4pm). Guided tours of The Homestead where she lived most of her life, and The Evergreens, home of her brother, leave from the visitors center. An audio tour of the grounds is available. Just off the spacious central green, **Amherst College**'s stately fraternity houses flank a campus quadrangle that is a classic of early 19th-century institutional architecture. At the college's **Mead Art Museum** (tel: 413-542 2000; www.amherst.edu/museums/mead; times vary, check the website; free), more than 16,000 works include a superb collection of American art, Russian modernist paintings, and West African sculptures. More than 2,500 Japanese woodblock prints make this one of the major collections of *ukiyo-e* ("pictures of the floating world") in the country.

The skeleton of a woolly mammoth is the centerpiece at the **Beneski**

Pioneer Valley

Brattleboro

Northfield
Warwick

0   10 miles
0   10 km

Green

91

Gill

Charlemont
Deerfield
Shelburne
Turner Falls
Farley
Orange
2

Hawley
Greenfield
2
Boston

⑪ Old Deerfield

Plainfield
Ashfield

Massachusetts
New Salem

⑩ South Deerfield
Locks Village
Leverett
Shutesbury

Magic Wings Butterfly Conservatory and Gardens

Goshen
North Amherst
202
Quabbin Reservoir

9
5

Williamsburg
Porter-Phelps-Huntington House
⑧ Amherst
Pelham

Ringville
Hadley ⑥
Emily Dickinson Homestead

112
Northampton
Smith College ⑤
South Amherst

Knightville
Knightville Reservoir
Hadley Farm Museum
J.A. Skinner SP
Mt Holyoke Range SP
9

Huntington
Easthampton
202
Belchertown

20
South Hadley ⑦ Mount Holyoke College
Ware

Southampton
91
32

Russell
Holyoke ④
Three Rivers

90
202
20
90
Palmer
Boston

Cobble Mtn Reservoir
Westfield
Chicopee Ludlow
Monson

West Springfield ② **Springfield** ①
Eastern States Exposition
East Longmeadow
32

West Granville
Agawam ③ Six Flags New England

Museum of Natural History, Amherst College (tel: 413-542 2165; www. amherst.edu/museums/naturalhistory; Tue–Fri 11am–4pm, Sat–Sun 10am–5pm; free), showcasing a trove of fossils and geological history.

South on Route 116, The **Eric Carle Museum of Picture Book Art** (125 W. Bay Road; tel: 413-658 1100; www.carlemuseum.org; Tue–Sat 10am–4pm, Sun noon–5pm) celebrates the first art most of us experience – the illustrations in children's picture books.

YIDDISH SPOKEN HERE

Hampshire College alumnus Aaron Lansky is the motivating force and director of the **National Yiddish Book Center** (1021 West Street, Hampshire College, Route 116; tel: 413-256 4900; www.yiddishbookcenter. org; Sun–Fri 10am–4pm; free guided tours available Sun at 11am and 1pm and Tue at 2pm). This is a collection of more than a million Yiddish books housed in a wooden complex designed to resemble an Eastern European *shtetl* (village). It's a heroic exercise in the preservation of an imperiled language and the tradition it represents.

Encompassing a 7-mile (11km) ridge that stretches from Hadley to Belchertown, **Mount Holyoke Range State Park** ❾ (Route 116; tel: 413-253 2883; www.mass.gov/locations/mount-holyoke-range-state-park; visitor center open daily) offers some of the Pioneer Valley's best scenery.

SOUTH DEERFIELD

Backtrack to Route 5 (or hop on I-91) and head north to **South Deerfield** ❿. Here it's always Christmas in the Disneyesque Bavarian Village and Santa's Workshop at "the world's largest candle store," **Yankee Candle Company** (Route 5; tel: 877-636 7707; www.yankeecandle.com; daily). This is one of the area's major attractions for children, who have the chance to dip

their own candles, colonial-style. Also, Chandler's Restaurant at Yankee Candle Company hosts a concert series through the summer and fall.

Less than 3 miles (5km) up Route 5 is **Magic Wings Butterfly Conservatory and Gardens** (tel: 413-665 2805; www. magicwings.com; daily 9am–5pm), where thousands of butterflies flutter about in an 18,400-sq-ft (1,710-sq-meter) indoor – and, in summer, outdoor – conservatory garden.

HISTORIC DEERFIELD

Farther northwest, just off Route 5, is the well-preserved pioneer village of **Old Deerfield** ⓫. Along Main Street, 12 museum houses make up Historic Deerfield (Main Street; tel: 413-774 5581; www.historic-deerfield.org; mid-Apr–late Dec daily 9.30am–4.30pm).

Deerfield has a fascinating history that dates from its settlement in 1669. The Pocumtuck Indians, who farmed the fertile valley, were not pleased to see their land usurped, and massacred the entire population (by then 125 strong) in 1675. That

Calvin Coolidge's reputation as a man of few words once prompted a matron at a society banquet to coax him: "Mr President, I have a wager with a friend that I can persuade you to say more than two words." His reply: "You lose."

The Wistariahurst Museum, Holyoke, a Beaux Arts gem.

deterred settlers, but the lure of the land was irresistible, and interlopers eventually won out, despite a French-instigated Indian raid in 1704 in which half the village was burned, 100 colonists carried off to captivity in Quebec, and 50 slaughtered.

Tomahawk marks can be seen on one sturdy wooden door, but the town's lurid history is not what attracts most visitors. The draw is an extraordinary architectural cache: the carefully restored Colonial and Federal structures along "The Street," Deerfield's mile-long main thoroughfare. The treasures inside the houses, representing decades of changing decorative styles, easily equal the exteriors.

Among the buildings open to the public are the **Ashley House** (1730), a former parson's home with intricately carved woodwork and antique furnishings; the **Asa Stebbins House** (1810) with early paintings, Chinese porcelain, and Federal and Chippendale furniture; and the **Hall Tavern** (1760), which serves as the information center. Deerfield doesn't offer the costumed interpreters and crafts demonstrations of a Sturbridge Village, but anyone enamored of the restrained elegance of colonial design will find it fascinating.

Memorial Hall Museum (Memorial Street; tel: 413-774 7476; https://deerfield-ma.org/about/memorial-hall-museum/; May–Oct daily, visit the website for details) houses a wonderful hodgepodge of folk art, American Indian relics, and local lore. The **Channing Blake Meadow Walk** (May–Dec; http://www.historic-deerfield.org/channing-blake-footpath/) passes by a working farm and through meadows to the Deerfield River.

The historic mill town of **Turner Falls** ⑫, north of Deerfield on Route 2, is an old mill town which is reinventing itself as an arts and outdoor recreation center. There are historic and geologic walking tours, the **Great Falls Discovery Center** (2 Avenue A; tel: 413-863 3221; www.greatfallsdiscoverycenter.org; Wed–Sun 10am–4pm) housed in an old mill complex, and an ongoing calendar of community arts events and festivals.

⊙ THE MAN WHO CREATED THE CAT IN THE HAT

The Dr. Seuss National Memorial Sculpture Garden is an enduring tribute to the wonderful and whimsical characters created by the beloved Springfield native, Theodor Geisel.

Beloved characters such as Yertle the Turtle, the Grinch and his dog Max, Horton the Elephant, Thidwick the Big-Hearted Moose, and the Lorax are clustered in a corner of the Quadrangle green in Springfield. The Cat in the Hat is there, too, looking over the shoulder of a sculpture of Geisel at work at his drawing board.

The son of German immigrants who wanted him to become a college professor, Geisel attended Dartmouth College, New Hampshire. He worked on the college newspaper, but when he was discovered drinking alcohol underage, he was forced to resign from his extra-curricular activities. To continue working for the college humor magazine, he wrote under the pseudonym Seuss. Geisel then entered Lincoln College, Oxford, intending to study for Doctorate in Literature, before deciding that academia was not for him. He returned the United States in 1927.

Working as a cartoonist, he designed advertisements and sold the occasional cartoon to *The Saturday Evening Post* and *Vanity Fair*. His first book, *And to Think that I Saw It on Mulberry Street*, was rejected 27 times before it found a publisher.

The Cat in the Hat was written on request, using words from a 225 "new reader" vocabulary list. He said his talent for rhyming came from his mother, who used to recite silly lists of rhyming words to him at bedtime, although it is also known that he used rhythmic inspiration from other encounters, including the pattern of noise from the ship's engine on a trans-Atlantic voyage.

Many of his Geisel's books have Springfield locations. The streams of Horton's Jungle of Nool are those of Forest Park. Mulberry Street is a Springfield thoroughfare, and the police officers ride red motorcycles, the color of Springfield's famed Indian motorcycles.

In 1984, Geisel was awarded a special Pulitzer prize in recognition of his contribution to the education and enjoyment of America's children. When he died in 1991, he had sold over 200 million copies of his 44 books, which have been translated into 15 languages.

Deerfield, Massachusetts.

THE BERKSHIRES

Berkshire County encompasses valleys dotted with shimmering lakes, rolling farmlands and orchards, deep forests abundant with deer, and powerful rivers that plunge into waterfalls.

◎ Main Attractions
Bash Bish Falls State Park
Norman Rockwell Museum
Ashintully Gardens
Tanglewood
Hancock Shaker Village
MASS MoCA, North Adams
Shelburne Falls

Map on page 205

Though less dramatic than the mountains of New Hampshire or Vermont, the Berkshire Hills were still formidable enough to insulate western Massachusetts from the rest of the state. The first settler didn't arrive until the relatively late date of 1725; the terrain, climate, and hostility of the tribes living in the area slowed the rate of development. The Industrial Revolution was a boon to the region, as its iron foundries smelted ore for factories and railroads and its marble graced the dome of the US Capitol. In the late 1800s, the

Berkshires' economic wave ebbed and it became a backwater region. During the Gay Nineties, the cool mountain breezes lured the Carnegies and Vanderbilts to build summer homes near Stockbridge and Lenox. Visitors today arrive for the renowned summer festivals, splendors of fall foliage, or fun of winter skiing.

Native Americans and early settlers used the Housatonic Valley from Connecticut to reach the Berkshires. Today's travelers can do the same, following US Highway 7 north along the Housatonic or by taking the Massachusetts Turnpike from the eastern part of the state.

THE SOUTHERN BERKSHIRES

Just inside the Connecticut border on Route 7A is **Ashley Falls ❶**, a village surrounded by hayfields and dairy farms. The village was named for Colonel John Ashley (1709–1802), a prominent lawyer and Revolutionary War officer.

Off Route 7A, the **Colonel John Ashley House**, built in 1735, is the oldest structure in Berkshire County. It was here that the Sheffield Declaration protesting British tyranny and advocating for individual rights was drafted (published 1773). It has been restored as a colonial museum (117 Cooper Hill Road; tel: 413-298 3239; www.thetrustees.org/places-to-visit/berkshires/ashley-house.html; grounds open year-round;

Fall foliage in the Berkshires.

guided house tours July–Aug Sun at noon, 1 and 2pm). Although the furnishings are not all true to the home's earliest period, it's worth a visit as an example of serenely proportioned early country Georgian architecture.

SHEFFIELD TO GREAT BARRINGTON

Up the road is the 329-acre (133-hectare) **Bartholomew's Cobble** (105 Weatogue Road; tel: 413-229 8600; http://www.thetrustees.org/places-to-visit/berkshires/bartholomews-cobble.html; daily, parking fee), a natural rock garden with hiking trails that meander along the banks of the Housatonic. It contains more species of fern – at their most prolific in June – than any other area in the continental United States. There's a small natural history museum.

Guided three-hour canoe tours, led by expert naturalists, explore Bartholomew's Cobble and the river in the summer. Children 12 and older are welcome, and advance reservations are mandatory.

North on Route 7, **Sheffield ❷**, established in 1733, is the oldest town in Berkshire County. In 1994 the state's oldest covered bridge, just off Route 7, was destroyed by vandals. A new one (pedestrians only) replaced it a few years later.

The Berkshires' true beauty lies in its backroads and small villages. **Mill River** and **New Marlborough**, small communities that prospered in the heyday of the Industrial Revolution, are gems.

The drive north along Route 7 skirts the Housatonic River, passing Sheffield Pottery and several antiques shops.

Great Barrington ❸ offers an excellent base from which to explore the towns and villages of the southern Berkshires. Although it does not have the architectural treasures of towns farther north such as Stockbridge and Lenox, Great Barrington has long been a popular vacation destination for sophisticated New Yorkers, and

upscale galleries, shops, and restaurants line the main and side streets.

Fans of singer Arlo Guthrie's *Alice's Restaurant Massacree* will want to see the **Guthrie Center** (2 Van Deusenville Road; tel: 413-528 1955; https://guthrie-center.org/), where Alice once lived. Built as a church in 1829, it is now an interfaith center.

Tom's Toys (297 Main Street; tel: 413-528 3330; www.tomstoys.com) is Santa's off-season warehouse. It's filled with toys, puzzles, games, dolls, and crafts – very few of which have commercial tie-ins.

Head west on Route 23 and south on Route 41 to the tiny hill hamlet of Mount Washington, in the state's southwestern corner. This smallest of Berkshires towns offers some of the finest fall-foliage viewing and the most dramatic natural waterfall in New England: at **Bash Bish Falls State Park ❹** (Falls Road; tel: 413-528 0330; www.mass.gov/locations/bash-bish-falls-state-park), in Mount Washington State Forest, water plummets 80ft (24 meters) into a deep gorge.

Kayaking on the Deerfield River.

STOCKBRIDGE

North of Great Barrington on Route 7 is **Monument Mountain** ➎, a craggy peak whose summit is a pleasant half-hour hike from the parking lot at its base. The mountain is a Berkshire literary landmark of considerable repute. The poet William Cullen Bryant sang its praises while practicing as a local attorney in the 1830s.

Stockbridge ➏ was incorporated as an Indian mission in 1739. Its first missionary was John Sargeant, a young tutor from Yale who lived among the Mohegan Indians for 16 years. He slept in their wigwams, shared their venison, and spoke their language while introducing them to the colonists' ways. Eventually, Sargeant helped them establish a town, build homes and cultivate the land. Some among the Mohegan tribe held public office, serving alongside whites in the town government. But as more colonists moved into the area, the tribes were slowly deprived of their land.

By 1783, the mission was history, and surviving Mohegans were forced to settle on the Oneida reservation in New York State. All that remains is the 1739 **Mission House**, now a museum on Stockbridge's Main Street (tel: 413-298 3239; www.thetrustees.org/places-to-visit/berkshires/mission-house.html; tours July–Aug Sat–Sun). It is furnished with a superb collection of 18th-century American furniture and decorative arts and has a unique Colonial Revival garden. There's a small museum about the Mohegans behind the house.

If Stockbridge's Main Street looks familiar, it may be because its New England essence was captured on the canvases of that remarkable illustrator of American life, Norman Rockwell, who created more than 300 covers for the Saturday Evening Post. He kept a studio and made his home here for a quarter of a century, until his death in 1978. Located on Route 183 is the stunning **Norman Rockwell Museum** (9 Glendale Road, Route 183; tel: 413-298 4100; www.nrm.org; daily 10am–4pm, until 5pm in summer). Designed by Robert A.M. Stern, it showcases his work and even recreates his Stockbridge studio.

Naumkeag Museum and Gardens, off Route 7 and Route 102 (Prospect Hill; tel: 413-298 3239; http://www.thetrustees.org/places-to-visit/berkshires/naumkeag.html; May 20–Columbus Day daily 10am–5pm, Columbus Day–Nov 26 Sat–Sun 11am–4pm, Apr–May 19 Sat–Sun 10am–5pm), is a 44-room, Norman-style mansion designed by Stanford White for Joseph Choate, the US ambassador to Great Britain, in 1899. It served as the summer home for three generations of the family. The furniture and artworks are outstanding, as are the 8 acres (3.2 hectares) of terrace gardens and grounds.

Chesterwood, the meticulously preserved summer home of sculptor Daniel Chester French (1850–1931), is 3 miles (5km) west of Stockbridge (4 Williamsville Road, off Route 183; tel: 413-298 3579; www.chesterwood.org; late May–early Oct daily 10am–5pm). It was

The Mission House, Stockbridge.

here that he created his masterpiece, *The Seated Lincoln*, focal point of the Lincoln Memorial in Washington DC. Many of his pieces are on exhibit, and displays in the Barn Gallery document his outstanding career.

TYRINGHAM

To the southeast, off Route 102, the tiny unspoiled village of **Tyringham** ❼ became an artists' colony in the early 20th century. **Ashintully Gardens** (Sodem Road; tel: 413-298 3239; www. thetrustees.org/places-to-visit/berkshires/ashintully-gardens.html; June–mid-Oct Wed and Sat 1–5pm), a charming assemblage of fountains, ponds, and statuary, is all that remains of the magnificent estate of the Egyptologist and politician Robb de Peyster Tytus (1875–1913), which was destroyed by fire. Recreating it was the 30-year project of composer John McLennan.

Bilbo Baggins would feel at home at **Santarella** (75 Main Road), the fairytale "gingerbread house" and studio of Sir Henry Hudson Kitson, sculptor of the *Minute Man* statue in Lexington.

Although only open for functions, it is worth a drive-by.

Jacob's Pillow (358 George Carter Road; tel: 413-243 0745; www.jacob-spillow.org; tickets go on sale in Feb), America's premier dance festival, is held every summer near **Becket** ❽. Over 50 dance troupes and performers, over 200 free performances, talks, events, and tours fill the schedule.

LENOX

Farther north, off Route 7, in **Lenox** ❾, are novelist Edith Wharton's grand neoclassical 1902 mansion and magnificent formal gardens at **The Mount** (2 Plunkett Street; tel: 413-551 5111; www. edithwharton.org; grounds year-round and house May–Oct daily, house winter

In the terraced grounds at Naumakeg, Steele's Blue Steps is a series of deep blue fountain pools flanked by four flights of stairs.

Sculpture at A Chapel for Humanity.

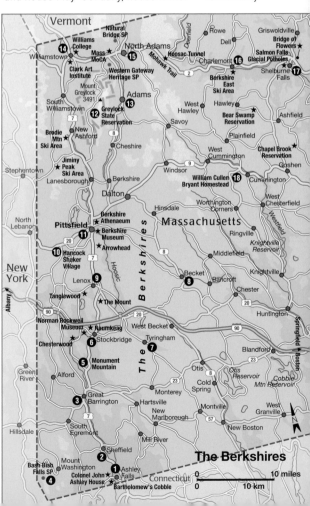

The Norman Rockwell Museum recreates the studio used by the Saturday Evening Post illustrator.

Small potteries are scattered around the Berkshires.

Sat–Sun 11am–4pm). After a $9 million restoration, they now look much as they did when she wrote *Ethan Frome*, *The House of Mirth*, and other works here.

Just out of town, **Tanglewood**, the 550-acre (220-hectare) summer home of the Boston Symphony Orchestra (297 West Street, Route 183; tel: 413-637 5180/888-266 1200; www.bso.org; July–Aug), has been a haven for performers, students, and music lovers since 1937. The BSO, the Boston Pops, and special guest artists also perform throughout the summer season in the 6,000-seat Music Shed, designed by architect Eero Saarinen. Tickets to Saturday morning rehearsals are offered at a reduced price.

There is a café and grille on the grounds, but picnicking is a huge part of the Tanglewood experience. The on-site Meals to Go offers several options, including the Picnic Tote for Two, which includes food, condiments, flatware, and bottled water.

Also in the grounds is a replica of the little red cottage where Nathaniel Hawthorne lived and wrote *The House of the Seven Gables* and *Tanglewood Tales*.

Continue on Route 183 past the entrance to Tanglewood to visit **Kripalu** (tel: 866-200 5203; www.kripalu.org), the country's largest center for yoga and holistic health. "Shadowbrook" was once the estate of Andrew Carnegie. Day passes – most generally available off-season and weekdays – include use of all facilities.

HANCOCK SHAKER VILLAGE

"'Tis a gift to be simple," says the old Shaker hymn, and the **Hancock Shaker Village ⑩** (tel: 413-443 0188; https://hancockshakervillage.org/; mid-Apr–June daily 10am–4pm, July–mid-Nov until 5pm, winter weekends only 10am–4pm), on Route US 20, 3 miles (5km) west of Pittsfield, testifies to the virtues of simplicity.

The Shakers settled in Hancock in the late 1780s. The community prospered through farming, printing, selling garden seeds and herbs, and making their distinctively designed furnishings. Shakers lived in Hancock until the 1950s, when the community had dwindled to a few staunch survivors, celibacy and changing times having led to their

decline. The 20 buildings in the village are open for self-guided tours.

PITTSFIELD

Returning to Route 7, continue north into **Pittsfield** ⓫, the Berkshire County seat and largest city (population 42,000). Herman Melville completed *Moby-Dick* (1851) while living at Arrowhead (off Route 7 at 780 Holmes Road; tel: 413-442 1793; www.mobydick.org; check the website for hours of guided tours). He lived in the 1780 farmhouse from 1850 to 1863; the view of the distant hills, he claimed, reminded him of the rolling ocean as he labored at his masterpiece.

A room in the **Berkshire Athenaeum** (1 Wendell Avenue; tel: 413-449 9480; www.pittsfieldlibrary.org; Mon–Sat) exhibits its photographs, documents and memorabilia of Melville.

Theater-lovers praise the **Barrington Stage Company** (30 Union Street, Pittsfield; tel: 413-236 8888; www.barrington stageco.org). The company supports two stages, one which presents familiar and classic works, the other dedicated to new plays and a musical lab.

The **Berkshire Museum** (39 South Street; tel: 413-443 7171; https://berkshiremuseum.org/; Mon–Sat 10am–5pm, Sun noon–5pm) presents an eclectic collection of natural science and history exhibits, ranging from a 143lbs (65kg) meteorite to shards of Babylonian cuneiform tablets. Its art collection is equally eclectic: it was the first gallery to exhibit Norman Rockwell, but it also showcased Andy Warhol and Robert Rauschenberg.

NORTH TO WILLIAMSTOWN

Off Route 7, just north of Lanesborough, turn right to **Greylock State Reservation** ⓬ (tel: 413-499 4262; www.mass.gov/locations/mount-greylock-state-reservation). Rising to 3,491ft (1,064 meters), Mt Greylock is the tallest peak in Massachusetts. At the top is a distinctive granite monument, the 92ft (28-meter) Veterans' Memorial Tower, commemorating the casualties of all America's wars.

From the top, the writer Nathaniel Hawthorne looked down upon Williamstown – "a white village and a steeple set like a daydream among the high

> **⊙ Tip**
>
> Lenox holds its annual Apple Squeeze Festival (www.lenoxapplesqueeze.com) the last weekend in September. It's a celebration of apples cooked in every imaginable way. North Adams, meanwhile, holds its Fall Foliage Festival and Parade (http://1berkshire.com/calendar/fall-foliage-parade) the same weekend.

Music makers celebrate fall in the Berkshires.

Food and music mix at Tanglewood.

The Hancock Shaker Village.

mountain waves." The visitor center at the base of the mountain is open daily.

Route 7 continues north past the turnoff for **Jiminy Peak**, with the highest skiing mountain in the state.

Susan B. Anthony, the 19th-century social reformer, abolitionist, and suffragist, was born in **Adams** . Her birthplace has been restored as a museum (67 East Road; tel: 413-743 7121; www.susanbanthonybirthplace.com; Memorial Day–Columbus Day Thu–Mon 10am–4pm, Columbus Day–Memorial Day Mon and Fri–Sat 10am–4pm, Sun 11am–4pm, call to arrange private tours) to her life and the history of the causes she espoused. The house itself was in excellent condition when the restoration began and much of it is original.

WILLIAMSTOWN

In the state's northwest corner, **Williamstown** , among the most beautiful of New England villages, is home to two excellent art museums. The **Williams College Museum of Art** (Main Street; tel: 413-597 2429; http://wcma.williams.edu; 10am–5pm Sept–May Fri–Tue, June–Aug Fri–Wed, Thu year round until 8pm), under the auspices of **Williams College** (founded in 1793), houses more than 12,000 works from diverse eras and cultures, with a special emphasis on modern and contemporary art.

Just down the street is the exceptional **Sterling and Francine Clark Art Institute** (225 South Street; tel: 413-458 2303; www.clarkart.edu; Tue–Sun 10am–5pm; children under 18 free). Between 1918 and 1956, the Clarks amassed a superb private collection that included silver and porcelain, as well as European and American paintings, including works by Botticelli, Goya, Gainsborough, and Fragonard. The museum is best known, however, for its French Impressionist collection. There are additional galleries in the new Stone Hill Center, designed by Japanese minimalist architect Tadao Ando.

ALONG THE MOHAWK TRAIL

The **Mohawk Trail** (Route 2; www.mohawktrail.com) winds for 63 miles (101km) eastward from Williamstown, across I-91 to Orange. The section

from North Adams to Greenfield (I–91) is a designated scenic drive. An old Indian path-turned-roadway, it offers some of the most rugged and romantic scenery in the Berkshires. It is a popular leaf-peeping route in the fall.

Stop in **North Adams** 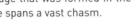 to visit one of the state's best museums, the **Massachusetts Museum of Contemporary Art (MASS MoCA)** (Junction Route 2 and Marshall Street; tel: 413-664 4481; www.massmoca.org; Summer from June Sun–Wed 10am–6pm and Thu–Sat 10am–7pm, rest of the year Wed–Mon 11am–5pm). The vast, renovated 19th-century factory complex houses a fine collection of contemporary art, including some pieces so large they've not been exhibited before. The large space is also a performance arts center, presenting a year-round program of dance, cabaret, films, and avant-garde theatre. The Museum's **Kidspace** is a contemporary art gallery and workshop for the kids.

Western Gateway Heritage State Park (115 State Street, Building 4; tel: 413-663 6312; www.mass.gov/locations/western-gateway-heritage-state-park; Thu–Mon 10am–4pm), in a restored freight yard, chronicles the town's history, including the building of the nearby 4.75-mile (7.6km) Hoosac railroad tunnel. An engineering marvel at the time, it was a deadly project. Two hundred men died during its construction.

Just north on Route 8, in **Natural Bridge State Park** (tel: 413-663 6392; www.mass.gov/locations/natural-bridge-state-park; Memorial Day–Columbus Day daily 9am–5pm), a water-eroded bridge that was formed in the last ice age spans a vast chasm.

CHARLEMONT

In **Charlemont** 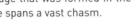, the Mohawk Trail winds past *Hail to the Sunrise*, a stirring statue of a Mohawk warrior performing his morning thanksgiving ritual. It was erected in 1932 to commemorate the American Indians who used the trail as a migration route back when it was a dirt road through the forest. A pool near the monument is lined with stones inscribed with messages from tribes and councils from across North America. Farther along, the **Berkshire East** ski area

The Veterans' Memorial Tower.

Fishing on the Deerfield River, best known for its trout.

☉ BERKSHIRES SUMMER FESTIVALS

Tanglewood is the best known of several Berkshires summer music and theatrical festivals, but is certainly not the only one. The South Mountain Concerts (tel: 413-442 2106; www.southmountainconcerts.org), featuring chamber music by renowned performers on most Sunday afternoons at 3pm in September and October, take place south of Pittsfield, on Route 7. For Renaissance and Baroque music, head for the Aston Magna Festival (tel: 413-528 3595; www.astonmagna.org), at St James Church in Great Barrington and at the Clark Museum in Williamstown.

When the Jacob's Pillow Dance Festival was launched in the early 1930s in the hill town of Becket, southeast of Pittsfield on State 8, modern dance was in its infancy. Today, it's a national institution and hosts a 10-week summer program (tel: 413-243 9919; www.jacobspillow.org).

The Williamstown Theater Festival (tel: 413-458 3253; www.wtfestival.org) stages summer theater from Greek tragedy to Restoration comedy, and from Chekhov to Pirandello, while at the Berkshire Theater Festival (tel: 413-997 4444; www.berkshiretheatregroup.org) in Stockbridge, the emphasis is on American classics. For fans of the Bard, there's Shakespeare & Co (tel: 413-637 3353; www.shakespeare.org) in Lenox, performing throughout the year. Film buffs attend the Berkshire International Film Festival (tel: 413-528 8030; www.biffma.org) in Great Barrington every June.

The Hail to the Sunrise sculpture depicts a Mohawk Indian raising his arms to the Great Spirit.

(http://berkshireeast.com) has summer activities as well as winter skiing.

Crab Apple Whitewater (Route 2; tel: 800-553 7238; www.crabapplewhitewater.com) offers half- and full-day rafting trips on the Deerfield and Millers rivers for all skill and courage levels.

BRIDGE OF FLOWERS

In **Shelburne Falls** , turn onto Route 2A East to visit the one-of-a-kind Bridge of Flowers, a trolley bridge until 1928, now pedestrian-only, which displays more than 500 varieties of flowers, vines, and shrubs. When the flowers are in bloom, it's truly worth a stop. At the **Shelburne Falls Trolley Museum** (tel: 413-625 9443; www.sftm.org; May–Oct Sat–Sun 11am–5pm), climb aboard for a spin on an 1896 trolley car that used the bridge. The glacial-carved **Salmon Falls Glacial Potholes** at the base of Shelburne Falls are no longer accessible, but you can view them from an overlook which explains the curious derivation of these geologic oddities.

Head south on Route 112, passing by the **Bear Swamp Reservation** (open

The potholes at Shelburne Falls.

year-round), a 285-acre (115-hectare) wilderness area with 3 miles (5km) of hiking trails, and **Chapel Brook Reservation**, whose Pony Mountain is popular with technical climbers. Both are properties of the Trustees of Reservations (tel: 478-921 1944; www.thetrustees.org). The pools that form at the base of Chapel Falls are a delightful spot to cool off on a hot summer's day.

THE BRYANT HOMESTEAD

Turn west where routes 112 and 9 merge to **Cummington** and the **William Cullen Bryant Homestead** ❶ (Bryant Road off Route 112; tel: 413-634 2244; house: tour schedules vary so call or visit www.thetrustees.org/places-to-visit/pioneer-valley/bryant-homestead.html; grounds daily). This was the boyhood home of Bryant (1794–1878), a widely published poet, editor/publisher of the *New York Evening Post*, and mentor to Walt Whitman. Bryant used the house as a summer retreat, converting it from Colonial style to Victorian. Today it is filled with objects he purchased while traveling overseas. There are footpaths and hiking trails round the property.

⦿ GLACIAL POTHOLES

Visitors to Shelburne Falls can view a fascinating geologic display in the form of potholes in the granite boulders at the base of Salmon Falls. About 50 near-perfect holes pockmark the rocks; the smallest is only 6 inches (15cm) in diameter, while the largest is 39ft (12 meters) in diameter. The "kettles" – to use their proper geologic name – were formed when stones were caught in the rushing waters of the falls at the end of the last ice age. The whirlpool effect caused trapped stones to slowly grind the circular indentations and continues to this day. Access to the boulders is prohibited, but you can get a good look at the rocks from an observation platform on nearby Deerfield Avenue.

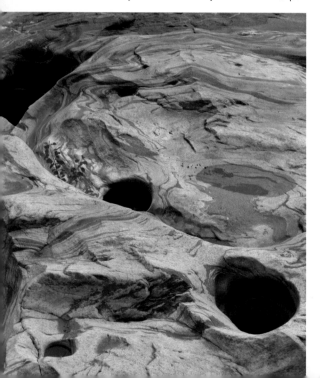

RHODE ISLAND

With Providence's cosmopolitan, collegiate, cultural energy; Newport's elegant opulence; and great stretches of ocean coast and inland countryside, the smallest state offers a long list of attractions.

Although the smallest state in the nation, Rhode Island always had a disproportionate influence in power, prosperity, and prestige. Free-thinking settlers inspired innovations in industry; vessels sailing from her ports brought wealth from fishing and trade; millionaires in the Gilded Age of the 19th century built stunning mansions on oceanside cliffs they called their summer "cottages."

Rhode Island's official founder was clergyman Roger Williams. Driven out of Salem in 1636 for preaching religious tolerance, Williams headed south to establish a settlement where all were free to practice their own faith. Traveling by canoe with a cadre of followers, he arrived at the head of Narragansett Bay and negotiated with the Wampanoag people for permission to start a settlement which he named Providence. In 1663, Charles II granted a charter to the rather wordily named Colony of Rhode Island and Providence Plantations – a name it still officially retains as a state. There's debate over where "Rhode Island" comes from. Explorer Giovanni da Verrazzano compared Aquidneck Island (the location of Newport) to the Greek isle of Rhodes. A less romantic, but more probable, claim may be by the practically minded Dutch explorer Adriaen Block. He noted that the soil in the islands was reddish in color or "Roode Eyland."

Soon many of the era's "outsiders" flocked to Rhode Island's shores. Quakers fleeing Puritan persecution made Newport their home, and as early as the 18th century, Jews from Portugal and Holland settled here. The first Baptist church, Quaker Meeting House, and Jewish synagogue in the colonies were all established in Rhode Island. In the ensuing centuries immigrants from Europe, the Mediterranean, China, and Cape Verde followed. With a population in excess of 1 million crowded into its 1,214 sq

Main Attractions

Waterplace Park and
  Riverwalk
RISD Museum
Brown University
Newport
Ocean Drive
Block Island

Maps on pages
214, 216, 220

Newport's Second Beach.

⊙ Tip

La Gondola (tel: 401-421 8877; www.gondolari.com) offers a unique way to tour the river: in a genuine Venetian gondola. Private rides for parties from two to six people are offered evenings Apr–Oct, and the gondoliers provide cheese, ice buckets, glasses, and, of course, music.

miles (3,143 sq km), Rhode Island is a bustling, multicultural cross-section of New England life.

REVITALIZED PROVIDENCE

Rhode Island's capital is wonderfully diverse. With five schools of higher education and a rejuvenated downtown, it hums with a creative vibe. It cherishes the outstanding 18th- and 19th-century architecture throughout its downtown and its appealingly diverse neighborhoods. It's also easily reached from Boston, a feasible day trip by car, train, or bus.

In its early days, **Providence ❶** struggled to survive. The hilly, rocky soil was not conducive to agriculture, and the same predisposition to dissent which

attracted many settlers led to arguments over any form of community goals or government. Still, its deepwater port thrived. By the 1760s, Providence and Newport were the busiest seaports in the New World. In the years following the Civil War, the Industrial Revolution became the economic driving force for the region. As a major manufacturing center, Providence was dubbed "the cradle of American industry." But with the Great Depression and the textile industry's exodus to the south, Providence lost its industrial pre-eminence. Today it is rebounding as a center for finance, health care, and higher education, while its designation as the state capital ensures strong government employment. As one of the

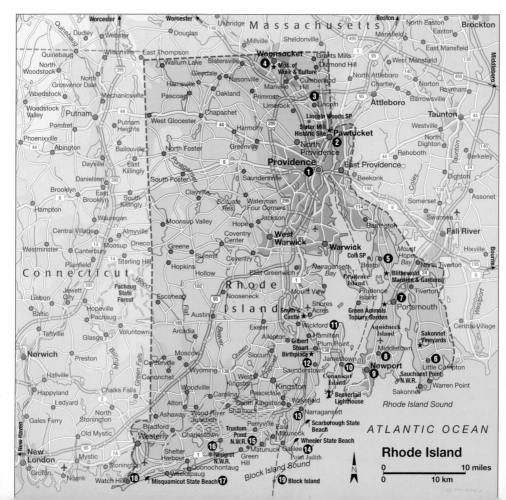

only two deepwater harbors in New England, it remains one of the busiest ports in the North East. But like most other cities in the region, it struggles with unemployment and poverty. The city has lavished restorative attention on its downtown. Massive redevelopment removed railroad tracks and roadways that covered the Providence River; old buildings received facelifts and found new tenants; parks became clean, safe, popular gathering places. Providence is a city best seen on foot. The street system follows no discernible pattern and can be a challenge even with GPS. Many residents forego cars altogether and walk to their destination. It's a compact, lovely city in which to stroll. Like Rome, it was built on seven hills, the three best-known being College (officially, Prospect), Federal, and Constitution.

CENTER OF TOWN

Constitution Hill is impossible to miss because of the **State Capitol** that dominates its crest (Smith Street; tel: 401-222 3983; reserve ahead for tours Mon–Fri 9am, 10am, 11am, 1pm, and 2pm; self-guided tour brochure available at entrance). Exhibits include a historic portrait of George Washington by Rhode Islander Gilbert Stuart.

Just across the way, **Providence Place** (www.providenceplace.com) has more than 180 stores, restaurants, and leisure options, including the six-story **Feinstein IMAX** theater (tel: 401-453-4629) in an enclosed three-story shopping mall.

The 4-acre (1.6-hectare) **Waterplace Park and Riverwalk** are the stars of Providence's waterside renaissance. The long-neglected riverside was cleaned up, equipped with an Italian-inspired piazza, cobblestone walkways, and boat landings. The **WaterFire** (https://waterfire.org) nights draw thousands of spectators and participants to downtown.

Kennedy Plaza is the site for a wide-ranging schedule of free concerts, outdoor art exhibits, and a

marketplace. In winter, there's an outdoor ice-skating rink (http://theprovidencerink.com) that's twice the size of the one in Rockefeller Center.

The plaza is set to undergo a major $17-million transformation beginning in 2018, upgrading it from a transportation hub into an impressive public space. The plan, unveiled by mayor Jorge Elorza in the fall of 2017, will redirect bus traffic to the Amtrak station and see the construction of new buildings, with the aim of making the square the "true civic heart" of the city.

THE MILE OF HISTORY

In historic East Side, **Benefit Street**, the "Mile of History," deserves walking from one end to the other. Originally it was a twisting dirt path that led to family graveyards. When a communal cemetery was created and ancestral remains moved there, the lane was widened and straightened "for the benefit of the people of Providence." It quickly became the haunt of the Provident elite. There are more than 200 restored 18th- and 19th-century

A statue of Roger Williams stands guard over the city he founded, Providence.

⊘ Tip

Cindy Salvato leads three-hour culinary walking tours (tel: 800 656 0713; www. savoringrhodeisland.com) of Federal Hill, which go behind the scenes at restaurants, butchers, and specialty Italian food shops. Watch ravioli being made, inhale lungsful of garlic, and sip some good Chianti.

buildings built by sea captains and merchants; many bear bronze plaques identifying their original owners and dates of construction. In the late 1960s and early 1970s the street was run down and nearly demolished as part of a renewal program; only the efforts of the Providence Preservation Society (www.ppsri.org) saved the day. Staff at the John Brown House Museum offer 90-minute walking tours (May–Oct Mon–Tue, Thu–Sat 10am).

In 1638 Roger Williams established the meeting house of the **First Baptist Church in America** Ⓔ (75 North Main Street; tel: 401-454 3418; www. firstbaptistchurchinamerica.org; guided tours Memorial Day–Columbus Day Mon–Fri 10am–3pm and after Sunday worship service). Built in 1774–5, it seated 1,200 people, over one-third of the population of Providence at the time. It is a premier example of traditional New England architecture. You can hear the magnificent Foley-Baker organ during Sunday service.

Prospect Terrace Ⓕ, on Congdon Street, is a tiny park that gives a fine view of the city. Roger Williams, the city's founder, is buried here. A statue of Williams stands on the bluff overlooking his city.

The bookstacks of **Providence Atheneum** Ⓖ (251 Benefit Street; tel: 401-421 6970; www.providenceathenaeum. org; summer Mon–Thu 10am–6pm, Fri 9am–5pm, Sat 10am–2pm, winter Mon–Thu 9am–7pm, Fri–Sat 9am–5pm, Sun 1–5pm) witnessed the demise of the courtship of Edgar Allan Poe and a local resident, Sarah Whitman (possibly the inspiration for "Annabel Lee"). While visiting the library, she learned he had broken his promise to stay sober. She broke their engagement, and they never saw each other again. The library is worth a visit for its collections of rare books, prints, and paintings.

Virtually opposite is the prestigious **Rhode Island School of Design (RISD) Museum** Ⓗ (224 Benefit Street; tel: 401-454 6500; www.risdmuseum.org; Tue–Sun 10am–5pm, third Thu of the month until 9pm; free Sun 10am–5pm and third Thu of the month 5–9pm). It has paintings by 19th-century American

Residents of Providence outside a Portuguese market.

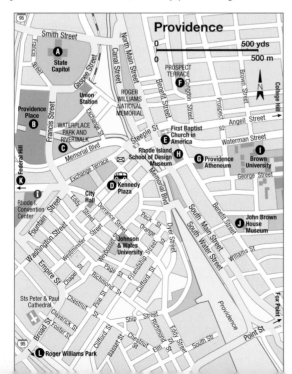

masters and French Impressionists, a major Oriental collection, Egyptian and Ancient art, 20th-century American furniture, and decorative arts.

Brown University  (College Hill) dominates this part of Providence. The independent, co-educational Ivy League establishment was founded as Rhode Island College in Warren in 1764, and moved to Providence in 1770. The name change came in 1804 in recognition of a $5,000 endowment from alumnus and Providence businessman Nicholas Brown. In 2010, it was recognized as "The Happiest College in the Country" for the student satisfaction in curriculum, cultural and campus life, community service opportunities, and athletics. Among the buildings of interest on the campus: the 1770 University Hall (on the Quadrangle), used as a barracks during the Revolutionary War; the 1904 Beaux Arts John Carter Brown Library (corner of George and Brown streets) with the largest collection of primary sources of pre-1825 Americana; and the Annmary Brown Memorial (21 Brown Street; Mon–Fri

1–5pm) with European and American paintings from the 16th to the early 20th centuries.

The heart of the **College Hill** shopping area is Thayer Street, which borders the eastern edge of the Brown campus. It caters to collegiate clientele with interesting restaurants, bars, shops, and bookstores. "The most magnificent and elegant private mansion that I have ever seen on this continent," said John Quincy Adams of the 1786 **John Brown House Museum** (52 Power Street; tel: 401-331 8575; Apr–Nov Tue–Fri 1–4pm with guided tours at 1.30 and 3pm, Sat 10am–4pm, free on first Thu of the month 5–8pm, Dec–Mar Sat 10am–4pm). Brown's life reflected the early years of the Republic. More than just viewing a collection of period furnishings, you learn about the genesis of the China tea trade, women's life and education, and Brown's participation in the slave trade. The museum staff also gives tours of Benefit Street.

Federal Hill , to the west of I-95, is Providence's "Little Italy." The

Marina on the Providence River. The river is 8 miles (13km) long and has a barrier near the city to guard it against tidal floods.

WaterFire is a festival that takes place on summer evenings on the Providence River.

⊘ WATERFIRE

WaterFire (www.waterfire.org for schedule of installations) is a unique expression of interactive installation art that graces Providence's riverfront on several nights throughout the year. More than 100 braziers in the river are lit at sunset, while torch-lit vessels drift down the river accompanied by sounds and music related to ritual, religious, and symbolic inspiration for the living artwork. Artist Barnaby Evans created the first WaterFire in 1994. A second in 1996 was so successful that a non-profit organization was created to support and fund future performances. The event draws thousands of people who are integral to the success of the living sculpture by their involvement with the music, the movement on and around the river, and their emotional response to the evening.

The resilient Rhode Island Red was originally bred in the 1830s in Adamsville, now part of Little Compton.

The green at Brown University.

sculpture of the pignola hanging from the arch across Atwells Avenue is one of the most recognizable landmarks in Providence. It is a traditional Italian symbol of welcome. Wander along Atwells Avenue and enjoy the aromas of crusty Italian breads, cheeses, herbs, and spices. DePasquale Plaza is lined with open-air cafés. It's a good stop for a meal and people-watching. In recent years, the area has added trendy boutiques and art galleries. South of Brown University and bordered by the Providence and Seekonk rivers, Fox Point is home to the city's Portuguese community. On holy days, celebrants parade with statues of the Virgin Mary while children dressed in their best suits and crinolines follow along. Early morning brings the tantalizing scent of Portuguese sweet bread wafting from small bakeries.

It's well worth a trek south on I-95 to exit 17 to see **Roger Williams Park** ❶ (Elmwood Avenue; tel: 401-785 9450), a 435-acre (176-hectare) complex filled with ponds, specimen trees, and outdoor sculpture. The acclaimed

Zoo (tel: 401-785 3510; www.rwpzoo.org; daily Apr–Sept 10am–5pm, Oct–Mar 10am–4pm) is home to nearly 1,000 animals, including some of the rarest, living in natural surroundings. The **Botanical Center** (Tue–Sun 11am–4pm) is the largest indoor display garden in New England. Outside, there is a wonderfully scented rose garden maze. The **Museum of Natural History and Planetarium** (daily 10am–4pm) concentrates heavily on items from Rhode Island, including fossils that pre-date the dinosaurs. For children, visit the **Carousel Village**, with a Victorian-style carousel and a barrier-free Hasbro playground.

Leave the park via the Montgomery Avenue exit, turn right on Narragansett, then turn left on Harborside. Foodies will salivate over the **Johnson and Wales Culinary Arts Museum** (315 Harborside Boulevard; tel: 401-598 2805; www.culinary.org; Mon–Tue 8am–9pm, Wed–Fri until 5.30pm). It bubbles over with gastronomic exhibits from the Roman Empire to the present day, including over 60,000 cookbooks and collections donated by chefs and restaurateurs.

BLACKSTONE RIVER VALLEY

America's Industrial Revolution began in the Blackstone Valley. Called "America's hardest working river," the Blackstone runs for 46 miles (74km) from Worcester MA to Providence.

The **John H. Chafee Blackstone River Valley National Heritage Corridor** links 24 communities along the river. The **Blackstone Valley Visitor Center** (175 Main Street; tel: 401-724 2200; www.centerbytheblackstone.com; daily 10am–4pm) in **Pawtucket** ❷, 5 miles (8km) northeast of Providence on I-95, has information on most of the sites along the route. There's a 20-minute orientation film about the rise and fall of the textile industry. The *Blackstone Valley Explorer* (tel: 401-724 2200; www.rivertourblackstone.

com; May–Oct), a 40-passenger riverboat, departs from Central Falls for a 45-minute narrated tour of the river's industrialized past and efforts to restore its ecosystem.

Techniques of mechanized textile production were pioneered in 1793 by Moses Brown. The riverfront **Slater Mill Living History Museum** (67 Roosevelt Avenue; tel: 401-725 8638; www.slatermill.org; Mar–Apr and Nov Sat–Sun 11am–3pm, May–June and Sept–Oct Wed–Sun and Mon holidays 10am–4pm, July–Labor Day Wed–Mon 10am–4pm) offers a rare look into the earliest days of the Industrial Revolution, showing how textiles progressed from being handcrafts to a major industrial undertaking.

LINCOLN

Seven miles (11km) to the northwest of Pawtucket, in **Lincoln** ❸, Lincoln Woods State Park (tel: 401-723 7892; www.riparks.com/Locations/LocationLincoln Woods.html; daily) has one of the largest freshwater beaches (with lifeguards on duty in summer) in the area, plus hiking, kayaking, and fishing. There's a relatively new covered bridge and trail rides. Blackstone River State Park (Lower River Road; tel: 401-723 7892; www.riparks.com/Locations/LocationBlack stoneBikeVisit.html) follows the course of the Blackstone Canal towpath. Adjacent to the path, the **Wilbur Kelly House Museum** (Lower River Road; tel: 401-333 0295; Apr–Oct daily 9am–5pm; free) narrates the history of the river and canal and how it was long used for transportation by Native Americans.

Twelve miles (19km) of the planned 48-mile (77km) **Blackstone River Greenway** (tel: 401-222 2450; https://blackstone heritagecorridor.org), which will eventually stretch from Providence to Worcester, are now completed between Lincoln and Pitman Square in Providence. NBX Bikes (tel: 401-434 3838; http://nbxbikes.com/) in Providence rents bikes and provides round trip and pick-up service.

WOONSOCKET

In **Woonsocket** ❹ on the Massachusetts border, visit the **Museum of Work and Culture** (42 South Main Street, Market Square; tel: 401-769 9675; www.rihs. org/museums/museum-of-work-and-culture; Tue–Fri 9.30am–4pm, Sat 10am–4pm, Sun 1–4pm). Interactive displays immerse visitors in the lives of the French Canadians who migrated from Quebec to work in the textile mills in the 1840s. In 1900, 60 percent of Woonsocket's population was French Canadian.

EAST BAY

Head east out of Providence on I-195 to Route 114 south (exit 7), which winds along the eastern shore of East Bay. **Bristol** ❺, about 15 miles (24km) south, held the nation's first Fourth of July parade in 1785. Its patriotic celebration continues all during July. Even the center line on Main Street is red, white, and blue. At the **Blithewold Mansion, Gardens & Arboretum** (101 Ferry Road; tel: 401-253 2707; www. blithewold.org; grounds and gardens: year-round Mon–Sat 10am–5pm, Sun

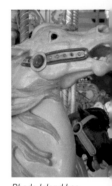

Rhode Island has several Victorian carousels, including the Crescent Park Looff Carousel in East Providence.

Old Slater Mill, Pawtucket.

Christmas lights illuminate Bowen's Wharf, Newport.

10am–3pm; mansion: mid-May–Oct, Tue–Sat 10am–4pm, Sun 10am–3pm), visitors can tour the 45-room mansion built by Pennsylvania coal magnate Augustus van Wickle in 1908 to resemble a 17th-century English country manor. (Blithewold is old English for "happy woodland.") The 33 acres (13 hectares) of landscaped grounds include rock, water, and rose gardens.

The Audubon Society's **Environmental Education Center** (1401 Hope Street/ Route 114; tel: 401-949 5454; https://asri. org/learn/environmental-education-center. html; mid-Apr–mid-Oct daily 9am–5pm, rest of the year Wed–Sat 9am–5pm, Sun noon–5pm) has some of the best bird watching in New England. The guided tours of the grounds and overlooks of Narragansett Bay are particularly nice for those unfamiliar with the region's flora and fauna.

The America's Cup Hall of Fame, more than 50 classic yachts, and over 500 scale models used by shipbuilder Capt. Nat Herreshoff, are displayed at **Herreshoff Marine and America's Cup Museum** (1 Burnside Street; tel:

401-253 5000; www.herreshoff.org; summer Wed–Sun 10am–5pm, winter pre-booked tours only). He's credited with designing eight consecutive defenders of the America's Cup. Visitors can step aboard many of the famous, vintage, and impeccably restored sailing and racing vessels.

Colt State Park (tel: 401 253 7482; www.riparks.com/Locations/LocationColt. html) on the west side of Bristol Harbor (Poppasquash Road off Route 114) is considered the gem of Rhode Island's state parks. The entire western boundary of the park is a panoramic vista of Narragansett Bay. The 464-acre (188-hectare) park has well-tended fruit trees, flowering plants, and putting-green-perfect lawns. There are over 100 picnic tables scattered across the grounds. The open-air **Chapel-by-the-Sea**, with a backdrop of the water, is a popular spot for weddings. The park is the location of **Coggeshall Farm Museum** (tel: 401-253 9062; www.coggeshallfarm.org; Memorial Day–Labor Day Tue–Sun 10am–4pm, times vary rest of the year, check the

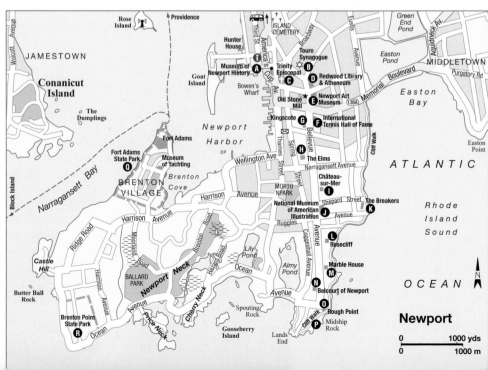

website). Southern New England's only hands-on, multisensory living history museum, it transports visitors back to a working farm in 1799. Accurately clothed interpreters working with equally authentic tools and heirloom plants and animals recreate Rhode Island's agricultural past.

LITTLE COMPTON AND THE EASTERN PENINSULA

A 30-minute detour to Rhode Island's less-visited eastern peninsula takes you to the state's oldest winery and one of its oldest towns. Leaving Bristol, take Route 114 N to Route 24 N. Take exit 5 (North Tiverton) on Route 138 and follow the turn onto Route 77 to head south. (This is Rhode Island. Distances are not great.)

Folks drive in from as far as Providence to get their recommended daily allowance of calcium at **Gray's Ice Cream** (tel: 401-624 4500; daily 6.30am–9pm) at the junction of Route 77 and Route 179.

The route passes through undeveloped countryside on its way to **Little Compton** ❻. The town was first settled by entrepreneurial Pilgrims eager to expand their land holdings. Many houses from the 17th to the 19th centuries surround the town common – the only communal grazing area left in the state – although you are more likely to see residents walking their Labradors than watching their Holsteins.

Just outside town is **Sakonnet Vineyards** (162 W. Main Road; tel: 401-635 8486; www.sakonnetwine.com; Columbus Day–Memorial Day daily 11am–5pm, rest of the year Sun–Thu 11am–6pm, Fri–Sat 11am–6pm). Founded in 1975, it takes advantage of soil and microclimate similar to the maritime climates of northern France to produce Vidal Blanc, Chardonnay, and Pinot Noir.

TOPIARY GARDENS

Returning to the Bristol area, just off Route 114 in **Portsmouth** ❼ is **Green Animals Topiary Garden** (380 Cory's Lane; tel: 401-847 1000; www.newportmansions.org/explore/green-animals-topiary-garden; mid-Apr–mid-Oct daily 10am–5pm; combined admission ticket with Newport mansions available). Eighty sculpted trees and shrubs represent everything from an ostrich to a camel.

MIDDLETOWN AND AQUIDNECK ISLAND

The major city on Aquidneck Island is Newport, but the rest of the island should not be ignored. The environs around **Middletown** ❽ are not much changed in appearance from the earliest years of settlement. In **Paradise Valley Park** (Paradise and Prospect avenues), **Boyd's Windmill** (1801), the only eight-vaned windmill in the country, is occasionally put into operation. **Paradise School** (1875) is a classic one-room schoolhouse with displays of area history. Docents are at both locations (both open July–Sept Sun 2–4pm; tel: 401-849 1870; voluntary donation).

Prescott Farm (2009 West Main Street; tel: 401-849 7300; grounds:

⊙ Tip

There are interesting shops along the Thames Street Landing on Bristol's downtown waterfront. The height of elegance is the Point Pleasant Inn and Resort (tel: 401-253-0627; http://pointpleasantinn.com), a 25-hectare (10-acre) restored English mansion overlooking the bay with luxurious accommodations.

Green Animals Topiary Gardens.

⊘ Tip

Fancy a game of tennis on courts once graced by Martina Navratilova and John McEnroe? You can rent a court from 30 minutes to 5 hours at the International Tennis Hall of Fame (tel: 401-846 0642; www.tennisfame.com) or visit the museum (Wed–Mon 10am–5pm, until 6pm in summer) open year-round.

A hoagie-style sandwich with salami, ham, turkey, cheese, lettuce, and tomato.

daily dawn–dusk) gives a glimpse of early Aquidneck Island life through its buildings and landscape. The 1812 windmill is original to the site, while several other structures were moved from other locations. The kitchen and herb garden is noted for its plantings of heirloom varieties and use of sustainable practices. The farm offers workshops in stone wall building, beekeeping, open hearth cooking, and gardening (summer and fall).

Whitehall Museum House (311 Berkeley Avenue; tel: 401-846 3116; www.whitehallmuseumhouse.org; late June–Aug Tue–Sun 10am–4pm, call to arrange visits outside season; voluntary donation) was the home of Dean (later Bishop) George Berkeley, who lived here from 1729 to 1731. He dreamed of starting a college where sons of colonists and American Indians could study together. When funds were not forthcoming, he returned to England, but not before donating his property and library to Yale University. His gift led to the creation of the Berkeley Divinity School at Yale. A century

later, when the University of California established a campus near San Francisco, they named the town where it would be built after him – Berkeley.

East of Paradise Park, **Norman Bird Sanctuary** (tel: 401-846 2577; http://normanbirdsanctuary.org/; daily 9am–5pm) has over 7 miles (11km) of trails and fabulous views of the ocean. Just beyond is **Sachuest Point National Wildlife Refuge** (tel: 401-847 5511; www.fws.gov/refuge/sachuest_point/; trails open daily dawn–dusk; visitor center daily 10am–4pm), with walking trails and viewing platforms. Third Beach is within the boundaries of the wildlife refuge. It is actually four separate public and semi-private beaches on Rhode Island Sound.

NEWPORT

Few places have the location, history, and ambience of **Newport** ⑨. The views of sailboats and yachts in Narragansett Bay are Hollywood-perfect; the atmosphere is imbued with Revolutionary and nautical history; the elegance of the Gilded Age mansions is tempered with casual gatherings

⊘ FOOD IN TRANSLATION

When ordering food in Rhode Island, you might need translations for some of the more unusual items on the menu. A grinder in New England is known in other parts of the world as a hoagie, po'boy, or submarine sandwich. Stuffies are clam stuffing appetizers baked in a clam shell, something like clams casino. If you order chourico, you'll get a dense and spicy Portuguese sausage. A frappe (pronounced *frap*) is milk, ice cream, and flavoring mixed together. (In other places, it would be a milk shake. In Rhode Island, a milk shake is just milk and flavoring mixed together without ice cream.) A cabinet is a coffee-flavored frappe. Coffee milk is sweet coffee syrup mixed with milk. Regardless of what you order, it will almost always be delicious.

at dockside bars. Known for its music and cultural festivals, its excellent dining, and its comfortable lodgings, it's a town where visitors linger.

A good place to begin a visit is downtown at the **Visitor Information Center** (23 America's Cup Avenue; tel: 401-845 9131; www.discovernewport.org; winter 9am–4pm, summer until 5 or 6pm). They have extensive information on the area, including maps. Be sure to pick up detailed directions to **Ocean Drive**, the stretch of Ocean Avenue that combines great Atlantic views with glimpses of Newport's grand mansions. Free 30-minute parking (have your ticket validated in the visitor center) is available in the parking lot adjacent to the center. There's also discounted parking when using public transportation.

Thames Street along the harbor is lined with shops and restaurants, many concentrated on **Bowen's Wharf**, lined with handsome craft tied up at yacht-club slips. Get your historical bearings at the award-winning **Museum of Newport History** Ⓐ (127 Thames Street; tel: 401-841 8770; daily 10am–5pm; voluntary donation) in Washington Square, in the restored 1762 Brick Market building. Engaging displays introduce the waterfront denizens, Gilded Age millionaires, religious rebels, and ambitious immigrants who've inhabited Newport. Museum staff offer walking tours of the city.

Whitehorne House (416 Thames Street; tel: 401-847 2448; closed until unspecified date in 2018, visits by appointment by calling Rachel Guadagni on 401-846 4152) houses the Doris Duke Collection of 18th-century Newport furniture. Some of the most outstanding examples of American furniture are displayed in the Federal mansion on the waterfront. The formal gardens behind the house recreate a period garden for an affluent, urban family. (You can purchase a combination ticket for Whitehorne House and Rough Point, Duke's mansion on Bellevue Avenue.)

The **White Horse Tavern** (26 Marlborough Street; tel: 401-849 3600; http://whitehorsenewport.com/) is the country's oldest operating tavern (1673). With its clapboard walls, gambrel roof, and interior beams, it is considered the very essence of 17th-century American architecture. Newport has a remarkable legacy of colonial architecture. Much of it is found around Washington Square. At 85 Touro Street, the Georgian **Touro Synagogue** Ⓑ (www.tourosynagogue.org) is the nation's oldest Jewish house of worship (1763). The adjacent **Ambassador Loeb Visitor Center** (tel: 401-847 4794; call for opening times) explores Rhode Island's tradition of religious tolerance, the history of Jews in colonial and Revolutionary America, and the nation's policy of separation of Church and State. A landmark of colonial Newport is the white clapboard 1725-6 **Trinity Episcopal Church** Ⓒ (tel: 401-846 0660; www.trinitynewport.org; late May–Nov Mon–Sat 10am–4pm, Sun after 10am liturgy 11.30am–12.30pm, only Sun in winter) on Queen

⊙ Tip

The Coastal Wine Trail maps out a route to the regional wineries from Newport to Cape Cod. Pick up a copy at the Newport Visitor Center or download it at www.coastalwinetrail.com.

Newport's Trinity Episcopal Church.

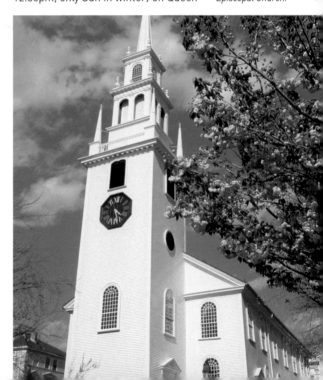

The Cliff Walk in Newport offers views of the water and the famous mansions.

One of the many bedrooms at Marble House.

Anne Square. The chandeliers seem to list to the north, but it is the building which leans, the result of 300 years of resisting winds blowing from the sea.

Many of Newport's attractions, including the famous mansions, line Bellevue Avenue. The 1748–50 **Redwood Library and Atheneum** (50 Bellevue Avenue; tel: 401-847 0292; www.redwoodlibrary.org; Mon–Sat 9.30am–5.30pm, Wed until 8pm, Sun 1–5pm; voluntary donation) is the oldest continuously used library building in the US and contains a collection of portraits of notable colonials.

The 1862 "Stick Style" **Newport Art Museum** (76 Bellevue Avenue; tel: 401-848 8200; www.newportartmuseum.org; Tue–Sat 10am–4pm, Sun noon–4pm) exhibits paintings by luminaries including Winslow Homer and George Innes as well as works by regional artists.

The state-of-the-art **International Tennis Hall of Fame** (194 Bellevue Avenue; tel: 401-849 3990; www.tennisfame.com; Wed–Mon 10am–5pm, until 6pm in summer) is the country's largest tennis museum. It's housed in the Newport Casino, which never had anything to do with gambling, but was America's most exclusive country club when it opened in 1880 and hosted the first US National Tennis Championships the following year. It displays memorabilia, trophies, art, and fashion dealing with tennis from the 12th century to the present. The Hall of Fame Tennis Championships are held in late July (the museum is open to ticket holders only during the tournament).

THE MANSIONS

The Vanderbilts, Astors, and other elite of America's 19th century chose the oceanside real estate of Newport for their summer "cottages." Exercises in conspicuous consumption, they were largely abandoned as fortunes and economics changed. By the 1960s, many were deteriorating shells. Rescued by the **Preservation Society of Newport** (424 Bellevue Avenue; tel: 401-847 1000; www.newportmansions.org; seasons and hours vary greatly, call or check website), many are now maintained as museums of another age. The Society sells a variety of tickets for admission to up to 11 properties. While all of the mansions have guided tours, several now have optional self-guided audio tours. The Society also sells tickets to the dockside **Hunter House** (54 Washington Street), a prosperous merchant's 1748 home, the Topiary Gardens, and organises underground tours of The Breakers mansion basements (see website for details).

Most of the mansions are located on Bellevue Avenue. Directional signs to the area often point to "the cottages," the term the wealthy used for their summer homes. **Kingscote** was the first of the summer cottages, built in Gothic Revival "Stick Style," making playful use of asymmetry and varied textures, sprouting a wealth of pendants, lattices, and gables. It is one of the most intact historical houses in the country, containing the furnishings,

art, and documents of over five generations of the King family.

The coal-rich Edward Julius Berwind commissioned **The Elms** ⊕, built in French Renaissance style, based on Château d'Asnières near Paris. It borrows from a range of styles, including Chinese, Venetian, and Louis XIV.

William S. Wetmore built **Château-sur-Mer** ⊕ in 1852, a confection of Victorian lavishness, and Newport's showiest mansion when built. For a break from the mansion trek, view works by Norman Rockwell, Maxfield Parrish, and N.C. Wyeth, among others, at the **National Museum of American Illustration** ⊕ (492 Bellevue Avenue; tel: 401-851 8949; www.americanillustration.org; Memorial Day–Labor Day 11am–5pm Thu–Sun, rest of the year Fri only; guided tour by advance reservation Fri 3pm).

The Preservation Society of Newport pays the grand sum of $1 a year to rent **The Breakers** ⊕. Considered the most magnificent of the Newport "cottages," this opulent Italian Renaissance palace contains 70 rooms extravagantly adorned with marble, alabaster, gilt, mosaic, crystal, and stained glass. The kitchen alone is the size of a small house. The tour here is more in-depth than most of the others, interpreting The Breakers and the Vanderbilts with respect to their place in America's architecture, society, and culture. Self-guided audio tours are available, which reduces the wait on busy summer days.

Farther along Bellevue Avenue, Mrs Hermann Oelrichs hired Stanford White to design **Rosecliff** ⊕, an imitation of Versailles' Grand Trianon. It has a huge French-style ballroom and a heart-shaped staircase.

Marble House ⊕, another of Hunt's designs, manages to upstage The Breakers for ostentation, although it is not as large. It was built in 1892 for William K. Vanderbilt and styled after the Grand and Petit Trianons of Versailles. A Chinese teahouse stands in the grounds.

Belcourt of Newport ⊕ (tel: 401-846 0669; www.belcourt.com; tours Mon, Wed and Fri at 10am by reservation only) is at 657 Bellevue Avenue. Styled after a Louis XIII hunting lodge at Versailles, the castle has the largest collection of objets d'art of any of the mansions, including a full-size gold coronation coach. Designer Carolyn Rafaelian, who bought the Belcourt in 2012, has instigated a program of renovations, including the installation of a 72-panel solar array. The site reopened in May 2017.

"The Richest Little Girl in the World" spent her summers at **Rough Point** ⊕ (680 Bellevue Avenue; tel: 401-847 8344; www.newportrestoration.org; early Apr–Nov Tue–Sun 9.30am–3.30pm). Doris Duke was the only child of tobacco baron James Duke. When he died in 1925, he left his 12-year-old daughter the bulk of his estate, estimated at somewhere around $80 million. The 49-room mansion was built in 1890, at the height of the Gilded Age. The landscape was created by Frederick Law Olmstead, who designed New York's Central Park. The house is as

Rough Point was one home of the heiress and horticulturalist Doris Duke (1912–93).

The Music Room at The Breakers.

Block Island sells itself as a hideaway destination, unsullied by developers and fast-food chains.

A family farm in Little Compton.

she left it, filled with French furniture, Chinese porcelains, and Turkish carpets. (You can purchase a combination ticket for Rough Point and Whitehorne House on Newport's waterfront, which holds Duke's collection of late-18th-century furnishings.)

Strollers can examine the backyards of the Bellevue Avenue mansions from the **Cliff Walk** (www.cliffwalk.com), a 3.5-mile (5.5km) path that overlooks Rhode Island Sound. Crusty local fishermen saved this path for public use by going to court when wealthy mansion owners tried to close it. Most of the walk is an easy, well-maintained public right-of-way, but the southern portion requires scrambling across rocks which are often slippery and subject to bracing winds. Visitors who don't wish to walk the entire length can start at the end of Narragansett Avenue and reach the water by way of the Forty Steps, partway along the route.

MUSIC EVENTS

During the summer, Newport hosts a number of major outdoor music events, such as the Newport Folk Festival (www.newportfolk.org) and the Newport Jazz Festival (www.newportjazz.org) at **Fort Adams State Park**  (Fort Adams Drive; tel: 401-841 2400; www.riparks.com/Locations/LocationFortAdams.html). Fortifications were first built in the early days of the Revolution; it remained the largest coastal fortification in the US until 1950.

A mile out to sea, the **Rose Island Lighthouse** (tel: 401-847 4242; www.roseislandlighthouse.org; Memorial Day–Labor Day 10am–4pm; $5 landing fee) was abandoned after the Newport Bridge was completed in 1969, restored to its 1912 appearance and using eco-sensitive energy generation. Visitors can spend the night or become "keepers" for a week.

OCEAN DRIVE

One of the region's most magnificent drives extends for 10 miles (16km) around Narragansett Bay to the tip, where the bay meets the Atlantic Ocean, at **Brenton Point State Park** ❸ (www.riparks.com/Locations/

⊙ SCENIC FERRY ROUTES

At Fort Adams, you can catch the Jamestown to Newport ferry (tel: 401-423 9900; www.jamestownnewportferry.com) for a peaceful trip across Newport Harbor to the historic town of Jamestown on Conanicut Island.

Some ferry boats stop off at Rose Island, where a historic lighthouse once guided ships into and around the harbor. Rose Island was once used to store live munitions for the local naval base, so parts of the island are off-limits to visitors. The lighthouse has been restored and offers excellent views of the area.

The ferries also stop at Perrotti Park and Market Square in Newport. Even if you're not traveling between locations, the ferry is a scenic route to see the harbor of Newport.

LocationBrentonPoint.html; sunrise–sunset). There are sweeping views and the rocky shores are great for exploring tidal pools and for sunset-watching.

JAMESTOWN

Just across the Newport Bridge (toll), follow signs to historic **Jamestown** . The southern tip of Conanicut Island offers New England scenery at its most picturesque. In **Beavertail State Park** (Beavertail Road; tel: 401-423 9941; www.riparks.com/Locations/LocationBeavertail.html), the Atlantic coast's third-oldest lighthouse is preserved at **Beavertail Lighthouse and Museum** (tel: 401-423 3270; www.beavertaillight.org; call or visit the website for opening hours).

The 275-acre (110-hectare) **Watson Farm** (455 North Road; tel: 401-423 0005; June–mid-Oct, Tue, Thu, and Sun 1–5pm) on Narragansett Bay has been a working farm since 1787. Visitors can take a self-guided tour, take part in an outdoor workshop, and hike 2 miles (3km) of scenic trails. Just down the road is the 1787 **Jamestown Windmill** (North Main Street; tel: 401-423 0784; http://jamestownhistoricalsociety.org/ptv-detail-windmill/; mid-June–mid-Oct weekends 1–4pm); climb to the top and see the inner workings. On "Windmill Day" – held every even year, the next being 21 July 2018 – the cloths are raised on the sails, which turn in the breeze.

SOUTH COUNTY

From Jamestown, continue west on Route 138 across the graceful Jamestown-Verrazano Bridge to Route 1A, and turn north to **Wickford** ⓫, whose historic waterfront, lined with galleries, shops, and restaurants, is one of the loveliest in Rhode Island. Many of the buildings in town date to the 18th century. A mile north of town is the inappropriately named **Smith's Castle** (55 Richard Smith Drive; tel: 401-294 3521; www.smithscastle.org; tours June–Aug Thu–Sun at noon, 1pm, 2pm and 3pm, May, Sept–mid-Oct Fri–Sun). The three-story clapboard house is one of the country's oldest plantation houses. Originally built in 1678 to garrison soldiers, it now preserves four centuries of Rhode Island history, which docents in period clothing bring to life.

The Jamestown Windmill ground corn from 1787 until 1895.

Newport Bridge leads to Jamestown.

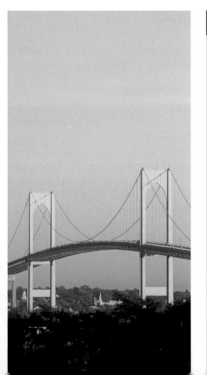

⊘ THE OCEAN STATE

Water dominates the geography of Rhode Island. Only 48 miles long and 37 miles wide (77km by 60km), it claims 400 miles (640km) of coastline. Rhode Island, in the singular, is a misnomer; there are 35 islands within the state, with names as varied as the islands are numerous: Aquidneck (also called Rhode), Block, Conanicut, and Prudence. Others include Hen, Hog, Rabbitt, Boat, Old Boy, Patience, Hope, and Despair.

Using Rhode Island as a base, pirates raided merchant ships in the North Atlantic until a clampdown in the 1720s. Later, Newport was the birthplace of the modern US Navy: President Chester Arthur developed a new fleet – built of steel, rather than wood – in Newport in the early 1880s.

Among the state's distinctions are: America's first textile mill, in Pawtucket, and America's only operational water-powered snuff mill, in Saunderstown. The state boasts the country's first synagogue, its first department store, and its oldest enclosed shopping mall.

Despite the concentrated population, parklands are plentiful. And precisely because the state is so small – it takes less than two hours to drive from one end to the other – a visitor can walk historic city streets in the morning, picnic in an idyllic grove at noon, and savor the delights of the seashore by moonlight.

SOUTH ALONG NARRAGANSETT BAY

Backtrack 5.5 miles (9km) south on Route 1A to **Saunderstown** ⓬. One of early America's most famous portrait artists was born in 1755 at the **Gilbert Stuart Birthplace** (815 Gilbert Stuart Road; tel: 401-294 3001; www.gilbertstuart museum.org; mid-June–Aug daily 10am–3pm, late Apr–mid-June and Sept–early Oct Thu–Mon 10am–3pm). The property encompasses an authentically restored and furnished workingman's house of the period, the country's first snuff mill, a grist mill, a colonial herb garden, and a fish ladder that teems with frantically migrating fish in spring.

To the south on Route 1A, at the town beach in **Narragansett** ⓭, you can stroll along the pier and admire the Twin Towers – the stone structures that are the remains of a casino destroyed by fire in 1900.

Between Narragansett and Point Judith is a skein of fine, sandy state-owned beaches (parking fee).

Whale-watching tours depart from **Point Judith** (for details visit

Block Island has a population of just over 1,000.

www.francesfleet.com). Backtrack a short distance on Route 108, past the entrance for **Captain Roger W. Wheeler State Beach** (tel: 401-789 3563; www.riparks.com/Locations/Location RogerWheeler.html; parking fee) and follow signs to **Galilee** ⓮, the departure point for the ferry to Block Island.

SOUTHWEST

Head north on Route 108 to US Route 1 and continue south along the Block Island Sound. In **South Kingston**, the **Trustom Pond National Wildlife Refuge** ⓯ (1040 Matunuck Schoolhouse Road; www.fws.gov/refuge/trustom_pond) protects the state's only undeveloped salt pond.

To the southwest, in **Charlestown**, more than 250 bird species regularly visit the diverse habitat at the **Ninigret National Wildlife Refuge** ⓰ (50 Bend Road; tel: 401-364 9124; www.fws.gov/refuge/nini).

In **Westerly**, the half-mile **Misquamicut State Beach** ⓱ (tel: 401-596 9097; www.riparks.com/Locations/LocationMis quamicut.html; parking fee) is one of the state's most popular; get there early on a hot summer day. The village of **Watch Hill** ⓲, with its Victorian cottage mansions, shops, and the c.1876 landmark **Flying Horse Carousel**, the oldest in the country, is well worth seeing.

BLOCK ISLAND

When Rhode Islanders want to get away from it all, they head for **Block Island** ⓳, a 3- by 7-mile (5km by 11km) island some 12 miles (19km) south of the entrance to Narragansett Bay. Whereas Newport is packed to the gills with hotels, shops, restaurants, and tourists, Block Island – named by the Nature Conservancy as one of the 12 "last great places" in the western hemisphere – remains a hideaway that holds its own, quite successfully, against developers and fast-food chains.

Narragansett Indians were the first inhabitants. They called it Manisses, which means "Island of the Little God." In 1614, Dutch explorer Adriaen Block spotted it and in an early example of shameless self-promotion, named it after himself. Captain Kidd visited occasionally, although there's no indication he deposited any of his ill-gotten treasures under the sand. Tourists sometimes arrive via planes out of Westerly RI (a 10-minute hop), but most people take the ferry.

The **Block Island Ferry** (tel: 401-783 7996/866-783 7996; www.blockisland ferry.com) offers passenger-only service from Point Judith and Newport's Fort Adams. The schedule changes seasonally. Although it's possible to visit as a day trip, it is worth staying at least overnight. The ferry docks in **Old Harbor**, the island's only town, a charming, small-scale resort. Charter fishing boats line the dock near the ferry.

Visitors come to Block Island for fine beaches, fishing, tranquility, and the romantic allure of aging Victorian hotels with huge verandas and a sense of bygone splendor. The **Spring House** (tel: 401-466 5844; www.springhousehotel. com), on a 15-acre (6-hectare) promontory, opened its doors in 1852; and the **National Hotel** (tel: 401-466 2901/800-225 2449), a majestic wooden ark of a building, opened in 1888 in the heart of Old Harbor. To spend time in either of these two lodgings is to be caught in a time warp.

The **Block Island Historical Society** (Old Town Road; tel: 401-466 2481; www. blockislandhistorical.org), in an 1850 farmhouse, does a good job of recreating the island's farming and seafaring history. Shipwrecks were a recurring event. Many luckless captains and their ships came to misery on the submerged rocks and sandbars around "The Block." The perils of the sea are elaborated upon at the interpretive center in **North Lighthouse** (Corn Neck Road; tel: 401-466 3200; www. newenglandlighthouses.net; late June–mid-Sept daily 10am–5pm, spring and fall weekends only).

The island's beaches include **Surfers Beach**, popular with surfers, as its name suggests; **State Beach** and others on the east are calmer and attract the most visitors. The westerly strands are wind-swept and usually deserted. The Nature Conservancy (www.nature.org) and local groups help to preserve more than 40 percent of the island. Hiking is also very popular. One trek not to be missed is the hike to the magnificently scenic **Mohegan Bluffs**, where the 1874 **Southeast Lighthouse** (www.newenglandlighthouses. net/block-island-southeast-lighthouse.html) perches above the cliffs. The legend that the Mohegan tribe was driven off the cliffs by a rival tribe is a fabrication. On the island's south side, **Rodman's Hollow** is a 230-acre (90-hectare) swath of conserved land formed more than 20,000 years ago by glacial meltwater.

When the kids have had enough ice cream and body surfing, visit **1661 Farm and Gardens** (1 Spring Street; tel: 401-466 2421), behind the 1661 Boutique Inn (https://blockislandresorts.com). It has an exotic menagerie, including camels, llamas, emus, sheep, and donkeys.

Block Island has many fine beaches. At Fred Benson Town Beach and Ballard's Beach there are lifeguards on duty.

⊙ ON THE WATER

The refreshing, salt-tinged air brings out the latent sailor in even the most untested landlubber. There are almost as many scenic cruises as there are seagulls in Narragansett Bay. Perhaps the most economical way to tour Narragansett Bay is on the Jamestown–Newport ferry. The boats follow a circuit across the bay, including three piers in Newport. An all-day round-trip ticket gets reduced admission to Rose Island, Fort Adams, and the Museum of Yachting. Narrated cruises tell the tales of Newport's role in merchant shipping, naval warfare, and competitive sailing.

Indulge in Newport's nefarious past with a tour on a motor yacht once used by bootleggers (www.cruisenewport.com), sample the thrill of the America's Cup with a sail on a Cup contender (www.12metercharters.com), or see 10 lighthouses up close on a narrated tour (www.rhodeislandbaycruises.com). Whale watchers should contact Frances Fleet (www.francesfleet.com) for July and August tours. You can rent sail and motor boats at Wickford Boat Rentals (tel: 401-295-0050; www.wickfordboatrentals.com). Those who want to learn how to sail should consider a multiday course at the Newport Sailing School and Tours (www.newportsailing.com) or Sail Newport (www.sailnewport.org).

NEWPORT'S MANSIONS

Newport, a 19th-century summer playground for the rich and famous, became a showplace for America's greatest architects and designers.

With the coming of the railways in the mid-19th century, vacationing became ever more popular, and the delights of Newport, set on an island with a fine summer climate, became readily accessible from New York and Boston. Wealthy and influential families began to spend their summers here. Many had made vast fortunes from industry and began to lavish unstinting funds on creating opulent summer homes, where they would entertain and impress all those who mattered.

The country's most innovative architects – names such as Stanford White and Richard Morris Hunt – were employed, creating designs that reflect the full range of styles in vogue at the time. Building materials and furnishings were often imported from Europe (for Marble House, for instance, different colored marbles were imported from Italy to be worked by Italian craftsmen in Newport). Interior decor frequently borrowed from European or Far Eastern styles; fine paintings, furnishings, and objets d'art collected from around the world filled the rooms.

Nine of these mansions are now maintained by The Preservation Society of Newport (www.newport mansions.org) and are open to the public.

The enormous dining room at The Breakers. The carved oak table was designed to seat up to 34 people and above it hang two Baccarat crystal chandeliers.

The Elms, at 367 Bellevue Avenue, replicates a two-story château near Paris, with the servants' quarters placed behind the roof balustrade and the kitchens located in a cellar. It was built in 1901 for the coal baron Edward Julius Berwind, the son of German immigrants.

Ochre Court, a Beaux-Arts mansion built in 1892. It is now owned by the local Salve Regina University. Only The Breakers is larger.

ball held at Beechwood.

A portrait of Cornelius Vanderbilt II by Daniel Huntington.

Legacy of the Vanderbilts

The Breakers was commissioned in 1893 by Cornelius Vanderbilt II to replace an earlier house destroyed by fire. Vanderbilt, chairman of the New York Central railway and a director of 49 other railways, was the head of America's wealthiest family. His younger brother, William, had inherited equal shares in the family fortunes, some part of which he spent building Marble House, on nearby Bellevue Avenue. A serious, modest, and gentle man, Cornelius II gave free rein and an unlimited budget to Richard Morris Hunt, the architect of Marble House and of the grand Vanderbilt houses on Fifth Avenue in New York. Hunt followed the Italian Renaissance layout adopted for 16th-century palaces, where rooms were grouped symmetrically around a central courtyard. With 70 rooms, including 33 for resident staff and visitors' servants, The Breakers is Newport's largest "cottage." Vanderbilt died in 1899, aged 55, four years after the house was completed.

The Breakers was designed by architect Richard Morris Hunt, who took his inspiration from the 16th-century palaces of Genoa and Turin, and employed an international team of builders.

CONNECTICUT

This historic state of Connecticut offers maritime traditions along its coast, rural charm in its hillside villages, and the sites of early patriotism and social reforms.

⊙ Main Attractions

Wadsworth Atheneum
  Museum of Art
Mark Twain House
The Litchfield Hills
Kent Falls State Park
Gillette Castle
Philip Johnson's Glass
  House
Yale University
Mystic Seaport

Maps on pages
234, 236

Connecticut's picturesque colonial villages, with their carefully kept, white clapboard homes and manicured lawns, evoke an image of quiet wealth, propriety, and old school ties. Its dollar-savvy Puritan founders left a legacy of sharp business acumen which has served the state well. But there is also a great pride in the place and a heartfelt sense of its history.

With Long Island Sound as its southern border, Connecticut roughly forms a rectangle measuring 90 miles (145km) from east to west and 55 miles

(89km) north to south. The Connecticut River bisects the state; along with the Thames and Housatonic rivers, they were vital avenues of settlement and industrialization.

THE STATE CAPITAL

The skyline of **Hartford ❶**, Connecticut's capital, is dominated by the towering headquarters of the nation's largest insurance companies. So many insurance firms are located here that the city calls itself the Insurance Capital of the World. Mergers and other economic factors have reduced the number in recent years; health care and education have filled the gap. Those two areas are responsible for approximately 25 percent of the jobs in the city.

Settled in 1635 and Connecticut's oldest city, Hartford has always maintained political, economic, and social pre-eminence. In 1662, a royal charter was drawn up uniting the colonies of Hartford and New Haven and guaranteeing their independence. Sir Edmund Andros, appointed governor of all New England in 1687, had the charter revoked. In defiance, colonists stole the charter and hid it in the trunk of an oak tree at the center of the town. Two years later, on the accession of William III, Andros was recalled to England, and the charter was reinstated.

The State Capitol.

A plaque at Charter Oak Place, in the south end of the city, marks the spot where the magnificent oak stood until 1856, when a windstorm felled it. That's the tree featured on the Connecticut state quarter.

The **Greater Hartford Convention and Visitors Bureau** (31 Pratt Street; tel: 860-728 6789) and the visitors' information desk at Old State House (800 Main Street; tel: 860-522 6766; Mon–Sat 9am–5pm, Sun noon–5pm) both distribute a free guide that includes a map and walking tour of the city.

OLD STATE HOUSE

Begin at the **Old State House A**, at the intersection of Main Street and Asylum Avenue (800 Main Street; tel: 860-522 6766; www.cga.ct.gov/osh/; 10am–5pm Columbus Day–July 3 Mon–Fri, rest of the year Tue–Sat; guided and self-guided tours). Built in 1796, it is one of the nation's oldest state house buildings, although it has been replaced as the active center of state government by the State Capitol building. The building was the site of the 1839 *La Amistad* slave-ship mutiny trial.

The interactive, multimedia presentation *History is All Around Us*, on the lower floor, is an introduction to 300 years of Connecticut history. In 1798, lawmakers shared the building with **Joseph Steward's Museum of Curiosities** (Mon–Fri 9am–5pm). The reconstruction of the room that displayed things like a two-headed calf and the alleged mummified hand of Ramses is on the second floor. The city's oldest historic site is the **Ancient Burying Ground B** (corner Gold and Main streets; maps at the Main Street gate; http://theancientburyingground.org/; self-guided walking tours available, see website for details). Between 1648 and the early 19th century, it was Hartford's first and foremost graveyard. Around 6,000 people are interred here, the oldest gravestones dating from 1648.

WADSWORTH ATHENEUM

Directly to the south, also on Main Street, is the **Wadsworth Atheneum Museum of Art C**, America's oldest continually operating public art museum (600 Main Street; tel: 860-278 2670; Wed–Sun 11am–5pm). Housed in five buildings – themselves historically and architecturally significant – the museum has Greek and Roman antiquities, Baroque, Impressionist, modernist, and surrealist paintings, Hudson River landscapes, and American decorative arts. Sculptor Alexander Calder's 50ft (15-meter) -high red stabile, *Stegosaurus*, dominates the plaza. The **Amistad Center for Art and Culture** (www.amistadcenter.org), located within the Atheneum, concentrates on the African-American experience from slavery through the civil rights movement.

THE STATE CAPITOL

Perched on Capitol Hill, the white marble, gold-domed **Connecticut State Capitol D** (210 Capitol Avenue; tel: 860-240 0222; tours Mon–Fri 8am–5pm; for more information go to https://

⊘ Tip

You can hop aboard the free downtown Hartford Star Shuttle, which passes every 12 minutes Mon–Fri 7am–11pm, and Sat 3–11pm. It stops at or within a short walk of most major attractions including Bushnell Park, the Atheneum, Convention Center, Riverwalk, Arts District, and Science Center. See its route at www.hartfordtransit.org.

A gallery in the Wadsworth Atheneum.

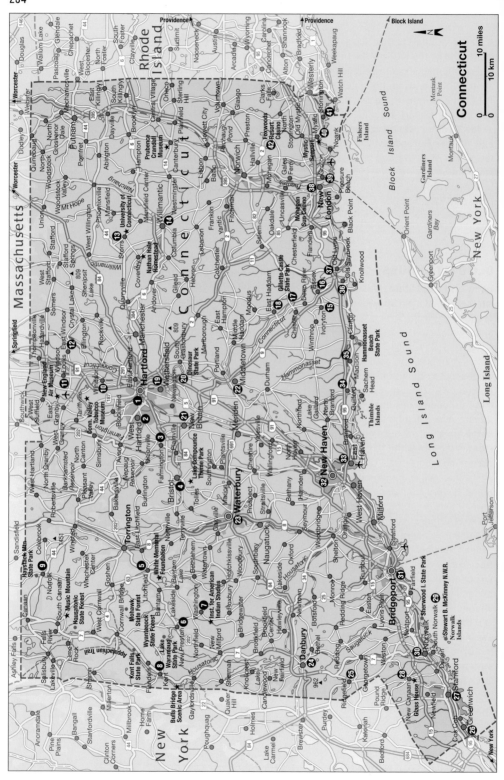

Connecticut

wp.cga.ct.gov/CapitolTours/) is an 1878 Gothic wedding cake of turrets, gables, porches, and towers. Its ornate interiors of hand-painted columns, marble floors, and elaborate stained-glass windows were designed to reflect the prosperity of the community it served. The Hall of Fame honors outstanding Connecticut locals like Jackie Robinson, Paul Newman, and Marian Anderson.

The Capitol overlooks 41-acre (17-hectare) **Bushnell Park** Ⓔ (tel: 860-232 6710; http://bushnellpark.org; historical tours of the park start in Apr), a pleasant urban oasis. The Gothic brownstone **Soldiers and Sailors Memorial Arch** (tel: 860-522 6400; free guided tours May–Oct Thu noon) honors the 4,000 Connecticut residents who fought in the Civil War. A climb up the 96 steps gives a panoramic view of the park.

In the late 19th century, there were nearly 3,000 carousels gracefully spinning in parks. The hand-carved horses were considered works of art, with Solomon Stein's and Harry Goldstein's among the best. Their **1914 carousel** (tel: 860-585 5411; May–mid-Oct Sat–Sun 11am–5pm), with 48 carved wooden steeds, carries riders accompanied by music from a Wurlitzer band organ. Free concerts are held in summer at the outdoor performance pavilion on the park's west side.

The **Bushnell Center for the Performing Arts** Ⓕ (166 Capitol Avenue; tel: 860-987 5900; www.bushnell.org), Connecticut's premier performing arts center, has an impressive program of concerts, ballet, opera, and theater all year. To the south of the Capitol is the **State Library** (a treasury of documents and archives for researchers) and the **Museum of Connecticut History** Ⓖ (231 Capitol Avenue; tel: 860-757 6535; www.museumofcthistory.org/hours.asp; Mon–Fri 9am–4pm, Sat 9am–2pm; free). Exhibits include the state's 1662 royal charter, the Mitchelson Coin Collection (with one of every coin ever minted in the US), and an extensive collection of Colt firearms.

Travelers' Tower Ⓗ, renovated at a cost of $30 million between 2012 and 2014, has an observation deck giving a good view of the Hartford area.

The **Butler-McCook House and Garden and Main Street History Center** Ⓘ (396 Main Street; tel: 860-522 1806; www.ctlandmarks.org/butler-mccook; noon–4pm May–Sept Thu–Sun and Oct–Dec Sat–Sun) was home to this family of physicians, missionaries, and social reformers from 1782 to 1971. It is one of the best-documented homes in America and shows how life along Main Street changed from the American Revolution through the mid-20th century.

The **Connecticut Science Center** Ⓙ (250 Columbus Boulevard; tel: 860-724 3623; www.ctsciencecenter.org; standard hours 10am–5pm, see website for details) has 150 hands-on activities which concentrate on sports science and inventing tools for people with visual or hearing obstacles.

MARK TWAIN HOUSE

Hartford's most famous resident, Samuel Langhorne Clemens, was better known

Bushnell Park, named after local pastor Horace Bushnell (1802–76).

Mark Twain House.

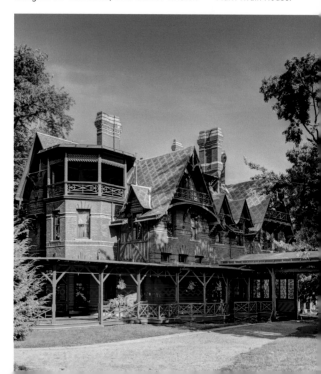

by his pen name, Mark Twain. Clemens thought Hartford was the loveliest city he'd ever seen and had a house built here in 1884. It is now the **Mark Twain House and Museum** Ⓚ (351 Farmington Avenue; tel: 860-280 3142; www.marktwainhouse.org; guided tours only daily 9.30am–5.30pm, last tour starts at 4.30pm, closed Tue Jan–Feb).

The 25-room mansion is a wonderful, whimsical display of Victorian Gothic indulgence. Outdoor porches and balconies give the impression of a Mississippi riverboat, while the grand interiors feature design elements by Tiffany. Clemens/Twain wrote his most famous works, *The Adventures of Huckleberry Finn*, *Tom Sawyer*, *The Prince and the Pauper*, and *A Connecticut Yankee in King Arthur's Court* in the handsome billiard room. The optional tour of the servants' wing gives insights into Victorian-era manners (additional charge). Tours fill quickly. They cycle generally every half-hour.

The museum features an introductory film by Ken Burns on Twain's life and influence on social issues and literature. There are displays of the family's personal items and a 12-volume set of his works in Russian. The building is the first museum in the country (and the first structure of any kind in Connecticut) to meet Leadership in Energy and Environmental Design (LEED) specifications, something Clemens, who deeply loved the natural world, would have appreciated.

HARRIET BEECHER STOWE CENTER

Clemens' neighbor was Harriet Beecher Stowe, author of *Uncle Tom's Cabin*. She lived next door in a 14-room Gothic Revival home built in 1871 by friend and abolitionist Franklin Chamberlin. She moved there in 1873 and wrote several of her later works in the house. Her restored house is a part of the **Harriet Beecher Stowe Center** Ⓛ (77 Forest Street; tel: 860-522 9258; www.harrietbeecherstowecenter.org; Mon–Sat 9.30am–5pm, Sun noon–5pm). The tour gives a glimpse into Stowe's personal life and her preference for informal homemaking, something at odds with prevailing Victorian pretence.

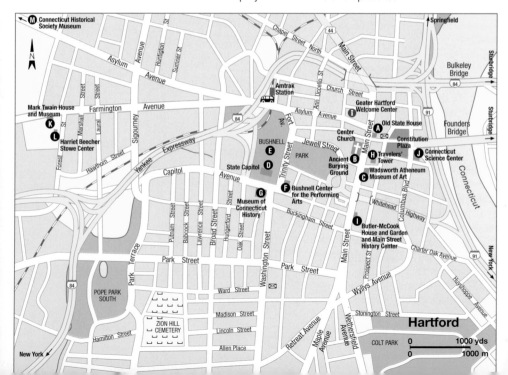

The neighborhood where Clemens and Stowe lived is called "Nook Farm." It was a fashionable community of abolitionists, suffragettes, actors, and social activists. The self-guided walking tour available at the Center introduces influential characters most people have never heard of.

The **Connecticut Historical Society Museum**  (1 Elizabeth Street; tel: 860-236 5621; https://chs.org/; Tue–Thu noon–5pm and Fri–Sat 9am–5pm) has a lot of interactive displays of Connecticut history from 1500 to the present. Visitors can work on a World War II assembly line, replace bobbins in a textile mill, and sew an American Indian moccasin.

WEST HARTFORD

In **West Hartford** ❷, a 2.5-acre (1-hectare) rose garden with 15,000 bushes is the centerpiece of **Elizabeth Park** (915 Prospect Avenue; tel: 860-757 9970; http://elizabethparkct.org; daily sunrise–sunset; donations appreciated). Rambling roses cover archways over paths that meander past borders and fences covered with climbing and shrub roses. The Heritage Garden was planted with 100 old rose varieties that fully bloomed in 2017 – the centennial of the Connecticut Valley Garden Club.

NOAH WEBSTER HOUSE

The author of the first American dictionary (1828) lived at what is now **the Noah Webster House and West Hartford Historical Society** (227 South Main Street; tel: 860-521 5362; www.noahwebsterhouse.org; guided tours daily 1–4pm). The dictionary, now revered, was not initially a big seller, and Webster had to mortgage his home to bring out a second edition. Informative displays examine Webster's influence on government and education, creation of a national language, and his personal life. Other exhibits look at the development of Hartford, with stations where you can sniff the aromas of the area's varied culinary traditions and listen to local musicians.

THE CHILDREN'S MUSEUM

The Children's Museum (950 Trout Brook Drive, exit 43 off I-84; tel: 860-231 2824; www.thechildrensmuseumct.org; Tue–Sat 9am–4pm, Sun from 11am) has lots of creative, hands-on exhibits, live animals, and space and science shows in the digital planetarium. Outside, a 60ft (18.2-meter) replica sperm whale sprays water through his blowhole on hot summer days.

WEST OF HARTFORD

Take I-84 south to exit 39 to **Farmington** ❸, 10 miles (16km) west of Hartford. Often called one of the loveliest towns in New England, its elegant 18th- and 19th-century mansions display untouched architectural detail.

A particular gem is the **Hill-Stead Museum** (35 Mountain Road; tel: 860-677 4787; www.hillstead.org; guided tours Tue–Sun 10am–4pm). The 19-room, Colonial Revival home on 150 acres (60 hectares) was the retirement home

Hartford's Riverfest, which includes concerts and parades, is held every July.

A summer festival in the grounds of Hill-Stead Museum.

Eat

If you're attending an Elizabeth Park concert either bring a picnic to the concert, or make reservations at the Pond House Café (tel: 860-231 8823; www.pondhousecafe. com; lunch and dinner Tue–Sat, Sat–Sun brunch). This moderately priced restaurant on the park grounds offers an eclectic menu and alfresco dining.

of industrialist Alfred Atmore Pope, a friend of the artist Mary Cassatt and a great admirer of French Impressionism. As much an art gallery as a residence, scattered throughout the mansion are a number of familiar canvases, including paintings from Monet's *Haystack* series, Manet's *The Guitar Lady*, and Degas's *The Tub*.

The **Stanley-Whitman House** (37 High Street; tel: 860-677 9222; www.stanleywhitman.org; Wed–Sun noon–4pm; last tour begins at 3.15pm) is a living-history center that invites visitors to immerse themselves in early colonial life by using everyday objects. The museum also maintains Memento Mori, the town's "ancient burying ground," with the earliest gravestone dating to 1685.

BRISTOL

Continue south on I-84 to exit 34 to **Bristol ❹**. The town was a 19th-century clockmaking capital, producing more than 200,000 clocks in a single year. The **American Clock and Watch Museum** (100 Maple Street; tel: 860-583 6070;

daily 10am–5pm) displays watches and clocks dating from 1595, including a two-story tower clock and the finest collection of American-manufactured timepieces in the world. The chiming and striking of the clocks on the hour is musical, synchronized audio chaos. Don't miss the sundial garden outside.

One of the most extensive collections of hand-carved, antique and contemporary carousel horses and band organs is featured at the **New England Carousel Museum** (95 Riverside Avenue; tel: 860-585 5411; www.thecarouselmuseum.org; Wed–Sat 10am–5pm, Sun noon–5pm). The museum is housed in the **Bristol Center for Arts and Culture**, which is also home to the **Museum of Fire History** (www.thecarouselmuseum.org/museum-of-fire-history), displaying firehouse memorabilia, and several art galleries.

Two wooden roller coasters and an antique 1911 carousel are the classic highlights among 50 rides at **Lake Compounce Theme Park** (186 Enterprise, exit 31 off I-84; tel: 860-583 3300; www.lakecompounce.com; hours vary daily – see website for calendar). There are also daredevil and kiddie rides and live shows. Splash Harbor Water Park, the state's only water park, is located here.

THE LITCHFIELD HILLS

In the northwest corner of Connecticut, the wooded Litchfield Hills are dotted with quintessential New England villages, covered bridges, and the tumbling stone walls of forgotten farms. Through it runs the **Housatonic River**, crystal clear and freckled with trout, and excellent for canoeing. Hikers may want to follow the Appalachian Trail from Kent to Salisbury and Mt Frissell.

Litchfield ❺, 35 miles (56km) from Hartford, is dominated by a spacious green, graced by the tall-steepled Congregational Church. During the Revolution, it housed Loyalist prisoners and was a depot for military supplies. The

The First Congregational Church of Litchfield.

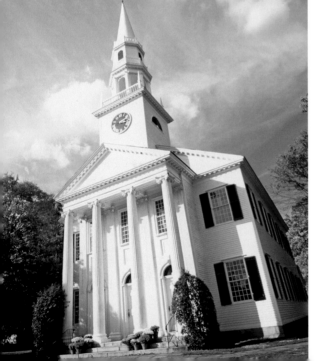

town's rich history is documented at the excellent **Litchfield History Museum** (7 South Street; tel: 860-567 4501; www. litchfieldhistoricalsociety.org; mid-Apr–Nov Tue–Sat 11am–5pm, Sun 1–5pm; free). Further along the same street is the **Tapping Reeve House and Litchfield Law School**, the nation's first school of law (82 South Street, Route 63; same hours as the Litchfield Museum; free), where visitors learn about student life in the early 19th century through role-playing and interpretive exhibits.

Just east of town, off Route 118, is Connecticut's first winery, **Haight-Brown Vineyard** (29 Chestnut Hill Road; tel: 860-567 4045; www.haight vineyards.com; Thu–Fri noon–5pm, Sat until 6pm, Sun until 5.30pm). They produce a wide range of wines, from a dry, barrel-fermented Chardonnay to late-harvest Vidals and Vignoles.

Head south out of Litchfield for 3.5 miles (6km) on Route 63 to **White Flower Farm** (167 Litchfield Road, Morris; tel: 800-503 9624; www.white flowerfarm.com; daily 9am–4.30pm during the gardening season), where something is always in bloom in the 5 acres (2 hectares) of display gardens.

White Memorial Foundation, 2 miles (3.2km) west of Litchfield on Route 202/Whitehall Road (tel: 860-567 0857; www.whitememorialcc.org; museum: Mon–Sat 9am–5pm, Sun noon–5pm; grounds and trails open year-round 24 hours a day), the state's largest nature conservation center, encompasses 4,000 acres (1,600 hectares) and includes 35 miles (56km) of trails. The Museum uses dioramas with mounted specimens to interpret local natural history.

LAKE WARAMAUG

Continue south on Route 202 for approximately 6 miles (10km) to **New Preston ⑥**, a tiny, picturesque town, and continue north on Route 45 for 5 miles (8km) to **Lake Waramaug State Park** (30 Lake Waramaug Road; tel:

860-868 0220; daily 8am–sunset), a tranquil hideaway with a swimming beach and canoe and kayak rentals.

WASHINGTON

To the southeast, on Route 47 is the magnificently preserved town of **Washington ⑦**, home to three historic districts, a select group of fine shops, and several private schools (including The Gunnery, founded in 1850 with students from 15 countries and 20 states).

Continue onto Route 199 to the turn-off for the **Institute for American Indian Studies** (38 Curtis Road; tel: 860-868 0518; http://iaismuseum.org/; Wed–Sat 10am–5pm, Sun noon–5pm), dedicated to the stewardship of American Indian culture. Exhibits trace the 10,000-year history of Connecticut's American Indian population. Outside, there's a model Algonquin village, a replicated archaeological dig, and a garden with medicinal plants.

WEST TO KENT

The Housatonic Valley has one of its most dramatic moments in the town

Lake Waramaug, named after an Indian chief of the Wyantenock tribe, has an average depth of 22ft (7 meters).

The West Cornwall Bridge, built in 1864.

You can canoe, kayak, or raft down the Housatonic from Clarke Outdoors' in West Cornwall (tel: 860-672 6365).

Serenity at Tyler Lake, Goshen.

of **Kent** at **Kent Falls State Park** (Route 7; tel: 860-927 3238; summer 8am–7pm, rest of the year 8am–sunset), where water tumbles 250ft (76 meters) down a natural stone staircase. There's also a covered bridge. In fall foliage season, the colors are extraordinary.

Dip south on Route 7, where an easy trail from the parking lot gives access to the handsome covered bridge, waterfalls, and rapids at **Bulls Bridge Scenic Area** (http://berkshirehiking.com/hikes/bulls_bridge.html). A hiking trail connects with the Appalachian Trail.

To the north on Route 7, in **West Cornwall**, a much photographed 1836 covered bridge spans the Housatonic.

At **Falls Village**, Music Mountain (Gordon Hall; tel: 860-824 7126; www.music mountain.org) hosts the country's oldest continuing summer chamber music festival. The 120-acre (48-hectare) property encompasses Gordon Hall, known for its excellent acoustics and a setting that allows concertgoers to enjoy the natural surroundings as well as the music. Most of the chamber music concerts are held on Sunday afternoons; Saturday evenings feature jazz.

Norfolk, on Route 44 almost on the border with Massachusetts, is another classic town with handsome 18th-century homes clustered around a tidy green. The **Ellen Battell Stoeckel Estate** (Routes 44 and 272; tel: 860-542 3000; charge for concerts) hosts Yale University's renowned **Norfolk Chamber Music Festival** (http://norfolk.yale. edu). Buy tickets well in advance, and bring a picnic.

On a clear day you can almost see forever – or at least to Long Island Sound and the Berkshires – from the top of the 34ft (12-meter) tower at the top of 1,716ft (523-meter) Haystack Mountain. A road in **Haystack Mountain State Park** (385 Burr Mountain Road, Route 272; tel: 860-482 1817; open 8am–sunset) goes halfway up the mountain, and from there it's a rather rugged half-mile hike to the summit.

NORTH OF HARTFORD

In the 1920s and 1930s, more than 35,000 acres (14,000 hectares) of land along the Connecticut River Valley between Hartford and the Massachusetts border were devoted to growing shade tobacco for cigar wrappers. Today, much of the land is covered by houses, but a few farmers carry on; Connecticut wrappers are still considered the world's best.

The importance of the now-declining industry to the region is well told in **Windsor** at the **Luddy/Taylor Connecticut Valley Tobacco Museum** (Northwest Park, 135 Lang Road; exit 38 off I-91; tel: 860-285 1888; www. tobaccohistsoc.org; Mar–mid-Dec Thu–Fri noon–4pm, Sat 10am–4pm). Nearby is "Elmwood," the beautifully preserved 1780 **Oliver Ellsworth Homestead** (778 Palisado Avenue, Route 159; tel: 860-688 8717; www.ellsworthhomesteaddar.org; mid-May–mid-Oct, check website for detailed information). Expelled from Yale for his "pranks," he made good,

eventually becoming the third Chief Justice of the US Supreme Court. His house is furnished with beautiful antiques of the period. The grounds of the 12-acre (5-hectare) estate are graced with stately oak, beech, and mulberry trees.

Cheek by jowl with Bradley International Airport in **Windsor Locks** ⓫ is the **New England Air Museum** (36 Perimeter Road, exit 40 off I-91; tel: 860-623 3305; www.neam.org; daily 10am–5pm), a must for aviation buffs. The three massive hangars hold over 125 aircraft – including WWII gliders, a B-29, a replica of the pudgy Gee Bee air racer, and a Lockheed Electra that's a twin of the one Amelia Earhart flew – and thousands of aviation artifacts from posters and charts to flight suits and simulators. Just down the road at the **Connecticut Firefighters Memorial** (34 Perimeter Road), an eternal flame burns atop a granite base to commemorate those who died in the line of duty. In **East Windsor** ⓬, the history of firefighting is chronicled at the **Connecticut Fire Museum** (230 Pine Street, Manchester; tel: 860-649 9436; www.thefiremuseum.

org; mid-Apr–mid-Nov Fri–Sat noon–4pm; voluntary donation). Appropriately housed in a 1901 firehouse, it's filled with pumpers and ladder trucks, as well as leather fire buckets and other firefighting memorabilia. A ticket to the museum also includes a visit to the **Connecticut Trolley Museum** (tel: 860-627 6540; www.ct-trolley.org; Apr–Dec, see website or call for opening times), located next door. The highlight is riding a variety of antique trolleys on a 3-mile (5km) journey (trolley rides start at 10.30am and run regularly throughout the day until 4pm).

THE QUIET CORNER

The Nutmeg State's relatively unheralded northeastern region has been dubbed the "Quiet Corner." The best way to enjoy the small, scenic villages is to "shun pike" – avoid the well-traveled highways and explore the meandering byways.

For a small town, **Storrs** ⓭ has much to offer. The extensive campus of the **University of Connecticut** is located here, and it encompasses numerous

The Connecticut River Museum.

The Thread City Crossing in Willimantic is known as Frog Bridge.

⊘ THE SCULPTURE MILE

Walk along the main streets of Madison and you'll enjoy a unique outdoor art exhibit. The Sculpture Mile brings world-class sculpture by nationally recognized artists to the "living museum" of a town. You expect to see artwork along the shopping district or in front of municipal buildings, but they have also been instituted beside parking lots and on the lawns of churches. The idea is to present art to people who would not usually visit art galleries or museums; "touching" the pieces is actually encouraged. The styles and materials are as varied as the locations: traditional to abstract; bronze to steel; granite to wood. The 30 pieces are refreshed annually. Other Connecticut towns are adopting the program. For information, visit www.hollycroft.org.

Sculpture Mile, Madison, CT.

William Gillette's will stated that his castle should not be sold to any "blithering sap-head who has no conception of where he is."

museums. The **William Benton Museum of Art** (245 Glenbrook Road; tel: 860-486 4520; http://benton.uconn.edu; Tue–Sun; voluntary donation) hosts a wide variety of temporary exhibits during the year. The **Connecticut Museum of Natural History** (2019 Hillside Road; tel: 860-486 4460; Tue–Fri 10am-4.30pm, Sat–Sun 1-4.30pm; voluntary donation) is the repository of a vast collection of Connecticut American Indian, colonial, and industrial artifacts. The **Archaeology Center** uses "story stations" to integrate Connecticut's natural and social history. The **Ballard Museum of Puppetry** (1 Royce Circle; tel: 860-486 8580; https://bimp.uconn.edu/; Tue–Sun 11am–7pm; donation) is a magical place filled with puppets, marionettes, and shadow figures from Bali, Italy, Java, and beyond. The **Jorgensen Center for the Performing Arts** (2132 Hillside Road, UConn campus; tel: 860-486 4226; https://jorgensen.uconn.edu/Online/default.asp) has a dynamic schedule of classical and contemporary music and dance.

Dip southwest to **Coventry** and the **Nathan Hale Homestead** (2299 South Street; tel: 860-742 6917; www.ctvisit.com/listings/nathan-hale-homestead-1776; May and Oct Sat–Sun noon-4pm, June–Sept Wed–Sat noon-4pm, Sun 11am–4pm), the family home of the official state hero, hanged as a spy by the British in 1776. Adjacent is the 1730 **Strong-Porter House Museum** (2382 South Street; tel: 860-742 1419; www.ctcoventryhistoricalsociety.org; June–Oct Sun noon–3pm; voluntary donation). A reconstructed two-story barn, carriage shed, and carpenter shop give a glimpse into rural life of the times. The museum is particularly proud of their "accurately reconstructed" privy. **Willimantic** , is home to the **Connecticut Eastern Railroad Museum** (55 Bridge Street; tel: 860-456 9999; www.cteastrrmuseum.org; May–Oct Sat 10am–4pm, Sun noon–4pm). Exhibits housed in vintage railroad buildings include locomotives, rolling stock, and a reconstructed roundhouse.

The **Windham Textile and History Museum** (411 Main Street; tel: 860-456 2178; www.millmuseum.org; Fri–Sun 10am–4pm) demonstrates how the experiences of craftspeople, workers, designers, and consumers influenced the technology, immigration, and culture of Connecticut.

To the east in **Canterbury**, the **Prudence Crandall Museum** (Junction Routes 14 and 169; tel: 860-546 7800; May–Oct Thu–Sun 10am–4pm, rest of the year by appointment) was the home of Connecticut's Official Heroine. In 1833, she admitted an African-American woman to her boarding school. The town reacted by passing a law forbidding her to accept African-American students. She was arrested for refusing to obey the law. When her conviction was overturned, a mob attacked the building, forcing her to close the school and leave Connecticut, eventually settling in Kansas. In 1886, the Connecticut legislature awarded her a pension, while the citizens of Canterbury signed a petition apologizing for their actions.

ALONG THE RIVER VALLEY

Beginning as a mountain stream near the New Hampshire–Canada border, the Connecticut River travels 410 miles (660km) through four states and ends its journey to the sea as a broad and majestic tidal estuary. The American Indians named it Quinnituckett, which means "the long, tidal river." Throughout history, the Connecticut River has linked valley residents with the outside world. A fertile floodplain nourishes crops, and water power has generated energy for small industries.

Begin a tour of the valley in **Ivoryton** ⑮, a center of piano-making 100 years ago which takes its name from the material used to make the keys.

The historic **Ivoryton Playhouse** (103 Main Street; tel: 860-767 7318; www.ivorytonplayhouse.org) was the first self-supporting stock theatre in the country. Katherine Hepburn, Alan Alda, and Marlon Brando, among other stars, have trod the boards here. Down the road, the **Museum of Fife and Drum** (62 North Main Street; tel: 860-767 2237; https://companyoffifeanddrum.org/museum/museum) presents a visual and musical history of America on parade from the Revolutionary War to the present. Free concerts are presented Tuesday evenings in July–August.

ESSEX

Essex ⑯, founded in 1645, was an important shipbuilding center during the 18th century. The *Oliver Cromwell*, America's first warship, was launched here in 1776. Yachts and cabin cruisers still berth here, and tall masts and yards of tackle lend the town a distinctly nautical air. The **Connecticut River Museum** (67 Main Street; tel: 860-767 8269; www.ctrivermuseum.org; 10am–5pm winter Tue–Sun, summer daily) highlights the importance of the Connecticut for transportation, recreation, and as a resource with exhibits, boats, and a replica of the *Turtle*, the nation's first submarine. A combination ticket includes a cruise on the museum's schooner, the *Mary E*. There are also eagle-watch cruises in February and March.

Take an old-fashioned journey by steam locomotive and riverboat by means of the **Essex Steam Train and Riverboat Ride** (1 Railroad Avenue; tel: 860-767 0103; www.essexsteamtrain.com; mid-May–Oct with varied schedule). You board a 1920s coach car and ride along the river through the villages of **Chester** and **Deep River**. At Deep River, passengers board a riverboat for a 90-minute cruise. The round trip takes about 2.5 hours.

Head north on Route 154 and east on Route 148 to the **Chester-Hadlyme Ferry** (54 Ferry Road; tel: 860-443 3856; weekdays 7am–6.45pm). It has been transporting people across the Connecticut River to East Haddam since 1769.

GILLETTE CASTLE

Crossing the river, you can't miss seeing the spectacularly eccentric **Gillette Castle** at **Gillette Castle State Park** ⑰ (67 River Road; tel: 860-526 2336;

◎ Drink

The Connecticut Wine Trail is a self-guided driving tour to 25 wineries in the state. One advantage of Connecticut's small size is that you are never more than 45 minutes from a vineyard. The brochure and map is available at wine shops, tourist centers, or at www.ctwine.com.

The Essex Steam Train.

Tarrywile Mansion, a community center in Danbury, is a large recreation area with picnic spots and 21 miles (34km) of hiking trails.

Dinosaur State Park.

castle Memorial Day–Labor Day Thu–Sun 11am–5pm; grounds daily year-round 8am–sunset; charge for castle tours). William Gillette (1853–1937) was a much admired American actor whose stage portrayal of Sherlock Holmes brought him fame and fortune.

For his dream house, the actor selected a hilltop aerie overlooking the Connecticut River and its surrounding countryside. Work on the 122-acre (49-hectare) site with its stone-and-concrete castle began in 1914, took five years, and cost more than $1 million. The results are whimsical and bizarre. He installed hidden mirrors so that he could spy on public rooms from the master bedroom. The park's 184 acres (75 hectares) have hiking trails and fine views of the river.

North on Route 82 is the charming Victorian town of **East Haddam** . The 1876 **Goodspeed Opera House** (tel: 860-873 8668; www.goodspeed.org), which sits majestically on the banks of the Connecticut River, was a popular stopover in the heyday of steamboat travel. Beautifully restored, it

is considered the incubator for new musicals. *Man of La Mancha* and *Annie* are just two shows which premiered here. Its schedule includes revivals of Broadway musicals, as well as original productions (productions Apr–Dec).

It's worth stopping for a quick visit at the one-room **Nathan Hale Schoolhouse** (29 Main Street; tel: 860-873 3399; Wed–Sun 11am–4pm; voluntary donation) where Connecticut's celebrated patriot once taught.

SOUTH OF HARTFORD

Take I-91 south to exit 25S, and CT 3S to **Wethersfield** , "Ye Most Auncient Towne" according to 1650 colonial records. The red onion, which features prominently on the town's logo, was developed in the farmland near here. More than 300 of the 17th- and 18th-century "downtown" homes have been preserved. Three can be toured at the **Webb-Deane-Stevens Museum** (211 Main Street; tel: 860-529 0612; www.webb-deane-stevens.org; May–Oct Wed–Mon 10am–4pm, Apr and Nov Sat 10am–4pm, Sun from 1pm, Jan–Mar tours by appointment only). George Washington planned the Yorktown campaign in the Webb House. Silas Deane, envoy to France during the Revolution, used his home as his political headquarters. The Stevens house shows middle-class life in the 1820s and 1830s.

The **Buttolph-Williams House** (249 Broad Street; tel: 860-529 0612; same hours as Webb-Deane-Stevens Museum) gives a rare look inside the life of the Puritans. It is also the setting for the novel, *The Witch of Blackbird Pond*.

The **Wethersfield Historical Society** (150 Main Street; tel: 860-529 7656; www.wethersfieldhistory.org; Tue–Sat 10am–4pm, from 1pm on Sun) has displays about the lives of ordinary people who created and built the town. It also maintains the adjacent 1790 Hurlbut-Dunham House, which is furnished to show life in the early 20th century, and maritime exhibits at the Cove

Warehouse (both places, June–Sept Sat–Sun).

Comstock, Ferre & Co. (263 Main Street; tel: 860-257 2790; Tue–Fri 8am–7pm, Sat–Sun 8am–4pm), housed in a collection of buildings dating as far back as the 1700s, was established as a seed house in 1811. Its inventory of heirloom seeds for sale in the store is one of the largest in the horticultural world. During renovation of the buildings, workers uncovered a hoard of agricultural treasures hidden under the dust and debris. Plans are to create a living history museum of agriculture in a setting that company founder William Comstock would recognize.

DINOSAUR STATE PARK

Continue south on I-91 to exit 23 to Rocky Hill and **Dinosaur State Park** ⑳ (400 West Street; tel: 860-529 8423; www.dinosaurstatepark.org; Oct–Dec Exhibit Center Thu–Sat 9am–4.30pm; grounds and trails: Tue–Sat 9am–4pm). Dinosaur tracks were found here in 1966 during building excavation. A massive geodesic dome protects some 500 of over 2,000 tracks found. An arboretum features plants descended from those the dinos munched.

NEW BRITAIN TO MIDDLETOWN

In **New Britain** ㉑, works from all eras and styles by artists including Cassatt, Whistler, and Sargent are on exhibit at the **New Britain Museum of American Art** (56 Lexington Street; tel: 860-229 0257; www.nbmaa.org; Sun–Wed and Fri 11am–5pm, until 8pm on Thu, Sat 10am–5pm). Free concerts, featuring everything from jazz to country to rock 'n' roll, are presented at the Davis Miller Band Shell in **Walnut Hill Park** (next to the museum) on Monday and Wednesday evenings in July and August.

Southeast of New Britain on Route 9, **Middletown** ㉒ is home to Wesleyan University and a romantic Main Street and town square.

WEST TO WATERBURY

In **Waterbury** ㉓, creative exhibits at the **Mattatuck Museum Arts and History Center** (144 West Main Street; tel: 203-753 0381; Tue–Sat 10am–5pm, Sun noon–5pm) document the industrial, social, architectural, and cultural history of the Naugatuck Valley. The exhibits include oral histories and family stories. Button-making was an important industry here; over 10,000 buttons made of cinnabar, ivory, and other materials and as diverse as those from George Washington's coat and floral bouquets made from human hair are on display. The art galleries focus on Connecticut landscapes and important figures from the 18th century to the present day.

The Renaissance Revival **Palace Theater** (100 East Main Street; tel: 203-346 2000; www.palacetheaterct.org) is the city's primary venue for performing arts.

DANBURY

To the west along I-84 at **Danbury** ㉔, the **Danbury Railway Museum** (120

Visitors from Long Island can cross the Sound to the Connecticut shore by ferry from Orient Point to New London.

The wealthy Gold Coast has a big appetite for antiques.

White Street, exit 5 off I-84; tel: 203-778 8337; www.danburyrailwaymuseum.org/; June–Aug daily, Sept–May Wed–Sun, standard hours 10am–4pm), with its 6-acre (2.43-hectare) switchyard, has over 70 engines – from steam to diesel – and rolling stock on display. Visitors can ride on a 90ft (27-meter) turntable. For an additional fee, there's a 20-minute ride through the rail yard in the cab with the engineer.

Danbury was the center of the millinery world in the 19th century. You can glimpse that era's fashionistas' fads at the **Danbury Museum and Historical Society** (43 Main Street; tel: 203-743 5200; www.danburymuseum.org; Tue–Sat 10am–4pm). The society also oversees the studio of the famous contralto Marian Anderson (call for openings).

To the south in **Ridgefield** ㉕, the **Aldrich Contemporary Art Museum** (258 Main Street; tel: 203-438 4519; www.aldrichart.org; Mon and Wed–Sat 10am–5pm, Sun noon–5pm; free admission third Sat of the month) is the only museum in Connecticut devoted to contemporary art. It has no permanent collection; exhibits are by emerging and mid-level artists.

Just down the street, at the **Keeler Tavern Museum** (132 Main Street; tel: 203-438 5485; www.keelertavernmuseum.org; Feb–Dec Wed and Sat–Sun 1–4pm), costumed guides conduct tours of exhibits which cover three centuries of Ridgefield history from the late 18th century to mid-20th century. A British cannonball from a skirmish between colonials and Redcoats in 1777 is embedded in an outer wall.

THE SOUTHWESTERN SHORE

China clippers and Yankee whalers sailed from the harbors of New Haven, New London, and Stonington out to seek their fortunes. People along Connecticut's coast still retain a fondness for the sea, and most towns have at least one marina. On a clear summer's day the horizon of Long Island Sound is filled with billowing sails.

THE GOLD COAST

"Greenwich, Cos Cob, Stamford, Darien, and Rowayton" – to the thousands of Connecticut residents who work in New York City, this is a railroad conductor's litany. About an hour from Manhattan by train, the Connecticut suburbs are among the nation's smartest bedroom communities.

The coastal area that parallels I-95 from Greenwich to Westport – lower Fairfield County – is sometimes referred to as the "Gold Coast" because of the many wealthy communities it encompasses.

In **Greenwich** ㉖, the **Bruce Museum** (1 Museum Drive; tel: 203-869 0376; https://brucemuseum.org; Tue–Sun 10am–5pm) features fine and decorative arts, natural science, and anthropology. Docent-led tours are on Fridays at 12.30pm. There's also a self-guided audio tour app.

Nearby, Cos Cob's **Bush-Holley Historic Site** (39 Strickland Road; tel: 203-869 6899; www.greenwichhistory.org/

Feeding time at South Norwalk's Maritime Aquarium.

visit.php; noon–4pm Mar–Dec Wed–Sun, Jan–Feb Sat–Sun; docent-led tours at 1pm, 2pm, and 3pm) explores two distinct historical periods. The first looks at the development of the community from 1790 to 1825. The other focuses on Cos Cob when it became the state's first art colony to attract Impressionist painters.

In **Stamford** ㉗, take a stroll through the **Bartlett Arboretum and Gardens** (151 Brookdale Road; tel: 203-322 6971; http://bartlettarboretum.org; daily until dusk; free), a 91-acre (37-hectare) swath of wildflower meadows, wetlands, boardwalks, and trails. Nature-lovers will also want to visit **Stamford Museum and Nature Center** (39 Scofieldtown Road; tel: 203-322 1646; www.stamford museum.org; museum and farm: Mon–Sat 9am–5pm, Sun 11am–5pm; observatory: Fri nights, closed Jan–Feb). Two very distinctive attractions are here. The Henri Willis Bendel Mansion was the realization of the residential dream of designer and department store owner Bendel. His elaborate house combined elements of Tudor manor homes he admired in England. It is lavishly furnished inside with

the epitome of interior design of the 1920s. Outside, Italian sculpture graces the grounds. The museum, housed in the mansion, has a small but excellent collection of American art, American Indian art and cultural objects, and objects of American history from the 17th century to World War II. The Nature Center has a completely different focus. The 118 woodland acres (48 hectares) include a working farm with cows and a creamery, pig pen, ducks, maple sugar house, and organic garden.

NEW CANAAN

Take Route 7N off I-95 to CT 123 and **New Canaan** ㉘ to visit **Philip Johnson's Glass House** (199 Elm Street; tel: 203-594 9884/866-811 4111; www. theglasshouse.org; tours May–Nov Thu–Mon, advance reservations recommended). This is the architect's minimalist masterpiece – once his private (if glass-walled) retreat – on 47 magnificently landscaped acres (19 hectares). The estate is operated to preserve and interpret modern architecture, landscape, and art. There are

Westport's Levitt Pavilion for the Performing Arts.

Seeing the sights of Bridgeport.

Sherwood Island State Park has facilities for shore fishing and saltwater swimming in Long Island Sound.

Marlon Brando, 1924–2004.

several different tours, which sell out quickly. Reservations are highly recommended. The **New Canaan Nature Center** (144 Oenoke Ridge; tel: 203-966 9577; https://newcanaannature.org; Mon–Sat 9am–4pm; voluntary donation), on a 40-acre (16-hectare) site with an unusual variety of habitats, has walking trails, a raptor exhibit, and a 4,000-sq-ft (372-sq-meter) greenhouse; the **New Canaan Historical Society** (13 Oenoke Ridge; tel: 203-966 1776; https://nchistory.org/; Tue–Fri 9.30am–4.30pm, Sat until 12.30pm) complex encompasses an 1845 pharmacy, an old schoolhouse, a sculpture studio, and a tool museum. The **Silvermine Guild Arts Center** (1037 Silvermine Road; tel: 203-966 9700; http://silvermine art.org; galleries: Wed–Sat noon–5pm, Sun 1–5pm) began as an artist colony in 1908 by visionary sculptor Solon Borglum (brother of Mt Rushmore sculptor Gutzon). Today, it is an association of over 300 juried artists, an award-winning school for visual arts, home to five galleries, and a venue for performing art productions.

THE NORWALKS

South Norwalk ㉙, with its upscale galleries and shops, has been dubbed "SoNo" for its emulation of New York's SoHo district.

The huge **Maritime Aquarium** (10 North Water Street; tel: 203-852 0700; www.maritimeaquarium.org; daily 10am–5pm) on the banks of the Norwalk River has more than 1,000 marine animals and plenty of hands-on displays relating to the marine life and maritime culture of Long Island Sound. The aquarium offers numerous educational activities including feeding programs and summer camps (see website for details). There's also an IMAX movie theater. The aquarium's research vessel takes passengers on a 2.5-hour excursion on Long Island Sound (for hours, see website).

You can hop on board the catamaran ferry at Hope Dock for a scenic cruise to **Sheffield Island** and a guided tour of an 1868, 10-room lighthouse (tel: 203-838 9444; Memorial Day–Sept daily). On a clear day, you can see the New York skyline from the lighthouse. The **Stewart B. McKinney National Wildlife Refuge** (www.fws.gov/refuge/stewart_b_mckinney/) is also here, and there are numerous marine-life encounter cruises on offer, too. In nearby **Norwalk** ㉚, tours are offered of "America's first château," the restored, 62-room Victorian **Lockwood-Mathews Mansion Museum** (295 West Avenue, Matthews Park; tel: 203-838 9799; www.lockwoodmathewsmansion.com; early Apr–early Jan Wed–Sun noon–4pm; tours, at noon, 1, 2, and 3pm weather permitting; audio tours if no docent is available). Tours show off the incredibly detailed woodwork and craftsmanship in the design and construction of the mansion, as well as the elaborate furnishings. Children 10 years old and younger will enjoy the hands-on activities at **Stepping Stones Museum for Children** (303 West Avenue; Matthews Park; tel: 203-899 0606; www.steppingstonesmuseum.org; 10am–5pm Memorial Day–Labor Day daily, rest of the year Tue–Sun).

WESTPORT

One of the country's most affluent communities, Westport is perhaps best known for its **Westport Country Playhouse** (25 Powers Court; box office tel: 203-227 4177/888-927 7529; www.westportplayhouse.org; season late-May–mid-Nov), which mounts award-winning experimental plays as well as reinterpretations of the classics. The outdoor **Levitt Pavilion for the Performing Arts** (40 Jesup Road; tel: 203-226 7600; www.levittpavilion.com) hosts more than 50 free events throughout the summer, including bands, movies, and children's shows.

Sherwood Island State Park by Long Island Sound is the location of the Connecticut Living 9/11 Memorial (Sherwood Island Connector off Route 1 in Westport; tel: 203-226 6983; charge in season). Before the attack, the Twin Towers were clearly visible from the beach. The monument and benches around it face the skyline.

BRIDGEPORT

To the east, **Bridgeport** ❸ is a major industrial center. The **Barnum Museum** (820 Main Street; tel: 203-331 1104; www.barnum-museum.org; Thu–Fri 11am–3pm) is a showcase for memorabilia connected to circus pioneer P. T. Barnum (1810–91), with a 4,000-piece miniature circus, clown props, bogus "oddities" like the Feejee Mermaid, and items relating to the diminutive Bridgeport native General Tom Thumb.

Highlights at Connecticut's **Beardsley Zoo** (1875 Noble Avenue; tel: 203-394 6565; www.beardsleyzoo.org; daily 9am–4pm), the state's only zoo, include over 300 North and South American species and a tropical rainforest.

NEW HAVEN

New Haven ❷, settled by Puritans in 1638, was an independent colony until 1662, when it merged with the Hartford settlement. At first a seafaring community, New Haven later embraced industry and pioneered such inventions

as the steel fish hook, the meat grinder, the corkscrew, and the steamboat.

New Haven is best known, however, for **Yale University** (visitor center, 149 Elm Street; tel: 203-432 2300; http://visitorcenter.yale.edu; tours Mon–Fri 10.30am and 2pm, Sat–Sun 1.30pm; self-guided tours for MP3 players available in English, Spanish, and Chinese). Founded in 1701 by a group of Puritan clergymen, it was originally located in nearby Saybrook. In 1716, the school was moved to New Haven, and two years later it took the name of benefactor Elihu Yale.

Alumni include, among others, both presidents Bush, Bill and Hillary Clinton, Supreme Court justices Sonia Sotomayor and Clarence Thomas, actors Paul Newman, Meryl Streep, Jodie Foster, Nobel-winner economist Paul Krugman, and composer Cole Porter. The buildings on campus evoke the British universities of Oxford and Cambridge.

Any visit to the university should include the **Beinecke Rare Book and Manuscript Library** at 121 Wall Street (tel: 203-432 2977; http://beinecke.library.yale.edu/; Mon–Thu 10am–7pm, Fri

Students heading to class at Yale University.

Joseph Cinque, leader of La Amistad slave revolt.

9am–5pm), where an edition of the Gutenberg Bible and original Audubon bird prints are displayed.

Two blocks south, the **Yale University Art Gallery** (1111 Chapel Street; tel: 203-432 0600; http://artgallery.yale.edu; Tue–Fri 10am–5pm, Sat–Sun 11am–5pm, Sept–June Thu until 8pm; free) has a comprehensive collection of American, African, and ancient art, and canvases by Manet, Van Gogh, Corot, Degas, and Matisse. Across the street is the **Yale Center for British Art** (1080 Chapel Street; tel: 203-432 2800; http://britishart.yale.edu; Tue–Sat 10am–5pm, Sun noon–5pm; free). It has the largest collection of British art outside the UK, donated in 1966 by industrialist Paul Mellon.

Collections at the **Peabody Museum of Natural History** (170 Whitney Avenue; tel: 203-432 5050; www.peabody.yale.edu; Tue–Sat 10am–5pm, Sun noon–5pm) include dinosaur fossils, native birds, meteorites, and minerals. Guided tours are offered on weekends and Thursdays at 12.30pm, 1.30pm, 2.30pm or 3.30pm (check website). An audio tour, via wand or MP3 download, is also available.

⊘ THE SAGA OF LA AMISTAD

In 1839, a group of slaves took over *La Amistad*, the vessel carrying them to sugar plantations in Cuba. They sailed up the East Coast, eventually arriving in Long Island Sound. The ship was towed to New Haven, where the fate of "the Amistads" became one of the first legal fights over slavery.

The protracted legal battles raised questions of morality and sovereignty. The Amistads insisted that as they were kidnapped, they were free. Spain, which ruled Cuba, countered that the US had no jurisdiction in the matter, as the "cargo" was loaded in Havana and destined for another Cuban port, and the mutiny occurred in international waters.

As it worked its way up the court system, each appeal found in favor of the Amistads, much to the annoyance of President Martin Van Buren, who was eager to appease Spain and keep face with the slave-holding South. But even the Supreme Court, with a majority of Southerners on the bench, decided against the Spanish claims. All people, it ruled, lived in a natural state of freedom and the Amistads were freed. It was the first antislavery decision by the Supreme Court. It took several years to raise the money to pay for their voyage home, but eventually the surviving Amistads returned home. Ironically, "amistad" means "friendship" in Spanish.

Over 1,000 musical instruments are displayed at the **Yale Collection of Musical Instruments** (15 Hillhouse Avenue; tel: 203-432 0822; Sept–July Tue–Fri 1–4pm, Sun 1–5pm; http://collection.yale.edu; free). It concentrates on Western art music. Concerts are given periodically throughout the year.

Adjacent to the university, New Haven Green is surrounded by a trinity of churches constructed in Gothic Revival, Georgian, and Federal styles.

New Haven's cultural offerings include Yale University's **Institute of Sacred Music** (409 Prospect Street; tel: 203-432 5180; https://ism.yale.edu/), which presents concerts, art exhibitions, and films; the award-winning **Yale Repertory Theater** (1120 Chapel Street; tel: 203-432 1234; www.yalerep.org), a professional company known for producing new plays and innovative interpretations of classics; the **Long Wharf Theater** on the downtown waterfront (222 Sargent Drive; tel: 203-787 4282; www.longwharf.org); and the **Shubert Theater** (247 College Street; tel: 203-562 5666; www.shubert.com), the "Birthplace of the nation's greatest hits". The **New Haven Symphony Orchestra** (tel: 203-865 0831; www.newhavensymphony.org) performs at Woolsey Hall on the Yale campus.

The **Grove Street Cemetery** (227 Grove Street; tel: 203-389 5403; www.grovestreetcemetery.org; daily; free tours early May–late Oct Sat 10am), also known as the New Haven Burial Ground, was established in 1797 to replace the common mass burial ground on the village green. It was the first in the country to have family plots instead of random interments. Eli Whitney and Noah Webster are two of the notables resting here. The database of known burials has over 14,000 entries.

THE EASTERN SHORE

Just off I-95 in **East Haven** ㉝, the **Shore Line Trolley Museum** (17 River Street; tel: 203-467 6927; http://shorelinetrolley.org/; 10am–5pm May–mid-June weekends only, late June–early Sept daily, rest of the year at weekends for special events only) preserves some 100 trolleys, the oldest rapid transit car, and a rare parlor car. Hop aboard for a 3-mile (5km) ride (10.30am–4.30pm) on one of the vintage cars.

East on Route 146 off Route 1 in **Branford**, cruises by Thimble Islands Cruise & Charter (tel: 203-488 8905), Capt. Bob Milne (tel: 203-481 3345; www.thimbleislands.com), and Capt. Dave Kusterer (tel: 352-978 1502/203-397 3921; www.thimbleislander.net) sail from the town's nearby **Stony Creek** dock for hour-long narrated tours of the **Thimble Islands**, a cluster of islands – 23 of them inhabited – just offshore.

Farther east on Route 146, **Guilford** ❸❹ was settled in 1639 by the Reverend Henry Whitfield. His home, the oldest stone dwelling in New England, is now the **Henry Whitfield State Museum** (248 Old Whitfield Road; tel: 203-453 2457; www.ctvisit.com/listings/henry-whitfield-state-museum; 10am–4.30pm May–Oct Wed–Sun, Nov–Apr Mon–Fri). The self-guided tour of the three-story building, whose thick stone walls served as a fort for the first colonists in the area, gives visitors a feel for how early settlers lived.

Guilford has one of the largest and prettiest town greens in New England. Nearby are several historic houses, including the 1690 **Hyland House** (84 Boston Street; tel: 203-453 9477; https://hylandhouse.org; June–Sept) and the 1774 **Thomas Griswold House** (171 Boston Street; tel: 203-453 3176; www.guilfordkeepingsociety.com; June and Sept Fri and Sat 11am–4pm, Sun noon–4pm, July–Aug Wed–Sat 11am–4pm, Sun noon–4pm), with a restored blacksmith shop and colonial garden. The **Dudley Farm** (2351 Durham Road; tel: 203-457 0770; www.dudleyfarm.com; May–Oct Thu–Sat 10am–2pm, Sun 1–4pm) is a working 1840 farmstead and living-history museum.

Five miles (8km) east, **Madison** ❸❺ has some of the state's most beautiful summer and year-round homes. The 1681 **Deacon John Grave House** (581 Boston Post Road; tel: 203-245 4798; http://deaconjohngrave.org; call for opening times), home for seven generations of the family, has been a school, wartime infirmary, inn, tavern, and courtroom.

Hammonasset Beach State Park (1288 Boston Post Road/Route 1; tel: 203-245 2785; parking fee mid-Apr–Memorial Day and Labor Day–Oct) is the state's longest public beach, with 2 miles (3km) of sand.

At **Old Saybrook** ❸❻, by the mouth of the Connecticut River, **Fort Saybrook Monument Park** (Saybrook Point/Route 154; tel: 860 395 3152; www.ctvisit.com/listings/fort-saybrook-monument-park) has storyboards chronicling Saybrook Colony from 1635. The monument is a statue of English military engineer Lion Gardiner, who built the fort in 1636 to protect the settlers from the Pequot Indians. The park offers fine estuary views, with opportunities for bird watching from the boardwalk. Stop in for excellent Italian ice-cream at **James Pharmacy** (2 Pennywise Lane; tel:

The Florence Griswold Museum has been restored to how it looked around 1910 when the local art colony was the center of Impressionism in America.

A breath of fresh air for a vintage vehicle.

860-395 1781; www.jamespharmacybnb.com), a historic building converted into a boutique Bed & Breakfast. The **Katharine Hepburn Cultural Arts Center**, or "The Kate" (300 Main Street; tel: 860-510 0473; www.katharinehepburntheater.org), is dedicated to honoring Old Saybrook's most celebrated resident with cultural and artistic presentations. There's a small museum (Tue–Fri 10am–4pm and one hour prior to performances; free) with her awards, costumes, and movie memorabilia.

OLD LYME TO NEW LONDON

Old Lyme ③⑦ boasts a rich artistic heritage – thanks in large part to Florence Griswold. The daughter of one of the town's many sea captains, she lived a privileged life until the Civil War and the rise of steam sea power reversed the family fortunes, and she was forced to take in boarders. One of them was painter Henry Ward Roger, recently returned from Europe and eager to start an art colony. A few years after his 1899 arrival, Old Lyme was the center for a new school of Impressionist landscape painting. It lasted for nearly three decades and included American artists like Childe Hassan, William Chadwick, and Matilda Browne. The "home" for many of them is now the **Florence Griswold Museum** (96 Lyme Street; tel: 860-434 5542; www.florencegriswoldmuseum.org; Tue–Sat 10am–5pm, Sun 1–5pm), which contains a stunning array of works by her illustrious American Impressionist boarders. Some were so moved by her hospitality that they left painted mementos on the doors, mantels, and paneled walls. The on-site café provides blankets and baskets for patrons who want to picnic in the fabulous gardens.

The **Lyme Art Association** (90 Lyme Street; tel: 860-434 7802; https://lymeartassociation.org/; Wed–Sun 10am–5pm) continues the support of artists started by "Miss Florence" by showcasing works by regional representational artists.

NEW LONDON

New London ③⑧ was one of America's busiest 19th-century whaling ports. Many a vast fortune was accumulated by its merchants. Evidence of this wealth can be seen on "Whale Oil Row" on Huntington Street, with its grand mansions.

When petroleum began to replace whale oil, manufacturing became New London's chief occupation. But the city maintained its ties to the sea and today is the home of the **US Coast Guard Academy** (31 Mohegan Avenue; tel: 800-883 8724; www.cga.edu; self-guided tours daily; cadet-led tours are available on Mondays, Fridays and some Saturdays; online registration required, see website for details). You will need a photo ID to enter the base and buildings. There is also a self-guided walking tour with maps available at the Coast Guard Museum and admissions office (both in Waesche Hall). The museum has 200 years' worth of Coast Guard history and memorabilia. The tall ship *Eagle*, the academy's training vessel, is open for tours when in port. A striking new museum building is set to be built at the

The whaling ship Charles W. Morgan at Mystic Seaport.

north end of Waterfront Park, thanks to $5 million of federal funding agreed by Congress in 2017. For updates, check www.coastguardmuseum.org.

New London was also the summer boyhood home of Eugene O'Neill (1888–1953), the Nobel Prize-winning playwright. The O'Neill family's **Monte Cristo Cottage** (325 Pequot Avenue; tel: 860-443 5378; www.theoneill.org/monte-cristo-cottage; June–Aug Thu–Sun noon–4pm) was the setting for his autobiographical work, *Long Day's Journey into Night*, and has been restored to reflect O'Neill's set directions and sketches for the play. Nearby, **Ocean Beach Park** (98 Neptune Avenue; tel: 860-447 3031; https://ocean-beach-park.com/; Memorial Day weekend–Labor Day daily), on Long Island Sound, has a large sugar-sand beach, huge pool, entertainment boardwalk, kid rides, a fully equipped fitness facility (additional charge), and a full-service restaurant. The two restored **Hempstead Houses** (11 Hempstead Street; tel: 860-443 7949; www.ctvisit.com/listings/hempstead-houses; May–Oct Sat–Sun 1–4pm) are far removed from the casual beach scene.

Joshua Hempstead lived his entire life in the frame house built in 1678. He was, at various times, a farmer, judge, gravestone carver, and shipwright. His grandson Nathaniel built the stone house next door in 1759. They are furnished with period pieces tracing the evolution of colonial lifestyles.

American Impressionist paintings and 18th- to 20th-century decorative arts are highlighted at the **Lyman Allyn Art Museum** (625 Williams Street; tel: 860-443 2545; www.lymanallyn.org; Tue–Sat 10am–5pm, Sun 1–5pm; free first Sat of the month).

USS NAUTILUS

Across the Thames River from New London is the city of **Groton** ⓷⓷, known as the "Submarine Capital of the World" – the manufacture of nuclear submarines is its major industry. Non-claustrophobes who wish to view the interior of a submarine may visit the USS *Nautilus* at the **US Naval Submarine Force Museum** (1 Crystal Lake Road at exit 86, off I-95; tel: 860-694 3174; www.ussnautilus.org; Wed–Mon May–Oct 9am–5pm, Nov –Apr until

Mystic Aquarium.

⊙ WHAT DID NATHAN HALE SAY?

Every schoolchild in New England learns the story of Nathan Hale, the 21-year-old soldier in the Continental Army hung as a spy by the British in 1776. As he stood by the gallows, Hale said, "I only regret that I have but one life to lose for my country."

No eyewitness account mentions the quote, although one British officer's memoir has Hale saying, "I am so satisfied with the cause in which I am engaged, that my only regret is, that I have not more lives than one to offer in its service." The much more repeatable and memorable version seems to stem from a newspaper article in 1799. In it, a British witness remembers Hale saying he regretted having only one life to lose for his country – not so much quoting Hale as paraphrasing his final words.

A graduate of Yale University, Hale was familiar with contemporary literature of his times. A play by Joseph Addison, *Cato*, was well known and contained a passage which directly applied to his situation and could have inspired him:

*How beautiful is death, when earn'd by virtue
Who would not be that youth?*

What pity is it that we can die but once to serve our country.

Much else about Hale's execution is equally mysterious. Three places in Manhattan vie for recognition as the site of the actual hanging; no one knows what happened to his body; and no one knows what Hale actually looked like. All of the statues of the patriot are idealized imaginings.

Hale has long been considered a hero of the American Revolutionary War, and in 1985 he was designated the official state hero of Connecticut. Although he never actually fought in battle, Hale was the only volunteer willing to travel behind enemy lines and spy on the British forces. Not much else is known about Nathan Hale. The only contemporary source is the diary of a British officer who was present at his execution, who wrote "He behaved with great composure and resolution, saying he though it the duty of every good Officer, to obey any orders given him by his Commander-in-Chief; and desired the Spectators to be at all times to meet death in whatever shape it might appear."

CONNECTICUT'S NICKNAMES

Like every other state, Connecticut has a nickname. Actually, it has several. Most often, it's called The Constitution State, but the Nutmeg State crops up occasionally, as do a few more colorful terms.

In 1638, the Connecticut Colony Council adopted the Fundamental Orders – generally considered the first written constitution anywhere in the world. Although the men who drafted the document were loyal British subjects, the Orders make no reference to the king or sovereign (nor to any government outside of Connecticut for that matter). The Orders created a General Assembly, determined how to elect officials, set terms of office, and determined how taxes would be decided and levied. At the time, these were all radical, if not revolutionary, concepts.

The Nutmeg State, another nickname, comes from traditional folklore. Thomas Haliburton, a Canadian author who used the pen name "Sam Slick," wrote humorous essays about rural Canada and New England in the 1830s. One of his stories

A statue on New London's City Pier shows playwright Eugene O'Neill as a boy.

claimed that Connecticut traders were so shrewd that they could convince gullible customers that knobs of wood were nutmegs.

But it's "The Land of Steady Habits" that has a fanciful origin that would make Sam Slick proud. The moniker shows up in a 1951 book, *The Dictionary of Americanism on Historical Principles*. The book says it's an allusion to the strict morals of the inhabitants enforced by the Connecticut "Blue Laws." The statutes were allegedly written in 1650 by Puritan clerics, printed in London on blue paper (hence the name "Blue Laws"), and distributed to households in New Haven. It sounds very authentic, but it's a great hoax. The real story is this: in 1781, Rev. Samuel Peters – a loyalist Anglican cleric who returned to England during the Revolution – published *A General History of Connecticut*. Far from an attempt to accurately describe Connecticut (or any other part of the rebellious colonies, for that matter), Peters' book is an over-the-top effort to make the Colonials appear backwards and foolish. He invented the Blue Laws story. In his *History*, he lists all 45 of the "laws." They include such decrees as "No woman shall kiss her child on the Sabbath" and "No one shall celebrate Christmas, make minced pies, dance, play cards, or play any instrument of music except drum, trumpet, and jaw harp." Despite their absurdity, the legend of the Blue Laws took root and – as seen by its use in the 1951 *Dictionary* – is an urban legend still widely accepted as truth.

In the real world, however, there really are Blue Laws. That's the term used for laws regulating activities on Sunday (probably coming from the Blue Laws legend). Most of them deal with gambling and liquor sales. Ironically, Connecticut is one of only three states which still prohibit Sunday liquor sales, and groups regularly work to see the repeal of Connecticut's one legitimate Blue Law.

Connecticut is also known as the "Provisions State," a term which originated during the Revolutionary War (1775–83) when the state equipped the Continental Army with food and cannons. It has also been dubbed the "Brownstone State" on account of the Portland Brownstone Quarries which provided stone for the state's most famous 19th-century buildings. Today the quarries are a National Historic Landmark.

4pm; free). The museum has the world's largest collection of submarine artifacts, photos, and documents. It chronicles the development of submarine technology and warfare from the Revolutionary War *Turtle* to today's super subs.

Fort Griswold Battlefield State Park (Monument Street and Park Avenue; tel: 860-449 6877; www.fortgriswold.org; museum and monument: Memorial Day–Labor Day Wed–Sun 9am–5pm) is the site of a notorious incident during the Revolution. British forces led by traitor Benedict Arnold overran the fort and massacred 88 of the 165 defenders after they surrendered. The ruins of the fortifications remain and the stone house where the wounded survivors were tended is a museum.

MYSTIC

Five miles (8km) east, at exit 90 off I-95, is **Mystic ⑩**, an old maritime community of trim white houses, sitting at the tidal outlet of the Mystic River. For generations, Mystic was the home of mariners and fishermen and was condemned by the British during the Revolution as a "cursed little hornets' nest" of patriots. The village teemed with activity during the Gold Rush days of 1849 when shipbuilders vied to see who could construct the fastest clipper ships to travel round Cape Horn to the boom town of San Francisco. The *Andrew Jackson*, a Mystic-built clipper launched in 1860, claimed the world's record: 89 days, 4 hours.

Beluga whales, sharks, penguins, sea lions, and sea otters are just a few of more than 3,500 creatures at the **Mystic Aquarium and Institute for Exploration** (55 Coogan Boulevard; tel: 860-572 5955; www.mysticaquarium.org; daily 9am–5pm). Visitors utilize the latest deep-sea technology, including live cameras, robots, and a live Web feed to dive under the sea, visit kelp beds, and watch sea otters romp. Another exhibit displays many of the treasures brought up from the ocean floor while researching the wreck of the *Titanic*.

MYSTIC SEAPORT

Down Route 27 just a mile, **Mystic Seaport, The Museum of America and the Sea** (75 Greenmanville Avenue; tel: 888-973 2767; www.mysticseaport.org; daily 10am–4pm), is a living replica of a 19th-century waterfront community during the heyday of sailing ships. The site includes over 60 buildings and is so authentic that it was used as the 1839 setting for New Haven's harbor in Steven Spielberg's 1997 movie *Amistad*, about a revolt aboard a slave ship sailing from Africa (see page 250).

A full day and plenty of stamina are required to tour the entire seaport properly. Visitors can wander along the wharves and streets of the village and taste the old seafaring way of life. Most buildings are set up to show their functions at the time. Others have special exhibits like a collection of carved ship figureheads or the story of women and the sea. A planetarium demonstrates how sailors used the stars for navigation.

The museum's collection of ships and boats from the age of sail and early machine power is unmatched.

Spinning a yarn at Mystic Seaport.

A rodeo on the Mashuntucket Pequot Reservation.

The *Charles W. Morgan*, the last surviving wooden whaling ship from a fleet which once numbered over 600, and the oldest American merchant ship afloat, is berthed here. In 2013, she was re-launched onto the Mystic River on the 172nd anniversary of her maiden voyage, and in 2014 she concluded her 38th, a trip of nearly three months around southern New England. Visitors can also board the tall ship *Joseph Conrad*, built in 1882 by the Danish as a training vessel. There are sloops, an island steamer, an open launch, and a Danish lighthouse tender used to smuggle Jews to Sweden during World War II.

From Memorial Day through Columbus Day, the museum offers cruises up the river on some of its historic fleet (additional fee). Visitors can also rent rowboats and sailboats. Each June, the seaport hosts an international Sea Music Festival, when the sound of sea chanteys floats across the docks.

STONINGTON

Five miles (8km) farther east is the charming old whaling port of

Dodson Boatyard, Stonington.

Stonington **④**. The **Old Lighthouse Museum** (7 Water Street; tel: 860-535 1440; www.stoningtonhistory.org; May–Oct Thu–Mon 10am–5pm) is inside an 1823 building. The light atop this sturdy stone edifice was visible 12 miles (19km) out to sea. The six rooms depict life of Stonington's residents: not just the fishermen, but boat builders, farmers, and tradesmen.

Admission to the museum includes a visit to the **Captain Nathaniel B. Palmer House** (40 Palmer Street, Route 1A; tel: 860-535 8445; Fri–Mon tours on the hour 1–4pm), built by the seal hunter and clipper ship designer who in 1820 discovered "land not yet laid down on my chart" – it turned out to be Antarctica. The house contains memorabilia of that trip as well as family portraits, artifacts, and furnishings.

MASSIVE CASINOS

Ten miles (16km) north of Stonington, on the **Mashantucket Pequot Reservation**, the massive **Foxwoods Resort Casino ④** (Route 2; open 24 hours; www.foxwoods.com) welcomes gamblers by the busload. On the grounds is the **Mashantucket Pequot Museum and Research Center** (110 Pequot Trail; tel: 800-411 9671; www.pequotmuseum.org; Apr–Dec Wed–Sat 9am–5pm). Using walk-through, life-size dioramas – starting with a descent into a sensorial-accurate glacial crevasse – visitors experience the Pequot people's history from the last ice age to the present. Interactive exhibits and videos create a comprehensive picture of the Natives of New England. The on-site restaurant serves American Indian fare as well as more familiar dishes. An annual powwow, usually held in mid-September, is one of the largest on the East Coast, with dancers, drumming, validated craftspeople, demonstrations, and a rodeo.

The **Mohegan Sun casino** (https://mohegansun.com), a worthy rival to Foxwoods, is just to the southwest in **Uncasville**.

THE COMING OF THE CASINOS

Considered sovereign entities under US law, American Indian tribes are permitted to run casinos on their own land, even in states where gambling is not otherwise permitted.

In 1972, Russell and Helen Bryan, a Chippewa couple living in a used house trailer on Indian land in rural Minnesota, received a property tax bill for $147.95. Since Indian reservations are considered lands belonging to a sovereign nation and are therefore not subjected to taxation, they refused to pay. The case eventually was heard by the Supreme Court, which issued a unanimous decision: not only could governments not tax reservation lands; they could not regulate what American Indians do on their tribal lands.

And thus began the age of the Indian casinos. It came at an ideal time for many tribes. Long considered at best an anachronistic remnant of another age and historically denied the economic and social opportunities of the larger society, in the 1980s American Indians were experiencing a new sense of identity and developing legal savvy to push forward their agenda of social, political, and economic advancement. The profits that could come from casinos would give them the financial clout to support their plans.

Eastern Connecticut's Mashantucket Pequots were the first New England tribe to gamble on casinos. They began developing hundreds of acres of tribal lands in sleepy Ledyard CT, creating a vast casino-and-hotel complex, Foxwoods (www.foxwoods.com). At 4.7 million sq ft (0.44 sq km), it is the second largest casino complex in the United States, with gambling, entertainment, shopping, and resort hotels. By 1998, just six years after it opened, Foxwoods was also the world's highest-grossing casino, raking in more than $1 billion annually, more than any single casino in Las Vegas or Atlantic City.

The money was a windfall undreamed of by the members of the tribe, which numbered fewer than 1,000 members. Most of them were employees of the casino or the other businesses the tribe soon opened. They received individual disbursements from the casino profits, in some cases over $100,000 a year. The money also funded a child development center, a tribal police force, post office, and employment, education, and social services for members. One of the biggest projects was the creation of the Mashantucket Pequot Museum and Research Center on the grounds of the casino resort. A state-of-the-art, excellent, and extensive facility, it is a point of pride for the tribe, grandly proving their long history, traditions, and culture.

Spurred by Foxwoods' success, the Mohegan tribe opened their own casino a few miles away. It's only slightly smaller than Foxwoods and is nearly as profitable. Both casinos give 25 percent of their gross to the state of Connecticut, with a minimum of $100 million annually.

But while the American Indian nations are exempt from many US laws, they are not exempt from the effects of worldwide economic collapse. The gambling industry as a whole is hurting. With less money to spend, fewer gamblers are at the tables and they are spending less. Foxwoods, in particular, had expanded exponentially during the boom years and by 2012 was deeply in debt, as was Mohegan Sun's. Like every other overextended and financially troubled company, both casinos have worked with lenders and applied for federal aid to survive the downturn.

Playing the tables at Mohegan Sun.

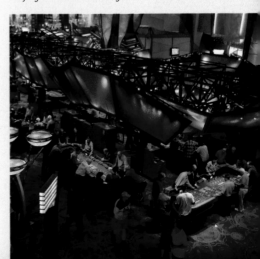

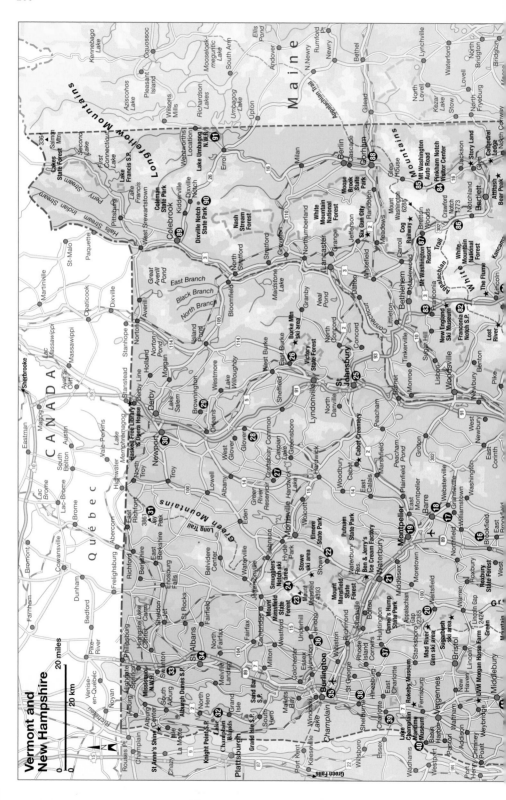

Vermont and New Hampshire

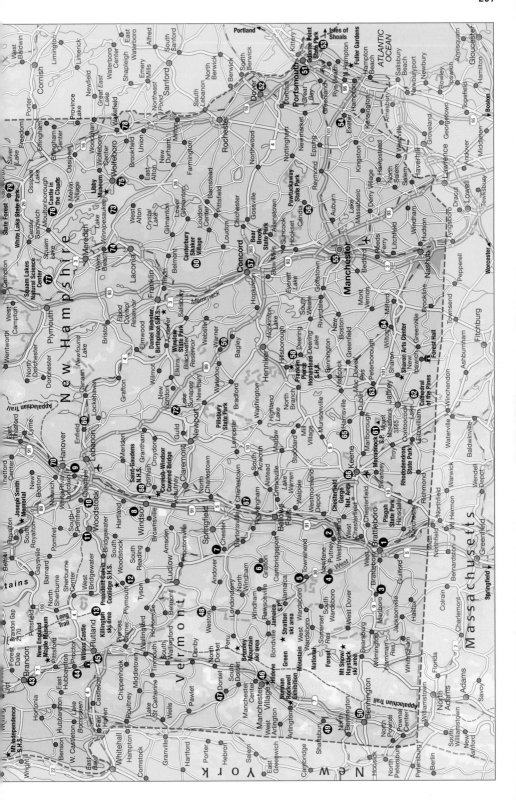

A classic farm scene in Reading on a beautiful October day.

VERMONT

The Green Mountain State is alive with the sound of leaves crunching underfoot, the sight of red barns and white steeples, the smell of country lanes, and the taste of freshly tapped maple syrup.

Imagine New England, and you will very likely imagine Vermont. When you round a bend to find a valley painted in a thousand shades of green, or stand atop Mount Mansfield to see a quilt of farm and forest rumpled against Lake Champlain, or drop down from the mountains into a white village framed in the glorious colors of autumn, your preconceptions become reality.

LAKESIDE RETREATS

Vermont's fresh air, fine scenery, and good fishing attracted tourists before the Civil War, but what really kicked the state's tourism industry into overdrive was the selling of winter. The ski boom began during the 1930s when the first mechanical lifts and cut trails appeared. By the early 1970s, dozens of ski areas had given rise to a burgeoning vacation-home industry and to worries over runaway development.

That same era brought an influx of new Vermonters, mostly young people looking for a simpler way of life. The cliché is that they were hippie communards, but the vast majority were tradespeople, artisans, and young professionals. What they shared was a sense that they had found someplace special and that they wanted to keep it that way.

In alliance with progressive natives, the new Vermonters crafted a far-reaching array of environmental regulations,

from a ban on highway billboards to controls on development in rural areas. It hasn't gone down smoothly; there is still considerable chafing between conservative natives and the "flatlanders" whom they feel have taken over the state.

THE LOWER CONNECTICUT RIVER VALLEY

The long, lazy Connecticut River forms the entire boundary between the states of Vermont and New Hampshire. Covered today by a hydroelectric dam, Vermont's first permanent settlement – Fort

⊙ Main Attractions
Brattleboro
Grafton
Quechee Gorge
Rock of Ages Quarry
Waterbury
Stowe
Lake Champlain
Shelburne
Bennington

Map on pages
258, 280

A sleigh ride near Stowe.

A farmer stirs the vats of maple sugar in a sugar house.

Watching for hawks on Putney Mountain.

Dummer, founded in 1724 – has been reduced to a mere marker on the shore.

A few miles north, however, **Brattleboro** , the town the fort was meant to protect, became an early resort when a local physician parlayed its pure springs into a "water cure." In the 1970s, some of the more dedicated "back-to-the-land" crowd settled here and sunk their roots deep into the community.

Some turned their talents to the arts, and the works of some 350 artisans from woodworkers to glass blowers are displayed at **Vermont Artisan Designs** (106 Main Street; tel: 802-257 7044; www.vtart.com; Mon–Thu and Sat 10am–6pm, Fri until 8pm, Sun 10am–5pm). The 1938 Art Deco **Latchis Building** on Main Street houses a movie theater which shows first-run and indie films. Upstairs from the theater is the 30-room, boutique **Latchis Hotel** (tel: 802-254 6300; www.latchishotel.com) providing a unique experience to stay in the town. The **Brattleboro Museum and Art Center** (tel: 802-257 0124; www.brattleboromuseum.org; Wed–Mon 11am–5pm; free first Fri of the month 5.30–8.30pm)

is in the Union Railroad Station. A "non-collecting" museum, it hosts changing art exhibits that offer unique views of the world by contemporary artists.

PUTNEY TO TOWNSHEND

Vermont's dairy industry owes its start to Charles Houghton, a Boston lawyer. In 1866, he started the first Holstein herd in the state on the family farm in **Putney** ❷, a few miles north on US 5.

Larger-than-life puppets, fantastic sets, and original scripts are featured at the **Sandglass Theater** (17 Kimball Hill Road; tel: 802-387 4051; www.sandglasstheater.org; call to arrange a tour). Performances are in the 60-seat theater in a converted barn as well as at venues throughout the region. It hosts a 10-day international puppet festival held on "even" years. Follow US 9 (also known as the Molly Stark Trail) west to **Marlboro** ❸, the hilltop home of small, liberal arts Marlboro College, which every summer hosts the world-renowned, chamber music **Marlboro Music Festival**, founded by the late Rudolf Serkin (book early for

tickets; tel: 802-254 2394; www.mar-lboromusic.org). Stop at the **Hogback Mountain Scenic Overlook** to savor the view and visit the **Southern Vermont Natural History Museum** (tel: 802-464 0048; www.vermontmuseum.org; Mon–Fri 10am–4pm; Sat–Sun until 5pm), where more than 600 mounted specimens of native mammals and birds are displayed in dioramas. A raptor center is home to birds which cannot be released into the wild.

A few miles farther west at Wilmington, turn north to reach **West Dover**, home to **Mount Snow/Haystack** (tel: 802-464 3333 or 800-245 SNOW; www.mountsnow.com), a behemoth ski area and summer resort. It's a popular spot for hikers and mountain bikers; on weekends throughout the summer and daily in fall, scenic chairlift rides are available.

Route 30 northwest out of Brattleboro follows the West River, past the 1872 West Dummerston Covered Bridge to the postcard-perfect town of **Newfane** ❹. Its broad common is lined with shady elms and surrounded by stately Greek Revival public buildings and the requisite high-steepled church.

Farther up Route 30, the handsome town of **Townshend** ❺ has a 2-acre common whose focal point is the 1790 Congregational Church. North on Route 30, Scott Bridge, the state's longest single-span covered bridge, was built in 1870.

Just past it is the turn for **Townshend Lake Recreation Area** (tel: 802-365 7703; late May–early Sept daily 8am–8pm). Created by a dam built in the 1960s, it's a fine spot to take a swim, picnic, or cook-out.

You can follow a trail to the 125ft (38-meter) Hamilton Falls at **Jamaica State Park** (off Route 30; tel: 802-874 4600; early May–Columbus Day 10am–sunset).

GRAFTON

About 10 miles (16km) north of Townshend on Route 35, **Grafton** ❻ is a Greek Revival town in an 1840s time warp. Once a thriving agricultural center, it was suffering the same fate as many other small Vermont towns until the Windham Foundation took it over. Interested in doing more than just preserving the setting, it re-established the businesses which once thrived here. The **Grafton Village Cheese Company** (tel: 800-472 3866; www.graftonvillagecheese.com; daily 10am–6pm) makes award-winning cheddar with milk from local cows; the Grafton Forge is a working blacksmithing forge. You can watch honeybees at work and dig for fossils at the small **Nature Museum** or view a miniature village made entirely from Vermont granite at the **Vermont Museum of Mining and Minerals**. The **Grafton Historical Society Museum** (tel: 802-843 2111; www.nature-museum.org; Thu–Fri 10am–4pm year-round; Memorial Day–Indigenous People's Day also Sat 10am–4pm) is housed in a homestead built in 1845 and relates the town's fascinating history. Collections range from soapstone objects to musical instruments.

The perfect piste – Mount Snow uses hundreds of fan guns that combine compressed air and water to create additional snow.

Mixed traffic in Grafton.

GREEN NEW ENGLAND

New Englanders cherish their environment – 33 million acres of forests; 30,000 family farms in pastoral valleys; and miles of rocky coasts.

Lobstermen and fishermen depend on unpolluted ocean waters to provide their catch. Even major cities recognize that the nearness of such unsullied lands adds to their quality of life, but it was not always so. The Industrial Revolution brought great economic development to the region, but at a great ecological price. Manufacturing plants ravaged the region's rivers and landscapes; urban development focused solely on rapid growth and quick profits; and logging operations harvested timber without considering reforestation. The ocean was a commodity with limitless supplies of fish and a convenient disposal site for garbage.

That is changing as the undeniable effects of thoughtless practices become clear. A combination of practicality, frugality, and New England's historic mistrust of authority has fueled a region-wide ecological movement. The goal is to find a balance between the financial benefits of development and the preservation and restoration of the environment.

There are as many issues as trails in the White Mountains: acid rain; the use of toxic chemicals in the

A wind turbine in Searsburg, Vermont.

environment; development; energy generation; garbage disposal; and transportation just for starters.

Many initiatives are grassroots and local, following the historic patterns of community action: a town in Massachusetts helps weatherize low-income housing; a village in Maine installs solar-powered street lights; a neighborhood in Boston plants vegetable gardens in vacant lots; a parent organization in Rhode Island works to remove toxic chemical cleaners from schools.

The closeness of communities – both geographically and philosophically – leads to networking and action on a larger scale. The New England Grassroots Environmental Fund (https://grassrootsfund.org/) has a vast database of groups, resources, and programs throughout the region and encourages connections between them. Conferences of "green" organizations are clearinghouses of ideas, strategies, and successful actions. There are councils of environmental businesses, a think-tank that studies the finances of environmental issues, and an association of "eco-friendly" lodgings and resorts. More than a dozen New England colleges and universities offer academic majors in environmental studies and are magnets for research projects. Job training for "green" careers is offered through community colleges. There's even EarthShare New England (www.earthsharenewengland.org), which oversees payroll contribution to environmental groups. On a larger scale, all six New England states are members of the Regional Greenhouse Gas Initiative (www.rggi.org), which has set goals for reducing greenhouse gas emissions. Additionally, four of them (Connecticut, Massachusetts, Vermont, and Rhode Island) joined the United States Climate Alliance (www.usclimatealliance.org) and pledged to uphold the Paris Agreement on climate change despite president Donald Trump's decision to withdraw the US from the deal in June 2017.

Not all ideas are popular. Wind energy has many opponents who consider the windmills a blight on the landscape and solar power is difficult, given the long, dark, snowy New England winters. Proposals to limit fishing and lobstering are met with fierce resistance by boat captains and crews. But no one doubts that solutions will eventually be found, especially as the private sector is realizing that investing in a healthy environment brings economic benefits, which will keep New England "green" in every sense of the word.

Claim a rocker on the porch of the 1801 **Old Tavern at the Grafton Inn** (92 Main Street; tel: 802-234 8707; www.graftoninnvermont.com), whose guests have included notables from Thoreau and Kipling to Ulysses S. Grant and Teddy Roosevelt.

There are more than 2,000 acres (800 hectares) of trails suitable for year-round use at the inn's **Grafton Ponds Outdoor Center** (783 Townshend Road; tel: 802-843 2350; www.graftoninnvermont.com/grafton-trails).

CHESTER

Route 35 winds north about 7 miles (11km) to **Chester** ❼, which straddles three branches of the Williams River. An 1850s stone village-within-a-village features 30 homes faced in gneiss ledgestone – a type of granite – built before the Civil War. The town is a good base for cyclists and boating enthusiasts. One easy bike ride runs from the delightfully named Popple Dungeon Road to Tater Hill Golf Course.

Chester is also the northern terminus for **the Green Mountain Flyer** (54 Depot Street; tel: 800-707 3530; www.rails-vt.com), a diesel-powered dinner train trip that travels to Ludlow and back and lasts two and a half hours (see website for schedule).

UPPER CONNECTICUT VALLEY

A center of invention during the 19th century, **Windsor** ❽ became home to Vermont's machine tool industry. **The American Precision Museum** (196 Main Street/Route 12 East; tel: 802-674 5781; www.americanprecision.org; late May–Oct daily 10am–5pm) is housed in a National Historic Landmark, the 1846 Robbins and Lawrence Armory. It has a fascinating array of the machinery that made "Yankee ingenuity" a byword: machine tools, an extensive firearms collection, sewing machines, and measuring devices.

Windsor is also famed as the birthplace of Vermont, because it was here in the **Old Constitution House** (tel:

802-672 3773; http://historicsites.vermont.gov/directory/old_constitution; late May–mid-Oct Sat–Sun and Mon holidays 11am–5pm) that delegates met in 1777 to draw up a constitution for the prickly little republic, which was as wary of the other states as of the Crown.

In the early years of the 20th century, the natural beauty of the area drew artists like Maxfield Parrish and Frederic Remington. Just up Main Street, the **Windsor-Cornish Covered Bridge** spans Connecticut River to lovely Cornish, New Hampshire. It's the longest covered bridge in the United States. Note that the Saint-Gaudens National Historic Site is just across the bridge in New Hampshire.

NORTH TO WOODSTOCK

Sixteen miles (26km) to the north, **White River Junction** ❾, at the intersection of Interstates 91 and 89, is developing into a major arts community. An old railroad town (Amtrak still stops here), the entire downtown is a registered National Historic District with buildings from the late 1800s and

The red-tailed hawk is one of three species colloquially known as the "chickenhawk."

early 1900s. The **Main Street Museum** (58 Bridge Street; tel: 802-356 2776; www.mainstreetmuseum.org; Tue–Wed 4–7pm) is quirky fun, filled with the sorts of things museums collected long ago. The **Northern Stage** is an award-winning, professional regional theater company, located in the modern **Barrette Center for the Arts** (74–6 Gates Street; tel: 802-296 7000; www.northernstage.org), inaugurated in 2015 and featuring a 240-seat theater, with state-of-the-art acoustics and sound system. A few miles west on Route 4 at **Quechee** , the 162ft (49-meter) -deep **Quechee Gorge**, "Vermont's Little Grand Canyon," is best viewed from the bridge which spans it, or from the 0.8-mile (1.3km) trail at the **Quechee State Park**. The mile-long gorge is a legacy of the last ice age. The name is from the Abenaki language and means "Great Chasm."

The **Vermont Institute of Natural Science** (149 Natures Way; tel: 802-359 5000; www.vinsweb.org; daily 10am–4pm, later in summer) rehabilitates and cares for injured raptors. There's also a songbird aviary featuring local birds. Numerous activities including walks and field trips, workshops and lectures, are designed to redefine the way people look and interact with the landscape.

Frustrated with the direction the traditional crafts were taking in Europe, Irish artisan Simon Pearce moved to Vermont in 1971. He transformed **The Mill at Quechee** (1760 Quechee Main Street; tel: 802-295 2711; www.simonpearce.com; daily 10am–9pm), an abandoned flannel factory, into an inviting complex where he and his fellow artisans create distinctive glassworks and pottery. No assembly lines here; each piece is made using traditional glassblowing skills. The pottery is also individually thrown and hand-glazed. The adjacent **Glassblower Café** offers fine dining overlooking the Ottauquechee River. The sprawling, very commercial **Quechee Gorge Village** (Route 4, tel: 802-295 1550; www.quechee-gorge.com) includes the Cabot Quechee store (with lots of cheese samples; daily 9.30am–5.30pm; www.cabotcheese.coop/cabot-quechee-store), an antiques mall, and several gift shops, including the **Vermont**

In theory, Vermont has enough land to produce all its food.

Toy & Train Museum (www.quecheegorge. com/vermont-toy-train-museum), a jumbled collection of antique and more recent playthings. An antique carousel operates on summer weekends through mid-October. The **Quechee Polo Club** (Dewey Mills Road; tel: 603-443 2000) holds occasional games in summer.

WOODSTOCK

Woodstock ⓫, just to the west, was one of the first Vermont towns to be discovered – and given a high polish – by outsiders.

A passion for maintaining a graceful balance between society and nature has long been the keynote to Woodstock's renown. Vermont native Frederick Billings returned from his lucrative law practice in San Francisco in the 1890s to become a pioneer in reforestation and a zealous model farmer. The slopes of Mount Tom and Mount Peg and the restored **Billings Farm and Museum** (Route 12 East; tel: 802-457 2355; www. billingsfarm.org; Apr–Oct daily 10am–5pm, Nov–Feb Sat-Sun 10am–4pm) are testaments to his love for rural Vermont. A working farm with draft horses, sheep, oxen, and a herd of milk-producing Jersey cows, it recreates life on an early 19th-century farmstead. In 1998 the Billings family mansion and its surrounding 500 acres (200 hectares) were bequeathed as the **Marsh-Billings-Rockefeller National Historical Park** (Route 12; tel: 802-457 3368; www.nps. gov/mabi; visitor center: Memorial Day–Oct daily 10am–5pm; grounds: open year-round; mansion tours by advance reservation Memorial Day–Oct; free). This is Vermont's only national park and the only park in the system to concentrate specifically on conservation. The Queen Anne-style mansion houses more than 400 paintings, including a superb collection of Hudson River art.

For further glimpses of Woodstock's past, visit the **Woodstock Historical Society** headquarters (26 Elm Street; tel: 802-457 1822; offices year-round,

Dana House Museum Tue–Sat 1–5pm, Sun 11am–3pm): nine rooms of period furnishings, fine art, clothing, textiles, silver, ceramics, photographs, and early American toys in the 1807 Dana House.

The **Woodstock Inn and Resort** (tel: 888-338 2745; www.woodstockinn.com) on the green is one of the state's finest lodgings, and its Robert Trent Jones golf course and **Suicide Six** ski area (tel: 802-457 6661; https://skivermont. com/suicide-six-ski-area) offer year-round amusements. Despite its ominous-sounding name, most of the ski trails are for beginners and intermediate skiers. On the other side of the green, a covered bridge leads to Mountain Avenue, a redoubt of old summer cottages, and a park at the base of Mount Tom.

THE COOLIDGE HOMESTEAD

The nation's 30th president was born and is buried at the **President Calvin Coolidge State Historic Site** (off Route 100A; tel: 802-672 3773; www. nps.gov/nr/travel/presidents/calvin_coolidge_homestead.html; late May–mid-Oct daily 9.30am–5pm) in **Plymouth** ⓬, 15

A country lane near Tunbridge, whose annual agricultural event is grandly known as "Tunbridge World's Fair."

Ⓞ INSTITUTE OF NATURAL SCIENCE

The Vermont Institute of Natural Science (www.vinsweb.org) is New England's premier avian wildlife rehabilitation center. Veterinarians and rehabilitators treat over 400 birds each year – not just hawks and eagles, but waterfowl, songbirds, even hummingbirds that are injured or orphaned. About 40 birds that cannot be released into the wild live permanently in outdoor enclosures which are as close to their natural habitat as possible.

Daily programs cover topics as diverse as the mechanics of avian flight, conservation issues, and the mysteries of seasonal migration. The most popular programs are those which show the raptors – eagles, hawks, falcons, and owls – in action and those demonstrating rehabilitation techniques. The Adopt a Raptor program provides donors with a photo of their bird, adoption papers, and a fact sheet about that species.

VINS's greater goal is to teach people to understand the wildlife and diverse natural habitats they encounter in daily life – even in urban settings – with empathy and intelligence. The field trips and walks along the VINS nature trails and the path to Quechee Gorge are designed to redefine how people look at the Vermont landscape, their impact on the natural world, and how to make that impact positive (or at least less damaging).

miles (24km) southwest of Woodstock. Coolidge (1872–1933) was a taciturn man, who became president after the sudden death of Warren Harding. Coolidge's father, a notary public, swore in his son in the middle of the night when they received the news.

One of the nation's most authentic presidential sites, the site preserves not only "Silent Cal's" home, but his entire boyhood village, including his father's general store, the dance hall which served as his summer White House, and a barn holding a superb collection of 19th-century agricultural equipment.

KILLINGTON

North and west via Routes 100 and 4, New England's largest ski area, **Killington** (4763 Killington Road; tel: 800-734 9435; www.killington.com), covers seven peaks and encompasses 200 trails. "The Beast of the East" also ranks top among the Northeast ski resorts for nightlife. With a 4,241ft (1,296-meter) peak reached by gondola for sightseers as well as skiers, the resort is active year-round – the skiing

Justin Morrill Homestead.

often lasts from October through June. In the summer, it joins with nearby Pico Peak to become an outdoor adventure center with mountain-biking trails, golf, an alpine slide, climbing walls, and lift rides.

The tiny village of **Strafford** was the birthplace of Vermont Representative and Senator Justin Smith Morrill, author of the 1862 Morrill Acts which established America's system of land grant colleges and universities. Sales of federal lands support 105 such schools. The **Justin Morrill Homestead** (Route 132; tel: 802-765 4288; Memorial Day–mid-Oct Wed–Sun and holiday Mon 11am–5pm) is a 17-room pink Carpenter Gothic home, built between 1848 and 1851.

MORMON CONNECTIONS

Joseph Smith, a visionary who founded the Mormon religion, was born in **South Royalton** in 1805. Just off Route 14, Mormons maintain the **Joseph Smith Memorial and Birthplace** (357 LDS Lane; tel: 802-763 7742; daily 9am–5pm, from 1pm on Sun), with a 38.5ft

(11.5-meter) obelisk – 1ft for each year of Smith's life – made from a single block of Barre granite, and a museum.

North of South Royalton on Route 110, five covered bridges span the First Branch of the White River in **Tunbridge** . Sadly the town's "Vermont History Expo" – the epitome of a country fair with ox pulls, sheepdog trials, and clog dancing – was discontinued as of 2017, but Tunbridge is still worth a visit for its nostalgic charm, which earned its entire center a place on the National Register of Historic Places.

BROOKFIELD

North on Route 14, the tranquil village of **Brookfield** ⑯ is in the geographical center of the state. In 1812, a 320ft (98-meter) floating bridge, supported by 380 tarred barrels, was built across Sunset Lake at the center of town. Replaced eight times so far, the current incarnation is supported by fiber-reinforced polymer pontoons. One of the last ice harvests in the East is now the occasion for an annual festival on the lake, held in late January with ice cutting, ice sculpting, and dog sledding.

ROCK OF AGES

About 10 miles (16km) to the north, on Route 14 between Brookfield and Barre, **Graniteville** ⑰ is site of the largest granite quarry in the world, the **Rock of Ages Quarry** (visitor center, 773 Graniteville Road; tel: 877-870 9057; May–Aug Mon–Sat 9.15am–3.35pm, Sept–Oct also Sun). There is a large array of quarry and factory tours, a sandblasting activity, and other features. The visitor center has all the details, times, and prices.

Mining began soon after the War of 1812 and boomed with the influx of skilled immigrant stoneworkers between 1880 and 1910. Fed up with poor wages and working conditions (many died of silicosis), the granite workers elected a Socialist mayor of Barre – many decades before liberal Burlington was ready to do the same.

BARRE

Many of the workers in the quarries were Italian immigrants, as evidenced by the names on the headstones at **Hope Cemetery** (off Route 14) in **Barre** ⑱ (pronounced *Barry*). Quarry workers commemorated their own with often-touching artwork. Among the standouts: a half-scale racing car and the life-size statue of labor leader Elia Corti, shot down in 1903 at a Socialist rally.

The workers' heritage and politics are much in evidence in downtown **Barre**. The larger-than-life statue of a mustachioed Italian stonecutter at the corner of North Main Street and Maple Avenue looks toward Granite Street, site of the old Socialist head-quarters, the **Old Labor Hall** (http://oldlaborhall.org), a National Historic Landmark renovated by the Barre Historical Society (46 Granite Street; tel: 802-331 0013).

The granite **Robert Burns Memorial** in front of the 1891 school on Washington

Coolidge State Historic Site.

Street was erected in 1899 by Scots who also worked in the quarries.

The **Vermont Granite Museum and Stone Arts School** (7 Jones Brothers Way; tel: 802-476-4605; www.vtgranite-museum.org; June–Oct Wed–Sat 10am–4pm, Nov–May Mon–Fri 9am–5pm) is an ambitious work-in-progress. Housed in a massive turn-of-the-century granite manufacturing plant, when completed it will detail the geologic, historic, technologic, and artistic impact of the state's granite industry. At the school, sculptors learn carving techniques from working professionals. Visitors are also very welcome to call for personal tours.

MONTPELIER

Home to about 8,000 people, **Montpelier** ⑲ (pronounced *Mont-peel-yer*) is the nation's smallest state capital. The lively little downtown is dominated by the gold-leaf dome of the **Vermont State House** (State Street; tel: 802-828-2228; guided tours on the half hour July–mid-Oct Mon–Fri 10am–3.30pm; self-guided and audio tours year-round).

Initially, Vermont's capital rotated through the state, but with the completion of the original nine-sided building in 1808 the seat of power settled here. When an imposing stone successor was gutted by fire, the portico and granite walls withstood the flames to form a shell for the present structure. The Senate Chamber is considered the most beautiful room in the state.

Adjacent to the State House is the **Vermont Historical Society and Museum** (109 State Street; tel: 802-828 2291; www.vermonthistory.org; Tue–Sat 10am–4pm). Housed in a re-creation of an Italianate Pavilion-inspired hotel which served early legislators, the award-winning museum is a virtual time-travel experience. Visitors walk through Vermont's history from Abenaki wigwams, the tavern hangout of the Green Mountain Boys, and military training camps of World War II.

Montpelier is home to the **New England Culinary Institute** (www.neci.edu), whose students and teachers staff two excellent dining spots on Main Street. Start the day off with European-style

Ⓞ NEW ENGLAND'S LAST FRONTIER

The Vermonter's streak of independence and the land's remoteness led to decades of self-sufficiency that define the peoples' character. Even to this day, Vermonters are known to be a hardy lot, ready to forge their own way, be it in politics or environmental policy.

Squeezed between New York, New Hampshire, and New France (as Colonial-era Canada was sometimes called), Vermont's wild territory was slow to be settled, and the people who took on the challenge were often as untameable as the terrain. The French and their Indian allies were one threat. Once those were eliminated, the Vermonters had to deal with the colonists to either side of them. Ethan Allen and his staunchly independent Green Mountain Boys, an informal militia, fought off "Yorker" surveyors in order to protect the interests of the Vermonters. In between, they dealt with repulsing the British invasion from Canada during the American Revolution.

Vermont's interest in getting rid of the British did not mean it was eager to join the new republic. It was not one of the original colonies and it remained the Republic of

Vermont, initially known as New Connecticut, from 1777 until finally becoming the 14th state of the Union in 1791. Uniquely, Vermont abolished slavery before joining the Union, and was the first state to have done so. The 1777 constitution also granted suffrage for men who did not own land and the provision of public education.

Things began to change in the mid-19th century. The 1849 California Gold Rush lured some young Vermonters from their farms, and the Civil War lured many more. As the nation expanded, it drew sturdy Vermonters to take on challenges far from the mountains. Between 1865 and 1960 Vermont's population declined and agricultural production dwindled. Today, it is rising again as the lure of the mountains and of living a simpler life closer to the land attracts people with same strong abilities and ambitions as the first settlers.

Vermont is unique in several ways, because it is the only state in New England that does not border the Atlantic Ocean. Without a strong maritime tradition, Vermonters have been forced to seek inspiration elsewhere, in the mountains and lakes of the beautiful landscape.

pastries at **La Brioche**, which also serves luncheon fare; **NECI on Main** serves lunch, afternoon light fare, and dinner, and its Sunday brunch buffet is justly famous. There are also two cafés: Dewey Café and National Life Cafeteria.

Lost Nation Theater (tel: 802-229 0492; http://lostnationtheater.org) is widely recognized as one of the top regional theaters in the US. Their Apr–Oct season features classic and contemporary shows for adults and youth at the **City Hall Arts Center** (39 Main Street). The **Savoy Theater** (26 Main Street; tel: 802-229 0598; www.savoytheater.com) is run by dedicated cinemaphiles. They screen a wonderful schedule of indie and world films nightly.

Tapping maple trees for their sap which is turned into syrup and sugar is an early-spring affair, but many of the "sugar works" are open year-round to demonstrate the process (and to sell you all varieties of the products). Two of them near Montpelier are the **Morse Farm Sugar Works** (1168 County Road/Main Street, 2.5 miles (4km) from town; tel: 800-242 2740; www.morsefarm.com; daily year-round, opening times vary with seasons) and **Bragg Farm** (Route 14, north of intersection of Route 14 and Route 2; tel: 802-223 5757/800-376 5757; www.braggfarm.com; daily 8.30am–6pm). Both offer free tours, tastings, activities for kids, and large gift shops.

SUGARBUSH TO WATERBURY

Some 20 miles (32km) west of Montpelier, the Green Mountain range attains heady heights that tempt skiers as well as mountain climbers and bikers. South of I–89 on Route 100 (exit 10), the Mad River Valley towns of **Waitsfield ❷⓪** and **Warren** support two ski areas. The challenging **Mad River Glen ski area** (www.madriverglen.com), opened in 1948, is strictly a winter destination. The more developed and extensive **Sugarbush** (www.sugarbush.com) is open year-round, with summer activities focusing on golf, hiking, and tennis. Both towns are full of inviting restaurants, cozy inns, gift shops, and galleries.

The folk art statue atop the State House is the Roman goddess of agriculture, Ceres, carved in 1938 by Dwight Dwinell, the building's chief usher.

Autumn comes to the area around Montpelier.

Mount Mansfield, Vermont's highest peak, has hiking trails and ski slopes, and alpine tundra survives here from the ice ages.

Vermont State House.

To get an unusual perspective on the countryside, consider a soaring excursion in a sailplane towed by **Sugarbush Soaring** (Warren-Sugarbush Airport, Route 100; tel: 802-496 2290; www.sugarbush.org; flights daily May–Oct). North on Route 100, the **Vermont Icelandic Horse Farm** (3061 North Fayston Road, Fayston; tel: 802-496 7141; www.icelandichorses.com) is home to a herd of the hardy, friendly, sure-footed pony-sized horses. You can take an hour's ride or up to a five-day trek.

For a more conventional scenic tour, head for one of the nearby "gaps" (glacially formed passes through the mountains). The road to **Lincoln Gap** begins on Route 100 south of Warren Village and climbs for 3 miles (5km) to 2,424ft (739 meters) before descending into tiny Lincoln. The road through **Appalachian Gap** begins on Route 17 and winds past Mad River Glen to the 2,365ft (721-meter) crest before its descent into the Champlain Valley. (Note: gaps can't accommodate trailers, and Lincoln Gap is closed in winter.)

WATERBURY

Fourteen miles (22km) northwest of Montpelier, by either I-89 or Route 2, is **Waterbury** , where a pair of "flatlander" entrepreneurs turned this famous dairy state into ice cream heaven. **The Ben & Jerry's Homemade Ice Cream Factory** offers tours and tastings daily (tel: 802-882 2047 for schedule; www.benjerry.com). If you want to actually see ice cream being made, schedule a weekday visit. On weekends, there's a video of the process. Either way, the 30-minute tour ends at the tasting room.

Amtrak still stops at the restored Victorian train station in Waterbury. It is also the visitor center and café of **Keurig Green Mountain Coffee Company** (www.keuriggreenmountain.com; Mon–Fri 7am–5pm, Sat–Sun from 8am). One of the first coffee companies to commit to "fair trade" principles, its free, self-guided, multimedia tour explains how coffee is grown and produced.

Continuing north on Route 100, stop for samples of the "Best Cheddar in the World" at the **Cabot Annex Store complex** (2657 Waterbury-Stowe Road; tel: 802-244 6334; www.cabot cheese.coop/cabot-farmers-store; daily 9am–6pm). Lake Champlain Chocolates, Vermont Teddy Bear, and Snow Farm Winery also have stores here. Watch fine-art glassblowing at **Ziemke Glassblowing** (3033 Waterbury-Stowe Road; tel: 802-244 6126; http://zglass blowing.com/; daily 10am–6pm). One mile (1.6km) farther north, watch cider being pressed, sneak a peek at the action inside a beehive, maybe watch apple jelly being made, and visit the Grand View Winery tasting room to try hard cider (if you are over 21) at the **Cold Hollow Cider Mill** (3600 Waterbury-Stowe Road; tel: 800-327 7537; www.coldhollow.com; daily 8am–6pm).

The headquarters of the **Green Mountain Club** (4711 Waterbury Road; tel: 802-244 7037; www.

greenmountainclub.org; Memorial Day–Labor Day Mon–Sat, rest of year Mon–Fri) is the best place to pick up information about the **Long Trail**, Vermont's "footpath in the wilderness," which follows the ridges of the Green Mountains for 270 miles (430km) from the Massachusetts border to the Canadian line, as well as other hiking trails. The Appalachian Trail shares about 100 miles (160km) of the Long Trail.

STOWE

Ten miles (16km) north on Route 100 is **Stowe** ㉒, one of the premier winter destinations in New England. The **Ski Museum** (1 South Main Street; tel: 802-253 9911; www.vtssm.com; Wed–Sun noon–5pm) chronicles the development of skiing in Vermont from the days of wooden skis and leather boots to the present. But even before skiing arrived in the 1930s, the town enjoyed a reputation as a stylish summer place. Summer or winter, sports opportunities abound, particularly along the **Stowe Recreation Path**. Ideally suited for skiers, cyclists (in

2017 bike-maintenance stations at the Lintilhac and Chase park were installed), wheelchair racers, runners, walkers, and stroller pushers, the 5.3-mile (8.5km) paved path skirts the West Branch river from town to **the Topnotch Resort and Spa** (www.topnotchresort.com), passing a number of appealing inns, restaurants, and shops en route. Another notable inn is the Austrian-style **Trapp Family Lodge** (tel: 800-826 7000; www.trappfamily.com). Founded by the Baroness Maria von Trapp of *Sound of Music* fame, the 2,700-acre (1,100-hectare) resort has Vermont's oldest cross-country ski trail system, part of one of the biggest networks in New England. Raising a beer stein in salute to the Austrian love of lager, the lodge has started its own on-site brewery producing European-style lagers. Visitors to the lodge can also enjoy European-style breakfast or dinner at the Main Dining Room.

Both **Eden Dog Sledding** (tel: 802-635 9070; www.edendogsledding.com) and **Peace Pups Dog Sledding** (tel: 802-888 7733; www.peacepupsdogsledding.

⊘ Tip

Stowe Performing Arts (tel: 802-253 7792; www.stoweperformingarts.com) has a schedule of several outdoor concerts every week in the summer, all with a backdrop of the mountains. Several of them, including the noonday series, are free.

Maria von Trapp.

⊘ THE VON TRAPP FAMILY

Orphaned before she was 7, Maria Augusta Kutschera was raised by her father's cousin as a socialist, atheist, and religious cynic. While in college, she heard a sermon by a visiting priest which changed her outlook. Newly devout, she joined a convent. Worried that the restrictions of convent life were damaging her health, her doctor recommended that she become the tutor of a daughter of a retired Austrian naval officer, Georg von Trapp. In true "this will be Hollywood material some day" fashion, they fell in love and were married in 1927. "The Trapp Family Choir" formed after Georg lost his fortune in a bank collapse. Their departure from Austria was not a dramatic escape across the mountains; they simply boarded a train to Italy on their way to a US concert tour. Vermont reminded them of Austria, so they purchased land near Stowe for what became the Trapp Family Lodge (www.trappfamily.com).

Maria sold film rights to a memoir she had written to a wily producer for just a few thousand dollars, effectively cutting herself out of the millions of dollars of profit. Far from the strict, unfeeling character portrayed on stage, Georg (who died in 1947) was a gentle, devoted father. After working in the South Pacific as a missionary, Maria returned to Vermont where she died in 1987. She is buried in the family cemetery next to the lodge.

⊙ **Tip**

Stowe's winter carnival, first held in 1921, is now a major nine-day fair in late January and early February. Events include a range of competitive sports (including snow golf and snow volleyball), icecarving, and "the world's coldest parade." For details, check http://stowewintercarnival.com.

com) have snow and dry-land mushing opportunities throughout the year.

On **Mount Mansfield**  Ralph Waldo Emerson had a bracing vacation in 1823 at the Summit House, where, he recounts, his "whole party climbed to the top of the [mountain's] nose and watched the sun rise over the top of the White Mountains of New Hampshire."

Hikers still favor this craggy human profile. Several trails of varying difficulty lead to the summit, including "Profanity Trail," which works its way along the ridgeline. A far easier ascent is to take the 4.5-mile (7.5km) **Auto Road** (fee), a century-old toll road that ends at a small visitor center. A moderate hike of 1.5 miles (2km) reaches the nose. Even easier is an eight-passenger gondola (Route 108; fee) which zips to 3,625ft (1,105 meters), close to the 4,393ft (1,338-meter) "chin," the state's highest point.

The handsome Cliff House at the upper terminus of the gondola serves an elegant lunch along with spectacular views when the lift is operating. The **Spruce Peak Performing Arts**

A hot-air balloon festival at Stowe.

Center (tel: 802-760 4634; www.sprucepeakarts.org) at the resort has the ambitious goal of establishing itself as the region's outstanding cultural venue.

Other big summertime draws are the Stoweflake Hot Air Balloon Festival (www.stoweflake.com/activities_balloon_festival.aspx) and a midsummer classic car rally; in mid-January, during the Stowe Winter Carnival, the whole town parties.

OVER SMUGGLERS' NOTCH

The nearby ski area at **Smugglers' Notch Resort** ② (Route 108 South; tel: 800-419 4615 or 802-332 6854; www.smuggs.com) was so named for its role during the War of 1812 when trade with Canada was forbidden. Wintertime visitors hoping to fit in a visit are in for a surprise – and a drive: the direct road from Stowe (Route 108) is closed in winter, and those who've traveled it in summer will understand why. Hundred-foot cliffs and giant boulders crowd the narrow, winding roadway.

You'll need to loop north on Route 100, west on Route 15, and south on Route 108 to get there. "Smuggs" offers downhill skiing on three peaks as well as cross-country trails and is popular with families for its well-thought-out children's programs. In summer the attractions are hiking, horseback riding, and an assortment of water slides.

The town closest to the resort, **Jeffersonville**, has a restaurant, the historic Smugglers' Notch Inn (www.smuggsinn.com), with a covered hot tub for six and a well-equipped general store with a liquor outlet.

THE NORTHEAST KINGDOM

The **Northeast Kingdom** is the name given to the region north of Route 15. It's a nearly 2,000-sq-mile (over 5,000-sq-km) swath of crystal lakes and deep forests, a region sparsely populated and with little industry. *Where* *the Rivers Run North* is the title writer Howard Frank Mosher gave his 1978 collection of short stories in honor of a region known for its backwater quirks.

Continue south on Route 15 through Morrisville and Hardwick. Turn south on Route 215 to **Cabot** and the **Cabot Creamery Co-operative** (2878 Main Street; tel: 800-837 4261; www.cabotcheese.coop; Jan–May Mon–Sat 10am–4pm, end of May–Oct daily 9am–5pm, Nov–Dec daily 10am–4pm). Founded in 1919, the co-op draws on some 1,200 member farms for the milk that goes into its award-winning cheddar cheese. Sadly creamery tours are no longer offered, but you can still enjoy a video tour of the cheese-making area, as well as sampling and purchasing Cabot cheese products.

ST JOHNSBURY

The city of **St Johnsbury** ㉕, the largest community in the Northeast Kingdom, remains a vibrant pocket of Victorian charm. From the bank buildings downtown to the Fairbanks mansion on the Plains overlooking the valley, the stamp of architect Lambert Packard (1832–1906) and his wealthy patrons is visible everywhere. Thaddeus Fairbanks started making the world's first platform scale here in the 1830s, and he and his sons were great civic benefactors.

The handsome **St Johnsbury Athenaeum** (1171 Main Street; tel: 802-748 8291; www.stjathenaeum.org; Mon, Wed, and Fri 10am–5.30pm, Tue and Thu 2–7pm, Sat 10am–3pm), built in 1871–73, houses both the city library and an art gallery. This is one of the oldest intact art collections in the country, with great attention paid to the Hudson River School. Works on display include the panorama *The Domes of the Yosemite* by Albert Bierstadt.

The Romanesque **Fairbanks Museum and Planetarium** (corner of Main and Prospect streets; tel: 802-748 2372; www.fairbanksmuseum.org; daily

9am–5pm) is northern New England's Museum of Natural History, with 4,000 mounted creatures (many in dioramas of natural settings) on display. The Museum is also home to the Lyman Spitzer Jr. Planetarium, the only public planetarium in Vermont, with a state-of-the-art projection system and an interactive "omniglobe" explaining geology and climate. East out of downtown St Johnsbury on Route 2, watch for the sign for **Stephen Huneck's Dog Mountain** (143 Parks Road off Spaulding Road; tel: 800-449 2580; www.dogmt.com; gallery: Mon, Wed, Fri 11am–4pm, Sat–Sun 10am–5pm; grounds open year-round dawn–dusk), where the late artist and woodcarver created a chapel to memorialize man's best departed friends. Dogs scamper up the hiking trails and splash in the pond on the property. Sales of his woodcuts and other artwork at the on-site gallery help maintain the property and keep it open.

Nearby, visit **Maple Grove Farms** (1052 Portland Street, Route 2; tel: 800-525 2540; www.maplegrove.com;

A hayride with a view of Burke Mountain.

The library in St Johnsbury's Athenaeum.

St Johnsbury, with a population of over 6,000, is known locally as St Jay.

Apr–May Mon–Fri 8am–5pm, June–Dec also Sat–Sun 9am–5pm; call for rest of the year) for a tour of the factory to learn how syrup and maple products are made.

EAST BURKE

About 10 miles (16km) north of St Johnsbury, in **East Burke** ㉖, **Kingdom Trails** (Route 114; tel: 802-626 0737; www.kingdomtrails.com) is a network of multi-use trails covering more than 100 miles (160km). It is consistently voted among the top trail systems for mountain biking, hiking, trail running, Nordic skiing, and snowshoeing. The welcome center is in town behind Bailey & Burke Store. **East Burke Sports** (tel: 802-626 3215; https://eastburkesports.com), across the street from the welcome center, rents bikes.

West and north of St Johnsbury via routes 15 and 16, **Greensboro**, on Caspian Lake, is a peaceful retreat long favored by writers, academics, and professionals. **Willey's Store** – the heart of the tiny village – dispenses local

information and carries an astounding inventory ranging from boots to Beaujolais to *The New York Times*.

THE CRAFTSBURYS

Northwest of St Johnsbury on Route 14, the **Craftsburys** begin. There are three: East Craftsbury, Craftsbury, and the Shangri-La of Vermont villages, **Craftsbury Common** ㉗, a tidy collection of beautifully preserved, 19th-century homes surrounding a town green on a ridge overlooking the valley. The trees around the village green were planted at the death of George Washington in 1799.

Back toward I-91, in **Glover** ㉘, the **Bread and Puppet Theater Museum** (Route 122; tel: 802-525 3031; http://breadandpuppet.org/museum; June–Oct daily 10am–6pm, July–Aug also tours Sun 1pm, plus before and after evening performances; voluntary donation) is home base for an amazing collection of huge and fantastical creatures created by German immigrant Peter Schumann to illustrate the horrors of war and the wonders

of life. Believing that art is to the soul what bread is to the body, he serves freshly baked bread to the audience. The company performs many Sunday afternoons throughout the summer: check their website for the schedule.

Farther north **Brownington** ㉙, a thriving community in the early 1800s when the Boston–Montreal stage stopped here, is best known for its elegant old homes and the **Old Stone House Museum** (off Route 58; tel: 802-754 2022; www.oldstonehousemuseum.org; mid May–mid-Oct Wed–Sun 11am–5pm). Its collection of local miscellanea is housed in the former county grammar school, built in 1827–30 by Alexander Twilight. He became the first African-American college graduate as a member of Middlebury College's class of 1823 and was the first African-American legislator when he was elected to the Vermont General Assembly in 1836.

NEWPORT

Straddling the US–Canada border, 30-mile (48km) -long **Lake Memphremagog** snakes between steep wooded hills. **Newport** ㉚, the "Border City" at the southern end of the lake, is noted for its easy mingle of Canadian day-trippers, locals, and sports fishermen in search of trout and landlocked salmon. There is a lovely boardwalk along the waterfront. The **MAC Center for the Arts** (158 Main Street; tel: 802-334 1966; www.maccenterforthearts.com; Mon–Sat 10am–5pm, June–Aug also Sun until 3pm) features a bright gallery with works by area artists inspired by the landscape and light.

Several outfitters rent canoes and kayaks for exploring the lake and the large **South Bay Wildlife Management Area** (http://fpr.vermont.gov). If you explore the northern part of the lake, be aware that the border with Canada bisects it at about the halfway point, and border regulations are enforced.

About 20 miles (32km) to the west of Newport, Route 242 climbs to the ski area of **Jay Peak** ㉛ (tel: 802-988 2611 or 800-451 4449; www.jaypeakresort.com). Massively extended and renovated over

Stained glass decorates the chapel at Stephen Huneck's Dog Mountain.

Ice windsurfing on Lake Champlain. Some years, the big lake freezes entirely across its 10-mile (16km) width at Burlington.

Farming chores in South Hero.

the last few years, it includes two new hotels, a large indoor water park, spa, indoor skating rink, upgraded snow-making equipment, Nordic Center, and a pro shop for summer golf.

THE NORTHWESTERN CORNER

Vermont's northwestern corner is defined by the Canadian border and the jagged, picturesque shoreline of **Lake Champlain**. The Vermont "mainland" here is gently rolling dairy country, growing flatter and more open as it nears the border and the great alluvial plain of the St Lawrence River. The big lake is bisected by the Alburgh peninsula descending from Quebec and by a 22-mile (35km) skein of islands, linked by bridges and causeways.

This is where Samuel de Champlain (1567–1635) first ventured out upon the waters that would bear his name, where Iroquois raiders canoed north to terrorize early French settlements, and where bootleggers' speedboats barreled south to the thirsty speakeasies of Prohibition days. Such excitement is

long past, and today's northwest corner is one of Vermont's most enticing watery playlands.

LAKE CHAMPLAIN ISLANDS

The **Lake Champlain Islands ❷** are strewn with Arcadian preserves, lakeshore drives, and sleepy little towns. The only town which is not on an island is Alburg. It's on a peninsula that's connected to the rest of the US only by a causeway. Several state parks have fine-sand swimming beaches, including **Sand Bar** (Route 2; Milton) and **Alburgh Dunes** (off Route 129 Alburgh; both Memorial Day–Labor Day 10am–sunset).

South Hero, on an island in the middle of Lake Champlain and on roughly the same latitude as Bordeaux, France, is home to Vermont's first winery, **Snow Farm Vineyard** (190 West Shore Road; tel: 802-372 9463; www.snowfarm. com; daily 11am–4pm). Bring a picnic or buy a salad or sandwich at the winery and enjoy a free concert under the stars at the farm's Thursday evening concert series (mid-June–late Aug). The Skinny Pancake Café (60 Lake St., Suite 1A, Burlington; tel: 802-540 0188; www.skinnypancake.com) is open daily from breakfast to dinner.

Turn onto South Street to visit **Allenholm Farms** (http://allenholm.com), where you can rent a bicycle to explore the country lanes, enjoy the petting zoo, and pick your own apples in the fall. At **Hackett's Orchards** (www.hackettsorchard.com) try a fresh cider doughnut at the bake shop.

Grand Isle is also home to the 1783 **Hyde Cabin** (Route 2; tel: 802-372 5440; July–mid-Oct, Sat–Sun 11am–5pm), the oldest log cabin in New England. The interior is arranged as a home setting of the period. Next to it is the 1814 **Corners Schoolhouse** with a small display of books and other articles.

The Vermont Shakespeare Company (tel: 877-874 1911; www.vermontshakespeare.org) performs in the Champlain

Islands and Burlington during the summer. Driftwood Tours (tel: 802-373 0022; www.driftwoodtoursvt.com) gives tours of Lake Champlain from its home base at the **North Hero House** (tel: 888-525 3644; www.northherohouse.com), one of the island's finest inns.

On **Isle La Motte**, "the oldest coral reef in the world" was left behind 10,000 years ago, when the Atlantic covered the Champlain Valley; the formations are visible at the **Goodsell Ridge Fossil Preserve** (Quarry Road; tel: 802 862 4150; trails dawn–dusk). Ever since the first French trappers said the first Mass on the island in 1666, Catholics have considered Vermont under the protection of St Anne. **St Anne's Shrine** (92 Saint Anne's Road; tel: 802-928 3362; www.saintannesshrine.org) attracts the faithful for pilgrimages and prayer among the pines.

SWANTON

East on Route 78 in **Swanton** ㉝, more than 200 avian species, including ospreys and blue heron, have been identified at the 6,345-acre (2,568-hectare) **Missisquoi National Wildlife Refuge** (29 Tabor Road; tel: 802-868 4781; www.fws.gov/refuge/mississuoi; grounds: daily dawn–dusk). Swanton is the tribal headquarters of the Abenaki people. The **Abenaki Tribal Museum** (100 Grand Avenue; tel: 802-868 2559; irregular hours, call) displays many items for daily and ceremonial use.

ST ALBANS

For many years **St Albans** ㉞, 10 miles (16km) south on Route 7, was headquarters of the Central Vermont Railway, and its glory days are reflected in its fine town green, imposing brick buildings, and handsome Victorian homes. St Albans was the scene of the Civil War's northernmost skirmish: in 1864 a band of Confederates infiltrated the town, robbed the banks, and hightailed it to Canada. Caught and brought to trial, their exploits were excused as "legitimate" acts of war. Billing itself as "The Maple Sugar Capital of the

A cabinetmaker carving scrollwork.

☉ VERMONT ARTS AND CRAFTS

More than 1,600 residents of Vermont identify themselves as professional artisans. That's one of the highest rates per capita in the country and makes Vermont the epicenter of the crafts revival in America. There are more than 130 galleries scattered throughout the state, including those singled out by the Vermont Crafts Council for showcasing work only by Vermont artisans. There are guilds for nearly every media, including fiber arts, painting, photography, weaving, furniture making, woodworking, and pottery.

From the first spring weekends through fall foliage, there are as many art festivals in Vermont as there are maple trees (www.vermontfairsandfes tivals.com). Every small town seems to hold a weekend art show, which usually features local talent. Major two-day festivals are scheduled from July through October. The largest of these is the Southern Vermont Arts & Fine Craft Festival, held every August in Manchester (www.craftproducers. com). Major festivals routinely attract from 200 to 400 artists who must send samples of their work to be reviewed before they are invited to participate. Acceptance in these juried shows means their work has been judged by other professionals as being of a very high standard. Meeting the artists and learning about their eclectic, and often eccentric, pasts is another insight into Vermont's unique character – and characters.

Bronze statue of Civil War General and local businessman William W. Wells (1837–92) in Burlington's Battery Park.

World," it hosts the Vermont Maple Festival, at the end of April (www.vtmaplefestival.org).

The city's history is ably recounted in exhibits at the **St Albans Historical Museum** (corner Church and Bishop streets; tel: 802-527 7933; http://stamuseum.org; mid-June–mid-Oct Wed–Fri 11am–4pm, Sat 10am–2pm).

A few miles east on Route 36 is the village of **Fairfield**, birthplace of President Chester A. Arthur (4588 Chester Arthur Road; tel: 802-828 3051; http://historicsites.vermont.gov/directory/arthur; July–mid-Oct Sat–Sun and Mon holidays 11am–5pm; donation). The son of an impoverished Baptist minister, he was born in 1829 or 1830 (Arthur himself was fuzzy on the date) in a primitive log cabin. (A granite monument marks the likely spot where it stood.) The parishioners quickly completed a modest parsonage for the family. A reconstruction of the house contains a pictorial record of Arthur's life and political career. He became president after the assassination of President James Garfield in 1881. Like another president born in rural poverty, Arthur advocated for civil rights.

BURLINGTON AND ENVIRONS

A picture-postcard setting, abundant recreational and cultural opportunities, five colleges and universities, and its position as Vermont's financial and industrial center make **Burlington** ❸❺ a lively city. With a population of over 42,000 – half of them students – Burlington is the smallest "state's largest city" in the country.

Burlington started as a trading post and port in 1775, but it didn't boom until the mid-1800s. Between shipping on Lake Champlain and along the Champlain Canal, the lumber industry, and water-powered mills and industries on the Winooski River, Burlington was a prosperous town with all the amenities that went with it. After World War II, it slipped into the same decline seen by many other New England cities as its waterfront decayed and was abandoned. But New England ingenuity

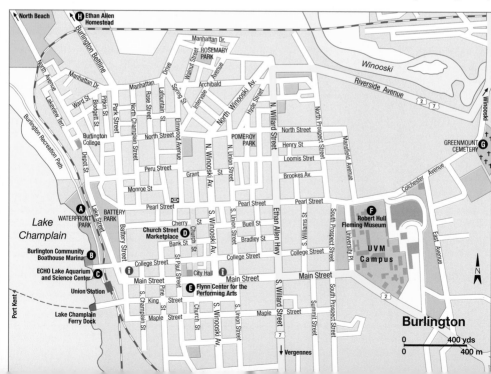

Burlington

0   400 yds
0   400 m

prevailed and the city is rebounding. Throughout the downtown, over 200 buildings have been restored. A growing influx of industry, notably IBM, and the new metropolitan tone mingle to keep Burlington turning up on polls as being one of the US's "most liveable cities."

Sunset over Lake Champlain and the Adirondacks from the heights above Burlington is enough to justify a visit. But along Lake and Battery streets, the old workaday waterfront has been reborn as **Waterfront and Battery parks** Ⓐ, with a smoke-free park, picnic tables, bandshell, and an 8-mile (12km) -long bike path developed along the old railroad right-of-way. The path underwent a major revamp in 2017, with new asphalt paving and extra pause places added. See https://enjoyburlington.com/type/recreational-paths-trails for other biking paths in and around Burlington.

Farther south from the Waterfront park, WND&WVS (688 Pine Street; tel: 802-540 2529; www.wndnwvs.com) is the place to rent essential equipment and hire an instructor to stand up paddleboard, windsurf or kitesurf.

If you'd rather someone else do the driving, the *Spirit of Ethan Allen III* (tel: 802-862 8300; www.soea.com) has 90-minute scenic cruises throughout the day, many with meals and entertainment. It departs from the **Burlington Community Boathouse Marina** Ⓑ. For an idea of what it was like "back then," the *Friend Ship* (tel: 802-825 7245; www.whistlingman.com) is traditional gaff-rigged sloop which offers up to five two-hour cruises per day in summer. It also leaves from the dock in the Community Boathouse Marina at the southern end of the Waterfront Park.

Just when you think you've seen enough nature centers to last a lifetime, you enter the **ECHO Lake Aquarium and Science Center** Ⓒ (1 College St.; tel: 877-324 6386; www.echovermont.

org; daily 10am–5pm). Even the most jaded adult can spend an entire day here, gazing over the waters of Lake Champlain from the observation deck if nothing else. But there is a lot of "else": hand-feeding of animals, a 3-D frog-call tracking station, exploring a submerged shipwreck via a remote control camera, learning the indigenous peoples' perspective on the lake. In the plaza outside, **the US Navy Memorial** features a statute of *The Lone Sailor*. It's a twin of the memorial statue in Washington.

The **Church Street Marketplace** Ⓓ (www.churchstmarketplace.com) in the center of the historic district is lined with shops, restaurants, and businesses. It's the site of events and celebrations from open-air art shows and jazz festivals to the "Festival of Fools" – a gathering of international street performers (usually in early August). (From Waterfront and Battery parks, walk east on Cherry Street. You'll pass the two-story, enclosed Burlington Town Center with the usual mix of chain retail stores.)

A local farmers' market.

Church Street Marketplace in Burlington, showing the First Unitarian Universalist Society Church.

The Ethan Allen Homestead.

The **Flynn Center for the Performing Arts** N (153 Main Street; tel: 802-863 5966; www.flynncenter.org), a 1930 Art Deco movie palace, hosts an impressive line-up of dance, music, and theater. The stage has seen k.d. lang, *South Pacific*, and the Zoppé Family Italian Circus.

Many of the buildings on and surrounding the University of Vermont campus are architectural gems. Preservation Burlington (http://preservation burlington.org) has brochures for self-guided tours of the waterfront and historic district. They can arrange for a guide. European and American paintings are displayed in UVM's **Robert Hull Fleming Museum** N (61 Colchester Avenue; tel: 802-656 0750; www.uvm.edu/~fleming/; Labor Day–mid-Dec and mid-Jan–June Tue and Thu–Fri 10am–4pm, Sat–Sun noon–4pm, Wed 10am–7pm, closed mid-Dec–mid-Jan). It includes more than 20,000 anthropological artifacts from around the world, a collection of American Indian artifacts, and works by painters of the Hudson River

School as well as Sargent, Homer, and Fragonard.

To the northeast of the campus on Colchester Avenue is **Greenmount Cemetery** N, the final resting place of Ethan Allen. His grave is easily found under an 8ft (2-metre) statute of Allen atop a 42ft (13-meter) granite shaft.

Five miles (8km) north of Burlington, off Route 127, is the **Ethan Allen Homestead** N (tel: 802-865 4556; www. ethanallenhomestead.org; May–Oct daily 10am–4pm). The flamboyant, belligerent, beloved backwoodsman-turned-soldier-turned-philosopher built this modest home just two years before he died. The restored 1787 farmhouse has an excellent exhibit on the state's history. There are also miles of walking trails along the Winooski River.

On Burlington's northern outskirts, near the bike path, **North Beach** (60 Institute Road) has a sandy beach, snack bar, and changing rooms. It is the largest beach in Burlington and the only one with active lifeguards during the summer months. In summer it is also possible to rent kayaks,

canoes, and stand-up paddleboards. Next to it is the North Beach Campground, with 137 sites.

In nearby **Colchester**, **Saint Michael's Playhouse** (1 Winooski Park; tel: 802-654 2281; http://saintmichaels playhouse.org), on the campus of Saint Michael's College, has mounted a professional summer theater from June to August since 1951.

Farther along Route 15 in the town of **Jericho** ㊱ is the **Old Red Mill** with the **Snowflake Bentley Exhibit** (tel: 802-899 3225; http://snowflakebentley. com/museum2.htm; Apr–Dec Mon–Sat 10am–5pm, Sun 11.30am–4pm, closed Sun July–Aug, Jan–Mar Wed and Sat 10am–5pm and Sun 11.30am–4pm). The lower level of the mill is devoted to the work of Wilson "Snowflake" Bentley. In the early years of the 20th century, he took thousands of microphotographs of snowflakes, proving the contention that no two snowflakes are alike. The exhibit is filled with copies of his photos of delicate ice crystals.

Southeast of Burlington on Route 2, take the turn south at Richmond and head for **Huntington** ㊲ and the **Birds of Vermont Museum** (tel: 802-434 2167; www.birdsofvermont.org; May–Oct daily 10am–4pm; Nov–Apr by appointment). Amazingly detailed and realistic carvings of 500 birds by master carver Bob Spear are displayed in realistic habitat settings. Each wing of the California Condor took over 100 hours to carve.

SHELBURNE

Head south out of Burlington on Route 7 to **Shelburne** ㊳ and one of Vermont's major destinations, the **Shelburne Museum** (tel: 802-985 3346; www.shel burnemuseum.org; 10am–5pm May–Dec daily, Jan–Apr Wed–Sun). This beautifully assembled 45-acre (18-hectare) complex reflects the tastes of one very passionate and well-funded collector. Electra Havemeyer Webb (1888–1960) developed an eye for Americana and folk art long before anyone else was paying attention. Her passion fills 39 galleries and buildings. Even the buildings are part of the collection, as they include barns, the Lake Champlain lighthouse, even a jail and the Lake Champlain side-wheeler *Ticonderoga*. Impressionist and American 19th- and 20th-century artists are well represented; there are displays of folk art, quilts, and carved bird decoys. One of the most popular exhibits is of two hand-carved miniature circuses, each with over 3,000 figures.

Just south of the museum is the **Shelburne Vineyard Winery and Tasting Room** (6308 Shelburne Road, Route 7; tel: 802-985 8222; http:// shelburnevineyard.com; tasting room daily 11am–5pm, May–Oct until 6pm; free tours of winery daily on the hour 1–4pm); the winter-hardy grapes are grown right at the vineyard.

Shelburne is home to a number of attractions including **Vermont Teddy Bear** (6655 Shelburne Road; tel: 802-985 3001; www.vermontteddybear.com; daily 10am–4pm, until 6pm in summer,

The Round Barn Visitor Center at the Shelburne Museum.

until 5pm in fall; factory tours: winter/spring 10.30am, 11.30am, 12.30pm, 1.30pm, 2.30pm; summer 10am 11am, 11.30am, noon, 12.30pm,1pm, 1.30pm, 2pm, 2.30pm, 3pm, 4pm; fall on the hour from 10am). Built in 1859, the **Shelburne Country Store** (29 Falls Road; tel: 800-660 3657; www.shelburnecountrystore.com; daily 9am–6pm) overflows with backpacks and books, toiletries and tools, antiques and art. On Bostwick Road off Route 7, **Shelburne Orchards** (tel: 802-985 2753; www.shelburneorchards.com; late Aug–Oct Mon–Sat 9am–6pm, Sun until 5pm) has apples, peaches, and cherries in season. They've perfected their apple cider recipe and are now making apple brandy and cider vinegar.

Another Shelburne landmark is the 100-room, lakefront Queen Anne-style "cottage" of Dr William Seward and Lila Vanderbilt Webb. Its surrounding estate was designed by Frederick Law Olmsted, designer of New York City's Central Park. This 1,400-acre (570-hectare) property, **Shelburne Farms** (off Route 7; tel:

802-985 8686; www.shelburnefarms.org; times vary, check the website) is a model ecological farmstead with an award-winning cheese-making facility, extensive grounds, and a children's farmyard. The mansion offers superb accommodations and dining throughout the summer.

SOUTH OF SHELBURNE

Charlotte ❸, 6 miles (10km) south of Shelburne, is home to the unusual **Vermont Wildflower Farm** (3488 Ethan Allen Highway; tel: 802-425 3641; www.vermontwildflowerfarm.com). Something colorful is always in bloom from May through September. A lovely self-guided tour meanders along a brook and pond. Charlotte is also a Lake Champlain crossing point; a ferry (www.ferries.com) to the little town of Essex NY operates several times a day year-round.

Quakers, farmers, abolitionists, authors, and artists – four generations of the Robinson family – lived in **Ferrisburg** at what is now the **Rokeby Museum** (4334 Route 7; tel: 802-877

Kayaking on Lake Champlain.

3406; www.rokeby.org; mid-May–mid-Oct daily 10am–5pm; guided tours of the house at 11am and 2pm; self-guided tour of outbuildings and farmstead). The farm is one of the best-documented "stations" on the Underground Railroad. The building overflows with 200 years' worth of furniture and belongings, and the guides enjoy relating the very rich history of this remarkable family. Outside, a self-guided hike, "How a Farm Becomes a Forest," is well worth the walk.

There are maple syrup and cheese-making operations galore in Vermont, but only one where you can visit a smokehouse as well. The **Dakin Farm** (5797 Route 7, Ferrisburg; tel: 800-99 DAKIN; www.dakinfarm.com; daily 8am–6pm) was established by Timothy Dakin in 1792. His descendants welcome visitors to see the operations (and buy the tasty results).

MARITIME ATTRACTIONS

Lake Champlain's maritime traditions are preserved just west of **Vergennes** at the **Lake Champlain Maritime Museum** ⓸ (4472 Basin Harbor Road; tel: 802-475 2022; www.lcmm.org; late-May–mid-Oct daily 10am–5pm). It's a fun take on the lake's history, with a replica 1776 gunboat, a nautical archaeological center researching over 300 wrecks on the lake bottom, and watercraft from early canoes to vintage steamboats on display. Divers can get information on wreck dives here.

Vermont spawned the world-famous Morgan horse, a barrel-chested steed which, as one celebrant boasted, "can outrun, outpull, and outlast any other breed, just as you would expect a Vermont horse to do." The **UVM Morgan Horse Farm** (www.uvm.edu/morgan), off Route 23 in the village of **Weybridge**, is a working farm with training demonstrations and tours (74 Battell Drive, Woodbridge off Route 23; tel: 802-388 2011; May–Oct daily 9am–4pm; tours

on the hour, last tour 3pm). The foals are irresistibly cute.

Middlebury ⓺, directly down Route 7 from Vergennes, is the ideal college town, a verdant campus of grand, well-spaced 19th-century buildings, accompanied by a lively community of pubs, shops, and restaurants. The traditional arts of Vermont are highlighted at the **Vermont Folklife Center** (88 Main Street; tel: 802-388 4964; www.vermont folklifecenter.org; Tue–Sat 10am–5pm). The shop features the work of artisans who carry on cultural traditions like quilting, basket weaving, and beeswax candle-making. A superb collection of late-18th- and 19th-century Vermontiana is housed in the **Henry Sheldon Museum of Vermont History** (1 Park Street; tel: 802-388 2117; www.hen rysheldonmuseum.org; Tue–Sat 10am–5pm, also May–mid-Oct Sun 1–5pm). Housed in a three-story residence built in 1829, recent exhibits trace leisure in the 19th century and Vermont's role in the Civil War.

Collections at the **Middlebury College Museum of Art** (Route 30 South;

The 19th-century steamboat Ticonderoga now sits on dry land. It provided passenger and freight services on lakes and rivers across the US.

The Vermont Marble Museum.

Taking aim at the Lake Champlain Maritime Museum.

tel: 802-443 5007; http://museum.middlebury.edu; Tue–Fri 10am–5pm, Sat–Sun noon–5pm) explore Asian and Western art from the 4th millennium BC to the present day. The 20th-century collection has a particular emphasis on photography and prints. There's a 45-minute audio walking tour (or brochure) of sculpture on the college campus.

A slightly different version of hand-crafted artwork is at **Otter Creek Brewing** (793 Exchange Street, Middlebury; tel: 802-388 0727; www.ottercreekbrewing.com; daily 11am–6pm; free self-guided tours and tastings). Their first beers were brewed in a storage garage at the edge of town. They now produce a range of popular seasonal and year-round brews from a much larger and more suitable location.

IN SEARCH OF ROBERT FROST

The poet Robert Frost spent his summers writing in a log cabin 7 miles (11km) east on Route 125 in **Ripton ⑫** in the northern section of the 400,000-acre (160,000-hectare) **Green**

The Robert Frost Cabin, Ripton.

Mountain National Forest, which stretches across two-thirds of the state. The cabin is not far from **Bread Loaf Inn**, home of the prestigious 10-day Bread Loaf Writers' Conference, founded in 1926.

The mile-long **Robert Frost Interpretive Trail**, beginning at his home, the Homer Noble Farm, is marked by several of his poems which are mounted at appropriate spots along the walk. For great scenery, continue on State 125, through steep **Middlebury Gap**; you can return to Route 7 by following Route 100 for 6 miles (10km) south and heading back west on equally scenic Route 73 through Brandon Gap. The route circumnavigates the **Moosalamoo National Recreation Area**. Covering 20,000 acres (8,000 hectares), it has over 70 miles (110km) of trails for biking, hiking, horseback riding, cross-country skiing, and enjoying marvelous vistas. Many trails have interpretative panels explaining the wildlife and environmental features. A birding guide, moose-viewing drive map, and other information are

available for free download (www.moosalamoo.org).

The entire core of **Brandon** ⓬ – more than 200 buildings – is listed on the National Register of Historic Places. Stephen A. Douglas was born in the white cottage next to the Baptist Church, north on Route 7; he was the Illinois senator whose famous seven debates with Abraham Lincoln, the rival for his seat in 1858, focused on the issue of slavery. His birthplace is now a small museum and visitor center (4 Grove Street; http://brandon.org/the-brandon-museum; mid-May–mid-Oct Mon–Sat 11am–4pm; free), where you can pick up the self-guided walking tour brochure.

At **Brandon Music** (62 Country Club Road; tel: 802-465 4071; www.brandon-music.net; open only during concerts and by appointment) Stephen and Edna Sutton maintain an arts oasis focused on music. It's home to their classical music recording company, a store specializing in hard-to-find artists and "boutique" labels, a café and proper British tearoom (they're transplants from the UK), an art gallery, and an antiques shop featuring – among other things – old phonographs. There are regular concerts with local and international artists.

Two historic sites near Brandon commemorate two important contributions by Vermont to the American Revolution. On the shore of Lake Champlain, west of Orwell, the fortification at **Mount Independence State Historic Site** (497 Mt. Independence Road; tel: 802-948 2000; http://historicsites.vermont.gov/directory/mount_independence; late May–mid-Oct daily 9.30am–5pm) was a massive structure designed to defend against a British invasion from Canada. Manned by 12,000 soldiers, it was one of the largest communities in North America in 1776. When the advancing British saw this fort and Fort Ticonderoga, they returned to Canada and prepared for a new invasion the following spring. The fort was evacuated in the face of the overwhelming British numbers. After Gen. Burgoyne's surrender in October 1777, the fort was no longer

Ⓞ Fact

The Vermont Fresh Network (www.vermontfresh.net) is a farm and chef partnership which works directly to source food from farms to restaurants with the connections directly strengthening the local economies and communities. Member restaurants display a green decal showing a barn bracketed by a knife and fork.

THE APPALACHIAN TRAIL

In 1921, Benton MacKaye, a regional planner and forester, proposed a trail system to "provide leisure, enjoyment, and the study of nature for people living in the urban areas of the Eastern United States."

By 1937, the Appalachian Trail (www.appalachiantrail.org) was completed. Stretching from Mt Katahdin in Maine's Baxter Park to Springer Mountain GA, the 2,175-mile (3,500km) footpath crosses 14 states, including five of the six in New England (Rhode Island misses out).

Each year, about 4 million people hike part of the Appalachian Trail. Almost 2,000 of them hike its entire length, traveling from South to North. Their odyssey takes an average of 5–6 months. Known as "thru-hikers" and going by such colorful trail names as Paul Bunion and Itchyfeet, they leave Georgia in early April, hoping to reach Mt Katahdin by late September, before the weather shuts trail access for the winter.

New England claims 734 miles (1,120km) of the Appalachian Trail. It has both the most stunning scenery and rugged terrain. While some stretches are testing for even the most experienced hiker, casual walkers can have a lot of fun, savor memorable views, and brag about hiking the trail when they return home.

An Appalachian Trail hiking sign.

When in New England and traveling from South to North as most of the thru-hikers do, hikers first cross into Connecticut, where the trail is relatively gentle. The trail goes from Kent to Salisbury, passing through the villages of Cornwall and Lime Rock. Moderate climbs up the foothills of the Berkshire Mountains are tempered by miles of trails along river banks and open farmland. Popular with day-hikers, it's a civilized adventure. After briefly meeting the mountains, you can return to your B&B, foregoing the dubious pleasures of freeze-dried spaghetti and a sleeping bag in favor of cocktails and the Jacuzzi.

The cascades of Sages Ravine dramatically announce the start of the Appalachian Trail in southwest Massachusetts. Moving deeper into the Berkshires, hikers face steeper climbs, but more panoramic vistas. In summer, the coolness of the mountains, including the summit of Mt Greylock (3,491ft, 1,064 meters), Massachusetts' highest peak, is a welcome relief from the sticky sweat of a day on the trail.

Vermont's 150 miles (241km) are probably the best for hikers looking for a bigger challenge but not ready for the fierce finale of the trail in New Hampshire and Maine. Entering Vermont near Bennington, the trail rises into the Green Mountains, joining with Vermont's Long Trail for nearly 100 miles (161km). The colors during fall foliage are unforgettable. During spring melts, known for good reason as mud season, the trail is an impassable, slippery morass. The trail brushes by Woodstock, another good base for hikers who want to explore only a small section.

The views along the trail in New Hampshire and Maine are breathtaking, and so is the effort required to reach them. Here, the Appalachian Trail is the domain of only the most seasoned, physically fit, and determined hikers. Much of New Hampshire's section is above the tree line in the White Mountains. Hikers are exposed to extreme, rapidly changing weather, with snow squalls or worse – even in summer – on Mt Washington (6,288ft, 1,917 meters). The climactic 282 miles (454km) in Maine sees hikers fording streams at the foot of steep, narrow trails, and making lung-gasping climbs through the Grafton and Mahoosuc notches – the latter a notorious mile-long scramble through a boulder-filled gorge – before the final climb to Mount Katahdin.

needed and was destroyed. Today it is one of the most valuable Revolutionary War military archaeological sites. The museum demonstrates how artifacts and modern technology explain the story of the fort.

Southwest of Brandon, the **Hubbardton Battlefield** (5696 Monument Road; tel: 802-759 2412; end May–mid-Oct Thu–Sun 9.30am–5pm, also Mon holidays) is the site of the only Revolutionary War battle fought entirely in Vermont. In July 1777, the Green Mountain Boys held off a much larger British force intent on splitting New England from the rest of the colonies. Although the British held the field at the end of the day, their losses were so great that they retreated. By October, the Redcoats had lost the battles of Bennington and Saratoga and Burgoyne had surrendered his army. The site includes a visitor center museum and walking trails on the battlefield. On most Sundays, there are interpretive programs.

In **Pittsford**, the **New England Maple Museum** (Route 7; tel: 802-483 9414; www.maplemuseum.com; daily 10am–4pm) bills itself as "the world's largest maple museum." One hundred feet (30 meters) of murals and scale-model dioramas show the process from sap collection to syrup production. There's a tasting room for the different grades of syrup, and a large gift shop sells syrup, maple candy, and cookies.

PROCTOR

Just off routes 7 and 3, the town of **Proctor ㊹** ("Marble Center of the World") is the logical spot for the **Vermont Marble Museum** (52 Main Street; tel: 800-427 1396; www.vermont-marble. com; late May–mid-Oct daily 10am–5pm). It offers a glimpse into the workings of the Vermont Marble Company factory which flourished here for more than 100 years, a hands-on exploration of geologic evolution, and a moving display on the history of the Tomb

of the Unknown Soldier. A nature path leads from the museum to the original Proctor Quarry overlook, a surprisingly lovely spot for a picnic.

Off Route 3 in Proctor, Dr John Johnson built a home for his wife, a wealthy English aristocrat, in 1867. **Wilson Castle** (West Proctor Road; tel: 802-773 3284; www.wilsoncastle.com; late May–mid-Oct daily 9am–6pm) is an opulent stone mansion with 32 rooms, 12 fireplaces, and 84 stained-glass windows.

Vermont's second-biggest city, **Rutland ㊺**, is filled with palatial Victorian homes, a restored Art Deco movie theatre, and an enclosed regional shopping mall (one of the largest in the state).

The **Chaffee Center for the Visual Arts** (16 South Main Street; tel: 802-775 0356; www.chaffeeartcenter.org) showcases the artistic expressions of local talent. The **Paramount Theater** (30 Center Street, tel: 802-775 0570; www. paramountvt.org), with its restored Victorian opera house interior, hosts film and live performances. Just outside

The Equinox Resort and Spa.

Visitors at the Norman Rockwell Museum.

Horse breeding is a well-established tradition in Vermont.

The Haskell Free Library and Opera House, which straddles the border between the US and Canada.

town, **Hathaway Farm** (741 Prospect Hill Rd.; tel: 802-775 2624; www.hatha wayfarm.com; Wed–Sun 10am–5pm) is a wonderful menagerie of barnyard animals. From late July through October, it operates the largest corn maze in Vermont: 12 acres (5 hectares) of twisting, meandering trails through head-high ripe corn.

East of Rutland on Route 4 is the **Norman Rockwell Museum** (654 Route 4 E; tel: 877-773 6095; www.normanrock wellvt.com; daily 9am–4pm). The prolific illustrator is best known for the covers of *The Saturday Evening Post*, which often showed a nostalgic, romanticized Americana. He lived in nearby Arlington from 1939 to 1953. The museum has several thousand of his illustrations, including the powerful four-part series *The Four Freedoms*.

THE MANCHESTERS

Franklin Orvis gave the local tourist industry a boost in 1849 when he began taking in summer guests at his father's house, located next to the 1769 Marsh Tavern in **Manchester Village**

, where Ethan Allen and his Green Mountain Boys plotted the Tories' overthrow. The hotel kept expanding until it grew into the **Equinox Resort and Spa** (3567 Main Street, Route 7A; tel: 800-362 4700; www.equinoxresort. com), a grand resort on more than 1,300 acres (530 hectares). Rooms are scattered among five buildings, including 19th-century farmhouses. Guests can indulge themselves in an array of unique outdoor experiences, like an introductory course in falconry or off-road driving on an 80-acre (32-hectare) track.

Franklin Orvis's younger brother, Charles, also had a clever idea – why not teach the leisured class to catch their supper along the banks of the abundant Battenkill River?

The store they opened to supply their students, Orvis (4180 Main Street, Route 7A; tel: 802-362 3750; www.orvis. com; Mon–Fri 9am–6pm, Sat 9am–7pm, Sun 10am–5pm), with its core emphasis on fly-fishing, has grown into an outdoor-lifestyle powerhouse. Its huge retail store is billed as "Vermont's

◎ THE HASKELL

The town of Derby Line is directly on the US–Canadian border, at the northernmost end of Route 5 or Interstate 91. On the other side, the town becomes Stanstead, Quebec. The Haskell Free Library and Opera House (http://haskell opera.com) sits astride the border; during performances, the audience is in the US while the stage is in Canada. The placement and location is quite deliberate; the building was donated by Martha Stewart Haskell with the intention of creating a center for learning and cultural enrichment for residents in both countries. The full schedule of plays, concerts, and international cultural performances supports the free library. The entrances to the building are on the American side, so you don't need your passport to see a performance.

largest retail attraction." There are indoor and outdoor trout ponds; at the latter, patrons can test equipment.

Next door to Orvis is the **American Museum of Fly Fishing** (Route 7A; tel: 802-362 3300; www.amff.com; Tue–Sat 10am–4pm). It is home to the world's largest collection of angling and angling-related items, including the fishing rods of Ernest Hemingway and Herbert Hoover. Orvis's success inspired a raft of other upscale companies such as Ralph Lauren, Brooks Brothers, Joan & David, and Giorgio Armani to open outlets in nearby **Manchester**, turning that one-time quaint town into a wall-to-wall shopping mall.

An artistic venue as expansive as the resort is the **Southern Vermont Arts Center** (West Road; tel: 802-362 1405; www.svac.org; Tue–Sat 10am–5pm, Sun noon–5pm; gallery and grounds free). Set on a 407-acre (165-hectare) estate, there are galleries with a permanent collection of nearly 800 pieces of 19th- and 20th-century art. A restored Georgian Revival mansion has 10 galleries selling works, and the grounds are an outdoor sculpture garden. A 400-seat auditorium, noted for its fine acoustics, is the site of live performances.

A contender for "most scenic drive in Vermont" is the 5-mile (8km) **Skyline Drive** toll road (Route 7A; tel: 802-362 1114; www.equinoxmountain.com; late May–Oct daily, weather permitting; toll for car and each passenger). The twisting road with 20 hairpin turns follows the ridgeline of Equinox Mountain to a visitor center at the summit. There are plenty of places to pull over and savor the view. Vintage sports cars race to the summit in an annual rally every summer. The mountain and road are owned by an order of monks who were bequeathed the property by the mountain's former owner.

Although Abraham Lincoln never visited Vermont, his wife and children did. Buoyed by fond memories of happier times, Lincoln's son, Robert Todd, returned many years later to build **Historic Hildene** (Route 7A; tel: 802-362 1788; www.hildene.org; daily 9.30am–4.30pm). The massive 8,000-sq-foot (700-sq-meter) mansion displays richly

The Hildene Mansion.

The Vermont Country Store in Weston.

Fly-fishing on the Housatonic near Manchester.

appointed Georgian Revival rooms, a 1,000-pipe organ (daily concert), observatory and telescope, and the 1928 Franklin Roadster that belonged to Robert Lincoln's daughter. The expansive grounds are open to cross-country skiers and summer strollers.

OUT OF MANCHESTER

The picturesque, marble-paved village of **Dorset** 47, 8.25 miles (13km) northwest of Manchester, is home to the **Dorset Playhouse** (tel: 802-867 5570; www.dorsetplayers.org). The community theatre group puts on productions from October to May. In the summer, it hosts a professional festival from June to August in a rustic barn with offerings as diverse as Agatha Christie and Stephen Sondheim. The **Dorset Inn** (tel: 802-867 5500) on the village green has welcomed guests since 1796. It's the oldest continually operating inn in Vermont.

Just 6 miles (10km) northeast of Manchester, on Route 11, is **Bromley Mountain** (tel: 802-824 5522; www.bromley.com). A popular winter ski resort, it

is a huge and hugely successful summer adventure park with thrill rides like a 5-story high, half-mile-long, 50mph (80kmh) zip-line; water slides; and climbing walls.

WESTON

Vermont's oldest summer playhouse is about 15 miles (24km) east of Bromley via routes 11 and 100, in the hill village of **Weston** 48. The first show at **Weston Playhouse** (tel: 802-824 5288; www.westonplayhouse.org; June–Sept) in 1937 featured a young actor by the name of Lloyd Bridges. The theatre building, which incorporates three old barns, has been newly renovated and updated. The Café at the Falls, overlooking the waterfall at the Playhouse, serves bistro fare on performance evenings.

The town is also home to another of the state's major attractions, the **Vermont Country Store** (657 Main Street; tel: 802-824 3184; www.vermontcountrystore.com), a purveyor of cracker-barrel atmosphere and useful (and arcane) merchandise since 1946. Raggedy Ann dolls, Fuller brushes, and Bonomo's Turkish Taffy evoke instant nostalgia.

In a 1769 stone house on Main Street in **Shaftsbury** 49, poet Robert Frost wrote *Stopping by Woods on a Snowy Evening* and *New Hampshire*, which concluded, "At present I am living in Vermont." His home is now the **Robert Frost Stone House Museum** (121 Route 7A; tel: 802-447 6200; www.frostfriends.org/stonehouse.html; May–Oct daily 10am–5pm, last admission to house 4.30pm). Exhibits are planned so that visitors feel as though they have met Frost. The grounds are much as he saw them, with the trees, stone walls, and landscapes which inspired his work unchanged.

BENNINGTON

Frost is buried just to the south on Route 7 in **Bennington** 50, at the Old Burying Ground. His epitaph reads simply, "I had a lover's quarrel with

the world." The cemetery is next to the 1805–06 **Old First Church** (tel: 802-447 1223; www.oldfirstchurchbenn.org; Mon–Sat 10am–4pm, Sun 1–4pm; voluntary donation), with its unusual three-tiered steeple.

Bennington, home to Bennington College, looms large in Vermont's history, and a crucial 1777 skirmish is commemorated by the 306ft (93-meter) **Bennington Battle Monument** (15 Monument Circle; tel: 802-447 0550; www.benningtonbattlemonument.com; mid-Apr–Oct daily 9am–5pm). The battle actually took place a few miles to the west in New York State, where General John Stark and 1,800 ragtag troops forced the Redcoats back across the Walloomsac River. But it was a colonial supply dump on this site that General John Burgoyne was after, and his failure to attain it proved a turning point in the British campaign. The tallest structure in Vermont, an elevator whisks visitors to the top for a spectacular view.

Nearby, the **Bennington Museum** (75 West Main Street, Route 9; tel: 802-447 1571; www.benningtonmuseum.org; July–Oct daily 10am–5pm, Nov–Dec and Feb–May Thu–Tue 10am–5pm) exhibits an exceptional collection of regional history and art, including the largest public collection of works by Grandma Moses and many portraits of early and sometimes prominent Vermonters. There are fine collections of Vermont furniture and the largest collection of Bennington pottery anywhere.

Near Route 67A in **North Bennington** is the 35-room **Park-McCullough House** (1 Park Street; tel: 802-442 5441; www.parkmccullough.org; guided tours mid-May–Sept Fri–Sat 10am–2pm, Sun noon–4pm). Pre-dating the mansions of Newport by a quarter-century (1865), it's equally opulent, showing how a fortune made in the California Gold Rush was expanded with railroads, steamships, and real estate investments. On the National Register of Historic Places, it is a time capsule of the family that lived here for more than 100 years. Its furniture and decorative arts are among the most outstanding in Vermont.

> ⊙ **Fact**
>
> No one is sure who discovered how to turn maple sap into maple syrup, but American Indians had perfected the process by the time the Europeans arrived. The process involves inserting a tube into the trunk of a maple tree (tapping) in early spring through which the warming sap can flow. It's caught in buckets hung onto the tubes. The sap is boiled down to the desired consistency, originally in big vats in sugar shacks.

The Bennington Battle Monument.

The Cornish-Windsor covered bridge, Cornish.

NEW HAMPSHIRE

This state serves outdoor pleasures on a platter, making the most of the dramatic and rugged White Mountains, with plenty of historical sites, romantic idylls, and charming villages thrown in for fun.

Tucked between the metro bustle of Boston, the vast wilderness of Maine, and the bucolic charm of Vermont, New Hampshire manages to absorb the best features of each of those states while maintaining its own sense of identity.

"Live Free or Die" is the state motto, and that sentiment permeates the attitude of its residents. The fierce streak of independence early settlers needed just to survive – much less thrive – in an unforgiving land shows up in sometimes diametrically different responses to modern issues.

A lower cost of living than in neighboring Massachusetts and no state income or sales tax encourages many people to live in New Hampshire and commute to jobs in Boston. But property taxes in the Granite State are among the highest in the country. In a traditionally liberal region, it is home to one of the most unapologetically conservative newspapers in the country, *The New Hampshire Union Leader* (www.unionleader.com). Justly proud of its mountain scenery, it allows billboard spatter on its highways. Practical New Englanders, they fell into deep mourning at the collapse of the Old Man of the Mountain. Dedicated to preserving history and tradition, it celebrates two native-born pioneers of the space age and science. And its tolerant nature

Stark, a typical small town.

dissolves into granite-hard resistance at the hint of the first presidential primary being held anywhere other than New Hampshire.

It's only about 175 miles from Dixville Notch in the north to Portsmouth and the Atlantic beaches. Along the way, visitors find elegant country resorts, B&Bs tucked into forest glades, and rustic lakeside cottages designed for making family memories. Hiking in the White Mountains is almost mandatory, as is reaching the top of Mt Washington in some fashion.

⊘ **Main Attractions**
Portsmouth
Isles of Shoals
McAuliffe-Shepard
  Discovery Center
Canterbury Shaker Village
White Mountain National
  Forest
Franconia Notch
Mount Washington Cog
  Railway

**Maps on pages
258, 296, 300**

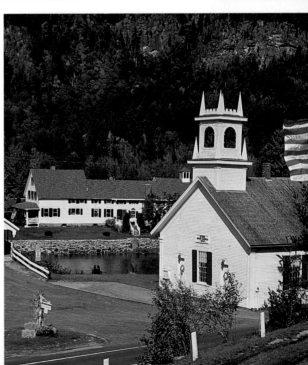

Boaters and anglers have an array of rivers and lakes to choose from; tidy villages lie on back roads; and that short but scenic coastline is strewn with state parks. Lovers of antiques and fine architecture enjoy the gracious world of the colonial elite in Portsmouth. And remember, if you want to take one of those antiques home, there isn't any sales tax.

PORTSMOUTH

Portsmouth ⑤ stands at the mouth of the Piscataqua River. Graced with a superb natural harbor, the town is the nation's third-oldest English settlement (after Plymouth and Jamestown).

The oldest continually occupied neighborhood in Portsmouth is **Strawbery Banke Ⓐ** (14 Hancock Street; tel: 603-433 1100; www.strawberybanke.org; May–Oct daily 10am–5pm; Nov weekend-only guided tours). A true living-history museum, it connects visitors with the past through interaction with costumed interpreters who stay in character as they recreate the lives of ordinary people from

1695 to the mid-1950s. There are 42 buildings, ranging from the humble to the grand, illustrating changes in architecture and society over time. The garden program preserves nearly four centuries of garden plants and methods. Just across from Strawbery Banke, **Prescott Park** stretches for more than 10 acres (4 hectares) along the Piscataqua River. The summer **Prescott Park Arts Festival** (tel: 603-436 2848; www.prescottpark.org) hosts family-friendly concerts, dance performances, and art shows. **Market Square Ⓑ** (at Congress and Pleasant streets) is lined with cafés and chic shops housed in stately brick buildings from the 17th and 18th centuries.

Lovers of historic houses will swoon in Portsmouth. The 1763 National Historic Landmark **Moffatt-Ladd House and Garden Ⓒ** (154 Market Street; tel: 603-436 8221; www.moffattladd.org; June–mid-Oct Mon–Sat 11am–5pm, Sun 1–5pm) is an imposing three-story Georgian mansion noted for choice examples of the furniture for which 18th-century Portsmouth was

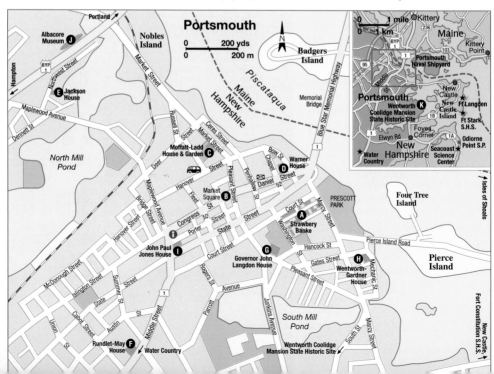

famous. The 1716 **Warner House**  (150 Daniel Street; tel: 603-436 5909; www.warnerhouse.org; June–Oct Wed–Sun 11am–4pm) was the first of Portsmouth's many brick houses. Each room is decorated in the style of one of the six generations who lived here. The 1614 **Jackson House** (76 Northwest Street; tel: 603-436 3205; www.historicnewengland.org/property/jackson-house/; June–mid-Oct first and third Sat of the month 11am–4pm) is the state's oldest surviving wood-frame house. The Federal-style **Rundlet-May House** (364 Middle Street; tel: 603-436 3205; www.historicnewengland.org/property/rundlet-may-house/; June–mid-Oct first and third Sat of the month), built by a wealthy textile merchant in 1807, is filled with many of the technological advances of the day like coal-fired central heating and an indoor well. George Washington considered the 1794 **Governor John Langdon House** (143 Pleasant Street; tel: 603-436 3205; www.historicnewengland.org/property/governor-john-langdon-house/; June–mid-Oct tours Fri–Sun) the finest house in the city. The 1760 Georgian **Wentworth-Gardner House** (50 Mechanic Street; tel: 603-436 4406; http://wentworthlear.org/wentworth-gardner/; June–Oct Thu–Mon 11am–4pm) is one of the finest examples of Georgian architecture in the country. The Tobias Lear House, immediately adjacent, was home to the private secretary to President George Washington. When Washington visited, a crowd outside peeked through the parlor windows. John Paul Jones did not own the house bearing his name **John Paul Jones House** (43 Middle Street; tel: 603-436 8420; May–Oct daily 11am–5pm). The Revolutionary War naval hero once rented a room here. The 1758 Georgian home has a fascinating portrait gallery of Portsmouth's notables.

The Silent Service – as the US Navy calls it submarine fleet – is recognized at **Albacore Museum** (600 Market Street; tel: 603-436 3680; www.ussalbacore.org; Memorial Day–Columbus Day daily 9.30am–5pm, Columbus Day–Dec daily 9.30am–4pm, Jan–Feb weekends 9.30am–4pm). Built in Portsmouth, she was a seagoing testing platform for technology from 1953 to 1972. The tour gives a glimpse into the lives of the 55-man crew in their sardine-can existence.

For a more pleasant experience on the water, consider a narrated, three-hour cruise on a replica 1900 ferryboat (Isle of Shoals Steamboat Company; tel: 603-431 5500/800-441 4620; www.islesofshoals.com; daily in season) to the **Isles of Shoals**, 9 miles (14km) offshore. The "barren piles of rock" were charted in 1614 by Captain John Smith and long haunted by pirates and other outcasts. Improbably enough, an arts colony blossomed here at the end of the 19th century. Kids can take a break from historic sites at one of New England's largest water parks, **Water Country** (2300 Lafayette Road; tel: 603-427 1111; www.watercountry.com; mid-June–Labor Day).

Strawbery Banke, in Portsmouth, is open for self-guided tours.

Tip

While in Portsmouth, visit the seaside Tugboat Alley shop on Bow Street (tel: 603-430 9556; www.tugboatalley.com), which stocks a wide selection of nautical-themed gifts.

New Hampshire's first royal governor, Benning Wentworth, chose a beautiful spot overlooking Little Harbor as the place to build his mansion. Two centuries later, artist and antiquarian John Templeman Coolidge restored the then-dilapidated building. The 40-room **Wentworth-Coolidge Mansion** (tel: 603-436 6607; http://wentworthcoolidge.org/; tours 10am–4pm May and Sept–mid-Oct Fri–Sun, June–Sept Wed–Sun; grounds are open year-round and free to enter) is an outstanding example of the life of colonial-era aristocracy.

NORTH TO DOVER

Dover ⑰, 10 miles (16km) northwest of Portsmouth, is the home of the **Children's Museum of New Hampshire** (6 Washington Street; tel: 603-742 2002; www.childrens-museum.org; Tue–Sat 10am–5pm, Sun noon–5pm and school holiday Mon, daily in the summer). Hands-on exhibits teach children about subjects from dinosaurs to flying machines. They can work in the museum's post office and play in a human-size kaleidoscope.

One of New Hampshire's most eclectic and eccentric museums is the **Woodman Institute Museum** (182 Central Avenue; tel: 603-742 1038; http://woodmanmuseum.org; Apr–mid-Dec Wed–Sun 10am–5pm). It's filled with antique powder horns, a saddle once used by Abraham Lincoln, a cougar killed in 1853, and many other interesting items.

SOUTH OF PORTSMOUTH

Three miles (5km) south of Portsmouth on Route 1A in **Rye**, is the 331-acre (134-hectare) **Odiorne Point State Park** ㊝ (570 Ocean Boulevard; tel: 603-436 7406; www.nhstateparks.org/visit/state-parks/odiorne-point-state-park.aspx). It has the largest undeveloped shoreline on the state's 16 miles (26km) of coastline.

The **Seacoast Science Center** (in the park; tel: 603-436 8043; www.seacoastsciencecenter.org; mid-Feb–Oct daily 10am–5pm, Nov–mid-Feb Sat–Mon 10am–5pm, also by appointment rest of the week) uses interactive exhibits to teach about the coastal environment.

An open-air theater in Prescott Park.

Continue south on Route 1A to **North Hampton and Fuller Gardens** (10 Willow Avenue; tel: 603-964 5414; www.fullergardens.org; mid-May–mid-Oct daily). This magnificent turn-of-the-20th-century estate garden has more than 1,700 rose bushes, English perennial gardens, and a tropical conservatory.

There are several fine public beaches along Route 1A from Portsmouth to the Massachusetts border, including **Wallis Sands State Beach** (Rye), **North Hampton State Beach**, and **Hampton Beach State Park**. You can find all the details including schedules and activities at the New Hampshire State Parks' website: www.nhstateparks.org.

HISTORIC EXETER

Five miles (8km) inland, just off Route 101, the handsome town of **Exeter** 🔟, one of the state's earliest settlements, was founded in 1638. It's home to Phillips Exeter Academy, a prestigious college preparatory school whose alumni include Daniel Webster.

The **American Independence Museum** (1 Governors Lane; tel:

603-772 2622; www.independencemuseum.org; May–Nov Tue–Sat 10am–4pm) is in a handsome 1721 building. Each room focuses on a different aspect of the Revolution and the creation of the new nation. The carefully restored **Folsom Tavern** was the center of Exeter's political scene during the Revolutionary era.

THE MERRIMACK VALLEY

Flowing south from the foothills of the White Mountains, the swift Merrimack River powered one of America's earliest and most successful industrial centers. Still the state's most populous region, the Merrimack Valley is a center of government, business, and the arts.

The **Budweiser Clydesdales** are among the most recognized corporate mascots in the world. A small herd of the big horses lives at the **Anheuser-Busch Brewery** (221 Daniel Webster Highway; tel: 603-595 1202; www.budweisertours.com; hours vary by season, call for times) in Merrimack. The brewery tour includes a tasting for those

The Market Square in Portsmouth, which was incorporated in 1653 and now has a population of more than 21,000.

Portsmouth sits along the Piscataqua River.

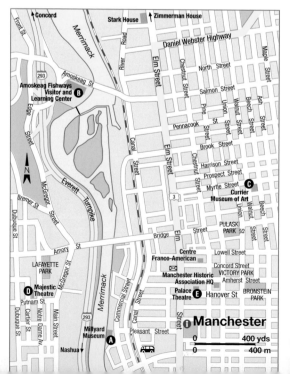

This 200-year-old stone chapel is on Star Island in the Isles of Shoals.

A tugboat at Portsmouth.

21 and over. A visit to the Clydesdale Hamlet (daily) gets you close to the horses. The first Saturday of every month is Camera Day from 1 to 3pm, when the horses pose for pictures.

MANCHESTER

Farther north on I-93 is **Manchester ⑤**, which along with Nashua and several other New Hampshire cities were centers of textile manufacturing. In the early 20th century, the massive, redbrick **Amoskeag Mills** was the world's largest textile enterprise, employing 17,000 workers in 64 buildings that stretched for 1 mile (1.6km) along the Merrimack River. As the industry declined, so did the town, but the Millyard District has become an example of adaptive reuse, with the buildings renovated as retail and office space, residences, classrooms, and high-tech incubators. The Chamber of Commerce (www.manchester-chamber.org) has a self-guided walking tour of the historic millyard (54 Hanover Street; tel: 603-792 4100). There are plenty of other tours focusing on

the arts, cemeteries, and chocolate. The **Millyard Museum ④** (200 Bedford Street; tel: 603-622 7531; www.manchesterhistoric.org/millyard-museum; Tue–Sat 10am–4pm) recounts the natural and social history of the area from the native peoples fishing here to the industry of the 20th century. Along with a massive collection of artifacts, there's a walk-through recreation of a "night on Elm Street," with lighted archways, store fronts with neon signs, and the State Theatre.

The **SEE Science Center** (above the museum; tel: 603-669 0400; www.see-sciencecenter.org; daily 10am–4pm) is a two-story, hands-on science learning center. If nothing else, it's worth seeing the scale model of the millyard made from over 3 million Legos.

Amoskeag Fishways Visitor and Learning Center ⑧ at Amoskeag Dam (4 Fletcher Street; tel: 603-626 3474; www.amoskeagfishways.org; Dec–Mar Mon–Sat 9am–4pm, until 5pm rest of the year; voluntary donation) is an environmental education center. During spawning season in late spring,

their fish ladder teems with herring, shad, and sea lamprey making their way upstream to spawn.

The **Currier Museum of Art** [150 Ash Street; tel: 603-669 6144; www.currier.org; Wed–Mon 11am–5pm] has fine collections of European and American paintings, New England decorative arts, and contemporary crafts. It also offers modern architecture buffs access to the **Zimmerman House** (tel: 603-669 6144; Wed–Mon 11am–5pm; no children under age 7; transportation is provided from the museum; reservations required), a 1950 design by Frank Lloyd Wright. The home, located on Manchester's outskirts and filled with the owners' modern art, pottery, and sculpture, is considered a work of art in itself. The museum offers tours.

You can catch a live performance at the **Majestic Theatre** (281 Cartier Street; tel: 603-669 7469; www.majestictheatre.net) or at the elegantly restored 1915 **Palace Theatre** (80 Hanover Street; tel: 603-668 5588; www.palacetheatre.org), which also presents a summer children's series.

CANDIA

First settled in 1742, **Candia** (north of Route 101, east of Manchester) was originally called Charmingfare. **Candia Vineyards** (702 High Street; tel: 603-867 9751; call for information on tours and tastings) is one of the smallest wineries in the northeast, but it has almost as many awards as it has wine corks.

Black bear, lynx, and porcupines as well as barnyard favorites are at **Charmingfare Farm** (774 High Street; tel: 603-483 5623; www.visitthefarm.com; May and Sept Sat–Sun 10am–4pm, June–Aug Tue–Sun 10am–4pm). Horse-drawn wagon tours cover the grounds; in winter, there are horse-drawn sleigh rides.

Candia Springs Adventure Park (446 Raymond Road; tel: 603-587 2093; http://candiasprings.com; late Apr–Aug daily, Sept–Oct weekends, opening times vary, see the website for details.) is a water park with challenge courses and ziplines in a beautiful setting.

CONCORD

Some 15 miles (24km) north of Manchester is **Concord**, New Hampshire's capital. The gold-domed 1819 **State House** (107 North Main Street; tel: 603-271 2154; www.gencourt.state.nh.us/nh_visitorcenter/default.htm; Mon–Fri 8am–4pm, call to make a tour reservation) was built of Concord granite by state prisoners and is fronted by statues of New Hampshire's political luminaries. Its Hall of Flags contains standards of over 100 New Hampshire military units from the Civil War to Vietnam.

The **Museum of New Hampshire History** (30 Park Street; tel: 603-228 6688; www.nhhistory.org; Tue–Sat 9.30am–5pm) has exhibits on the state's history and traditions. Most impressive is an original Concord Coach, the 19th-century vehicle built

⊘ Fact

"Live Free or Die" is the official motto of New Hampshire. It was written by Gen. John Stark, the hero of the Revolutionary Battle of Bennington VT. Unable to attend a commemoration of the battle, he sent a toast to be read to his former colleagues: "Live Free or Die; Death is not the Worst of Evils." It was adopted by New Hampshire as its motto in 1945, during World War II.

A farming community near Manchester.

here and known as "the coach that won the West," although the brightly painted and very clean coach on display doesn't look much like the battered, dust-coated stagecoaches familiar from Western movies. **The League of New Hampshire Craftsmen** gallery (36 North Main Street; tel: 603-228 8171; Mon–Fri 8.30am–4.30pm) is one of eight in the state selling work by its members. On Saturdays from June through September, check out the Concord Arts Market (1 Bicentennial Square, near the State House; tel: 603-229 2157; www.concordartsmarket.net; Sat 9am–3pm), a juried outdoor artisan and fine arts market.

Only one New Hampshire native has been elected president: Franklin Pierce. Elected in 1852, he tried unsuccessfully to find a compromise to the question of slavery. His administration was successful in other areas: reducing the national debt by 60 percent, establishing the office of the United States Attorney General, and opening trade with Japan. The **Pierce Manse** (14 Horseshow Pond Lane; tel: 603-225

4555; www.piercemanse.org; mid-June–Labor Day Tue–Sat 11am–3pm, early Sept–Oct Fri–Sat noon–3pm; rest of the year by appointment, for reservations call 603-224 2939), where Pierce and his family lived from 1842 to 1848, depicts domestic life in the pre-Civil War era.

The wonders of the universe and the dedication of those who explore it are the focus at the **McAuliffe-Shepard Discovery Center** (2 Institute Drive; tel: 603-271 7827; www.starhop.com; mid-Apr–Aug daily 10.30am–4pm, first Fri of the month also 6.30–9pm, rest of the year times vary), named after the first teacher in space, Christa McAuliffe, who died in the space shuttle *Challenger* disaster, and the first American in space, Alan Shepard, who was launched in May 1961. Both were natives of New Hampshire. You can plan an expedition to Mars and take a virtual walk across the sun. The observatory brings galaxies that are far, far away up close and personal. Special filters even allow you to look at sunspots.

Concord stagecoaches were described by Mark Twain as "a cradle on wheels."

⊙ JACKSON, NH

If you are short on time, but still want the entire "New England Experience," consider staying in Jackson. With covered bridges, white-steepled churches in quaint towns, galleries, mountain vistas, trails with requisite waterfalls, winter sleigh rides, and postcard-perfect pastures, Jackson and the surrounding area are a microcosm of New England. A big attraction is the variety of outdoor activities for non-experts. While serious devotees find excellent skiing, mountain biking, and challenging hikes, there is an equal number of beginner, intermediate, and "curious enough to try it once" activities. Great Glen Trails (Route 16, Pinkham Notch; tel: 603-466 2333; www.greatglentrails.com) rents equipment and has all sorts of information. Their kayak tours on the Androscoggin River are a peaceful way to enjoy the region.

The planetarium shows (additional charge) explore black holes and celestial objects. There are special programs for younger kids.

Nature and art celebrate each other at the **Mill Brook Gallery and Sculpture Garden** (236 Hopkinton Road; tel: 603-226 2046; http://themillbrookgallery.com/; May–Dec Thu–Sun 11am–5pm, rest of the year by appointment). The gallery represents some 70 artists, with the work of sculptors set on the grounds amid blooming gardens, ponds, and woodland trails.

Near **Deering ⑱**, southwest of Concord, by Deering Lake, the **New Hampshire School of Falconry** (183 Deering Center Road; tel 603-464 6213; www.nhschooloffalconry.com) offers a two-hour Falconer's Workshop. Participants learn about the art and history of falconry and how to approach and handle a peregrine falcon. Reservations are mandatory; book well in advance. Non-participants are welcome to watch and take photos.

NORTH OF CONCORD

Take I-89 to **Warner ⑲** and the **Mt Kearsarge Indian Museum** (18 Highlawn Road; tel: 603-456 2600; www.indianmuseum.org; May–Oct daily 10am–5pm, Sun from noon, Jan–Apr by appointment). Seven galleries demonstrate the culture, foodways, and ceremonies of the native nations of North America.

Head north on I-93 about 17 miles (27km) to exit 18 and follow signs to **Canterbury Shaker Village ⑳** (288 Shaker Road; tel: 603-783 9511; www.shakers.org; mid-June–Aug Tue–Sun 10am–5pm, Sept–Oct daily 10am–5pm, Nov weekends 10am–4pm), an eloquent testament to the ingenuity and gentle faith of the Shakers. More than two dozen restored and reconstructed buildings show how the Shakers put their faith into practice. Traditional crafts like broom-making, wood-turning, and spinning are demonstrated by costumed craftspeople. There are excellent trails through the 700 acres (285 hectares) of grounds. The shop has excellent wares, particularly of goods made at the Village.

The orator and statesman Daniel Webster (1782–1852) was born in a tiny farmhouse near **Franklin**. Today the restored **Daniel Webster Birthplace** (131 North Road, off Route 127; tel: 603-934 5057; www.nhstateparks.org/visit/Historic-Sites/daniel-webster-birthplace-state-historic-site.aspx; late May–mid-Oct Sat–Sun 9am–5pm; free), filled with period furnishings and family memorabilia, gives visitors an idea of the rigors of 18th-century farm life.

MT MONADNOCK REGION

Mt Monadnock is a rocky 3,165ft (968-meter) peak whose 360-degree views attract record numbers of climbers. The relatively gentle ascent is surpassed in popularity only by Japan's Mount Fuji and China's Mount Tai.

Trails to the peak begin at **Monadnock State Park ㉑** (169 Poole Road, off Route 12, Jaffrey; tel: 603-532 8862;

⊙ Tip

You can traverse New Hampshire fast by driving I-95. But the state's seacoast is best discovered by meandering along the slower Route 1A, with its ocean vistas and state park beaches.

Crafting a traditional broom at Canterbury Shaker Village, founded in 1969.

Concord's 1819 State House.

The Monadnock Merlin team participates in a bird-sighting competition.

www.nhstateparks.org/visit/state-parks/monadnock-state-park.aspx; year-round). Hikers need to stay on the trails, wear proper shoes, and bring along enough water and bug spray.

This is a region of meandering back roads past prim white churches, innumerable antiques stores, and historic inns. **Rhododendron State Park** (Route 119W, Fitzwilliam; tel: 603-532 8862; year-round) boasts a 16-acre (6-hectare) grove of the flowers, which bloom in mid-July. Some of the bushes are 20ft (6-meter) high. Other flowers start blooming as the rhododendrons fade, so there is color on the hills through autumn. To the east, the small town of Rindge is the location of the 750-seat **Cathedral of the Pines** ⑫ (10 Hale Hill Road; tel: 603-899 3300; www.cathedralofthepines.org; May–Oct daily; voluntary donation). Sibyl and Douglas Sloane built the open-air memorial to their son, Sandy, and all others who died in World War II. Their cathedral without walls welcomes people of all faiths in a spirit of unity and mutual respect. The view of Grand Monadnock

Mountain is awe-inspiring. In the former mill town of New Ipswich, the elegant Federal c.1800 **Forest Hall** (the Barrett House; 79 Main Street; tel: 603-436 3205; www.historicnewengland.org/property/barrett-house/; June–mid-Oct second and fourth Sat; guided tours 11am–4pm on the hour) was built by Charles Barrett Sr as a wedding gift for his son and new daughter-in-law. Its grand scale was reportedly suggested by her father. There's even a ballroom on the third floor. The house sits in 70 acres (28 hectares) of elegant lawns and gardens.

PETERBOROUGH

To the north, the handsome town of **Peterborough** ⑬ is home to the country's most prestigious artists' retreat, the MacDowell Colony.

The **Peterborough Historical Society** (19 Grove Street; tel: 603-924 3235; https://monadnockcenter.org; Wed–Sat 10am–4pm) exhibits early American furniture, decorative arts, and pewter. The renowned **Sharon Arts Center** (30 Grove Street; 603-836 2591; www.nhia.

edu/campus-life/sharon-arts-center; daily 10am–6pm) has two exhibition galleries featuring the artwork of regional and nationally recognized artists. A separate Fine Craft Gallery (20–40 Depot Street; tel: 603-836 2591; daily) features the work of more than 100 juried artists in a variety of media.

"When children are raised with respect and curiosity towards other cultures, the world will know more peace and less war." That philosophy is behind the **Mariposa Museum and World Culture Center** (26 Main Street; tel: 603-924-4555; http://mariposamuseum.org; Tue–Sun 11am–5pm). The museum is very hands-on with thousands of examples of folk art, toys, wedding gowns, and instruments from six continents.

To the east, **Frye's Measure Mill** (12 Frye Road; tel: 603-654 6581; www.fryesmeasuremill.com) in **Wilton** ❻❹ is one of the country's few remaining water-powered mills and its only active measure mill. Since 1858, Frye's has been making boxes designed for accurate measurement of quantities of items such as nails. A 90-minute tour of the mill shows off the water-powered system and box-making machinery. Reservations are recommended (check the website for details).

Head west on Route 101 from Peterborough to **Dublin**, home of *Yankee Magazine* and the *Old Farmer's Almanac*, America's oldest continuously published periodical. This road is particularly scenic during the fall foliage season. The nearby village of **Harrisville** ❻❺ is one of New Hampshire's best-preserved 19th-century mill towns.

Twelve miles (20km) to the west, **Keene** ❻❻, the largest city in this region, was a thriving mill town at the turn of the 19th century. Today, the town attracts visitors for its growing arts scene and natural beauty. Keene claims to have America's widest Main Street, crowned at one end by the handsome spire of the United Church

of Christ. The handsome 1806 Federal home at the **Horatio Colony House Museum & Nature Preserve** (199 Main Street; tel: 603-352 0460; http://horatiocolonymuseum.org/; May–mid-Oct Wed–Sun 11am–4pm; rest of the year by appointment; free) overflows with early-18th- to late-19th-century American and European furnishings. The **Nature Preserve** is 3.5 miles (5km) to the west off Route 9 (Daniels Hill Road). There are 3.5 miles (5km) of trails winding through the 415-acre (168-hectare) preserve. In April 1775, 29 Minutemen departed from the 1762 **Wyman Tavern** (339 Main Street; tel: 603-357 3855; June–Aug Thu–Sat 11am–4pm) to join the battles in Lexington and Concord MA. The tavern reflects the 1770–1820 period. The **Historical Society of Cheshire County** (246 Main Street; tel: 603-352 1895; https://hsccnh.org/; Tue, Thu–Fri 9am–4pm, Wed 9am–9pm, first and third Sat of the month 9am–noon) concentrates on local glass, pottery, and toymaking, which were leading industries in Keene.

Dublin's 1852 Community Church. A hurricane in 1938 snapped the steeple off the building.

A covered bridge at Swanzey.

Amor Caritas in the garden of Augustus Saint-Gaudens' home. The sculptor created many variations on this motif.

The Cornish-Windsor covered bridge connects Vermont and New Hampshire.

The city is home to **Keene State College**, whose **Thorne-Sagendorph Art Gallery** (tel: 603-358 2720; http://www.keene.edu/tsag/; Sept–May Sat–Wed noon–5pm, Thu–Fri noon–7pm) exhibits works by 19th-century artists who worked around Mt Monadnock, and more contemporary artists. The school's **Redfern Arts Center** (tel: 603-358 2168; www.keene.edu/arts/redfern/) has a lively, innovative schedule of performing professional artists as well as shows by students and faculty.

You can experience the life of a New Hampshire dairy farmer at the 250-year-old **Keene Stonewall Farm** (242 Chesterfield Road; tel: 603-357 7278; www.stonewallfarm.org; Mon–Fri 10am–4.30pm, Sat–Sun 10am–6pm). The morning milking is at 4.30am and you're invited to help. The rest of the day you can visit the barnyard animals and meander along the nature trails.

Just few miles to the south, **Swanzey** has the state's largest collection of covered bridges. Runners participating in the annual Covered Bridges Half-Marathon (usually in September; http://cbhalfmarathon.blogspot.com/) run through four of them.

CONNECTICUT RIVER VALLEY

Like its counterpart on the Vermont side of the river, New Hampshire's portion of the Connecticut River Valley is a realm of small towns, meandering roads, and rolling meadows but with an Ivy League college at its heart.

In colonial times, **Charlestown** ⑰, about 22 miles (35km) northwest of Keene, was a center of law and lawyers second only to Boston. So many fine houses and buildings were constructed that the entire **Main Street** has been designated a National Historic Landmark.

The early years of the settlement were marked with vicious attacks by the French and American Indians determined to drive the English settlers out. The **Fort at Number 4 Living History Museum** (Route 11 West; tel: 603-826 5700; www.fortat4.org; May–Oct Wed–Sun 10am–4.30pm) recreates a 1740s settlement. Within its stockade, interpreters demonstrate such crafts

as candle-dipping, weaving, and the molding of musket balls and, at certain dates, re-enact skirmishes.

Some 10 miles (16km) farther north on Route 12A in **Cornish**, the **Cornish-Windsor bridge** (www.nh.gov/nhdhr/bridges/p39.html) on the Connecticut River connects New Hampshire to Vermont and is the world's longest two-span covered bridge.

Cornish was a thriving artists' colony at the turn of the 20th century. One of the most prominent artists was Augustus Saint-Gaudens (1848–1907), the celebrated classical sculptor whose works included Boston's *Robert Gould Shaw Memorial*. Today, his handsome home, gardens, and studios are the **Saint-Gaudens National Historic Site** ❻❽ (139 Saint-Gaudens Road, off Route 12A; tel: 603-675 2175; www.nps.gov/saga/index.htm; Memorial Day–Oct daily 9am–4.30pm). Over 100 of his works are displayed in the galleries and throughout the grounds. There is an audio tour app for smartphones.

ENFIELD

In Lebanon, jog east on routes 4 and 10 to **Enfield** ❻❾ and the **Enfield Shaker Museum** (447 Route 4A; tel: 603-632 4346; daily, opening times vary, for details see www.shakermuseum.org), which preserves the settlement that existed here from 1793 to 1923. Far more modest than the Canterbury Shaker Village, the preserved buildings hold a collection of artifacts and displays. The six-story "Great Stone Dwelling" was designed by Ammi Burnham Young, later the architect for the US Treasury in Washington DC. The Mary Keane Chapel was built by a religious order which occupied the land after the Shakers left. It has a 26-rank Casavant pipe organ and magnificent German stained-glass windows.

DARTMOUTH COLLEGE

Another 5 miles (8km) north along the Connecticut River is **Hanover** ❼⓿, home of Ivy League **Dartmouth College**. Dartmouth was founded in 1769, primarily for "the education and instruction of youth of the Indian tribes in this land." It is known for its business, engineering, and medical programs. One-hour, student-led campus tours show off the buildings and history and give some insight into student life.

The collections at the **Hood Museum of Art** (tel: 603-646 2808; http://hoodmuseum.dartmouth.edu/; Wed–Sat 11am–7pm, Sun 1–5pm) run from Assyrian relief to Revere silver to Winslow Homer. If the **Hopkins Center for the Arts** (tel: 603-646 2422; http://hop.dartmouth.edu), reminds you of Lincoln Center in New York, that's probably because they were both designed by Wallace Harrison. It's an exemplary performing arts center, with over 100 live performances a year in every genre.

Just across the river in **Norwich**, VT, the wonderful **Montshire Museum of Science** (1 Montshire Road, Norwich VT; tel: 802-649 2200; www.montshire.org; daily 10am–5pm) has over 140 hands-on exhibits on natural history,

The Baker-Berry Library graces the campus of Dartmouth College.

The Jackson Honeymoon covered bridge, built in 1876.

⊙ Tip

If you take the 11am cruise on the *Mount Washington* from Weirs Beach, you can stop off at one of the other lakeside towns for lunch and shopping and return by a later cruise. The vessel operates from early May through the end of October (tel: 603-366 5531; www.cruisenh.com).

physics, and astronomy. Many of them are on the nature trails.

Fifteen miles (24km) north on Route 10 in **Orford** ⑦, the entire length of Main Street is on the National Register of Historic Places. Mansions, residences, and public buildings built between 1773 and 1889 stretch along "The Ridge" in one of the state's loveliest towns. The 3-mile (5km) **Orford–Indian Pond Heritage Trail** is an easy walking trail with lovely scenery.

THE LAKES REGION

Canoes, loons, rustic family camps along wooded shores – all of the classic icons of easy days in the lake-dappled New England forest – are found in New Hampshire's "Lakes Region." It straddles the state's central section and boasts dozens of inviting lakes and ponds. One of the prettiest, **Lake Sunapee** ⑦ in Newbury, has been a summer resort since the late 1800s. **Sunapee State Beach** (tel: 603-763 5561; www.nhstateparks.com/sunapee beach.html; mid-May–mid-June weekends only, mid-June–Labor Day daily)

Keeping cool at Lake Sunapee.

has a swimming beach, bathhouse, and canoe and kayak rentals. **Mount Sunapee Resort** (Route 103; tel: 603-763 3500; www.mountsunapee.com) is a popular ski area, but is a summer destination as well. It is the venue for the nine-day **League of NH Annual Craftsmen's Fair** (www.nhcrafts.org), usually held in August, which draws over 350 artisans. The chairlift ride during the fall foliage season gives a spectacular view of the colors. From the summit, a short trail makes the most of the views across to Mt Washington and other points some 75 miles (135km) distant.

About halfway between Lake Sunapee and Lake Winnipesaukee, **Tarbin Gardens** (321 Salisbury Road/ Route 127 S; tel: 603-934 3518; www. tarbingardens.com; May–Sept Tue–Sun 10am–6pm) is an oasis of tranquility from the often commercial and hectic vibe of the lake resorts. There are acres of blooming perennial English gardens which attract birds and butterflies.

LAKE WINNIPESAUKEE

To the northeast, **Lake Winnipesaukee** ⑦ sprawls in convoluted splendor with 183 miles (294km) of shoreline. Local folklore says there are 365 islands on the lake – one for each day of the year – but local trivia addicts can only come up with 253.

A number of towns dot the shoreline. **Weirs Beach** ⑦ (named for the weirs, or fishnets, which Indians once stretched across a narrow channel there) brings a touch of Atlantic City to Winnipesaukee's western shore, with its boardwalk, marina, and elaborate miniature golf links.

Weirs Beach is homeport for the **M/S Mount Washington** (tel: 603-366 5531; www.cruisenh.com), which offers day, evening dinner dance, and island cruises. For a unique tour of the lake, consider hopping aboard the mail boat **Sophie C** (tel: 603-366 5531; http://www. cruisenh.com/sophie.php) as she makes

her daily rounds of five islands. A few miles to the north, the resort town of Meredith is home to the **Winnipesaukee Railroad** (154 Main Street; tel: 603-745 2135; www.hoborr.com; late May–late Oct), which offers a scenic ride alongside the lake to Lakeport. Trains also leave from Weirs Beach. There are several galleries and antiques shops waiting to be browsed.

WOLFEBORO

One of the M/V *Mount Washington*'s ports of call is **Wolfeboro** , on the eastern shore, the oldest summer colony in the nation. In 1769, John Wentworth, the last of New Hampshire's colonial governors, built a summer home here, and comfortable old money has been following his example ever since. A stroll around reveals a wealth of architectural styles.

The **Wolfeboro Historical Society** (233 Main Street; tel: 603-569 4997; www.wolfeborohistoricalsociety.org; July–Aug Wed–Fri 10am–4pm, Sat 10am–2pm, rest of the year by appointment) maintains three buildings which look

at daily life, daily work, and education, respectively. The "Ladies' Emporium" is a slice of the Victoriana fashionista's bling. The state's rich boating history is preserved at the **New Hampshire Antique and Classic Boat Museum** (397 Center Street; tel: 603-569 4554; www.nhbm.org; Memorial Day–Columbus Day Mon–Sat 10am–4pm, Sun noon–4pm). Exhibits include a magnificent collection of vintage mahogany and antique boats, canoes, and sailboats.

The first-rate **Wright Museum of World War II** (77 Center Street; tel: 603-569 1212; www.wrightmuseum.org; May–Oct Mon–Sat 10am–4pm, Sun noon–4pm) documents World War II with cleverly assembled exhibits. There's great emphasis on the home front.

Throughout the summer, **Great Waters Music Festival** (tel: 603-569 7710; www.greatwaters.org) presents a diverse series of entertainment at the state-of-the-art Kingswood Arts Center.

Three miles (5km) north of town on Route 109, exhibits at the small, lakeside **Libby Museum** (tel: 603-569 1035; www.thelibbymuseum.org; June–mid-Oct

A dock on Lake Winnipesaukee, which has more than 250 islands.

A trip on Lake Winnipesaukee.

Tue–Sat 10am–4pm, Sun noon–4pm) are like exploring your grandmother's attic. It was voted the "Best Eclectic Little Museum" in a state poll.

ELSEWHERE ON THE LAKE

Looking down over the lake from the north near Moultonborough, the **Castle in the Clouds** ⑦ (off Route 171; tel: 603-476 5900; www.castleintheclouds. org; May weekends only, June–Oct daily 10am–4pm) stands as an imposing monument to one man's vision of a tranquil idyll. Built in an inventive amalgam of styles by shoe machinery magnate Thomas Gustave Plant, this 1910 mansion, which he called "Lucknow," is set in a 5,200-acre (2,100-hectare) estate with waterfalls, miles of forest trails, and magnificent views. Visitors approach the mansion via a trolley.

At **Moultonborough**, the **Old Country Store** (1011 Whittier Highway; tel: 603-476 5750; http://nhcountrystore.com/; daily), built as a stagecoach stop in 1781, makes a strong argument that it's the "Oldest Country Store" in the

A lakeside concert at Wolfeboro.

country. It sells just about everything, including a trove of New Hampshire-made products.

The Loon Center (183 Lee's Mill Road; tel: 603-476 LOON; www.loon. org; mid-May–June Mon–Sat 9am–5pm, July–Columbus Day daily; Columbus Day–mid-May Thu–Sat 9am–5pm; voluntary donation) is devoted to the speckled birds with penetrating red eyes. The award-winning center is on one of the largest areas of natural shoreline left on the lake. Twelve miles (19km) southwest, in **Holderness**, exhibits at the 200-acre (80-hectare) **Squam Lakes Natural Science Center** ⑦ (Route 113; tel: 603-968 7194; www.nhnature. org; May–Nov 1 daily 9.30am–5pm) include a nature preserve for injured animals, including black bears, mountain lions, and bobcats, unable to survive in the wild. Visitors can also take a 90-minute lake cruise mid-May–mid-October.

To the east of Lake Winnipesaukee, Route 153 winds north along the Maine border toward the White Mountains,

☉ THE OLD MAN

The Old Man of the Mountain, also known as the Great Stone Face, was the state symbol of New Hampshire. The natural rock formation with its jutting brow, regal nose, and sharp line of the bearded chin produced not merely a likeness, but a real sense of character.

Ten thousand years of weathering finally proved too much for the Old Man. Long held together by cables and iron braces, he finally slid down the mountainside and disappeared in a pile of rubble on May 3, 2003. The cleverly designed monument at Profile Lake "recreates" the formation twice. Five granite monoliths are arranged so that the profile is seen when viewed from a platform. A similar arrangement of metal "profilers" places the face back on the mountain when viewed from the lake's shore.

threading together a skein of tidy small towns set amidst rolling countryside.

The New Hampshire Farm Museum (1305 White Mountain Highway/Route 125 off Route 153; tel: 603-652 7840; www.farmmuseum.org; June–Labor Day Thu–Sat 10am–4pm and Sun noon–4pm, Labor Day–end of Oct Sat 10am–4pm and Sun noon–4pm) in **Milton** preserves three centuries of farm life in New Hampshire. A blacksmith and wood-shaver demonstrate essential skills; you can crack corn, feed the chickens, and sample freshly pressed apple cider. In the winter, there are horse-drawn sleigh rides.

WAKEFIELD

More than 200 years ago **Wakefield ⑱**, "the center of New England," was the intersection of two stagecoach routes. Twenty-six of the 18th- and 19th-century buildings are listed in the National Register of Historic Places.

Continue through the Effinghams to Effingham Falls, and turn onto Route 25, which skirts **Ossipee Lake** as it merges with Route 16 and heads northwest to the turnoff for Route 113 and **Tamworth ⑲**. Grover Cleveland, US president in 1885–9 and 1893–7, summered here. In 1931, his son founded **Barnstormers Theatre** (tel: 603-323 8500; www.barnstormerstheatre.org). It is the country's oldest professional summer theater and puts on eight well-chosen plays every season.

The **Remick Country Doctor Museum and Farm** (58 Cleveland Hill Road; tel: 603-323 7591; www.remickmuseum.org; May–mid-June Mon–Sat 10am–4pm, late June–Aug Mon–Fri 9am–5pm, Sat 9am–4pm, Sept Mon–Sat 10am–4pm, Oct–May Mon–Fri 10am–4pm) is a working farm museum which concentrates on the life of a country doctor from 1790 to the present.

THE WHITE MOUNTAINS

Continuing north on Route 16, you enter the **White Mountain National Forest**, a vast tract of almost 800,000 acres (320,000 hectares) of scenic, rugged wilderness. The Franconia and Presidential mountain ranges are both located here, as is Mt Washington, New England's highest peak. Long a forbidding wilderness, the White Mountains have evolved into an enormously popular tourist region for hikers and motorists (particularly at foliage time).

For all of their massive beauty, most of these peaks are not too demanding. Most summits can be reached within a couple of hours at a fairly leisurely pace. One of the most rewarding excursions (in terms of view obtained relative to energy expended) is the 3.2-mile (5.1km) moderate hike up **Mount Willard**. Those reaching the summit are rewarded with a magnificent panorama of **Crawford Notch** – particularly splendid at sunrise.

There are too many trails – some 1,200 miles (1,900km) all told – to attempt even a partial description here; details can be obtained from White Mountain National Forest offices

Ice climbing in the White Mountains.

A rock house in the White Mountains.

(various locations in the area; tel: 603-528 8721; www.fs.usda.gov/whitemountain) and the Appalachian Mountain Club (AMC; www.outdoors.org). The AMC maintains two lodges with comfortable accommodations and meals at the Pinkham Notch Visitors Center (361 Route 16, Gorham, at the base of Mount Washington; tel: 603-466 2721; www.outdoors.org/lodging-camping/Lodges/pinkham/index.cfm), and at Crawford Notch (Route 302, Bretton Woods; tel: 603-278 HIKE; www.outdoors.org/lodging-camping/Lodges/highland/index.cfm). The AMC also maintains a network of "huts" (some fairly large) offering hikers bunk lodgings and hearty meals; it's wise to reserve (tel: 603-466 2727) well ahead for both lodges and huts. The AMC's *White Mountain Guide* is the "walker's bible."

CONWAY

Alternatively, you can just enjoy the scenery from the car. One of the most rewarding routes begins in **Conway** ⑳, best known as the southern end of a stretch of shopping outlets that

The view from Mt Willard.

extends 5 miles (8km) to the bustling tourist town of North Conway, home to the **Conway Scenic Railroad** (tel: 800-232 5251; www.conwayscenic.com). The railroad runs day-long excursions. Call for schedule and pricing information.

To the north of North Conway, at **Glen**, is **Story Land** (850 Route 16; tel: 603-383 4186; www.storylandnh.com; Memorial Day–mid-Oct). There's enough here to keep children aged 2–12 occupied most of a day. Plenty of food options, some of them healthy, but who can resist Oreo funnel cake?

THE KANCAMAGUS HIGHWAY

Conway is the eastern terminus for the 35-mile (56km) **Kancamagus Highway** (Route 112), a designated National Scenic Byway. The "Kanc" winds alongside the Pemigewasset and Swift rivers, passing numerous trailheads offering anything from short strolls through the forest to major upland hikes. Seek out the Kancamagus, Pemi, and Hancock overlooks at the western end. Views are at their best when the fall foliage reaches its most brilliant phase, but then you may find the traffic bumper to bumper. Worthwhile short walks include the Champney Falls Trail and the Boulder Loop Trail, while pleasant roadside picnic areas are at Rocky Gorge and Sabbaday Falls.

Lincoln ㉛, at the western terminus, is home to **Loon Mountain ski area** (60 Loon Mountain Road; tel: 603-745 8111; www.loonmtn.com). During the summer and fall a gondola whisks visitors to the summit, where there's an artisans' village, hiking trails, and observation tower.

This well-developed tourist area offers several other attractions, including one of the state's oldest, **Clark's Trading Post** (Route 3; tel: 603-745 8913; www.clarkstradingpost.com; mid-May–mid-Oct; check the website for hours), where black bears put on a performance; the **Whale's Tale Water Park** (Route 112; tel: 603-745 8810;

www.whalestalewaterpark.net; mid-June–Labor Day); and **Hobo Railroad** (64 Railroad Street, Lincoln; tel: 603-745 2135; www.hoborr.com), which runs excursions late May–late October, plus Santa Trains in November–December.

FRANCONIA NOTCH

Route 3/I–93 north from **Lincoln** winds through **Franconia Notch State Park** ❽ (tel: 603-823 8800; www.nhstateparks.org/visit/state-parks/franconia-notch-state-park.aspx), between Kinsman and Franconia mountain ranges. A highlight of the park is **The Flume** (tel: 603-745 8391; visitor center and flume early May–late Oct; charge for flume), an 800ft (240-meter) gorge with granite walls rising 90ft (27 meters) and ending at a waterfall. It was reportedly discovered in 1803 by 93-year-old Aunt Jess Guernsey, who happened upon it while out fishing. It's no longer quite as she found it – boardwalks and viewing platforms have been added to accommodate the busloads of sightseers – but it is still an awesome sight. The Pool and Avalanche Falls – two other fine waterfalls – and a covered bridge are also in the park.

Pull into the parking lot at **Profile Lake** at the monument to the **Old Man of the Mountain**, the rock formation that loomed just above the lake.

Directly to the north is **Cannon Mountain** (tel: 603-823 8800; www.cannonmt.com). A ski area in winter, in summer it has a lovely view of four states and Canada from the **Aerial Tramway** (tel: 603-823 8800; late May–mid-Oct daily 8.30am–5pm). There are walking trails and a cafeteria at the summit. At the base, the **New England Ski Museum** (11 Franconia Notch Parkway; tel: 603-823 7177; www.newenglandskimuseum.org; Memorial Day–early Apr daily 10am–5pm; free) exhibits historical paraphernalia, such as handcrafted wooden skis from the 19th century, and audio-visual exhibits.

BEYOND THE NOTCH

To the west, **Franconia** ❽ was home to poet Robert Frost in 1915–20. Here he "farmed a little, taught a little and

The Conway Scenic Railroad has been in operation since 1974.

New Hampshire farmers and consumers have an unusually close relationship. A much higher percentage of the harvest is sold directly to consumers in New Hampshire compared to rates in the rest of the country.

Much of the produce and dairy, and even some meat, is sold at farmers' markets, weekly institutions which are often as important as community gatherings as they are for stocking up the larder. Also popular are Community Supported Agriculture groups (CSAs). Members pay for a "share" at the beginning of the year and receive a weekly delivery of produce from the farm. For the farmer, it provides a guaranteed income which helps their otherwise notoriously unpredictable cash flow. Members share the risk of a bad growing season or failed crops, which adds to the appreciation of what's involved in putting food on their table.

One of the pleasures of traveling New Hampshire's back roads is stopping at roadside produce stands. Blueberries and sweet corn, plump tomatoes and slender carrots, rich red peppers and shining green beans create an organic still life. Many of the stands

Squash for sale at a New England orchard during autumn.

are unattended; there's just a table for the produce and a cigar box to hold payment. Some stands post prices, others leave it up to the customer to decide what to pay. Rarely is the food just taken and equally rarely are the contents of the honor box stolen.

Pick-your-own farms are about as "back to nature" as most urbanites can get. From May through October, these farms welcome guests to harvest berries, peaches, and apples as they come into season. Places charge either by the pound or by the basket, and they are generally liberal in their tolerance for quality control taste testing while picking. If you don't have your own container, they'll provide one.

The ease of connection with local farmers and the great variety of crops, dairy products, and meat locally available in New Hampshire have encouraged a strong locavore movement. Locavores purchase only foods grown within a self-selected radius, usually between 50 and 150 miles (80–241km). Not all are purists; many have a limited number of groceries that come from beyond that circle; coffee, tea, and spices usually head the list. In those cases, they try to buy fair-trade items – products harvested, marketed, and sold in a way that supports the native farmers and growers.

The movement started as a dare by four California women who decided to see if they could live off local foods for a month. The challenge appeals to people who see it as a positive way to do several things: support their local farmers and, by extension, their local community and economy; to eat healthier foods, since many farms use sustainable practices with minimum application of pesticides and artificial fertilizers; to promote humane practices in raising livestock and poultry; and to reduce their carbon footprint by minimizing transportation of their food. In comparison, most produce in US groceries travels between 1,300 and 2,000 miles (2,100–3,200km) from farm to store.

Restaurants have enthusiastically embraced the concept. Chefs have arrangements with nearby growers and some maintain their own gardens. The New Hampshire Farm to Table Restaurant Connection creates partnerships between the restaurants and growers and has a list of certified restaurants. For more information on sustainable restaurants, visit www.nhfarmtorestaurant.com.

wrote a lot." Looking out towards his favorite three New Hampshire mountains is the modest **Robert Frost Place** (158 Ridge Road, off Route 16; tel: 603-823 5510; www.frostplace.org; Memorial Day–Columbus Day; check the website for opening hours; voluntary donation). It is maintained as the quiet refuge where the young poet found inspiration and could concentrate on his art.

Route 117 from Franconia winds south to the upscale hill town of **Sugar Hill**, home to several elegant country inns, and the **Sugar Hill Historical Museum** (Main Street; tel: 603-823 5336; www.sugarhillnh.org; late May–mid-Oct Fri–Sat 11am–3pm; voluntary donation). The museum is a repository of local history, with a re-creation of a local tavern and a sleigh once owned by actress Bette Davis.

Heading north toward Mt Washington, detour to the town of **Bethlehem** and **The Rocks Estate** (Route 302; tel: 603-444 6228; www.therocks.org; hours vary with season). Originally a summer estate in the Gilded Age, it is now the Forest Society's North Country Conservation and Education Center. A self-guided walking tour includes 13 buildings on the National Register of Historic Places. Among other things, it is a sustainable Christmas tree farm. The "tree trail" explains tree farming.

MT WASHINGTON

The **White Mountains** cover approximately one-quarter of New Hampshire and are the most rugged mountains in New England. The most difficult terrain of the 2,180-mile (3,508km) Appalachian Trail slices diagonally across them. Though hardly reaching the heights of the Rockies, the White Mountains claim 48 summits which are over 4,000ft (1,219 meters) high. Topping them all is **Mt Washington**. At 6,288ft (1,917 meters), it is the tallest summit north of the Carolinas and east of the Rockies. Its sheer bulk is

impressive, at least from the bottom, but to really appreciate its height, one must tackle the peak.

There are three ways to "climb" Mt Washington: on foot, by car, or by train. The first two options are accessible from **Pinkham Notch**. A trail to the summit via **Tuckerman Ravine**, a large glacial cirque famous for its spectacular scenery and dangerous but thrilling spring skiing, begins at the Appalachian Mountain Club's **Pinkham Notch Visitor Center** ㉞ (tel: 603-466 2721). The 8-mile (13km) climb up the **Mt Washington Auto Road** ㉟ (tel: 603-466 3988; http://mtwashingtonautoroad.com; opens sometime in May when the snow melts, closes in Oct when flurries start; hours vary with season), via endless switchbacks, can be hell on radiators, the return journey tough on the best of brakes. While it is a rough trip for drivers, the views along the way – when your car is higher than the clouds – and at the summit make the effort worthwhile. You'll slap on the "This Car Climbed Mount Washington" bumper sticker with pride. For those

Above the clouds on Mount Washington. The mountain's erratic weather makes it popular with glider pilots.

Heading up the mountain.

Accumulated rime ice at the weather observatory on the summit of Mt Washington.

The Old Man of the Mountain prior to its collapse on May 3, 2003.

who'd rather spare their vehicles the ordeal, a tour van departs from the base for a 90-minute tour (in winter there are also SnowCoach tours, for details check the website). There's also a one-way shuttle for hikers. Be sure to bring a jacket or sweater since it can be bitterly cold in August. Sandals are not such a good idea, either.

The summit bears chilling markers commemorating those who, like 23-year-old Lizzie Bourne in September 1855, died of exposure only a few hundred yards from the top. The destination she sought, a rustic hotel called the **Tip Top House** (Memorial Day–Columbus Day 10am–4pm), survives as a small museum, with the cramped dormitories where travelers bunked down on crude beds cushioned with moss.

Climatically, the summit is classified as arctic. Higher than any other mountain east of the Rockies with nothing to stop the howling winds sweeping down from Canada or across the continent, its topographic isolation results in alarmingly abrupt changes in weather, including blizzards even in summer. The highest-velocity winds ever recorded – 231mph (372kmh) – were measured here in 1934. Some buildings are chained down to keep them from blowing away.

The **Sherman Adams Summit Building** is surrounded by a deck with 70-mile (110km) views; inside is the small but fascinating **Extreme Mount Washington** centre (tel: 603-356 2137; www.mountwashington.org/visit-us/extreme-mount-washington.aspx; mid-May–mid-Oct daily). It's a comprehensive display of geology, meteorology, and ecology delivered through high-tech hands-on exhibits.

THE COG RAILWAY

The third way to reach the summit is almost as famous and popular as driving. The **Cog Railway** leaves from **Crawford Notch**. Turn off Route 302 onto the access road for 6 miles (10km). The 1869 **Cog Railway** (tel: 603-278 5404; www.thecog.com; Apr–Nov, see the website for schedules and hours, booking recommended) is a testament to American ingenuity in the pursuit of diversion. Powered by tough little steam locomotives, the train – the world's first mountain-climbing cog railway – carts passengers 3.5 miles (5.5km) up and down the mountain, relying on a failsafe rack-and-pinion system.

CRAWFORD NOTCH

Head west on Route 302 through **Crawford Notch** , a narrow pass named for two notable early entrepreneurs. The notch was "discovered" in 1771 (more or less accidentally) by Timothy Nash, who was tracking a moose at the time. When Nash informed Governor Wentworth of his discovery, the disbelieving governor offered him a tract of land including the notch if Nash could bring a horse through it and present the animal at Portsmouth. Nash met the challenge, incidentally opening up the White Hills (as the mountains were then called) to a steady influx of settlers and eventually tourists.

Among the first to anticipate and capitalize on the area's potential were Abel Crawford and his son, Ethan Allen Crawford. They blazed the first path to the summit of Mt Washington in 1819, advertised both it and their services as tour guides, and established inns to accommodate travelers, thereby masterminding the White Mountains' debut as a tourist attraction.

BRETTON WOODS

Route 302 through **Crawford Notch State Park** (tel: 603-374 2272; www.nhstateparks.org/visit/state-parks/crawford-notch-state-park.aspx) passes by two waterfalls you can see from your car: Silver Cascades and Flume. Nearby, the colossal **Omni Mount Washington Resort at Bretton Woods** **87** (tel: 888-444 6664; www.omnihotels.com), which first opened in 1902, welcomes well-heeled visitors in a manner to which most people could easily become accustomed.

Circled by a 900ft (270-meter) veranda set with white wicker chairs and topped with red-tiled turrets, this elongated, white stucco wedding cake contains some 200 rooms and suites, and a voluminous lobby with 23ft (7-meter) ceilings supported by nine sets of columns and illumined with crystal chandeliers.

GORHAM

It's fitting that **Gorham** **88** has a **Railroad Museum** (25 Railroad Street; tel: 603-466 5338; http://gorhamnewhampshire.com/Railroad_Museum.html; Memorial Day–Columbus Day Tue–Sat 10am–3pm), since railroads brought the first tourists to the area. Among the displays are a 1911 steam engine and a 1920s-era railroad snow plow.

If it's moose you want to see, sign on for a trip with **Gorham Moose Tours** at the kiosk in the town center

(tel: 877-986 6673/603-466 3103; www.gorhammoosetours.org; end May–Sept, times vary). They boast a 94 percent success rate in spotting moose, with an average of eight moose an hour.

Learn to mush at **Muddy Paw Sled Dog Kennel** (32 Valley Road, Jefferson; tel; 603-545 4533; https://dogslednh.com/). Trips run from 1.5 to 3 hours, or take a three-hour sledding class. In summer, there are rolling sled dog rides and a licensed **white-water rafting** operation for all levels of experience and nerve.

The importance of the logging industry gets its due at the **Northern Forest Heritage Park** (961 Main Street; tel: 603-752 7202) in **Berlin**. There's a full-size replica of a logging camp. Guided boat tours on the Androscoggin River are offered (http://androscogginvalleychamber.com/). In October, there's a weekend lumberjack festival.

THE NORTH COUNTRY

This isolated, sparsely populated region is one of New Hampshire's better-kept secrets. The landscape

Golf and skiing at the Mount Washington Resort, Bretton Woods.

Mount Washington Cog Railway.

Motorists stop to photograph a young bull moose – but collisions are not uncommon.

The Balsams Hotel in Dixville Notch.

is stunning: vast stretches of forest which provide its primary industry – logging. A lacework of lakes and waterways offers a delicate counterpoint to the craggy hills and mountains. The Connecticut River begins in a string of lakes just a few miles from the Canadian border, in a corner so out of the way that its allegiance was not decided, nor its boundary fixed (and then, by force), until 1840. The wilderness is a magnet for fishermen in search of salmon and trout. In winter, snowmobilers are attracted by miles of trails.

Route 3 is the road north past the Connecticut Lakes to the border. Just south of **Colebrook** ⑲, where the Mohawk and Connecticut rivers meet, the Oblate Fathers once oversaw the **Shrine of Our Lady of Grace**. Sadly, the shrine was closed in 2014; rumours that it could be turned into a transitional shelter for homeless veterans seem – so far – to be unfounded.

From here north to Canada, it's a world of forest, water, and scattered hunting and fishing camps. Folks at

The Glen (tel: 603-538 9995; www.atbeartree.com/the-glen), a handsome lakeside retreat on the western shore of the First Connecticut Lake, will be glad to provide information (as well as great home cooking), as will the **Connecticut Lakes Tourist Association** (www.nhconnlakes.com).

Route 26 east out of Colebrook follows the Mohawk River through **Dixville Notch State Park** ⑳ (tel: 603-538 6707; www.nhstateparks.org/visit/state-parks/dixville-notch-state-park.aspx; year-round). There are several yurts available for overnight camping, and the view from the top of the fire tower takes in three states and Canada. Watch for moose; the park is home to much of the state's population of these behemoths. That provides a peg for the Moose Festival (tel: 603-237 8939; www.chamberofthenorthcountry.com/moose-festival.html) each August, with various events in Colebrook, Pittsburg, and across the state line in Canaan VT.

In the heart of the Notch is **The Balsams Grand Resort Hotel** (tel: 603-255 2500; www.thebalsams.com; currently closed under a $170 million restoration and expansion plan, call or check website for updates).

LAKE UMBAGOG

At the junction of routes 26 and 16 in **Errol**, turn north for 5.5 miles (9km) to visit the headquarters of the 13,000-acre (5,300-hectare) **Lake Umbagog National Wildlife Refuge** ㉑ (tel: 603-482 3415; www.fws.gov/refuge/umbagog/), which spreads across New Hampshire and Maine. Access is primarily by boat. Created in 1992 to conserve wetlands and protect migratory birds, its bird watching list is over 200 species long. You can also expect to spot mink, otter, and bobcat. "**Moose Alley**" is another name for Route 3. Look for low-lying marshy places beside the road or watch from a platform on Route 26 in Errol.

PIONEERS AND REVOLUTIONARIES

The diverse landscapes of New England were ideal for the hardy pioneers.

From the seashore to the mountainous forests, New Englanders have found a way to live and work in harmony with the land, taking advantage, and protecting their greatest resource.

Like the rest of New England, New Hampshire had little to offer in the way of good soil or easy farming. The main assets of the region at the beginning of the colonial period were the deepwater port and surrounding shores of what is now Portsmouth, and the tall, straight pines, used in the construction of ships. Fisheries along the coast prospered from the sale of salt cod and other catches hauled from the Atlantic as far north as the Grand Banks off Newfoundland.

The impetus behind these first forays was provided by Sir Ferdinando Gorges, head of the council established by King James to govern all of New England, and Captain John Mason, an early governor of Newfoundland. They obtained grants to an ill-defined territory lining the coast and extending roughly 60 miles (100km) inland. They proposed a variety of commercial enterprises and promised healthy dividends to investors. Lack of supplies limited the scheme's progress, and the company eventually collapsed. The settlers simply divided the land up among themselves and proceeded to amass their own fortunes, without giving very much thought to the niceties of property laws.

Strong-willed settlers, gradually pushing their way inland from Portsmouth and up the Connecticut River from the south, laid claim first to the lush valleys, then to the harsher hillsides, and finally to the forbidding mountains in the north. Despite frequent attacks by the French and their Huron, Mohegan, and Ottowa allies, determined to rid the region of the British, settlement by British pioneers took tenuous root. John Wentworth, the first colonial governor, worked to stabilize the province by encouraging settlement and promoting commerce. When the Revolution came, New Hampshire joined early in the fight. It was the first colony to assert its independence from England (establishing its own government on January 5, 1776) and the first to suggest independence to the Continental Congress in 1775. Of the original 13 colonies, it was the only one which saw no skirmishes or battles within its boundaries.

Following the Revolution, the push inland continued, extending up into the White Mountains, where the logger's axe was more useful than the plow. Even early in the 19th century, though, the success of rough hostelries such as the one run by Ethan Allen Crawford in Crawford Notch pointed the way for the mountains' eventual economic direction – tourism. The first retreats were modest affairs, but as railroads reached farther into the mountains, palatial resort hotels were built to serve wealthy clients who would arrive with servants and steamer trunks in tow, ready to spend the summer days in the lap of luxury. Those were followed by rustic lakeside cabins enjoyed by families and the less affluent, in keeping with New Hampshire's egalitarian approach to life and leisure. By the 1850s, "summer people" were as much a part of the mountain scenery as loons and moose.

Meanwhile, along the Merrimack River in the south, textile mills grew in output, creating a new economic power base, centered in Manchester and Nashua. This urban New Hampshire would become an extension of the industrial and commercial centers in Massachusetts. Between the "two" New Hampshires was a buffer of small towns and farms. That amalgam gives New Hampshire a broad economic base.

First settlers of Maine drying and salting fish.

📷 FLORA AND FAUNA

New England's wilderness areas are one of its big draws, attracting campers, hunters, fishermen, photographers, and nature lovers.

Trees cover more than three-quarters of New England, cloaking the mountains of New Hampshire, Maine, and Vermont. These woods and mountains ring with birdsong and are carpeted with wild flowers; particularly enthralling are the alpine flowers on Mt Washington.

The most exciting animals to see in the forests are moose. Desperately ungainly, and sporting hairy dewlaps beneath large snouts, they can often be spotted in northern New England, especially in and around lakes and marshes – or licking the salt that runs off the roads in winter. A bull can grow to well over 6ft (2 meters) tall, with huge antlers, and can weigh half a ton – give him a wide berth. You may see moose as you drive around, particularly at dawn or dusk; if not, join one of many moose-watching trips organized locally.

Black bears are shy denizens of the deep forests. They seldom attack humans, but don't feed them or leave food scraps on the ground. Keep food in sealed containers and never approach cubs – their mothers are fiercely protective.

In the lakes and streams that lace the forests, beavers fell trees with their teeth, building dams and creating ponds. Their lodges built of mud and sticks may be up to 6ft (2 meters) tall. Also look out for raccoons, chipmunks, squirrels, porcupines, and skunks.

Black bears are most common in Maine, which has over 35,000. Hunters in the state shoot ("harvest") an average of 2,900 a year.

Signs along Route 3 from Pittsburg, New Hampshire, to the Canadian border read: "Brake for Moose. It Could Save Your Life. Hundreds of Collisions." They're not kidding: attracted by salt on the road, dozens of the state's 4,000 moose can be seen just before dusk strolling along "Moose Alley." These docile beasts, said to outnumber humans in parts of Vermont's Northeast Kingdom, have spread as far south as Connecticut.

The fact that a Massachusetts company called Beaver Solutions dedicated itself to "resolving human/beaver conflicts and flooding-related beaver problems" indicate how North America's largest rodent wreaks havoc. Slow-moving, they take refuge in the ponds they create by building intricate dams.

A cairn (pile of stones) signifying the trail on an alpine hike.

Alpine attractions

This cairn on Mt Washington, in New Hampshire, marks an alpine hike across this rugged arctic zone. The treeline occurs as low as 1,400ft (420 meters). The area supports mammals such as voles and shrews, living in deep crevices, and 100 species of alpine plants, many of which grow only here, on Mt Katahdin in Maine's Baxter State Park, and in Labrador and the Arctic. They have adapted to desiccation (dryness resulting from the removal or lack of water) caused by biting winds, poor soil, minimal sunlight, and a short growing season. Some take 25 years to flower. These exquisite plants, growing in and around the lichen-covered rocks with sedges and dwarfed balsam firs, include gold thread, fireweed, alpine bearberry, starflower, arnica, mountain cranberry, wren's egg cranberry, skunk currant, and the dwarf cinquefoil Potentilla robbinsiana, unique to Mt Washington. Their vibrant colors are best seen from mid-June to August. The Alpine Gardens Research Natural Area (www.nrs.fs.fed.us/rna/nh/white-mountain/alpine-gardens/) on Mt Washington is a 100-acre (40.5-hectare) protected area reserved for study of the sensitive, generally hard-to-reach environment.

he loon is the state bird of New Hampshire. Some believe it the oldest bird on earth, though scientists say this is a ase of mistaken identity. They are known in Europe as divers," and their American name derives from the aquatic irds' yodel-like cry. They can live for up to 30 years.

lmost four in five of New England's red foxes were wiped ut in the 1990s, hit by rabies and distemper and outflanked y coyotes. But, to the alarm of chicken farmers, they have een making a comeback. They can most easily be seen in ummer when they hunt food for their young.

Waders include American egret (pictured) and black-crowned night heron. Forest birds include pine siskin, blue jay, golden crowned kinglet, and chickadee.

Marshall Point Lighthouse.

MAINE

Maine is a land of jagged coastlines and vast pine woods, of remote peninsulas and fresh lobster, inimitably captured in the soft canvases of Winslow Homer.

Beyond its heavily trafficked southern coast, Maine remains a vast wilderness. Larger in area than the other five New England states combined, the "Pine Tree State" – nine-tenths covered with forest and with a savage beauty – bears little resemblance to its comfortably settled neighbors. Residents pride themselves on their rugged independence and turn a bemused eye on the strange habits of "summer people" – or, in the still-used 19th-century term, "rusticators."

THE TWO MAINES

Maine's geography dictated its economic development. Coastal Mainers made ample use of the fine natural harbors, and virtually all commerce within Maine and between Maine and the outside world was conducted by sea.

Along with trading and boatbuilding, the seaside communities of Maine depended heavily upon the fishing industry and eventually became home to New England's biggest lobster fleet. Inland Maine, where settlement was thin, became a timber empire. The "paper plantations" have kept much of northern Maine a wild paradise for campers, canoeists, hunters, and anglers, although the industry is turning more land over to potential development and shuttering mills in towns such

A tribute to the region's fishing heritage.

as East Millinocket, where the overpowering aroma of paper manufacture has long been the perfume of prosperity.

THE SOUTH COAST

The best way to see Maine is to start at the southern tip and head northeast along the old coastal highway, US 1. Although geographically the coast represents only a tiny fraction of the state, 45 percent of Maine residents call it home, and the overwhelming majority of visitors are also headed for the shore.

Main Attractions

Kennebunkport
Portland
Brunswick
Wiscasset
Boothbay Harbor
Pemaquid Point
Mount Desert Island
Bar Harbor

Maps on pages 324, 328, 340

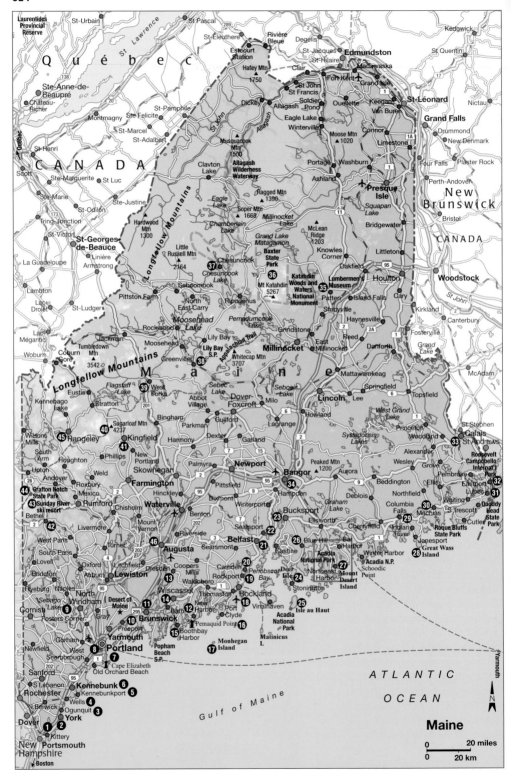

Maine

The southernmost segment, extending from Kittery to Freeport, attracted the earliest settlers and to this day is the most heavily traveled, blending historic enclaves with built-up beaches and discount shopping malls. Just across the New Hampshire border from Portsmouth is **Kittery ❶**, home to Kittery Outlets (exit 3 off I–95; tel: 888-548 8379; www.thekitteryoutlets. com), one of the state's largest concentrations of outlet malls. More than 120 stores are clustered around the **Kittery Trading Post** (tel: 888-587 6246; www. kitterytradingpost.com; daily), a shopping destination for outdoor equipment and clothing since 1926.

The town is also home to **Portsmouth Naval Yard**, the nation's first, founded in 1806. **Kittery Historical and Naval Museum** (200 Rogers Road Extension; tel: 207-439 3080; www.kitterymuseum. com; Wed and Sat 10am–4pm) documents the shipyard's history, from the construction of Ranger (the first ship ever to fly the Stars and Stripes, under the command of John Paul Jones in 1777) to today's submarines.

Nearby **Fort McClary State Historic Site** (off Route 103, 28 Oldsfield Road, Kittery Point; tel: 207-439 2845; Memorial Day–Columbus Day daily 10am until sunset) was first fortified in 1715 and rebuilt repeatedly right up until the 1898 Spanish–American War. All that remains is the 1846 hexagonal wooden blockhouse, a powder magazine and the granite seawall with a scenic view of Portsmouth Harbor and Whaleback Light at the mouth of the Piscataqua River.

YORK

A few miles to the north, **York ❷**, one of Maine's first settlements, was a center of dissent during the Revolutionary era. The local chapter of the Sons of Liberty decided to hold their own tea party when a British ship carrying tea anchored in **York Harbor**. Being practical Mainers, however, they "liberated" the tea rather than threw it in the harbor.

The **Museums of Old York** (tel: 207-363 1756; www.oldyork.org; June–Aug Tue–Sat 10am–5pm, Sun 1–5pm, Sept–Oct Thu–Sat 10am–5pm, Sun 1–5pm)

⊘ Tip

Route 1 from Ogunquit through Wells is studded with antiques shops, from multi-shop flea markets to upscale galleries. There are also several excellent used-book stores, including the sprawling Douglas N. Harding Rare Books (2152 Post Road, Route 1; www.hardingsbooks. com), which also sells old maps and prints.

The calm waters of Maine make for perfect harbors.

⊘ MAINE'S HARBORS

The "rock-bound coast of Maine" extends only 400 miles (640km) as the gull flies, but 3,500 miles (5,600km) if all the coves, inlets, and peninsulas were magically ironed out. Geologists refer to Maine's shoreline as a "drowned" coastline. The original coast sank thousands of years ago; its valleys became Maine's harbors, its mountains the islands lying offshore. As the coastline sank, receding glaciers exposed vast expanses of granite, which not only gave Maine's mountains their peculiar pink coloration, but also provided settlers with a valuable source of building material.

The first known residents were Paleolithic hunters and fishers who lived along the coast 11,000 years ago. Archaeologists debate evidence that Norse explorers visited. The earliest European explorers, in the 15th and 16th centuries, were greeted by the Abenaki tribe, whose name means "easterners" or "people of the dawn." John Cabot visited Maine in 1497–99, and his explorations established all future British claims to the land, but it wasn't until after Captain John Smith sounded "about 25 excellent harbors" in 1614 that the "Father of Maine," Sir Ferdinando Gorges, was granted a charter to establish British colonies. Rival French explorers also claimed parts of Maine and Canada, provoking territorial disputes that were resolved only by the French and Indian Wars of the 18th century.

maintains nine historic sites, including the **John Hancock Warehouse**, the 1750 **Jefferds Tavern**, and the **Old Gaol**, built in 1719 and restored to its 1790s appearance, complete with dungeon. It provides an interesting window on penal attitudes of yore. The **Elizabeth Perkins House** is a prime example of Colonial revivalism.

York Beach is a narrow, mile-long strip of fine sand, lined with every imaginable type of fast-seafood shack and family-entertainment facility. The **Cliff Walk** off York Harbor's boardwalk affords beautiful views of the coastline, and of Cape Neddick's 1879 **Nubble Light** (Lighthouse and grounds closed to public).

OGUNQUIT AND WELLS

Take scenic **Shore Road** north from York's Main Street to **Ogunquit ❸** ("beautiful place by the sea" in the Abenaki language). Artist and teacher Charles Woodbury arrived in 1898 and was soon followed by other artists drawn to the dramatic landscape. The **Ogunquit Museum of American Art** (543 Shore Road; tel: 207-646 4909; www.ogunquit-museum.org; May–Oct daily 10am–5pm) is devoted exclusively to 20th-century American paintings, sculpture, photography, and graphics, including Maine-inspired Edward Hopper.

Today, tourists crowd the galleries, shops, and eateries that have taken over the fishing shacks and frolic in the surf at the 3-mile (5km) town beach (parking charge). In summer the town is so packed with visitors that reproduction trolleys are the easiest way to get around. Ethel Barrymore, Sally Struthers, and Lorenzo Lamas all trod the boards at the **Ogunquit Playhouse**, a highly regarded summer theater founded in 1933 (Route 1; tel: 207-646 5511; www.ogunquitplayhouse.org; mid-May–Oct).

Turn right just past the museum to Perkins Cove in Ogunquit, the southern terminus for Marginal Way, a spectacular, 1-mile (1.6km) seaside walk along the cliffs.

A few miles north on Route 1 brings you to **Wells ❹** and the **Wells National Estuarine Research Reserve** at

The harbor at Kennebunkport.

Laudholm (342 Laudholm Road; tel: 207-646 1555; www.wellsreserve.org; year-round daily 7am–sunset). Exhibits explore estuarine environments and developing coastal management. The preserve has 7 miles (11km) of hiking trails along coastal marsh, uplands, and pristine beach.

THE KENNEBUNKS

East of Wells on Route 9, **Kennebunkport** ➎, once the shipbuilding center of York County, has embraced tourism; upscale shops, galleries, and restaurants are clustered around downtown **Dock Square**. The **Kennebunkport Historical Society** (125 North Street; tel: 207-967 2751; www.kporthistory.org) maintains several properties. The buildings at the North Street location include a blacksmith shop, school, and exhibit gallery. In town, an 1853 Greek Revival building, known as White Columns, houses the First Families Kennebunkport Museum (8 Maine Street; Memorial Day–Columbus Day). Displays relate stories of former residents, from sea captains and rusticators to former President George H.W. Bush, Kennebunkport's most famous summer resident.

From Dock Square head up North Street (which becomes Log Cabin Road) 3 miles (5km) to the **Seashore Trolley Museum** (195 Log Cabin Road; tel: 207-967 2800; www.trolleymuseum.org; mid-May–Oct daily 10am–5pm, early May and late Oct Sat–Sun 10am–5pm, first two weekends of Dec Fri–Sun 10am–5pm). One of the world's largest collections of antique trolley cars, it offers a 1.5-mile (2.5km) ride on vintage streetcars.

From town, take a drive along Ocean Avenue, past Walker's Point, the summer home of the first President Bush. After the road converges with Route 9, continue on to visit the charming fishing village of **Cape Porpoise**, site of the region's first settlement. Route 9, which passes the turnoff for **Goose Rocks Beach**, is a scenic – and less crowded – route to Old Orchard Beach.

Kennebunk ➏, 4 miles (6km) northwest of Kennebunkport, has a rich shipbuilding heritage. This is the focus of the **Brick Store Museum** (117 Main Street; tel: 207-985 4802; www.brickstoremuseum.org; Tue–Fri 10am–5pm, Sat 10am–4pm, Sun noon–4pm). There's a cell phone-based audio tour of the exhibits. The museum also offers tours of the architecturally diverse downtown Historic District. At 105 Summer Street (Route 9A/35) look for the unmistakable 1826 **Wedding Cake House**, festooned with elaborate carved wooden scrollwork. Legend has it that a sea-bound captain who married in haste had it built to compensate his wife for the lack of a cake at their rushed ceremony. In reality, it was a way to unify disparate designs of several buildings.

NORTH TO PORTLAND

Farther up the coast is **Old Orchard Beach**, a seaside resort popular among French Canadians. The 7-mile (11km) beach is flanked with motels and condos and, at the Ocean Pier, an old-style amusement park.

The Wedding Cake House at Kennebunk. It is said that its creator, shipbuilder George Washington Bourne (1801–56), was inspired by Milan's cathedral.

Rachel Carson National Wildlife Refuge.

Eastward, just south of Portland on **Cape Elizabeth** , is the oldest lighthouse on the eastern seaboard, and quite possibly the most photographed, the Portland Head Light (1791). The history of lighthouses is documented at the **Museum at Portland Head Light** (1000 Shore Road, Fort Williams Park; tel: 207-799 2661; www.portlandheadlight.com; Memorial Day–Oct daily 10am–4pm; Nov–first weekend of Dec Sat–Sun).

PORTLAND

With a population of more than 520,000 in its greater area, **Portland** is home to almost one-fourth of the state's population. Founded as Casco in the middle of the 17th century, the city has the advantage of being 100 miles (160km) closer to Europe than any other major US seaport and is blessed with a sheltered, deep-water harbor.

Three times the city was burned completely to the ground – by Indians in 1675, by the British in 1775, and by accident in 1866. After the last fire, it was reconfigured. Streets were widened, and an elaborate network of municipal parks instituted. The **Portland Trolley** (tel: 207-774 0808; www.portlanddiscovery. com; May–Oct) provides a 105-minute tour of the city's highlights.

The atmospheric **Old Port** district, a salty warren of old brick buildings and cobbled streets, is packed with sophisticated shops and restaurants. Several whale-watch and cruise ships depart from the docks along Commercial Street. Spread out beyond the harbor are the Calendar Islands – so named because John Smith reported that there were 365 of them.

Portland remains a thriving cultural crossroads. Congress Street is the main thoroughfare of the Arts District, with museums and theatres, art galleries and studios, and plenty of chic shops and cafés. The I.M. Pei-designed **Portland Museum of Art** (7 Congress Square; tel: 207-775 6148; www.portlandmuseum.org; winter Wed, Sat–Sun 10am–6pm, Thu–Fri 10am–8pm, summer also Mon–Tue; free Fri 4–8pm; check website for details) is strong on locally inspired artists such as Winslow Homer, Edward Hopper, and Andrew

The Flat Iron Building, Portland.

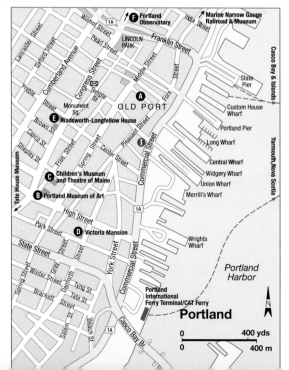

Wyeth. Among the well-represented European masters are Van Gogh, Degas, Mary Cassatt, and Picasso.

Next door is the imaginative **Children's Museum and Theatre of Maine**  (142 Free Street; tel: 207-828 1234; www.kitetails.org/; Tue–Sun 10am–5pm). Kids can climb inside a humpback whale, play in a dress-up theatre, and crew on a kid-size lobster boat.

The **Institute of Contemporary Art** at Maine College of Art (522 Congress Street; tel: 800-699 1509; Wed–Sun 11am–5pm, Thu 11am–7pm; www.meca. edu/about/institute-of-contemporary-art/; free) presents cutting-edge works by regional and international artists.

The **State Theatre** (609 Congress Street; tel: 207-956-6000; www.statetheatreportland.com) has a rich schedule of musical performances; **Portland Stage Company** (27A Forest Avenue; tel: 207-774 0465; www.portlandstage.org) is the town's professional theatre troupe. **Merrill Auditorium** (Myrtle Street; tel: 207-842 0800; www.porttix.com) is the city's premier performing arts center. Concerts on the 5,000-pipe Kotzschmar organ are performed periodically during the year.

Several Portland neighborhoods warrant strolling – especially the Western Promenade, a parade of 19th-century architectural styles. By far the most elaborate dwelling in town is the 1859–63 brownstone Italianate villa **Victoria Mansion** (109 Danforth Street; tel: 207-772 4841; www.victoriamansion. org; May–Oct Mon–Sat 10am–3.45pm, Sun 1–4.45pm). Also known as the Morse-Libby House, it is considered one of the country's premier examples of pre-Civil War opulence.

In contrast is the somewhat restrained 1785–6 **Wadsworth-Longfellow House** (489 Congress Street; tel: 207-774 1822; www.hwlongfellow.org; daily May noon–5pm, June–Oct Mon–Sat 10am–5pm, Sun noon–5pm), built by Longfellow's grandfather, a Revolutionary War officer. Inside are the parlor where the poet's parents were married and the room where he wrote "The Rainy Day." Behind the house lies a beautifully landscaped garden with meandering paths (May–Oct daily 10am–5pm; free), a beloved green oasis in the heart of downtown. Next door, exhibits at the **Maine Historical Society** (www.mainehistory.org; hours as for Wadsworth-Longfellow House) span more than five centuries of Maine life.

Built in 1807 as a maritime signal tower, the 86ft (26-meter) -high **Portland Observatory** (138 Congress Street; tel: 207-774 5561; http://portlandlandmarks.org/observatory; Memorial Day–Columbus Day daily 10am–4.30pm by 45-minute guided tour) offers one of the most magnificent views in town.

Hop aboard one of the 2ft-gauge trains that once connected rural Maine to the rest of the world at the **Marine Narrow Gauge Railroad and Museum** (58 Fore Street; tel: 207-828 0814; www. mainenarrowgauge.org, www.facebook.com/ mainenarrowgauge; 9.30am–4pm Apr Sat–Sun, May–Oct daily; trains depart on the hour between 10am–3pm; Polar

Statue to the poet Henry Wadsworth Longfellow (1807–82) in Portland's Longfellow Square.

Maine has a 400-year history of boatbuilding.

The Androscoggin River rapids at Brunswick.

A vintage locomotive in Yarmouth Station in Maine.

Express runs from Ocean Gateway on selected days from Thanksgiving through Christmas, check Facebook page for details). The train ride rumbles along the shore of Casco Bay in an antique rail car pulled by a steam or diesel engine.

Overlooking the Fore River is the **Tate House Museum** (1267 Westbrook Street; tel: 207-774-6177; www.tatehouse.org; June–Oct Wed–Sat 10am–4pm, Sun 1–4pm; tours on the hour; museum store open year-round. Built in 1755 for George Tate, the senior mast agent for the Royal Navy who was in charge of cutting and shipping white pines to England, it's the only pre-Revolutionary house in Portland that's open to the public.

THE LAKES REGION

With its easy access from Portland via Route 302, **Sebago Lake 9** is the state's second-largest lake and the most popular of the Western Lakes, offering swimming, boating, camping, and fishing in 1,400-acre (160-hectare) **Sebago Lake State Park** (State Park Road, between Naples and South Casco; tel: 207-693 6613; year-round 9am–sunset.

The ***Songo River Queen II*** (Route 302; tel: 207-693 6861; www.songoriverqueen. net), a replica Mississippi River paddle-wheeler, provides one and two-hour tours on Long Lake. Several marinas rent canoes, powerboats, pontoon boats, and Jet Skis.

FREEPORT

The little town of **Freeport 10** is known worldwide, thanks to the legendary **L.L.Bean** outdoor equipment store (95 Main Street; tel: 877-755 2326; www. llbean.com), open 24 hours, 365 days a year. A middle-of-the-night browse is worth the lost sleep. Their Outdoor Discovery program (see website for details) has courses and outings for biking, fly-fishing, kayaking, sporting clays, stand-up paddling, cross-country skiing, and snowshoeing. Many of them have same-day, walk-in registration at the store. The village of Freeport (www.freeportusa.com) is crammed with about 200 outlets, shops, galleries,

⊘ MOOSE-SPOTTING

The moose is as much a symbol of Maine as lighthouses and lobster. Standing at about 6ft (1.8 meters) at the shoulder and weighing up to 1,000lbs (455kg), the bull moose is a majestic creature. Spotting one of the behemoths is a highlight of the trip for many visitors.

They roam freely in the North Woods and young males sometimes wander hundreds of miles from their home in search of females. In the Moosehead Lake area, Route 15 near Rockwood, Route 201 from Forks to the Canadian border, and Lazy Tom Bog near Kokadjo north of Greenville are all prime moose habitat. Keep an eye out for them in the bogs. In the summer, they are most active in the early morning and late afternoon. Keep your camera close, but do not approach them. Generally placid, they will charge if they feel threatened.

and cafés. Local zoning ordinances are surprisingly effective at maintaining a small-town appearance. Even the McDonald's looks like an old house.

Private boat operators run trips to Eagle Island, the former home of North Pole explorer Admiral Robert E. Peary (www.pearyeagleisland.org; mid-June–Labor Day 10am–5pm), as well as seal and osprey watch cruises, and a day-long excursion to Seguin Island Lighthouse.

Ten minutes from the heart of town, **Wolfe's Neck Woods State Park** (426 Wolfe Neck Road; tel: 207-865 4465; daily 9am–sunset) has hiking trails through copses of pine and hemlock, the saltwater estuary, and the shoreline along Casco Bay and the Harraseeket River. It's a good place for whale sightings, too.

THE MID-COAST

Brunswick ⓫ is best known as the home of **Bowdoin College** (tel: 207-725 3100 for tour information; www.bowdoin. edu). Founded in 1794, Bowdoin was originally slated to be built in Portland, but the college's benefactors found that the city offered too many "temptations to dissipation, extravagance, vanity and various vices of seaport towns." Nathaniel Hawthorne and Henry Wadsworth Longfellow were alumni, class of 1825.

On campus, the **Bowdoin College Museum of Art** (Walker Art Building; tel: 207-725 3275; www.bowdoin.edu/ art-museum; Tue–Sat 10am–5pm, Thu until 8.30pm, Sun 1–5pm; voluntary donation) houses paintings by Stuart, Copley, and Winslow Homer; the Warren Collection of classical antiquities; and works by European masters.

Also on campus, the fascinating **Peary-MacMillan Arctic Museum** (Hubbard Hall; tel: 207-725 3416; www. bowdoin.edu/arctic-museum/; Tue–Sat 10am–5pm, Sun 2–5pm; voluntary donation) heralds the accomplishments of North Pole explorers Robert E. Peary and Donald MacMillan, who achieved their objective in 1909.

The **Pejepscot Historical Society** (159 Park Row; tel: 207-729 6606; http:// pejepscothistorical.org; Memorial Day–Columbus Day Wed–Sat 10am–4pm, Columbus Day–Memorial Day Wed–Fri

A bull moose.

⊙ Tip

The Bowdoin International Music Festival (tel: 207-373 1400; www.bowdoin festival.org), from late June through July, features chamber music concerts at sites throughout Brunswick.

10am–4pm; voluntary donation) has a fine collection of material dealing with the area's history.

The Pejepscot Society oversees the **Skolfield-Whittier House** (next door to the museum; Memorial Day–Columbus Day Wed–Sat 10am–4pm; guided tours on the hour). The house is a time capsule of three generations of a Brunswick family that was prominent in seafaring, medicine, and education. The **Joshua L. Chamberlain Museum** (226 Maine Street; tel: 207-725 6958; Memorial Day–Columbus Day Tue–Sat 10am–4pm, Sun 1–4pm, mid-Oct–mid-Nov Fri–Sat 10am–4pm, Sun 1–4pm, guided tours on the hour) exhibits memorabilia of Chamberlain, a hero at the Battle of Gettysburg, who later served four one-year terms as Maine's 32nd governor and became Bowdoin's president.

BATH

East of Brunswick on US 1, **Bath ⑫** was once the nation's fifth-largest seaport and still builds ships. For a time in the 19th century, Maine's shipyards were responsible for one-third to one-half

There are more than 2 million lobster traps in Maine waters.

of all ships on the high seas. When the days of wooden ships ended, the old yards gave way to the **Bath Iron Works**, today a busy producer of Navy ships.

Visitors can tour the Iron Works aboard a trolley run by the **Maine Maritime Museum** (243 Washington Street; tel: 207-443 1316; www.mainemaritime museum.org; daily winter 9.30am–5pm, until 7.30 in summer). The 20-acre (8-hectare) campus on the Kennebac River preserves the history of shipbuilding in Bath, and Maine's relationship with the sea. Exhibits on nautical tools and gadgets capture the flavor of seafaring days, while a working boatyard demonstrates shipbuilding techniques. The museum also offers history- and nature-themed cruises.

Bath's historic district has fine examples of Greek Revival, Georgian, and Italianate architecture among its mansions, cozy inns, and restaurants. **Sagadahoc Preservation** (880 Washington Street; tel: 207-443 2174; www.sagadahocpreservation.org) has a self-guided walking tour and podcast tours of the historic district (map

available on the website and at Main Street Bath office, 4 Centre Street). Fourteen miles (22km) south of Bath on Route 209 on the **Phippsburg Peninsula** is **Popham Beach State Park** (tel: 207-389 1335; https://visitbath.com/attractions/popham-beach-state-park/), a 4.5-mile (7km) stretch of sand that is one of the prettiest and most popular beaches in the state.

Just across the Kennebec River from Bath, in **Woolwich**, visitors have several options: turn north on Route 128 for approximately 10 miles (16km) to the **Pownalborough Courthouse** (23 Courthouse Road; tel: 207-737 2504; Memorial Day–Columbus Day Sat 10am–4pm, Sun noon–4pm, also July–Aug Tue–Fri 10am–4pm; www.lincolncountyhistory.org) in **Dresden** ⓭. The state's only remaining pre-Revolutionary courthouse is a handsomely restored and magnificently detailed three-floor riverfront building with a fascinating period cemetery on the grounds. (Note: if continuing north, to avoid backtracking, continue north past the courthouse for 2.5 miles/4km

to Route 27 and head south about 9 miles/14km to Wiscasset.)

WISCASSET

Wiscasset ⓮ claims, with some justification, to be the "prettiest village in Maine." Two handsome houses reflect the style of life of successful sea captains: the Federal-era **Nickels-Sortwell House** (121 Main Street; tel: 207-882 7169; June–mid-Oct Fri–Sun 11am–4pm; tours on the half-hour; www.historicnewengland.org/property/nickels-sortwell-house/) and the 1807 **Castle Tucker** (2 Lee Street; tel: 207-882 7169; June–mid-Oct Wed–Sun 11am–4pm; tours on the half-hour; www.historicnewengland.org/property/castle-tucker/). Built in 1807, its furnishings are an intact vision of Victorian life.

Another offbeat tourist attraction is the **Old Lincoln County Jail and Museum** (133 Federal Street; tel: 207-882 6817; June–early Oct Sat–Sun noon–4pm). This is an 1811 hoosegow with granite walls up to 41ins (over 1 meter) thick. Considered a model of humane treatment in its day because prisoners were

Bath claims to have a slower pace and a friendly pedestrian atmosphere.

⊘ THE LIFE OF A GROWING CRUSTACEAN

The colorful lobster buoys dotting the coast of Maine highlight a multi-million business. In 2016, lobstermen caught over 130 million lbs (57 million kg) of the crustaceans, with a value of over $533 million. Most lobsters are caught by independent fishermen in small boats.

The hardy fishermen head out long before dawn, when the waters are calmer and before the wind has picked up, and return in the late afternoon after a hard day on the nets. Called "highliners," these lobstermen have 1,000 to 1,500 traps which need to be checked at least once a week. Although proximity to shore makes lobstering safer than other commercial fishing, it is still a dangerous profession, and is particularly grueling in the bitter Maine winter.

Lobsters are crustaceans whose external skeletons do not grow. They go through the process of molting, or shedding their old shells and growing into new, larger ones. This process happens in late June or early July. Conveniently for highliners, molting brings the lobsters closer to shore, making them easier to catch.

Without shells, the soft lobsters are vulnerable to

predators such as codfish and sharks, so they migrate to shallow waters for safety. Here, they hide, expanding 15 to 20 percent in size. Over four to six weeks, the lobsters produce new shells, then return to deep water. The lobsters are now known as "soft-shell," as opposed to the "hard-shell" they have just before molting. A hard-shell lobster's meat can be up to 33 percent of its body weight, while a soft-shell's is only 25 percent, so hard-shell lobster tends to be more expensive. The taste is slightly different, and each Maine connoisseur has a preference. Some say soft-shell is sweeter, some prefer hard-shell for its stronger taste.

The New England Aquarium is studying ways of harvesting lobsters through aquaculture, but as of yet have not found a reliable method of raising lobster in a contained environment. Lobsters are cannibalistic, and will eat each other if given the opportunity. They are also incredibly slow growing, meaning that the investment has a long return, when most fishermen need a quick turnaround of their cash.

The Nickels-Sortwell House, Wiscasset, built in 1807 by Captain William Nickels, a ship owner and trader.

afforded individual cells, this grim repository was used until 1953 and has the graffiti to prove it.

BOOTHBAY HARBOR

North on Route 1, just over the Sheepscot River, turn onto Davis Island to visit **Fort Edgecomb State Historic Site**, an octagonal fort completed in 1809 with commanding views of the river and beyond. It's a particularly nice place to picnic and spot harbor seals and osprey (tel: 207-882 7777; Memorial Day–Labor Day daily 9am–sunset).

Although certainly subdued compared to the commercial excesses of the south coast, **Boothbay Harbor ⑮**, to the south on Route 27, is decidedly touristy. In summer, tens of thousands of visitors throng the streets of this former fishing village to inspect the shops, sample seafood delicacies, charter boats to explore offshore islands with names such as the Cuckolds and the Hypocrites, and book passage on whale watches and deep-sea fishing trips. There are yacht and golf clubs, flower shows, auctions, and clambakes.

Antiques for sale in Wiscasset.

At **Boothbay Railway Village** (Route 27, 586 Wiscasset Road, Boothbay; tel: 207-633 4727; www.railwayvillage.org; end of May–mid-Oct daily 10am–5pm, trains operate 11am–4pm on the hour), the main attraction is a narrow-gauge, coal-fired railroad, encircling a range of reconstructed buildings of yesteryear, including a barbershop, bank, and country store.

In **West Boothbay Harbor**, the **Maine State Aquarium** (194 McKown Point Road; tel: 207-633 9559; 10am–5pm Memorial Day–Labor Day daily, Sept Wed–Sun) has an 850-gallon (3,200-liter) fish tank and a gallery echoing the rocky Maine coast. Kids can pet live sharks and meet a giant blue lobster.

PEMAQUID POINT

Farther to the north off Route 1, Route 130 cuts south through Damariscotta to **Pemaquid Point ⑯**. Turn onto Route 130 the **Colonial Pemaquid State Historic Site** (tel: 207-677 2423; Memorial Day–Labor Day 9am–5pm). Ongoing archaeological digs are turning up American Indian pottery, a 17th-century building foundation, and lots of pottery shards and clay pipe stems. Guides give interpretive tours around the site.

Admission also includes **Fort William Henry**, a 1907 replica on the site of several failed Colonial stockades. The view from the roof of the fort is fabulous. At the tip of this peninsula on Route 130, in **Lighthouse Park** (parking charge) stands the **Pemaquid Point Lighthouse**, commissioned in 1827 by John Quincy Adams. Visitors can climb the tower and visit the 1857 keeper's house, now a **Fishermen's Museum** (tel: 207-677 3540; Memorial Day–Labor Day; daily 9am–5pm; www.thefishermensmuseum.org; free) filled with a hodgepodge of nets, traps, tools, hull models, and other fishing paraphernalia. With powerful surf constantly breaking on the rocks, the point is a favorite spot for painters and photographers, as well as

families who enjoy poking around the tide pools. The lighthouse is shown on the Maine quarter coin.

The large white mansion on the hill overlooking the St George River at the junction of routes 1 and 131 in **Thomaston** is the **General Henry Knox Museum** (tel: 207-354 8062; June–Sept Tue–Fri 10am–4pm and Sat 10am–1pm, Sept–Oct Fri 10am–4pm, Sat 10am–1pm; http://knoxmuseum.org/visit/). It's a replica of Montpelier, the home built by the Revolutionary War hero after the war. Architecturally, it compares to Monticello and Mount Vernon. Historically, it teaches about the gentleman farmer and instinctively talented artillery commander who was vital to America's struggle for independence.

MONHEGAN ISLAND

Lured by tales of marvelous people and cities in the New World, a group of Germans settled **Waldoboro** in 1748. A plaque at the center of town attests, "the promise and expectation of finding a prosperous city, instead of which they found nothing but wilderness."

One tale which was accurate, however, was the description of an island that looked like a whale. The cliffs of **Monhegan Island** 17, 12 miles (19km) south of Port Clyde, do indeed lend the island the appearance of a whale. An otherworldly air still pervades this 700-acre (280-hectare) isle, little changed in the past century. There are no cars or paved roads, and not all dwellings have electricity. Most of the 65 or so year-round residents make their living from the sea as fishermen or lobstermen. It's a favorite for artists in the summer. The most famous summer resident is the painter Jamie Wyeth, son of Andrew Wyeth. There are 12 miles (19km) of steep, strenuous trails circling the island. Monhegan is served by several ferries that leave from Port Clyde (tel: 207-372 8848; www.monheganboat.com), Boothbay Harbor (tel:

207-633 2284; www.balmydayscruises.com), New Harbor (tel: 207-677 2026; www.hardyboat.com), and Muscongus (tel: 207-380 5460; www.sailmuscongus.com). Although it's possible to make the round-trip in one day, an overnight is advised for those who wish to ease back into a less stressful age.

WEST OF PENOBSCOT BAY

On the west end of Penobscot Bay is the town of **Rockland** 18, once a great limestone producer and now the world's largest distributor of lobsters, as well as the "Schooner Capital of Maine." These two- or three-masted schooners are a wonderful way to discover the coast as the earliest explorers encountered it. Weekend and weeklong excursions may be booked aboard more than a dozen vessels, some vintage and others quite new. The Maine Windjammer Association is the central directory of the ships (tel: 800-807 WIND; www.sailmainecoast.com). The **Maine State Ferry Service** (tel: 207-624 3000; http://maine.gov/mdot/ferry/) transports passengers and

A photographer's favorite: Pemaquid Point Lighthouse.

Boothbay Harbor, a popular yachting destination.

Rowing teams in training.

vehicles to **Matinicus**, a small, quiet island populated primarily by lobstermen and their families; **Vinalhaven**, where old granite quarries make fine swimming holes and the paved roads are ideal for day-tripping bicyclists; and **North Haven**, mainly given over to vacation homes. The main village has several shops, restaurants, and galleries. It's usually easy to board as a foot passenger; but taking a car means advance planning and often a wait in line.

Thanks to the 1935 bequest of "Aunt" Lucy Farnsworth, a frugal spinster who lived in but three rooms of her family mansion and left the town $1.3 million to start a museum, Rockland has a world-class collection of art. The **Farnsworth Art Museum and Wyeth Center** (16 Museum Street; tel: 207-596 6457; www.farnsworthmuseum. org; June–Oct daily 10am–5pm, Nov–Dec and Apr–May Tue–Sun 10am–5pm, Jan–Mar Wed–Sun 10am–4pm, Wed and first Fri of the month 10am–8pm; www.farnsworthmuseum.org; free on Wed 5–8pm July–Sept) has many noted 19th- and 20th-century works, including paintings by Winslow Homer and John Marin, and sculpture by Louise Nevelson, who grew up in a Bath lumberyard.

Paintings by all three Wyeths (N. C., Andrew, and Jamie) are exhibited in a former church across from the **Farnsworth Homestead**, an 1850 Greek Revival home next to the museum. The museum's **Olson House** (Hathorne Point Road; tel: 207-354 0102; late May–Oct Wed–Sun noon–5pm), 14.5 miles (23km) from Rockland in Cushing, was home to Christina Olson, immortalized in Andrew Wyeth's painting, Christina's World.

The traditions and history of lighthouses, life saving, lifesaving services, and the US Coast Guard are lovingly preserved at the **Maine Lighthouse Museum at the Maine Discovery Center** (1 Park Drive; tel: 207-594 3301; www.mainelighthousemuseum.com; Mon–Fri 9am–4.30pm, Sat–Sun 10am–4pm; closed Sun–Wed in winter and early spring).

The **Owl's Head Transportation Museum** (117 Museum Street, Owls Head, off Route 73; tel: 207-594 4418; www.owlshead.org; daily 10am–5pm) is housed in a spiffed-up hangar at the Owl's Head airport south of Rockland. It displays a splendid collection of vehicles: 50 cars, 28 planes, plus bikes and motorcycles – ranging from an 1885 Benz to a 1939 Packard to a Model F plane, a Wright Brothers prototype. On summer weekends, some displays are taken off their blocks and sent for a spin – a worthwhile departure from usual museum practice.

Works by some of the state's finest contemporary artists are in the **Center for Maine Contemporary Art** (21 Winter Street; tel: 207-7015005; www.cmcanow. org; Nov–May Wed–Sat 10am–5pm, from noon on Sun; check the website for summer hours), 6 miles (10km) up the coast in the quiet village of **Rockport ⑲**. The collection is housed in a

strikingly modern building, with an iconic sawtooth roofline designed by Toshiko Mori, inaugurated in 2016. The excellent Strand Theatre (www.rockland strand.com) is within walking distance.

CAMDEN

Camden ⑳, "Where the Mountains Meet the Sea," has enjoyed a long reign as the ultimate in genteel summering spots. Its picturesque harbor is lined with shops and restaurants; many of the finely preserved, gracious homes of 19th-century ship captains have been converted into upscale B&Bs.

Numerous excursion boats and windjammers (www.sailmainecoast.com) sail from the harbor from late May to mid-October. Rockland native Edna St. Vincent Millay penned one of her verses after climbing to the summit of 800ft (240-meter) Mt Battie in the **Camden Hills State Park** (north of town off Route 1; tel: 207-236 3109; daily 9am–sunset). The summit is accessible on foot or via a toll road; the view of Penobscot Bay and the distant islands is one of Maine's loveliest.

BELFAST AND SEARSPORT

The 19th-century captains and ship-builders of **Belfast** ㉑ built their stately mansions in a variety of architectural styles that makes the town at the mouth of the Passagassawaukeag River a fascinating place to take a stroll.

A few miles north on Route 1, **Searsport** ㉒, lined with dazzling-white sea captains' homes, calls itself "the antiques capital of Maine." Between 1770 and 1920, this one town produced more than 3,000 vessels, and evidence of its rich history, along with China Trade treasures, can be found on Route 1 in **Penobscot Marine Museum** (5 Church Street; tel: 207-548 2529; http://penobscotmarinemuseum.org; Memorial Day–mid-Oct Mon–Sat 10am–5pm, from noon on Sun). The sprawling complex has a fine collection of marine and folk art, ship models, nautical paintings, and watercraft.

Farther along the coastal road, the outskirts of **Bucksport** ㉓ are dominated by the **Penobscot Narrows Bridge** (tel: 207-469 6553; daily May–June and Sept–Oct 9am–5pm,

⊙ Tip

Windjammer cruises, lasting a day to a week, depart from Rockland and nearby Camden. For information, contact the Maine Windjammer Association (tel: 800-807 9463; www.sail mainecoast.com).

Camden seen from Mount Battie.

The annual Maine Lobster Festival features parades, a Sea Goddess contest, and cooking competitions.

Recruits from the Maine Maritime Academy, Castine.

July–Aug until 6pm, until midnight near full moon; charge for observatory includes admission to Fort Knox; http://maine.gov/mdot/pnbo/). Visitors can ride an elevator to the world's tallest bridge observatory, 420ft (128 meters) above sea level, and view sweeping panoramas. The only way to reach the observatory is from the vast **Fort Knox State Park** (Route 174 off Route 1; tel: 207-469-6553; May–Oct 9am–sunset). It was built in 1844–69; troops were stationed there during the Civil War through the Spanish–American War.

EAST OF PENOBSCOT BAY

Intent on getting to the justly famed Mount Desert Island, many tourists never veer from US 1 and miss one of the most scenic areas in Maine. The peninsulas along the eastern side of Penobscot Bay warrant some poking around, but be forewarned: the roads can be confusing, even with a road map and GPS.

From Route 1 in Bucksport, wind your way down routes 175 and 166 (or 166A) to **Castine**. Established as a

trading post by the Plymouth Pilgrims, the tiny town became one of the most hotly contested chunks of property in New England. Changing hands nine times, it was taken from the American Indians by the French, Dutch, British, and, eventually, Americans. Plaques around town, as well as a free walking tour brochure available at most local merchants, fill in the details, but it's enough to wander around, beneath a canopy of elms, taking in the array of fine white houses.

Some of these houses belong to the **Maine Maritime Academy** (www.main emaritime.edu), founded in 1941 and one of five such schools nationwide that train merchant mariners. The academy's 1952 ship, the decommissioned T/S *State of Maine*, serves as a floating classroom when she is not being inspected at the drydock.

Take a detour off this detour to make a circuit of **Deer Isle ㉔**, where the principal occupations are lobstering and fishing. On the eastern side of the isle is the prestigious Haystack Mountain School of Crafts (88 Haystack

⊘ THE MAKING OF ACADIA

Society notables discovered this remote spot in the mid-19th century, and by the time the stock market crashed in 1929, millionaires had constructed more than 200 extravagant "cottages." (Only a few survive, some as institutions or inns: many were destroyed in 1947's devastating fire.) Harvard University president Charles W. Eliot had the foresight to initiate the park in 1916, and many of his peers contributed parcels. John D. Rockefeller Jr threw in 11,000 acres (4,400 hectares) crisscrossed with 50 miles (80km) of bridle paths he built to protest against the admission of horseless carriages onto the island in 1905. The trail network encourages mountain-biking, cross-country skiing, and just plain walking. And Frenchman Bay, to the northeast, is great for sailing.

School Drive; tel: 207-348 2306; www.
haystack-mtn.org), housed in a cluster of
small modern buildings perched pre-
cipitously on a piney bank overlooking
Jericho Bay. The school periodically
puts on exhibits. On the southern
coast of the island, the **Stonington
Opera House** (tel: 207-367 2788; www.
operahousearts.org), on the commercial
fishing pier, is nationally recognized as
a community performing arts center.
For a true getaway, take the **Isle au
Haut Mail Boat** (tel: 207-367 5193; www.
isleauhaut.com; bicycle rentals available)
from the picturesque port of Stonington to the sparsely inhabited 5,800-
acre (2,300-hectare) **Isle au Haut** Ⓩ, 6
miles (10km) out to sea. The company
also offers lobster fishing and lighthouse cruises, and a cruise to Seal
Island with its colony of nesting puffins.

Half of Isle-au-Haut is privately
owned and occupied primarily by lobstermen and their families; the other
half is part of **Acadia National Park**.
Heading northeast to hook up with US
1 again, you'll pass through **Blue Hill**
Ⓩ, long the choice of blueblood "rusticators" – summer vacationers – who
didn't care for the showy social season
in Bar Harbor. It's still well-heeled,
with many galleries, antiques shops,
and studios. The shipbuilding town is
also renowned for its pottery, finished
with glazes made from nearby copper
mines and quarries. **Rackliffe Pottery**
(132 Ellsworth Road, Route 172; tel:
888-631 3321; http://rackliffepottery.com/)
welcomes visitors.

MOUNT DESERT ISLAND

Spotting the 17 exposed pink granite
peaks of **Mount Desert Island** in 1604,
Samuel de Champlain described the
place as "l'île des monts déserts" – and
the French pronunciation still holds,
more or less, so accentuate the final
syllable, as in "dessert."

The reason there's so much territory
to explore on **Mount Desert Island** Ⓩ
is that 41,409 acres (16,765 hectares)

of the 16- by 13-mile (26km by 21km)
island belong to **Acadia National Park**
(tel: 207-288 3338; www.nps.gov/acad;
park: year-round 24 hours; Thompson
Island visitor center mid-May–mid-
Oct, hours vary), which draws more
than 5 million visitors a year.

Stop at the **Mount Desert Island
Information Center** (18 Harbor Drive,
in the Yachtsmen's Building; tel: 207-
276 5040; www.mountdesertchamber.org;
May–Sept daily) to get general information for the entire island. The park
visitor centers have park maps and a
schedule of naturalist activities here;
there are excellent hiking maps on sale.

Most visitors will want to experience the view from Cadillac Mountain,
whose form dominates the park, and
to drive or cycle the Park Loop Road,
but there are many other possibilities,
including horse-and-carriage tours
from **Wildwood Riding Stables** (www.
acadiamagic.com/wildwood-stables.html)
and kayaking, sailing, and hiking in
the less frequented areas. Even the
shorter trails tend to be over uneven
rock, so suitable footwear is essential.

*Camden's Chestnut
Street Baptist Church.*

Mount Desert Island.

Totems for sale in Belfast.

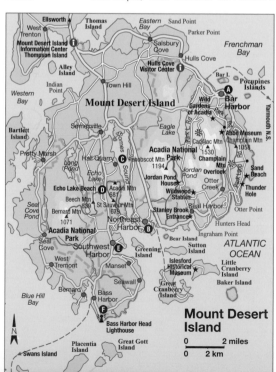

Riding out on Mount Desert Island.

Car traffic is kept under control by a permit system covering the mostly one-way 27-mile (43km) **Park Loop Road**, a toll road which makes a clockwise circuit of all the more scenic spots along the eastern coast; the reasonably priced permits are good for a week (major portions closed Dec–mid-Apr; may be closed other times in inclement weather). Another excellent option is the Island Explorer Shuttle (tel: 207-667 5796; www.exploreacadia.com; late June–Columbus Day). This free bus service has nine intersecting routes through the island. Maps and schedules are available at the visitor centers and on the website.

Sieur de Monts Spring is a lovely spot dubbed "The Sweet Waters of Acadia" by the park's first superintendent. There are three attractions worth visiting clustered here. The **Wild Gardens of Acadia** (year-round), which shows nearly 300 labeled flora arranged in several display areas; the adjacent **Nature Center** (mid-June–late Sept); with exhibits on Acadia's cultural and natural history; and a branch of the **Abbe Museum** (www.abbemuseum.org; late May–Oct daily 10am–5pm). The museum is devoted to Maine's American Indian heritage. The Bar Harbor location of the museum is open year-round.

Sweeping views follow, from the Champlain Mountain Overlook across Frenchman Bay to the distant Gouldsboro Hills. The road passes the start of the **Precipice Trail**, which has iron rungs and ladders for the steep sections, and farther on are Sand Beach – edged by low cliffs and Acadia's one sandy beach – and the **Beehive Trail**, which has superb panoramas but involves some potentially dizzying sections. Thunder Hole needs a wind to stir things up; in the right conditions, the spray blasts up through this chink on the coastline. Otter Point provides another memorable coastal outlook before the road heads inland, past Jordan Pond with walks along the lakeside, or on the short trail past Bubble Rock, a huge boulder transported and dumped by glacier,

Mount Desert Island

0   2 miles

0   2 km

to South Bubble Summit. The Jordan Pond House on the shore is the only full-service restaurant in the park. A tea break with the restaurant's popovers is a park tradition.

Reached by the toll road or on foot, the tallest peak, 1,530ft (466-meter) **Cadillac Mountain**, is the highest point along the Atlantic coast north of Rio de Janeiro. The glorious 360-degree views stretch inland as far as Mt Katahdin, Maine's highest summit, and seaward to encompass myriad smaller islands – a particularly lovely vista when bathed in the glow of sunrise (a surprisingly large number of people arrive at this early hour) or sunset.

BAR HARBOR

Bar Harbor Ⓐ is Mount Desert Island's main town – a bit over-commercialized, but with a pretty town green, a marvelous Art Deco cinema, a lovely ocean walk, some exceptional crafts stores, appealing restaurants, and a good choice of accommodations. The **Bar Harbor Historical Society** (33 Ledgelawn Avenue; tel: 207-288 0000; www.barharborhistorical. org; mid-June–Oct Mon–Fri 1–4pm, winter by appointment; free), in the former St Edwards Convent, does a fine job of chronicling the resort town's rich history.

Numerous whale watches, cruise boats, and sailing charters set sail from the town's wharf. **Abbe Museum Downtown** (26 Mount Desert Street; tel: 207-288 3519; www.abbemuseum. org; May–Oct daily 10am–5pm, Nov–Apr Thu–Sat 10am–4pm) displays an extensive collection of Indian artifacts from the Wabanaki, the state's native people.

ELSEWHERE ON THE ISLAND

The "quiet side" of the island is just as lovely, but a lot less traveled. Head out of Bar Harbor on Route 3 to **Northeast Harbor** Ⓑ, known for its scenic,

yacht-filled, protected harbor. Visit the spectacular seaview **Asticou Azalea Garden** (tel: 207-276 3727; May–Oct daylight hours; www.gardenpreserve. org/asticou-azalea-garden) and **Thuya Garden and Lodge** (tel: 207-276 3727; garden: late May–Oct daily during daylight hours, Lodge: mid-June–Sept daily 10am–4.30pm), the 215-acre (87-hectare) garden and home of landscape artist Joseph Henry Curtis. The **Asticou Terraces Trail** is a moderate climb with scenic overlooks ending at the gardens.

The *Sea Princess* (tel: 207-276 5352; www.barharborcruises.com) offers nature cruises around the park and through **Somes Sound** Ⓒ, the only fjord on the East Coast. The sunset dinner cruise travels to a waterside restaurant on **Little Cranberry Island**, a scenic, 400-acre (160-hectare) island 20 miles (32km) offshore.

Head south on Route 102 to **Echo Lake Beach** Ⓓ, part of Acadia National Park, one of the best spots for freshwater swimming. There's a hiking trail up 839ft (256-meter) -high **Beech Mountain**.

The dockmaster's shed at Bar Harbor.

Maine's private and state-run ferries provide a vital link to many island communities.

Puffins on Machias Seal Island.

The charming little town of **Southwest Harbor** at the entrance to Somes Sound has art galleries and restaurants, plus the **Wendell Gilley Museum of Bird Carving** (4 Herrick Road; tel: 207-244 7555; www.wendell gilleymuseum.org; Sept–Oct Tue–Sat 10am–4pm, Nov–Dec Fri–Sat 10am–4pm, see website for summer hours). It exhibits the magnificent works of the world-renowned bird carver. The "Brass Era" of automotive history – the earliest years from the 1880s to 1920 – is documented in the **Seal Cove Auto Museum** (1414 Tremont Road; tel: 207-244 9242; www.seal-coveautomuseum.org; May–Oct daily 10am–5pm, Nov–Apr by appointment). Nearly 100 rare and exquisitely preserved autos, motorcycles, and pumpers are on display.

Cranberry Cove Ferry (Southwest Harbor and Manset; tel: 207-460 1981; www.cranberryisles.com) operates a ferry to the Cranberry Isles, Isleford, and the Sutton Islands. If you'd rather be captain, rent a power boat at Manset Yacht Services (113 Shore Road, Manset; tel: 207-244 4040; www.manset yachtservice.com).

Isleford, also known as Little Cranberry Island, has restaurants, lodgings, and a few crafts shops. The **Isleford Historical Museum** (tel: 207-288 3338; mid-June–Aug daily 11am–4pm, Sept 9am–3pm; www. islesfordhistoricalmuseum.info; free) documents the lives of the hardy inhabitants with everything from harpoon guns and sextants to store ledgers and storage barrels. Capt. Stefanie Alley takes up to six passengers out on her working lobster boat as she checks her traps among the outer islands. The 90-minute trips run mid-June–Sept (tel: 207-244 7466).

Bass Harbor Head Lighthouse (www.acadiamagic.com/BassHarborLight. html) presents a classic Maine cameo. The view from the trails is magnificent.

TO THE CANADIAN BORDER

Back on the mainland, continue north on Route 1 and turn south onto Route 186 to the small, unspoiled fishing village of **Winter Harbor**, so named because it does not freeze in the winter, and home to a fleet of lobster boats, and nearby **Schoodic Point**, a little-visited portion of Acadia National Park with fine views of Cadillac Mountain across the bay.

North on Route 1, Washington County is also known as "Sunrise County" for its easterly location. Tourism takes a back seat to lobstering, blueberry cultivation, and Christmas trees.

Head south off Route 1 on Route 187 about 12 miles (19km), continue through the fishing villages of Jonesport and Beals to the 1,540-acre (623-hectare) **Great Wass Island** **28**. The Nature Conservancy property, with several somewhat difficult but very rewarding trails through the woods and along the coast, is one of the state's natural treasures.

Just off Route 1 in **Columbia Falls** **29**, tour the elegant 1818 **Ruggles**

House (146 Main Street; tel: 207-483 4637; www.ruggleshouse.org; guided tours June–mid-Oct Mon–Sat 10am–4pm, Sun noon–4pm), which has a magnificent flying staircase and intricately carved woodwork. A few miles north, turn south onto Roque Bluffs Road for about 5 miles (8km) to **Roque Bluffs State Park** (tel: 207-255 3475; mid-May–Sept daily 9am–sunset) for fabulous views, a beach (with incredibly cold water), and a much warmer freshwater pond. Bird watching is particularly good here.

Machias ㉚, on Route 1, was the site of the first naval battle of the Revolutionary War. In June 1775, a month after the Battle of Lexington, the British vessel Margaretta anchored off Machias to stand guard over a freight ship collecting wood with which to build British barracks in Boston. After debating their course of action at **Burnham Tavern** (Main and Free streets; tel: 207-733 4577; www.burnhamtavern.com; July–Aug Mon–Tue and Fri 10am–3pm), the townspeople successfully attacked and captured the Margaretta. A re-enactment is held every June.

Approximately 90 percent of the world's blueberry crop is harvested in the area around Machias. "The Wild Blueberry Capital of the World" celebrates with a four-day blueberry festival every August.

North on Route 1 and east on Route 189 about 18 miles (29km), **Lubec** ㉛ is the easternmost town in the United States. **Tours of Lubec and Cobscook** (135 Maine Street; tel 207-733 2997; www.toursoflubecandcobscook.com) offers interpretive history, farm, art, and nature tours with guides who are particularly knowledgeable. Some of the tours go into New Brunswick, Canada. You will need a passport to participate in those. The easternmost American soil is **West Quoddy Point**, a dramatic landscape of rocky cliffs and crashing surf graced with a candycane-striped 1858 lighthouse. The lighthouse tower can be visited in summer on scheduled tours. The visitor center is in the lighthouse keeper's house (tel: 207-733 2180; Memorial Day–mid-Oct daily 10am–4pm; donation).

A pie-eating contest at the Machias Wild Blueberry Festival.

The Allagash Historical Museum.

The lighthouse is part of 600-acre (240-hectare) **Quoddy Head State Park** (tel: 207-733 2180; mid-May–mid-Oct 9am–sunset). Hiking trails wander past a peat bog and through stands of wild roses and day lilies. Whales are often spotted offshore, and you can look across the Quoddy Channel to Canada.

CAMPOBELLO PARK

From Lubec, you can cross over the Franklin D. Roosevelt Memorial Bridge to **Roosevelt Campobello International Park** ❷ in Canada (tel: 506-752 2922; www.fdr.net; visitor center and cottage: daily mid-May–mid-October sunrise–sunset, trails: year-round; free). Franklin Delano Roosevelt summered on New Brunswick's Campobello Island from 1905 to 1921, when the island was a fashionable summer resort for well-off Americans and Canadians. He returned here only briefly during his presidency. After a self-guided tour of the 34-room Roosevelt house (audio tour can be downloaded to MP3 players), which remains as the family left it, visitors can enjoy 16 miles (26km) of

Statue of lumberjack Paul Bunyon in Bangor park.

walking trails, including a 2-mile (3km) stroll along the ocean. (Note: You will pass through Canadian and US passport control stations. You will need a passport or passport card. Also note that New Brunswick is one hour ahead of Maine's time zone.)

CALAIS

Farther north on Route 1, **Calais** ❸ has three border crossings into Canada. It is the site of **St Croix Island International Historic Site**, the only such joint site (Route 1, 8 miles/13km south of Calais; tel: 207-454 3871; daily sunrise–sunset; ranger station manned daily mid-May–Columbus Day, visitor centre daily July–Aug 9am–5pm, rest of the year, see www.nps.gov/sacr/planyourvisit/basicinfo.htm). It commemorates the ill-fated French settlement of Pierre Dugua on the island in 1604. The bitter winter claimed the lives of nearly half of the 79 colonists. The mainland site has an interpretive trail peopled by bronze statues representing the settlers and the Passamaquoddy tribespeople who tried to help them. A model of the settlement overlooks the island. Access to the island itself is limited and discouraged.

The **Moosehorn National Wildlife Refuge** is the easternmost wildlife refuge on the Atlantic flyway, the primary avian migration route. There are two sections: the 1,700-acre (690-hectare) Baring Division just southwest of Calais on Route 1 and the 7,200-acre (2,900-hectare) Edmunds Division on Route 1 between Dennysville and Whiting, bordering the tidal waters of Cobscook Bay. Between them, there are over 50 miles (80km) of trails with observation decks for better viewing of waterfowl, shorebirds, upland game birds, and raptors. Fishing is good for smallmouth bass and yellow perch. Some areas are open for deer hunting. In the summer, there are

ranger-led programs at both locations. Refuge Headquarters (tel: 207-454 1700; Mon–Fri 8am–4pm) is at the Calais location. The refuge itself is open daily from a half-hour before sunrise to a half-hour after sunset.

BANGOR

In the 1830s, **Bangor** ❸❹, Maine's third-largest city, was the lumber capital of the world, with more than 300 sawmills. Today little remains of those glory days except for the huge houses built by lumber barons that line its wide avenues, and a 31ft (9-meter) statue of legendary lumberjack Paul Bunyan on the outskirts of town.

As the retail, cultural and service center for northeastern Maine and the Maine highlands, Bangor has a busy downtown which takes advantage of the Penobscot River waterfront. The quality and variety of its performing arts and museums rival those in larger cities, while the shopping is a delightful mix of sophisticated fashion and outdoor practicality. Restaurants take advantage of Maine's seafood and local brewing.

The **Thomas A. Hill House Museum** (159 Union Street; tel: 207-942 1900; www.bangorhistoricalsociety.org/; June–Sept Mon–Sat 10am–4pm, Oct–May Tue and Thu 10am–4pm) is a repository for more than 10,000 early photographs and daguerreotypes, plus an exhaustive collection of 19th-century clothing – gowns, walking-suits, day and evening dresses, shoes, hats, and accessories. The center's Civil War Museum displays a sword owned by Joshua Chamberlain and soldiers' diaries and letters.

A legendary modern author makes his home in the city. Stephen King's house on West Broadway is easy to spot – it's the handsome 1856 Italianate mansion surrounded by a wrought-iron fence decorated with bats and spiders. The **Maine Discovery Museum** (74 Main Street, tel: 207-262 7200; www.mainediscoverymuseum.org; summer Mon–Sat 10am–5pm, Sun noon–5pm, rest of the year see website) is the largest children's museum north of Boston. It has three floors packed with hands-on activities.

Viewing Mount Katahdin in Baxter State Park.

MAINE'S LIGHTHOUSES

The craggy coast of Maine is only 250 miles (402km) long as the seagull flies, but when you straighten out the coves, harbors, inlets, and estuaries, it adds up to an impressive 3,478 miles (5,597km).

It's no surprise that 57 active lighthouses pepper the treacherously rocky shoreline from Whaleback Light, guarding the Piscataqua River on the Maine–New Hampshire border in the south, to Whitlocks Mill on the St Croix River to the north and the East Quoddy Lighthouse on Campobello Island in Canada.

Although many of the lighthouses have been replaced by ocean buoys and other modern aids to navigation, the iconic image of the tall sentinels bravely sending out beacons of protection as they stand atop granite cliff pummeled by angry waves remains both dramatic and romantic. While their purpose was uniform – to guard ships through dangerous waters – each has a unique story. Portland Head Light, the oldest in Maine, was authorized by President George Washington in 1791. East Quoddy Lighthouse protected legitimate shipping, but cramped the style of smugglers operating between the US and Canada. It's accessible at low tide by

The reputedly haunted Owl's Head Light.

those willing to scramble over the rocks and seaweed to reach it. Owls Head Light near Rockland is reputedly haunted by a lighthouse keeper still watching over his station.

The coastline along Bar Harbor, Bristol, and Machias is dotted with lights on shore and the nearby islands. Only a handful of lighthouses allow visitors inside, although several have museums. One which provides both is Pemaquid Point near Bristol. If it looks familiar, that's because it's the light used on the Maine quarter. The tower and small fishermen's museum are open from May to October.

Rockland Breakwater Light is another good stop. The breakwater was built to protect the town's harbor from storm damage, but it became a hazard to navigation so the lighthouse was built to guide ships safely into the harbor. It's also open for tours in the summer and is the location of the Maine Lighthouse Museum (tel: 207-594 3301; www. mainelighthousemuseum.org). Just down the coast in Port Clyde, the keeper's house at Marshall Point has another small display about lighthouse life.

It's possible to stay at some lighthouses. Goose Rocks Light (tel: 203-400 9565; www.beaconpreservation. org) in the waters of the Fox Islands, and reachable only by boat, can take up to six people for an overnight stay. The light is free-standing, without an island or anywhere to go except the light itself.

There's a one-bedroom apartment in the keeper's house at Pemaquid Point (tel: 207-563 6500; www. mainecoastcottages.com) that's available for weekly rental. You bring your own linens and food when you stay at Little River Light (tel: 877-276 4682; www. littleriverlight.org) near the unspoiled fishing village of Cutler. You'll be ferried out to the island; after that, you're on your own to cook out, read a book, and savor the stars at night.

The Whitehead Light Station (tel: 207-200 7957; www.whiteheadlightstation.org) 8 miles (13km) southwest of Rockland runs a variety of courses, ranging from cookery to meditation, and is available for rent during June, August, and September. The house has seven bedrooms with en-suite bathrooms, plus two sitting rooms, a dining room, and a fully equipped kitchen.

The **Hudson Museum** (first floor of the Collins Center for the Arts; tel: 207-581 1904; www.umaine.edu/hudson-museum; Mon–Fri 9am–4pm, Sept–May also Sat 11am–4pm; visitor's parking permit available from basement of student union building), at the Orono campus of the University of Maine approximately 10 miles (16km) north of Bangor, focuses on ethnographic and archaeological collections, with a huge inventory of Pre-Columbian ceramics and gold pre-dating the arrival of the Spanish. Its American Indian and Native Alaskan collection is one of the most comprehensive in the country. The gleaming **Collins Center for the Arts** (tel: 207-581 1755; www.collinscenterforthearts.com) is home to the Bangor Symphony and hosts a continuing, wide-ranging schedule of visiting performers.

THE NORTH WOODS

Much of the northernmost part of Maine consists of millions of acres of softwood forest. For an overview of the logging boom that swept the area in the mid-19th century, visit the **Patten Lumbermen's Museum** ❸❺ (61 Shin Pond Road, Patten; tel: 207-528 2650; www.lumbermensmuseum.org; Memorial Day–June Fri–Sun 10am–4pm, July–mid-Oct Tue–Sun 10am–4pm). Nine buildings of exhibits include a reconstructed 1860s cabin and a blacksmith shop.

Continue west on Route 159 to **Baxter State Park** ❸❻ (tel: 207-723 5140; 8am–4pm summer daily, winter Mon–Fri; https://baxterstatepark.org/), the legacy of Percival Baxter, governor from 1920 to 1925. When the state legislature refused to purchase and protect this land, he bought a total of 201,018 acres (81,211 hectares) and deeded them to the state, requiring only that the tract remain "forever wild." The northern terminus of the 2,175-mile (3,500km) Appalachian Trail is the 5,267ft (1,605-meter) Mt Katahdin.

Dozens of trails, from easy meanders to tough technical climbs, lace the park. Adjacent Katahdin Woods and Waters National Monument (www.nps.gov/kaww/planyourvisit/maps.htm) is de facto America's 413th national park. It was created in Penobscot County in 2016 by the former president, Barack Obama. Comprising 87,500 acres, it boasts splendid cross-country trails with plenty of opportunities for hiking, camping, mountain biking and fishing throughout the year.

Running northward from the northwest corner of Baxter State Park, the **Allagash Wilderness Waterway** provides 92 miles (150km) of America's most scenic canoeing; the trip takes a week to 10 days. South of the park, the Penobscot River's West Branch offers hair-raising white-water rafting, through granite-walled **Ripogenus Gorge**. Katahdin Outfitters (tel: 207-723 5700; www.katahdinoutfitters.com) and Penobscot Adventures (877-356 9386; www.penobscotadventures.com) both offer a variety of canoeing and white-water trips.

⊙ **Tip**

Casco Bay Lines (56 Commercial Street; tel: 207-774 7871; www.cascobaylines.com) offers sightseeing, sunrise, sunset, moonlight, and party cruises, as well as a leisurely three-hour ride aboard a mailboat, which delivers mail to islands throughout Casco Bay. The Odyssey offers whale-watching, bird-watching, birdwatching, and deep-sea fishing cruises (170 Commercial Street; tel: 207-775 0727; www.odysseywhalewatch.com).

Moosehead Lake.

Old Fort Western.

Vintage cars in Bethel.

To the west of the park, accessible only by boat or float plane, is the preserved 19th-century logging town of **Chesuncook** . The **Chesuncook Lake House** (tel: 207-745 5330) in this lovely little village welcomes outdoors-oriented guests eager to leave the 21st century behind.

Several dozen such "camps," unchanged for decades, are tucked away in this region pocked with lakes and ponds, where fish are plentiful and moose outnumber people. Many cluster around **Moosehead Lake**, the largest body of fresh water entirely in New England, with 320 miles (510km) of shoreline.

Although tiny **Greenville** , at the southern end of the lake, has grown into a year-round vacation destination with several fine B&Bs, fishing resorts, and restaurants, it still retains its air of a wilderness hideaway. Three- and four-hour cruises on the lake and to Mt Kineo are offered aboard the National Historic Landmark Katahdin (tel: 207-695 2716; www.katahdincruises.com), a restored 1914 lake steamboat, the last of a fleet of over 50 vessels that once steamed up the lake carrying passengers, mail, and supplies. The **Moosehead Marine Museum** (tel: 207-695 2716; Memorial Day–Columbus Day Tue–Sat 10am–4pm and selected Sundays July–Sept), next to the boat dock, holds steamboat memorabilia and early photographs of the Greenville area.

Another great way to get a full grasp of this mammoth lake is to take a float-plane tour; try Currier's Flying Service (Greenville Junction; tel: 207-695 2778; www.curriersflyingservice.com).

Lily Bay State Park (tel: 207-695 2700; daily 9am–sunset), 8 miles (13km) north of Greenville, has a fine sandy beach and a 2-mile (3km) lakeside walking trail.

WHITEWATER RAFTING

About 20 miles (32km) southwest of Greenville as the crow flies (or thrice that distance by car), **West Forks** attracts thousands of adventurers eager to try whitewater rafting along the Kennebec and Dead rivers. Suitable for anyone over 10 and in reasonably good health, these thrilling descents take only a day and alternate roiling rapids with placid floats.

Several outfitters organize trips and provide lodging and meals. Among them: North Country Rivers (Bingham; tel: 800-348 8871; www.ncrivers.com), Magic Falls Rafting (West Forks; tel: 800-207 7238; www.magicfalls.com), and Dead River Expeditions (West Forks; tel: 877-301 2040; www.deadriverexpeditions.com).

WESTERN LAKES AND MOUNTAINS

In the heart of Carrabassett Valley, the ski area at **Sugarloaf** (Route 27; tel: 207-237 2000/800-THE LOAF; www.sugarloaf.com), on Maine's second-highest peak, has a treeless top offering superb views (including Mt Katahdin and Mt Washington) and boasts a greater vertical descent (2,820ft/860 meters) than any other winter resort in New England. The area is a year-round resort; its 18-hole golf course is considered the best in Maine. It also has fly-fishing, and hiking and mountain-biking trails.

A useful base for Sugarloaf is **Kingfield** ㊶, 18 miles (29km) to the south, which has been a magnet for sporting types since the mid-19th century. It's been called the most beautifully preserved ski town east of Aspen, with all of the requisite cafés, shops, and sports-massage therapists. The town fostered a family of homegrown geniuses, whose accomplishments are showcased in the Stanley Museum (40 School Street; tel: 207-265 2729; www.stanleymuseum.org; Nov–Apr Tue–Fri 11am–4pm, May–Oct Tue–Sun 11am–4pm). The twins, F.O. and F.E., invented the Stanley Steamer, which wowed enthusiasts at the first New England auto show in 1898 and set a land-speed record of 127mph (203kmh) in 1906. Three restored, working samples are garaged in this Georgian-style schoolhouse, which the family built for the town in 1903.

GRAFTON NOTCH

Some of Maine's prettiest and least visited scenery is near the New Hampshire border. **Bethel** ㊷ takes its name, which means "House of God," from the Book of Genesis. It gained prominence as a spa town when Dr John Gehring attracted to his clinic many Harvard academicians suffering from nervous disorders. The hotel he built in 1913 on the pretty town green, the **Bethel Inn** (tel: 800-654 0125; www.bethelinn.com), is an elegant, upscale, all-season resort.

Also in town is the National Historic Register **Moses Mason House** (10–14 Broad Street; July–Aug Thu–Sat 1–4pm, rest of the year by appointment, tel 207-824 2908). This 1813 Federal manse is a treasure house of American primitive painting; the itinerant muralist Rufus Porter decorated the entryway and second-floor landing with, respectively, a seascape and a forest tableau. The 1821 **O'Neil Robinson House** (adjacent; Tue–Fri 10am–4pm, also Sat 1–4pm July–Aug) has on-going, developing displays about the area's history. Both houses are owned by the Bethel Historical Society (tel: 207-824 2908; www.bethelhistorical.org).

North of town, in **Newry**, the **Sunday River ski resort** ㊸ (Sunday River Road; tel: 800-543 2754; www.sundayriver.com) covers seven mountains and has the largest snow-making system in New England. Off-season, chairlifts (late June–mid-Oct Sat–Sun) carry visitors to the top for an exhilarating ride and spectacular views. The nearby 1872 **Artists' Covered Bridge** (closed to traffic) is a delightful spot for a swim or a picnic. It's named for its popularity among painters and photographers.

Head north on Route 26, which climbs into the fabulously scenic

> **⊙ Tip**
>
> Visitors crossing between Maine and Canada must show a passport or certified birth certificate and photo ID at the border. Single parents, grandparents, or guardians traveling with children may need proof of custody or notarized letters from the other parent authorizing travel.

The State House and the Governor's residence, Blaine House.

Grafton Notch State Park  (tel: 207-824 2912; mid-May–mid-Oct 9am–sunset), known for its rugged-back country hiking trails. Less strenuous trails lead to impressive waterfalls and gorges. The cascades are most impressive during the spring snow melt.

RANGELEY LAKES REGION

Although both routes 4 and 17 leading to the town of **Rangeley** ㊺, overlooking the 9-mile (14km) -long Rangeley Lake, are designated National Scenic Byways, Route 17 has the more spectacular scenery. The **Rangeley Lakes region** is actually a collection of 112 lakes and ponds, and has been popular with outdoors enthusiasts for more than a century. Not surprisingly, fishing and paddle sports are the big draws here, but hikers find plenty to do and, in winter, **Saddleback Ski Area** (http://majellagroup.com/saddlebackmaine/) welcomes downhill and cross-country skiers.

THE CAPITAL CITY

Augusta ㊻, Maine's modest-sized capital (population 19,000), stands on the Kennebec River and began its days in 1628 as a trading post. Its gold-domed State House (State and Capitol streets; tel: 207-287 2301) was designed by Charles Bulfinch in 1832. A connecting tunnel between the State House and the adjacent Cross Office building features a granite mural with text in English, French, and the Penobscot, Passamaquoddy, and Abenaki languages.

The superb **Maine State Museum** in the State House complex (tel: 207-287 2301; Tue–Fri 9am–5pm, Sat 10am–4pm; www.mainestatemuseum.org) is the repository for artifacts and documents from prehistory to the present – from bark canoes and silver spoons to a three-story, water-powered working mill. You can easily spend a full day exploring the extensive galleries and exhibits.

The **Children's Discovery Museum** (171 Capitol Street; tel: 207-622 2209; www.childrensdiscoverymuseum.org; Tue–Thu 10am–4pm, Fri–Sat until 5pm, Sun 11am–4pm) has a bank, grocery store, and restaurant designed to teach children how to cope with such places in later life, and there's a rainforest play area for toddlers.

The city's other major sight is **Old Fort Western**, built on the shore of the Kennebec River in 1754 and America's oldest wooden fort (16 Cony Street; tel: 207-626 2385; Memorial Day–Oct Wed–Mon, Labor Day–Columbus Day Sat–Sun). The stockade and blockhouses have been evocatively recreated, complete with replica cannons.

The only active Shaker community in the world is the **Sabbathday Lake Shaker Community** (Route 26, 12 miles/19km west of Exit 12 off the Maine Turnpike, 70 Shaker Road; tel: 207-926 4597; http://maineshakers.com/; museum: Memorial Day–Columbus Day Mon–Sat 10am–4.30pm). The museum is in several buildings on the grounds; the daily life of the Shakers continues around them.

Augusta waterfront at sunrise.

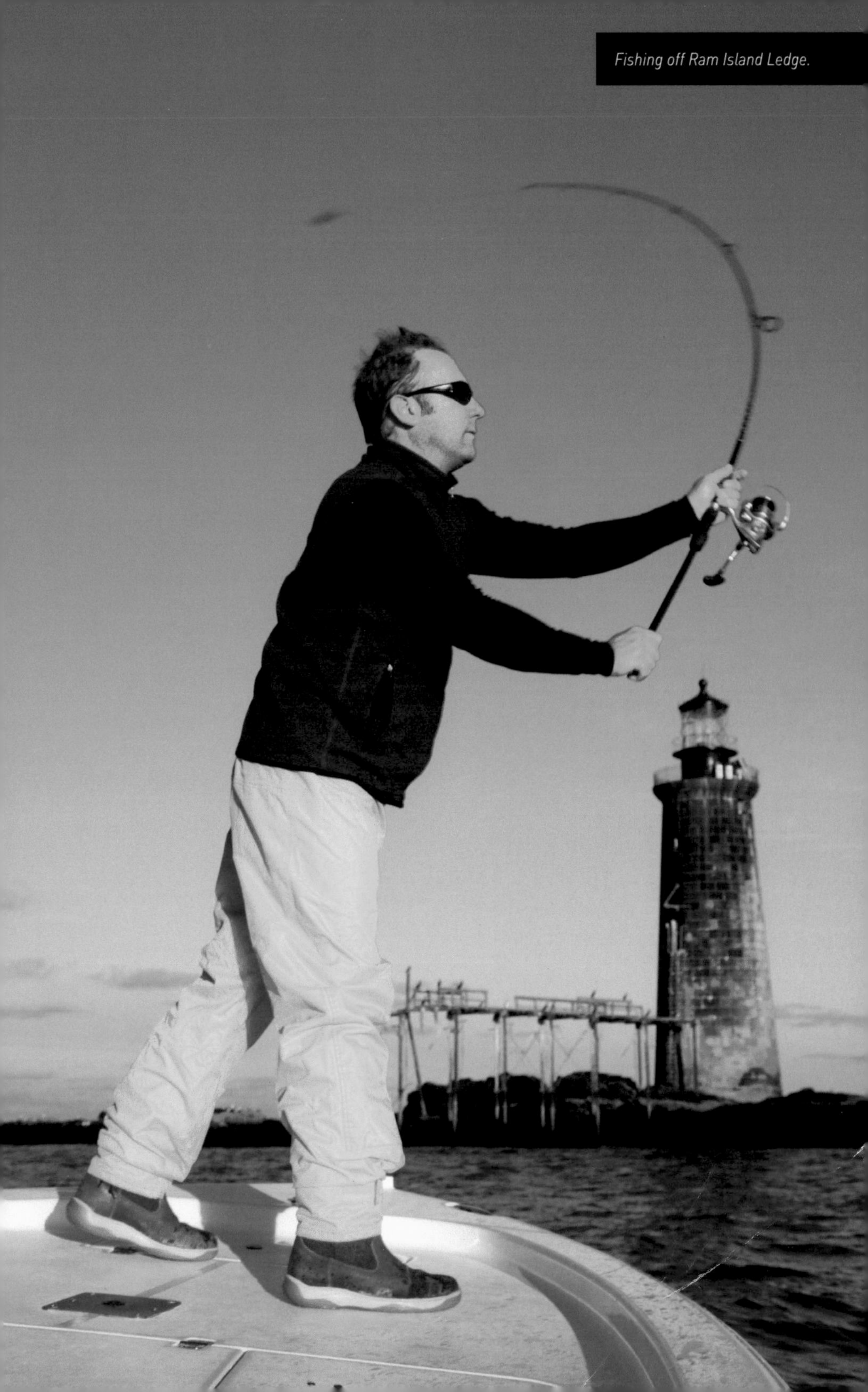

Fishing off Ram Island Ledge.

View of Penobscot Bay from the
Owl's Head peninsula.

NEW ENGLAND

TRAVEL TIPS

TRANSPORTATION

Getting there **354**
   By air.....................................**354**
   By train.................................**354**
   By boat **354**
Getting around **354**
   Boston...................................**354**
   New England.........................**355**

A – Z

Accommodations **357**
Age restrictions **357**
Budgeting for your trip **357**
Children.....................................**358**
Climate.......................................**358**
Crime and safety.......................**359**
Customs regulations.................**359**
Disabled access **359**
Eating out **360**
Electricity **360**
Embassies and consulates **360**
Emergencies **360**
Festivals **360**
Health and medical care...........**361**
Internet **361**

LGBTQ travelers........................**361**
Media..**361**
Money..**362**
Opening hours............................**362**
Pets **363**
Postal services...........................**363**
Public holidays...........................**363**
Religious services **363**
Shopping **363**
Smoking **364**
Tax **364**
Telephones.................................**364**
Time zone....................................**364**
Tourist information **364**
Tour operators and
   travel agents **364**
Visas and passports **365**
Websites.....................................**365**

FURTHER READING

History and culture **366**
Landscape and natural history.**366**
Architecture **367**
Fiction **367**
Movies set in New England.......**367**
Other Insight Guides.................**367**

TRANSPORTATION

GETTING THERE

Flying is by far the easiest way to get to New England from abroad. If you come overland from elsewhere in the US, cars are the preferred mode of travel. Trains are less frequent than flights, and although buses connect most cities and several major towns, they are not much cheaper than a discount airfare, take significantly longer, and are less comfortable.

By air

Virtually all international flights arrive at Boston's Logan Airport. Most major European locations have non-stop flights to Boston. If coming from Australia or Asia, you will probably land in Los Angeles or New York. There are shuttle flights from New York with Delta, JetBlue, Republic Airlines (American Eagle), and United. You may find it easier and more economical to rent a car and drive.

Most major US carriers service the New England states. A variety of discount fares and special deals are offered, and many of the lowest are available on their own websites.

Smaller airports are in Hartford CT, Portland and Bangor ME, Manchester NH, Burlington VT, and Providence RI.

During holidays it may be difficult to find a flight, especially at Thanksgiving, when most of the US seems to be on the move.

Clearing customs can take a very long time, depending on how many flights have arrived at the same time and the current level of security enforcement. If you have a connecting flight, the more time between flights, the better. Sometimes, you can jump the queue if you can prove to the security people that you are on a tight schedule, but there's no guarantee of that.

By train

Amtrak (tel: 800-USA RAIL/800-872 7245; www.amtrak.com) provides rail services to New England from Washington DC, Philadelphia, and New York, routing through coastal Connecticut and Rhode Island and terminating in Boston. The Acela Express, which travels at speeds of up to 150mph (240kmh), costs more than regular trains but is much quicker. Another route extends from Washington and New York to New Haven CT, Springfield MA, and St Albans VT. Amtrak's Downeaster (tel: 800-872 7245; www.amtrakdown easter.com) runs between Boston and Portland ME (and beyond to Brunswick). Commuter trains link Boston with smaller towns in Massachusetts and Rhode Island.

International travelers (but not Canadians) planning to travel extensively on Amtrak can purchase a USA Rail Pass, good for 15,30 or 45 days. Rates are reduced; children ages 2–12 are half-price (under 2, free) when accompanied by a full fare-paying adult. Pass holders cannot use the Acela, and advance tickets and reservations are needed.

By boat

The Cruiseport Boston (www.mass port.com/cruiseport) in South Boston is the port for transatlantic passenger ships as well as cruise vessels for the Norwegian Cruise Line, Holland America, and Royal Caribbean.

GETTING AROUND

Boston

To and from the airport

Boston's Logan Airport (www.mass port.com/logan-airport), 3 miles (5km) from downtown, is easily accessible by public transportation. A free shuttle marked "Massport" transports passengers from all airline terminals to the MBTA Airport station (Blue Line); it's also reached by the Silver Line buses, which stop at every terminal, and the Inner Harbor Ferry (tel: 800-392 6100/617-222 3200; www.mbta. com/schedules/ferry) which runs to Long Wharf; The Rowes Wharf Water Transport (tel: 617-406 8584; www.roweswharfwatertransport.com) provides water taxi service to the entire Boston waterfront. The 1.6-mile (2.6km) Ted Williams Tunnel (toll payable) starts close to the car rental area and connects the airport easily with downtown and the Massachusetts Turnpike (also toll). Scheduled van services include Boston-Loan Super Shuttle (tel: 800-258 3826; www.supershuttle. com) and Star Shuttle (tel: 617-230 6005; www.starshuttleboston.com). Taxis from the airport to central Boston cost about $25 per person.

By bike

The Hubway (tel: 855-948 2929; www.thehubway.com; spring–fall) bike sharing system has more than 1,800 bikes at 185 sidewalk kiosks (to increase to 245 by the end of 2018) throughout Boston, Brookline, Cambridge, and Somerville. Most of the kiosks are near MBTA stops. Twenty-four-hour, three-day, and annual passes are available entitling the user to unlimited rides less than 30 minutes in duration. Boston has over 62 miles (100km) of bike lanes.

By car

Boston is not particularly car-friendly. Its narrow streets are congested and parking is often hard to find and expensive. The city center is compact enough that walking is generally a good idea.

By public transportation

Boston's public transportation system, universally called the "T," provides excellent coverage of the city and surrounding suburbs. A map is posted at many locations, particularly near tourist areas. Fees vary with time and distance (at the time of writing a one-way subway ticket cost $2.75 ($2.25 with CharlieCard) and bus ticket $2 ($1.70 with CharlieCard). The "Charlie Card" pass is a pre-paid, rechargeable card useable on all "T" services. Information on the "T," including route maps and schedules, is available at www.mbta.com.

New England

By air

Flying makes sense only if time is essential.

Cape Air (tel: 800-227 3247; www.capeair.com) is a regional carrier.

The following New England locations have airports with scheduled regional services:

Massachusetts: Hyannis, Martha's Vineyard, Nantucket, New Bedford, Worcester

Maine: Bangor, Portland, Bar Harbor

Connecticut: Bradley Airport (near Hartford), Bridgeport, Groton, New Haven

Vermont: Burlington, Rutland

New Hampshire: Lebanon-Hanover, Manchester

Rhode Island: Providence

By bus

Peter Pan (tel: 800-343 9999; www.peterpanbus.com) operates the most extensive New England service. Many bus services coordinate connections with Amtrak rail schedules. **C&J Trailways** (tel: 800-258 7111; www.ridecj.com). Northeastern

Parking regulations are clearly posted and are enforced.

Massachusetts, New Hampshire, southern Maine, Boston's South Station and Logan Airport.

Concord Trailways (tel: 800-639 3317; www.concordcoachlines.com). Maine, New Hampshire, Newburyport MA, Boston's South Station and Logan Airport.

Greyhound (tel: 800-231 2222; www.greyhound.com). From New York to larger cities only.

Plymouth & Brockton (tel: 508-746 0378; www.p-b.com). Cape Cod and Massachusetts' South Shore to Boston and Logan Airport.

By train

Amtrak (tel: 800-872 7245; www.amtrak.com) services New England.

Connecticut is served by **Metro-North** (tel: 877-690 5114; www.mta.info/mnr), with trains between New York City's Grand Central Station and New Haven, New Canaan, Danbury, and Waterbury.

Boston has numerous commuter lines operated by the Massachusetts Bay Transport Authority (MBTA; www.mbta.com), from Boston to outlying towns.

By car

Although the network of airplanes, buses, trains, ferries, and taxis is reliable, having your own car is the easiest way to get around (except in the congested heart of Boston), and it also offers the greatest opportunity for getting off the beaten path.

Highways

Interstate highways make distance traveling easy. You can travel from Boston to Burlington VT, a distance of 216 miles (348km) in about 4 hours.

Secondary roads

Travel on secondary roads is much more scenic, if slower. However, beware of dirt roads – usually represented by a broken line – in mud season (typically, March into late April), when melting snow turns them into rutted and slippery quagmires. Mountain roads may be closed in winter.

Car rental

All major international companies have branches across New England, at airports and frequently in town at major cities. It's best to book ahead and take advantage of deals. Often they tie in with hotel discounts.

Legal requirements

Most car-rental agencies require drivers to be at least 25 and to hold a major credit card and a driver's license that is current and has been valid for at least a year; some will accept a cash deposit, sometimes as high as $500, in lieu of a credit card.

Foreign travelers will need to show an international driver's license or a license from their own country.

Insurance

Liability is not included in the terms of your lease, so advertised rates usually do not include additional fees for insurance. Collision Damage Waiver (CDW) is recommended, as it covers you if someone else damages your car. Check your own car insurance coverage; sometimes it covers rental cars. Some credit cards offer coverage on rental cars, something the car-rental firms do not tell you.

Rules of the road

States and municipalities have specific laws and regulations regarding parking, speed limits, and the like; most are clearly posted. Speed limits on some country roads may not be well posted, and can range from 20 to 50mph (32–80kmh): be sure to find out what the local regulations are.

The speed limit on interstate highways is mostly 65mph (100kmh) although portions in built-up areas may be limited to 55mph (90kmh) or lower. Enforcement, though sporadic, can be strict, with high penalties. Drunk-driving penalties are very severe in all states.

Roads with solid lines down the middle are "no passing" zones. But in Vermont passing is legal at any time except where explicitly posted as "no passing" (this is a nod to the state's rural character, where tractors and farm vehicles often travel at slow speeds).

Moose and deer are particularly active at dawn and dusk, and are a hazard to drivers on country roads, particularly in northern New England. If a deer runs in front of your car, slow down or stop – they often travel in groups and a second or third one may not be far behind. Moose, however, don't usually run. Generally weighing between 800 and 1,200lbs (360–545kg), they don't need to. Give them the right of way, too.

Beware of dirt roads in mud season, when they become impassable for ordinary cars. Some mountain roads are closed in winter.

Seatbelts

These are obligatory for all occupants. In some states the police may stop vehicles and ticket unbelted passengers. Children under 6 must be buckled into safety seats or a proper child restraint, and in some states children must sit in the back seat. Many rental firms supply child seats for a small extra cost.

Fuel

Fuel is lead-free and stations are plentiful, and often open 24 hours a day near major highways (otherwise, usually 5 or 6am until 10 or 11pm). Many pumps can be activated by credit cards. British travelers should note the US gallon is 17 percent smaller than the English equivalent. Metric users note that 1 gallon equals 3.8 liters.

Special considerations

Unless otherwise posted, a right-hand turn at a red light is permitted. On sighting a school bus that has stopped to load or unload children, drivers in both directions must stop completely before reaching the bus and may not proceed until the flashing red warning signals on the school bus have been switched off.

Ambulances, fire engines, and police cars with emergency lights on always have right of way. Pull over, and wait until they've passed before proceeding.

Rotaries (roundabouts), especially in Boston, require caution. The official rule is that the cars already in

Ferry boats line up at Portland, Maine.

the circle have the right of way in exiting, but this rule is often ignored in practice. It's best to proceed carefully, whether entering or exiting.

Hitchhiking and car-jacking

Hitchhiking is discouraged; so is picking up hitchhikers. Car-jackings are rare, but not unheard of. When you pick up your rental vehicle, ask the clerk which areas to avoid.

Breakdown

Some highways have emergency phones every few miles. You can also call tel: 911 on your cell phone for help. Otherwise, park with the hood raised and a police patrol car will stop. The **American Automobile Association** (tel: 800-222 4357; www.aaa.com) offers reciprocal breakdown services with some affiliated firms in other countries, and provides members with excellent information on road conditions.

Parking

You must park in the direction of traffic, and never by a fire hydrant. A yellow or red line on the curb means no parking is allowed. In some towns a white line along the curb shows where you can park.

Traffic/road conditions

For all New England States, visit www.usroadconditions.com.

Boston: For up-to-the-minute traffic information, tel: 877-623 6846; www.mass.gov/orgs/massachusetts-department-of-transportation. WBZ radio provides traffic updates at 10:30am and at http://boston.cbslocal.com/station/wbz-news-radio/.

By water

Ferries can save travelers hours of driving time, and, in Massachusetts and Maine, provide transportation to many of the islands. Some ferries service both passengers and vehicles; others are passenger-only. Reservations are highly recommended at all times and mandatory during peak tourist season when you're planning to transport a vehicle. During off-season, ferries may have limited schedules or may suspend operations.

Popular ferry routes

It is fairly easy to travel around New England by ferry, if you don't mind taking the scenic route.

Some of the most popular routes take you from Boston out to Cape, or from Long Island back to the mainland.

Boston's Logan Airport to downtown Boston, including stops along Boston Harbor and at Long Wharf (MBTA; tel: 800-392 6100/617-222 3200; www.mbta.com). A free bus shuttle (Route 66 bus) runs between all airport terminals and the airport dock. Other MBTA ferry routes include Long Wharf to Charlestown Navy Yard; and Hull to Long Wharf and Logan Airport.

Boston to Provincetown (Cape Cod): ferries include the passenger-only **Provincetown Fast Ferry** from Long Wharf (tel: 617-748 1428; www.baystatecruisecompany.com/schedule-fares.php) and **Bay State Cruise Ferry** (tel: 888-274 3050; www.baystatecruisecompany.com), which is accessed by the MBTA's Silver Line.

Woods Hole (Falmouth, Cape Cod) to Martha's Vineyard: **Steamship Authority** (tel: 508-477 8600; www.steamshipauthority.com).

Hyannis (Cape Cod) to Nantucket: **Steamship Authority** (tel: 508-477 8600; www.steamshipauthority.com).

Hyannis to Martha's Vineyard: passenger-only **Hy-Line Fast Ferry** (tel: 800-492 8082; www.hylinecruises.com).

New Bedford MA to Martha's Vineyard: **Sea Streak Martha's Vineyard** (tel: 800-262 8743; www.seastreak.com).

Orient Point, Long Island NY to New London CT: **Cross Sound Ferry** (tel: 860-443 5281; www.longislandferry.com).

Montauk, Long Island NY to Block Island RI (passengers only): **Viking Fleet** (tel: 631-668 5700; www.vikingfleet.com).

Quonset Point RI to Martha's Vineyard (shuttle from Amtrak and Providence Airport): **Vineyard Fast Ferry** (tel: 401-295 4040; www.vineyardfastferry.com).

Port Jefferson, Long Island to Bridgeport CT: **Bridgeport & Port Jefferson Steamboat Company** (tel: 888-44FERRY/888-443 3779; www.88844ferry.com).

Maine State Ferries (tel: 207-624 3000; http://maine.gov/mdot/ferry/).

Lake Champlain Ferries from Charlotte, Burlington, and Grand Isle VT to Essex, Port Kent, and Plattsburg NY (tel: 802-864 9804; www.ferries.com).

A

Accommodations

Many lodgings – particularly those in resort areas – close for at least part of the winter, unless they're in ski territory. Some – particularly in Vermont, Maine, and New Hampshire – close for "mud season," generally mid-March through April, and in November between autumn foliage and ski seasons. And a few in particularly buggy areas will delay opening until July, when black flies and mosquitoes taper off.

In general, the least expensive time to travel is November–April, although December–early March is a peak time for lodgings at or near ski areas. High seasons are during summer months and during foliage season, generally late September–mid- to late October. During these times many lodgings add a premium to their rates and may require a minimum stay of two or three nights. Most city hotels charge $20–50 a night for parking.

Country inns and B&Bs

If you are tired of motels and hotels, these lodgings are a wonderful option. They range from weathered farmhouses with huge fireplaces and homemade muffins at breakfast to grand elegance. Some require sharing a bathroom and others "require" you to relax by not providing TVs or in-room phones. Most are warm and welcoming, though a few can seem slightly pretentious. If traveling with children, be sure to check minimum age requirements.

Inns and Resorts of New England (www.newenglandinnsandresorts.com) has a site specially designed for visitors from the UK, Canada, France, Spain, Germany, and Japan.

Other resources include **Bed & Breakfast Agency of Boston** (tel: 617-720 3540, www.boston-bnbagency. com), **Rental Homes** (tel: 888-216-4649; www.rentalhomes.com), and **Bed and Breakfast Associates Bay Colony** (tel: 888-486 6018 in US and Canada, 01-617-720 0522 outside US; www.bnbboston.com), for reservations in Boston, eastern Massachusetts, and Cape Cod.

Holiday homes

If you're planning to stay a week or longer in one location, it may be more affordable to rent a home or condominium. Popular websites for this service include www.vrbo.com and www.homeaway.com.

Hostels and other budget lodgings

Although most prevalent in the Boston area, several cities and towns throughout New England also offer budget accommodations at hostels, YMCAs, and YWCAs. Facilities might include shared common spaces and baths and/or dormitory-style rooms, but are generally clean and relatively inexpensive. Many of the YMCA/YWCA lodgings do not charge lodging or room taxes.

HostelWorld.com (www.hostelworld.com) makes reservations for YMCAs, budget lodgings, and hostels throughout New England. For more information on hostels, contact:
Hostelling International Boston
19 Stuart Street
Boston MA 02116
Tel: 617-536 9455
www.hiusa.org

Budget lodgings in the mountains
Appalachian Mountain Club
10 City Square
Boston MA 02129
Tel: 617-523-0636
www.outdoors.org
    The **Appalachian Mountain Club** operates six roadside lodges with a variety of sleeping and meal options in Maine and New Hampshire. They also have eight huts a day's hike apart along the Appalachian Trail in the White Mountains.

Age restrictions

The legal age for both the purchase and consumption of alcoholic drinks is 21. Liquor stores are state-owned or franchised in Vermont, New Hampshire, and Maine; privately owned in southern New England. Laws on Sunday purchase vary between states.

Some restaurants have a license restricting them to serve only beer and wine. Restaurants without a liquor license usually permit customers to bring their own beer or wine (BYOB); some may charge a "corkage" or "set-up" fee. When driving, keep bottles of alcohol unopened and out of sight in the car.

B

Budgeting for your trip

Industry research estimates that the average visitor spends about $300–400/day. This breaks down to:
Double room per night in a three-star hotel in high season: $160–260; in a city, parking may be an additional $20–50 per night.
Simple lunch for two (without alcohol, with tax and 15 percent gratuity) is approximately $30–35.
Three-course dinner for two (without alcohol, with tax and 20 percent gratuity): $80–120.
Car hire per week (excluding taxes and fees): from $210.
Admission charges for two: about $50 per day.
Miscellaneous (drinks, taxis, etc): $75–100 per day.

There are many discount plans available: family passes, and reduced admission for students and senior citizens. These are sometimes offered by a destination and sometimes by a group of attractions. Their availability changes annually, if not seasonally, but if you can browse the tourism websites and those of attractions of interest, you can probably find some very nice options. Some of those include accommodation, meals, and entrance charges. They are always posted at the admission booth of attractions, which will usually also post information about combination passes with other attractions.

Passes: In Boston, CityPass (tel: 888-330 5008; www.citypass. com) is good for nine consecutive days, and saves about 50 percent at five popular attractions: the Museum of Science, New England Aquarium, Skywalk Observatory, Harvard Museum of Natural History or Boston Harbor Cruises. Passes are sold at all five venues. What is more, the pass lets you skip most of the ticket lines, and also offers discounts at museum shops.

The **GoBoston Card** (tel: 866-628 9027; www.gobostoncard.com), available for one to seven days, and gives visitors unlimited access to more than 40 attractions as well as restaurant and shopping discounts, and excursions outside the city.

Many other cities with multiple attractions also offer combination rates: be sure to ask in advance of ticket purchase. Mystic CT has a Mystic Pass Card (https://mystic.org/purchase/) with reduced admissions to several attractions and meal deals. Newport RI has discounts to the mansions (www.newportmansions.org).

Disabled persons: US citizens and permanent residents with disabilities can apply for a free access pass (documentation required) to all US National Parks (www.nps.gov).

Accommodations: Discounted lodgings and airfare are available on numerous websites including hotwire.com, travelocity.com, kayak. com, and priceline.com. Discount hotel and motel coupons and books with last-minute hotel reservations are distributed free of charge at most Interstate rest stops and tourist information centers.

Seniors: Many businesses and attractions offer discounts of 10–15 percent to senior citizens; the qualifying age can range from 60 to 65, although ID is seldom requested.

Students: Both the Student Advantage Card (tel: 800-333 2920; www.studentadvantage.com) and the STA Travel Discount Card (tel: 0333 321 0099; www.statravel.com) provides students with substantial discounts while travelling in the US.

C

Children

It's quite easy to travel in New England with children. There are hands-on museums, theme parks, and toy and book stores throughout the region. With proper planning, driving distances between destinations can be kept quite short. Almost all attractions which charge admission have a discounted rate for children, and many change nothing at all for very young kids, often 5 and under.

Many restaurants offer children's menus, but some – particularly the more expensive – may not welcome young children at dinner. Lodgings generally welcome children and do not charge for those under 18, although they may add on $10 or $15 for a cot or crib. It is quite common for bed-and-breakfasts to have age restrictions, so be sure to check in advance.

Many hotel concierges will provide lists of local agencies which provide sitters; this can be quite costly, as the agencies charge a referral fee plus an hourly fee, but

the sitters are carefully screened. Two agencies in Boston include **Care** (formerly Parents in a Pinch) (77 Fourth Avenue, 5th Floor Road, Waltham 02451; tel: 855-781 1303; www.parentsinapinch.com) and **Boston's Best Baby Sitters** (513 East Broadway, Boston; tel: 617-455 7171; www.bostonsbestbabysitters.com).

Laws in each state are quite specific about driving with children in a car. If you are renting, be sure to tell the agency in advance how old your children are so that they will have the proper size car seats available, and check with them about state requirements.

Climate

New England's climate is as varied as its landscape, with large variations from state to state, from season to season, and even from one hour to another. A local saying, "if you don't like the weather, wait 10 minutes," aptly illustrates this fact. Massachusetts and Connecticut have very similar temperature patterns. In the west, the summer temperatures will be around 80°F (27°C), 85°F (32°C) in Boston, and about 81°F (27°C) on Cape Cod and the islands and along the Connecticut coast. The winters can be quite cold; temperatures in the mountains are frequently 20°F (–7°C) or colder. They will be warmer in Boston; 32°F (0°C) is about the norm. Along the water, the air temperature may be either side of freezing, but the "wind chill" makes it seem much colder.

Rhode Island: Temperatures are similar to those in Boston and Cape Cod. Block Island has an average January temperature of about 31°F (–1°C) and an average July temperature of about 70°F (21°C).

Vermont and New Hampshire have considerable variations in temperature depending on proximity to the mountains. In general, winter temperatures in the mountains are 17°F (–8°C) and average July temperatures are 70°F (21°C). In the central areas of both states, the mean January temperature is 22°F (–6°C) with a mean July temperature of 70°F (21°C).

Atop Mt Washington, which has its own weather pattern, the average July temperature is 50°F (10°C) and the mean January temperature

CLIMATE CHART

Boston

Maximum temperature
Minimum temperature
Rainfall

6°F (-14°C). In April 1934, winds of 231mph (372kmh) were recorded on the summit of Mt Washington.

Maine: The coastal part of the state has a maritime climate. Winter temperatures are much milder than those inland; summer temperatures are cooler. Northern Maine, however, is extremely cold with a high snowfall. In 1925, Maine's lowest recorded temperature of -48°F (-44.4°C) was observed. The south is the warmest part of the state.

What to wear

Clothing styles in New England vary from state to state, as well as from region to region. In rural areas, people tend to dress in casual clothes geared towards outdoor life, whereas attire in cities in Massachusetts, Connecticut, and Rhode Island is more traditional. A few formal restaurants may require a jacket and tie for men. "Business casual" is an often-quoted dress code. For men, that means a short-sleeved shirt or polo shirt and khaki or twill trousers. Women's attire should have a similar accent. Denim jeans are usually permitted if they are not obviously faded, worn, or patched. While "relaxed" is the norm, some bars and nightclubs ban jeans and T-shirts.

Some warm clothing, such as jumpers, jackets, and windbreakers, should be packed even during the summer, when evening temperatures tend to dip in the mountains and on the coast. Winters generally necessitate heavy outerwear, including hats, scarves, gloves, and boots. The best advice for winter dressing is to dress in layers in order to adapt to immediate situations. Keep in mind that denim, once wet, becomes very heavy, provides no insulation, and is nearly impossible to dry.

When to visit

Generally, the tourist season runs from early June through the first weekend in September. It's particularly crowded along the coastline of Maine, Cape Cod, Martha's Vineyard, Nantucket, and Newport. Make reservations as early as possible. The other very busy time is fall foliage season, from mid-September through October. Reservations are required

everywhere, even in areas which otherwise see few tourists.

In the summer, humidity, even in the mountains, can be draining, and there will often be afternoon thunderstorms, which can often cause downpours. While New England is rarely affected by hurricanes, the storms can strike, as Hurricane Irene did in August 2011, causing massive flooding. Less damaging were tropical storms Jose and Philippe which haunted New England's coast in 2017. The latter caused massive power outages across the region. Hurricane season runs from June through November, with August and September the most active months. Coastal areas may be evacuated ahead of an approaching storm.

Winter blizzards are much more likely. New England is generally ready for them, but massive storms can shut down the region and cause power outages. Most resorts and hotels have their own generators which kick in if the power grid turns off. If driving, make sure you have plenty of gas, carry a blanket in case you are stuck and cannot be reached immediately, and keep your cell phone charged.

Early spring, from March through April, is often called "mud season", and for good reason. The melting snow turns many unpaved roads into morasses that challenge even four-wheel drive vehicles. Many of the seasonal tourist attractions are still closed, although those in cities are usually open, if with limited hours.

Crime and safety

Boston is one of the safest cities in the US, but visitors should always be vigilant. Areas where crime is a problem offer few tourist attractions and are on the fringes of the city. Equally, New England's urban areas are among the safest in the US. Nevertheless, always lock car doors, and don't leave valuables visible in your car or hotel room.

Customs regulations

Visitors aged 21 or over may bring the following to the US, providing they are staying in the country for at least 72 hours and have not declared

the same amounts within the past six months:

1 liter of duty-free alcohol

200 duty-free cigarettes or 100 cigars (non-Cuban) or 2kg of smoking tobacco

Gifts worth $100

Up to $10,000 in US or foreign cash, or travelers' checks; any more must be declared.

Import of meat, seeds, plants, and fruit is forbidden. For more information, contact US Customs (tel. 877-227 5511; www.cbp.gov). If returning to your country from the US, contact:

Australian citizens: Department of Immigration and Border Protection Service (tel: 1300 363 263 www.border.gov.au).

Canadian citizens: the Canada Border Services Agency (tel: 800-461 9999 in Canada [24-hour computer information; live operators Mon–Fri 8am–4pm], or outside Canada, tel: 204-983 3500 or check their website: www.cbsa-asfc.gc.ca).

UK citizens: HM Revenue and Customs (tel: 0300-200-3700 [8am–6pm Mon–Fri]; www.gov.uk/government/organisations/hm-revenue-customs).

D

Disabled access

The Americans with Disabilities Act requires handicapped access for most buildings used by the public, but there are exceptions. Most attractions, restaurants, and lodgings comply, but it's a good idea to check in advance, particularly when visiting older historic sites which may be physically unable to provide access.

Resources include the **Society for Accessible Travel and Hospitality** (tel: 212-447 7284; www.sath.org); **Mobility International USA** (MIUSA; tel: 1 541 343-1284; http://www.miusa.org/resource/tipsheet/disability-resources), which offers travel tips for the disabled; and the informative website **Flying Wheels Travel** (tel: Tel: 612-381-162; http://flyingwheelstravel.com/).

For access on public transportation throughout Boston, contact the **Massachusetts Bay Transportation Authority's Office for Transportation Access** (tel: 617-222 3200; www.mbta.com).

E

Eating out

Visitors to New England will have no trouble finding old standbys, such as Yankee pot roast, creamy clam or fish chowder, and Indian pudding. The latter, a baked corn porridge affair, is usually served – as it definitely wasn't during colonial times – with vanilla ice cream. But these time-honored dishes have largely been relegated to the menus of restaurants that make a specialty of them, and of "ye olde" colonial decor too.

New England has long since joined the trend toward a cuisine greatly influenced by European and Asian concepts of super-fresh ingredients, lighter stocks and sauces, and a contrast of flavors and textures. There is, moreover, the element of authentic ethnic dining; most cities and college towns offer a broad range of world cuisines. Boston, in particular, is known for its Chinatown eateries and the Italian restaurants that populate the North End.

Abundant seafood

A drive along the Maine coast can become a movable feast of lobster; you can have it boiled and served roadside "in the rough," cubed or shredded with lashings of mayonnaise or melted butter in bulging rolls, or in rich bisques and stews. Wellfleet oysters, Chatham scallops from Cape Cod, freshly caught swordfish and bluefish are all considered to be among the world's greatest saltwater treats.

You should not miss out on trying authentic chowder packed with clams. You will also come across "steamers," soft-shelled clams so called because they are steam-cooked. Hard-shell clams come in several varieties, such as littlenecks, cherrystones, and quahogs.

Local treats

When it comes to culinary curiosities, New England certainly has its share. All of the following can be found in the region: French Canadian-style breakfasts, with baked beans crowding eggs and sausages; clam pizza in Connecticut; vinegar-marinated Portuguese pork and seafood dishes that are especially common in southeastern Massachusetts; and muffins (or pancakes) packed with blueberries, which can frequently be purchased from roadside outlets in Maine.

Where to eat

New England has its fair share of fancy restaurants in Boston to the more relaxed, cutting-edge operations of Portland, Maine, or Portsmouth, New Hampshire.

If you are after a quick, cheap bite, you can hardly do better – or have a more authentic American dining experience – than at a diner. The diner phenomenon was born in Providence, Rhode Island, and matured in Worcester, Massachusetts, where the Worcester Lunch Car Company churned out more than 600 pre-fabricated units up until the early 1960s.

Electricity

Most wall outlets have 110-volt, 60-cycle, alternating current plug bays. If using European-made appliances, step down the voltage with a transformer and bring a plug adaptor as sockets are two-prong. These can be purchased at stores in airports and some office supply stores (Staples and Office Depot) and at AAA stores, but are otherwise not easy to find.

Embassies and consulates

For a listing of embassies in the US, log onto: www.embassy.org/embassies. Many countries have a consulate office in New England, usually in Boston. For a complete list: www.state.gov/s/cpr/32122.htm.

Australia: No consulate. Embassy: 1601 Massachusetts Avenue, Washington DC; tel: 202-797 3000; http://usa.embassy.gov.au/.

Canada: 3 Copley Place, Boston; tel: 1-844-880-6519. Embassy: 501 Pennsylvania Avenue, Washington DC; tel: 1-844-880-6519; https://travel.gc.ca/assistance/embassies-consulates/united-states.

India: No consulate. Embassy: 2107 Massachusetts Avenue, Washington DC; tel: 202-939 7000; www.indianembassy.org.

Ireland: 535 Boylston Street, Boston; tel: 617-267 9330. Embassy: 2234 Massachusetts Avenue, Washington DC; tel: 202-462 3939; www.dfa.ie/irish-embassy/USA/.

Israel: 20 Park Plaza, Boston; tel: 617-535 0200; http://embassies.gov.il/boston/Pages/default.aspx. Embassy: 3514 International Drive NW, Washington DC; tel: 202-364 5500; http://www.israelemb.org/washington/ConsularServices/Pages/consular-services.aspx.

United Kingdom: 1 Broadway, Cambridge MA; tel: 617-245 4500. Embassy: 3100 Massachusetts Avenue, Washington, DC; tel: 202-588 6500; www.gov.uk/world/organisations/british-embassy-washington.

Emergencies

For all emergencies, tel: 911. If you can be very clear about your location, it will help responders reach you more quickly.

F

Festivals

Ethnicity and history; agriculture and the arts – New England has a unique cultural depth. And it celebrates it all with festivals. Throughout the year, every weekend sees some exciting, entertaining, or delicious salute to what makes New England special. These are just a very few of the annual events:

Patriot's Day, Boston, Lexington, Concord: Held the Monday closest to April 19. www.bostoncentral.com.

Newport Flower Show: The largest flower show in New England. June. www.newportmansions.org.

Boston Harborfest: Week-long, city-wide festival culminating on the Fourth of July. www.bostoncentral.com.

New Hampshire Craftsman's Fair: 10 days in August. www.nhcrafts.org.

Feast of the Blessed Sacrament, New Bedford: Largest Portuguese festival in the country. August. http://feastoftheblessedsacrament.com/.

Newport Folkfest: Prestigious folk festival. www.newportfolk.org.

Maine Lobsterfest, Rockland: 20,000oz (9,000kg) of lobster. Late July/early August. www.mainelobsterfestival.com.

Mashpee Wampanoag Pow Wow, Mashpee MA: One of the largest in the country. July. www.mashpeewampanoagtribe-nsn.gov/.

Madawaska Acadien Festival, Madawaska ME: Celebration of French Canadian and American roots. Some events are in Canada; bring your passport. August. www. acadianfestival.com.

The Big "E", West Springfield MA: 17-day-long agricultural festival. Mid-September through early October. www.thebige.com.

Connecticut Renaissance Faire, Hebron CT: The largest Renfest in New England. Weekends late September–late October. http://ctfaire.com/.

Haunted Happenings, Salem MA: If it's ghostly, haunted, or can appear so, it will happen here during October. www.hauntedhappenings.org.

Thanksgiving in Plymouth: A celebration of Pilgrim life and early relations with the Algonquins. Held the weekend before Thanksgiving. www.usathanksgiving.com.

Health and medical care

Most visitors to New England have no health problems during their stay; sunburn is the main nuisance for the majority. Even so, non-Americans should never leave home without travel insurance to cover themselves and their belongings. It's not cheap to get sick in the United States. Your own insurance company or travel agent can advise you on policies, but shop around, as rates vary. Make sure you are covered for accidental death, emergency medical care, cancellation of trip, and baggage or document loss.

Pharmacies stock most standard medication (though some painkillers that are available over the counter in other countries may be prescription-only in the US), and staff are trained to help with most minor ailments.

Hospitals are signposted on highways with a white H on a blue background. Major hospitals have 24-hour emergency rooms – you may have a long wait before you get to see the doctor, but the care and treatment are thorough and professional.

Walk-in clinics are commonplace in cities, where you can consult a nurse or doctor for a minor ailment without an appointment. If cost is a concern, turn first to clinics offering free or pro-rated care (look under "Clinics" in the Yellow Pages).

A couple of serious health hazards exist in the region, including Lyme disease (borne by deer ticks hiding in high grass), which is a potentially dangerous chronic condition. Starting with a rash, it develops into flu-like symptoms and joint inflammation, and possible long-term complications such as meningitis and heart failure. When hiking, wear light-colored pants tucked into socks, and spray the clothing with an insecticide. Inspect your skin afterwards: if a tick has attached itself, it should be removed very carefully, using tweezers. Place the tweezers as low on the tick's body as possible, and remove slowly and deliberately; tick mouth parts left in the skin can still deliver the infection. Disinfect the area with alcohol, and visit a doctor or clinic if a red rash begins to appear.

Another potential danger is poison ivy, although it causes only temporary discomfort, but this can be avoided by keeping an eye out for the shiny three-leaf clusters and washing immediately upon accidental contact. Calamine lotion is good for soothing the skin.

Tap water is safe to drink, but avoid stream water as it can cause giardia, an intestinal disorder spread by wild animal wastes. Use a filter or purification tablets, or boil water, when hiking or camping.

Bear, moose, and other wildlife are unpredictable and can be very dangerous. Never try to approach any wild animal. They can charge at you without warning, particularly if you disturb a female with young (who may be hidden nearby) or a male in rutting season. Before hiking, ask about sightings.

If an animal acts particularly friendly – raccoon or fox, for example – it may have rabies. Do not touch it. If you do, get to a medical facility immediately and report the contact. The animal does not have to be having convulsions or foaming at the mouth to be contagious, and the bacteria is extremely virulent.

There are both rattlesnakes and copperheads in the woods, although they try to avoid us as much as we try to avoid them. If bitten, put a firm binding around the bite – do not use a tourniquet – keep the bitten limb below the level of the heart, and get to a medical facility as soon as possible.

Internet

Wi-fi access is nearly universal. Restaurants, visitor centers, even gas stations often have access, usually at no charge. In small towns, access may be limited. Most lodgings have service, although in more rural areas the connection may be weak. Larger hotels often have in-room connections, but many of them charge a fee, which can be as much as $20/day. Others have business centers, which are generally free of charge. Most public libraries will let you use their computers for free or a small fee.

LGBTQ travelers

Boston has a vibrant LGBTQ community, as do Cambridge, Springfield, and Northampton MA and Portland ME. Provincetown on Cape Cod is the country's best-known gay summer vacation spot. Most college towns have some kind of LGBTQ community.

Information concerning gay-oriented activities can be found at the Massachusetts LGBTQ site www.lgbtmassvacation.com and in alternative weeklies such as Boston-based *Rainbow Times* (www.therainbowtimesmass.com); northern Vermont's *Seven Days* (www.sevendaysvt.com); western Massachusetts' and Connecticut's *The Valley Advocate* (http://valleyadvocate.com); and Boston's *Bay Windows* (http://www.baywindows.com).

Boston Pride organizes many events and activities for the LGBTQ community in Greater Boston and beyond (tel: 617-262 9405; www.bostonpride.org).

Media

Newspapers and magazines

As well as the US nationals such as *USA Today* and the financial *Wall*

Street Journal and *The New York Times*, New England has many local newspapers. Larger cities have their own dailies. *Boston Magazine* (www.bostonmagazine.com) and free daily *Metro Boston* (www.metro.us/news/local-news/boston) cover the city's life and entertainment. In western Massachusetts the free, weekly *Valley Advocate* (www.valleyadvocate.com) is an excellent resource for the Pioneer Valley. Alternative papers, often with excellent events and entertainment listings, thrive in college towns. Foreign magazines and papers are sold on newsstands in the larger cities.

Radio stations

AM radio is geared toward talk, news, and information programming. (Saturday and Sunday mornings are often when local stations in small towns broadcast local news – including obituaries and anniversaries – and on-air "flea markets" with people selling everything from non-functioning snowmobiles and dining room sets to dairy cows.) FM stations tend to offer specific music formats, such as country or classic rock. Red Sox games are broadcast on 68 stations throughout New England, anchored in Boston by WRKO (680 AM; www.wrko.com) and WEEI (850 AM; www.weeradioonline.com). New England Patriot games are aired on WBCN (104.1 FM).

National Public Radio, known for in-depth news coverage, classical music, and special programming, has affiliates throughout New England. Among them: 88.5 FM in western Massachusetts, 89.5 FM in southern Vermont, 89.7 FM in the Boston area, and 89.1 FM in Concord, NH. WBUR (90.9 FM; www.wbur.org) is NPR's news source in Boston.

Station formats can change to reflect listener ratings. What was classic rock today can be Top 40 tomorrow. The easiest way to find what you are listening for is to use the "scan" button on your radio setting.

Television stations

Cable and satellite television is ubiquitous, although how many channels you receive depends on the plan your accommodation pays for. At the very least, you will get "local" stations – although in rural areas, that can mean a city 50 miles (80km) away – which carry the major networks (ABC, NBC, CBS), The Weather Channel, CNN, Fox, ESPN (sports), at least one movie channel, most likely HBO, and probably a Public Broadcasting System (PBS) channel, which is advertisement-free and has some of the better-quality programs.

Money

Paper money is issued in $1, $2 (very rare), $5, $10, $20, $50, and $100 denominations.

Coins come in seven denominations: 1¢ (a penny); 5¢ (a nickel); 10¢ (a dime); 25¢ (a quarter); 50¢ (a half dollar; infrequently seen); gold-colored coins worth $1 (which are nearly the same size and hue as the quarter and are universally despised and rarely used); and the rarely-seen silver dollar.

ATMs are ubiquitous in all but the smallest of towns throughout New England, and, although they charge a fee, they are an extremely convenient way to get cash as you need it. They will convert your transaction automatically at a generally good rate. Unlike Europe, most places in the US are not equipped to handle currency exchange, even in major cities.

Credit cards are almost universally accepted, except in some very small towns and a few eateries. Some are more welcome than others. Visa and MasterCard are taken almost everywhere, but American Express is occasionally not accepted. Discover is another card with relatively wide acceptance. Most cards charge a fee of 3 percent for international transactions and do not convert at a favorable rate. Almost all retailers accept debit card purchases and pre-paid debit cards.

If your credit card is lost or stolen, report it to the company immediately. Visa's US emergency number: tel: 800-847 2911. For American Express cardholders: tel: 800-992 3404. American Express traveler's check holders: tel: 800-221 7282. For MasterCard: tel: 800-627 8372. Discover: tel: 800- 347-2683.

International visitors can exchange funds at exchange booths at Logan Airport: Sovereign Bank BCE Travelex Foreign Exchange (tel: 877-414 6359; www.travelex.com) booths are open daily at terminals B and E, and they have an office open daily at 745 Boylston Street in downtown Boston. There is a Bank of America Exchange at terminal C. All exchanges charge a processing, service, and/or administration fee.

Up-to-the-minute exchange rates are posted on www.x-rates.com.

Banks are generally open Monday through Friday from 9am until 5pm. Some may remain open later on Thursdays and Fridays, and others may open Saturday mornings (but don't count on it).

Though they are becoming less and less popular, travelers' checks are accepted by many businesses, although smaller establishments may be hesitant to accept, and make change for, larger denominations. When exchanging checks for cash, you will get the best rate at banks: hotels generally give a poor rate. Most financial establishments will charge a commission fee when cashing travelers' checks.

Tipping

Tip appropriately (unless the service is poor) or it will be interpreted as an insult. For meals, hairdressers, bartenders, and taxi drivers, around 15 percent is the norm (20 percent for exceptional waiter service or if the bill is $100 or more). Don't tip on the tax portion of the bill.

Give a few dollars to the doorman if he performs a service such as hailing a cab, $1 per bag to the bellhop, and $1 to the parking attendant each time you use valet parking; housekeepers should get $2–5 per day.

O

Opening hours

Government, and most business, offices are open weekdays from 9am to 5pm. Most large retail stores open at 9am and stay open at least until 5pm; many stay open until 6pm, and often later on Thursday and Friday nights. Stores in malls generally open at 10am and close at 9pm Monday through Saturday, although many stay open later in the evening; on Sundays malls generally open at noon and close at 6–8pm.

Smaller shops throughout New England, particularly in tourist areas, are usually open in the summer from 10am until at least 5 or 6pm. But these hours vary tremendously with location and season.

Many museums are open daily from 9–10am to 5pm in the summer, but others are closed on Monday or Tuesday. Off-season hours will vary a great deal, particularly in smaller towns.

In larger cities many gas stations and convenience stores remain open 24 hours, as do those close to Interstate exits.

P

Pets

In recent years, travel with pets has become increasingly popular in New England, and some lodgings are now setting aside "pet-friendly" units. Many charge a cleaning fee ranging from $25 to $35 a night; and some will request a damage deposit, returnable at the end of a stay provided the pet did no permanent harm. Pets are not permitted in restaurants, but are generally welcome at establishments with outdoor seating, providing the pet does not have to go through the restaurant to get in.

Some stores will permit pets. Burlington VT is particularly pet-friendly, and stores welcoming them have signs posted in their windows.

Car interiors can heat up rapidly in summer. Do not leave your pet unattended in a car on a warm day, even with windows ajar. The heat can quickly cause brain damage or death, and at the least may cause a concerned passerby to break your window to rescue your pet. Many states and local governments have made such negligence a crime; you can be fined and, if the situation is extreme, jailed.

Postal services

There are post offices in most New England villages and towns. They are generally open daily Monday through Friday, and Saturday mornings.

If you do not know where you will be staying in a particular town,

you can receive mail simply by having it addressed to you, care of General Delivery, at the main office in that town – but you must pick up such mail personally (within 30 days). Check with postal officials about charges and the variety of mail-delivery services available.

Stamps may be purchased at hotel desks. There are occasionally vending machines in shops and airports. Many grocery stores also sell stamps. For domestic and international rates, log onto www. usps.com.

To facilitate quick delivery within the US, include the five-digit zip code when addressing communications. Zip code information may be obtained from any post office or on: www.usps.com.

Public holidays

During the holidays listed below, some or all state, local, and federal agencies are closed. Local banks and businesses may also close on the following days:
New Year's Day
Third Monday in January: Martin Luther King's Birthday
Third Monday in February: Presidents Day, marking Lincoln's and Washington's birthdays
Third Monday in April: Patriots' Day (Massachusetts only)
Last Monday in May: Memorial Day
July 4: Independence Day
First Monday in September: Labor Day
Second Monday in October: Columbus Day
November 11: Veterans Day
Fourth Thursday in November: Thanksgiving
December 25: Christmas Day

R

Religious services

The US Government officially observes separation of Church and State. In practice, though, since its founding, America has attracted numerous immigrants fleeing religious persecution in their home country, and religious freedom is an aspect of American life that is never taken for granted. The majority of Americans believe in god and many attend religious

or spiritual services regularly in their communities. Both high- and low-church Christianity is usually the most visible religious expression across the US, but you'll also find Jewish temples, Mormon tabernacles and temples, Baptist chapels, Quaker meeting houses, Buddhist zendos, pagan Wicca ceremonies, evangelical tent revivals on Indian reservations, and other religious gathering places in the unlikeliest places. Visitors are welcome at most church services.

S

Shopping

What to buy

Although shopping isn't usually the prime reason people visit New England, the region offers a large and diverse number of options ranging from giant malls to tiny shops selling homemade specialty foods including chocolates, maple syrup, salsas, and artisanal cheeses. Some retail giants, such as Maine's L.L. Bean (https:// global.llbean.com/) and the Vermont Country Store (www.vermontcountry store.com), have become tourist destinations in their own right. Several states, including Connecticut with its Wine Trail (www.ctwine.com) and Vermont with its Cheese Trail (www. vtcheese.com), have developed touring routes for visitors.

Boston, home to Pilgrims and, later, Boston's upper-crust Brahmins, has never been famous for high fashion. But retailers such as Saks Fifth Avenue (www.saks fifthavenue.com), Neiman Marcus (www.neimanmarcus.com), Barney's New York (www.barneys.com), and Lord & Taylor (www.lordandtaylor. com) have established outposts in the city, offering shoppers a wide range of upscale merchandise. New England's factory outlets are well known to bargain hunters. Once places where manufacturers sold discounted wares to employees, today the towns of Kittery and Freeport in Maine and Manchester Center VT have converted themselves into giant outlet centers, vying to offer shoppers discounts on big names such as Reebok, Armani, Anne Klein, and Crate & Barrel.

Other sprawling outlet complexes have opened up throughout the region, including in Manchester and North Conway NH, where the absence of a state sales tax makes the deals even sweeter.

Taxes

All states except New Hampshire have a sales tax of 5 to 7 percent. Some cities such as Vermont's Burlington and Williston, add an additional 1 percent on top of the state tax.

Smoking

The legal age in New England to buy tobacco is 18. Although the laws vary somewhat between states, in general smoking is banned in most indoor public places, restaurants, workplaces, and on transport. Hotels have non-smoking rooms; many inns and B&Bs ban smoking. Marijuana is now legal for medical and recreational use in Maine and Massachusetts. In Connecticut, New Hampshire, Rhode Island, and Vermont marijuana is legal for medical use only.

T

Tax

All states levy taxes on meals and accommodation, and all but New Hampshire on all sales. When restaurants and hotels quote prices, these taxes are not normally included – so ask, as they can bump up the cost by up to 12 percent. Ticket prices for transport have the tax included.

Telephones

Although scarce, public telephones can still be found in some hotel lobbies, restaurants, garages, and convenience stores. Local calls require a deposit of 50¢–$1 (coins only) before you dial the number. If your call lasts longer than three minutes, the operator will require an additional deposit to continue the call. For **emergencies**, dial tel: 911; coins are not needed.

The charge for using a phone in your hotel room can vary greatly from one lodging to another: some will charge an access and per-minute fee even if you use a calling card; some may charge for local calls; and others will offer the service at no charge. This information is usually posted in your room.

If you are visiting from outside the US and your cell (mobile) phone plan does not cover international calls, consider renting a phone when you arrive. The cost is generally under $50 a week for unlimited incoming and outgoing calls. Providers in the US include **All Cell Rentals** (tel: 877-724 2355; www.allcellrentals.com) and **Travel Cell** (tel: 877-235 5746; www.travelcell.com).

All 800, 877, 866, and 888 numbers are toll-free.

Directory assistance for any location from any location: tel: 411.

To dial a long-distance number, dial 1, then the area code, then the number.

Time zone

All New England is on Eastern Standard Time: three hours ahead of Los Angeles, one hour ahead of Chicago, five hours behind London, and 15 hours behind Tokyo. New England is one hour behind the Canadian provinces of New Brunswick and Nova Scotia. Daylight Saving Time is in effect between specified dates in early April and early November; turn clocks ahead one hour in spring, back one hour in fall.

Tourist information

Larger cities have tourist information centers; in smaller towns, the Chamber of Commerce or town hall fills that role. State tourist agencies all have their tourism brochures available on their websites.
Connecticut: tel: 888-288 4748; www.ctvisit.com
Maine: tel: 800-767 8709; www.visitmaine.com
Massachusetts: tel: 617-973 8500; www.massvacation.com
New Hampshire: tel: 603-271 2665; www.visitnh.gov
Rhode Island: tel: 800-326 6030; www.discovernewport.org
Vermont: tel: 802-223 3443; www.visitvt.com
Discover New England (www.discovernewengland.org) supplies telephone numbers and accommodation, plus maps of each state.

The Massachusetts Office of Travel and Tourism (MOTT) has a comprehensive website (www.massvacation.com) with information on things to see and do in the region, plus listings for hotels and restaurants.

Tour operators and travel agents

New England has the most physically fit population in the US. That's not surprising, since the area begs to be explored by hiking, kayaking, riding, biking, and camping – for starters. The tour operators listed here are some of the best outdoor outfitters. However, the best advice when traveling to someplace new is to ask about conditions and changes at outdoor stores, the tourism office or Chamber of Commerce, or the locals at the general store or diner.

Massachusetts

Appalachian Mountain Club
Boston; tel: 603-466 2725; www.amc-nh.org
Offers organized trips, courses, and instruction on waterways throughout New England.
Orvis Saltwater School
Chatham; tel: 888-235 9763; www.orvis.com
Saltwater fly-fishing on Cape Cod, with a course that teaches basic saltwater techniques.
Patriot Party Boats
Falmouth Harbour; tel: 508-548 2626; www.patriotpartyboats.com
Excellent deep-sea fishing trips.
Zoar Outdoor
Charlemont; tel: 800-532 7483; www.zoaroutdoor.com
In western Massachusetts, based along the Mohawk Trail in Charlemont, Zoar Outdoor runs whitewater rafting expeditions for all levels on the Deerfield River, and two- or three-day learn-to-kayak and canoe clinics.

Rhode Island

Kayak Centre
Wickford; tel: 401-295 4400; www.kayakcentre.com
Coastal sea kayaking is popular and the Kayak Centre leads a variety of excursions, including a Newport tour with ocean glimpses of mansions; the company also runs a multi-day trip to Block

⊘ Weights and measures

32°F = 0°C; 60°F = 15.5°C;
80°F = 26.7°C; 100°F = 37.8°C
1 US gallon = 0.85 Imperial
gallon or 3.79 liters
1 mile = 1.6km
1 inch = 2.54cm
1ft = 0.3048 meter
65mph = 105kmh
1 acre = 0.4 hectares
1lb = 0.45kg

Island. At their Charlestown location (tel: 401-364 8000; www.kayak centre.com), they offer kayaking on Ninigret Pond.

Rhode Island Audubon Society
Smithfield; tel: 401-949 5454; https://asri.org
Well-regarded independent organization that leads nature hikes.

The Wayfarers
Newport; tel: 800-249 4620; https://www.thewayfarers.com
Packages inn-to-inn hiking tours.

Connecticut

Clarke Outdoors
Housatonic River; tel: 800-672 63265; www.clarkeoutdoors.com
Clarke Outdoors organizes Housatonic rafting trips.
Macedonia Brook State Park in Kent and **Sleeping Giant State Park** in Hamden run scenic day hikes. Contact the **Connecticut State Bureau of Parks and Recreation** (tel: 860-424 3000; www.ct.gov/dep/stateparks) for details.

Vermont

Discovery Bicycle Tours
Woodstock; tel: 800-257 2226; www.discoverybicycletours.com
Puts together tours in all six states.
True North Kayak Tours
Lake Champlain; tel: 802-238 7695; www.vermontkayak.com
Runs good kayak tours in Vermont. To mix serious hiking with country-inn comforts, contact **Country Inns**

Along the Trail (tel: 802-247 3300; www.inntoinn.com), which organizes inn-to-inn tours. **The Wayfarers** (tel: 800-249 4620; www.thewayfarers.com/about-us/sp2018) also packages inn-to-inn hiking (and biking) tours in Vermont, New Hampshire, Rhode Island, and Maine.

New Hampshire

Great Glen Trails
Near Mt Washington; tel: 603-466 3988; www.greatglentrails.com
Great Glen Trails offers learn-to-mountain-bike courses, ranging from a short introductory class to more in-depth skill-building. They can also organize introductory fishing classes and arrange guided fly-fishing trips.

Maine

Back Roads
Office Berkeley CA; tel: 800-462 2848; www.backroads.com/trips/BMNI
One of several companies offering bicycle tours in the state of Maine.
Devils Den
Portland; tel: 207-773 7632; http://dimillosmarina.com/
For ocean fishing excursions, Devils Den runs half- and full-day trips from DiMillo's Marina in Portland.

Visas and passports

Immigration and visitation procedures can change rapidly depending on real and perceived threats to security.

To enter the United States, foreign visitors need a passport and many also need a visa. You may be asked to provide evidence that you intend to leave the United States after your visit is over (usually in the form of a return or onward ticket).

You may not need a visa if you are a resident of one of 27 countries that participate in the Visa Waiver Program (VWP) and are planning to stay in the US for less than 90 days. You must, however, log onto the Electronic System for Travel Authorization's unmemorably named website, http://www.cbp.gov/travel/international-visitors/esta at least 48 hours before traveling and provide personal information and travel details; either your application will be accepted (and will be valid for multiple visits over two years) or you will be told to apply for a visa. As of 2016, you must have an e-passport (with embedded electronic chip) to use the VWP. Anyone wishing to stay longer than 90 days must apply for a visa in any case. This can be done by mail to the nearest US Embassy or Consulate. Visa extensions can be obtained in the US from United States Immigration and Naturalization Service offices. Applications can be downloaded at www.travel.state.gov.

Canadian citizens traveling to the US by air or across the land border need a passport to enter the country.

The US Department of Homeland Security maintains a website at: www.dhs.gov.

HIV: Travelers who are HIV-positive may not enter the US under the Visa Waiver Program. They must file for a visa. For information, log onto: www.travel.state.gov.

Immunization requirements
Log onto www.travel.state.gov for a complete list of immunization requirements by country.

W

Websites

For general tourist information about New England, see www.visit-newengland.com and www.discovernewengland.org.

FURTHER READING

HISTORY AND CULTURE

Builders of the Bay Colony, by Samuel Eliot Morison. New England's most celebrated historian tells the story of the men – and one woman – who gave New England its intellectual underpinnings.

A Week on the Concord and Merrimack Rivers, Walden, The Maine Woods, and Cape Cod, by Henry David Thoreau. Thoreau's four greatest works describe his travels on foot and by canoe – and his sojourn at Walden Pond; detailed descriptions of mid-19th-century landscape and people combine with the blunt, often ornery musings of an archetypal New England intellect.

Paul Revere's Ride, by David Hackett Fischer. Historian Fischer explains what really happened on that April night, which is a lot juicier and more interesting than what's generally taught in school.

The Encyclopedia of New England, by edited by Burt Feintuch and David H. Watters. A magisterial compendium of New England persons, places, and accomplishments (in the same vein, look for New England University Press's **The Vermont Encyclopedia**, by edited by Duffy, Hand, and Orth. A very readable Green Mountain gather-all.

The Proper Bostonians, by Cleveland Amory. Not satire or skewering, but a lighthearted yet near-anthropological study of a Brahmin elite with "grandfather on the brain."

The Prince of Providence, by Mike Stanton. The story of very colorful Providence mayor Buddy Cianci, who oversaw the rebirth of his city and was convicted of corruption while still in office.

The Enduring Shore: A History of Cape Cod, Martha's Vineyard, and Nantucket, by Paul Schneider. Natural and social history, with an emphasis on human impact on a fragile, ultimately ephemeral environment.

The Outermost House: A Year of Life on the Great Beach of Cape Cod, by Henry Beston. Beston's classic rivals Thoreau's Walden as an account of a year of blissful solitude in the loveliest of natural surroundings.

String Too Short to Be Saved: Recollections of Summers on a New England Farm, by Donald Hall. A poet's warm, elegiac recollections of life on his grandfather's small New England farm in the 1940s.

The Survival of the Bark Canoe, by John McPhee. An account of a Maine river trip in a modern bark canoe, interwoven with the story of an uncompromising New Englander who builds the timeless craft.

⊘ Send us your thoughts

We do our best to ensure the information in our books is as accurate and up-to-date as possible. The books are updated on a regular basis using local contacts, who painstakingly add, amend and correct as required. However, some details (such as telephone numbers and opening times) are liable to change, and we are ultimately reliant on our readers to put us in the picture.

We welcome your feedback, especially your experience of using the book "on the road". Maybe you came across a new attraction we missed.

We will acknowledge all contributions, and we'll offer an Insight Guide to the best letters received.

Please write to us at:
Insight Guides
PO Box 7910
London SE1 1WE

Or email us at:
hello@insightguides.com

The Lobster Chronicles: Life on a Very Small Island, by Linda Greenlaw. New England's iconic fishery, seen from the inside by one of the first women captains to break a famously rigid gender barrier.

All Souls, by Michael Patrick MacDonald. A searing memoir of an anguished childhood growing up in Boston's Irish housing projects.

Mayflower, by Nathaniel Philbrick. A well-researched, entertainingly written, unvarnished, and unromantic account of the Pilgrims.

A Civil Action, by Jonathan Harr. Story of Woburn MA and its suits against two large firms held responsible for polluting the town's water source and causing illness and death.

Hackers, by Steven Levy. Largely focusing on MIT, it explores how hackers are responsible for the increasing sophistication of computer technology.

LANDSCAPE AND NATURAL HISTORY

A Guide to New England's Landscape, by Neil Jorgensen. Written in layperson's English, a comprehensive look at how today's mountains, lakes, farmland, and coastline evolved in deep and recent geologic time.

Hands on the Land: A History of the Vermont Landscape, by Jan Albers. The story of human interaction with the land the glaciers left – a never-easy process that yielded a remarkably beautiful balance between the natural and built environments.

In Season: A Natural History of the New England Year, by Nona Bell Estrin. In a region with some of the world's sharpest seasonal divisions, the drama of life's winter ebb and summer flow.

Cod, by Mark Kurlansky. A surprisingly fascinating account of how codfish and the fishing industry impacted New England and the rest of the world.

The Secret Life of Lobsters, by Trevor Corson. Told from the perspectives of lobstermen and marine biologists, it explores the near-collapse of the lobster industry in the 1980s and unravels the mysteries of a lobster's life cycle, living arrangements, and mating habits, often in hysterical detail.

Not Without Peril, by Nicholas Howe. Stories of climbers in New Hampshire's Presidential range from 1849 to 1994.

ARCHITECTURE

Houses of Boston's Back Bay: An Architectural History, 1840–1917, by Bainbridge Bunting. A social as well as an architectural history, this amply illustrated book describes the evolution – and living style – of Boston's fist planned neighborhood.

New England's Architecture, by Wallace Nutting. A fine collection of sketches and photographs drawn from books on the architecture of individual New England states by the late antiquarian Nutting, who pioneered the preservation of the region's vintage homes and furnishings.

Spenser's Boston, by Robert Parker. A photographic journey in and around the city with the author of the popular mystery series as your guide. Quite a few settings from the novels, of course, but it's really a love letter from Parker to his city.

FICTION

Writing New England: An Anthology from the Puritans to the Present, edited by Andrew Delbanco. This carefully chosen collection of New England authors represents nearly four centuries of the region's intellectual development.

The Late George Apley, by John P. Marquand. A deft and wry portrayal of a Brahmin trapped within his class, as its grip on Boston weakens.

The Last Hurrah, by Edwin O'Connor. The ethnic-based machine politics of 20th-century Boston shape the career of a protagonist based on Boston's roguish Mayor James Michael Curley.

Northern Borders, by Howard Frank Mosher. A coming-of-age tale, set among Mosher's vanishing breed of back-country Vermonters equally at home with sawmills and Shakespeare.

Empire Falls, by Richard Russo. The Pulitzer Prize-winning novel of a mill town's deterioration.

Blues, by John Hersey. An old fisherman and a youth explore Cape Cod, life, and the New England outdoors.

An Arsonist's Guide to Writers' Homes in New England, by Brock Clarke. A wonderful send-up of memoirs, mystery fiction, and the adulation of New England's literary icons.

Townie: A Memoir by Andre Dubus III. A moving memoir about growing up in a depressed Massachusetts mill town.

Mark Wahlberg and George Clooney in The Perfect Storm.

MOVIES SET IN NEW ENGLAND

Manchester by the Sea (2016) is a widely acclaimed drama, starring Casey Affleck and Michelle Williams, about an emotionally crippled handyman who, after his brother's sudden death, is unexpectedly named his teenage nephew's guardian.

Spotlight (2015) is an Oscar-winning film starring Mark Ruffalo and Micheal Keaton as *Boston Globe* journalists who investigate cases of widespread and systemic child sex abuse in the Boston area.

Ted (2012) is a comedy starring Mark Wahlberg as a Boston native whose childhood teddy bear Ted suddenly comes alive.

The Ghost Writer (2010), starring Ewan McGregor and Pierce Brosnan, and directed by Roman Polanski, is a political thriller adapted from Robert Harris' novel set in a fictional Massachusetts village.

Revolutionary Road (2008), based on the Richard Yates novel, depicts the disaffections of striving Connecticut suburbanites in the 1950s.

The Departed (2006) is Martin Scorsese's Oscar-winning take on the Boston underworld. Jack Nicholson's character was allegedly based on fugitive gangster Whitey Bulger.

Little Children (2006) stars Kate Winslet as the matriarch of a family surviving a tumultuous summer in a Boston suburb.

Mystic River (2003), director Clint Eastwood's retelling of the Dennis Lehane novel, examines lives tightly intertwined in a working-class Irish Boston neighborhood.

The Perfect Storm (2000), starring George Clooney and based on the real-life *Andrea Gail* tragedy, is a paean to the 10,000 Gloucester men who have lost their lives in the North Atlantic fishery.

Where the Rivers Flow North (1994) features Rip Torn in a Howard Frank Mosher tale of fierce Yankee independence run to ground in 1920s Vermont.

Dead Poets Society (1989), set in a New England prep school, centers on Robin Williams's performance as an inspiring English teacher.

The Bostonians (1984), an elegant Merchant-Ivory production, screens Henry James's tale of propriety's clash with social activism in the 19th-century Hub.

On Golden Pond (1981), filmed at New Hampshire's Squam Lake, was Henry Fonda's final role, as crusty Yankee professor Norman Thayer.

The Last Hurrah (1958), a political drama based on the career of Boston Mayor James M. Curley, features Spencer Tracy as a master of machine politics.

Northwest Passage (1940) features Spencer Tracy as French-and-Indian War hero Major Robert Rogers, in one of cinema's better New England historical dramas; they even got the geography right.

OTHER INSIGHT GUIDES

Insight Guide titles cover every major travel destination in North America, from Alaska to Arizona. City titles include *Boston, New York, Chicago,* and *San Francisco*. Regional and state titles include *Colorado, USA on the Road, USA Southwest, Florida, California, Texas,* and *Alaska*.

CREDITS

PHOTO CREDITS

123RF 187T
Abraham Nowitz/Apa publications
10B, 14/15, 19T, 19B, 52, 53, 55, 76,
106, 113, 115B, 122T, 122B, 134, 135,
139BR, 146, 147, 154T, 155B, 156T,
172B, 354
Aiken1986. 286/287B
Alamy 84, 132, 248B, 319
APA 64, 74, 240T
AWL Images 1, 16/17, 100/101,
104/105
BCRC 205B
Bigstock 307B, 344B
Bostonian Society Library 37
Corbis 11B, 65, 69, 120B, 138/139T,
197B, 212, 218B, 220, 224B, 225B,
230MR, 233, 301, 302, 303, 310
Equinox Resort and Spa 289T
Fotolia 139ML, 160BL
Getty Images 30, 31, 36, 61, 66, 67, 75,
78R, 79, 92, 128B, 138BR, 149, 169,
175, 189B, 201, 210B, 211, 230/231T,
257, 273, 279, 290B, 304B, 316B, 318B
iStock 4, 6, 7ML, 12/13, 20, 21, 22, 23,
24R, 25, 46, 63, 68, 73, 85, 93, 94L,
94R, 95, 97, 98, 119, 154B, 158B,
160/161T, 161B, 161ML, 161TR, 168B,
186MR, 186/187T, 186/187B, 187B,
193, 215, 217T, 217B, 218T, 219T, 222,
225T, 227T, 232, 235T, 235B, 239B,

244T, 245T, 256, 260, 263T, 264, 265,
271B, 278T, 280, 282T, 288, 293, 295,
300T, 304T, 305T, 305B, 311T, 311B,
313, 314, 315T, 316T, 318T, 320/321T,
320BR, 320BL, 321ML, 321BR, 321BL,
321TR, 322, 325, 329B, 330T, 330B,
331, 333, 339T, 341, 342T, 345, 347,
350, 356, 366
JERRY DOUGHERTY'S CONNECTICUT
242T
John Phelan 177
Kindra Clineff 6BL, 6ML, 6BR, 7B,
7TL, 7MR, 9TR, 11T, 18, 48, 50/51, 54,
58, 62, 81, 86, 87, 88, 89L, 89R, 91, 140,
141, 145, 148, 151B, 152, 156B, 158T,
159, 162, 163, 166, 167, 168T, 170, 171,
172T, 173T, 173B, 174T, 174B, 176, 178,
179, 180T, 180B, 181, 182B, 183T,
183B, 184, 185, 188, 189T, 190B, 192,
194, 195, 197T, 199B, 202, 203, 204,
205T, 206T, 206B, 207, 208T, 208B,
209T, 209B, 210T, 213, 216, 219B, 221,
223, 224T, 226B, 226T, 227B, 228, 229,
230BL, 231BL, 231BR, 237T, 237B,
238, 239T, 240B, 241B, 241T, 243,
245B, 246, 247T, 247B, 248T, 249, 251T,
251B, 252, 253, 254, 255T, 255B, 261,
262T, 262B, 263B, 266, 267, 268, 269,
271T, 272T, 272B, 274, 275, 276T,
276/277B, 277, 278B, 281, 282B, 283,

284, 285B, 285T, 286T, 290T, 292B,
292T, 294, 297, 298, 299T, 299B, 300B,
306T, 307T, 308, 309T, 309B, 312, 315B,
317T, 323, 326, 327B, 327T, 328, 329T,
332, 334T, 334B, 335T, 335B, 336, 337,
338T, 338B, 339B, 340T, 340B, 342B,
343, 346, 348B, 348T, 349, 352
Library of Congress 26/27, 39, 77R,
150
Mass Audubon 190T
MOTT 96
Mount Washington Cog Railway 317B
Norman Rockwell Museum 289B
npa.gov 344T
Public domain 7TR, 24L, 28, 32, 34, 35,
38, 40, 41, 43, 44, 45, 59, 60, 77L, 78L,
116, 155T, 182T, 191, 199T, 231TR, 250
Richard Nowitz/Apa publications
7ML, 8B, 9TL, 29, 33, 42, 47, 49, 56, 57,
70, 71, 72, 80, 82, 83, 90, 102/103, 107,
112, 114, 115T, 117B, 117T, 118, 120T,
121, 123T, 123B, 124T, 124B, 125, 126T,
126B, 127, 128T, 130T, 130B, 131, 133T,
133B, 136, 138BL, 139TR, 143, 144,
151T, 157, 355, 356/357
Robert Harding 9BR, 160BR, 306B, 351
Rolf Müller 291
Shutterstock 10T, 99, 129, 242B
SuperStock 8T, 244B
Warner Bros/Kobal Collection 367

COVER CREDITS

Front cover: The Portland Head
Lighthouse in Maine *iStock*
Back cover: Fall countryside *iStock*
Front flap: (from top) Lobster buoys

iStock; Lobster *iStock*; Church in
Greenfield *iStock*; Skier in Stowe
iStock
Back flap: The colours of fall *iStock*

INSIGHT GUIDE CREDITS

Distribution
UK, Ireland and Europe
Apa Publications (UK) Ltd;
sales@insightguides.com
United States and Canada
Ingram Publisher Services;
ips@ingramcontent.com
Australia and New Zealand
Woodslane; info@woodslane.com.au
Southeast Asia
Apa Publications (SN) Pte;
singaporeoffice@insightguides.com
Worldwide
Apa Publications (UK) Ltd;
sales@insightguides.com
Special Sales, Content Licensing and
CoPublishing
Insight Guides can be purchased in
bulk quantities at discounted prices.
We can create special editions,
personalised jackets and corporate
imprints tailored to your needs.
sales@insightguides.com
www.insightguides.biz

Printed in China by CTPS

All Rights Reserved
© 2018 Apa Digital (CH) AG and
Apa Publications (UK) Ltd

First Edition 1984
Eleventh Edition 2018

No part of this book may be
reproduced, stored in a retrieval
system or transmitted in any form or
means electronic, mechanical,
photocopying, recording or otherwise,
without prior written permission from
Apa Publications.

Every effort has been made to provide
accurate information in this
publication, but changes are
inevitable. The publisher cannot be
responsible for any resulting loss,
inconvenience or injury. We would
appreciate it if readers would call our
attention to any errors or outdated
information. We also welcome your
suggestions; please contact us at:
hello@insightguides.com

www.insightguides.com

Editor: Helen Fanthorpe
Author: Fran Severn and Maciej
Zglinicki
Head of Production: Rebeka Davies
Update Production: Apa Digital
Picture Editor: Tom Smyth
Cartography: original cartography
Mapping Ideas, updated by Carte

CONTRIBUTORS

This edition of one of Insight Guides'
classic titles was thoroughly updated
by **Maciej Zglinicki**. It builds on earlier
editions produced by **Magdalena
Helsztynska, Fran Severn**, and **Bill**
and **Kay Scheller**.
The book was managed by **Helen
Fanthorpe**, and copyedited by her and

Sîan Marsh.
Much of the eye-catching
photography in this book is the work of
Kindra Clineff. Many other
photographs come from **Richard,
Abraham**, and **Daniella Nowitz**.
Penny Phenix indexed the book.

ABOUT INSIGHT GUIDES

Insight Guides have more than 45
years' experience of publishing high-
quality, visual travel guides. We
produce 400 full-colour titles, in both
print and digital form, covering more
than 200 destinations across the
globe, in a variety of formats to meet
your different needs.
Insight Guides are written by local
authors, whose expertise is evident in
the extensive historical and cultural

background features. Each destination
is carefully researched by regional
experts to ensure our guides provide
the very latest information. All the
reviews in **Insight Guides** are
independent; we strive to maintain an
impartial view. Our reviews are
carefully selected to guide you to the
best places to eat, go out and shop, so
you can be confident that when we say
a place is special, we really mean it.

3 1502 00851 0222

Legend

City maps

	Freeway/Highway/Motorway
	Divided Highway
	Main Roads
	Minor Roads
	Pedestrian Roads
	Steps
	Footpath
	Railway
	Funicular Railway
	Cable Car
	Tunnel
	City Wall
	Important Building
	Built Up Area
	Other Land
	Transport Hub
	Park
	Pedestrian Area
	Bus Station
	Tourist Information
	Main Post Office
	Cathedral/Church
	Mosque
	Synagogue
	Statue/Monument
	Beach
	Airport

Regional maps

	Freeway/Highway/Motorway (with junction)
	Freeway/Highway/Motorway (under construction)
	Divided Highway
	Main Road
	Secondary Road
	Minor Road
	Track
	Footpath
	International Boundary
	State/Province Boundary
	National Park/Reserve
	Marine Park
	Ferry Route
	Marshland/Swamp
	Glacier Salt Lake
	Airport/Airfield
	Ancient Site
	Border Control
	Cable Car
	Castle/Castle Ruins
	Cave
	Chateau/Stately Home
	Church/Church Ruins
	Crater
	Lighthouse
	Mountain Peak
	Place of Interest
	Viewpoint

INDEX

MAIN REFERENCES ARE IN BOLD TYPE

A

Abenaki tribe 279, 325
Acadia National Park, ME 97, 338, 339, 342
accommodations 357
activist movements 67
Adams, John 119, 154, 155
Adams, John Quincy 155
Adams, MA 208
Adams, Samuel 38, 119, 121, 152
African-Americans 71, 125, 183, 233, 277
African-American Heritage Trail (Martha's Vineyard, MA) 178
Agawam, MA
Six Flags New England 197
age restrictions 357
agriculture 24, 170, 262. See also farms
Community Supported Agriculture (CSAs) 314
New Hampshire food producers 314
Alcott, Amos Bronson 188
Alcott, Louisa May 124, 153, 153
Algonquin tribes 30, 31, 32, 34, 53, 185
Allagash Wilderness Waterway, ME 96, 347
Allen, Ethan 270, 282, 290
Alvarez, Julia 79
American Indians 340
Amesbury, MA 149
Boat Shop 149
Whittier Home 149
Amherst, MA 198
Amherst College 72, 198
Beneski Museum of Natural History 199
Emily Dickinson Museum 198
Eric Carle Museum of Picture Book Art 199
Mead Art Museum 198
National Yiddish Book Center 199
Amistad slave ship incident 250
Ando, Tadao 91
Anthony, Susan B. 66, 208
Appalachian Gap, VT 272
Appalachian Trail 238, 240, 273, 288, 315, 347
Appleseed, Johnny 191
aquariums
ECHO Lake Aquarium and Science Center (Burlington, VT) 281
Maine State Aquarium (West Boothbay Harbor, ME) 334
Maria Mitchell Association (Nantucket town, MA) 183
Maritime Aquarium (South Norwalk, CT) 248

Mystic Aquarium and Institute for Exploration (Mystic, CT) 255
New England Aquarium (Boston, MA) 116
Woods Hole Science Aquarium (Woods Hold, MA) 176
Aquidneck Island, RI 213, 221
architecture 86, 247
gingerbread houses 87
Arthur, Chester A. 280
art museums and collections
Aldrich Contemporary Art Museum (Ridgefield, CT) 246
Art Complex Museum (Duxbury, MA) 156
Birds of Vermont Museum (Huntington, VT) 283
Bowdoin Museum of Art (Bowdoin College, ME) 331
Brattleboro Museum and Art Center (Brattleboro, VT) 262
Bristol Center for Arts and Culture (Bristol, CT) 238
Cahoon Museum of American Art (Cotuit, MA) 174
Cape Cod Museum of Art (Dennis, MA) 167
Carpenter Center for the Visual Arts (Harvard University, MA) 135
Chaffee Center for the Visual Arts (Rutland, VT) 289
Currier Museum of Art (Manchester, NH) 301
DeCordova Sculpture Park (Lincoln, MA) 154
Eric Carle Museum of Picture Book Art (Amherst, MA) 199
Farnsworth Art Museum and Wyeth Center (Rockland, ME) 335
Florence Griswold Museum (Old Lyme, CT) 252
George Walter Vincent Smith Art Museum (Springfield, MA) 196
Gogswell's Grant (Essex, MA) 148
Granary Gallery at the Red Barn (West Tisbury, MA) 179
Harvard art museums (Harvard University, MA) 135
Hood Museum of Art (Dartmouth College, NH) 307
Institute of Contemporary Art (Boston, MA) 118
Institute of Contemporary Art (Portland, ME) 329
List Art Gallery (Providence, RI) 91
Lyman Allyn Art Museum (New London, CT) 253
Lyme Art Association (Old Lyme, CT) 252

MAC Center for the Arts (Newport, VT) 277
Massachusetts Museum of Contemporary Art (MASS MoCa) (North Adams, MA) 209
Mattatuck Museum Arts and History Center (Waterbury, CT) 245
Michele and Donald D'Amour Museum of Fine Arts (Springfield, MA) 196
Middlebury College Museum of Art (Middlebury, VT) 285
Mill Brook Gallery and Sculpture Garden (Concord, NH) 303
Mills Gallery (Boston, MA) 129
Museum of Fine Arts (MFA) (Boston, MA) 40
National Museum of American Illustration (Newport, RI) 225
New Britain Museum of American Art (New Britain, CT) 245
Newport Art Museum (Newport, RI) 224
Norman Rockwell Museum (Stockbridge, MA) 204
Norman Rockwell Museum (Stockbridge, VT) 290
Ogunquit Museum of American Art (Ogunquit, ME) 326
Portland Museum of Art (Portland, ME) 328
Provincetown Art Association and Museum (Provincetown, MA) 171
Rhode Island School of Design (RISD) Museum (Providence, RI) 216
Sackler Museum (Harvard University, MA) 91
Saint-Gaudens National Historic Site (Cornish, NH) 307
Sharon Arts Center (Peterborough, NH) 304
Silvermine Guild Arts Center (New Canaan, CT) 248
Snowflake Bentley Exhibit (Jericho, VT) 283
Southern Vermont Arts Center (Manchester, VT) 291
Sterling and Francine Clark Art Institute (Williamstown, MA) 208
St. Johnsbury Athenaeum (St, Johnsbury, VT) 275
Thorne-Sagendorph Art Gallery (Keene, NH) 306
Vermont Artisan Designs & Gallery (Brattleboro, VT) 262
Visual Arts Center (Massachusetts Institute of Technology (MIT), MA) 134

Wadsworth Atheneum Museum of Art (Hartford, CT) 233
Wendell Gilley Museum of Bird Carving (Mount Desert Island, ME) 341
Whistler House Museum of Art (Lowell, MA) 150
Worcester Art Museum (Worcester, MA) 191
Yale Center for British Art (Yale University, CT) 250
Yale University Art Gallery (Yale University, CT) 250
Ashley, Col. John 202
Ashley Falls, MA 202
Colonel John Ashley House 202
Atlantic White Cedar Swamp Trail, MA 169
Augusta, ME 350
Children's Discovery Museum 350
Maine State Museum 350
Old Fort Western 350
State House 350

B

Bangor, ME 344
Collins Center for the Arts 347
Hudson Museum 345
Maine Discovery Museum 345
Thomas A. Hill House Museum 345
Bar Harbor, ME 341
Abbe Museum Downtown 341
Bar Harbor Historical Society 341
Barnstable, MA 167
Coast Guard Heritage Museum 167
Great Marsh 167
Barre, VT 269
Hope Cemetery 269
Old Labor Hall 269
Robert Burns Memorial 269
Vermont Granite Museum and Stone Arts School 270
Bash Bish Falls State Park, MA 203
Bass Harbor Head Lighthouse, ME 342
Bates, Katherine Lee
America the Beautiful 175
Bath, ME 332
Bath Iron Works 332
historic district 332
Maine Maritime Museum 332
Battle of Bunker Hill 39
Battle of Concord 151
Battle of Lexington 151
Battle Road 151, 152
Battle Road Trail 153
Baxter Park, ME 288
Baxter State Park, ME 321, 347
beaches
Cape Cod 162, 166, 168
Cape Cod, MA **168**, 172, 174
Connecticut 251, 253
Maine 325, 326, 327, 332, 341
Martha's Vineyard, MA 176, 180
Nantucket Island, MA 180, 184

New Hampshire 299, 308
Rhode Island 222, 228, 229
Vermont 278, 282
Bear Swamp Reservation, MA 210
Beech Mountain, ME 341
Belfast, ME 337
Benjamin, Asher 90
Bennington, VT 292
Bennington Battle Monument 293
Bennington Museum 293
Old First Church 293
Bentley, Wilson 'Snowflake' 283
Berkshire East, MA 209
Berkshire Mountains, MA 288
Berkshires, The, MA 202
Beston, Henry
The Outermost House 169
Bethel, ME 349
Bethel Inn 349
Moses Mason House 349
O'Neil Robinson House 349
Bethlehem, NH 315
Rocks Estate 315
Biddeford, ME 57
Blackstone River Bikeway 92, 219
Blackstone River Greenway 189
Blackstone River State Park, RI 219
Blackstone River Valley 218
boat tours 218
Block, Adriaen 213, 229
Block Island, RI 228
1661 Farm and Gardens 229
Block Island Historical Society 229
ferry 229
hotels 229
Mohegan Bluffs 229
North Lighthouse 229
Old Harbor 229
Rodman's Hollow 229
Southeast Lighthouse 229
State Beach 229
Surfers Beach 229
Blue Hill, ME 339
Rackliffe Pottery 339
Bohjalian, Chris 79
Boothbay Harbor, ME 333
Boothbay Railway Village 334
Boston Bruins 98, 131
Boston Celtics 98, 131
Boston Harbor Island National Recreation Area 137
Boston Landmarks Orchestra 133
Boston, MA 37, 45, 46, 69. See also Brookline; Cambridge
200 Clarendon Street **129**
Athenaeum 40, 121
Back Bay 45, 125
Bay Village 121
Beacon Hill 45, 123, 124
Berklee College of Music 73
Big Dig 130
bike rentals 92
Black Heritage Trail 125
Boch Center 121
Boston Center for the Arts 129
Boston College 72
Boston Common 91, 114, 122
Boston Public Library 42, 91

Boston Tea Party Ships & Museum 117
Bunker Hill Monument 114, 116
Charles River 131
Charles Street and Meeting House 125
Charlestown and Navy Yard 115
Children's Museum 117
Chinatown 119, 120
Christian Science Center 127
Columbus Park 116
Commonwealth Avenue 126
Copley Place 126
Copley Square 128
Copp's Hill Burying Ground 115
Custom House Tower 118
Downtown Crossing 120
Faneuil Hall 118
Fenway Park 131
festivals 139
Freedom Trail **113**
Gibson House Museum 126
Government Center 119
Hancock Tower 91
harbor cruises and ferries 116, 137
HarborWalk 116
Harrison Gray Otis House 124
Hatch Memorial Shell 133
Haymarket Square 119
Hollis Street Church 91
Institute of Contemporary Art 118
Irish Famine Memorial 120
Isabella Stewart Gardner Museum 130
John F. Kennedy Presidential Library and Museum 133
Johnson and Wales University 73
King's Chapel 121
literary sites 132
Long Wharf 116
Louisburg Square 124
Mapparium 127
Museum of African-American History 125
Museum of Fine Arts (MFA) 40, 129, 130
Museum of Science and Science Park 131
National Historical Park **138**
Newbury Street 126
New England Aquarium 116
New England Conservatory of Music 40, 73
New England Holocaust Memorial 118
New England Telephone Company 120
Nichols House Museum 124
North End 113
Old City Hall 121
Old Granary Burying Ground 121
Old North Church 114
Old South Meeting House 119
Old State House 119
Opera House 121

Park Street Church 122
Paul Revere House **114**
Prudential Center 127
Prudential Tower 127
Public Garden 123
Public Library **128**
Quincy Marketplace 90, 118
restaurants 83, 118, 119
shopping 118, 126, 127
Shubert Theater 121
South End 129
State House 89, 91, **123**
Symphony Hall 129
TD Garden 131
Theater District 121
Trinity Church 90, 128
USS Constitution 55, 115
Wang Center for the Performing
   Arts 121
Waterfront 116
Boston Marine Society 115
Boston Massacre 37, 119, 121
Boston Pops 40, 133, 206
Boston Red Sox 98, 131
Boston Symphony Orchestra 40,
   206
Boston Tea Party 38, 117, 119,
   120
re-enactment 120
Bourne, MA
Aptucxet Trading Post and
   Museum 165
Briggs-McDermott House 165
Bowdoin College, ME 72, 331
Bowdoin Museum of Art 331
Peary-MacMillan Arctic
   Museum 331
Bradstreet, Anne 74
Brandon Gap, VT 286
Brandon, VT 287
Brandon Music 287
Hubbardton Battlefield 289
Branford, CT 251
Brant Point, MA 183
Brattleboro, VT 262
Latchis Building 262
Latchis Hotel 262
Vermont Artisan Designs 262
Brenton Point State Park, RI 226
Brewster, MA 167
Cape Cod Museum of Natural
   History 168
Nickerson State Park 168
Stony Brook Mill 167
Bridgeport, CT 249
Barnum Museum 249
Bristol, CT 238
American Clock and Watch
   Museum 238
Bristol Center for Arts and
   Culture 238
Museum of Fire History 238
New England Carousel Museum
   238
Bristol, RI 219, 221
Blithewold Mansion, Gardens
   Arboretum 219
Chapel-by-the-Sea 220
Coggeshall Farm Museum 220
Environmental Education
   Center 220

Herreshoff Marine America's
   Cup Museum 220
Bromley Mountain, VT 292
Brookfield, VT 269
Brookline, MA
John F. Kennedy National
   Historic Site 137
Brooks, Geraldine
Caleb's Crossing 32
Browne, Charles Farrar.
See Ward, Artemus
Brownington, VT 277
Old Stone House Museum 277
Brown, John 217
Brown University, RI 40
Brown, William Wells 76
Brunswick, ME 331, 332. See
also Bowdoin College
Joshua L. Chamberlain
   Museum 331
Pejepscot Historical Society 331
Skolfield-Whittier House 331
Bryant, William Cullen 75, 204,
   210
Bucksport, ME 337
Fort Knox State Park 337
Penobscot Narrows Bridge 337
Bulfinch, Charles 89, 90, 91, 123,
   124
Bulls Bridge Scenic Area 240
Burgess, Thornton 166
Burlington, VT 280
Church Street Marketplace 281
cruises 281
ECHO Lake Aquarium and
   Science Center 281
Ethan Allen Homestead 282
festivals and events 281
Flynn Center for the Performing
   Arts 282
Greenmount Cemetery 282
North Beach 282
Robert Hull Fleming Museum
   282
University of Vermont 72
US Navy Memorial 281
Waterfront and Battery Parks
   281
buses 355
Buzzards Bay, MA 165
National Marine Life Center 165

C

Cabot, John 31, 325
Cabot, VT 275
Cabot Creamery Co-operative
   275
Cadillac Mountain, ME 339, 340
Cahoon, Ralph and Martha 174
Calais, ME 344
Calendar Islands, ME 328
Cambridge, MA 133
Cambridge Common 136
Harvard Square 134
Longfellow House-Washington
   Headquarters National
   Historic Site 137
Radcliffe College. See Harvard
   University, MA
Camden, ME 336

Camden Hills State Park 337
camping 93
Cape Cod, MA 168
Maine 330
New Hampshire 318
Candia, NH 301
Candia Springs Adventure Park
   301
Candia Vineyards 301
Charmingfare Farm 301
Cannon Mountain, NH 313
Aerial Tramway 313
New England Ski Museum 313
Canterbury, CT 242
Prudence Crandall Museum 242
Canterbury, NH 43
Canterbury Shaker Village, NH
   303
Cape Cod Canal, MA 162, 163, 63
Cape Cod Highland Lighthouse,
   MA 170
Cape Cod, MA 62, 60, 181
Cape Cod National Seashore, MA
   166, 62, **168**, 177
biking trails 92
Salt Pond Visitor Center 169
Cape Cod Rail Trail, MA 168, 177
Cape Cod School of Art, MA 171,
   182
Cape Elizabeth, ME 328
Cape Porpoise, ME 327
Captain Roger W. Wheeler State
   Beach, RI 228
carousels 155, 159, 166, 178, 195,
   197, 218, 228, 235, 238
Carter, Stephen L. 79
Casco Bay, ME
cruises 347
casinos 256
Castine, ME 338
Maine Maritime Academy 338
Catamount Trail, VT 98
Chapel Brook Reservation, MA
   210
Chapman, John. See Appleseed,
   Johnny
Chappaquiddick Island, MA 179
Cape Poge Wildlife Refuge 179
Wasque Reservation 179
Charlemont, MA 209
Charlestown, MA 69
Charlestown, NH 306
Fort at Number 4 Living History
   Museum 306
Charlestown, RI 228
Ninigret National Wildlife
   Refuge 228
Charlotte, VT 284
Vermont Wildflower Farm 284
Chatham, MA **173**
Chatham Light 173
Chatham Marconi Maritime
   Center 173
Chatham Railroad Museum 173
Monomoy National Wildlife
   Refuge 173
Cheeshahteaumuck, Caleb 32
Cheever, John 78
Chester, CT 243
Chester, NH
Chester College 73

Chester, VT 265
Green Mountain Flyer 265
Chesuncook, ME 347
children 358
Chilmark, MA 180
churches and meetinghouses 86,
90, 213
Charles Street Meeting House
(Boston, MA) 125
Christian Science Center
(Boston, MA) 127
First Congregational Church
(Nantucket town, MA) 182
Holden Chapel (Harvard
University, MA) 135
Hollis Street Church (Boston,
MA) 91
King's Chapel (Boston, MA) 121
Meeting House of the First
Baptist Church in America
(Providence, RI) 216
Memorial Church (Harvard
University, MA) 135
MIT Chapel (Massachusetts
Institute of Technology (MIT),
MA) 133
Old First Church (Bennington,
VT) 293
Old Indian Meetinghouse
(Mashpee, MA) 174
Old North Church (Boston, MA)
114
Old Ship Meetinghouse
(Hingham, MA) 87
Old South Meeting House
(Boston, MA) 119
Old Whaling Church
(Edgartown, MA) 178
Park Street Church (Boston,
MA) 122
Quaker Meetinghouse
(Nantucket town, MA) 182
Seamen's Bethel (New Bedford,
MA) 159
Touro Synagogue (Newport, RI)
223
Trinity Church (Boston, MA) 90,
128
Trinity Episcopal Church
(Newport, RI) 223
Trinity Park (Oak Bluffs, MA)
177
Union Chapel (Oak Bluffs, MA)
178
West Parish Meetinghouse
(Barnstable, MA) 167
Civil War 42, 279
Clemens, Samuel Langhorne.
See Twain, Mark
climate 358
Colebrook, NH 318
Shrine of Our Lady of Grace
318
Colechester, VT 283
Saint Michael's Playhouse 283
Columbia Falls, ME 342
Ruggles House 342
Columbus, Christopher 31
Comstock, Anthony 116
Concord, MA 35, 38, 151, **152**
Concord Museum 152

North Bridge Visitor Center
151
Old Manse 153
Old North Bridge 153
Orchard House 153
Ralph Waldo Emerson House
154
Sleepy Hollow Cemetery 154
Walden Pond 67, 75, 153, 154
Wayside, The 153
Concord, NH 301
League of New Hampshire
Craftsmen gallery 302
McAuliffe-Shepard Discovery
Center 302
Mill Brook Gallery and
Sculpture Garden 303
Museum of New Hampshire
History 301
Pierce Manse 302
State House 301
Connecticut 107, 288
nicknames 254
Connecticut River 195, 243, 261,
265, 318, 319
Chester-Hadlyme Ferry 243
Connecticut River Valley 243,
306
Connecticut Wine Trail 243
Conway, NH 312
Coolidge, Calvin 197, 268
Cornish, NH 307
Saint-Gaudens National Historic
Site 307
Cornwall, CT 288
Cos Cob, CT 246
Bush-Holley Historic Site 246
**Coskata-Coatue Wildlife Refuge,
MA** 184
cotton 40, 41
Cotuit, MA
Cahoon Museum of American
Art 174
Coventry, CT
Nathan Hale Homestead 242
Strong-Porter House Museum
242
covered bridges 90, 203, 219, 240,
263, 265, 267, 269, 302, 306,
307, 313, 349
Covered Bridge Society 187
crafts 165, 183, 197, 266, 272, 285,
302, 339
Craftsburys, The, VT 276
Craigville Beach, MA 174
Cranberry Bog Trail, MA 170
Cranberry Isles, ME 341, 342
Crandall, Prudence 242
Crawford, Abel and Ethan Allen
317
Crawford Notch, NH 311, 316
Crawford Notch State Park
317
Omni Mount Washington Resort
at Bretton Woods 317
crime and safety 359
Cummington, MA 210
William Cullen Bryant
Homestead 210
Curley, James Michael 45
customs regulations 359

D

Danbury, CT 245
Danbury Museum and Historical
Society 246
Danbury Railway Museum 245
Dartmouth College, NH 40, 70, 71,
307
Hood Museum of Art 307
Dawes, William 37, 38, 114
de Champlain, Samuel 278, 339
Declaration of Independence 38
Dedham, MA 35
Deep River, CT 243
Deerfield, MA 199. See also Old
Deerfield, MA; South Deerfield,
MA
Deer Isle, ME 338
Haystack Mountain School of
Crafts 338
Stonington Opera House 338
Dennis, MA 167
Cape Cod Museum of Art 167
Cape Playhouse 167
Scargo Hill Tower 167
Dennis, MA
Cape Playhouse 167
Derby Line, VT 290
Haskell Free Library and Opera
House 290
Dickinson, Emily 76, 71, 198
Dinosaur State Park, CT 245
disabled access 359
Dixville Notch, NH 55
Balsams Grand Resort Hotel
318
Dixville Notch State Park 318
Dorchester, MA 69
Dorchester, NH 35
Dorset, VT 292
Dorset Inn 292
Douglas, Stephen A. 287
Dover, NH 298
Children's Museum of New
Hampshire 298
Woodman Institute Museum 298
Dresden, ME 332
Pownalborough Courthouse 332
driving 355
Dublin, NH 305
Duxbury, MA 156
Alden House 156
Art Complex Museum 156
King Caesar House 156
Myles Standish Monument State
Reservation 156
Old Burying Ground 156

E

Eagle Island, ME 331
East Burke, VT 276
Kingdom Trails 276
East Haddam, CT 244
Goodspeed Opera House 244
Nathan Hale Schoolhouse 244
Eastham, MA 168, 177
one-room schoolhouse 168
Swift-Daley House 168
East Haven, CT 250
Shore Line Trolley Museum 250

East Sandwich, MA 86
East Windsor, CT 241
  Connecticut Trolley Museum
    241
eating out 360
economy 44, 45, 46, 47, 48
  of New Hampshire 318
Eddy, Mary Baker 127
Edgartown, MA 178
  Edgartown Lighthouse 179
  Martha's Vineyard Museum 178
  Old Whaling Church 178
  Vincent House Museum 178
education 46, 62, 65, 66, 69, 214
electricity 360
Eliot, Charles William 73
Eliot, Reverend John 32
embassies and consulates 360
emergencies 360
Emerson, Ralph Waldo 38, 67,
  113, 153, 154, 182, 274
Emerson, Ralph Waldo 75
Enfield, NH 307
  Enfield Shaker Museum 307
environmental issues 23, 48, 261,
  264
  EarthShare New England 264
  forest conservation 48
  forest restoration 25, 177
  green energy 48, 49
  locavore movement 82, 314
  New England Grassroots
    Environmental Fund 264
Errol, NH 318
Essex Coastal Scenic Byway 145
Essex, CT 243
  Connecticut River Museum 243
  Essex Steam Train and
    Riverboat Ride 243
  Sculpture Mile 241
Essex, MA 148
  Gogswell's Grant 148
  Shipbuilding Museum 148
Essex National Heritage Area
  145
Evans, Barnaby 217
Exeter, NH 299
  American Independence
    Museum 299
  Folsom Tavern 299

F

Fairfield, CT
  Fairfield University 72
Fairfield, VT 280
fall foliage 57, 92, 94, 203, 209,
  240, 261, 288, 305, 308
Fall River, MA 159
  Battleship Cove 159
  Fall River Heritage State Park
    159
  Marine Museum 159
Falls Village, CT 240
Falmouth, MA 175
  Museums on the Green 175
  Spohr's Gardens 175
Farmington, CT 237
  Hill-Stead Museum 237
  Stanley-Whitman House 238
farms 42, 83

1661 Farm and Gardens (Block
  Island, RI) 229
Allenholm Farms (South Hero,
  VT) 278
Billings Farm and Museum
  (Woodstock, VT) 267
Bragg Farm, VT 271
Charmingfare Farm (Candia,
  NH) 301
Coggeshall Farm Museum
  (Bristol, RI) 220
Dakin Farm (Ferrisburg, VT) 285
Dudley Farm (Guilford, CT) 251
Hathaway Farm (Rutland, VT)
  290
Keene Stonewall Farm (Keene,
  NH) 306
Maple Grove Farms (St.
  Johnsbury, VT) 275
Morse Farm Sugar Works, VT
  271
Prescott Farm (Middletown, RI)
  221
Remick Country Doctor
  Museum and Farm
  (Tamworth, NH) 311
Shelburne Farms (Shelburne,
  VT) 284
Shelburne Orchards
  (Shelburne, VT) 284
UVM Morgan Horse Farm
  (Weybridge, VT) 285
Vermont Icelandic Horse Farm
  272
Vermont Wildflower Farm
  (Charlotte, VT) 284
Watson Farm (Jamestown, RI)
  227
White Flower Farm (Litchfield,
  CT) 239
ferries 356
Ferrisburg, VT 284
  Dakin Farm 285
  Rokeby Museum 284
festivals and fairs 57, **360**
  Ancient and Honorable Artillery
    Company parade (Boston,
    MA) 139
  art and crafts events, VT 279
  Battle of Bunker Hill
    re-enactment (Boston, MA)
    139
  Blessing of the Fleet
    (Gloucester, MA) 147
  blueberry festival (Machias, ME)
    343
  Boston Harborfest (Boston, MA)
    139
  Boston Massacre Day (Boston,
    MA) 139
  Boston Tea Party re-enactment
    (Boston, MA) 139
  Bowdoin International Music
    Festival, Brunswick, ME 332
  chamber music festival (Falls
    Village, CT) 240
  classic car rally (Stowe, VT) 274
  Eastern States Exposition (West
    Springfield, MA) 196
  Festival of Fools (Burlington,
    VT) 281

Fourth of July (Bristol, RI) 219
Great Waters Music Festival
  (Wolfeboro, NH) 309
ice harvest (Brookfield, VT) 269
international puppet festival
  (Putney, VT) 262
in The Berkshires 209
Jacob's Pillow Dance Festival
  (Becket, MA) 205
Maine Lobster Festival
  (Rockland, ME) 336
Marlboro Music Festival
  (Marlboro, VT) 262
Newport Folk Festival (Newport,
  RI) 226
Newport Jazz Festival
  (Newport, RI) 226
Norfolk Chamber Music Festival
  (Norfolk, CT) 240
Patriots' Day (Boston, MA) 139
PowWow (Mashantucket Pequot
  Reserve, CT) 256
Prescott Park Arts Festival
  (Portsmouth, NH) 296
Sea Music Festival (Mystic
  Seaport, CT) 256
Southern Vermont Arts & Fine
  Craft Festival (Manchester,
  VT) 279
Stoweflake Hot Air Balloon
  Festival (Stowe, VT) 274
Stowe Winter Carnival (Stowe,
  VT) 274
Tanglewood Music Festival, MA
  40, 206
Vermont Maple Festival (St.
  Albans, VT) 280
WaterFire festival (Providence,
  RI) 215, 217
WaterFire (Providence, RI) 45
financial services industry 46, 214
First Encounter Beach, MA 168
fishing industry 41, 48, 59, 61, 81,
  265, 323, 335, 342
food and drink 81, 314
  blueberries and cranberries 82,
    85, 170, 342, 343
  Boston baked beans 82
  cheese 42, 83, 263, 272, 284,
    285, 312
  cider 272, 284
  clambakes 81
  culinary walking tours
    (Providence, RI) 216
  ice cream 85, 221, 272, 313
  locavore movement 314
  maple syrup 82, 85, 271, 275,
    285, 289
  microbreweries 273, 286
  New England Culinary Institute
    (Montpelier, VT) 270
  Rhode Island specialities 222
  seafood 81, 148
  Vermont Fresh Network 287
  vineyards and wineries 221, 223,
    239, 243, 278, 283, 301, 312
  Whoopie Pies 85
Fort Adams, RI 226
Fort Dummer, VT 262
fossil finds 30
Franconia, NH 313

Robert Frost Place 315
Franconia Notch State Park, NH
313
The Flume 313
Franklin, James 74
Franklin, NH 303
Daniel Webster Birthplace 303
Freeport, ME 330
Wolfe's Neck Woods State Park
331
French and Indian Wars 325
French Canadians 219
French, Daniel Chester 204
Frost, Robert 78, 286, 292, 313
further reading 366

G

Gage, Gen. Thomas 38, 39
Galilee, RI 228
gardens. See parks and gardens
Gardner, Isabella Stewart 131
Garrison, William Lloyd 66, 75,
122, 125
geology 21, 180, 210, 325
Getting Around 354
Getting There 354
Gilbert, Sir Humphrey 31
Gillette Castle State Park, CT 243
Gillette, William 244
Glen, NH 312
Story Land 312
Gloucester, MA 147
Beauport/Sleeper-McCann
House 147
Blessing of the Fleet 147
Cape Ann Museum 147
Gloucester Fishermen's Wives
Memorial 147
Maritime Gloucester 147
Glover, VT 276
Bread & Puppet Theater
Museum 276
Goddard, Dr. Robert 190
Goose Rocks Beach, ME 327
Gorges, Sir Ferdinando 34, 319,
325
Gorham, NH 317
Railroad Museum 317
Gosnold, Bartholomew 181
Grafton Notch State Park, ME
349
Grafton, VT 263
Grafton Historical Society
Museum 263
Grafton Ponds Outdoor Bike
Center 265
Grafton Village Cheese
Company 263
Nature Museum 263
Old Tavern at Grafton 265
Vermont Museum of Mining and
Minerals 263
Grand Island, VT 278
Hyde Cabin and Corners
Schoolhouse 278
granite and marble 21, 46, 263,
269, 270, 289, 325
Graniteville, VT 269
Rock of Ages Quarry 269
Great Barrington, MA 203

Guthrie Center 203
Tom's Toys 203
Great Depression 47
Great Glen Trails, NH 98
Great Wass Island, ME 342
Green Mountain Flyer 265
Green Mountain National Forest
286
Green Mountains, VT 271, 273, 288
Greensboro, VT 276
Greenville, ME 348
Moosehead Marine Museum
348
Greenwich, CT 246
Bruce Museum 246
Greylock State Reservation 207
Griswold, Florence 252
Gropius, Walter 91, 154
Groton, CT 253
Fort Griswold Battlefield State
Park 255
US Naval Submarine Force
Museum 253
USS Nautilus 253
Guilford, CT 251
Dudley Farm 251
Henry Whitfield State Museum
251
Hyland House 251
Thomas Griswold House 251

H

Hadley, MA 198
Hadley Farm Museum 198
Porter-Phelps-Huntington
Historic House Museum 198
Hale, Nathan 253
Hale, Sara Josepha 158
Haliburton, Thomas 254
**Hammonasset Beach State Park,
CT** 251
Hammond Castle, MA 145
Hampton Beach State Park, NH
299
Hancock, John 39, 119, 121, 152
Hancock, MA 43
Hancock Shaker Village, MA 206
Handel and Haydn Society 40
Hanover, NH 307. See
also Dartmouth College, NH
Harrisville, NH 305
Hartford, CT 33, 57, 90
Amistad Center for Art and
Culture 233
Ancient Burying Ground 233
Bushnell Park 235
Butler-McCook House and
Garden and Main Street
History Center 235
Charter Oak Place 233
Connecticut Historical Society
and Museum 237
Connecticut Science Center 235
Connecticut State Capitol 233
Greater Hartford Convention
and Visitors Bureau 233
Harriet Beecher Stowe Center
236
Joseph Steward's Museum of
Curiosities 233

Mark Twain House and Museum
236
Museum of Connecticut History
235
Old State House **233**
Soldiers and Sailors Memorial
Arch 235
State Library 235
transportation 233
Travelers' Tower 235
Wadsworth Athenaeum 42
Wadsworth Atheneum Museum
of Art 233
Harvard, MA
Fruitlands Museum 188
Harvard, Rev. John 69
Harvard University, MA 32, 35, 40,
46, 65, 73, 91, **134**
Botanical Museum 136
Carpenter Center for the Visual
Arts 135
Harvard Museum of Natural
History 136
Holden Chapel 135
Massachusetts Hall 135
Memorial Church 135
Mineralogical and Geological
Museum 136
Museum of Comparative
Zoology 136
Peabody Museum of
Archaeology and Ethnology
136
Radcliffe Institute for Advanced
Study 136
Sackler Museum 91
Semitic Museum 136
Sever Hall 135
tours 135
University Hall 91, 135
Widener Library 135
Harwich and Harwich Port, MA
173
Hawthorne, Charles 170
Hawthorne, Nathaniel 76, 153,
206, 207
Haystack Mountain State Park, CT
240
health and medical care 361
Herring Cove, MA 172
Higgins, George V. 79
Hingham, MA 155
Old Ship Meetinghouse 87
World's End Reservation 155
historic houses 230. See
also architecture
Abigail Adams Birthplace
(Weymouth, MA) 155
Adams National Historical Park
(Quincy, MA) 154
Alden House (Duxbury, MA)
156
Arrowhead (Pittsfield, MA) 207
Asa Stebbins House (Old
Deerfield, MA) 200
Ashley House (Old Deerfield,
MA) 200
Atwood Higgins House
(Wellfleet, MA) 169
Beauport/Sleeper-McCann
House (Gloucester, MA) 147

Belcourt Castle (Newport, RI) 225

Blithewold Mansion, Gardens Arboretum (Bristol, RI) 219

Briggs-McDermott House (Bourne, MA) 165

Butler-McCook House and Garden and Main Street History Center (Hartford, CT) 235

Buttolph-Williams House (Wethersfield, CT) 244

Captain Bangs Hallett House (Yarmouth Port, MA) 167

Captain Nathaniel B. Palmer House (Stonington, CT) 256

Capt. Penniman House (Wellfleet, MA) 169

Castle in the Clouds (Moultonborough, NH) 310

Castle Tucker (Wiscasset, ME) 333

Château-sur-Mer (Newport, RI) 225

Chesterwood (Stockbridge, MA) 204

Colonel John Ashley House (Ashley Falls, MA) 202

Cushing House (Newburyport, MA) 149

Daniel Webster Birthplace (Franklin, NH) 303

Deacon John Grave House (Madison, CT) 251

Ebenezer Fiske House Site (Lexington, MA) 152

Edward Gorey House (Yarmouth Port, MA) 167

Elizabeth Perkins House (York, ME) 326

Ethan Allen Homestead (Burlington, VT) 282

Farnsworth Homestead (Rockland, ME) 336

Forest Hall (New Ipswich, NH) 304

Gardner-Pingree House (Salem, MA) 89

General Henry Knox Museum (Thomaston, ME) 334

Gilbert Stuart Birthplace (Saunderstown, RI) 228

Glass House (New Canaan, CT) 91

Governor John Langdon House (Portsmouth, NH) 297

Gropius House (Lincoln, MA) 154

Hadwen House (Nantucket town, MA) 182

Hall Tavern (Old Deerfield, MA) 200

Hancock-Clarke House (Lexington, MA) 152

Harriet Beecher Stowe Center (Hartford, CT) 236

Harrison Gray Otis House (Boston, MA) 124

Hempstead Houses (New London, CT) 253

Henry Whitfield State Museum (Guilford, CT) 251

Hill-Stead Museum (Farmington, CT) 237

Historic Hildene (Manchester, VT) 291

House of the Seven Gables (Salem, MA) **145**

Hoxie House (Sandwich, MA) 166

Hunter House (Newport, RI) 224

Hyde Cabin and Corners Schoolhouse (Grand Island, VT) 278

Hyland House (Guilford, CT) 251

Jackson House (Portsmouth, NH) 297

Jared Coffin House (Nantucket town, MA) 182

Jethro Coffin House (Nantucket town, MA) 182

John Paul Jones House (Portsmouth, NH) 297

John Whipple House (Ipswich, MA) 148

Justin Morrill Homestead (Strafford, VT) 268

King Caesar House (Duxbury, MA) 156

Kingscote (Newport, RI) 224

Lockwood-Mathews Mansion Museum (Norwalk, CT) 248

Longfellow House-Washington Headquarters National Historic Site (Cambridge, MA) 137

Marble House (Newport, RI) 230, 225

Maria Mitchell home (Nantucket town, MA) 183

Mark Twain House and Museum (Hartford, CT) 236

Moffatt-Ladd House and Garden (Portsmouth, NH) 88

Moffatt-Ladd House & Garden (Portsmouth, NH) 296

Monte Cristo Cottage (New London, CT) 253

Moses Mason House (Bethel, ME) 349

Nathan Hale Homestead (Coventry, CT) 242

Nickels-Sortwell House (Wiscasset, ME) 333

No. 99 Main Street (Nantucket town, MA) 183

Noah Webster House & West Hartford Historical Society (West Hartford, CT) 237

Old Manse (Concord, MA) 153

Oliver Ellsworth Homestead (Windsor, CT) 240

Olson House (Rockland, ME) 336

O'Neil Robinson House (Bethel, ME) 349

Orchard House (Concord, MA) 153

Paper House (Rockport, MA) 148

Park-McCullough House (North Bennington, VT) 293

Parson Capen House (Topsfield, MA) 86

Paul Revere House (Boston, MA) **114**

Pierce Manse (Concord, NH) 302

Porter-Phelps-Huntington Historic House Museum (Hadley, MA) 198

Preservation Society of Newport 224

Ralph Waldo Emerson House (Concord, MA) 154

Robert Frost Place (Franconia, NH) 315

Rocks Estate (Bethlehem, NH) 315

Roosevelt Campobello International Park (Canada) 344

Rosecliff (Newport, RI) 225

Rotch-Jones-Duff House & Garden (New Bedford, MA) 159

Rough Point (Newport, RI) 225

Ruggles House (Columbia Falls, ME) 342

Rundlet-May House (Portsmouth, NH) 297

Saint-Gaudens National Historic Site (Cornish, NH) 307

Skolfield-Whittier House (Brunswick, ME) 331

Smith's Castle (Wickford, RI) 227

Stanley-Whitman House (Farmington, CT) 238

Swift-Daley House (Eastham, MA) 168

Tate House Museum (Portland, ME) 330

The Breakers (Newport, RI) 225

The Elms (Newport, RI) 225

The Mount (Lenox, MA) 205

Thomas Griswold House (Guilford, CT) 251

Three Bricks (Nantucket town, MA) 182

Tobias Lear House (Portsmouth, NH) 297

Two Greeks (Nantucket town, MA) 182

Victoria Mansion (Portland, ME) 329

Wadsworth-Longfellow House (Portland, ME) 329

Warner House (Portsmouth, NH) 297

Wayside, The (Concord, MA) 153

Wedding Cake House (Kennebunk, ME) 327

Wentworth-Coolidge Mansion (Portsmouth, NH) 88, 298

Wentworth-Gardner House (Portsmouth, NH) 297

Whitehall Museum House (Middletown, RI) 222

Whitehorne House (Newport, RI) 223

White Horse Tavern (Newport, RI) 223

Whittier Home (Amesbury, MA) 149

William Cullen Bryant
Homestead (Cummington, MA) 210
Wilson Castle (Proctor, VT) 289
Witch House (Salem, MA) 143
Zimmerman House
(Manchester, NH) 301
history 30, 36
Holderness, NH 310
Squam Lakes Natural Science
Center 310
Holyoke, MA
Children's Museum 197
Holyoke Heritage State Park 197
Volleyball Hall of Fame 197
Wisteriahurst Museum 197
Homer, Winslow 323
Hopper, Edward 170
Housatonic River 203, 238, 240
Housatonic Valley 202
Howells, William Dean 78
Huguenots 34
**Humane Society of the
Commonwealth of
Massachusetts** 63
Huntington, VT 283
Birds of Vermont Museum 283
Hyannis, MA 174
Cape Cod Central Railroad 177
classic sports car collection 174
John F. Kennedy Hyannis
Museum 174
Pirate Adventure on Sea Gypsy
174

I

immigrants 67, 120, 213
Portuguese 181
immigration 44, 56
illegal immigrants 56
Independence Day 54, 57
Indians. *See* Native Americans
Industrial Revolution 54, 66, 107,
150, 189, 203, 214, 218, 219,
264
Internet access 361
**Intra-coastal Waterway (Cape
Cod, MA)** 63
Ipswich, MA 35, 148
Ipswich Museum 148
John Whipple House 148
Irish-Americans 44, 54, 71
Irving, John 79
Isle au Haut, ME 338, 341
Isleford, ME 342
Isleford Historical Museum 342
Isle La Motte, VT 279
Goodsell Ridge Fossil Preserve
279
St. Anne's Shrine 279
Isles of Shoals, NH 297
Italian-Americans 54, 218
Ivoryton, CT 243
Ivoryton Playhouse 243
Museum of Fife and Drum 243

J

Jackson, NH 302
Jamaica State Park, VT 263

James, Henry 78
Jamestown, RI 226, 227
Beavertail Lighthouse and
Museum 227
Beavertail State Park 227
Jamestown Windmill 227
Watson Farm 227
J.A. Skinner State Park 198
Jay Peak, VT 98, 277
Jeffersonville, VT 274
Jericho, VT 283
Old Red Mill and Snowflake
Bentley Exhibit 283
Jewett, Sarah Orne 77
Jewish community 34, 213, 223
Jiminy Peak 208
**John H. Chafee Blackstone River
Valley National Heritage
Corridor** 189, 191, 218
Johnson, Philip 90, 91, 247
Joseph Sylvia State Beach, MA 176

K

Kancamagus Highway, NH 312
Katahdin, ME 98
**Katahdin Woods and Waters
National Monument, ME** 347
Keene, NH 305
Historical Society of Cheshire
County 305
Horatio Colony House Museum
& Nature Preserve 305
Keene State College 306
Keene Stonewall Farm 306
Redfern Arts Center 306
Thorne-Sagendorph Art Gallery
306
Wyman Tavern 305
Kennebunk, ME 327
Brick Store Museum 327
Wedding Cake House 327
Kennebunkport, ME 57, 327
Dock Square 327
Kennebunkport Historical
Society 327
Seashore Trolley Museum 327
Kennedy, John F. 133, 137, 168,
174
Kent, CT 240, 288
Kent Falls State Park 240
Kerouac, Jack 79, 150
Killington, VT 98, 268
Kincaid, Jamaica 79
Kingfield, ME 349
Stanley Museum 349
King Philip's War (1675–76) 35
King, Stephen 79, 345
Kittery, ME 325
Fort McClary State Historic Site
325
Kittery Trading Post 325
Portsmouth Naval Yard 325
Kripalu, MA 206
Kutschera, Maria Augusta 273

L

Lahane, Dennis 79
Lahiri, Jhumpa 79
Lake Champlain Islands, VT 278

Lake Champlain, VT 22, 24, 261,
278, 279, 284, 285, 287
cruises 281
Lake Champlain Maritime
Museum (Vergennes, VT)
285
Lake Compounce Theme Park, CT
238
Lake Memphremagog, VT 277
Lakes Region, NH 308
Lake Sunapee, NH 308
**Lake Umbagog National Wildlife
Refuge** 318
Lake Waramaug State Park, CT
239
Lake Winnipesaukee, NH 308
cruises 308
Lawrence, MA 150
Lawrence Heritage State Park
150
Le Corbusier 91
Lee, Ann 43
Lenox, MA 205
The Mount 205
Lexington, MA 37, 38, 151, **152**
Battle Green 152
Buckman Tavern 152
Ebenezer Fiske House Site 152
Hancock-Clarke House 152
Munroe Tavern 152
Scottish Rite Masonic Museum
& Library 152
Visitor Center 152
LGBTQ issues 170
LGBTQ travelers 361
libraries 42
American Antiquarian Society
(Worcester, MA) 190
Athenaeum (Boston, MA) 40
Beinecke Rare Book and
Manuscript Library (Yale
University, CT) 249
Berkshire Athenaeum
(Pittsfield, MA) 207
Boston Athenaeum (Boston,
MA) 121
Boston Public Library 91, **128**
Forbes Library (Northampton,
MA) 197
Goddard Library (Worcester,
MA) 190
Haskell Free Library and Opera
House (Derby Line, VT) 290
John F. Kennedy Presidential
Library and Museum (Boston,
MA) 133
Nantucket Atheneum
(Nantucket town, MA) 182
National Yiddish Book Center
(Amherst, MA) 199
Providence Atheneum
(Providence, RI) 216
Redwood Library and Atheneum
(Newport, RI) 224
State Library (Hartford, CT) 235
St. Johnsbury Athenaeum (St.
Johnsbury, VT) 275
Widener Library (Harvard
University, MA) 135
lighthouses 229
Connecticut 248, 256

Maine 326, 328, 331, 334, 336, 339, 342, 343, **346**
Massachusetts 156, 169, 170, 173, 178, 179, 180, 181, 183, 184
Rhode Island 226, 227, 229
Lime Rock, CT 288
Lincoln, Abraham 158
Lincoln Gap, VT 272
Lincoln, MA 154
DeCordova Sculpture Park 154
Gropius House 154
Hartwell Tavern 151
Minute Man Visitor Center 151
Lincoln, NH 312
Clark's Trading Post 312
Hobo Railroad 313
Loon Mountain ski area 312
Whale's Tale Water Park 312
Lincoln, RI 219
Lincoln Woods State Park 219
Wilbur Kelly House Museum 219
liquor laws 67, 254
Litchfield, CT 238
Haight-Brown Vineyard 239
Litchfield History Museum 239
Tapping Reeve House and Litchfield Law School 239
White Flower Farm 239
White Memorial Foundation 239
Litchfield Hills, CT 238
literature 74, **79**, 132, 153
Little Compton, RI 221
Sakonnet Vineyards 221
lobsters. See fishing industry
Longfellow, Henry Wadsworth 76, 137
Long Point Wildlife Refuge, MA 179
Lovecraft, H. P. 77
Lowell, Francis Cabot 40
Lowell, MA 57, 150
Boott Cotton Mills Museum 150
Kerouac Memorial 150
Lowell National Historical Park 150
Mill Girls and Immigrants Exhibit 150
National Streetcar Museum 151
New England Quilt Museum 151
Whistler House Museum of Art 150
Lubec, ME 343

M

Machias, ME 342
blueberry festival 343
Burnham Tavern 343
MacMillan, Donald 331
Madison, CT 241, 251
Deacon John Grave House 251
Sculpture Mile 241
Mad River Glen ski area, VT 271
Maine 25, 107, 288, 323
Mamet, David 79
Manchester, CT
Connecticut Fire Museum 241
Manchester, NH 300, 319

Amoskeag Fishways Visitor and Learning Center 300
Amoskeag Mills 300
Currier Museum of Art 301
Majestic Theatre 301
Millyard District 300
Millyard Museum 300
Palace Theatre 301
SEE Science Center 300
Zimmerman House 301
Manchester, VT 290
American Museum of Fly Fishing 291
Equinox Resort & Spa 290
Historic Hildene 291
Orvis 290
shopping 291
Southern Vermont Arts & Fine Craft Festival 279
Manuel F. Correllus State Forest, MA 177
marble. See granite and marble
Marblehead, MA 141
Old Burial Hill 143
Marconi Beach, MA 169
Marconi, Guglielmo 169, 173
maritime trade 39, 41, 59, 60, 323
Marlboro, VT 262
Hogback Mountain Scenic Overlook 263
Marlboro Music Festival 262
Marsh, George Perkins 23
Martha's Vineyard, MA 57, **176**
African-American Heritage Trail 178
East Chop Lighthouse 178
Mashantucket Pequot Reservation, CT 256
Foxwoods Resort Casino 256
Mashantucket Pequot Museum and Research Center 256, 257
Mashpee, MA
Old Indian Meetinghouse 174
Mason, Capt. John 319
Massachusetts 141, 162, 188, 195, 107
Massachusetts Bay Colony 33
Massachusetts Institute of Technology (MIT), MA 46, 72, 91, **133**
Hart Nautical Gallery 134
Kresge Auditorium 134
MIT Chapel 133
MIT Museum 134
Visitor Center 134
Visual Arts Center 134
Mather, Cotton 65, 34
Mather, Increase 67, 65
Matinicus, ME 335
Mayflower 21, 23, 33, 61, 121, 158, 171, 181
Mayhew, Thomas 176
McIntire, Samuel 89
media 361
Melville, Herman 77, 183, 207
Mencken, H. L. 64
Mendon, MA
Southwick's Zoo 192
Menemsha, MA 180
Meredith, NH 309

Winnipesaukee Railroad 309
Merrimack, NH
Anheuser-Busch Brewery and Budweiser Clydesdales 299
Merrimack River 41, 299, 302, 319
Middlebury Gap, VT 286
Middlebury, VT 285
Henry Sheldon Museum of Vermont History 285
Middlebury College 72
Middlebury College Museum of Art 285
Otter Creek Brewing 286
Vermont Folklife Center 285
Middletown, CT 245
Wesleyan College 72
Middletown, RI 221
Boyd's Windmill 221
Norman Bird Sanctuary 222
Paradise School 221
Paradise Valley Park 221
Prescott Farm 221
Sachuest Point National Wildlife Refuge 222
Millay, Edna St. Vincent 336
Miller, Arthur 65
The Crucible 65
Mill River, MA 203
Milton, NH 311
New Hampshire Farm Museum 311
Minute Man National Historical Park 151
Minutemen 37, 38, 151, 152, 153, 305
Mitchell, Maria 183
Mohawk Trail 208
Monadnock State Park, NH 303
money matters 362
Monhegan Island, ME 335
Monomoy, MA 184
Montpelier, VT 270
City Hall Arts Center 271
Lost Nation Theater 271
New England Culinary Institute 73, 270
restaurants 270
Vermont Historical Society and Museum 270
Vermont State House 270
Monument Mountain 204
Moosalamoo National Recreation Area, VT 286
Moosehead Lake, ME 348
cruises 348
float-plane tour 348
Morgan horse 285
Morgan, William G. 197
Morison, Samuel Eliot 61
Mormons 268
Morrill, Justin Smith 268
Mosher, Howard Frank 79
Where the Rivers Run North 275
Moultonborough, NH 310
Castle in the Clouds 310
Loon Center 310
Old Country Store 310
Mount Battie, ME 336
Mount Desert Island, ME 337, **339**. See also Bar Harbor
Abbe Museum 340

Asticou Azalea Garden 341
Asticou Terraces Trail 341
Beehive Trail 340
cruises 341
Echo Lake Beach 341
Mount Desert Island
  Information Center 339
Nature Center 340
Northeast Harbor 341
Park Loop Road 339
Precipice Trail 340
Seal Cove Auto Museum 341
Sieur de Monts Spring 340
Southwest Harbor 341
Thuya Garden and Lodge 341
Wendell Gilley Museum of Bird
  Carving 341
Wild Gardens of Acadia 340
Wildwood Riding Stables 339
Mount Holyoke College, MA 66,
  71
Mount Holyoke Range State Park,
  MA 199
Mount Independence State
  Historic Site, VT 287
Mount Katahdin, ME 289, 288,
  347
Mount Mansfield, VT 261, 274
Mount Monadnock, NH 21, 303
Mount Sunapee Resort, NH 308
Mount Tom State Reservation, MA
  198
Mount Washington, NH 288, 295,
  315
Auto Road 315
Cog Railway 316
Extreme Mount Washington
  316
Sherman Adams Summit
  Building 316
Tip Top House 316
tour van 316
weather conditions 316
Mount Willard, NH 311
movies 367
Amistad 255
Jaws 180
The Perfect Storm 147
The Raid 275
museums
Abbe Museum Downtown (Bar
  Harbor, ME) 341
Abbe Museum (Mount Desert
  Island, ME) 340
Abenaki Tribal Museum
  (Swanton, VT) 279
Albacore Museum (Portsmouth,
  NH) 297
Amazing World of Dr. Suess
  Museum (Springfield, MA)
  196
Ambassador Loeb Visitor
  Center (Newport, RI) 223
American Clock and Watch
  Museum (Bristol, CT) 238
American Independence
  Museum (Exeter, NH) 299
American Museum of Fly
  Fishing (Manchester, VT) 291
American Precision Museum
  (Windsor, VT) 265

Amistad Center for Art and
  Culture (Hartford, CT) 233
Aptucxet Trading Post and
  Museum (Bourne, MA) 165
Archaeology Center (University
  of Connecticut, CT) 242
Ballard Museum of Puppetry
  (University of Connecticut,
  CT) 242
Barnum Museum (Bridgeport,
  CT) 249
Battleship Cove (Fall River, MA)
  159
Beneski Museum of Natural
  History (Amherst, MA) 199
Bennington Museum
  (Bennington, VT) 293
Berkshire Museum (Pittsfield,
  MA) 207
Block Island Historical Society
  (Block Island, RI) 229
Boott Cotton Mills Museum
  (Lowell, MA) 150
Boston Tea Party Ships &
  Museum (Boston, MA) 117
Botanical Museum (Harvard
  University, MA) 136
Bread & Puppet Theater
  Museum (Glover, VT) 276
Brick Store Museum
  (Kennebunk, ME) 327
Bruce Museum (Greenwich, CT)
  246
Bunker Hill Museum (Boston,
  MA) 116
Cape Ann Museum Gloucester,
  MA) 147
Cape Cod Museum of Natural
  History (Brewster, MA) 168
Chatham Marconi Maritime
  Center (Chatham, MA) 173
Chatham Railroad Museum
  (Chatham, MA) 173
Children's Discovery Museum
  (Augusta, ME) 350
Children's Museum (Boston, MA
  117
Children's Museum (Holyoke,
  MA) 197
Children's Museum of Maine
  (Portland, ME) 329
Children's Museum of New
  Hampshire (Dover, NH) 298
Children's Museum (West
  Hartford, CT) 237
Coast Guard Heritage Museum
  (Barnstable, MA) 167
Coast Guard Museum (New
  London, CT) 252
Concord Museum (Concord, MA)
  152
Connecticut Eastern Railroad
  Museum (Willimantic, CT) 242
Connecticut Fire Museum
  (Manchester, CT) 241
Connecticut Historical Society
  and Museum (Hartford, CT)
  237
Connecticut Museum of Natural
  History (University of
  Connecticut, CT) 242

Connecticut River Museum
  (Essex, CT) 243
Connecticut Science Center
  (Hartford, CT) 235
Connecticut Trolley Museum
  (East Windsor, CT) 241
Cottage Museum (Oak Bluffs,
  MA) 178
Custom House Maritime
  Museum (Newburyport, MA)
  149
Danbury Museum and Historical
  Society (Danbury, CT) 246
Danbury Railway Museum
  (Danbury, CT) 245
ECHO Lake Aquarium and
  Science Center (Burlington,
  VT) 281
Emily Dickinson Museum
  (Amherst, MA) 198
Enfield Shaker Museum
  (Enfield, NH) 307
Essex Shipbuilding Museum
  (Essex, MA) 148
Extreme Mount Washington
  (Mount Washington, NH)
  316
Fairbanks Museum and
  Planetarium (St. Johnsbury,
  VT) 275
Fishermen's Museum
  (Pemaquid Point, ME) 334
Fort at Number 4 Living History
  Museum (Charlestown, NH)
  306
Fort Griswold Battlefield State
  Park (Groton, CT) 255
French Cable Station Museum
  (Orleans, MA) 172
Fruitlands Museum (Harvard,
  MA) 188
Gibson House Museum (Boston,
  MA) 126
Grafton Historical Society
  Museum (Grafton, VT) 263
Hadley Farm Museum (Hadley,
  MA) 198
Hart Nautical Gallery
  (Massachusetts Institute of
  Technology (MIT), MA) 134
Harvard Museum of Natural
  History (Harvard University,
  MA) 136
Henry Sheldon Museum of
  Vermont History (Middlebury,
  VT) 285
Heritage Museums & Gardens
  (Sandwich, MA) 166
Higgins Armory Museum
  (Worcester, MA) 191
Highland House Museum
  (Truro, MA) 170
Historical Society of Cheshire
  County (Keene, NH) 305
Horatio Colony House Museum
  & Nature Preserve (Keene,
  NH) 305
Hudson Museum (Bangor, ME)
  345
Hull Lifesaving Museum
  (Nantasket, MA) 156

Institute for American Indian Studies (Washington, CT) 239

Ipswich Museum (Ipswich, MA) 148

Isabella Stewart Gardner Museum (Boston, MA) 130

Isleford Historical Museum (Isleford, ME) 342

John Brown House Museum (Providence, RI) 216, 217

John F. Kennedy Hyannis Museum (Hyannis, MA) 174

John F. Kennedy Presidential Library and Museum (Boston, MA) 133

Johnson and Wales Culinary Arts Museum (Providence, RI) 218

Joseph Smith Memorial and Birthplace (South Royalton, VT) 268

Joseph Steward's Museum of Curiosities (Hartford, CT) 233

Joshua L. Chamberlain Museum (Brunwick, ME) 331

Katherine Hepburn Museum (Old Saybrook, CT) 252

Keeler Tavern Museum (Ridgefield, CT) 246

Kittery Historical and Naval Museum (Kittery, ME) 325

Lake Champlain Maritime Museum (Vergennes, VT) 285

Libby Museum (Wolfeboro, NH) 309

Litchfield History Museum (Litchfield, CT) 239

Luddy/Taylor Connecticut Valley Tobacco Museum (Windsor, CT) 240

Lumberman's Museum (Patten, ME) 347

Lyman and Merrie Wood Museum of Springfield History (Springfield, MA) 196

Maine Discovery Museum (Bangor, ME) 345

Maine Historical Society (Portland, ME) 330

Maine Lighthouse Museum at the Maine Discovery Center (Rockland, ME) 336

Maine Maritime Museum (Bath, ME) 332

Maine State Museum (Augusta, ME) 350

Main Street Museum (White River Junction, VT) 266

Marblehead Museum & Historical Society (Marblehead, MA) 141

Maria Mitchell Natural Science Center (Nantucket town, MA) 183

Marine Museum (Fall River, MA) 159

Marine Narrow Gauge Railroad and Museum (Portland, ME) 330

Mariposa Museum and World Culture Center (Peterborough, NH) 305

Maritime Gloucester (Gloucester, MA) 147

Mark Twain House and Museum (Hartford, CT) 236

Martha's Vineyard Museum (Edgartown, MA) 178

Mashantucket Pequot Museum and Research Center (Mashantucket Pequot Reservation, CT) 257

Mashantucket Pequot Museum and Research Center (Mashantucket Pequot Reservation, CT) 256

Mattatuck Museum Arts and History Center (Waterbury, CT) 245

McAuliffe-Shepard Discovery Center (Concord, NH) 302

Mead Art Museum (Amherst, MA) 198

Memorial Hall Museum (Old Deerfield, MA) 200

Millyard Museum (Manchester, NH) 300

Mineralogical and Geological Museum (Harvard University, MA) 136

Mission House (Stockbridge, MA) 204

MIT Museum (Massachusetts Institute of Technology (MIT), MA) 134

Montshire Museum of Science (Norwich, NH) 307

Moosehead Marine Museum (Greenville, ME) 348

Mt. Kearsarge Indian Museum (Warner, NH) 303

Museum at Portland Head Light (Portland, ME) 328

Museum of African-American History (Boston, MA) 125

Museum of African American History (Nantucket town, MA) 182

Museum of Comparative Zoology (Harvard University, MA) 136

Museum of Connecticut History (Hartford, CT) 235

Museum of Fife and Drum (Ivoryton, CT) 243

Museum of Fine Arts (MFA) (Boston, MA) 129, 130

Museum of Fire History (Bristol, CT) 238

Museum of Natural History and Planetarium (Providence, RI) 218

Museum of New Hampshire History (Concord, NH) 301

Museum of Newport History (Newport, RI) 223

Museum of Russian Icons (Clinton, MA) 200

Museum of Science and Science Park (Boston, MA) 131

Museums on the Green (Falmouth, MA) 175

Mystic Seaport, The Museum of America and the Sea (Mystic, CT) 255

Nantucket Lightship Basket Museum (Nantucket town, MA) 183

Nantucket Shipwreck and Life-Saving Museum (Nantucket Island, MA) 184

National Streetcar Museum (Lowell, MA) 151

Nature Center (Mount Desert Island, ME) 340

Nature Museum (Grafton, VT) 263

Naumkeag Museum and Gardens (Stockbridge, MA) 204

New Bedford Whaling Museum (New Bedford, MA) 60, 159

New Canaan Historical Society (New Canaan, CT) 248

New England Air Museum (Windsor Locks, CT) 241

New England Carousel Museum (Bristol, CT) 238

New England Maple Museum (Pittsford, VT) 289

New England Pirate Museum (Salem, MA) 144

New England Quilt Museum (Lowell, MA) 151

New England Ski Museum (Cannon Mountain, NH) 313

New Hampshire Antique and Classic Boat Museum (Wolfeboro, NH) 309

New Hampshire Farm Museum (Milton, NH) 311

Nichols House Museum (Boston, MA) 124

Old Lighthouse Museum (Stonington, CT) 256

Old Lincoln County Jail and Museum (Wiscasset, ME) 333

Old State House (Boston, MA) 119

Old Stone House Museum (Brownington, VT) 277

Old Sturbridge Village (Sturbridge, MA) 192

Owl's Head Transportation Museum (Rockland, ME) 336

Peabody Essex Museum (Salem, MA) 42, 60, **144**

Peabody Museum of Archaeology and Ethnology (Harvard University, MA) 136

Peabody Museum of Natural History (Yale University, CT) 250

Peary-MacMillan Arctic Museum (Bowdoin College, ME) 331

Pejepscot Historical Society (Brunswick, ME) 331

Penobscot Marine Museum (Searsport, ME) 337

Pilgrim Hall Museum (Plymouth, MA) 157

Porter-Phelps-Huntington Historic House Museum (Hadley, MA) 198
Provincetown Museum (Provincetown, MA) 171
Prudence Crandall Museum (Canterbury, CT) 242
Railroad Museum (Gorham, NH) 317
Robert Frost Stone House Museum (Shaftsbury, VT) 292
Robert Hull Fleming Museum (Burlington, VT) 282
Rokeby Museum (Ferrisburg, VT) 284
Sabbathday Lake Shaker Community museum, ME 350
Salem Witch Museum (Salem, MA) 143
Sandwich Glass Museum (Sandwich, MA) 165
Science Museum (Springfield, MA) 196
Scottish Rite Masonic Museum & Library (Lexington, MA) 152
Seacoast Science Center (Rye, NH) 298
Seal Cove Auto Museum (Mount Desert Island, ME) 341
Seashore Trolley Museum (Kennebunkport, ME) 327
SEE Science Center (Manchester, NH) 300
Semitic Museum (Harvard University, MA) 136
Shelburne Falls Trolley Museum (Shelburne Falls, MA) 210
Shelburne Museum (Shelburne, VT) 283
Shore Line Trolley Museum (East Haven, CT) 250
Ski Museum (Stowe, VT) 273
Slater Mill Living History Museum (Pawtucket, RI) 219
Smith College Museum of Art (Smith College, MA) 197
Springfield Armory National Historic Site (Springfield, MA) 195
Springfield Museums at the Quadrangle (Springfield, MA) 195
St. Albans Historical Museum (St. Albans, VT) 280
Stamford Museum and Nature Center (Stamford, CT) 247
Stanley Museum (Kingfield, ME) 349
Stepping Stones Museum for Children (Norwalk, CT) 248
Storrowton Village Museum (West Springfield, MA) 196
Strong-Porter House Museum (Coventry, CT) 242
Sugar Hill Historical Museum (Sugar Hill, NH) 315
Susan B. Anthony Birthplace (Adams, MA) 208

Tapping Reeve House and Litchfield Law School (Litchfield, CT) 239
The Peterborough Historical Society (Peterborough, NH) 304
Thomas A. Hill House Museum (Bangor, ME) 345
Tip Top House (Mount Washington, NH) 316
Titanic Historical Society (Springfield, MA) 196
US Naval Submarine Force Museum (Groton, CT) 253
USS Constitution Museum (Boston, MA) 115
Vermont Granite Museum and Stone Arts School (Barre, VT) 270
Vermont Historical Society and Museum (Montpelier, VT) 270
Vermont Marble Museum (Proctor, VT) 289
Vermont Museum of Mining and Minerals (Grafton, VT) 263
Vermont Toy & Train Museum (Quechee, VT) 267
Village of Canterbury, NH 43
Village of Hancock, MA 43
Vincent House Museum (Edgartown, MA) 178
Wadsworth Athenaeum (Hartford, CT) 42
Webb-Deane-Stevens Museum (Wethersfield, CT) 244
Wethersfield Historical Society (Wethersfield, CT) 244
Whaling Museum (Nantucket town, MA) 60, 181
White Memorial Foundation (Litchfield, CT) 239
Whydah Pirate Museum (Provincetown, MA) 171
Wilbur Kelly House Museum (Lincoln, RI) 219
William Benton Museum of Art (University of Connecticut, CT) 242
Windham Textile and History Museum (Willimantic, CT) 242
Wisteriahurst Museum (Holyoke, MA) 197
Witch Dungeon Museum (Salem, MA) 143
Witch History Museum (Salem, MA) 143
Wolfeboro Historical Society (Wolfeboro, NH) 309
Woodman Institute Museum (Dover, NH) 298
Woods Hole Oceanographic Institution (Woods Hole, MA) 175
Woodstock Historical Society (Woodstock, VT) 267
Worcester Historical Museum (Worcester, MA) 189, 190
Wright Museum of World War II (Wolfeboro, NH) 309

Yale Collection of Musical Instruments (Yale University, CT) 250
music venues 245, 273, 291. See also theaters and performing arts centers
Hatch Memorial Shell (Boston, MA) 133
in Springfield, MA 196
Institute of Sacred Music (Yale University, CT) 250
Symphony Hall (Boston, MA) 129
Tanglewood, MA 206
Truro Center for the Arts (Truro, MA) 170
Woolsey Hall (Yale University, CT) 250
Mystic, CT 255. See also Mystic Seaport, CT
Mystic Aquarium and Institute for Exploration 255
Mystic Seaport, CT 255
Charles W. Morgan (ship) 60, 256

N

Naismith, Dr James 195
Nantasket, MA 155
Fort Revere Park 156
Hull Lifesaving Museum 156
Paragon Carousel 155
Nantucket Island, MA 180
Black Heritage Trail 183
Nantucket Shipwreck and Life-Saving Museum 184
transportation 184
Nantucket town, MA 60, 180, 181
First Congregational Church 182
Hadwen House 182
Jared Coffin House 182
Jethro Coffin House 182
Maria Mitchell Association 183
Museum of African American History 182
Nantucket Atheneum 182
Nantucket Historical Association 181
Nantucket Lightship Basket Museum 183
National Landmark Historic District 181
No. 99 Main Street 183
Old Gaol 182
Old Mill 182
Old South Wharf 181
Quaker Meetinghouse 182
shopping 181
Straight Wharf 181
Three Bricks 182
Two Greeks 182
Upper Main Street 181
Whaling Museum 60, 181
Narragansett, RI 228
Narragansett tribe 34, 35, 228
Nash, Timothy 316
Nashua, NH 319
national and state parks
Acadia National Park, ME 97, 338, 339, 342

Bash Bish Falls State Park, MA 203
Baxter State Park, ME 347
Beavertail State Park, RI 227
Blackstone River and Canal Heritage State Park (Uxbridge, MA) 192
Blackstone River State Park 219
Brenton Point State Park, RI 226
Cape Cod National Seashore, MA 92, 166, 62, 168, 177
Crawford Notch State Park, NH 317
Dinosaur State Park, CT 245
Dixville Notch State Park (Dixville Notch, NH) 318
Fall River Heritage State Park, MA 159
Fort Adams State Park, RI 226
Fort Griswold Battlefield State Park, CT 255
Franconia Notch State Park, NH 313
Gillette Castle State Park, CT 243
Grafton Notch State Park, ME 349
Hammonasset Beach State Park, CT 251
Hampton Beach State Park, NH 299
Haystack Mountain State Park, CT 240
Holyoke Heritage State Park, MA 197
Jamaica State Park, VT 263
J.A. Skinner State Park, MA 198
Kent Falls State Park, CT 240
Lake Waramaug State Park, CT 239
Lawrence Heritage State Park, MA 177
Lily Bay State Park, ME 348
Lincoln Woods State Park, RI 219
Manuel F. Correllus State Forest, MA 177
Marsh-Billings-Rockefeller National Historical Park (Woodstock, VT) 267
Monadnock State Park 303
Mount Holyoke Range State Park, MA 199
Natural Bridge State Park, MA 209
Nickerson State Park, MA 168
Odiorne Point State Park, NH 298
Quechee State Park, VT 266
Quoddy Head State Park, ME 343
Rhododendron State Park, NH 304
Roque Bluffs State Park, ME 342
Sherwood Island State Park, CT 249
Western Gateway Heritage State Park, MA 209
White Mountain National Forest, NH 311

Native Americans 23, 31, 34, 53, 71, 172, 209, 239, 257. See also names of tribes
Natural Bridge State Park, MA 209
nature reserves
Bear Swamp Reservation, MA 210
Broad Meadow Brook Wildlife Sanctuary (Worcester, MA) 189, 191
Cape Poge Wildlife Refuge (Chappaquiddick Island, MA) 179
Chapel Brook Reservation, MA 210
Coskata-Coatue Wildlife Refuge (Nantucket Island, MA) 184
Great Wass Island, ME 342
Horatio Colony House Museum & Nature Preserve (Keene, NH) 305
Lake Umbagog National Wildlife Refuge 318
Long Point Wildlife Refuge (Martha's Vineyard, MA) 179
Loon Center (Moultonborough, NH) 310
Missisquoi National Wildlife Refuge (Swanton, VT) 279
Monomoy National Wildlife Refuge (Chatham, MA) 173
Moosehorn National Wildlife Refuge, ME 344
Mount Tom State Reservation, MA 198
National Estuarine Research Reserve at Laudholm (Wells, ME) 327
Ninigret National Wildlife Refuge (Charlestown, RI) 228
Norman Bird Sanctuary (Middletown, RI) 222
Parker River National Wildlife Refuge, MA 149, 150
Sachuest Point National Wildlife Refuge (Middletown, RI) 222
Squam Lakes Natural Science Center 310
Stewart B. McKinney National Wildlife Refuge, CT 248
Trustom Pond National Wildlife Refuge (South Kingston, RI) 228
Wasque Reservation (Chappaquiddick Island, MA) 179
Wellfleet Bay Wildlife Sanctuary (Wellfleet, MA) 170
World's End Reservation (Hingham, MA) 155
Nauset Beach, MA 172
Nauset Light Beach, MA 169
New Bedford, MA 57, 60, 158
New Bedford Whaling Museum 60, 159
New Bedford Whaling National Historical Park 158
Rotch-Jones-Duff House & Garden 159
Seamen's Bethel 159

New Britain, CT 245
New Britain Museum of American Art 245
Walnut Hill Park 245
Newburyport, MA 45, 89, 149
Cushing House 149
Custom House Maritime Museum 149
Joppa Flats Education Center 148
Market Square 149
New Canaan, CT 247
Glass House 91
New Canaan Historical Society 248
New Canaan Nature Center 248
Philip Johnson's Glass House 247
Silvermine Guild Arts Center 248
New England Patriots 98
Newfane, VT 263
New Hampshire 107, 288, 295
motto 295, 301
New Hampshire Ice Cream Trail 313
New Hampshire School of Falconry 303
New Hampshire Wine and Cheese Trails 312
New Haven, CT 33, 246, 249. See also Yale University
Grove Street Cemetery 250
Long Wharf Theater 250
Shubert Theater 247, 250
New Haven Symphony Orchestra 250
New Ipswich, NH 304
Forest Hall 304
New London, CT 46, 252
Hempstead Houses 253
Lyman Allyn Art Museum 253
Monte Cristo Cottage 253
Ocean Beach Park 253
US Coast Guard Academy and Museum 55, 252
New Marlborough, MA 203
Newport, RI 63, 222, 213
Ambassador Loeb Visitor Center 223
Belcourt Castle 225
Bowen's Wharf 223
Château-sur-Mer 225
Cliff Walk 226
Fort Adams State Park 226
Hunter House 224
International Tennis Hall of Fame 222, 224
Kingscote 224
Marble House 230, 225
Museum of Newport History 223
National Museum of American Illustration 225
Newport Art Museum 224
Newport Folk Festival 226
Newport Jazz Festival 226
Ocean Drive 223, 226
Preservation Society of Newport 224
Redwood Library and Atheneum 224

Rosecliff 225
Rose Island lighthouse 226
Rough Point 225
The Breakers 225
The Elms 225
Touro Synagogue 223
Trinity Episcopal Church 223
Visitor Information Center
    Visitor 223
Whitehorne House 223
White Horse Tavern 223
Newport, VT 277
MAC Center for the Arts 277
South Bay Wildlife Management
    Area 277
New Preston, CT 239
Newry, ME 349
Artists' Covered Bridge 349
Sunday River Ski Resort 349
Nipmuc tribe 35
Norfolk, CT 240
Ellen Battell Stoeckel Estate 240
North Adams, MA 209
Massachusetts Museum of
    Contemporary Art (MASS
    MoCa) 209
Western Gateway Heritage State
    Park 209
Northampton, MA 197. *See
    also* Smith College, MA
Forbes Library 197
Smith College 72
North Bennington, VT 293
Park-McCullough House 293
North Conway, NH 98, 312
Conway Scenic Railroad 312
Northeast Kingdom, VT 274
Northern Forest Canoe Trail 96
North Hampton State Beach, NH
    299
North Haven, ME 335
Norwalk, CT 248
Lockwood-Mathews Mansion
    Museum 248
Stepping Stones Museum for
    Children 248
Norwich, NH 307
Montshire Museum of Science
    307

O

Oak Bluffs, MA 177
Cottage Museum 178
Flying Horses Carousel 178
Trinity Park 177
Union Chapel 178
Obama, Barak 176
Ogunquit, ME 326
Marginal Way 326
Ogunquit Museum of American
    Art 326
Ogunquit Playhouse 326
town beach 326
Old Deerfield, MA 88, 199
Asa Stebbins House 200
Ashley House 200
Channing Blake Meadow Walk
    200
Hall Tavern 200
Memorial Hall Museum 200

Old Lyme, CT 252
Florence Griswold Museum
    252
Lyme Academy College of Fine
    Arts 73
Lyme Art Association 252
Old Man of the Mountain, NH 295,
    310, 313
Old Orchard Beach, ME 327
Old Saybrook, CT 251
Fort Saybrook Monument Park
    251
James Pharmacy 251
Katharine Hepburn Cultural
    Arts Center 252
Olmsted, Frederick Law 155
O'Neill, Eugene 78, 253
opening hours 362
Oppenheim, James
Bread and Roses 150
Orford, NH 308
Orford–Indian Pond Heritage
    Trail 308
Orleans, MA 172
French Cable Station Museum
    172
Orvis, Charles 290
Orvis, Franklin 290
Ossipee Lake, NH 311
Otis, Harrison Gray 90, 124
Otis, James 119

P

**Pairpoint Glass Works, Cape Cod,
    MA** 165
**Parker River National Wildlife
    Refuge, MA** 149, 150
Parker, Robert B. 79
Parker's Island, ME
Fort St George 32
parks and gardens
Ashintully Gardens (Tyringham,
    MA) 205
Asticou Azalea Garden (Mount
    Desert Island, ME) 341
Bartholomew's Cobble
    (Sheffield, MA) 203
Bartlett Arboretum and
    Gardens (Stamford, CT) 247
Blithewold Mansion, Gardens
    Arboretum (Bristol, RI) 219
Boston Common (Boston, MA)
    122
Bridge of Flowers (Shelburne
    Falls, MA) 210
Bushnell Park (Hartford, CT)
    235
Columbus Park (Boston, MA)
    116
Dr. Seuss National Memorial
    Sculpture Garden
    (Springfield, MA) 196
Elizabeth Park (West Hartford,
    CT) 237, 238
Forest Park (Springfield, MA)
    196
Fort Revere Park (Nantasket,
    MA) 156
Fort Saybrook Monument Park
    (Old Saybrook, CT) 251

Green Animals Topiary Garden
    (Portsmouth, RI) 221
Heritage Museums & Gardens
    (Sandwich, MA) 166
Magic Wings Butterfly
    Conservatory and Gardens
    (South Deerfield, MA) 199
Naumkeag Museum and
    Gardens (Stockbridge, MA)
    204
North Hampton and Fuller
    Gardens (Rye, NH) 299
Paradise Valley Park
    (Middletown, RI) 221
Prescott Park (Portsmouth, NH)
    296
Prospect Terrace (Providence,
    RI) 216
Public Garden (Boston, MA) 123
Roger Williams Park
    (Providence, RI) 218
Rotch-Jones-Duff House &
    Garden (New Bedford, MA)
    159
Smith College arboretum,
    gardens and Lyman
    Conservatory (Smith College,
    MA) 197
Spohr's Gardens (Falmouth,
    MA) 175
Tarbin Gardens, NH 308
Thuya Garden and Lodge
    (Mount Desert Island, ME)
    341
Walnut Hill Park (New Britain,
    CT) 245
Waterfront and Battery Parks
    (Burlington, VT) 281
Waterplace Park and Riverwalk
    (Providence, RI) 215
White Flower Farm (Litchfield,
    CT) 239
Wild Gardens of Acadia (Mount
    Desert Island, ME) 340
Passamaquoddy tribes 344
Patriots Day 54
Patten, ME
Lumberman's Museum 347
Pawtucket, RI 40, 218, 227
Blackstone Valley Explorer 218
Blackstone Valley Visitor Center
    218
Slater Mill Living History
    Museum 219
Peary, Robert E. 331
Pei, I.M. 91, 129, 133, 328
Pemaquid Point, ME 334
Colonial Pemaquid State
    Historic Site 334
Fishermen's Museum 334
Fort William Henry 334
Lighthouse Park 334
people 53
Pequot tribes 35, 256, 257
Peterborough, NH 304
MacDowell Colony 304
Mariposa Museum and World
    Culture Center 305
Peterborough Historical Society
    304
Sharon Arts Center 304

Peters, Rev. Samuel 254
pets 363
Phippsburg Peninsula, ME 332
Pico Peak, VT 268
Picoult, Jodi 79
Pierce, Franklin 302
Pilgrims 21, 23, 30, 33, 53, 54, 156, 158, 172
Pinkham Notch, NH 98, 315
  Visitor Center 315
pioneers 319
Pioneer Valley, MA 195
Pittsfield, MA 207
  Barrington Stage Company 207
  Berkshire Museum 207
Pittsford, VT 289
  New England Maple Museum 289
plantlife 320, 321
Plimoth Plantation, MA 157
Plum Island 148
Plymouth, MA 33, 61, 156
  Burial Hill 157
  Coles Hill 157
  Jenney Grist Mill 157
  Mayflower II (replica) 157
  Pilgrim Hall Museum 157
  Plymouth Rock 156
Plymouth Rock, MA 33
Plymouth, VT 267
  President Calvin Coolidge State Historic Site 267
Poe, Edgar Allan 216
Point Judith, RI 228
politics 44, 45, 47, 49, 55, 66
Popham Beach State Park, ME 332
Port Clyde, ME 335
Portland, ME 45, 328
  Children's Museum of Maine 329
  Institute of Contemporary Art 329
  Maine Historical Society 330
  Marine Narrow Gauge Railroad and Museum 330
  Merrill Auditorium 329
  Old Port 328
  Portland Museum of Art 328
  Portland Observatory 330
  Portland Stage Company 329
  Portland Trolley 328
  State Theatre 329
  Tate House Museum 330
  Victoria Mansion 329
  Wadsworth-Longfellow House 329
Portsmouth, NH 296
  Albacore Museum 297
  cruises 297
  Governor John Langdon House 297
  Jackson House 297
  John Paul Jones House 297
  Market Square 296
  Moffatt-Ladd House and Garden 88, 296
  Portsmouth Harbor Trail 296
  Prescott Park 296
  Prescott Park Arts Festival 296
  Rundlet-May House 297

Strawbery Banke 296
  Tobias Lear House 297
  Warner House 297
  Water Country 297
  Wentworth-Coolidge Mansion 88, 298
  Wentworth-Gardner House 297
Portsmouth, RI 221
  Green Animals Topiary Garden 221
Portuguese-Americans 54, 218
postal services 363
Prescott, Col. William 39
Prescott, Dr. Samuel 37
Proctor, VT 289
  Vermont Marble Museum 289
  Wilson Castle 289
Profile Lake, NH 313
Providence, RI 34, 45, 57, 72, 213, 214
  Arcade 90
  Atheneum 216
  Benefit Street 215
  Brown University 70, 217
  College Hill 217
  Federal Hill 217
  John Brown House Museum 216, 217
  Johnson and Wales Culinary Arts Museum 218
  Kennedy Plaza 215
  List Art Gallery 91
  Little Italy 217
  Meeting House of the First Baptist Church in America 216
  Museum of Natural History and Planetarium 218
  Prospect Terrace 216
  Providence Place 215
  restaurants 215
  Rhode Island School of Design (RISD) 73
  Rhode Island School of Design (RISD) Museum 216
  Roger Williams Park 218
  shopping 215, 217
  State Capitol 215
  WaterFire festival 45, 215, 217
  Waterplace Park and Riverwalk 215
Provincetown, MA 170, 181
  art colony 182
  Dune Shacks 172
  Pilgrim Monument 171
  Province Lands Visitor Center 172
  Provincetown Art Association and Museum 171
  Provincetown Museum 171
  shopping 170
  transportation 170
  Whydah Pirate Museum 171
public holidays 363
Puritans 23, 32, 33, 34, 64, 66, 67, 116
Putney, VT 262
  international puppet festival 262
  Sandglass Theater 262
Pynchon, Thomas 77
Pynchon, William 116

Q
Quabbin Reservoir 192
Quakers 34, 213
Quechee, VT 266
  Quechee Gorge 266
  Quechee Gorge Village 266
  Quechee Polo Club 267
  Quechee State Park 266
  The Mill at Quechee 266
  Vermont Institute of Natural Science 266, 267
  Vermont Toy & Train Museum 267
Quincy, MA
  Adams National Historical Park 154
Quoddy Head State Park, ME 343

R
Race Point Beach, MA 172
Radcliffe College, MA 66
Rangeley Lakes region, ME 350
Rangeley, ME 350
restaurants 83
Revere, Paul 37, 38, 114, 121, 152
Revolutionary War 38, 325
  in Maine 343
  in Massachusetts 122, 151, 185
  in New Hampshire 299, 319
  in Vermont 270, 287, 293
Rhode Island 107
Rhododendron State Park, NH 304
Richardson, Mary
  The Capture and Restoration of Mrs. Mary Richardson 35
Ridgefield, CT 246
  Aldrich Contemporary Art Museum 246
  Keeler Tavern Museum 246
Rindge, NH 304
  Cathedral of the Pines 304
Ripton, VT 286
  Bread Loaf Inn 286
  Robert Frost Interpretive Trail 286
Robinson, Edward Arlington 78
Robinson, Rowland 77
Rockland, ME 335, 336
  Farnsworth Art Museum and Wyeth Center 335
  Farnsworth Homestead 336
  Maine Lighthouse Museum at the Maine Discovery Center 336
  Olson House 336
  Owl's Head Transportation Museum 336
Rockport, MA 148
  Paper House 148
Rockport, ME 336
Rockwell, Norman 204, 290
Rocky Neck Art Colony, MA 147
Roger, Henry Ward 252
Roosevelt Campobello International Park (Canada) 344
Roosevelt, Franklin Delano 158, 344
Roque Bluffs State Park, ME 342

Rose Island, RI 226
Roth, Philip 79
Russo, Richard 79
Rutland, VT 45, 289
  Chaffee Center for the Visual
    Arts 289
  Hathaway Farm 290
  Paramount Theater 289
Rye, NH 298
  North Hampton and Fuller
    Gardens 299
  Odiorne Point State Park 298
  Seacoast Science Center 298
  Wallis Sands State Beach 299

S

Saarinen, Eero 91, 133, 206
Sabbathday Lake Shaker
  Community, ME 43, 350
Saddleback ski area, ME 350
Sages Ravine, MA 288
Salem, MA 33, 34, 89, **143**. See
  also witches
  Chestnut Street National
    Historic Landmark 89
  Gardner-Pingree House 89
  House of the Seven Gables **145**
  New England Pirate Museum
    144
  Peabody Essex Museum 42, 60,
    144
  Pioneer Village **145**
  Salem Maritime National
    Historic Site 144
  Salem Witch Museum 143
  Salem Witch Trials Tercentenary
    Memorial 143
  Witch Dungeon Museum 143
  Witch History Museum 143
  Witch House 143
Sandwich, MA 165
  Dexter Grist Mill 166
  Greenbriar Nature Center 166
  Heritage Museums & Gardens
    166
  Hoxie House 166
  Sandwich Glass Museum 165
Sandy Neck Beach, MA 166
Sargeant, John 204
Saugus Iron Works National
  Historic Site, MA 141
Saunderstown, RI 228
  Gilbert Stuart Birthplace 228
Schoodic Point, ME 342
Schumann, Peter 276
Seal Island, ME 339
Sears, Clara Endicott 188
Searsport, ME 337
  Penobscot Marine Museum 337
Sebago Lake, ME 330
Sebago Lake State Park, ME 330
Shaftsbury, VT 292
  Robert Frost Stone House
    Museum 292
Shakers 43, 206, 350
Sheffield Island, CT 248
Sheffield, MA 203
  Bartholomew's Cobble 203
Shelburne Falls, MA 210
  Bridge of Flowers 210

Salmon Falls Glacial Potholes
  210
Shelburne Falls Trolley
  Museum 210
Shelburne, VT 283
  restaurants 284
  Shelburne Country Store 284
  Shelburne Farms 284
  Shelburne Museum 283
  Shelburne Orchards 284
  Shelburne Vineyard Winery and
    Tasting Room 283
  Vermont Teddy Bear 283
shellfish 82
Sherwood Island State Park, CT
  249
Shining Sea Bikeway, MA 175,
  177
shipbuilding 41, 47, 59, 61, 148,
  149, 243, 255, 323, 327, 332,
  337
shopping 67, **363**
  antiques 149, 203, 296, 325
  discount malls 325
  L.L.Bean (Freeport, ME) 330
  Orvis (Manchester, VT) 290
  used books 325
Siasconset, MA 184, 185
Skaket Beach, MA 173
Skyline Drive, VT 291
Slater, Samuel 40
slavery, abolition of 66, 75, 122
Smith College, MA 66, 197
  Smith College arboretum,
    gardens and Lyman
    Conservatory 197
  Smith College Museum of Art
    197
Smith, John 32
Smith, Joseph 268
smoking 364
Smugglers' Notch Resort, VT 274
Somes Sound, ME 341
Sons of Liberty 37
South Beach, MA 176
South Deerfield, MA 199
  Magic Wings Butterfly
    Conservatory and Gardens
    199
  Yankee Candle Company 199
South Dennis, MA 173
South Hadley, MA 198
  Mount Holyoke College 72, **198**
South Hero, VT 278
  Allenholm Farms 278
  Snow Farm Vineyard 278
South Kingston, RI 228
  Trustom Pond National Wildlife
    Refuge 228
South Norwalk, CT 248
  Maritime Aquarium 248
South Royalton, VT 268
  Joseph Smith Memorial and
    Birthplace 268
sports and activities 92
  America's Cup 63
  basketball 195
  biking 92, 168, 175, 177, 178,
    219, 263, 265, 268, 273, 276,
    281, 286, 302, 330, 335, 338,
    348

canoeing, kayaking, rafting 96,
  192, 203, 210, 219, 238, 277,
  302, 308, 317, 330, 339, 347,
  348
climbing 303, 347
diving 285
dog-sledding 93, 273, 317
fishing 95, 173, 184, 192, 219,
  277, 296, 318, 330, 334, 338,
  344, 347, 348, 350
geocaching 94
golf 268, 271, 334, 348
hiking 94, 271, 273, 274, 276,
  286, 295, 304, 311, 315, 288,
  302, 327, 331, 339, 340, 341,
  343, 347, 348
horseback riding 95, 219, 274,
  286, 339
hunting 344
polo 267
sailing 97, 181, 229, 338, 341
skiing 189, 188, 97, 208, 210,
  261, 263, 265, 267, 268, 271,
  273, 274, 276, 277, 286, 292,
  302, 308, 312, 313, 330, 338,
  348, 349
snowmobiling 98, 318
spectator sports 98
surfing 184, 229
tennis 222, 224, 271
volleyball 195, 197
yacht racing 62
sports and outdoor activities 92
Springfield, MA 195. See also West
  Springfield, MA
  Amazing World of Dr. Suess
    Museum 196
  Basketball Hall of Fame 195
  Dr. Seuss National Memorial
    Sculpture Garden 196
  entertainment venues 196
  Forest Park 196
  George Walter Vincent Smith
    Art Museum 196
  Lyman and Merrie Wood
    Museum of Springfield
    History 196
  Michele and Donald D'Amour
    Museum of Fine Arts 196
  Science Museum 196
  Springfield Armory National
    Historic Site 195
  Springfield Museums at the
    Quadrangle 195
  Symphony Hall 196
  Titanic Historical Society 196
Squanto 33
St. Albans, VT 275, 279
  St. Albans Historical Museum 280
  Vermont Maple Festival 280
Stamford, CT 247
  Bartlett Arboretum and
    Gardens 247
  Stamford Museum and Nature
    Center 247
Standish, Capt. Myles 33, 156
Stark, Gen. John 301
St. Croix Island International
  Historic Site, ME 344
Stellwagen Bank National Marine
  Sanctuary, MA 147

Stephen King Trail 79
Stewart B. McKinney National
    Wildlife Refuge, CT 248
Stirling, James 91
St. Johnsbury, VT 275
    Fairbanks Museum and
        Planetarium 275
    Maple Grove Farms 275
    Stephen Huneck's Dog
        Mountain 275
    St. Johnsbury Athenaeum 275
Stockbridge, MA 204
    Mission House 204
    Naumkeag Museum and
        Gardens 204
    Norman Rockwell Museum 204
Stonington, CT 246, 256
    Captain Nathaniel B. Palmer
        House 256
    Old Lighthouse Museum 256
Stonington, ME 338
Storrs, CT 241
Stowe, Harriet Beecher 76, 236
    Uncle Tom's Cabin 66
Stowe, VT 98, 273
    festivals and fairs 274
    Ski Museum 273
    Spruce Peak Performing Arts
        Center 274
    Stowe Performing Arts 273
    Stowe Recreation Path 273
    Topnotch Resort and Spa 273
    Trapp Family Lodge 273
Strafford, VT 268
    Justin Morrill Homestead 268
Sturbridge, MA
    Old Sturbridge Village 192
Sugarbush, VT 271
Sugar Hill, NH 315
    Sugar Hill Historical Museum
        315
Sugarloaf ski area, ME 98, 348
Sunapee State Beach, NH 308
Swanton, VT 279
    Abenaki Tribal Museum 279
    Missisquoi National Wildlife
        Refuge 279
Swanzey, NH 306

T

Tamworth, NH 311
    Barnstormers Theatre 311
    Remick Country Doctor
        Museum and Farm 311
Tanglewood, MA 206
Tarbin Gardens, NH 308
tax 364
Taylor, Edward 74
technology industry 46, 72, 127
telephones 364
textiles industry 150, 159
Thanksgiving (origin) 33, 158
theaters and performing arts
    centers. See also music venues
    Barnstormers Theatre
        (Tamworth, NH) 311
    Barrington Stage Company
        (Pittsfield, MA) 207
    Boch Center (Boston, MA) 121
    Boston Center for the Arts 129

Bread & Puppet Theater
    Museum (Glover, VT) 276
Bushnell Center for the
    Performing Arts (Hartford,
    CT) 235
Cape Playhouse (Dennis, MA)
    167
City Hall Arts Center
    (Montpelier, VT) 271
Collins Center for the Arts
    (Bangor, ME) 347
Dorset Playhouse (Dorset, VT)
    292
Flynn Center for the Performing
    Arts (Burlington, VT) 282
Goodspeed Opera House (East
    Haddam, CT) 244
Haskell Free Library and Opera
    House (Derby Line, VT) 290
Hopkins Center for the Arts
    (Dartmouth College, NH) 307
Ivoryton Playhouse (Ivoryton,
    CT) 243
Jorgensen Center for the
    Performing Arts (University
    of Connecticut, CT) 242
Katharine Hepburn Cultural
    Arts Center (Old Saybrook,
    CT) 252
Levitt Pavilion for the
    Performing Arts (Westport,
    CT) 249
Long Wharf Theater (New
    Haven, CT) 250
Lost Nation Theater
    (Montpelier, VT) 271
Majestic Theater (West
    Springfield, MA) 196
Majestic Theatre (Manchester,
    NH) 301
Merrill Auditorium (Portland,
    ME) 329
Northern Stage (White River
    Junction, VT) 266
Ogunquit Playhouse (Ogunquit,
    ME) 326
Opera House (Boston, MA) 121
Palace Theater (Waterbury, CT)
    245
Palace Theatre (Manchester,
    NH) 301
Paramount Theater (Rutland,
    VT) 289
Redfern Arts Center (Keene,
    NH) 306
Saint Michael's Playhouse
    (Colechester, VT) 283
Sandglass Theater (Putney, VT)
    262
Shubert Theater (Boston, MA)
    121
Shubert Theater (New Haven,
    CT) 247, 250
Silvermine Guild Arts Center
    (New Canaan, CT) 248
Spruce Peak Performing Arts
    Center (Stowe, VT) 274
State Theatre (Portland, ME)
    329
Stonington Opera House (Deer
    Isle, ME) 338

Symphony Hall (Springfield, MA)
    196
Theater District (Boston, MA)
    121
Wang Center for the Performing
    Arts (Boston, MA) 121
Weston Playhouse (Weston, VT)
    292
Westport Country Playhouse
    (Westport, CT) 249
Yale Repertory Theater (Yale
    University, CT) 250
theaters and performing arts
    centers
    Cape Playhouse (Dennis, MA)
        167
Thimble Islands, CT 251
Thomas, Isaiah 75, 190
Thomaston, ME 334
    General Henry Knox Museum 334
Thoreau, Henry David 67, 75, 153,
    154
Thumb, Tom 249
tipping 362
Topsfield, MA
    Parson Capen House 86
tourism 57, 62
    Cape Cod, MA 181
    Nantucket Island, MA 185
    New Hampshire 319
    Vermont 261
tourist information 364
Townshend, VT 263
    Townshend Lake Recreation
        Area 263
trains 355
transportation 354
Truro, MA 170
    Highland House Museum 170
    Truro Center for the Arts 170
Tuckerman Ravine, NH 98, 315
Tunbridge, VT 269
Turner Falls, MA 200
    Great Falls Discovery Center
        200
Twain, Mark 71, 236
Twilight, Alexander 277
Tyringham, MA 205
    Santarella 205

U

Uncasville, CT
    Mohegan Sun casino 256
Underground Railroad 159, 285
University of Connecticut, CT 241
    Archaeology Center 242
    Ballard Museum of Puppetry
        242
    Connecticut Museum of Natural
        History 242
    Jorgensen Center for the
        Performing Arts 242
    William Benton Museum of Art
        242
Updike, John 78
US Coast Guard 63, 149, 252
Uxbridge, MA 191
    Blackstone River and Canal
        Heritage State Park 192
    River Bend Farm 189, 192

V

Vanderbilt, Cornelius II 231
Vaughan, Alden T. 32
Vergennes, VT
  Lake Champlain Maritime
    Museum 285
Vermont 25, 107, 261
Vermont Crafts Council 279
Vermont Icelandic Horse Farm,
  VT 272
Vermont Shakespeare Company
  278
Vikings 30
Vinalhaven, ME 335
Vineyard Haven, MA 176
  Black Dog Tavern 176
visas and passports 349, 365
von Trapp family 273

W

Wachusett State Reservation and
  Ski Area, MA 189
Waitsfield, VT 271
Wakefield, NH 311
Walden Pond, MA 22
Waldoboro, ME 335
Wampanoag tribes 35, 53, 158,
  172, 181, 213
Ward, Artemus 34
Warner, NH 303
  Mt. Kearsarge Indian Museum
    303
War of 1812 39, 61, 115, 185,
  274
Warren, VT 271
Washington, CT 239
  Institute for American Indian
    Studies 239
Washington, George 39, 137, 195,
  244
Watch and Ward Society 116
Watch Hill, RI 228
Waterbury, CT 245
  Mattatuck Museum Arts and
    History Center 245
  Palace Theater 245
Waterbury, VT 272
  Cabot Annex Store complex
    272
  Cold Hollow Cider Mill 272
  Green Mountain Club 272
  Keurig Green Mountain Coffee
    Company 272
  The Ben & Jerry's Homemade
    Ice Cream Factory 272
  Ziemke Glassblowing 272
Watertown, MA 35
Webster, Daniel 303
Webster, Noah 198, 237, 250
weights and measures 365
Weirs Beach, NH 308
Wellesley, MA
  Wellesley College 66, 72
Wellfleet, MA 169, 177
  Atwood Higgins House 169
  Capt. Penniman House 169
  Drive-in movies 169
  Wellfleet Bay Wildlife Sanctuary
    170

Wells, ME
  National Estuarine Research
    Reserve at Laudholm 327
Wemouth, MA
  Abigail Adams Birthplace 155
Wentworth, Benning 298
Wentworth, John 319
West Barnstable, MA
  West Parish Meetinghouse
    167
West Boothbay Harbor, ME 334
  Maine State Aquarium 334
West Cornwall, CT 240
West Dover, CT 263
  Mount Snow/Haystack 263
Westerly, RI 228
  Misquamicut State Beach 228
West Forks, ME 348
West Hartford, CT 237
  Children's Museum 237
  Elizabeth Park 237, 238
  Noah Webster House & West
    Hartford Historical Society
    237
Weston, VT 292
  Vermont Country Store 292
  Weston Playhouse 292
Westport, CT 249
  Levitt Pavilion for the
    Performing Arts 249
  Westport Country Playhouse
    249
West Quoddy Point, ME 343
West Springfield, MA 196
  Majestic Theater 196
  Storrowton Village Museum 196
West Tisbury, MA 179
  Granary Gallery at the Red Barn
    179
Wethersfield, CT 33, 244
  Buttolph-Williams House 244
  Comstock, Ferre & Co. 245
  Wethersfield Historical Society
    244
Weybridge, VT 285
  UVM Morgan Horse Farm 285
whale watching. See wildlife
whaling 41, 59, 158, 181, 185
Wharton, Edith 78, 205
Whistler, James Abbott 150
White Mountains, NH 295, 311,
  319, 288
White River Junction, VT 265
  Main Street Museum 266
  Northern Stage 266
Whitman, Sarah 216
Whittier, John Greenleaf 76, 149
Wickford, RI 227
  Smith's Castle 227
wildlife 320
  bears 320
  beavers 320
  birds 173, 192, 220, 228, 251,
    263, 266, 267, 286, 310, 318,
    344, 347
  bobcats 318
  moose 318, 286, 317, 329,
    348
  whale watching 63, 97, 117, 147,
    149, 167, 170, 228, 229, 328,
    331, 334, 341, 343, 347

Williams, Roger 34, 213, 216
Williamstown, MA 207, 208
  Sterling and Francine Clark Art
    Institute 208
  Stone Hill Center 91
  Williams College 72
Willimantic, CT 242
  Connecticut Eastern Railroad
    Museum 242
  Windham Textile and History
    Museum 242
Wilton, NH 305
  Frye's Measure Mill 305
Windsor, CT 33, 240
  Luddy/Taylor Connecticut Valley
    Tobacco Museum 240
  Oliver Ellsworth Homestead
    240
Windsor Locks, CT 241
  Connecticut Firefighters
    Memorial 241
  New England Air Museum 241
Windsor, VT 265
  American Precision Museum
    265
  Old Constitution House 265
  Windsor-Cornish Covered
    Bridge 265
Winter Harbor, ME 342
Winthrop, John 33, 40, 65, 121,
  122
Wiscasset, ME 333
  Castle Tucker 333
  Nickels-Sortwell House 333
  Old Lincoln County Jail and
    Museum 333
witches 65, 143, **146**
Wolfeboro, NH 309
  Libby Museum 309
  New Hampshire Antique and
    Classic Boat Museum 309
  Wolfeboro Historical Society
    (Wolfeboro, NH) 309
  Wright Museum of World War II
    309
Woodbury, Charles 326
Woods Hole, MA 62, 175, 176
  Woods Hole Oceanographic
    Institution 175
  Woods Hole Science Aquarium
    176
Woodstock, VT 267, 288
  Billings Farm and Museum 267
  Suicide Six ski area 267
  Woodstock Historical Society
    267
  Woodstock Inn and Resort 267
Woolwich, ME 332
Woonsocket, Ri
  Museum of Work and Culture
    219
Worcester, MA 72, **190**
  American Antiquarian Society
    190
  Broad Meadow Brook Wildlife
    Sanctuary 189, 191
  College of the Holy Cross 72
  EcoTarium 191
  Goddard Library 190
  Higgins Armory Museum 191
  Worcester Art Museum 191

Worcester Historical Museum 189, 190
Worcester Polytechnic Institute 46, 72
writers 74

Y

yacht racing
Herreshoff Marine America's Cup Museum 220
Yale, Elihu 69
Yale University, CT 40, **249**
Beinecke Rare Book and Manuscript Library 249
Institute of Sacred Music 250
Kline Science Center 91

Peabody Museum of Natural History 250
Yale Center for British Art 250
Yale Collection of Musical Instruments 250
Yale Repertory Theater 250
Yale University Art Gallery 250
Yankee Doodle 141
Yarmouth Port, MA 167
Captain Bangs Hallett House 167
Edward Gorey House 167
Hallett's Store 167
York, ME 325
Cliff Walk 326
Elizabeth Perkins House 326
Jefferds Tavern 326
John Hancock Warehouse 326

Old Gaol 326
Shore Road 326
York Beach 326
York Harbor 325

Z

zoos and animal parks
Beardsley Zoo (Bridgeport, CT) 249
Roger Williams Park (Providence, RI) 218
Southwick's Zoo (Mendon, MA) 192
Vermont Institute of Natural Science (Quechee, VT) 266, 267

Boston Subway Ⓣ

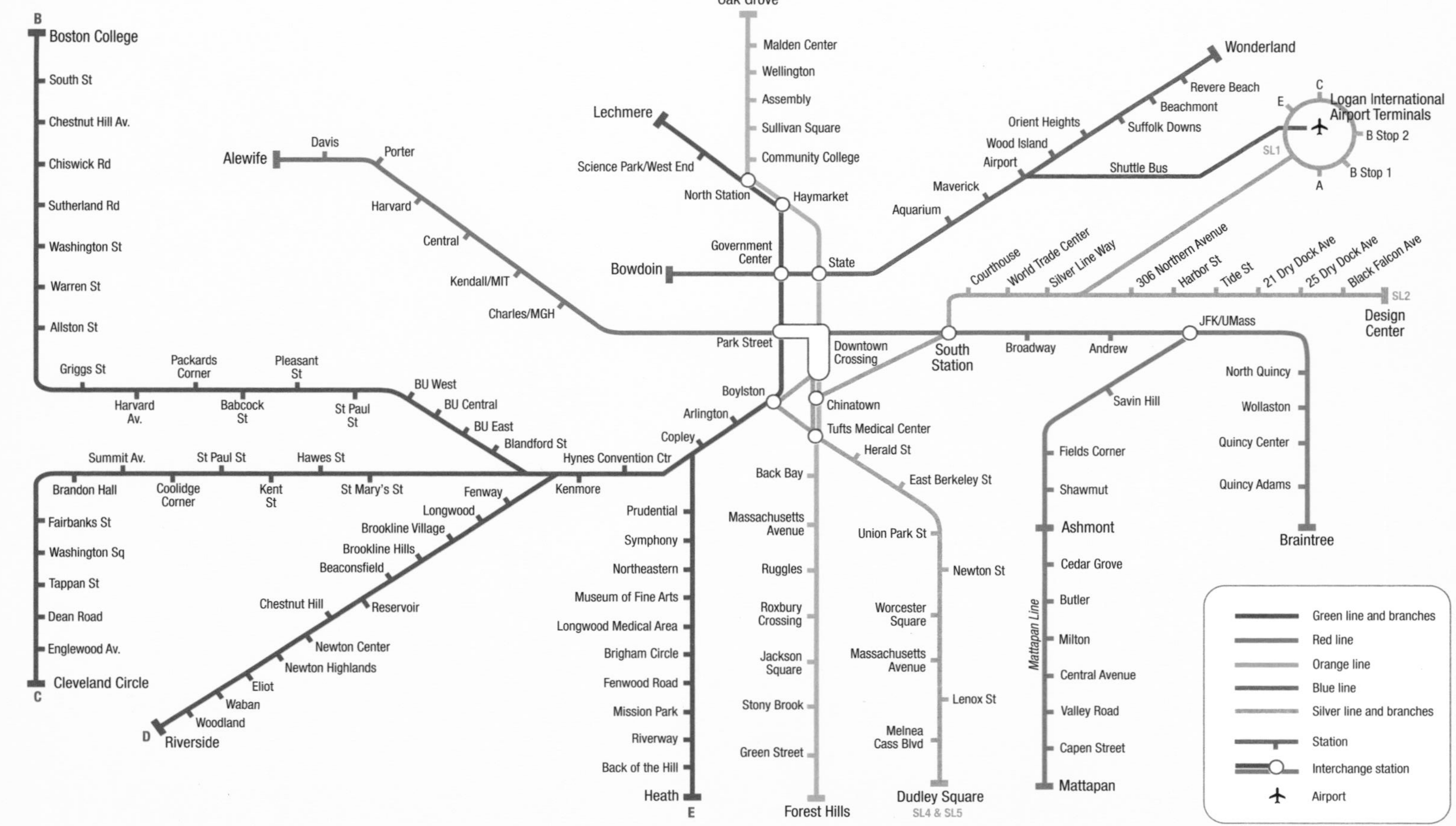

Logan International Airport Terminals

B Stop 2
B Stop 1
C
A
E
SL1
SL2

Design Center

Black Falcon Ave
25 Dry Dock Ave
21 Dry Dock Ave
Tide St
Harbor St
306 Northern Avenue
Silver Line Way
World Trade Center
Courthouse

Wonderland
Revere Beach
Beachmont
Suffolk Downs
Shuttle Bus
Orient Heights
Wood Island
Airport
Maverick
Aquarium

Malden Center
Wellington
Assembly
Sullivan Square
Community College
Oak Grove

Haymarket
State
North Station
Government Center
Bowdoin
Science Park/West End
Lechmere

Downtown Crossing
Park Street
Boylston
Chinatown
Tufts Medical Center
Herald St

JFK/UMass
Andrew
Savin Hill
Broadway
South Station

North Quincy
Wollaston
Quincy Center
Quincy Adams
Braintree

Fields Corner
Shawmut
Ashmont
Cedar Grove
Butler
Milton
Central Avenue
Valley Road
Capen Street
Mattapan
Mattapan Line

East Berkeley St
Newton St
Lenox St
Union Park St
Worcester Square
Massachusetts Avenue
Melnea Cass Blvd
Dudley Square
SL4 & SL5

Back Bay
Massachusetts Avenue
Ruggles
Roxbury Crossing
Jackson Square
Stony Brook
Green Street
Forest Hills

Arlington
Copley
Hynes Convention Ctr
Prudential
Symphony
Northeastern
Museum of Fine Arts
Longwood Medical Area
Brigham Circle
Fenwood Road
Mission Park
Riverway
Back of the Hill
Heath
E

Blandford St
BU East
BU Central
BU West
Kenmore
Fenway
Longwood
Brookline Village
Brookline Hills
Beaconsfield
Reservoir
Chestnut Hill
Newton Centre
Newton Highlands
Eliot
Waban
Woodland
Riverside
D

St Paul St
Hawes St
Kent St
St Mary's St
St Paul St
Coolidge Corner
Summit Av.
Brandon Hall
Fairbanks St
Washington Sq
Tappan St
Dean Road
Englewood Av.
Cleveland Circle
C

Boston College
South St
Chestnut Hill Av.
Chiswick Rd
Sutherland Rd
Washington St
Warren St
Allston St
Griggs St
Harvard Av.
Packards Corner
Babcock St
St Paul St
Pleasant St
B

Charles/MGH
Kendall/MIT
Central
Harvard
Porter
Davis
Alewife

Legend
Green line and branches
Red line
Orange line
Blue line
Silver line and branches
Station
Interchange station
Airport

Boston

0 ——— 500 yds
0 ——— 500 m

N

Cambridge Street

Cambridge Street

Cambridge Street

Broadway

Palermo St

Elm Street

Lincoln Street

Columbia Street

Willow Street

Webster Street

York Street

Otis St

Spring Street

Thorndike Street

Otis St

Sacred Heart

Lechmere

Lechmere Square

Twin City Plaza

Monsignor O'Brien Highway

Winter Street

Gore Street

Holy Cross Polish Church

Middlesex County Courthouse

Cambri Gall

EAST CAMBRIDGE

DONNELLY FIELD

AHERN FIELD

Hurley Street

Charles Street

Bent Street

Binney Street

Sciarappa

6th Street

5th Street

Rogers Street

Binney

Munroe

Potter St

3rd

2nd

1st

Athenaeum St

Cambridge

Land

Prospect St

Tremont St

Norfolk Street

Elm Street

Columbia Street

Market St

Windsor Street

Hampshire Street

Broadway

Harvard Street

H. Cardinal Medeiros Av.

Berkshire Street

Bristol Street

Fulkerson Street

Binney Street

5th Street

EDWARD J. SENNOTT PARK

Harvard St

Worcester St

Suffolk St

Washington St

Pine

Cherry

Washington Street

Harvard Street

Technology Square

Broadway

Kendall/MIT

Main Street

Longfellow

Central

Harvard

Massachusetts

Green Street

Franklin Street

Brookline Street

Sidney St

Blanche

Pine

Landsdowne

Purlington St

Pacific St

Albany

Vassar Street

State St

Smart St

Osborn St

Albany Street

Massachusetts Av.

Vassar

Main Street

CAMBRIDGE

MIT Museum

Ray and Maria Stata Center

List Visual Arts Center

Carleton St

Ames

Wadsworth St

Amherst St

Harvard Boat Club

CAMBRIDGEPORT

Massachusetts Institute of Technology (MIT)

Great Court

MIT Chapel

Hart Nautical Gallery

Steinbrenner Stadium

Kresge Auditorium

Vassar Street

Memorial Drive

Memorial Drive

Memorial Drive

Charles

Esplanade

Lagoon

G Ins

Clarendon St

Storrow

Storrow Drive

Storrow Drive

Beacon Street

Marlborough

Fairfield

Dartmouth

Ames-Webster Mansion

Hunnewell Mansion

First Baptist Church

Harvard Bridge

Back Street

Bay State Road

Beacon Street

Gloucester Street

Hereford Street

Commonwealth

Newbury

Exeter Street

BACK BAY

John F. Andrews House

Old South Church

Boston Public Library

Copley

Copley Square

Boston University East

Commonwealth Avenue

Kenmore Square

Commonwealth

Commonwealth Avenue

Newbury

Boylston Street

Institute of Contemporary Art

Lord & Taylor

Copley Place

Blandford St

Kenmore

Turnpike

Hynes Convention Center

Berklee Performance Center

Dalton Street

Burrage House

Prudential Center

Sak's

Prudential Tower

Back Bay

Beacon Street

Landsdowne Street

Ipswich Street

Fenway Park

Yawkey Way

Van Ness Street

FENWAY

Park Dr.

Massachusetts Av.

Edgerly Rd

St Germain St

Belvidere Street

Prudential

Newton St

CARLETON COURT

PARK

John F. Kennedy NHS

Fenway

Landmark Center

Brookline Avenue

Boylston Street

Peterborough Street

Park Dr.

BACK BAY FENS

Hemenway

Fenway

Norway St

Burbank St

Westland Av

Horticultural Hall

Mother Church

Christian Science Center

Publishing Co. Bldg

Symphony Hall

Huntington

St Botolph Street

HARRIET TUBMAN PARK

Columbus Av

West Newton St

Warr

Museum of Fine Arts, Isabella Stewart Gardner Museum

Symphony